Reading for Results

Twelfth Edition

Laraine E. Flemming

Jordan Fabish, Long Beach City College
Contributing Consultant

"When it comes to reading, words are only
the tip of the iceberg."

WADSWORTH
CENGAGE Learning·

Australia · Brazil · Japan · Korea · Mexico · Singapore · Spain · United Kingdom · United States

WADSWORTH
CENGAGE Learning·

Reading for Results, Twelfth Edition
Laraine Flemming

Director of Developmental Studies:
Annie Todd

Executive Editor: Shani Fisher

Senior Development Editor:
Kathy Sands-Boehmer

Editorial Assistant: Erin Nixon

Media Editor: Christian Biagetti

Brand Manager: Lydia LeStar

Market Development Manager:
Erin Parkins

Marketing Communications Manager:
Linda Yip

Senior Content Project Manager:
Aimee Chevrette Bear

Art Director: Faith Brosnan

Print Buyer: Betsy Donaghey

Rights Acquisition Specialist:
Ann Hoffman

Production Service: Books By
Design, Inc.

Text Designer: Books By Design, Inc.

Cover Designer: Saizon Design

Cover Image: shutterstock.com
© Scrugglegreen

Compositor: S4Carlisle Publishing
Services

For product information and technology assistance, contact us at
Cengage Learning Customer & Sales Support, 1-800-354-9706

For permission to use material from this text or product,
submit all requests online at **www.cengage.com/permissions**.
Further permissions questions can be e-mailed to
permissionrequest@cengage.com

Library of Congress Control Number: 2012946775
ISBN-13: 978-1-133-58996-9
ISBN-10: 1-133-58996-0

Wadsworth
20 Channel Center Street
Boston, MA 02210
USA

Cengage Learning is a leading provider of customized learning solutions with office locations around the globe, including Singapore, the United Kingdom, Australia, Mexico, Brazil, and Japan. Locate your local office at **international.cengage.com/region.**

Cengage Learning products are represented in Canada by Nelson Education, Ltd.

For your course and learning solutions,
visit **www.cengage.com.**

Purchase any of our products at your local college store or at our preferred online store **www.cengagebrain.com.**

Instructors: Please visit **login.cengage.com** and log in to access instructor-specific resources.

Printed in the United States of America
1 2 3 4 5 6 7 16 15 14 13 12

Contents

6 Focusing on Supporting Details in Paragraphs 256

7 Focusing on Supporting Details in Longer Readings 314

8 Focusing on Inferences in Paragraphs 358

9   Understanding the Role of Inferences in Longer Readings   426

10   Learning from Organizational Patterns in Paragraphs   489

Putting It All Together 683

Preface

Known for her ability to turn abstract reading theory into concrete reading practice, Laraine Flemming is back with a host of new explanations and exercises that show students, step-by-step, how to read and respond to textbook writing.

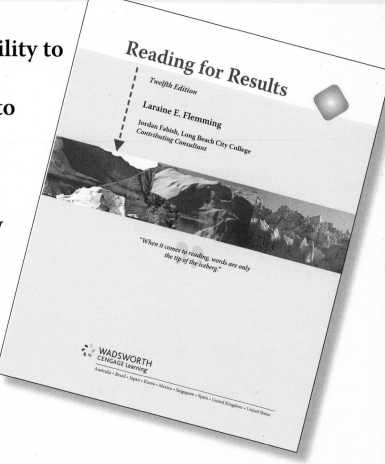

Reading for Results

Twelfth Edition

Laraine E. Flemming

Jordan Fabish, Long Beach City College
Contributing Consultant

"When it comes to reading, words are only the tip of the iceberg."

WADSWORTH
CENGAGE Learning

Australia • Brazil • Japan • Korea • Mexico • Singapore • Spain • United Kingdom • United States

"I actually learned some new things about explaining comprehension skills to students in new and different ways. I think every reading teacher should have a copy of this book . . ."
—Carla Bell, Henry Ford Community College

"LOVE IT!"
—Victor Sandoval, Riverside City College

A New Approach to Academic Reading

◆ Focus on Explanatory Patterns Typical of Textbooks.

This edition of *Reading for Results* focuses on textbook templates, or explanatory patterns, that consistently turn up in academic writing. Chapter 4, for instance, **Getting to the Point of Paragraphs**, offers examples of the "That Was Then, This Is Now" template. Guided by this explanatory pattern, readers learn what was once standard practice or thought *before* getting to the real point of the paragraph—a current and more up-to-date perspective. Continuing the focus on textbook templates, Chapter 5, **Getting to the Point of Longer Readings**, shows how common it is for thesis statements to conclude the paragraphs that open chapter sections.

◆ Strategy Matched to Subject Matter

Chapters 4 through 8 emphasize the ways in which subject matter influences both the writer's approach and the reader's response. While writers of business texts like starting paragraphs with topic sentences, authors of psychology and sociology texts are fond of posing questions that lead to the main idea. Writers of history texts, for their part, are just as likely to imply the main idea as state it. The reader who shifts expectations and strategies with the material has the edge.

◆ Reading Protocols Help Students Spot What's Relevant

The eleventh edition showed students how to track the chains of repetition and reference that lead to the main idea. The twelfth edition expands and refines that explanation, offering many more concrete examples of the different ways repetition and reference bind the writer's thoughts together and, at the same time, help the reader follow the writer's train of thought.

"I think that emphasizing the importance of repetition to finding emerging main ideas is a good one and will be a great lead into unstated main ideas."

—Mary Nielson, Dalton State College

---

4 Getting to the Point of Paragraphs

IN THIS CHAPTER, YOU WILL LEARN

- more about identifying topics, main ideas, and supporting details in paragraphs.
- about some variations on the explanatory patterns writers frequently use to present their ideas.
- how to use repetition and reference to identify both the topic and the main idea in paragraphs.

"Understanding depends on mutual empathy, on reader and writer appreciating each other's task."
—Larry Wright, professor, philosopher, and author of *Critical Thinking: An Introduction to Analytical Reading and Reasoning*

Chapter 4 reviews and enlarges what you learned about paragraphs in Chapter 3 (pp. 135–47). It further describes and illustrates the kinds of explanatory patterns textbook writers use when combining general and specific sentences in paragraphs. The chapter also gives you an additional strategy for dealing with paragraphs where you can't quite get a handle on the author's meaning, despite your understanding of how general and specific sentences relate to one another.

Additional Ways Authors Introduce Topic Sentences

As you know from Chapter 3, authors sometimes introduce the topic sentence by offering background or context about the topic *before* presenting the main idea. But what you may not realize is that those introductions can be longer than a single sentence. In the following paragraph, for example, two sentences—rather than one—pave the way for the topic sentence expressing the main idea.

164

Following the Chains of Repetition and Reference ◆	**The Writer's Link: Word Repetition** The second sentence opens with a word that comes at the end of the previous sentence.	[1]Warren G. Harding could not be nominated today when, at the first mention of his name, a hundred reporters would be digging for <u>dirt</u> in his past. [2]<u>The dirt</u> was there. (Conlin, *The American Past*, p. 642.)
	The Writer's Link: Transition Words The sentence that comes after opens with a transition, which explicitly identifies its relationship to the previous sentence.	[1]Already as a young child, the writer knew that becoming fluent in English was separating him from his Spanish-speaking grandmother. [2]<u>Thus,</u> he tried to hide how well he had mastered the language of his new country and made a point of not speaking it at home, even when his parents, proud of his achievement, encouraged him to.
	The Writer's Link: An Implied Example or Clarification The following sentence supplies a specific illustration of some idea, attitude, theory, or opinion that has just been mentioned.	[1]Warren G. Harding could not be nominated today when, at the first mention of his name, a hundred reporters would be digging for dirt in his past. [2]The dirt was there. [3]<u>For fifteen years in Marion, Ohio, he carried on a sexual affair with a neighbor.</u>

◆ Marginal Think-Alouds Provide Models of Skilled Reading

Throughout the text, marginal think-alouds help students see how experienced readers use both text and format to construct meaning.

"BRAVO! Our mission is to give students the skill to handle the textbooks they will be reading in their content area courses."

Dawn Sedik, Valencia College, West Campus

In Persuasive Writing, Both Sides Rarely Get Equal Time

Writers whose intention is to inform will present both sides of an argument just about equally so that readers can draw their own conclusion, for example:

Notice that the title does not take a stand. All it tells you is the topic.

The authors consistently use a question and answer format to make it clear that they are not endorsing any one point of view.

To avoid taking a stand themselves, the authors pose a question without providing an answer.

Paragraph 3 offers the opposing point of view. And again the authors don't take a stand, suggesting both sides have merit.

Drug Use and Pregnancy

1   Court cases with policy implications for whether a woman can or should be arrested if she exposes a fetus to illegal drugs are continuing to be debated at the highest judicial levels, including the Supreme Court in the United States. Is this an effective way to reduce the likelihood of drug use and any of its accompanying risks for the fetus? That depends on your point of view.

What Are the Opposing Arguments?

2   Some say a concerned society should impose criminal or other charges on a pregnant woman who uses a drug that may be dangerous to the fetus. A number of jurisdictions in the United States and provinces in Canada have implemented laws permitting a newborn to be removed from a parent on the grounds of child abuse or neglect because of drug exposure during pregnancy. In some cases, the woman has been ordered to be confined to a drug-treatment facility during pregnancy. After all, anyone found to provide such illegal substances to a child would certainly expect to face criminal or other charges. Are the circumstances that much different in the case of a pregnant woman and her fetus?

3   Others believe the situation is vastly different and further claim that criminal charges, imprisonment, or mandatory treatment are counterproductive (Beckett, 1995; Farr, 1995). Legislation specifically targeted to pregnant drug users might actually drive prospective mothers, out of fear of being prosecuted, away from the care and treatment needed for both themselves and their fetuses. Moreover, the tendency to rely on criminal procedures could limit the resources available for the implementation of innovative, well-funded public health efforts for treating addiction and its consequences for the fetus (Chavkin, 2001). (Adapted from Bukatko and Daehler, *Child Development*, 5th ed., pp. 123–24.)

Greater Emphasis on Combining Reading with Writing

◆ Writing Assignments That Link Reading and Writing

Every chapter includes *From Reader to Writer* assignments, showing how skills and concepts introduced in the context of reading also apply to writing.

> **From Reader to Writer**
>
> Pick a person, an animal, or a location that you know well. Write down all the specific details about that person or place that make it meaningful to you. Then make the last sentence the general statement that expresses the meaning of the details, for instance, "He was a dog whose loyalty knew no limits" or "It was a room no child could resist."

◆ More Concrete Tips on How to Paraphrase

Because paraphrasing is essential to both reading and writing from sources, Chapter 1, **Strategies for Learning from Textbooks**, offers a new discussion of this key academic skill. New paraphrasing pointers also accompany several exercises in the book and offer advice geared to specific sentence types and relationships.

◆ New Discussion of Summary Writing

This edition provides students with everything they need to know about writing a summary. This includes showing them how the content of a summary changes with the purpose, becoming shorter if it's destined to be an introduction, longer if it's the sole objective of an assignment.

> **Pointers for Summary Writing**
> ◆
>
> 1. Summaries are *paraphrased* and *abbreviated* versions of original text. Thus, your summary should never be as long as the original article, essay, or chapter section.
>
>   Summaries, however, don't have a fixed length. How long or short they are depends on the audience and the purpose of the summary
>
> 2. In a summary, the language and length of the original changes, the meaning does not.
>
> 3. The number of major or minor details you include in a summary will vary with the purpose and audience.
>
> 4. If the reading you are summarizing implies but doesn't state the main idea, your summary should express the implied main idea directly in a thesis statement.
>
> 5. If you are writing a summary for someone other than yourself, always assume that person hasn't read the original. Then decide what major and minor details are essential to making the main idea of the reading clear to the reader.
>
> 6. While a summary should not change the meaning of the original, it can change the order in which ideas are presented. Notice in the sample summary above that the detail about Franklin's men resorting to cannibalism comes earlier in the summary than it does in the original.
>
> 7. When you are considering what can be eliminated, look closely at illustrations or examples. Often one example will do for a summary and you can eliminate the rest. Quotations, for the most part, can usually be left out of the summary. Quotations almost always provide emphasis, and in a summary you don't need to say things in different ways. Once is enough.
>
> 8. Unlike examples, reasons for a particular idea or action should not be cut although they can be trimmed down. Reasons are there to prove a point in the original text and should always make their way into a summary.
>
> 9. Authors sometimes use repetition for emphasis. But repetition has no place in a summary. Eliminate any sentences that serve

Revised Discussion of Using the Web While Reading

◆ In-Depth Explanations of How to Search the Web

Chapter 1 offers a completely revised and simplified discussion of how to be a savvy Web searcher, someone who knows that (1) search terms make a difference, (2) all websites aren't equally trustworthy, and (3) YouTube has more to offer than cat videos.

◆ Web Quest Assignments Build Search Expertise *and* Background Knowledge

Every chapter contains two or more Web Quest assignments that encourage students to think about the best search term for the best results. The Web Quest assignments have also been carefully designed to enhance students' knowledge of culturally significant people, places, and events.

WEB QUEST
Why was Alcatraz chosen as the site of AIM's protest?

_____

_____

_____

A More Flexible Sequence of Instruction

◆ A Brand-New Chapter Sequence

The chapter sequence has been expanded and revised to accommodate different reading levels. Students struggling to master concepts like identifying the topic and main idea can still, if they need to, get plenty of practice with paragraph-length excerpts. However, students who grasp these same concepts quickly can move right into determining the topic and main idea of longer, multi-paragraph readings.

"**Reading for Results** *successfully scaffolds for readers an awareness of the writer by explaining typical moves writers make.*"

—Christine Barrilleaux,
Tallahassee Community College

"**Reading for Results** *is the most complete text suited for entry level reading. The paragraphs are appropriately written with varied types and organization. What Ms. Flemming has done is provide a great framework for the instructor to work with.*"

—Victor Sandoval, Riverside City College

◆ All New Three-Part Format for Questions in *Putting It All Together*

There are three sets of questions for the extended readings that conclude the book: *Getting the Gist* consists of multiple-choice questions typical of those found on a standardized reading test. *Taking a Closer Look* poses more complex questions about content and form and requires written responses. The critical thinking segment, *Reading with a Critical Eye*, includes short answer and multiple-choice questions about argument, tone, and bias.

"I had a student who did not respond to a question I asked and she said, 'Oh, I'm so sorry. I was so interested in reading this on the next page I didn't hear you.' This is what I like the most about this book—high interest readings. . . ."

—Mary Rouse,
Bluegrass Community and
Technical College

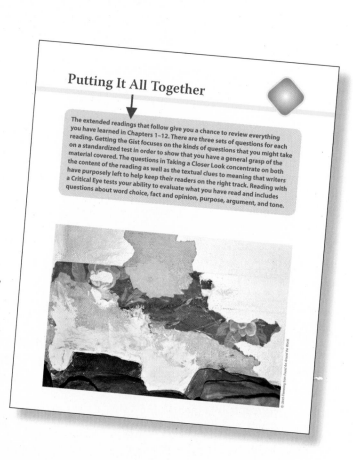

Putting It All Together

The extended readings that follow give you a chance to review everything you have learned in Chapters 1–12. There are three sets of questions for each reading. Getting the Gist focuses on the kinds of questions that you might take on a standardized test in order to show that you have a general grasp of the material covered. The questions in Taking a Closer Look concentrate on both the content of the reading as well as the textual clues to meaning that writers have purposely left to help keep their readers on the right track. Reading with a Critical Eye tests your ability to evaluate what you have read and includes questions about word choice, fact and opinion, purpose, argument, and tone.

More Visual Instruction

◆ Visual Images of Key Concepts

Diagrams that reinforce the explanations encourage dual processing of key concepts.

Specific Sentences

1. In Brazil's celebration of Carnival, there are samba contests, with all the dancers wearing brightly colored costumes dripping in sequins and feathers.

2. In Italy, Carnival is the big winter festival, celebrated with colorful parades, but also with private parties and balls.

3. In the Netherlands, Carnival is the last chance to eat and drink before Easter, and much of the celebrating is done indoors in pubs, or bars.

4. In Croatia, the celebration of Carnival did not get started until 1982, but it is now an established tradition, with face masks being an essential part of the celebration.

5. The festival of Carnival is celebrated all across the Caribbean with steel-band music playing a huge role in the outdoor festivities.

General Statement

6. Carnival, once mainly a Christian tradition, has lost many of its religious associations, but it is still celebrated around the world, with each country adding its own individual touch.

© Bettmann/Corbis.

Emiliano Zapata was a horse trainer by profession but ended up becoming a heroic leader of the Mexican revolution.

◆ New Photos That Expand Cultural Literacy

This edition of *Reading for Results* has more photos than ever before. The photos were carefully chosen to stimulate student interest in the topic under discussion and expand their background knowledge about important people and events.

New Format for Vocabulary Round Ups

◆ More Detailed Definitions and Examples

As in the eleventh edition, the twelfth edition provides vocabulary footnotes in each chapter, a round up of the definitions, and a final review test. But new words are now accompanied by expanded definitions and sample sentences that better prepare students for the vocabulary tests that conclude each chapter.

VOCABULARY ROUND UP 1

Below are six words introduced in pages 000–000. The words are accompanied by more detailed definitions, the page on which they originally appeared, and additional sample sentences. Spend time reviewing the words and their meanings because you will see them again in review tests at the end of the chapter. Use the online dictionary Wordnik to find more sentences illustrating the words in context. (*Note:* If you know of another dictionary, online or in print, with as many examples of the words in context, feel free to use that one instead.)

1. **strident** (p. 000): loud, angry, harsh. "For some reason women who are outspoken are likely to be called *strident*, but men who speak their minds are labeled confident and forceful."

2. **innuendo** (p. 000): a hint, something that is not directly said but still suggests something unpleasant. "His opponent did not say it outright but the *innuendo* was there; as a twice-married man, he was immoral and unfit for office."

"The integration of reading and vocabulary totally eliminates the idea of adopting two separate textbooks."

—Felicia Grimes,
Tarrant County College District

And Some Things Never Change

As in prior editions, the following highly acclaimed features remain:

● Every chapter starts with an overview.

● Each concept and skill is followed by numerous chances for practice and review.

● An entire chapter (Chapter 2) is devoted to vocabulary building.

● The explanations remain clear and concrete.

● Reading tips are sprinkled throughout the chapters.

● The terms *general* and *specific* get a chapter all to themselves (Chapter 3).

● *Digging Deeper* multi-paragraph readings conclude each chapter.

● *Summing Up the Key Points* and *Check Your Understanding* reviews help students and instructors monitor comprehension.

● As always, the readings focus on topics guaranteed to stimulate student interest.

Additional Resources

◆ For Students

Aplia Developmental Reading, an online reading and learning solution, helps students become better readers by motivating them with compelling material, interactive assignments, and detailed explanations. In-text vocabulary features new and challenging words. Students receive immediate, detailed explanations for every answer, and grades are automatically recorded in the instructor's Aplia gradebook.

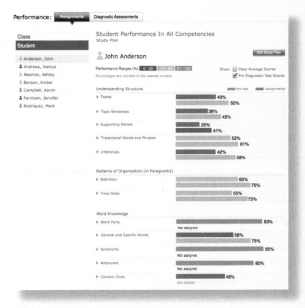

The Student Companion Website offers interactive practice quizzes, tips for reading and studying, advice for preparing for class and exams, along with links to Online Reading Resources and Writing Centers.

Interactive vocabulary flashcards provide definitions to the vocabulary in the text and can be used to refresh students' memory.

◆ For Instructors

The Instructor's Resource Manual and Test Bank offers suggestions for teaching each chapter and supplementary exercises for skills introduced in *Reading for Results*. These suggestions and exercises are great for the new instructor looking for support or the more experienced teacher looking for ideas. The Instructor's Resource Manual also provides a list of all the vocabulary words introduced in the book, along with a sample midterm and final.

Examview® Test Bank, a text-specific test bank that features automatic grading, allows you to create, deliver, and customize tests and study guides (both print and online) in minutes. Instructors can see assessments onscreen exactly as they will print or display online, and build tests by entering an unlimited number of new questions or editing existing questions.

The Instructor Companion Website features a wide variety of teaching aids, including chapter-specific PowerPoint presentations, the Instructor's Manual and Test Bank, a semester final exam, and more. Instructors who want to use the companion website should go to login.cengage.com, where they can use the access code provided by their Cengage representative or find out how to get one.

Acknowledgments

A huge thank you goes to all of the following reviewers, whose suggestions and comments contributed so much to the twelfth edition:

Phillis Aaberg, University of Central Missouri; Lisa Barnes, Delaware County Community College; Christine Barrilleaux, Tallahassee Community College; Carla Bell, Henry Ford Community College; Deira Benton, St. Louis Community College at Forest Park; Kathleen Carlson, Brevard Community College; Sharon Cellemme, South Piedmont Community College; Marlys Cordoba, College of the Siskiyous; Julia Erben, Gulf Coast State College; Felicia Grimes, Tarrant County College District–South Campus; Valerie Hicks, Community College of Baltimore County; Harry Holden, North Lake College; Tiare Hotra, Long Beach City College; Judith Isonhood, Hinds Community College; Paula Khalaf, Lone Star College–CyFair; Kearney Kok, Bluegrass Community & Technical College; Mary Nielsen, Dalton State College; Beth Penney, Monterey Peninsula College; Mary Rouse, Bluegrass Community & Technical College; Victor Sandoval, Riverside City College; Dawn Sedik, Valencia College–West Campus; Jerry Stevens, Kent State University–Trumbull; Shari Waldrop, Navarro College; Patricia Weak, College of the Ouachitas (Ouachita Technical College); and Jenni Wessel-Fields, Black Hawk College.

Although not official reviewers for this edition of *Reading for Results*, the following people have contributed mightily to the final product: Denice Josten, St. Louis Community College; Dee Robbins, Black Hawk College; Kathy McCourt, Camden County College; Judi Breinin, Miami Dade College; and Susan Fawcett, formerly of Bronx Community College and now textbook author extraordinaire.

In addition to all the reviewers, who were so instrumental in shaping this revision, I would also like to thank my editor Shani Fisher, whose thoughtful suggestions and unfailing good humor contributed enormously to this new edition; my developmental editor Kathy Sands-Boehmer, whose wit and high spirits kept me from a meltdown as deadlines loomed; Nancy Benjamin, from Books By Design, who, for twenty years now, has treated all of my books as if she had written them herself; Mary Schnabel, who proofreads every word I write and keeps me looking respectable in print; and lastly Ulrich Flemming, who said to me in 1976, "Don't be silly, of course you can write a book," making this edition and all the others possible.

Strategies for Learning from Textbooks

IN THIS CHAPTER, YOU WILL LEARN

- how to use *SQ3R*, a reading method specifically created for learning from textbooks.

- why paraphrasing is an essential reading skill.

- which methods of reading and review might work best for you.

- how to match your reading rate to the material.

- how to use the Web to expand your background knowledge.

"Skeptics say college is overrated, but those with degrees make more even when their jobs don't require higher education."

—"Even for Cashiers, College Pays Off,"
New York Times, June 26, 2011

Created more than half a century ago, *SQ3R*, the study system for learning from textbooks described in this chapter, has sometimes been called obsolete, or out of date. Yet, in fact, it's anything but.

Francis P. Robinson, the educational psychologist who created *SQ3R* in the 1940s, spent years teaching both college students and military personnel how to learn from textbooks. Due to his extensive teaching experience and his training in psychology, Robinson had an in-depth understanding of how people learn. For that reason, his system,† used consistently and with some modifications, still offers big benefits.

Chapter 1 also emphasizes the importance of writing while reading as a way of improving both comprehension and remembering. It pays particular attention to **paraphrasing**, or translating someone else's words into your

---

†*SQ3R* has spawned numerous similar study systems like *PQRST*—i.e., *Preview, Question, Read, Summary, Test*. If you have used another system that gets the results you want, feel free to stick with it.

own. Because paraphrasing is a critical academic skill, you'll hear about it in several chapters. Chapter 1, however, gives you the basics.

Finally, Chapter 1 tells you how to use the Web to expand your background knowledge and improve your comprehension of textbook assignments.

Introducing *SQ3R*: Survey, Question, Read, Recall, Review

If you are reading a bestseller by a writer like Dean Koontz[†] or Charlaine Harris,[†] you probably let your mind drift along with the story, almost like you were dreaming it. However, this dreamy, unfocused approach, perfect for leisure reading isn't particularly effective with textbooks.

With textbooks, you need a systematic but flexible system that can take into account the difficulty of the material, the author's writing style, and the goals of your assignment. *SQ3R* is flexible enough to include all three elements. What follows are the steps in the system, all of which can and should be adapted to your needs.

S: Survey to Get a General Overview and Make Predictions

When you start a textbook assignment, don't just open your textbook and begin reading. Instead, **survey** or preview the material using the general sequence of steps described in the following box. The purpose of the survey is for you to develop expectations about the content. That way, when you start reading, you will have a **purpose**. You'll be reading to confirm or revise your expectations. Having a purpose improves both comprehension and remembering.

Although the steps in a survey may increase or decrease according to text difficulty and your knowledge of the material, these seven steps are almost always essential.

[†]Dean Koontz is the author of numerous thrillers like *Odd Thomas* and *Frankenstein: The Dead Town*. If you like crime novels, you will love his.
[†]Charlaine Harris is the author of *The Southern Vampire Mysteries* series of novels, on which the hit HBO series *True Blood* is based, and the books are as good as the HBO series.

Seven Basic Steps in a Survey

◆

1. Read the title. Consider what it suggests about the chapter's contents.

2. Read all introductory material. That includes opening anecdotes, or stories, chapter outlines, lists of questions, goals, and objectives. These are all ways in which textbook authors identify what the author expects readers to learn.

3. Use the title and introduction to form a general question or two about what's covered in the chapter. Check your memory to see if you have any prior knowledge, or previous experience, with the topic discussed.[†]

4. Read the headings and opening sentence of chapter sections. If the material is especially difficult or unfamiliar, expand this step: Read the last sentence of every chapter section or even the first and last sentence of every paragraph. Use this material as the basis for focus questions that will guide your reading and help you maintain concentration.

5. Look at all visual aids. Visual aids include pictures, photos, maps, charts, boxes, icons, or visual symbols, and graphs. If captions, or explanations, accompany the visual aids, read them, too. Ask yourself what each visual aid suggests about the chapter's content. If specific icons are used consistently in the chapter, see if you can detect a pattern in the kinds of information they identify.

6. Pay attention to words printed in boldface or in the margin of the page. With particularly important or difficult courses, expand this step to include jotting boldface or italicized terms in the margins. As you read, add brief definitions to the terms noted in the margins.

7. Read end-of-chapter summaries and questions. If there is no end-of-chapter summary or list of questions, read the last page of the chapter.[†]

[†]More on developing prior knowledge using the Web on pages 42–45.
[†]You'll be surveying a chapter excerpt on pages 56–58. Note how the survey steps get adapted to the material.

The Four Goals of a Survey

Whatever the length and depth of the survey, it should always give you the following: (1) a general overview of the content covered; (2) a feeling for the writer's style; (3) an idea or sense for what's important; and (4) a sense of the chapter's (or article's) natural breaks or divisions, which you can then use to decide the number and length of your study sessions. While most articles assigned for outside reading can be read and at least generally understood in a single study session, chapter assignments should be divided up so that you read in chunks, completing only ten or so pages in each study session.

Ten Questions to Consider During Your Survey
◆

1. What does the title suggest about the author's emphasis or focus?

2. According to the heading and highlighted terms, what issues or topics will the author address?

3. Are any visual aids included? What do they suggest about the chapter's content and emphasis?

4. Do any chapter sections look especially difficult?

5. Does any of the material look familiar?

6. What method does the author consistently use for emphasis? Does the author favor **boldface** and marginal annotations? Or does she make heavy use of opening questions and boxed information? Textbook authors are likely to favor a particular method of presenting important information. Try to determine the author's preference.

7. How many pages should I plan to complete during each study session?

8. Do I have any background knowledge about the topics or issues addressed in this chapter?

9. Do the headings include any questions I can use to focus my attention while reading?

10. Is there a summary I can use to figure out what's central to the chapter?

The Importance of Reading Flexibility

"A how-to-study program must be individualized to each student's needs."
—Francis P. Robinson

Before moving to the next step in *SQ3R*, it's time to talk about the importance of **reading flexibility**, or the willingness to change reading strategies to match the material. If, for example, flexible readers are studying a textbook chapter on marriage and the family and don't feel that the material is especially difficult, they might abbreviate their survey: They would read just the introduction and the headings while ignoring the pictures and other visual aids. They would probably also increase their reading rate from the average rate of 250 words per minute to a rate more appropriate to familiar material, around 350 words per minute.

But if those same readers were studying a difficult biology chapter, they would make their survey longer and more detailed. They would look at every clue to meaning in the chapter. They might even read the first and last sentence of every paragraph.

Flexible readers feel the same way about taking notes or reviewing. Difficult texts get a separate sheet of detailed notes and numerous reviews. Less difficult texts might get just marginal notes and underlining, followed by one or two reviews.

READING TIP

Be a flexible reader who consciously adapts reading strategies to the text. If, for instance, reading your history and health texts at the same rate of speed leaves you feeling confused, adapt to the more difficult material by slowing down your reading rate.

SUMMING UP THE KEY POINTS

1. Surveying a chapter before you read it should fulfill four objectives: Your survey should (1) give you a general overview of the chapter, (2) give you a feel for the writer's style and method of organization, (3) help you figure out what's important in the chapter, and (4) identify chapter breaks that will help you decide how many pages you want to read in each study session.

2. Flexibility is crucial to surveying and every other aspect of reading. Each new reading assignment calls for a different set of reading strategies that reflect the kind of material you are reading, the author's style, and your own reading purpose.

◆ EXERCISE 1   Surveying for Advance Knowledge

DIRECTIONS   Survey the reading *Cognitive Learning* on pages 56–58, using the steps listed below. Then, based on the information drawn from your survey, answer the questions that follow by circling the correct answer.

1. Read the title and all the topic headings.
2. Read the definitions following all **boldface** terms and anything written in italics.
3. Pose questions based on the title, headings, boldface terms, and visual aids.
4. Read the opening and closing paragraphs.
5. Because this is a fairly detailed and complex textbook excerpt, read the first and last sentence of every paragraph.

Questions Based on Your Survey of Pages 56–58

1. *True* or *False*. Cognitive learning refers to the way our emotions influence our thinking.

2. *True* or *False*. Cognitive maps are inside your head; they aren't held in your hand.

3. *True* or *False*. For some students drawing pictures of what they are reading helps them understand the material.

4. *True* or *False*. The meaning of latent learning can be summed up in the expression "practice makes perfect."

5. *True* or *False*. People don't learn without being rewarded for it.

6. *True* or *False*. "Understanding" is a synonym for cognitive learning.

7. *True* or *False*. "Memorization" is another way of describing rote learning.

8. *True* or *False*. A model is someone who serves as an example.

9. *True* or *False*. We don't learn by observation. We learn only by doing.

10. *True* or *False*. If we pick the right model, there is no limit to what we can accomplish.

✔ **CHECK YOUR UNDERSTANDING**

1. What are the four goals of a survey?

_____

_____

_____

_____

2. What does the term *reading flexibility* mean?

_____

_____

_____

_____

Q: Ask and Answer Questions While Reading

Many students struggle to maintain concentration while reading. This isn't unusual. We all struggle when we try to absorb new and difficult material for an extended length of time.

Still, the problem of failing concentration can be considerably reduced. One way to reduce it is to ask questions while reading. Raising and answering questions during a study session will help you remain mentally active throughout. Using questions to maintain your concentration can also alert you to key points addressed in the chapter. What follows are several methods you can use to develop questions that guide your attention and keep you focused.

Use Opening Lists

Many textbook chapters open with a list of ready-made questions that the author or authors expect to answer in the chapter. Use these lists to focus your reading. Questions based on introductory lists of questions will keep you alert to especially important passages. Here, for instance, are three questions that could open a chapter of a psychology text:

- What Are the Basic Brain Structures and Their Functions?

- How Does the Nervous System Operate?

- How Does the Brain Change?

With questions like these to guide your reading, you are bound to be alert to passages that provide an answer. You are also more likely to stay alert because you won't be reading aimlessly and wondering what you should be looking for.

Some textbook chapters open with a list of specific objectives that tell you what you should know after reading the chapter. When that's the case, use words like *what*, *why*, and *how* to turn the objectives into focus questions. For an illustration, look at the list of objectives from a health textbook titled *An Invitation to Health* and compare the objectives on the list to the questions they evoke:

Objectives	Questions
Define health and wellness	What does it mean to be healthy? What does it mean to be well?
Name three ways in which gender impacts health	How does gender affect health?
Describe the Healthy People 2010–2020 initiative	What is the Healthy People 2010–2020 initiative?
List three to five attributes of credible medical information websites	What are three to five ways medical information websites indicate that they are trustworthy?

However you develop your questions, it pays to jot down an abbreviated version of the questions or objectives on a piece of paper *before* you begin reading. The list will make you more alert to places in the text where questions get answered or objectives are met.

Each time you find a passage that answers a question or meets an objective, put a check mark next to the passage. Then cross the question or objective off your list. That way you will have a record of what's really significant in the chapter.

Taking the time to check off the questions and objectives gives your brain extra time to mull over what you have read. That extra time will help anchor the information in your long-term memory.

Turn Headings into Questions

Most textbook chapters are divided by major and minor headings. **Major headings** introduce the topics or issues addressed within the chapter. **Minor headings** further subdivide topics and issues introduced by the major headings. Here's an example of both:

The major heading introduces the topic under discussion.

It should also make readers pose the question, "What are the causes of violence?"

The minor heading suggests questions such as "Are the two causes always in combination?" "Can someone become violent due to psychological causes without there being a biological one?"

The Causes of Violence

What sets off a violent person? Criminologists have a variety of views on this subject. Some believe that violence is a function of human traits and makeup. Others point to improper socialization and upbringing.

Psychological/Biological Abnormality
On March 13, 1996, an ex-Boy Scout leader named Thomas Hamilton took four high-powered rifles into the primary school of the peaceful Scottish town of Dunblane and slaughtered 16 kindergarten children and their teacher. This horrific crime shocked the British Isles into implementing strict controls on all guns. Bizarre outbursts such as Hamilton's support a link between violence and some sort of mental and biological abnormality. (Siegel, *Criminology*, 10th ed., p. 302.)

Most textbook writers make use of major and minor headings to divide up chapters. You should make use of them too. Use them to help you make predictions about what will follow. Use them as well to create questions that will focus your attention on the text even when the material is new and complex.

Form Questions Based on Key Terms

Authors make it a point to highlight vocabulary words essential to their subject matter. They highlight the words using **boldface**, *italics*, colored ink, and marginal notes. Often they use a combination of visual devices to get your attention.

When you spot those highlighted terms during a survey, use them as the basis for questions. For example, the following words, *mnemonic* and *acronym* appear as marginal notes in a chapter on memory. Together they provide the basis for the two questions listed below.

Mnemonic[†] a device for improving memory

Acronym[†] a word composed of the first letter of a series of words

Questions: 1. What are some examples of mnemonics, and are they useful for all kinds of remembering?

2. What are some examples of acronyms, and how can they aid memory?

Use Whatever's Available as the Basis for Questions

Some textbook chapters won't use headings, icons, or marginal annotations, etc., to highlight key points. This is particularly true of history books. When your textbook doesn't offer many visual clues to significance, be a flexible reader. Use whatever is available as the basis for your questions.

You could, for instance, read the first sentence and last sentence in each paragraph of a chapter section to see if they provide a basis for questions. Note the questions that can be derived from the opening and closing sentences of each paragraph in this excerpt from a history text.

[†]An example of a mnemonic would be the expression "Spring forward and fall back" to remember how to wind your clocks with the change of season.
[†]Some examples of acronyms are ASAP for As Soon As Possible and SCUBA for Self-Contained Underwater Breathing Apparatus.

Mexican-American Activism

How did migrant workers start a movement for social justice?

The national Mexican-American movement for social justice began with migrant farm workers. From 1965 to 1970, labor organizers César Chávez and Dolores Huerta led migrant workers in a strike (*huelga*) against large grape growers in California's San Joaquin Valley.

How did Chávez and the union draw attention to these conditions?

Chávez and the AFL-CIO affiliated United Farm Workers (UFW), drew national attention to the working conditions of migrant laborers, who received as little as 10 cents an hour (the minimum wage in 1965 was $1.25) and were often lodged by employers in squalid housing without running water or indoor toilets. A national consumer boycott of table grapes brought the growers to the bargaining table, and in 1970 the UFW won better wages and working conditions. The union resembled nineteenth century *mutualistas*, or cooperative associations. Its members founded cooperative groceries, a Spanish-language newspaper, and a theater group. (Adapted from Norton et al., *A People and a Nation*, 8th ed., pp. 892–93.)

Do all of these still exist?

César Chávez and Dolores Huerta were central figures in the movement to improve the working conditions of migrant workers.

William James Warren/Science Faction/Getty Images.

SUMMING UP THE KEY POINTS

1. Readers who pose questions are less likely to lose their concentration while reading. They are also more likely to spot the most important passages in a chapter.

2. Questions used to guide your reading can be based on (1) introductory lists of questions and objectives, (2) major and minor headings, (3) key words highlighted in the text, (4) first and last sentences in paragraphs, and (5) whatever is available.

◆ **EXERCISE 2**   **Using Questions to Focus Your Attention**

DIRECTIONS   Survey the following selection. Pose a question or questions in the margins for each heading or underlined sentence. The first two questions are examples of the kinds of questions you might ask.

What is a "sense" of maleness or femaleness?

Does that mean that before the age of three, children don't know if they are male or female?

_____

_____

_____

_____

Gender Identity: Our Sense of Maleness or Femaleness

By the age of three, most children have acquired a firm sense of their gender identity, of being either male or female. But what determines gender identity? The answer is not yet clear. Some research points to biological influences. Investigators suspect that prenatal hormones sculpt the developing brain in ways that influence the later development of gender identity (Reiner & Gearhart, 2004). But research suggests that gender identity may not be fully stamped in at birth. In this research, children who were born with ambiguous[†] genitalia because of inherited birth defects developed a gender identity that was consistent with the gender to which they were assigned and raised accordingly, even when the assigned gender conflicted with their chromosomal (XY or XX) sex (Slijper et al., 1998). All in all, most scientists believe that gender identity arises from a complex interaction of nature (biology) and nurture (rearing influences) (Diamond, 1996).

Whatever the sources of gender identity may be, it is almost always consistent with one's biological sex. But for a few individuals, their gender identity and their biological sex are mismatched. These individuals have the gender identity of one gender but the sexual organs of the other.

_____

†ambiguous: unclear because a choice has not been made.

Transsexualism: A Mismatch of Identity and Biology

People with transsexualism feel trapped in the body of the opposite gender by a mistake of nature. A transsexual man is anatomically a man but has the gender identity of a woman. A transsexual woman is anatomically a woman but possesses a male gender identity. Myths around transsexualism abound.

Transsexual men and women may be repulsed by the sight of their own genitals. Many undergo gender reassignment surgery to surgically alter their genitals to correct what they see as nature's mistake. Gender reassignment surgery transforms the genitalia to a workable likeness of those of the opposite gender. But since it cannot transplant the internal reproductive organs that produce the germ cells—the testes in the man and the ovaries in the woman—reproduction is impossible. Thus, surgery does not change a man into a woman or a woman into a man, if what it means to be a man or a woman depends on having the internal reproductive organs of their respective sex. Nonetheless, gender reassignment surgery generally permits the individual to perform sexual intercourse. Hormonal replacement therapy is used to foster growth of the beard and body hair in female-to-male cases and of the breasts in male-to-female cases. (Adapted from Nevid, *Psychology: Concepts and Applications*, 3rd ed., pp. 406–7.)

Chastity, now known as Chaz, Bono is someone for whom changing genders was worth the physical pain and mental readjustment a sex change requires.

Ron Galella/WireImage/Getty Images.

Barry King/FilmMagic/Getty Images.

✔ CHECK YOUR UNDERSTANDING

1. Why is posing questions while reading important?

_____

_____

2. What are some of the sources readers can use as the basis for questions?

_____

_____

_____

R1: Read in Sections or Chunks

Once you finish your survey and have a sense of what you need to look for, you are ready to start reading. But that doesn't mean you should sit down and read an entire chapter. Instead, assign yourself a specific number of pages to cover during the time you have set aside for study.

Each time you return to the text to read the next group of pages, try to recall what was said in the previous ones. These spaced reviews of the previous material *before* you process what's new will help you remember what you read.

The number of pages you read per session should be determined by (1) how difficult the material is and (2) how much you already know about it. If you don't know anything about the subject under discussion, if the content is complex and the style difficult, consider reading only eight to ten pages per session. Just make sure you plan on at least three or four study sessions to get through the chapter.

Think about reading a whole chapter in one sitting *only* if the material is familiar and the style easy to read.

For Really Difficult Textbook Assignments, Consider the 10/5 Approach

When a textbook assignment is filled with new terms, concepts, and facts, reading can seem like torture. What can help is a variation on the technique productivity gurus like Alan Lakein call *The Swiss Cheese Method*. The principle behind the Swiss Cheese method is to accomplish a large task by completing small pieces of it step by step. The name comes from the idea of poking holes into a cheese until the cheese disappears.

To apply this principle to reading, set a stop watch on your computer or your phone—if you don't have either, use a kitchen timer—for ten minutes. Read during every minute of the ten. No interruptions allowed, so turn off your cell phone.

But when the timer goes off, stop and take five minutes to take a quick stroll from say your desk to the kitchen. While you stroll think about what you've read, summing it up in your mind. You don't necessarily have to be right. All you have to do is to paraphrase, or put into your own words, what you think the author said. The more you read of the chapter, the more the pieces will fall into place, and you may well revise your first thoughts about the author's message. When the five minutes are up—time them too—go back to reading for another ten.

Follow this routine for at least an hour. If you can, push it to an hour and fifteen minutes. Do this every day until you finish the chapter. When you are done, you will be surprised at how much you know, and the process will be much less painful than laboring over a hard-to-read chapter for thirty-minute or hour-long stretches.

Vary Your Assignments to Stay Sharp

If you've set aside an hour and a half to study, vary your assignments so that you aren't spending all your study time on one subject. Changing from assignment to assignment helps concentration and remembering. Each time you switch to new material, your brain will feel refreshed and more alert simply because it's working on something different.

For best results, alternate between related subjects so that one reinforces the other. If you are reading a psychology chapter on the parts and functions of the brain, follow it with a health chapter on injuries and diseases of the brain. If you have set aside an hour and half to study, spend forty-five minutes on each subject. If you set aside two hours, give each subject an hour.

READING TIP

A willingness to re-read is critical to understanding a difficult textbook. But just as important is a willingness to re-read *in a different way*. If a first reading left you confused, do the second reading at a slower rate. You might also try reading aloud. If the text describes a physical event or process, try visualizing. Again be flexible and adapt to the material.

Write While You Read

"I write all over the pages of every book I read. It helps me have a conversation with the author and allows me to keep track of my thinking while I am reading."
—Teacher and blogger, John Howell

If I could personally give every student who reads this book one piece of advice, it would be this: Keep a pen or pencil in hand while you read, and use it—*a lot*. For somewhat familiar material written in an easy-to-absorb style, underline key words and jot brief notes in the margins of pages. With more complicated texts, especially those essential to your college career, do both—take brief marginal notes and make a more detailed set of notes in a separate notebook.

If you are reading a print text, keep a highlighter close by. Use the highlighter for sentences that seem especially significant—for example, ideas that might turn up on exams or prove useful for term papers. Because writing while reading is critical to academic success, you'll hear more on this subject later on in the chapter.

E-Books Are No Exception

If you are using an e-book, it probably allows you to highlight, attach sticky notes, and jot your own notes in pop-up boxes, etc. Use every single one of the features available to you. Maybe even develop your own special system with sticky notes for term paper ideas and note boxes for test questions. Whether print or digital, writing in a book is a way of personalizing the information and making it your own. The more you personalize new information, the better you will understand and remember it.

Writing and the Brain

In addition, more recent research on the brain shows how truly specialized it is. Different parts of the brain respond to different language activities. When you read new material and write about it at the same time, your brain is absorbing the information via two separate pathways, one devoted to reading, the other to writing. The double processing involved in reading and writing about the same passage makes the material in that passage more memorable.

Personal Experience Counts

The more you know about a subject, the more learned your marginal notes are going to be. Take a government and an economics course, and you might be able to jot a note that compares Supply Side and Keynesian solutions[†] to an economic crisis. But initially, college textbooks introduce largely unfamiliar subjects about which you know very little. That doesn't mean, however, that you can't comment on the author's statements in order to deepen your understanding of them. Often, you can compare what the author says to something you know about in your own life, for instance:

This is just like fraternities and sororities where people get mistreated and forever after treasure their membership.

They can't face thinking they went through it for nothing.

In 1959, researchers Elliot Aronson and Judson Mills, published a groundbreaking article titled "Severity of Initiation and Liking for a Group." In it, the two researchers argued "that persons who go through a great deal of trouble or pain to attain something tend to value it more highly than persons who attain the same thing with a minimum of effort." To prove their point, Aronson and Mills described the behavior of 63 college women, who had to take an "embarrassment test" in order to join a discussion group about sexual behavior that had been touted as highly informative. The tests had been designed by the researchers to range from mildly to very embarrassing. Some women, for example, had to listen to descriptions of moderately sexual situations. Others had to listen to four-letter words and stories of an explicitly sexual nature. Whatever the nature of the material, they were told not to show embarrassment. If they did, they wouldn't be allowed to attend the discussion group. Those who passed the test, which many later described as humiliating, were then allowed into the discussion group. What they didn't know was that the discussion group had been designed to be as boring as possible. Yet the women who had suffered the severest humiliation during "testing" were the ones who most strongly insisted the discussions were really interesting.

As the poet and textbook author John Frederick Nims said so correctly, "When a new piece of information is fed into the brain, it is whirled around the circuits until it finds its place with similar things."[†] When you make marginal comments that compare new information to your own personal experiences, you are ensuring that your brain holds on to the new by connecting it to what you already know or have experienced.

[†]The Supply Side school claims tax cuts stimulate the economy, whereas Keynesians would ask that the government create jobs.
[†]John Frederick Nims and David Mason, *Western Wind: An Introduction to Poetry*, 4th ed. (Boston: McGraw-Hill, 1999), p. 18.

Match Your Reading Rate to the Material

"Readers make choices in the kinds of attention they give to texts—from scanning, skimming, and speed reading to deep reading and re-reading."
—Catherine L. Ross, professor, University of Western Ontario

Unless you are reading a very difficult text, where the complexity of the material forces you to maintain a low, phrase-by-phrase reading rate (see the following chart), the speed with which you read should vary. While re-reading the introduction you already surveyed, for instance, you can speed up to 500 or 600 words a minute. You need to slow down, though, when you start a chapter section, reducing your rate to around 250 or 300 words a minute.

With material that is familiar and not too difficult—introductions in textbooks, for instance, are often lists of single sentences rather than paragraphs—your reading rate can be on the boundary between skimming—that is, very fast reading to understand just a few main points—and study reading. If you are reading a chapter on childhood nutrition, for example, and already know much of the information from another course, then keep your reading rate fairly high, between 350 and 400 words a minute. If the text becomes difficult, don't be afraid to slow down and do an analytical, or close, reading, probably at 100 or 150 words a minute.

Reading Rates
◆

Good readers are flexible about reading rate. They vary it to suit the material and their reading purpose.

Reading Strategy	Purpose	Type of Assignment	Rate
Scanning	To locate a specific piece of information	You are searching for a specific fact, statistic, or study.	700 to 1,000 words a minute
Skimming	To get a very general overview of an article or a chapter	You are preparing to read a chapter and previewing it to determine how much time and how many study sessions you will need to master the material.	400 to 800 words a minute
Study Reading	To understand an author's message or follow the plot of a novel or short story	You are reading a detailed but clearly written chapter in preparation for class.	250 to 400 words a minute
Close or Analytical Reading	To understand a very difficult passage or unfamiliar and complex material	You are trying to understand a chapter filled with new material and written in a hard-to-read style.	100 to 250 words a minute

◆ **EXERCISE 3**   **Reviewing What You've Learned**

DIRECTIONS   Fill in the blanks by explaining what each piece of advice introduced in the previous chapter section means. The first one is done for you.

1. Read in sections or chunks.	Don't try to read the whole chapter. Divide it into sections and read a section at a time.
2. When material is difficult, consider the 10/5 approach.	
3. Vary your assignments to stay sharp.	
4. Write while you read.	
5. Match your reading rate to the material.	

SUMMING UP THE KEY POINTS

1. Unless the material is really easy to learn, don't think you have to read entire chapters in one sitting. Break the chapter up into sections with a limited number of pages that you can read in about an hour.

2. Varying your assignments during a study session is a good way to maintain concentration.

3. Whether your textbook is print or digital, write while you read. Writing while reading gives your brain a chance to double-process the new material, making it easier to remember.

4. Vary your reading rate according to the difficulty of the material and your knowledge of the subject. Slow down when a text is difficult and unfamiliar. Speed up when you are dealing with material that is familiar or uncomplicated.

R2: Recall[†] Right After Reading

When an author's words are right in front of us, we usually think we understand them. Yet if we look away from the page and try to recall what we've read, we often discover that our understanding is muddled or incomplete. That's what makes the recall step of *SQ3R* so important. It's a way of monitoring your understanding before going on to the next section of a chapter or an article.

There's another reason why recalling immediately after reading is critical: Most people are inclined to forget new information right after reading it. But with the passage of time, the rate of forgetting slows down, and we forget less as time goes by. That means anything we do to fix newly absorbed information into long-term memory *right after reading*—when the rate of forgetting is highest—improves our chances of remembering it, weeks or even months later.

As always with *SQ3R*, there are different ways to complete this step. The one you choose depends on the kind of material you are reading and the depth of understanding you want to achieve. Here again, flexibility is key. Here are just some of the ways you can fulfill this key step in *SQ3R*.

[†]Francis Robinson used the word *recite*, but he included under that term "mentally reviewing the answer or writing it out," which is another way of saying "recall."

1. Recite the Answers to Your Questions

With material that's not too difficult or too unfamiliar, try mentally reciting answers to the following questions: What topic, or subject, was discussed? What point did the author make about the topic? How did the author illustrate or argue the point? The last question of the three is usually the toughest to answer. If you can think of one illustration or reason after a first reading, you are doing just fine.

You might also consider reciting the answers aloud. That would give your brain an external and internal repetition of key material. The more pathways your brain uses to receive information, the greater your chances of remembering it.

2. Write Out the Answers to Your Questions

Robinson believed that readers were inclined to fool themselves if they only recited answers to their questions. In his opinion, it was too easy to accept a vague and confused answer. Posing questions about the material and writing out the answers was, from Robinson's perspective, a better comprehension check.

3. Make an Informal Outline

Some students panic when they hear the word *outline.* They panic because they think they have to create formal outlines in which every *a* is followed by a *b*, and strict rules dictate how the outline has to be completed. But the outlines you use for the recall step of *SQ3R* don't have to be formal ones. They just have to provide a quick review of the content covered and show the relationship between ideas.

Start your outline by looking only at the heading of the chapter section and asking yourself, "What was the main idea or central message of this section?" Write the heading and your answer down at the top of the page. Then indented underneath the main idea, in your own words, list any reasons, illustrations, studies, facts, or figures that the author used to explain or prove that overall point.

Here to illustrate is a brief textbook excerpt about "Convenience Products" followed by an outline. Read the text first. Then look over the outline to see how it matches up.

Convenience products are goods and services consumers want to purchase frequently, often immediately, and with minimal effort. Milk, bread, and toothpaste are convenience products. Convenience services include 24-hour quick-stop stores, walk-in hair or nail salons, copy shops, and dry cleaners.

Marketers further subdivide the convenience category into impulse items, staples, or emergency services. **Impulse goods and services** are purchased on the spur of the moment—for example, visit a car wash or buy a pack of gum while at the super market register. . . . **Staples** are convenience goods and services consumers constantly replenish to maintain a ready supply: gasoline, shampoo, and dry cleaning are good examples. **Emergency goods and services** are bought in response to unexpected and urgent needs. A snow blower purchased during a snowstorm and a visit to a hospital emergency room to treat a broken ankle are examples. (Adapted from Boone and Kurtz, *Contemporary Marketing*, 15th ed., pp. 348–49.)

Convenience Products: Marketers divide into three categories.
1. impulse buys like grabbing a candy bar when you reach the cash register.
2. staples like gas
3. emergency purchases like batteries during a tornado

Informal outlines are a great way to figure out just how much you have understood of what you've read. They will also serve you well when you want to review for exams. Just make sure to leave plenty of space between the items in your outline so you can add to it during early reviews.

4. Draw Rough Diagrams and Pictures

If you think you are a **visual learner**, that is, you remember what you see even better than what you hear, consider translating words into pictures or diagrams during the recall step of your reading. Then check your drawing against the actual text to see what you've missed.

Just be aware that not every text will easily translate into a picture. If you are reading about the developmental stages of frogs in biology, then a picture might well be worth a thousand words. But if you are trying to remember the meaning of "probable cause"† in criminology, making a drawing will be tough because the definition is more **abstract** (i.e., an idea that can't take visual form), than **concrete** (i.e., something that can be physically seen and touched).

---

†probable cause: refers to the circumstances under which law enforcement can obtain a search warrant.

What follows is a passage about the layers of the earth. It's perfect for the reader-made diagram that follows it.

Four different layers make up the Earth: the inner core, outer core, mantle, and crust. The rocky and brittle crust is the outermost and thinnest layer. In contrast, the thickest part of the Earth's mass is in the mantle, which is composed of iron (Fe), magnesium (Mg), aluminum (Al), silicon (Si), and oxygen (O) silicate compounds. Below the mantle lies the core, composed mostly of iron so hot that it's molten, or so hot that it has turned to liquid. The inner portion of the core, however, is under such intense pressure, it remains solid.

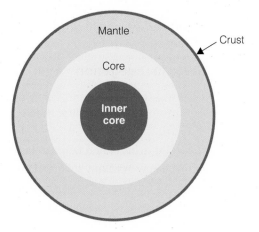

5. Work with a Friend

If you can work with someone who is serious about studying, consider completing assignments in pairs. Read each chapter section at the same time. Then take turns doing the recall. While one person does the recall, the other should look at the chapter section. When the person doing the recall finishes up, the person doing the reading should add anything missed that seemed important.

SUMMING UP THE KEY POINTS

1. Recalling right after reading is important for two reasons. First, it's a way of monitoring your understanding. It tells you how well you have or have not understood what you've read. Completing the recall step in *SQ3R* also slows down the rate of forgetting and increases your chances of remembering what the text actually said.

2. Flexibility is important in choosing the method of recall. In addition to mentally reciting after reading, you should also consider the following: (1) reciting the key points aloud, (2) writing out answers to the questions you came up with during your survey, (3) creating an informal outline, (4) making rough diagrams or drawing pictures, and (5) working with a friend. The method you choose depends on the kind of material you are reading and your understanding of how you learn most easily.

◆ **EXERCISE 4**   **Recalling After Reading**

DIRECTIONS   Read the following excerpt. Then, from memory, fill in the boxes.

Steps in Delegation

The process of **delegation** essentially involves three steps. First, the manager assigns **responsibility**. That is, the manager defines the employee's duty to perform a task. For example, when a manager tells someone reporting to him to prepare a sales report, order additional raw materials, or hire a new assistant, he is assigning responsibility.

Second, the manager must also grant the **authority** necessary to carry out the task. Preparing a sales report may require analyzing previous sales reports, ordering raw material may require negotiations on price and delivery dates, and hiring a new assistant may mean submitting a hiring notice to the human resource department. If these activities are not a formal part of the group member's job, the manager must give her the authority to do them anyway.

Finally, the manager needs to create **accountability**. This suggests that the group member incurs, or takes on, an obligation to carry out the job. If the sales report is never prepared, if the raw materials are not ordered, or if the assistant is never hired, the group member is accountable to her boss for failing to perform the task. Indeed, if the manager is not careful, it is possible for some personnel to lose sight of their major task because they become focused on the wrong objectives. (Adapted from Van Fleet and Peterson, *Contemporary Management*, 2nd ed., pp. 252–53.)

Delegation Process

✔ **CHECK YOUR UNDERSTANDING**

1. What are two reasons why recalling right after reading is useful?

_____

_____

_____

2. What are some of the methods readers can use to recall what they've read after finishing a chapter section?

_____

_____

_____

R3: Review Right After Completing the Assignment

Robinson's suggestion to review right after reading is a good one. But it needs some modification and clarification. Perhaps because he assumed students were also outlining chapters while they read, Robinson allotted only five minutes for review. Actually, you need at least fifteen to make this step productive.

Robinson also didn't always make it clear that the third *R* in his system represented only *the first* of several reviews. Trained as an educational psychologist, Robinson knew full well that *mastery of new material occurs with repeated reviews that extend over time.* He never assumed that the first review would be the reader's last.

The Goal of the First Review: See the Big Picture

The first goal is to understand how the individual parts of the chapter fit together. For example, in a chapter titled "The Professional Sports Business," you would need to determine the author's overall intention or objective. Is the author trying to give you a historical overview of how sports have become more about making money than a celebration of athletic prowess? Or perhaps the chapter focuses on the various elements that make up the business of sports, such as scouts, agents, contracts, owners, trainers, and endorsements.

Once you have the larger chapter objective in mind, it becomes easier to see what each chapter section contributes to that objective.

Pick a Review Method That Suits You and Your Assignment

For some assignments and some readers, outlining is an ideal learning strategy. But that's not always the case. Fortunately, there are other ways to complete a first review. The following are some suggestions.

Draw Diagrams and Charts. If you remember pictures or images more readily than words, you might consider reviewing with diagrams. One popular diagram used for study purposes is called a **concept map**.

With a concept map, you put the overall point of the chapter or article in the middle of the page or top of the page and enclose it in a circle or box. Then using arrows and indentation, you can show how ideas relate to one another. Here, for instance, is a concept map that gives visual form to the ideas and relationships introduced in a chapter about the internment of Japanese Americans during World War II:

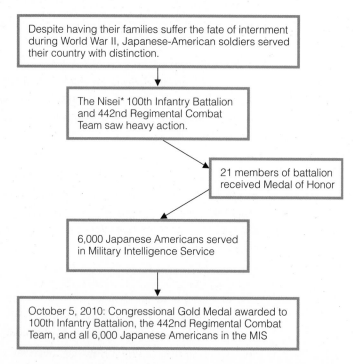

Despite having their families suffer the fate of internment during World War II, Japanese-American soldiers served their country with distinction.

The Nisei* 100th Infantry Battalion and 442nd Regimental Combat Team saw heavy action.

21 members of battalion received Medal of Honor

6,000 Japanese Americans served in Military Intelligence Service

October 5, 2010: Congressional Gold Medal awarded to 100th Infantry Battalion, the 442nd Regimental Combat Team, and all 6,000 Japanese Americans in the MIS

*Nisei: refers to children born of Japanese parents who immigrated to other countries and raised their children in those countries, rather than in Japan.

Don't think, however, that you are restricted to concept maps. If another format suits the text and your purpose, use it. Here, for instance, is part of a chart created for a chapter on disorders of the digestive system. Note how the reader has tried to fill in some of the details about the headings and left question marks under headings about which she recalled little or nothing.

Common Disorders of the Digestive System

stomatitis	hiatal hernia	pyloric stenosis	gastritis	enteritis	peptic ulcers	IBD[†]
inflammation of soft tissue in mouth	stomach protrudes above diaphragm into esophagus opening	?	chronic inflammation of stomach lining	?	lesion in stomach lining, most bacterial caused	Crohn's disease and ?

Look at All the Major Headings. Go through the chapter page by page or screen by screen. Look at each major heading and then look away to see how much you remember about what's included under that heading. Give yourself just a few seconds to respond. If nothing comes to mind at the end of ten or fifteen seconds, mark the chapter or article section for another reading.

While being able to recall the main point introduced under each heading is wonderful, recognizing that you can't recall much of anything is also useful. Your lack of recall tells you that the chapter section needs a second reading.

Work with a Classmate. Here again, think about working with someone in your class. Ask him or her to say the major headings aloud. Then respond by reciting what you remember about each one. Any time you draw a blank or remember very little, your partner should mark the passage for another reading.

Whittle Recall Cues Down to Size

Reviews done right after reading and the follow-up reviews you do for exam preparation have slightly different goals. Your first review should tell you what the chapter covers and how the different parts fit together.

[†]IBD: inflammatory bowel disease.

Are they ordered, for instance, according to sequence in time? Or do they tell you how different parts of the United States related to the same key event? It should also help you determine what you do and don't know about the material you've just finished reading.

However, the reviews you do in preparation for exams should focus on creating **recall cues**, words or phrases that call up the information you have learned. Although you may well start out reviewing with notes or diagrams based on complete sentences—"Gender identity refers to our sense of being male or female" or "Delegation involves three basic steps"—you should end up with notes that include only a few key words and phrases, for example, "gender identity," or "steps in delegation." You can tell you are prepared for exams when just glancing at those key words and phrases triggers the explanations they represent.

SUMMING UP THE KEY POINTS

1. The third *R* in *SQ3R* refers to the review that takes place after a chapter is completed. However, Robinson knew that several reviews over an extended period of time were essential to mastery of new material. He never assumed that one review right after finishing a chapter would be enough.

2. The first goal of a review is to get a sense of how the parts of a chapter connect. Are they all effects of one cause, for instance, or do they describe a progression of events? Like the first step of *SQ3R*, the survey, use the review step to establish a sense of the chapter's general, or overall, goal.

3. Robinson suggested readers should review by looking over their informal outlines, but other methods can be used as well. You can look at all the major headings and then look away to see how much information you recall about each heading. You can make a concept map, which shows the chapter's central point in the center along with the sub-topics or issues used to explain it. Or you can go over the chapter with a classmate who asks you what each major heading contributes to the overall point of the chapter.

Writing and Reading

"Your memory is not a product of what you want to remember or what you try to remember; it's a product of what you think about."
—Daniel T. Willingham, *Why Don't Students Like School*, p. 53.

Whether you are reading a print or digital book, writing while reading will help you understand and remember what you read. When you underline or jot notes in the margin, you analyze the text, trying to decide what's important and what's not. It's the thought involved that deepens your understanding and anchors new facts and ideas in long-term memory.

What follows are suggestions about how you can write and read at the same time. Over the course of several study sessions, try them all to see which ones work best, and which ones are appropriate to specific kinds of texts. Underlining key words, for instance, probably works well with any kind of material from history to science. Diagramming, in contrast, is usually more effective with descriptions of physical events or processes.

Suggestions for Writing While Reading ◆

1. As you do a first reading, underline in pencil key words in selected sentences that you think are essential to the author's explanation.

2. When you do a second reading (or even a third one) for exam reviews, make final decisions about what's essential and what's not. This time, underline in pen.

3. Use boxes, circles, or stars to highlight key names, dates, and events.

4. If you have any personal knowledge about the subject matter, make personal comments in the margin.

Uncle Bob went to Wild West show this summer.

Examples:

Between 1872 and 1878, William "Buffalo Bill" Cody alternated between his career as a scout for the U.S. Cavalry and his starring roles in a series of melodramas popular in the East. By 1882, he had founded the enterprise that brought him even greater fame and shaped the country's view of itself, "Buffalo Bill's Wild West."

5. Use numbers to itemize individual parts of a definition, process, or procedure.

6. Paraphrase, or restate, the author's ideas in your own words.

Examples:

4 parts of emotions:

1. how you feel

2. how body responds

3. thoughts

4. purpose of

<u>Emotions</u> have several <u>components</u>: feelings ①, physiological ② responses ③, cognitions, and goals ④.

7. Use the margins to identify points of view that agree or disagree with the author's.

8. Use the top margin to summarize the contents of the page.

9. Use two different-colored pens, one to underline, another for marginal notes.

Examples:

Marshall Plan Provides Massive Aid

Comp. Howard Zinn on role of Marshall Plan.

The Marshall Plan was a <u>four-year program proposed by U.S. Secretary of State George C. Marshall</u> on June 5, 1947. Its goal was to <u>provide foreign assistance</u> to seventeen western and southern <u>European nations</u> as part of post–World War II reconstruction. Between 1948 and 1951, over <u>$13 billion</u> was <u>dispensed</u> through the Marshall Plan.

10. Whenever you find yourself struggling to understand an author's meaning for more than two or three sentences, mark the passage for a second and slower reading (e.g., *RR, x2, ??*).

11. Use arrows, labels, and abbreviations to make relationships between sentences clear.

12. Double underline, star, or otherwise highlight definitions.

Examples:

If you boil water on a stove, you can see a steamy mist above the kettle, and then higher still the mist seems to disappear into the air. Of course, the water molecules have not been lost.

Step ❶ →   Step ❷

In the pan, water is in the liquid phase, and in the mist above

→   Step ❸   →

the kettle, water exists as tiny droplets. These droplets then

Step ❹

evaporate, and the water vapor mixes with air and becomes

invisible. Air generally contains some water vapor. ****Humidity**

is a measure of the amount of water vapor in air. (Turk and Turk,

Physical Science, p. 410.)

13. Put quotation marks or rectangles around statements you think are particularly significant.

14. Mark a statement or passage you think might be a test question (e.g., *T.Q.*).

15. Use double lines in the margins to identify any statements you think could be the jumping-off point for a paper. Try to comment on the statement in a way that suggests how the paper might be developed.

Examples:

Effect of 1918 Influenza

How lethal was the 1918 influenza? It was twenty-five times

more deadly than ordinary influenzas. This flu killed 2.5

percent of its victims. Normally just one-tenth of 1 percent

of people who get the flu die. And since a fifth of the world's

population got the flu that year, including 28 percent of

Americans, the number of deaths was stunning. So many

died, in fact, that the average lifespan in the United States

fell by twelve years in 1918. If such a plague came today, kill-

ing a similar fraction of the U.S. population, 1.5 million Ameri-

cans would die. (Adapted from Kolata, *Flu,* p. 216.)

T.Q.
Paper: There are signs bird flu could be worse than 1918.

Effect on mortality: average lifespan decreased.

◆ EXERCISE 5   Marking a Text

DIRECTIONS   Read each marked excerpt. Circle the letter of the one that better illustrates the advice given on pages 29–31. Then, in the blanks at the end, explain why you chose one over the other.

a. How Short-Term Memory Works

1   Most psychologists refer to short-term memory as *working memory*, since information held in short-term memory is actively "worked on," or processed, by the brain (Baddeley, 2001; Braver et al., 2001). Working memory is a kind of mental workspace or blackboard for holding information long enough to process it and act on it (Stoltzfus, Hasher, & Zacks, 1996). For example, we engage working memory when we form an image of a person's face and hold it in memory for the second or two it takes the brain to determine whether it is the face of someone we know. We also employ working memory whenever we perform arithmetical operations in our heads or engage in conversation. In a conversation, our working memory allows us to retain memory of sounds long enough to convert, or change, them into recognizable words.

2   In the 1950s, psychologist George Miller performed a series of groundbreaking studies in which he sought to determine the storage capacity of short-term memory. Just how much information can most people retain in short-term memory? The answer, Professor Miller determined, was about seven items, plus or minus two (Kareev, 2000). Miller referred to the limit of seven as the "magical number seven."

3   The magic number seven appears in many forms in human experience, including the "seven ages of man" in Shakespeare's *As You Like It*, the Seven Wonders of the World, the Seven Deadly Sins, and even the seven dwarfs of Disney fame (Logie, 1996). Investigators find that people can normally repeat a maximum of six or seven single-syllable words they have just heard (Hulme et al., 1999). Think about the "magical number seven" in the context of your daily experiences. Telephone numbers are seven-digit numbers, which means you can probably retain a telephone number in short-term memory just long enough to dial it. (Nevid, *Psychology: Concepts and Applications,* 3rd ed., p. 221.)

b. How Short-Term Memory Works

1   Most psychologists refer to short-term memory as *working memory*, since information held in short-term memory is actively "worked on," or processed, by the brain (Baddeley, 2001; Braver et al., 2001). Working memory is a kind of mental workspace or blackboard for

*Form images,
holding in memory
to see if familiar*

EX

holding information long enough to process it and act on it (Stoltzfus, Hasher, & Zacks, 1996). For example, we engage working memory when we form an image of a person's face and hold it in memory for the second or two it takes the brain to determine whether it is the face of someone we know. We also employ working memory whenever we perform arithmetical operations in our heads or engage in conversation. In a conversation, our working memory allows us to retain memory of sounds long enough to convert, or change, them into recognizable words.

T.Q.

2   In the 1950s, psychologist George Miller performed a series of groundbreaking studies in which he sought to determine the storage capacity of short-term memory. Just how much information can most people retain in short-term memory? The answer, Professor Miller determined, was about seven items, plus or minus two (Kareev, 2000). Miller referred to the limit of seven as the "magical number seven."

*Miller says we hold
about 7 items in s.t.
memory.*

3   The magic number seven appears in many forms in human experience, including the "seven ages of man" in Shakespeare's *As You Like It*, the Seven Wonders of the World, the Seven Deadly Sins, and even the seven dwarfs of Disney fame (Logie, 1996). Investigators find that people can normally repeat a maximum of six or seven single-syllable words they have just heard (Hulme et al., 1999). Think about the "magical number seven" in the context of your daily experiences. Telephone numbers are seven-digit numbers, which means you can probably

*Keep phone number
in mind.*

retain a telephone number in short-term memory just long enough to dial it. (Adapted from Nevid, *Psychology: Concepts and Applications*, 3rd ed., p. 221.)

READING TIP Using a variety of page-marking techniques will keep you focused on what's important. Marking pages as you read them will also help you remember what you read.

Putting the Spotlight on Paraphrasing

While you may think of paraphrasing as something you do only when you write papers, paraphrasing, or putting someone else's ideas into your own words, is actually an essential part of reading and note-taking.

When we really want to understand something, we paraphrase, using our words to express the author's ideas.

Think about it. Even if you are just reading instructions for how to put a simple bookcase together, you're going to paraphrase. The directions say "Place board 1 at a right angle to board 2," and you say to yourself, "This board goes on the corner of this one." What you've done is automatically paraphrase, or re-word, the directions to make sure you have understood them.

But paraphrasing while reading isn't just essential to concrete tasks like building a bookshelf. It's critical for reading textbooks as well. Paraphrasing while reading acts as a **comprehension check**. It tells you how well you have understood what you've just read. If you can paraphrase it, you can rest easy. You and the author have made contact. But if you can't, a re-reading is in order.

When the author's words are right in front of your eyes, it's easy to think you've understood their message. But if you can't recap the meaning in your own words, you probably haven't really understood the author's point.

Clearly, you don't want to make that discovery the day before a test. On the contrary, you need to identify passages you don't understand *while* you are reading. That way you can (1) adjust your reading rate and re-read the passage more slowly, (2) mark it for a later re-reading, or (3) ask someone for help understanding the passage.

Equally important, paraphrasing gives your brain a chance to store what you have learned from your reading in long-term memory. As you search your mind for word substitutes that allow you to paraphrase, your brain is re-processing what you have just read. The double processing is a memory booster.

◆ EXERCISE 6   Practice with Paraphrasing

DIRECTIONS   Read the following quotations from famous people. Put each one into your own words. *Note:* Your paraphrase may be longer than the original. All the people quoted are famous writers and that was part of their gift—to say a lot in few words.

EXAMPLE   "Many of the things you can count, don't count. Many of the things you can't count, really count." —Albert Einstein

Concrete things like possessions and money are not what's important. What's

important are more abstract things like happiness, love, and a sense of well-being.

EXPLANATION   The original text has two parts. The first half tells you about the kind of things that don't truly count in life. The second half tells you about the things that do. The goal of the paraphrase, then, is to find the words that would describe each category. "Possessions and money" are good substitutes for things we can count. What about things we can't count? In the paraphrase shown above, the words "happiness, love, and a sense of well-being" were used. But actually, for both sides of the sentence, there were other choices as well. And that's typical for paraphrasing. Each person's paraphrase is likely to be different.

1. "Genius is born, not paid." —Oscar Wilde, writer

   _____

   _____

2. "The cure for boredom is curiosity." —Dorothy Parker, writer

   _____

   _____

3. "A good hockey player plays where the puck is. A great hockey player plays where the puck is going to be." —Wayne Gretzky, hockey player, also known as "The Great One"

   _____

   _____

4. "The most unpardonable sin in society is independence of thought." —Emma Goldman, political activist

   _____

   _____

Pointers on Paraphrasing for Reading

The more you practice paraphrasing, the better you will get at doing it, even when you have more than one sentence to translate into your own words. But your ability to paraphrase will also improve if you know some basic pointers about how to go about it. Some general suggestions are presented here. Later chapters will add more specifics to these instructions. However, these pointers will get you off to a good start.

Be Selective

The goal of paraphrasing for reading is to see how well you have understood the author's overall message. Thus the most you want to paraphrase would be the sentence (or sentences) that express the main idea, or point, and a supporting detail or two. If you can do that, you know that you have not only understood the author's message but can explain it to someone else.

Use Language That Is Equally General or Equally Specific

As you search for words that can replace the author's, try to match the level of generality or specificity in the original language. Don't, for instance, replace the specific word *train* with the more general phrase *mode of transportation*. By the same token, *dog* is a good replacement for *canine*. *Animal* is not.

Accept the Fact That Some Words Don't Translate

Some words have no substitutes. You won't find replacements for names and scientific terminology, so don't waste time looking for them. In a sentence like this one, you can probably find replacements for every word except Freud's name and the name of his book: "Based on new studies of the brain, Sigmund Freud's famous book *The Interpretation of Dreams* is no longer considered relevant to an understanding of what happens when we dream." It follows, then, that a paraphrase would retain those words without any change: "Given what we currently know about the brain, Sigmund Freud's once-important text *The Interpretation of Dreams* is now considered hopelessly out of date."

Feel Free to Change the Order of Ideas

A paraphrase shouldn't alter the original meaning. Sometimes, though, it helps to change the order of ideas, putting, say, the beginning of the original sentence at the end of your paraphrase.

Changing the order of ideas is especially useful if words for the end of a sentence come to mind more readily than those for the beginning. Once you complete the part of the sentence that's easier for you to paraphrase, you may find that the puzzling piece has become clear too. Notice here how the original order has been reversed in the paraphrase:

Original: There are two major changes that occur in the central nervous system.

Paraphrase: Within the central nervous system, two key changes take place.

Look Away from the Text When You Paraphrase

When the original words are right in front of you, it's tempting to use them. But that leads to copying the author's words without really understanding them. When you find a sentence or passage you want to paraphrase, read it carefully. Maybe even read it twice. Underline key words. Then, without looking at the sentence or passage, jot the paraphrase in the margins of your textbook or in your notebook.

Don't Confuse Paraphrasing for Reading Notes with Paraphrasing for Term Papers

Reading paraphrases don't require you to be as complete and grammatically correct in the same way paraphrasing for term papers do. For reading paraphrases all you have to do is re-create, in your own words, a bare bones version of the main idea or key point. For an illustration, here are some original statements followed by reading and writing paraphrases.

Original	In the nineteenth century, baseball emerged as the most popular new urban sport.
Reading Paraphrase	19th century baseball big in cities.
Writing Paraphrase	Baseball became a favorite urban sport in the nineteenth century.

Original	The Antarctic seals, however, after almost becoming extinct, have made an astonishing comeback, and the population is now rapidly increasing.
Reading Paraphrase	After almost dying out, Antarctic seals make big comeback.
Writing Paraphrase	Once almost extinct, Antarctic seals are rebounding and their numbers are increasing.
Original	Although much of the behavior of lower animals appears to be regulated by instincts, this is not true of human behavior.
Reading Paraphrase	Instinct doesn't control our behavior like in animals.
Writing Paraphrase	Instinct regulates almost all behavior among lower animals, but it does not have the same control over human actions.
Original	For a period of about seventy-five years (1765–1840), the Gothic novel, an early relative of the modern horror story, was popular throughout Europe.
Reading Paraphrase	1765–1840, Gothic horror novels big sellers.
Writing Paraphrase	Between 1765 and 1840, the ancestor of the modern-day horror story, the Gothic novel, was widely read throughout Europe.

SUMMING UP THE KEY POINTS

1. Paraphrase to check your understanding. But paraphrase selectively. Pick out a few sentences to paraphrase rather than huge chunks of text.

2. If a paraphrase for an entire sentence doesn't come to you immediately, try paraphrasing in pieces. Paraphrase one half of the sentence and then the other. Or else, paraphrase the parts of the sentence enclosed in commas.

3. Look away from the text while you paraphrase so that you are not tempted to copy the original.

4. Feel free to change the order of ideas and words as long as you don't change the meaning.

5. In choosing words to replace the original ones, come up with words that are equally specific rather than being more general.

6. Remember, names, titles, and many terms have no replacements. Thus they can be used in your paraphrase.

◆ **EXERCISE 7**   **Picking the Better Paraphrase**

DIRECTIONS   Circle the letter of the better paraphrase. Then explain what's wrong with the one you didn't choose.

Original   **EXAMPLE**   When we are in our twenties, we are confronted with the question of how to take hold in the adult world. (Adapted from Gail Sheehy, *Passages*, p. 25.)

Paraphrase   a. As we age, we have to learn how to function as adults.

b. Once we reach our twenties, we have to learn how to function as adults.

EXPLANATION   The opening words in the original text were quite specific about the time frame. "When we are in our twenties. . ." Thus paraphrase *a* is incorrect. It makes the time frame, "As we age," too general. Sentence *b* is the better paraphrase because it keeps the opening phrase specific.

Original   1. Although they must be painted in a very short time, frescos, i.e., paintings done in plaster, will last a very long time—that is their great advantage. (Adapted from Adam Goodheart, *Civilization*, p. 100.)

Paraphrase   a. The great advantage of frescos, or paintings in plaster, is that they last forever, despite the fact that they take only minutes to produce.

b. The great advantage of frescos, or paintings done in plaster, is how long they last, despite their being created fairly quickly.

The ancient Egyptians were already painting frescos on the walls of their temples.

John Copland/Shutterstock.com.

Explanation _____

_____

_____

Original 2. The processes to which a dead body may be subjected are, to some extent, restricted by law.

Paraphrase a. The law places some restrictions on the handling of dead bodies.

b. The law restricts all handling of dead bodies that are being processed for burial.

Explanation _____

_____

_____

Original 3. When Ulysses S. Grant and Robert E. Lee met in the parlor of a modest house at Appomattox Court House, Virginia, on April 9, 1865, to work out the terms for the surrender of Lee's Army of Northern Virginia, a great chapter in American life came to a close, and a great new chapter began. (Bruce Catton, *Grant and Lee: A Study in Contrasts. The American Story*, p. 56.)

Paraphrase a. An important chapter in life closed when Ulysses S. Grant and Robert E. Lee met in Virginia in 1865, while a brand new and more promising chapter got started.

b. One chapter opened and another one closed when Ulysses S. Grant and Robert E. Lee met at Appomattox Court House in Virginia to determine the conditions under which Lee's Army of North Virginia would admit defeat.

Explanation _____

_____

_____

Original 4. Psychologists try to diagnose chronic boredom with questionnaires: the Boredom Proneness Scale, for instance, was developed in 1986 and asks subjects twenty-eight separate questions about boredom.

Paraphrase a. Psychology researchers use questions to measure chronic boredom. The Boredom Proneness Scale, for example, tests how consistently bored people are by asking twenty-eight different questions.

b. The Boredom Proneness Scale is the major test psychologists use to determine the number of years people have been experiencing intense and constant boredom.

Explanation _____

_____

_____

✔ CHECK YOUR UNDERSTANDING

1. Why should you paraphrase while reading?

_____

_____

2. Should you try to paraphrase everything you read? Please explain.

_____

_____

3. What should you do if the paraphrase for a key sentence doesn't occur to you immediately?

_____

_____

4. When you paraphrase, can you change the order of ideas? Please explain.

_____

_____

5. When you paraphrase, is it acceptable to make the words you use more general than the original ones? Please explain.

_____

_____

 ## Mining the Web for Background Knowledge

Around 1970, reading researchers began focusing on the relationship between background knowledge and comprehension. Almost unanimously they came to one conclusion: The more readers know about a subject *before* they begin reading, the more their comprehension improves.

In the 1970s, though, student readers couldn't really put this insight into practice. It would have required too much time searching for sources. Fortunately the arrival of the Internet and the World Wide Web has changed all that.

The Web Makes a Difference

Today, if you survey a textbook chapter and think, "Oh no, this reads as if it were written in a foreign language, that's how little I know about the subject," you can turn to the Web, a huge network of computerized documents linked together in cyberspace. The Web has information on just about any topic you can think of. With the Web to assist you, it is possible to develop some basic background knowledge about whatever subject you are studying, and you can do it in minutes.

Build Background Knowledge Before Reading

You can add a Web step to your survey by quickly jotting down some headings that describe unfamiliar people or events. Say, for instance, in a chapter titled *Early American Reformers*, you spotted the name Dorothea Dix and thought to yourself, Who's she?

You can find out in less than a minute by typing her name into a search engine box. Within seconds the screen will show you a list of websites, any one of which will tell you that Dorothea Dix was an activist who fought to protect the rights of the poor and the mentally ill.

Your Timing Matters

It's fine to look up names and events while you read as well. If that works for you, wonderful. But be careful. It's easy to get distracted and start aimlessly browsing the Web *while* you are supposed to be reading your textbook. If you find that you are easily distracted when you do a Web search, then make it a point to look up unfamiliar names, events, and terms *before* you actually settle down to start reading.

Be a Savvy Searcher

Web searches are a great way to quickly build background knowledge. But they can also waste time as you sift through lists of irrelevant, or unrelated, websites. To avoid that pitfall, keep the following pointers in mind.

Pointers on Choosing a Website
◆

1. **Give your search term a sharp focus.** Make your search term state, as precisely as possible, what you are looking for. If, for instance, you are trying to find out more about the Battle of Saratoga in the Revolutionary War and the heading of your chapter section reads, "Saratoga—A Watershed," don't use the heading. The word *watershed* is going to make the search too **general**, or broad in meaning. You will end up sifting through websites about water drainage.

   Instead, make your search term more **specific**, or restricted in meaning. Use, for instance, the search term "Battle of Saratoga." That will get you a much more relevant list of websites. It will also eliminate all references to bodies of water. Overall, making your search term a phrase rather than a single word is likely to improve your search results.

2. **Be selective.** Whatever you do, don't just start at the top of the list that comes up on the screen and work your way down. Instead, give the list a quick once-over to get a sense of which sites might be most appropriate to your purposes. Don't make the mistake of thinking that the order of the sites represents their quality. For the most part it doesn't. The first website on the list that comes up on the screen is not necessarily the best. So evaluate the websites before hitting any Web links.

3. **Check for relevance.** Look for references to words used in your search term. Keep an eye open, too, for references to people and events related to your chapter assignment. Search engines introduce each link with a title, description, and Web address. The most relevant links will usually include at least one or two words from your original search term. The least relevant won't contain any words from your search term or your chapter assignment.

4. **Review the language.** If the website description is hard to read, skip it altogether. The website probably won't be easier to understand.

5. **Stay focused on your topic.** Avoid websites that mention your search term as a sub-topic of some larger, more general discussion. If you are researching the role José Martí played in winning Cuba's independence from Spain, don't get sidetracked by a site that mentions his name as one of several Latin American poets. Martí was a poet. But his poetry is not your focus. You want to learn about his role as a revolutionary.

6. **Skip sites referring to documents, conference proceedings, addresses, interviews, and journal articles.** These will probably be too limited in scope to enlarge your general background knowledge adequately. Hold off clicking on websites identified as outlines or timelines. These kinds of sites work better for later reviews. Because outlines and timelines reduce information to the bare minimum, they are usually too abbreviated to be valuable as pre-reading preparation.

7. **Ignore sponsored sites or sites selling products.** Sponsored sites weren't just found by the Web crawler searching the Web. Someone paid a fee to make them come up in response to a particular set of search terms. They are likely to be **biased**, or inclined to show favoritism. With Google, sponsored sites generally appear on the right-hand side of the screen and at the very top. But they can also make their way into the list of sites compiled randomly, or without plan, by the Web crawler. If a site seems to be selling products of any kind, don't use it for background knowledge.

8. **Use any shortcuts that let you view the website before hitting the link.** If there's a magnifying glass to the right of the website description, hit that icon. You'll get a brief snapshot of the opening Web page. If the snapshot shows a long piece of text with few paragraph breaks or pictures, pick another site to preview. Your goal is to get as much information as quickly as you possibly can. Stay away from sites that are still putting Word files on the Web without making them appropriate for Web reading.

READING TIP

If the chapter you are ready to read has an unfamiliar name or date in the heading, do a quick Web search for background knowledge before you start to read.

◆ **EXERCISE 8**   Searching the Web

DIRECTIONS   Read the description of the search goal. Then look over the accompanying list of websites that came up in response to the search term "sentencing circles," a heading drawn from a criminology textbook. Answer the questions that follow.

Search Goal: The purpose of the search is to get a clear sense of what "sentencing circles" are and how they are used in the U.S. justice system.

| Search | Images | Maps | Play | YouTube | News | Gmail | Documents | Calendar | More ▾ |

Google   Sentencing Circles   [🔍]   [Sign in]

Advanced search

Web   About 1,070,000 results (0.17 seconds)

[1] **Sentencing Circles** | National Institute of Justice [+1] 🔍
www.nij.gov/topics/courts/restorative.../**sentencing**-cricles.htm - Cached
Dec 5, 2007 – A **sentencing circle** is a community-directed process, conducted
in partnership with the criminal justice system, to develop consensus on an ...

[2] Restorative Justice: **Sentencing Circles** [+1] 🔍
www.november.org/razorwire/rzold/13/1310.html - Cached
"The **Sentencing Circle** concept originated in the Yukon Territory of Canada, and
is based on ancient tribal traditions. Barry Stuart, a Yukon Circuit Judge, ...

[3] **Sentencing Circles**: What are they and how do they work? - Posted [+1] 🔍
network.nationalpost.com/.../**sentencing-circles**-what-are-the... - Canada
- Cached
Feb 27, 2009 – A: **Sentencing circles** were introduced nearly two decades ago
in a bid to ... A **sentencing circle** held last month for Christopher Pauchay, ...

[4] **Circle Sentencing**: Part of the Restorative Justice Continuum [+1] 🔍
www.lirp.org/article_detail.php?article_id=NDQ3/ - Cached
Aug 9, 2002 – Heino Lilles, Territorial Judge, Whitehorse, Canada, discusses his
experiences as a judge working with **circle sentencing**: a restorative ...

[5] **Sentencing Circles** for Aboriginal Offenders in Canada [+1] 🔍
www.lirp.org/library/mn02/mn02_spiteri.html - Cached
It is one of these initiatives, circle sentencing, which is the focus of ...

[6] Restorative Justice - Wikipedia, the free encyclopedia [+1] 🔍
en.wikipedia.org/wiki/Restorative_justice - Cached
Jump to **Sentencing circles**: **Sentencing circles** (sometimes called
peacemaking circles) use traditional circle ritual and structure to involve all ...

[7] **[PDF]** **Sentencing Circles**   [+1] 🔍
www.courts.ca.gov/documents/**SentencingCircles**.pdf
File Format: PDF/Adobe Acrobat - Quick View
A **sentencing circle** is a community-directed process, conducted in
partnership with the ... Sentencing circles — sometimes called peacemaking
circles — ...

[8] **[PDF]** **SENTENCING CIRCLES** FOR ABORIGINAL OFFENDERS IN CANADA:
FURTHERING ... [+1] 🔍
citeseerx.ist.psu.edu/viewdoc/download?doi=10.1.1.135.4245...
File Format: PDF/Adobe Acrobat
by M Spiteri - 2001 - Cited by 2 - Related articles
justice initiatives, such as **sentencing circles**, are operating within the Western
..... **sentencing circles**). As of yet, there have only been a handful of ...

The word "circles" is misspelled in the URL for site 1. This is how it appeared on the original
Google screen. It is not a typo.

1. Look over the first three websites on the list. Of those three, which one seems most appropriate to the search purpose? _____ Please explain your choice.

_____

_____

_____

_____

_____

2. If none of the first three sites got you the information you needed, would you try site 4? _____ Please explain.

_____

_____

3. A savvy Web searcher probably would not even bother with site 5. Why is that?

_____

_____

4. Do you think the Wikipedia site, number 6, would be a good first choice to find out, as quickly as possible, what sentencing circles are and how they are used in the United States? _____ Please explain.

_____

_____

_____

_____

5. In your own words, what is a sentencing circle and how is it used?

_____

_____

_____

_____

_____

Evaluating Websites

Once you zero in on the websites to look at, you'll still need to evaluate each site individually. The following suggestions will help you decide if you have made the right choice or need to keep looking.

"On the Internet, nobody knows you're a dog."

Know Who's Supplying the Information

If you find a site that seems to have good information, but it isn't managed by an educational institution (look for ".edu" at the end of the Web address) or linked to a traditional news source (for instance, the Public Broadcasting Service or the *New York Times*), look for a link that says *About Us*, *About the Author*, *Biography*, or *Home*. If you can't find any indication of who's responsible for keeping the material on the website accurate and up-to-date, go back to your original list. You need to know the source of the information you are getting in order to decide if it's credible, or trustworthy.

Look for Sources

Some information—like the dates of the American Civil War or the fate of the *Titanic*— is so widely known that **documentation**, or the citing of sources used, isn't necessary. However, as soon as a writer, on the Web or anywhere else, starts judging or evaluating people and events—"The Civil War was more about economic interests than it was about the abolition of slavery"; "Had the *Titanic* been built with better materials, it never would have sunk"—then you need to see some sources. The only time this isn't absolutely necessary is if the person is such a well-known expert on the topic, it's highly unlikely he or she would be making unsupported claims.

If, for instance, the economist Paul Krugman mentions in his blog that Congress raised the debt limit seven times under George W. Bush and doesn't cite a source, you can probably still trust that Krugman isn't passing on inaccurate information.[†] He is, after all, one of the most well-known and respected economists in the United States.

However, if a Web writer who is not a well-known expert expresses an opinion and cites facts to support that opinion but doesn't cite sources *or* credentials, then you probably need to use a different website for gathering background knowledge.

Don't Absorb the Opinions with the Facts

Using words that have strong, positive or negative **connotations**, or associations, writers can weave opinions into statements that might seem like **facts** but aren't. In other words, the statements haven't been and cannot be **verified**, or proven true, by reference to outside sources, which is the hallmark of factual information. Statements that cannot be

---

[†]In fact, Krugman did make this claim, and it was correct.

verified are a matter of **opinion**, or personal preference, and can vary from person to person.

Here, for instance, is one writer's negative take on Hugo Chávez, the president of Venezuela: "Hugo Chávez masquerades as a democratic leader but behaves like a dictator." Compare that statement to this one, which **implies**, or suggests, a positive judgment: "Relieved that he had survived cancer surgery, the people of Venezuela celebrated the return of Hugo Chávez to power." Both statements are more opinion than fact, and you need to be aware of that, rather than taking in the opinions with the information.

If the website you choose to use for background knowledge turns out to be heavy with connotative language like the previous examples, you have two choices. You can simply hit another link on the list. Or—and this is my preference—you can read what the author says and then look at another site on the same topic to see if the language or opinions differ. That approach will probably give you a deeper understanding of the topic, even though it's going to take a bit more time.

Be Aware That Photos Can Convey a Bias

Sometimes **bias**, or prejudice for or against someone or something, is conveyed through photos even more than words. For instance, a website that recounts the controversial trial of Julius and Ethel Rosenberg, a couple executed for spying in the fifties, may reveal a hidden bias in the photographs used. Pictures of the couple's courtship, wedding, and two small sons may have been selected to favorably influence your impression of the pair, who some people believe, to this day, were railroaded into the electric chair.

If that's the only site you use to get background knowledge about this controversial case, you might end up sharing the bias expressed in the pictures, and you don't want to do that until you can be sure you have formed your own opinion, rather than unthinkingly absorbing someone else's.

Don't Ignore YouTube

In some ways, YouTube has a reputation it doesn't completely deserve. Many people think of it as the site to visit for videos about a goose scaring off a Doberman or a cat romancing a pig. But YouTube offers much more than crazy pet antics. Do you need to understand the meanings of the two numbers you get when the doctor takes your blood pressure? Do you want to hear the Gettysburg Address? Or maybe you want to see a dramatization of the Poe short story you are reading for American Literature class. You can find all this and more on YouTube, so do not rule it out, *especially* when you are in need of background knowledge. It's a fabulous resource.

SUMMING UP THE KEY POINTS

1. The more background knowledge you have about a textbook topic before you begin reading, the easier it will be for you to understand and remember the material.

2. The Web is an excellent source of background knowledge. Just make sure you use a search term specific enough to generate a list of websites related to your topic. Usually that means a phrase rather than a single word.

3. Once you get a list of websites on the screen, be selective about which ones you actually look at. Check the website descriptions to be sure the site is relevant to your search purpose.

4. Don't assume that the top spot on a list of websites provided by a search engine is an indication of the site's quality. It is not.

5. If the website you have chosen uses emotionally charged language, you should switch to a different site. Even better, compare two (or three) different sites on the same topic.

6. When your goal is building up background knowledge, You-Tube is a better resource than you might think.

◆ **EXERCISE 9**   **Using the Web for Background Knowledge**

DIRECTIONS   Answer the questions by filling in the blanks or circling the correct response.

1. What's the point of using the Web before or during reading?

    _____

    _____

2. The letters *edu* indicate that a website is affiliated with, or connected to,

    _____ .

3. If you are using a personal website for background knowledge, what do you need to look for?

    _____

4. If you are searching the Web *while* you read, what should you be cautious about?

_____

5. During World War II, there was a resistance organization in Germany made up of teenagers who fought the Nazis until the entire group of young people was rounded up and executed. The group was called the "White Rose." Imagine that you are looking for more information about this organization. Would the search term "White Rose" be a good one? After circling your answer, please explain it.

   Yes or *No*. Please explain.

_____

_____

6. If this were the heading in a chapter you were assigned—"The Chesapeake Bay—an Estuary[†] in Trouble" (from *Living in the Environment*)—you should search the Web using as your search term

   a. the heading.

   b. the phrase "Chesapeake Bay."

   c. the phrase "estuaries in trouble."

   Please explain your answer.

_____

_____

7. When a list of websites comes up in response to your search term, read the description to see if it contains _____

_____.

8. Imagine that you were looking for background information on President Franklin Delano Roosevelt and you landed on a website

-----

[†]Estuary: a partially enclosed body of water along a coastline.

where you found the following description. Would this be a good site to use for background knowledge? Please circle your answer. Then explain your reasoning.

> Franklin Delano Roosevelt held office during a time of financial crisis and economic instability: the Great Depression of the 1930s. Roosevelt, however, rose to the occasion. Gathering around him some of the finest minds in the country, known as "Roosevelt's brain trust," the president introduced a radical economic program called the "New Deal." At the heart of the New Deal was Roosevelt's willingness to intervene in the free market through government funding of programs that would create jobs and, at the same time, improve the goods and services available to U.S. citizens. The Works Progress Administration (WPA) was the largest federal agency in the government's program of economic relief. It provided close to 8 million jobs. The WPA affected almost every section of the country and was responsible for the building of much-needed bridges and roads still in use today. More than any president before or since, Roosevelt successfully used the government to enact essential social and political reforms.

Yes or *No*. Please explain.

_____

_____

9. What about this site? Do you think it could be useful for background knowledge about another president, Andrew Jackson (1829–1837), and his role in what's come to be called "The Trail of Tears"?

> President Andrew Jackson has been justly criticized for forcing Native Americans to walk the "Trail of Tears," which pushed Indian tribes off of their lands and relocated them to lands that white settlers did not want. Many Indians died on the almost thousand-mile walk, and the "Trail of Tears" represents a truly shameful chapter in America's history. But it's also true that Jackson's reasons for being a proponent of what was called "Indian Removal" are often inaccurately described.
>
> Jackson was not an Indian-hater. He had fought in wars against the Indians and had a military man's respect for their skills as warriors. The fact that he adopted an Indian child and cared for him also

provides evidence for a more complex view of his character. If it had been up to Jackson, he would have sent the child to West Point, but West Point would not accept someone of Native-American heritage.

Jackson was, however, a man of his time. He lived in an era when white superiority was simply assumed. If white settlers needed more land, then Jackson, like many other Americans, believed that the Indians had to leave theirs and make room for white "civilization." No one with any sense of justice could defend Jackson's actions. Still, his motives and attitudes toward the Indians are often inaccurately represented as his personal failing rather than a reflection of the times in which he lived. (Source of this interpretation of Jackson's behavior: http://histclo.com/pres/lnd19/jackson.html.)

Yes or *No*. Please explain.

_____

_____

_____

10. *True* or *False*. When you are searching for background knowledge, it doesn't pay to waste time looking at the photos on websites. Please explain.

_____

_____

✔ CHECK YOUR UNDERSTANDING

1. What role can the Web play in helping you complete your reading assignments?

_____

_____

2. When using a search term, why is it better to use a phrase instead of a single word?

_____

_____

3. Why wouldn't a personal blog be the best place to look when you are trying to gain background knowledge about topics in a textbook assignment?

_____

_____

_____

_____

4. When a list of websites comes up in response to your search term, should you start at the top and look at each website until you find one that is useful? Please explain.

_____

_____

DIGGING DEEPER Cognitive Learning

Looking Ahead This reading, from a psychology text by Dennis Coon and John Mitterer, defines and illustrates cognitive learning. It describes in detail various ways we can go about mastering new information and skills.

Getting Focused Based on your survey, you already know that this reading illustrates different types of cognitive learning. As you read, jot definitions and examples for each kind of learning.

1 There is no doubt that human learning includes a large *cognitive* component, or mental dimension. As humans, we are greatly affected by information, expectations, perceptions, mental images, and the like.

2 Loosely speaking, cognitive learning refers to understanding, knowing, anticipating, or otherwise making use of information-rich higher mental processes. Cognitive learning extends into the realm of memory, thinking, problem solving, and language.

Cognitive Maps

3 How do you navigate around the town you live in? Have you simply learned to make a series of right and left turns to get from one point to another? More likely, you have an overall mental picture of how the town is laid out. This cognitive map acts as a guide even when you must detour or take a new route.

4 A cognitive map is an internal representation of an area, such as a maze, city, or campus. Even the lowly rat—not exactly a mental giant— learns where food is found in a maze, not just which turn to make to reach the food. If you have ever learned your way through some of the levels of video games, you will have a good idea of what a cognitive map is. In a sense, cognitive maps also apply to other kinds of knowledge. For instance, it could be said that you develop a "map" of psychology or history, when you read a textbook in one of these disciplines. That's why students sometimes find it helpful to draw diagrams of how they envision concepts fitting together.

Latent Learning

5 Cognitive learning is also revealed by latent (hidden) learning. **Latent learning** occurs without obvious reinforcement and remains hidden until the right situation turns up to reveal what's been learned. Here's

an example from a classic animal study. Two groups of rats were allowed to explore a maze. The animals in one group found food at the end of the maze. Soon, they learned to rapidly make their way through the maze when released. Rats in the second group were unrewarded and showed no signs of learning. But later, when the "uneducated" rats were given food, they ran the maze as quickly as the rewarded group. Although there was no outward sign of it, the unrewarded animals had learned their way around the maze. Their learning, therefore, remained latent at first.

6   *How did they learn if there was no reinforcement?* Just satisfying curiosity can be enough to reward learning. In humans, latent learning is related to higher-level abilities, such as anticipating future reward. For example, if you give an attractive classmate a ride home, you may make mental notes about how to get to his or her house, even if a date is only a remote future possibility.

Discovery Learning

7   Much of what is meant by cognitive learning is summarized by the word "understanding." Each of us has at times learned ideas by **rote** (mechanical representation and memorization). Although rote learning can be efficient, many psychologists believe that learning is more lasting and flexible when people discover facts and principles on their own. In discovery learning, skills are gained by insight and understanding instead of by rote.

8   *As long as learning occurs, what difference does it make if it is by discovery or by rote?* Here's the difference. Two groups of students were taught to calculate the area of a parallelogram[†] by multiplying the height by the length of the base. Some were also encouraged to discover on their own that a "piece" of the parallelogram could be "moved" to create a rectangle. Later, based on that information, members of this group were able to solve unusual problems in which the height x base formula did not work. The students who simply memorized the formula, however, were unable to solve the unusual problems.

9   When possible, people should try to discover their own strategies and solutions during learning. However, this doesn't mean that students are supposed to stumble around and rediscover established principles of English, math, physics, and chemistry. The best teaching strategies are based on *guided discovery*, in which students are given enough

---

[†]parallelogram: A four-sided flat shape where the sides are equal in length and parallel, having the same distance continuously between them.

freedom to actively think about problems, and enough guidance so that they gain useful knowledge.

Modeling—Do as I Do, Not as I Say

10 Many skills are learned by what Albert Bandura called *observational learning* or *modeling*. Watching and imitating the actions of another person or noting the consequence of the person's actions can lead to **observational learning**. We humans share the capacity for observational learning with many mammals. The value of learning by observation is obvious: Imagine trying to tell someone how to tie a shoe, do a dance step, or play a guitar. Bandura believes that anything that can be learned from direct experience can be learned by observation. Often, this allows a person to skip the tedious trial-and-error stage of learning.

11 **Observational Learning.** *It seems obvious that we learn by observation, but how does it work?* By observing a model (someone who serves as an example), a person may (1) learn new responses, (2) learn to carry out or avoid previously learned responses, or (3) learn a general rule that can be applied to various situations.

12   For observational learning to occur, several things must take place. First the learner must *pay attention* to the model and *remember* what was done. Next the learner must be able to reproduce the modeled behavior. Finally, once a new response based on observation is attempted, normal reinforcement or feedback determines whether the behavior being observed will be correctly repeated thereafter. A word of caution, though, is in order when it comes to observational learning: Sometimes learning is a matter of practice, but it may be that the learner will never be able to perform the behavior at the highest level. We may admire the feats of world-class gymnasts, but most of us could never reproduce them, no matter how much we practiced. (Adapted from Dennis Coon and John O. Mitterer, *Introduction to Psychology: Gateways to Mind and Behavior*, 12th ed., pp. 241–44. © Cengage Learning.)

Sharpening Your Skills

DIRECTIONS   Answer the following questions by filling in the blanks or circling the letter of the correct response.

1. If someone brings up cognitive skills, what kinds of skills are they talking about?

2. Which one of the following would not involve much cognitive learning?

   a. learning from a textbook

   b. mastering a new language

   c. reviewing for an exam

   d. dreaming during sleep

3. Why do some students make it a point to diagram what they read?

   _____

4. In paragraph 5, what does the rat experiment illustrate?

   _____

   _____

5. What are two causes of latent learning?

   _____

6. What's the benefit of discovery learning?

   _____

   _____

7. How does the experiment with the parallelogram illustrate that benefit?

   _____

   _____

8. What's the first rule that has to be followed for observational learning to take place?

   _____

9. If you told Albert Bandura that you wanted to learn how to build a bookcase, he would probably tell you to

   a. read a book about household carpentry.

   b. buy some wood, get some tools, and follow your instincts.

   c. get a friend to show you how to make one.

10. What's a favorite device the authors of this selection used to focus readers' attention on important points?

   _____

Share Your Thoughts If someone asked you, what motivates you to learn. How would you respond?

Building Word Power

IN THIS CHAPTER, YOU WILL LEARN

- how a word's context, or setting, can help you develop a definition.

- how a knowledge of word parts can help you define an unfamiliar word.

- how to recognize specialized vocabulary words in textbooks.

- how context can change word meaning.

- how to choose a dictionary definition by matching meaning to context.

- when to use a print or an online dictionary.

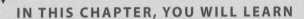

"Words and eggs must be handled with care."

—Poet Anne Sexton

Enlarge your vocabulary while sharpening your comprehension skills and you'll be amazed at your increased ability to understand and remember what you read. As Wilfred Funk, one of the great dictionary makers of all time, aptly expressed it, "The more words you know, the more clearly and powerfully you will think…the more ideas you will invite into your mind."

Making the Meanings "Automatic"

The pages that follow are going to give you numerous strategies for improving your reading vocabulary.[†] However, as you learn those techniques, keep in mind the ultimate, or final, goal of vocabulary work:

[†]Reading vocabulary includes all the words you know on sight when you read, but you may or may not use those same words when you write. The word *cognition*, for instance, refers to the mental processes you engage in to understand something. To read psychology textbooks, you have to know the word, but you may never use it in your writing.

to develop **automatic word recognition**. That means seeing the word and knowing its meaning, automatically, without having to consciously think about it.

Learning researchers call this *automaticity*. That's a fancy way of saying your grasp of word and meaning is so firmly embedded in your memory that you don't have to mentally search for a definition. It's just there.

Understanding words at this automatic level is like driving a car for a long time. You have practiced your driving skills to such a degree that, after a certain point, they feel like a natural instinct rather than a learned activity.

But like driving, having word meanings automatically at your disposal doesn't come without practice. You'll need to do several reviews to develop that level of word recognition.

Active Reviews and Memory Pegs

As soon as you get ten new words together, write them in a notebook or on flash cards.[†] On a regular basis, actively review both words and meanings. That means look at the word first and then try to come up with the meaning. If you can't recall the meaning from memory, make up a memory peg that will help you in later reviews.

Memory pegs are connections you make between what you already know and what you are trying to learn. When it comes to words, memory pegs can take many different forms. Here are just a few to get you started:

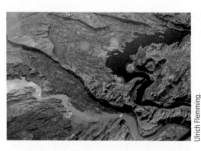

Ulrich Flemming.

This aerial photo shows the striking topography of southern Utah.

Topography refers to the physical appearance of an area or region, particularly the elevations or heights.

Memory Peg: A *top*ography map shows you what's on *top* of the land like trees, bushes, rocks, and mountains.

[†]I'd vote for online flash cards, where you won't be tempted to turn the card over and look at the definition. You won't get the definition until you get to another screen.

Depiction refers to a representation of something, for instance, in a drawing, painting, or sculpture.

Memory Peg: A de*pict*ion is a *pict*ure of something.

Alleviate means to improve, reduce, or eliminate some difficulty or pain.

Memory Peg: *Alleve* is a commonly used medication for *alleviat*ing pain.

◆ **EXERCISE 1**   **Using Memory Pegs**

DIRECTIONS   Here are three words that commonly turn up in textbooks, particularly history texts. Make up a memory peg for each one.

Impromptu means unrehearsed or done spontaneously without being planned beforehand. "The candidate gave an impromptu speech and as usual said the wrong thing."

Memory Peg:

Ramifications refers to the results or consequences of an action. "The discovery of the explorer's long-buried journal was going to have widespread ramifications for historians."

Memory Peg:

Enigma describes someone or something who is always mysterious and can never be completely understood. "Because no one could ever predict his actions, Thomas Jefferson, America's third president, was called 'The Great Enigma.'"

Memory Peg:

◆ Using Context Clues

What do you do when you come across an unfamiliar word? Do you just skip over it? Or do you pick up your dictionary and look for the definition? You probably already know that the first method is not recommended. Yet actually, the second one—turning to the dictionary every time—also has drawbacks. Looking up too many words can hurt your concentration. Look up too many words and you can lose track of where you were on the page.

Developing Approximate Definitions

Fortunately, there are other alternatives to ignoring new words or looking them up. One alternative is to search the *context*, or setting, of the word to see if it contains a clue or clues to word meaning. Frequently, the sentence or passage in which the word appears can help you determine an **approximate definition** that allows you to keep reading without interruption. An approximate definition may not perfectly match a dictionary's definition. Still, it is close enough so that you can continue reading without interruption, and that's what's essential.

> When Russia was under the control of Josef Stalin, *dissidents* were routinely shot or imprisoned in hospitals for the mentally ill. Stalin did not allow anyone to express disagreement or discontent with his policies.

If you didn't know what the word *dissidents* in the first sentence meant, you could probably **infer**, or figure out, a definition from the sentence that follows. That sentence offers an example of what dissidents do: They disagree with their government.

Although there are several different kinds of context clues, most fall into one of four categories: *example, contrast, restatement,* and *general knowledge.*

Example Clues

As you already know from the previous illustration, the context of an unfamiliar word sometimes provides you with an example of the behavior or thinking associated with the word. Here's another sentence in which an example can lead you to a definition:

> His feelings for his cousin were *ambivalent*: Sometimes he delighted in her company; at other times, he couldn't stand the sight of her.

What's an example of *ambivalent* feelings? They are in conflict with one another. Because this is an example of what it feels like to be ambivalent, we can infer the following approximate definition: To be ambivalent is to experience conflicting emotions.

Contrast Clues

Context clues can also tell you what a word does not mean. Fortunately, knowing what a word doesn't mean can often lead you to a good approximate definition. Here's an example of a passage that provides a contrast clue:

> As a child, she liked to be alone and was fearful of people; but as an adult, she was remarkably *gregarious*.

This sentence suggests that someone who is *gregarious* does not exactly flee the company of others. In fact, the sentence implies just the opposite: People who are gregarious like to be in the company of others. Thus, "liking the company of others" would be a good approximate definition.

Words That Signal Contrast Clues

In addition to knowing what a contrast clue is, you should also know that words such as *but*, *yet*, *nevertheless*, and *however* frequently introduce contrast clues. These words are all **transitions**—verbal bridges that help readers connect ideas. The transitions mentioned here tell readers to be on the lookout for a shift, reversal, or change in thought. Look at the word *however* in the following example. Do you see how it changes the author's train of thought and paves the way for a contrast clue that helps define the word *frivolous*?

> After having had a really bad day, she wanted to read something *frivolous*. Normally, *however*, she preferred serious novels.

So what does the word *frivolous* mean? "Silly," "light," or "not serious" are all good approximate definitions.

Restatement Clues

To avoid tedious word repetition, authors often use a word and then follow it with a **synonym**, a word or phrase similar in meaning:

> The journalist had the *audacity* to criticize the president to his face. Oddly enough, her boldness seemed to amuse rather than irritate him.

In this case, the author doesn't want to overuse the word *audacity*, so she follows it with a synonym, *boldness*. For readers not sure what *audacity* means, the synonym *boldness* restates the word in language they can understand and provides them with a definition.

Restatement Clues in Textbooks

Intent on supplying readers with the **specialized vocabulary** essential to mastering an academic subject, textbook authors often introduce a word and then carefully define it. For example, the authors of the following passage want to be sure that their readers have exact definitions for the terms *brand recognition* and *ad recognition*. To make sure their readers have no doubt what these two terms mean, the authors define them in parentheses:

> Two important types of recognition in marketing are *brand recognition* (we remember having seen the *brand* before) and *ad recognition* (we remember having seen the *ad* before). (Hoyer and MacInnis, *Consumer Behavior*, 5th ed., p. 17.)

In addition to parentheses, authors use other devices to tell readers, "Here is the definition for the word I just introduced." Colons and dashes, for instance, are also common.

> Most people have experienced brain freeze: This is the painful sensation in the temples that follows the consumption of food or drink that is very cold.

> Reconversion—the transition from wartime production to the manufacture of consumer goods—ushered in a quarter century of ever-expanding prosperity. (Boyer et al., *The Enduring Vision*, 7th ed., p. 790.)

In addition to colons, dashes, and parentheses, textbook authors often signal a restatement clue by first introducing the word being defined, in either boldface or italics. Then they follow the word with a comma and a definition. Here's an example:

> A major buzzword in leadership and management is *vision*, the ability to imagine different and better conditions and the ways to achieve them. (Dubrin, *Leadership*, 5th ed., p. 6.)

Here, the author is well aware that readers might think they know the meaning of the word *vision*—the ability to see. Yet within this particular context, the author has a specialized definition in mind. To avoid any confusion, he provides that definition right after he introduces the word.

Textbook authors go to great lengths to make sure you have the right definitions for the words essential to their academic field. In turn, your job as a reader is twofold: (1) pay attention to the devices that signal the presence of restatement or definition clues; and (2) when those definitions appear, read them carefully.

Consider as well jotting both words and definitions in a notebook for later review. The chances are good that the definitions will not reappear in later chapters, though the words themselves will.

General Knowledge Clues

Example, contrast, and restatement context clues are important. However, some context clues are not so obvious. Often your knowledge of the situation or events described will be your only real clue to word meaning. The following passage illustrates this point:

> For months he had dreamed of being able to *redeem* his medals. He had been unable to think of anything else. Now, with the vision of the medals shimmering before him, he hurried to the pawnshop.

None of the context clues previously discussed appears in the passage. However, your general knowledge should tell you that the word *redeem*, in this context at least, means "reclaim" or "recover." Most people go to a pawnshop to buy or to sell, and the man described as hurrying to the pawnshop probably wouldn't be in such a rush to sell something he had dreamed of for months. He is going to buy back what he has already sold.

1.	**Example Clue**	"The discussion was becoming increasingly *belligerent*; no matter what was said, someone in the group would challenge it in an angry voice."
2.	**Contrast Clue**	"At first the smell was almost flower-like, but in a matter of minutes it became harsh and *acrid*."
3.	**Restatement Clue**	"*Cognition*—thinking or knowing—has been the subject of numerous studies."
4.	**General Knowledge Clue**	"Football and basketball coaches are frequently known for their *volatile* tempers."

SUMMING UP THE KEY POINTS

1. The goal of learning new vocabulary is to make your understanding of the word automatic.

2. Memory pegs are links between what you already know and what you want to learn.

3. Often, the sentence or passage in which an unfamiliar word appears can tell you what the word means. The words or sentences that supply the meaning are called *context clues*.

4. Context clues don't necessarily give you an exact dictionary definition, but they can supply an "approximate definition" that allows you to keep reading without interruption.

5. Of the many different kinds of context clues, four are particularly common: example, contrast, restatement, and general knowledge.

6. An example clue describes the behavior, attitude, event, or experience associated with a word.

7. A contrast clue provides the reader with a word that is opposite in meaning.

8. A restatement clue follows the unfamiliar word with a synonym substitute. In textbooks, authors explicitly define the word, often within dashes or parentheses.

9. General knowledge clues are descriptions of events or experiences that are likely to be familiar to readers because they are familiar with both the events and the experiences.

◆ **EXERCISE 2**   **Using Context Clues**

DIRECTIONS   Use context clues to develop an approximate meaning for each italicized word.

EXAMPLE   To the old dog lying under the table, the smell of frying bacon was almost unbearably *tantalizing*, and he stared at the pan with obvious doggy longing.

Tantalizing means <u>appealing, exciting; desirable but out of reach</u>.

EXPLANATION   In this case, the sentence offers a general knowledge clue. Even readers who don't have pets would undoubtedly know that to a dog, the smell of frying bacon is extremely appealing or exciting.

1. According to the myth, the hero Achilles was *vulnerable* in just one area of his body. He could be killed only if he was wounded in the heel.

   Vulnerable means _____.

2. The candidate had expected to win, but instead she was *trounced* by her opponent, who won by a landslide.

   Trounced means _____.

3. Forced to sell their lands and homes at whatever prices they could obtain, Japanese Americans were herded into detention camps in the most desolate areas of the West. Sadly, few Americans protested the *incarceration* of their Japanese-American countrymen. (Boyer et al., *The Enduring Vision*, 7th ed., p. 778.)

   Incarceration means _____.

4. Before allowing someone to deliver a personal opinion on the air, most television news programs issue a *disclaimer* denying all responsibility for the views expressed.

   Disclaimer means _____.

5. Killed by an obsessed fan in 1995, the Latina entertainer Selena was deeply mourned because she was so much more than an entertainer: Selena was the *embodiment* of Mexican-American culture—representing devotion to the family, hard work, and a sense of community. (Adapted from Hoyer and MacInnis, *Consumer Behavior*, 5th ed., p. 295.)

   Embodiment means _____.

6. Unjustly accused of spying, Captain Alfred Dreyfus[†] (1859–1935) was convicted and sentenced to life in prison on the ill-famed Devil's Island; pardoned in 1899, Dreyfus was fully *exonerated* of all charges in 1906.

   Exonerated means _____.

[†] What came to be known as the "Dreyfus Affair" polarized the French people. Many rightly suspected that Dreyfus was being persecuted because he was Jewish. That fact appalled some and pleased others.

7. The novelist Alice Hoffman is an amazingly *inventive* writer: her plots range from teenage coming-of-age novels to historical fiction.

   Inventive means _____.

8. Confusion and *delusions* (false and distorted beliefs) are typical signs of sleep deprivation. (Coon, *Essentials of Psychology*, p. 34.)

   Delusions means _____.

9. Queen Marie Antoinette's *hedonistic* lifestyle was one of the things that made her hated by the people of France; close to starvation themselves, they could not love a queen who seemed to care about nothing but pleasure.

   Hedonistic means _____.

10. If she wants to get her finances under control, she will have to *consolidate* her debt; she can't continue paying all of her debts and interest individually.

    Consolidate means _____.

◆ **EXERCISE 3**   **Using Context Clues**

DIRECTIONS   Use context clues to write an approximate meaning for each italicized word.

1. The reporters were sent out to cover the fighting that had broken out in the streets, but under no condition were they to get involved in the *upheaval*.

   Upheaval means _____.

2. The millionaire did not expect the judge to hand down such a *punitive* sentence, and his face went white with shock when he heard the verdict.

   Punitive means _____.

3. All over the country, people were starving and desperately *scavenging* for food.

   Scavenging means _____.

4. Looking filthy and *disreputable* after an all-night bender, the reporter tried to spruce up in the men's room before going into work.

   Disreputable means _____.

5. Her boss didn't need to make an effort to be nasty; he was *inherently* so and thought nothing of publicly humiliating his employees.

   Inherently means _____.

6. Because I can't spell very well, I was happy to learn there is no apparent *correlation* between the ability to spell and a high IQ.

   Correlation means _____.

7. The jockey hoped that *submersing* himself in the hot tub would soothe his aching body.

   Submersing means _____.

8. Inventors don't necessarily care if their inventions are *lucrative*; often they just have an idea they are desperate to make a reality, and money doesn't matter.

   Lucrative means _____.

9. Research on people who have lived to be more than eighty years old has consistently revealed a connection between low body weight and *longevity*.

   Longevity means _____.

10. How is it that so many doctors who *advocate* diet and exercise are overweight couch potatoes?

    Advocate means _____.

◆ EXERCISE 4   Using Context Clues

DIRECTIONS   Use context clues to write an approximate definition for each italicized word.†

EXAMPLE   People driven by *intrinsic* motivation don't need external rewards such as praise from others; instead, they find satisfaction in simply completing a task.

Intrinsic means <u>internal, inside or within oneself</u>   .

EXPLANATION   In this case, the sentence offers a contrast clue. If people do not need external rewards, they must be motivated by rewards that are internal, or inside themselves.

Famous as a writer and civil rights activist, James Baldwin ended up with his face on a stamp.

1. African-American novelist James Baldwin was an outspoken advocate of civil rights, who did not believe that racism would disappear on its own. Friends enjoyed relaying *anecdotes* about Baldwin's fiery and often funny responses to anyone claiming it would.

   Anecdotes means   .

2. In the sixth century, Emperor Justinian turned Rome's disorganized laws into a *coherent* legal system.

   Coherent means   .

3. Corporate raiders spend their days figuring out how to acquire new companies while offering the previous owners as little *compensation* as possible.

   Compensation means   .

4. By embracing drug use, rock music, "free love," and non-Western religions, the rebellious hippies of the 1960s and 1970s rejected *conventional* rules.

   Conventional means   .

---

† The italicized words in Exercises 4 and 5 are all from the Academic Word List developed by the School of Linguistics and Applied Language Studies at Victoria University of Wellington in New Zealand.

5. If *preliminary* testing of a new drug indicates potential benefits, the drug is then tested again for a longer period of time and on a larger sample population.

   Preliminary means _____.

6. Electricity is *generated* from a variety of energy sources, including coal, oil, wood, nuclear reactors, wind, sunlight, and water.

   Generated means _____.

7. *Proponents* of the bill were disheartened when the vote was put off until spring; the bill's critics, however, were thrilled.

   Proponents means _____.

8. Milton Hershey certainly didn't invent chocolate, but his *innovations* to the recipe and manufacture of it turned a luxury for the wealthy into an affordable treat for all.

   Innovations means _____.

9. The lawyer's *cogent* argument convinced the court, and she was allowed to submit the fibers as evidence.

   Cogent means _____.

10. After the Twenty-second Amendment to the U.S. Constitution took effect in 1951, all *ensuing* presidents were limited to two terms each.

    Ensuing means _____.

◆ **EXERCISE 5**   **Using Context Clues**

DIRECTIONS   Use context clues to write an approximate definition for each italicized word.

1. Although global warming has been *attributed* to the burning of fossil fuels, a few scientists argue that it's actually caused by natural climate cycles.

   Attributed means _____.

After the bombing of Hiroshima and Nagasaki in 1945, a huge mushroom cloud bloomed in the sky.

2. U.S. military officials believed that dropping atomic bombs on Japan was the only way to save millions of American lives and end World War II; however, others have argued that there was no *justification* for killing more than 140,000 Japanese citizens and injuring another 100,000.

Justification means _____.

3. Based on research and observation, scientists propose theories, or explanations, of events; then they conduct experiments that either prove a theory's *validity* or reveal its inaccuracy.

Validity means _____.

4. In the U.S. Army, a general is the highest rank of officer, whereas the most *subordinate* officer rank is second lieutenant.

Subordinate means _____.

5. The final event of the American Civil War occurred on April 9, 1865; Confederate General Robert E. Lee officially *terminated* the conflict by surrendering to Union commander Ulysses S. Grant at the Appomattox, Virginia, courthouse.

Terminated means _____.

6. Medical research rules require that human subjects know they are participating in an experiment; therefore, scientists must obtain each subject's *consent*, or permission, before giving him or her any treatment.

Consent means _____.

7. When scientists attempt to create a clone, they *extract* the DNA from the cell of one organism and then insert it into the egg cell of another organism of the same species.

Extract means _____.

8. The kilometer is a unit of length used in Europe, Canada, and other countries; it is *equivalent,* or equal, to 0.62 miles.

    Equivalent means _____.

9. Because they can explode when mixed together, *incompatible* chemicals spelled with the same first letter, like cadmium chlorate and cupric sulfide, must be kept apart; they should never be stored alphabetically in a laboratory.

    Incompatible means _____.

10. The *Oxford English Dictionary* aims to present all words from the earliest records to the present day. Its over 600,000 entries make it our language's most *comprehensive* dictionary.

    Comprehensive means _____.

Context and Meaning

"Words mean different things in different contexts, often totally different things."
—Language researcher Walter Kintsch

Generally speaking, there are few situations in life where context isn't important. Words are no exception. Change a word's context and you very likely change its meaning. For instance, if you are buying a new air conditioner, you might ask the salesperson how big a room the unit can *cool.* Here the word means "lower the temperature." But if someone asks your opinion of the Foo Fighters' new CD, you might say, "It's cool," and you wouldn't be talking about the group's temperature.

From Reader to Writer

What follows are four uncommon words. Look them up in a print or online dictionary. Then create sentences for each one in which the context makes the meanings clear. The first one is done for you.

gossamer   nostrum   palaver   redolent

She wore a white shawl made of some gossamer material that was so sheer he could

see her pale freckles beneath it.

Based on the context, could you tell that *gossamer* refers to material that is easy to see through?

CHECK YOUR UNDERSTANDING

1. When readers get definitions from context, should the definition be almost the same as the one that appears in a dictionary? Please explain your answer.

   _____

   _____

2. What are the most common kinds of context clues?

   _____

3. The following sentence gives what kind of context clue for the italicized word?

   "*Stressors*, the external events that disrupt our daily functioning, are unavoidable but still manageable."

   Type of context clue: _____

4. The following sentence gives what kind of context clue for the italicized word?

   "The administration offered the older teachers *incentives* for taking early retirement: They could have one full year of health benefits and a three-hundred-dollar bonus."

   Type of context clue: _____

5. The following sentence gives what kind of context clue for the italicized word?

   "In the 1960s, members of opposing political parties in Congress worked together, but today members of Congress are much more *polarized*."

   Type of context clue: _____

6. The following sentence gives what kind of context clue for the italicized word?

   "After all the cars leaving the game streamed onto the highway, there was complete *gridlock* going north and away from the stadium."

   Type of context clue: _____

7. What are memory pegs?

   _____

   _____

Defining Words from Their Parts

In addition to using context clues to determine approximate meanings for unfamiliar words, check to see if you know any of the word's parts. For example, imagine you read this sentence and were initially puzzled by the word *dermatitis*: "The deadly disease began with a seemingly minor symptom—a light *dermatitis* on the arms and legs." Even if you had never heard or used the word *dermatitis*, you could come up with a definition simply by knowing that *derma* means skin and *itis* means inflammation, or outbreak. Given the context and your knowledge of the word's parts, you would be correct to say that *dermatitis* means "inflammation of the skin," or "rash."

Learning Roots, Prefixes, and Suffixes

To determine meaning from word parts, you need to know some of the most commonly used roots and prefixes, along with a few suffixes. The exercises in this chapter will introduce you to a good many. It's worth your while to learn a few new word parts every day, averaging about twenty a week. If you review them regularly, you will be amazed at how quickly your vocabulary expands.

1. **Roots** give words their fixed meaning. Prefixes and suffixes can then be attached to the roots to form new words. For example, the following words are all based on the root *spec*, which means "look" or "see": re*spec*t, in*spec*tion, *spec*tacles, *spec*ulation.

2. **Prefixes** are word parts that appear at the *beginning* of words and modify the root meaning, as in *in*clude and *ex*clude or *in*voke and *re*voke.

3. **Suffixes** are word parts that appear at the *end* of many words. Although suffixes do occasionally affect word meaning, they are more likely to reveal what part of speech a word is, as in quick*ness* and quick*ly*. Words ending in *ness* are usually nouns. Those ending in *ly* are usually adverbs.

STUDY TIP

When you make a list of word parts, put the definitions on the far right. Each time you review, cover one side of the list and *recall from memory* either the word part or the definition.

◆ **EXERCISE 6**　　**Learning Word Parts**

DIRECTIONS　　Read each sentence and note what meaning the missing or partial word should convey. Then fill in the blanks with one—or, in some cases, two—of the word parts listed below.

Prefixes	Roots
bi = two	*chron* = time
im = not	*gam* = marriage
per = through	*lat* = side
poly = many	*mob* = move
	pel = force
	popul = people
	rect = straight, straighten

EXAMPLE　　When we talk about events being ordered according to time, we are talking about events that are described in <u>chron</u> ological order.

EXPLANATION　　The partially completed word needs to say something about "time." Thus, we need a word part that brings that meaning to the blank. The obvious choice would be the root *chron*, meaning "time."

1. When a situation can't be fixed or straightened out, we say that it cannot be _____ ified.

2. If a city is filled with people, it can be described as _____ ous.

3. When a disease goes away and repeatedly comes back over time, it is called _____ ic.

4. Human skin is called _____ meable because substances, both good and bad, can pass through it.

5. An interesting book that almost forces you to keep reading is often described as com _____ ling.

6. An agreement that has to be signed by two sides is called ____ ____ eral.

7. Being married to two people at the same time is called ____ _____y.

8. Being married to several people at the same time is called _____ _____y.

9. If someone or something can move, we say that he, she, or it is _____ ile.

10. In contrast, someone or something that cannot move would be described as ____ _____ile.

STUDY TIP

Because the word parts introduced in Exercise 6 appear in many different words, you should start learning them right now. Repeated reviews done over an extended period of time are the key to mastery.

Combine Forces: Use Context Clues *and* Word Parts

Recognizing word parts and using context clues are, by themselves, effective methods of determining meaning. However, they are even more powerful when combined. Take, for example, the following sentences:

> I can't imagine a more *credulous* person. He actually believed I saw a flying saucer on the way home.

To a degree, knowing that the root *cred* means "belief" and the suffix *ous* means "full of" are helpful clues to meaning. We can start off, then, by saying that to be *credulous* is to be "full of belief." Yet what exactly does that mean? You can imagine a bottle full of juice or wine. But how can a person be "full of belief"?

This is where context comes in. Look at the example clue the author offers: "He actually believed I saw a flying saucer on the way home." Apparently, a credulous person is likely to believe a story that most people might laugh at or question. After a closer look at the context, we can come up with a more precise definition of *credulous*: "gullible" or "easily fooled."

A knowledge of word parts can also help you sharpen or improve an approximate definition derived from context. Suppose you are not sure how to define the word *ambiguous* in a sentence like this one: "The finest poems are usually the most *ambiguous*, suggesting that life's big questions defy easy answers."

Relying solely on context, you might decide that *ambiguous* means *puzzling* or *difficult*. Those definitions are certainly acceptable. But once you know that the prefix *ambi* means "both," you could make your definition more precise by defining *ambiguous* as "open to more than one interpretation."

SUMMING UP THE KEY POINTS

1. Recognizing the meaning of prefixes or roots within a word can unlock a word's meaning, especially if you can combine that knowledge with context clues.

2. Roots give words their central, or core, meaning. Attaching new beginnings (prefixes) or endings (suffixes) to the word will change the meaning of the whole word, but the essential meaning of the root won't change. Just think, for instance, of how the meaning of *invent* stays the same in the following sequence, *reinvent, inventor, invention*, even though the words as a whole assume different (but related) meanings.

3. Prefixes modify root meanings, and they can do so rather dramatically. Consider, for example, the difference between the words "do" and "*undo*."

4. Suffixes can tell you something about word meaning. Suffixes like *er* and *or* at the end of a word indicate that the word refers to a

2. The new recruits were disappointed to discover that their drill sergeant was a _____.

3. In the rock world of the 1970s and 1980s, Freddie Mercury, lead singer of the group Queen, was a _____, but fame did not save him from AIDS, and he died in 1991.

4. As a tourist, he was inclined to be a _____; any deviation from what he was accustomed to in his own country just had to be bad.

5. After a pair of male penguins stole eggs from some of the other birds, replacing them with stones, the two birds were _____ by the rest of the flock.

LEARNING TIP

Associate new words with images or examples; connect them to sample sentences or to people, e.g., "The word *anecdote* reminds me of how my dad gives advice. He always starts with an anecdote."

WEB QUEST

What links these three men together: Samuel Johnson, Noah Webster, and James Murray?

_____

Connotations and Denotations of Words

"The meaning of a word is not a set, cut-off thing like the move of a knight or pawn on a chessboard. It comes up with roots, with associations."
—Poet Ezra Pound

The more words you add to your reading vocabulary, the more inclined you will be to try them out in your own writing. However, to use words effectively, you need to know more than their **denotation**, or dictionary definitions. You also need to know whether a word carries with it any connotations. **Connotations** are the associations or implications some words develop over time with repeated use. Consider, for instance, the different connotations of the words *house* versus *home*. *House* has neutral connotations. It calls up few associations or feelings. *Home* is different. It's associated with positive feelings about family and safety.

The sense of a word's connotations will become clearer the more you see it in different contexts. That's one of the reasons why you usually need a good deal of experience with new words before you use them in your writing.

Matching Up Connotation with Context

For example, the words *house* and *domicile* both refer to a place where people live. Thus a nonnative speaker who looked the two words up might think they were interchangeable. But a native speaker who had seen and heard the words repeatedly would know they require different contexts. Yes, a "domicile" is a house or a building where people live. However, it's likely to turn up in a formal context, like tax, travel, or insurance forms, e.g., "Indicate your legal domicile on the second page of the passport form."

It would be very unusual, though, to see the word *domicile* in a sentence like the following. "The dog hated to sleep in his new dog domicile; he much preferred the living room couch." In this context, only *house* is appropriate because its connotations are more informal than those attached to the word *domicile*.[†]

Changing the Connotation with the Context

Words don't necessarily have positive *or* negative connotations. Some words have strong connotations in one context and negative or no connotations in another.

Take, for example, the words *cans* and *bags* in the following sentence, "He threw the empty cans and bags into the trash." In that sentence, the two words have no emotional impact. They pretty much call up only their dictionary definitions.

But that changes dramatically when the two words appear in the context of this poem called "Hard Evidence," written by poet and textbook author Carol Kanar.

[†] The house versus domicile example is thanks to my friend and colleague Joan Hellman of Catonsville Community College.

Hard Evidence

for Wolf

> I'm stumbling on signs of life
> throughout the empty house,
> bones buried under rugs,
> a leash snared by a table leg.
>
> These and other of your effects—
> cans and bags of uneaten food,
> assorted toys and grooming aids—
> a legacy now for homeless dogs.
>
> Habits die, but need remains:
> the walk I will not take today.
> Silence whimpers at my door.
> I still can smell you in the rain.[†]

See how the connotations of those ordinary words change with the context? Now the words *cans* and *bags* are hard evidence of a beloved dog's death. They carry with them associations of sadness and loss. Changing the context of a word often changes not just its meaning but its emotional impact as well.

SUMMING UP THE KEY POINTS

1. The term *etymology* refers to the history or story behind a word. The etymologies of words can often serve as memory pegs. Learn the history of the word and the history will anchor the meaning in your memory.

2. The more you want to use the words you learn, the more attentive you need to be to their context. The dictionary will give you a word's *denotation*, or formal meaning. But the *connotations*, or associations, the word carries only become clear after you have seen it used in multiple contexts.

3. Context can dramatically shift a word's meaning along with its connotations. Teachers telling "stories" to children are just doing their job. But an employee who tells "stories" about co-workers

---

[†]Poem used by permission of Carol Kanar.

probably doesn't have many friends. Context makes all the difference.

4. When you learn a new word, it's a good idea to get some experience with how it is used in context (or contexts) before using it in your own writing. A sense of the correct context only comes with practice.

◆ **EXERCISE 8**   **Understanding Connotation**

DIRECTIONS   Underline the word with more positive connotations.

1. (Crude, Direct) in the way he expressed himself, he often offended people even when he meant no harm.

2. She (giggled, guffawed) her amusement at her husband's quick-witted response.

3. Today's fashion models are almost always tall and (slender, skinny).

4. He didn't expect to pay such a high price for a (preowned, used) vehicle.

5. Clothes for (overweight, husky) boys are located on the second floor.

◆ **EXERCISE 9**   **Understanding Connotation**

DIRECTIONS   Underline the word with more negative connotations.

1. The student (called, blurted) out the answer before the teacher had finished reading the question.

2. The couple spent days (deliberating, disputing) how to spend their tax refund.

3. She was (stubborn, determined) and refused to change her mind.

4. His (carelessness, recklessness) caused the accident.

5. He (tossed, hurled) her suitcase out the window.

CHECK YOUR UNDERSTANDING

1. What does the word *etymology* refer to?

_____

2. What's the difference between a word's *connotation* and its *denotation*?

_____

_____

3. Once you learn a new word, can you assume that it means the same thing in every context? Please explain your answer.

_____

4. Why is it a good idea to see a new word used repeatedly before you use it in your own writing?

_____

Turning to the Dictionary

The specialized vocabulary words necessary to understanding a particular subject are often defined in **annotations**, or notes in the margins of textbooks. Or they can be found in the **glossary**, or list of key terms located in the back of your textbook. Context clues can also provide you with approximate definitions for both specialized and non-specialized vocabulary.

However, despite help from marginal annotations, the glossary, and context, there still will be times when you have to turn to the dictionary to learn the meaning of a word. Here's a quick review of what you can expect from a dictionary.

Getting Down the Basics: Syllable Count, Pronunciation Guide, and Parts of Speech

Whether you are using an online or a print dictionary, you can expect the **entry word**, or word being defined, to appear in boldface. The entry word will be divided into syllables. It might be divided by dots (jus·ti·fi·ca·tion) or hyphens (jus-ti-fi-ca-tion). Dots or hyphens fulfill the same function. They indicate where the syllable breaks appear. That way you know how many syllables there are in a word.

Electronic and print dictionary entries both provide a sequence of letters with symbols in parentheses (ĭn-strŭkt'). The letters and symbols tell you what sounds to give the vowels[†] and consonants that make up the word. Consonants almost never present any pronunciation difficulty. But long and short vowel sounds occasionally do. That's why dictionaries provide pronunciation keys, even online, where you can usually hear the word pronounced.

An accent mark (dī-dăk'-tĭk') or **boldface** (dahy-**dak**-tic)[‡] tells you what syllable gets the stronger emphasis. Following the guide to pronunciation enclosed in brackets or parentheses comes the part of speech either spelled out (*noun, adjective*) or abbreviated (*n, adj, adv*). Often at the very end of an entry, enclosed in brackets, you'll also find a brief etymology of the word.

READING TIP

If you are a student of English as a second language (ESL), pronunciation of new words is especially important to you. Anytime you can access an online dictionary you should use it. Hit the audio link ◀)), which will allow you to hear the words pronounced, over and over again if need be.

◆ **EXERCISE 10** **Using the Dictionary**

DIRECTIONS Use a dictionary to answer the following questions. It can be an online or a print dictionary.

1. The word *heinous*, meaning "horribly wicked," is often *mispronounced*. Should the first syllable rhyme with *hey* or *hi?* _____

[†]Long vowel sounds: wāy, wē, bīte, nō, cūte. Short vowel sounds: săt, lĕt, lĭt, lŏt, bŭt.
[‡]The word is spelled *didactic* and means "intended to instruct."

2. What part of speech is the word *heinous*? _____

3. How many syllables are there in the word *prevaricate*, meaning to mislead or lie? _____

4. *Hyssop* is a woody plant with small blue flowers. How many syllables does the word have, and which one gets the strongest accent? _____ Is the *y* in *hyssop* pronounced like the *i* in "hi" or the *i* in "him"? _____

5. During World War II, a *kamikaze* was a pilot trained to make a suicidal attack, usually on ships. How many syllables does the word have? _____ Which one gets the strongest accent? _____ Is the *e* at the end of the word silent or spoken? _____ Are the *a*'s in the word pronounced like the *a* in *father* or the *a* in *pat*? _____ The word is a noun, but it can also play what other part of speech? _____

Sorting Through Multiple Meanings

As you already know, a word can have multiple meanings. Those different meanings, however, can seem confusing when they appear together in a dictionary entry.

To avoid feeling overwhelmed when faced with multiple meanings, keep in mind that your goal is to determine what an unfamiliar word means *within a specific context*. That specific context will help you sort through any number of definitions and find the right one. Say, for instance, that the word *scald* in the following sentence sent you to the dictionary. "The dental instruments need to be *scalded* before being re-used." Here are some of the meanings you would find:

1. to burn with hot liquid or steam

2. to cook slightly

3. to criticize harshly

4. to sterilize, or clean thoroughly, by washing in boiling water

5. *Botany*: a disease that affects some grasses

Faced with so many different definitions, you may feel unsure about which meaning to pick. Yet, usually, you can find the meaning through the simple process of elimination. For example, you can immediately eliminate the definition following the word "Botany," which is a **special context label**. Special context labels tell you that the meaning provided is only appropriate within discussions of a particular subject, for instance, law, medicine, or architecture.

The special context label shown on page 91, tells you that the word *scald* means "a disease that affects some grasses" *only* when used in discussions of botany, the study of plants. Because our sample sentence has nothing to do with plants, we can safely ignore this definition.

Once you eliminate this meaning, you have four left. However, notice that meaning 3 applies to people whereas the sample sentence talks about "dental instruments." That means that this definition also won't work with the sample sentence. Nor will definition 2, since you cook in order to eat and you are not going to eat dental instruments.

Of the five meanings, the fourth one makes the most sense. No self-respecting dentist is going to use dirty dental instruments. He or she is going to sterilize them so they don't spread germs and disease. Thus meaning 4 perfectly fits the sentence in which *scald* appears and that's what you are aiming for.

◆ **EXERCISE 11   Choosing the Correct Meaning**

DIRECTIONS   Read each sentence and look carefully at the italicized word. Then look at the various meanings and pick the one that best fits the context.

1. *Sentence:* The young reporter volunteered to act as a *conduit* between the rebels and the government.

    Meanings: **con•duit** *n.* **1.** a pipe that carries liquids, such as water **2.** a tube or duct that covers or encases electric wires or cable **3.** a means by which something is communicated or transmitted: *Throughout the war, she had been a conduit for the enemy's messages* **4.** *Archaic*† a fountain

    What is the best meaning for the word *conduit* in the above sentence? _____

---

†archaic: used to describe an early meaning no longer in use.

2. *Sentence:* The prime minister generally had a *sanguine* temper but there were times when the weight of his duties plunged him into depression.

> *Meanings:* **san•guine** *adj.* **1.** having the color red **2.** having a healthy reddish skin tone **3.** inclined to be cheerful **4.** bloody

What is the best meaning for the word *sanguine* in the above sentence? _____

3. *Sentence:* The so-called financial analyst was a *patent* liar, but he had powerful friends and those who knew him were afraid to challenge him.

> *Meanings:* **pat•ent 1.** *n.* a grant by a government acknowledging exclusive ownership of an invention **2.** *v.* to obtain an exclusive right to ownership **3.** *adj.* open, obvious, unconcealed **4.** *Biology. adj.* open, unblocked

What is the best meaning for the word *patent* in the above sentence?

_____

4. *Sentence*: After his *vital* organs shut down, only machines were keeping him alive.

> *Meanings*: **vi•tal 1.** *adj.* pertaining or related to life **2.** necessary to the continuation of life **3.** being full of life **4.** destructive to life

What is the best meaning for the word *vital* in the above sentence?

_____

READING TIP

Next time you turn to a dictionary to look up an unfamiliar word and find several definitions, quickly eliminate any meanings that have no bearing on the word's context. Then look for the meaning that makes the most sense within the context of the sentence or passage.

Figurative and Literal Word Meanings

Because most of the definitions for *scald* on page 91 involved heat in some form, you may have been surprised by the meaning "to criticize harshly." That definition seems to have nothing to do with the other definitions listed. There's a reason for that. The meaning "to criticize harshly" doesn't completely fit the others because it's figurative rather than literal.

Words used in a **figurative sense** don't describe a real experience, event, or object. Instead, they suggest a resemblance. It's through the resemblance or comparison that a meaning is conveyed. If we say we were *scalded* by harsh criticism, we are talking about a person saying something so hurtful it feels *as if* the words could burn.

For another example of words used figuratively, we can go to the other end of the temperature scale. Take, for instance, the word *frozen*. We can certainly use it to describe ice cream. That would be using the word **literally**, or realistically, to describe the actual state or consistency of ice cream.

But we can also say that someone's opinions have "frozen with time." That phrase uses the word *frozen* figuratively. It suggests that a person's opinions haven't changed in any way with the passage of time, much like frozen ice cream hasn't changed from its original state to a more liquid one. With figurative language, there is always an implicit comparison tucked somewhere in the words.

SUMMING UP THE KEY POINTS

1. In addition to providing definitions, dictionary entries tell you how a word is pronounced, broken into syllables, and used in a sentence.

2. Special context labels tell you that certain meanings apply only within a particular setting such as botany, architecture, or law.

3. Many dictionaries include a word's etymology at the end of the entry, usually enclosed in brackets.

4. If you are looking up an unfamiliar word from your reading, don't panic if the entry contains several definitions. Just sort through them using the original context of the word as a guide to your selection. Different definitions are often somewhat related in meaning, so even if you don't pick the exactly right one, you may still be able to get an approximate definition. That approximate definition will allow you to continue your reading.

5. Words used in a figurative sense convey their meaning by implying, or suggesting, a resemblance. Thus, in the following sentence, the man's face is not made of wood. But it resembles wood due to the lack of movement: "The stroke had turned his face into a wooden mask."

◆ **EXERCISE 12   Going from Literal to Figurative Language**

DIRECTIONS   Fill in the blanks with the word that matches the literal and figurative description of each word.

1. Used literally the word describes something you take when you are ill, but you could also use it figuratively to say that someone is really annoying. The word is _____ .

2. Used literally the word describes something you put in tea or on fish, but you could also use it figuratively to describe something that doesn't work well. The word is _____ .

3. Used literally the word describes a male cow, but you could also use it to describe a story you think has been made up. The word is

    _____ .

4. Used literally the word describes a legless creature that slithers through grass and can contain poison, but you could also use it to describe someone who can't, under any conditions, be trusted. The word is _____ .

CHECK YOUR UNDERSTANDING

1. The opening of a dictionary entry usually introduces three elements. What are the three?

   _____

2. If an entry contains several different definitions, what should guide your choice of meaning?

   _____

3. What does etymology refer to?

   _____

4. Look over the pairs of sentences that follow and circle the letters of the sentences that use the italicized words figuratively.

   a. The coach had to call a "time out," when two parents of the players got into a *heated* argument.

   b. The little boy *heated* the soup on the stove and then carried the pot to the table.

   a. The cookies were on a very *high* shelf where the dog could not reach them.

   b. The Tejano singer was *high* on nothing more than the enthusiasm of the crowd.

5. Look over the pairs of sentences that follow and circle the letters of the sentences that use the italicized words literally.

   a. The young girl had learned how to *weave* from her Cherokee grandmother.

   b. Unlike writers in the nineteenth century, modern writers are not inclined to *weave* morals, or lessons, into their short stories.

   a. The surgeon *cut* a hole on the top of the man's head in order to relieve the pressure on his brain.

   b. The police captain told his lieutenant to *cut* the chatter and get to the point.

Web-Based Dictionaries and Definitions for Reading

For reading purposes,[†] a Web-based definition will probably serve you as well as a definition from a print dictionary. Web definitions tend to be easier to read and, here again, the context of the word you are looking up will ensure that you don't choose a completely inappropriate meaning. Also entries on the Web are inclined to be briefer than those in print dictionaries.

That being said not all the dictionaries on the Web are equally complete or equally easy to use. In some cases, the layout of the web page is so cluttered, it's hard to find the entry word among all the ads for products and services.

Also, some dictionaries seem to have been created just for the Web, and they occasionally have meanings that don't seem to appear anywhere except on that website. Thus, if you are looking up a word

---

[†]Where writing is concerned, I'd be inclined to avoid using words I had to look up before I used them. But if you absolutely need to look up a word for something you are writing, a print dictionary is going to give you more reliable definitions and more information about correct usage.

because you need to define it while you are reading, you might be better off using your search engine, for instance, Google, Yahoo, or Bing, to get a brief definition. (Type *define*: plus the word you are looking up into your search engine box.)

READING TIP Web-based definitions fall under the same rule as those in print. Turn to the Web only when you can't continue reading without determining the meaning of an unfamiliar word.

Collecting Examples of Words in Context

If you define a word and think, "I should add that to my vocabulary," then you should visit Wordnik.com. This site offers numerous examples of words in sentences. In fact, that is the stated purpose of Wordnik: "to show you as many example sentences as we can find for each word."

Wordnik.com also gives you several different lists of definitions from three or four different dictionaries. That way if one set of definitions is unclear, another set may provide some clarification. There's probably no better way to learn new words than to see them in lots of different contexts.

However you choose to use the Web to define words, make sure the site you're drawing definitions from fulfills these criteria:

1. The web page should be easy to read. If you have to study the page to separate the entry from the ads and promotional sidebars, keep looking. Busy web pages can prove a distraction. You may end up browsing weight loss ads and forget what word you were looking up.

2. The various elements in the entry—for example, pronunciation guide, audio link, and word history—should be clearly laid out. If you have to look at the page for a long time to determine where, say, the meanings leave off and the history begins, this is not the site you want to be using.

3. The definitions of words should be clearly written. If you have to puzzle over how a definition is worded because it doesn't quite make sense, it's probably the definition and not you.

4. The definitions should come from several different sources so that you can compare the meanings from various sources.

5. If an online dictionary uses only one source for its definitions, the meanings listed in the entry should be fairly similar to the meanings listed in other dictionary entries for the same word. (Yes, this means you have to do some cross-referencing.) If you find a definition for a word that doesn't appear anywhere else, you should probably not use this site again.

6. The best sites for looking up words will give you actual examples of the word used in sentences. The sentences will illustrate the range of meanings.

In addition to definitions, most Web dictionaries have examples of the words in context and audio links that let you hear the words pronounced.

READING TIP

If possible, try to have access to the Web while you read. When an unfamiliar, general vocabulary word appears and you feel you can't understand the sentence without its meaning, type the command "define" plus a colon (:) followed by the word, for instance, "define: sensory."[†] You'll get a brief definition that will let you finish your assignment without having to turn to the dictionary.

[†]sensory: of or relating to the physical senses.

DIGGING DEEPER Words on Words

Looking Ahead Famous and not-so-famous people have pondered the use and effect of words for centuries. The quotations that follow offer various thoughts on what words can or cannot do.

Getting Focused If you have any trouble determining what a quotation means, say it aloud. Often when you hear what's written on the page, it becomes more meaningful, and that applies to paragraphs as much as it does to brief quotations. Reading aloud is an important aid to comprehension.

Sharpening Your Skills

DIRECTIONS Translate each of the following quotations into your own words.

1. "One great use of words is to hide our thoughts." —Voltaire, French philosopher

   _____

   _____

2. "If you look after them [words], you can build bridges across incomprehension and chaos....They deserve respect." —Tom Stoppard, playwright

   _____

   _____

3. "No visual image is as vivid as the image created by the mind in response to words." —Norman Cousins, writer

   _____

   _____

4. "No word can be judged as to whether it is good or bad, correct or incorrect, beautiful or ugly, or anything else that matters to a writer, in isolation." —I. A. Richards, literary critic

_____

_____

5. "The basic tool for the manipulation of reality is the manipulation of words." —Philip K. Dick, science fiction writer

_____

_____

6. "What words say does not last. The words last. Because words are always the same, and what they say is never the same." —Antonio Porchia, poet

_____

_____

WEB QUEST
Do a Web search for quotations about words. Come up with two or three quotes about words that fit your personal view of how important they are or are not in your life.

◗ **TEST 1**   **Reviewing Key Concepts**

DIRECTIONS   Complete the following sentences by filling in the blanks.

1. If you don't know what a word means, before turning to the
   _____ , see if _____ will provide
   a(n) _____ .

2. There are many different kinds of context clues, but these four
   are particularly common: _____
   _____ .

3. The _____ of a word will give you its core meaning.
   But a(n) _____ can still dramatically change that
   meaning.

4. A _____ doesn't tell you much about word meaning, but it says a lot about _____ the word is.

5. Whenever possible, try to use _____ and
   _____ to determine the meaning of an unfamiliar
   word.

6. Words like *nitwit*, *gorgeous*, and *snarl* have strong _____ .

7. Words that have strong associations in one _____
   may not have the same associations in another.

8. If a dictionary entry gives you several meanings for the same word,
   make sure the meaning you pick fits the _____ of
   the unfamiliar word.

9. The history of a word is its _____ .

10. In this sentence—"The rock hit the window and shattered it" —is
    the word *rock* used literally or figuratively? _____
    What about in this sentence? Is the word *rock* used literally or figu-
    ratively? "She took her husband's death hard; he had been her *rock*
    for almost thirty years" _____

▶ **TEST 2**   **Using Context Clues**

DIRECTIONS   Use context clues to select an approximate meaning for each italicized word.

1. In the face of real danger, he didn't even try to display his usual *bravado.* When the bull charged, he ran like a scared rabbit.
   a. extreme shyness
   b. love of animals
   c. false bravery
   d. quick wit

2. With age, the financial wizard and penny pincher Hazel Green grew increasingly eccentric: She wore *bizarrely* unfashionable clothes, trusted no one, went on strange diets, and generally seemed to be out of step with the world.
   a. stingily
   b. weirdly
   c. colorful
   d. cleverly

3. In *The Country of the Pointed Firs*, the nineteenth-century writer Sarah Orne Jewett created the remarkable and compelling Mrs. Todd, a country woman who uses her vast store of herbal *lore* to cure the ailing and aging.
   a. knowledge
   b. mystery
   c. myths
   d. poisons

4. After her face was *disfigured* by an automobile accident, the supermodel realized that there really were people in the world who could love her for who she was rather than what she looked like.
   a. enriched
   b. abandoned
   c. rebuilt
   d. ruined

5. In order to justify his claim to visitation rights, Adam was willing to undergo a *paternity* test that would prove David was indeed his son.

a. relative
b. brotherhood
c. fatherhood
d. chemical

6. In the nineteenth century, girls and boys were rigidly *socialized*: Girls were encouraged to be subordinate to boys, and boys were told they could conquer the world.
   a. restricted by class
   b. punished for misbehavior
   c. taught to obey
   d. taught appropriate social roles

7. Although the curse of Tutankhamen's tomb has never been scientifically proven, the *irrational* belief persists that those who discovered the tomb met an early death.
   a. dishonest
   b. sensational
   c. fast-spreading
   d. illogical

8. In the fairy tale, the wolf tried to disguise his *predatory* nature by dressing up as Little Red Riding Hood's elderly grandmother.
   a. insensitive
   b. youthful
   c. dangerous
   d. wild

9. He wanted to work on their relationship by regularly seeing a therapist; she opted for a more *radical* solution and filed for divorce.
   a. insignificant
   b. drastic
   c. quiet
   d. expensive

10. The lawyer *systematically* worked his way through the document and eliminated all references to the coauthor.
    a. casually
    b. slowly
    c. quickly
    d. carefully

▶ **TEST 3**　　　　**Using Context Clues**

DIRECTIONS　　Use context clues to develop an approximate meaning for each italicized word.

1. The artist, who is clearly a Democrat, uses his *satirical* cartoons to expose the follies of Republican politicians.

   Satirical means _____.

2. They decided against buying the house because of its *proximity* to the airport.

   Proximity means _____.

3. Having a child outside of marriage no longer carries the punitive *stigma* it did a half century ago.

   Stigma means _____.

4. On the highway running through the city, a vehicle accident can cause *gridlock* that stretches for miles.

   Gridlock means _____.

5. To provide her children with intellectual *stimulation*, the young mother often took them to museums, bookstores, and concerts.

   Stimulation means _____.

6. When Martha asked her husband if she was getting fat, he said "yes" without thinking and quickly regretted his *candor*.

   Candor means _____.

7. George Washington was the first and last U.S. president to govern from Philadelphia; all *subsequent* presidents have resided in the White House in Washington, D.C.

   Subsequent means _____.

8. When the *Apollo 11* astronauts landed on the moon, they found a rocky, *barren* landscape.

   Barren means _____.

9. The diplomat had a *supercilious* expression on his face and seemed to be looking down his nose at the other guests.

   Supercilious means _____.

10. The Rev. Martin Luther King Jr.'s *charismatic* leadership inspired millions of people to demand civil rights for black Americans.

    Charismatic means _____.

▶ **TEST 4** **Using Context Clues**

DIRECTIONS Use context clues to develop an approximate meaning for each italicized word.

1. The 1938 Fair Labor Standards Act signed by Franklin D. Roosevelt prevents the *exploitation* of children; it prohibits anyone under the age of thirteen from working in most jobs.

   Exploitation means _____.

2. The Louisiana Purchase, President Thomas Jefferson's *acquisition* of 530 million acres of French territory in 1803, doubled the size of the United States.

   Acquisition means _____.

3. Wilbur and Orville Wright succeeded in building the first "flying machine" because they systematically *modified* their design, making changes and improvements following each test flight.

   Modified means _____.

4. By the end of the twentieth century, America's economy had begun to shift from one based *predominantly* on manufacturing to one based mostly on employees' knowledge and skills.

   Predominantly means _____.

5. The Common Era, also known as the Christian Era, began with the year Jesus was believed to have been born; the years *preceding* this date are followed by *BC*, an abbreviation for "Before Christ."

   Preceding means _____.

6. The American Civil War *commenced* on April 12, 1861, when the South fired the first shots at Union troops in Charleston, South Carolina, and ended on April 9, 1865.

   Commenced means _____.

7. According to one *hypothesis*, the impact of an asteroid 65 million years ago led to the extinction of the dinosaurs, but this explanation is not a proven fact.

   Hypothesis means _____.

8. The legal document known as a "living will" provides *explicit* instructions about what caregivers should and should not do in the event that a person goes into a coma and requires long-term life support.

   Explicit means _____.

9. According to many scientists, global warming could have dangerous *implications* for the future, including a destructive rise in sea levels, damage to ecosystems and agriculture, and an increase in extreme weather events like hurricanes.

   Implications means _____.

10. In economics, *fluctuations* in the prices of goods are caused by similar increases and decreases in the availability of and demand for those goods.

    Fluctuations means _____.

▶ TEST 5   Using Word Analysis and Context Clues

DIRECTIONS   Use context clues and word parts to develop an approximate meaning for each italicized word.

Prefixes	Roots
anti = against	*cred* = belief
extra = over, outside, beyond	*dict* = say or speak
dis = apart from, not, without	*sect* = cut, divide
ad = to, toward	*here* = stick

1. The doctors were fearful the boy would die because they had no *antidote* for the snakebite.

   Antidote means _____.

2. The girl refused to *dissect* the frog because she couldn't bear the thought of wasting a frog's life just so some student could cut up the body.

   Dissect means _____.

3. Because the Shaker religion forbade sex even in marriage, it had a hard time keeping *adherents*.

   Adherents means _____.

4. The report included too much *extraneous* information: The committee wanted only the essential facts of the situation, not silly gossip about dress and personal behavior.

   Extraneous means _____.

5. If she wants to run in the next campaign, she needs to *disassociate* herself from well-known gamblers and gangsters.

   Disassociate means _____.

6. Dr. Sorenson thinks of himself as an expert on ocean environment, but he lacks the proper *credentials*: He's a dentist, not a marine biologist.

   Credentials means _____.

7. My mother always told me to follow the *dictum* "neither a borrower nor a lender be," but I am always borrowing money from my friends.

   Dictum means _____.

8. The bank official desperately tried to *extricate* himself from the financial crisis he had helped to create, but all his influence couldn't get him out of trouble this time.

   Extricate means _____.

9. Once the suspect gave a *credible* account of his actions the night before, the police decided to let him go.

   Credible means _____.

10. Even with the glue in place, the pictures simply would not *adhere* to the shiny wallpaper.

    Adhere means _____.

▶ **TEST 6**   **Using Word Analysis and Context Clues**

DIRECTIONS   Use context clues and word parts to develop an approximate meaning for each italicized word.

Prefixes	**Roots**
in, im = in, into, not	*clin* = lean
multi = many	*plac* = calm, please
omni = all	*ven* = come
circum = around	*sci* = know
	vor = eat

1. As my uncle got older, he became less *implacable*; more mellow with age, he was much easier to please.

   Implacable means _____.

2. The entertainer Lena Horne was determined to *circumvent* the racism that once ruled Las Vegas. When hotel owners told her they didn't allow African Americans to rent rooms, Horne told them no room, no performance. As usual, Horne got her way.

   Circumvent means _____.

3. President Lyndon B. Johnson's first *inclination* in a difficult situation was to sweet talk whomever he needed on his side; if that didn't work, he could quickly turn into a bully.

   Inclination means _____.

4. In George Orwell's famous novel *1984*, "Big Brother" is an *omniscient* political leader, so all-knowing that privacy simply doesn't exist in the world he controls.

   Omniscient means _____.

5. The United States had a *multiplicity* of reasons for not entering World War II, but after Japan bombed Pearl Harbor, every one of those reasons disappeared like smoke.

   Multiplicity means _____.

6. When millions died during the civil war in Rwanda, both Europe and the United States were harshly criticized for not *intervening* early on, when lives might have been saved.

   Intervening means _____.

7. Roaches have survived for centuries because they are *omnivorous*; they eat anything and everything—from paste to nail filings.

   Omnivorous means _____.

8. While the angry *multitudes* shouted outside the gates of the palace, the frightened king and queen tried to leave in secret, knowing full well that there was no way to calm their starving subjects.

   Multitudes means _____.

9. The mother *placated* the child with a chocolate chip cookie; in a matter of seconds, he went from tears to giggles.

   Placated means _____.

10. Not anxious to return to work, the boy took the most *circuitous* route he could think of and managed to make a fifteen-minute trip take three-quarters of an hour.

    Circuitous means _____.

▶**TEST 7** **Using Word Analysis and Context Clues**

DIRECTIONS Use context clues and word parts to develop an approximate meaning for each italicized word.

Prefixes	Roots
pre = before or preceding, prior to	*locut, loqu* = speech
	voc = voice, call
super = over, beyond, above	*fic, fact, fect* = to make, to do
sub = under, from below, put under	*gen* = to give birth to, to produce, to cause

1. She has an amazing mind; in a single class session, she can *generate* one original idea after another, and most of them are quite good.

   Generate means _____.

2. After having their reports censored by military officials, the reporters were *vocal* in their complaints; they told anyone who would listen that their right to free speech had been ignored by the high command.

   Vocal means _____.

3. As a *prelude* to his speech, the scientist told a silly joke; as he had hoped, the comic introduction warmed up the audience and made them more attentive.

   Prelude means _____.

4. Patricia Henley's novel *Hummingbird House* wonderfully *evokes* the lush and beautiful landscape of Guatemala; she is particularly good at describing the country's colorful birds and gorgeous flowers.

   Evokes means _____.

5. What exactly is the *genesis* of the word "bedlam"? I've heard two different stories about its origin, and I am not sure which one is accurate.

   Genesis means _____.

6. Although the two men work together very well, they couldn't be more different: Bob is relaxed and *loquacious*, whereas Will is tense and silent most of the time.

   Loquacious means _____.

7. To avoid being followed by reporters, the famous couple used *fictitious* names when they checked into the hotel, but they used their real names after they had crossed over the border into Mexico.

   Fictitious means _____.

8. In an effort to trim her speech down to no more than fifteen minutes, the union organizer carefully crossed out any *superfluous* details that weren't directly related to her message.

   Superfluous means _____.

9. The previous group leader encouraged independent thought; unfortunately, the current leader tries to *subdue* all signs of it.

   Subdue means _____.

10. Sometimes truth is stranger than *fiction*, and the real world can be odder than the one you find in books.

    Fiction means _____.

Prefixes, Roots, and Suffixes You Should Know

♦

Prefixes

a, ad = to, toward

anti = against

bene = well, good

bi = two

circum = around

dis = apart from, not, without

extra = over, outside, beyond

im = not

in, im = in, into, not

mal = bad

mono = one

multi = many

omni = all

per = through

phil = love

poly = many

pre = before, preceding, prior to

pseudo = false

re = again, back

sub = under, from below, put under

super = over, beyond, above

syn, sym = together

Roots

bellum = war

chron = time

clin = lean

cred = belief

derma = skin

dict = say or speak

fic, fact, fect = to make or to do

for = to bore into

gam = marriage

gen = to give birth to, to produce, to cause

here = stick

lat = side

locut, loqu = speech

mob = move

pe, pull = push, force

plac = calm, please

popul = people

rec, rect = straight, straighten

sci = know

sect = cut, divide

the = god

ven = come

vi, vit, viv = life

voc = voice, call

vor = eat

Suffixes

ism = state, condition, or quality

ist = person who does what's described in the root

itis = inflammation

ize = to cause to be, to treat or affect

onym = name, word

ous = full of

General and Specific Sentences Work Together

3

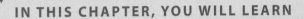

IN THIS CHAPTER, YOU WILL LEARN

- how to tell the difference between general and specific sentences.

- how general and specific sentences work together to communicate a writer's message or meaning.

- about three common patterns of general and specific sentences that appear in your textbooks.

"To generalize means to think."

—Georg Wilhelm Friedrich Hegel, philosopher

"The truth, if it exists, is in the details."

—Anonymous

Throughout this book you'll see repeated references to sentences being *general* or *specific*. Because these terms need to be absolutely clear in your mind, Chapter 3 provides a detailed explanation of how general and specific sentences differ from one another. Equally important, the chapter describes how the two kinds of sentences combine to make sure paragraphs communicate the author's message or meaning to readers.

The Difference Between General and Specific Sentences

To test your understanding of the terms *general* and *specific* when they are applied to sentences, read the following examples. See if you can explain what makes the first sentence more general than the second.

General Sentence   **1.** People express anger in different ways.

Specific Sentence   **2.** Some people get quiet when they get angry, others scream and shout.

Notice how the more general sentence, when viewed on its own, could be understood in a number of ways? Based on sentence 1, we could assume that anger might be expressed in tears, shouts, silence, or laughter. It all depends on how readers understand the key phrase "in different ways."

Look now, though, at the more specific sentence. Sentence 2 puts limits on the number of ways the general sentence can be interpreted. It restricts expressions of anger to just two responses: being quiet or noisy.

The pattern illustrated by these two sentences is very common in writing. It's particularly common in textbooks, where the author's **primary purpose**, or goal, is to inform. Writers use a general sentence to sum up a number of individual events, e.g., "Body piercing has a long cultural history." Then they clarify that general point by illustrating or explaining it with a specific sentence. The more specific sentence points to some individual person, event, group, or experience, for instance, "The ancient Mayans[†] used lip piercing to indicate social rank or status."

Here's another pair of sentences. Now it's your turn to label them. Put a *G* in the blank next to the more general sentence. Put an *S* next to the more specific one.

1. When they are in a classroom, many people are afraid to ask questions or disagree. _____

2. Our behavior is often affected by the presence of others. _____

If you labeled sentence 1 as *specific* and sentence 2 as *general*, you are correct on both counts. Sentence 2 says that our behavior is affected by the presence of others. But it doesn't zero in on any one situation. Instead, it sums up and includes any and all situations where people are present.

Sentence 1, in contrast, focuses on one particular setting—the classroom. It also identifies two particular kinds of behavior—asking questions or disagreeing. Here again, the more specific sentence helps us correctly understand the more general one by restricting the meanings the general sentence can suggest to readers.

[†]ancient Mayans: people living in Central America, whose civilization was strikingly advanced in its complexity and sophistication.

READING TIPS

1. Be alert to general sentences that are further clarified by specific sentences. General sentences sum up the point of a paragraph and therefore deserve extra attention. Above all, make sure you understand how the more specific sentences clarify the general one.

2. Writers of business textbooks are particularly fond of making the first sentence of a paragraph the most general one. That first sentence sums up the point or message, leaving the rest of the sentences to explain it.

WEB QUEST

Where do many of the descendants of the Mayans now live?

_____ **Based on the Mayan calendar, what claims were made about the year 2012?** _____

Ceremonies celebrating Mayan culture remain popular today.

John and Lisa Merrill/The Image Bank/Getty Images.

SUMMING UP THE KEY POINTS

1. General sentences cover a number of individual events, ideas, or people. Therefore, they can be understood in different ways. While general sentences are essential to summing up events and experiences, they often require specific sentences for clarification.

2. Specific sentences don't sum up as many events or experiences as general ones do. Their focus is narrower. They describe or sum up fewer events and experiences. As a result, they are less open to different interpretations.

3. General and specific sentences work together to ensure that communication between writer and reader takes place. Without specific sentences to place restrictions on key words and phrases, general sentences can be easily misunderstood because they are open to different interpretations.

4. In textbooks, writers rely heavily on general and specific sentences because their primary purpose is to inform.

◆ **EXERCISE 1**   **Recognizing General and Specific Sentences**

DIRECTIONS   Read each pair of sentences. Then label the general sentence *G* and the specific one *S*.

EXAMPLE

a. The focus in elementary schools has switched from girls to boys, and researchers now have a new set of educational concerns. __G__

b. In the 1990s, educational research focused on how to help girls excel in science and math, but currently there is a greater emphasis on helping boys become better readers and writers. __S__

EXPLANATION   Sentence *a* is more general because we don't have specific meanings for the words *focus* and *concerns*. Note how sentence *b*, the more specific sentence, defines both terms and puts limits on how they can be understood.

1. a. Early newspapers made no pretense of being without political bias. _____

   b. In the eighteenth century, American politicians funded and controlled newspapers. _____

2. a. In Japan, revealing one's emotions to others is not encouraged, but in America the opposite is true. _____

   b. Culture affects behavior in a number of ways, particularly within the context of personal relations. _____

3. a. Like many of his victims, Jesse James was shot in the back. _____
   b. The outlaw Jesse James met what some have called a fitting end. _____

4. a. By 2050, the U.S. Census Bureau predicts that the number of Hispanic individuals living in the United States will increase from 50.5 million to 132.8 million. _____
   b. People of Hispanic origin make up about 16 percent of the total population in the United States, but the U.S. Census Bureau expects a dramatic increase in that number over the course of time. _____

5. a. The cow known as Molly B is a true survivor who refused to accept her miserable fate. _____
   b. Destined for the slaughterhouse, Molly B made her escape by leaping over the slaughterhouse gate and swimming across the Missouri River. _____

◆ EXERCISE 2   Connecting General and Specific Sentences

DIRECTIONS   For each general sentence, circle the letter of the specific sentence that further clarifies it.

EXAMPLE

General Sentence Pit bulls are not, by nature, vicious dogs, who attack for no reason; their reputation is undeserved.

Specific Sentences (a.) Before pit bulls were trained as fight dogs by being subjected to repeated abuse and cruelty, they were considered the ideal family pets due to their loyal and gentle nature.
   b. People who are convicted of breeding and training pit bulls to fight one another should be sent to jail for a minimum of five years.
   c. The poet and philosopher Vicki Hearne spent her life defending the rights of animals, using her poetry and prose to express her belief that animals are capable of both compassion* and loyalty.

_____

*compassion: a feeling for the suffering and pain of others.

Raised by the right owner, pit bulls make wonderful pets.

© Image Source/Jupiter Images.

EXPLANATION   Only sentence *a* offers a more specific explanation of why pit bulls don't deserve their reputation as vicious dogs. If they were considered loyal and affectionate pets before those who trained them to fight entered the picture, then they cannot be vicious by nature. Including this specific explanation is another way of clarifying the point expressed in the general sentence.

General Sentence **1.** Despite strong security efforts, pirates have become bolder in their attacks on vessels sailing off the African coast.

Specific Sentences
    a. Pirates attack private boats in the hope of taking prisoners who can be held for ransom.

    b. Pirates have increased attacks off the coast of East Africa in recent years despite an international flotilla* of warships dedicated to protecting vessels and stopping the pirate assaults.

    c. The government of Somalia is barely functioning, which is one of the reasons the waters off the coast of Somalia are a hot spot for pirate attacks.

General Sentence **2.** Betty Ford, the wife of President Gerald Ford, died in 2011 and was mourned by many who admired her courage and her commitment to helping others.

---

*flotilla: fleet of small ships.

Specific Sentences

a. Unlike many first ladies, Betty Ford supported herself before getting married, and she knew the meaning of hard work: She was a women's clothing buyer for a large department store and an assembly-line frozen-food factory worker.

b. When Betty Ford had breast cancer and a mastectomy, she broke with tradition and publicly disclosed the details of her surgery because she believed knowing about her experiences would help other women feel less alone in their struggle.

c. In his inaugural address, Gerald R. Ford was the first president to ever credit his wife for his extraordinary political success.

General Sentence

3. Medical research has saved billions of lives through the development of vaccines and medicines that protected against or cured once deadly diseases, but at times medical research has done tragic, even deadly, harm.

Specific Sentences

a. Researchers are reporting that the sexually transmitted disease gonorrhea has become resistant to even the strongest antibiotics, a fact that is causing great concern in the medical community.

b. Professor of Surgery at the Jefferson Medical College from 1856 to 1882, Professor Samuel Gross was one of the most famous surgeons of the nineteenth century, and his textbook *A System of Surgery* (1859) provided the basis for surgeries performed during the Civil War.

c. During World War II, researchers looking for treatments infected prisoners in American correctional facilities* with typhoid, dysentery, malaria, and a number of other dangerous diseases.[†]

WEB QUEST

Betty Ford had a profound and lasting effect on two health-related areas. What were those two areas and how did she influence them?

_____

_____

---

*facilities: spaces and/or equipment for performing some specific activity.
[†]From the blog of Leonard Glantz, professor of bioethics at Boston University (http://primr.blogspot.com/2011/01/another-look-at-guatemala-research.html).

◆ **EXERCISE 3**   **Making the General More Specific**

DIRECTIONS   Make the general sentence more specific and turn it into a common English saying.

EXAMPLE

General Statement It's impossible to determine the meaning of reading matter from its external appearance.

You can't tell a book by its cover.

EXPLANATION   The word *book* is a more specific type of "reading matter" in the same way that the word *cover* is more specific than "external appearance." Plug in those more specific words and what emerges is the old cliché, or oft-repeated saying,[†] about outward appearances.

1. Don't count your winged creatures before they come to light.

   _____

2. Avoid being emotional over a wasted dairy product.

   _____

3. A single work of art is equal to a lot of language.

   _____

From Reader to Writer Pick three well-known sayings and translate them into more general language. Read them aloud and see if your classmates can recognize the more specific point hidden in the general language.

◆ **EXERCISE 4**   **Connecting General and Specific Sentences**

DIRECTIONS   Read the three specific sentences. Then look at the more general sentences that follow. Put a check in the blank next to the one that could sum up the specific sentences.

_____

[†]Beware of using clichés in writing. They have been repeated so often they lack all originality. Their presence in a paper suggests a writer who isn't thinking very hard about his or her subject matter.

EXAMPLE

Specific Sentences
a. Before 1980, most doctors were self-employed, but today more than half are salaried employees who work in medical groups.

b. The number of general practitioners has been steadily declining as more and more medical students choose to become specialists.

c. Increasingly, doctors are the subject of lawsuits for medical malpractice, and the damages awarded in many of those lawsuits have increased sharply over the last decade.

General Sentences
_____ **1.** The number of women and minorities applying to medical school has increased greatly.

✓ **2.** The professional life of physicians has changed dramatically over the past few decades.

_____ **3.** Most people who enter medical school do so because they have been influenced by family doctors.

EXPLANATION   General sentences 1 and 3 are not good choices because the specific sentences do not mention medical schools or why people apply to them. Only sentence 2 is broad enough in meaning to include all three specific sentences.

Specific Sentences
1. a. The tradition of using candles at funerals began with the Romans, who used them to frighten away evil spirits.

b. Tombstones originated as a way of keeping the dead in the underworld.

c. The original purpose of coffins was to keep the dead safely underground.

General Sentences
_____ **1.** Anthropologists have found evidence that funeral traditions existed during the Neanderthal age (100,000–40,000 BCE).

_____ **2.** Different cultures have different ways of mourning their dead.

_____ **3.** Many of the modern customs associated with mourning came from a fear of what the dead might do to the living.

Specific Sentences 2. a. The citizens of Sparta, a city-state of ancient Greece, were not allowed to become farmers; they were made to train as warriors instead.

b. Family life in Sparta was severely limited because both boys and girls spent long hours in physical training.

c. From age seven to age thirty, the boys received instruction in the art of waging war.

General Sentences _____ 1. The Spartans were obedient to the laws of their land.

_____ 2. Spartan life was hard and devoted to war.

_____ 3. Spartan men and women were known for their heroism in war.

Specific Sentences 3. a. During World War II, German invaders destroyed Russia's richest agricultural regions.

b. According to official reports, more than seven million Russians were killed while defending their country against German attacks.

c. Although precise figures are hard to come by, Russia seems to be the country with the greatest number of casualties during World War II.

General Sentences _____ 1. The Russians suffered heavy losses in World War II.

_____ 2. Russia suffered more than any other country during World War II, largely because it began the war on the side of Adolf Hitler and then switched sides in 1941.

_____ 3. Russia has never recovered from the tragedy of World War II.

Specific Sentences 4. a. During World War II, the U.S. War Department finally approved the training of African-American pilots.

b. In 1941 Benjamin O. Davis Jr. became the first African American to lead a squadron of pilots.

c. President Franklin D. Roosevelt's Executive Order 8802 required employers in defense industries to make jobs available "without discrimination* because of race, creed* or color."

---

*discrimination: the act of showing prejudice in favor of or against a particular group.
*creed: set of beliefs, religious beliefs.

Initially barred from flight training because of his race, Benjamin O. Davis Jr. went on to become the first African American to achieve the rank of general in the Air Force.

© Corbis.

General Sentences _____ **1.** For many African Americans, World War II offered a chance to break down racial barriers.

_____ **2.** During World War II, racial violence broke out on several military bases.

_____ **3.** When they returned home, many African-American veterans of World War II were shocked to discover that they were still being treated as second-class citizens.

Specific Sentences **5.** a. Between 1933 and 1939, about 150,000 square miles of U.S. farmland in the Great Plains baked to dusty clay as a result of a killing drought.

b. During the same period, more than 500 million tons of rich earth dried out and turned to powder.

c. Huge dust storms repeatedly turned day into night all over the Great Plains.

General Sentences ——— **1.** American land has been over-plowed and over-planted for decades.

——— **2.** In the 1930s, a large part of the United States turned into what came to be called the "Dust Bowl."

——— **3.** Poor farming techniques cause hardships for many countries, including the United States.

Specific Sentences **6.** a. So many people use the search engine Google that "to google" has become a verb.

b. Xerox Corporation produced the first plain paper photocopier in 1959, which became so famous, "xeroxing" became a synonym for "photocopying."

c. The company Kimberly-Clark came up with the brand name Kleenex in the 1920s; now many people refer to facial tissues as "kleenex," even if they are not talking about a Kimberly-Clark product.

General Sentences ——— **1.** In the twentieth century, American companies earned a reputation for creativity and originality by creating products and services that revolutionized daily life.

——— **2.** Over time, some brand-name products became so popular, people began using the brand name to describe the thing being sold or used.

——— **3.** Google is not the only company unhappy about having its trademark used as a general descriptive term.

Specific Sentences **7.** a. When actor Robert Coates liked the lines in one of Shakespeare's death scenes, he would repeat the scene over and over until angry theatergoers pelted him with oranges.

b. Coates forgot his lines every night, so he made up his own for well-known plays such as *Hamlet* and *King Lear*.

c. England's theater critics laughingly called the actor "Romeo" Coates because he would stop the show to wave to friends and chat with people in the audience.

General Sentences ____ **1.** Robert Coates, a nineteenth-century stage performer, was one of the worst Shakespearean actors to ever step on a stage.

____ **2.** Actor Robert Coates played many of Shakespeare's most famous characters during the early 1800s.

____ **3.** Handsome costumes mattered very much to British actor Robert Coates.

Specific Sentences **8. a.** A blue fireball exploded above central Siberia when an asteroid, or small planet, hit near the Tunguska River on June 30, 1908.

b. A mushroom cloud blossomed in the air, and trees were uprooted and scorched for dozens of miles.

c. An entire herd of reindeer died because of the heat the asteroid produced, while its impact shattered windows as far away as 600 miles.

General Sentences ____ **1.** Scientists believe that asteroids are ancient chunks of matter that never clumped together to become planets.

____ **2.** Most asteroids are grouped into belts that hang in space.

____ **3.** When an asteroid crashed to earth in 1908, it caused a shocking amount of damage.

Specific Sentences **9. a.** In sign language, we use hands and other body parts to make gestures that stand for letters, words, and concepts.

b. Morse code requires a wire telegraph machine to produce sounds— dots and dashes—that are translated into letters, numbers, and punctuation.

c. Often seen at airports, the semaphore, or flag signaling system, works this way: A person stands holding a flag in each hand, and then moves his or her arms to positions that indicate letters and numbers.

General Sentences ____ **1.** Mass communication means that messages are sent to large audiences.

____ **2.** Some communication methods do not rely on written language.

____ **3.** Simple writing systems date back to the Sumerians of 3000 BCE.

Specific Sentences **10.** a. In the city of Dubai small boys who have been sold by or stolen from their parents are forced to work as camel jockeys: held captive and half-starved they are tied to camels, who can race at speeds of up to thirty miles per hour.

b. In Southern Asia "bonded workers" are tricked into incurring a large debt, and then they have to lay bricks or pick vegetables for years until they have paid what they owe.

c. On February 22, 2012, a New York judge determined that Shanti Gurung was owed 1.5 million dollars by her employer, who had forced her to work sixteen-hour days without pay for a period of three years.

General Sentences _____ **1.** Childhood is supposed to be a carefree happy time, but for many children around the world, life consists of little more than hard work and fear of punishment.

_____ **2.** Throughout the war in the Sudan, armed militias sold women and children in order to raise money for weapons.

_____ **3.** The 1926 slavery convention outlawed slavery around the world, but in one form or another, slavery still exists the world over.

✔ CHECK YOUR UNDERSTANDING

1. What's the function of general sentences, and why is it a good idea to follow them with more specific sentences?

_____

_____

_____

2. What's the primary purpose of textbook writing? _____

VOCABULARY ROUND UP 1

Below are five words introduced in pages 119–24. The words are accompanied by more detailed definitions, the page number on which they originally appeared, and additional sample sentences. Spend time reviewing the words and their meanings because you will see them again in review tests at the end of the chapter. Use the online dictionary Wordnik to find additional sentences illustrating the words in context. (Note: If you know of another dictionary, online or in print, with as many examples of words in sentences feel free to use that one instead.)

1. **compassion** (p. 119): a feeling for the suffering and pain of others, pity, inclination to give help or support. "The social worker knew she was dealing with a hardened criminal but given the man's horrific childhood, she still felt *compassion* for him."

2. **flotilla** (p. 120): a fleet of small ships, any small group. "By two o'clock in the morning, the *flotilla* of taxis that normally waited at the railroad station had thinned out considerably."

3. **facilities** (p. 121): spaces and equipment for performing some specific activity. "The library *facilities* were closed for the two weeks of vacation."

4. **discrimination** (p. 124): the act of showing prejudice in favor of or against a particular group; the ability to see fine differences. (1) "When the young woman first joined the police force, she felt that she was the victim of *discrimination*." (2) "The chef did not believe that the restaurant's guests had any sense of *discrimination* when it came to recognizing the difference between a great meal and a mediocre one."

5. **creed** (p. 124): set of beliefs, religious beliefs. "Respect for the natural world was part of the Apache *creed*."

Recognizing Different Levels of General and Specific Sentences

As you can probably guess, writers don't alternate, or go back and forth, between general and specific sentences in any rigid pattern. Sometimes they introduce an idea with a series of general sentences before switching to a more specific illustration or explanation. At other times, they might start an explanation with one general sentence and make each succeeding sentence slightly more specific.

Look, for example, at the following diagram. It shows you how a writer moves an explanation forward from the very general to the very specific, with a series of increasingly specific sentences about temperament in artists.

Based on sentence 1, the reader can assume that the writer is making a point about all artists, from sculptors to musicians.

1. Many artists are as famous for their temperament as they are for their talent.

By sentence 2 the reader can eliminate people who work in the fine arts, painting, architecture, etc.

2. Popular entertainers are no exception to this rule.

Sentence 3 reduces possible interpretations even further. The author has one particular popular entertainer in mind.

3. Super-talented rapper and singer-songwriter, Nicki Minaj has made headlines more than once for letting her temper get the best of her.

Sentence 4 is even more specific than sentence 3. It focuses on defining what the author means by "letting her temper get the best of her."

4. In the space of a few months, Minaj's maid and facialist accused her of having screaming temper tantrums.

Sentences 4 and 5 are equally specific. Both help explain how the rapper has let temper "get the best of her."

5. When the singer felt the sting of criticism on Twitter, she retaliated by closing her account.

In this case, the writer becomes increasingly specific in order to explain the point of the opening general sentence. However, it's also possible to do the reverse. Writers sometimes build up to a larger, more general point by listing a series of more specific sentences:

Specific Sentences

1. In Brazil's celebration of Carnival, there are samba contests, with all the dancers wearing brightly colored costumes dripping in sequins and feathers.

2. In Italy, Carnival is the big winter festival, celebrated with colorful parades, but also with private parties and balls.

3. In the Netherlands, Carnival is the last chance to eat and drink before Easter, and much of the celebrating is done indoors in pubs, or bars.

4. In Croatia, the celebration of Carnival did not get started until 1982, but it is now an established tradition, with face masks being an essential part of the celebration.

5. The festival of Carnival is celebrated all across the Caribbean with steel-band music playing a huge role in the outdoor festivities.

General Statement

6. Carnival, once mainly a Christian tradition, has lost many of its religious associations, but it is still celebrated around the world, with each country adding its own individual touch.

The carnival in Rio de Janeiro may be the most colorful of them all.

General and specific sentences can be combined in different ways. How they combine depends on the author's topic, purpose, and audience. What's important is that you, the reader, keep track of how the writer shifts back and forth between different levels of generality.

Why Recognizing Shifts in Level Is Important

As you read, you certainly don't have to make written diagrams of the sentences to indicate when the author is shifting from general to specific. But you do have to notice where the author has shifted to a different *level of specificity or generality*. When you figure out that a shift has taken place, you then have to consider what purpose the shift to a more general or specific level of language serves.

A change toward the more general level usually means that the author is introducing a new point. In contrast, a shift to a more specific level of language usually indicates the author is still discussing the previous point but explaining it in greater detail, much like the first example shown above (p. 130). By the same token, a series of sentences that are equally specific often means that the author is building up to a larger point, as shown in the second example.

Overall, recognizing the relationships between general and specific sentences in writing is one of the main ways the reader tracks the writer's train of thought. It's also one of the ways readers decide what's essential information and what's not. But we'll discuss that in more detail in later chapters.

READING TIPS

1. If you are reading a business text, then more often than not, the first sentence is the most general sentence in the paragraph, and it will be explained by the more specific sentences that follow.

2. But if you are reading a history textbook, then you have to re-tool your expectations. Yes, the first sentence might introduce the general point of the paragraph, but so might the last.

SUMMING UP THE KEY POINTS

1. Writers combine general and specific sentences in different ways depending on the subject matter, the kind of information they want to convey, and their purpose or reason for writing.

2. Readers need to be alert to shifts in general and specific language. Noticing when the language shifts can help readers stay tuned in to the writer's train of thought.

3. Different disciplines are likely to combine general and specific sentences in different ways. Business texts start out general and become more specific. History texts, in contrast, are just as likely to start out specific and become more general.

◆ **EXERCISE 5**   **Recognizing Shifts in General and Specific Language**

DIRECTIONS   Fill in the accompanying diagrams with the appropriate letters. The letter of the most general sentence goes on the top level. The letter of the most specific sentence goes on the bottom level.

EXAMPLE

a. We use our teeth to prepare food for digestion.

b. To prepare food for digestion, *molars* crush and grind food; *incisors* cut large pieces of food into smaller ones.

c. In the process of preparing food for digestion, different teeth have different functions.

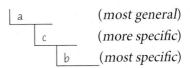

EXPLANATION   Sentence *a* is the most general. It tells us that our teeth prepare food for digestion. Sentence *c* tells us more about the way the teeth prepare the food for digestion. Sentence *b* is the most specific sentence. It identifies specific kinds of teeth and their functions.

1. a. The biggest change in the American workforce involves gender.

    b. The American workforce is changing.

    c. Since 1960, the number of women in the American workforce has nearly doubled.

2. a. In mathematics, for example, some words have meanings that are different from their usual ones.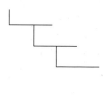

    b. In mathematics, a *curve* is the path between two points, and a curve can be straight rather than rounded.

    c. Changing the context of a word can change its meaning.

3. a. There are many ways to fight insomnia and fall asleep more easily.

    b. The more carbohydrates—sugars, starches, and grains—you eat at night, the more easily you will fall asleep.

    c. Diet can help you fight insomnia.

4. a. In *The Net Delusion*, Morozov shows how the Internet can actually make it easier for repressive* governments to spy on activists who promote democracy.

   b. Not everyone is convinced that the Internet can be used to promote democracy around the world.

   c. Journalist Evgeny Morozov has insisted that those in the West need to liberate* themselves from the belief that the Internet can only be used to support democratic freedom.

5. a. While our own culture considers mutilation* of the body to be a sign of a psychiatric disorder, other cultures do not necessarily share this view.

   b. The culture we are born into has a strong influence on how we view or interpret behavior.

   c. In some African cultures, boys entering manhood have six cuts made into their forehead as a mark of their new status.

Connecting General and Specific Sentences: Three Common Templates, or Patterns

Textbook writers have a definite **purpose**, or goal, in mind when they write. Their goal is to **inform** their readers. They want to supply their

---

*repressive: inhibiting or restraining freedom.
*liberate: free, break away from.
*mutilation: cutting or injuring the body.

audience with information it hasn't encountered before, or at least not encountered in quite the same way.

Writers know that much of the content they want to give their readers is unfamiliar and complex. They also know their audience is pressed for time.

Taking into account both their purpose and the needs of the audience, textbook authors generally write in the most straightforward way possible. They also tend to rely on standard, or common, **textbook templates**. These are explanatory patterns, which combine general and specific sentences in familiar ways.

While essay or novel writers might temporarily leave readers in the dark as they try out new styles of writing or build up suspense, textbook authors take a much more direct approach. Less concerned with originality of style and more concerned with familiarity of form, they want their readers to recognize standard patterns of explanation and make use of them to determine the text's intended meaning.

What follows are three of the most common textbook templates, or explanatory patterns. Becoming familiar with them will enhance, or improve, your ability to understand textbook material.

Explanatory Pattern 1: Starting Off with the Topic Sentence

Topic sentence

Specific details

Textbook authors frequently start off paragraphs with what's called a **topic sentence**.[†] Topic sentences can be long, short, or somewhere in between. But they always perform two functions. First, they refer to the topic of the paragraph. The paragraph's **topic** is the person, place, idea, or experience the author wants to discuss. It's the subject that is mentioned, referred to, or suggested throughout the paragraph, usually from beginning to end.

However, writers don't just introduce a topic and then list a number of facts and figures related to that subject. They usually have a point or **main idea** they want their readers to grasp or share, and that's where the second essential function of the topic sentence comes in: The topic sentence always tells you, in general terms, what the main idea of the paragraph is. It tells you what the author wants to say *about* the topic. If someone were to ask you what the paragraph was meant to communicate to readers, you could answer by paraphrasing the topic sentence.

[†]This pattern isn't restricted to textbook writing, but it is probably most common in textbooks.

Here's a typical example of a paragraph that opens with a topic sentence:

The word theory *doesn't get mentioned again. However, the remaining sentences all describe it, so we can call "Hilgard's theory of hypnosis" the topic.*

The topic sentence tells us that Hilgard's theory emphasized something called "split awareness."

The more specific sentences illustrate "split awareness."

The best-known theory of hypnosis was proposed by Ernest Hilgard (1904–2001), who argued that hypnosis causes a dissociative state, or "split in awareness." To illustrate, he asked hypnotized subjects to plunge one hand into a painfully cold bath of ice water. Subjects told to feel no pain said they felt none. The subjects were then asked if there was any part of their mind that did feel pain. With their free hand, many wrote. "It hurts," or "Stop it, you're hurting me," while they continued to act pain-free. In this split awareness state, one part of the hypnotized person says there is no pain and acts as if there is none. Another part, which Hilgard calls the hidden observer, is aware of the pain but remains in the background. The **hidden observer** is the detached* part of the hypnotized person's awareness that silently observes events. (Coon and Mitterer, *Introduction to Psychology*, 11th ed., p. 194.)

Paragraphs like this one are extremely common in textbooks. The author opens with a general topic sentence that (1) mentions or refers to the topic and (2) makes a point about the topic.

Understanding the Supporting Details

But as you already know, general sentences, like general words, cover a lot of territory. For precisely that reason, topic sentences need more specific follow-up to successfully convey their message to readers. Left totally on their own, they can cause confusion.

It follows, then, that textbook authors, intent on informing their readers, need to provide more specific sentences, called **supporting details**. These sentences "support" the main idea by anticipating and answering questions readers might raise in response to reading it. In the case of the sample paragraph on hypnosis, the supporting details answer the obvious question: What exactly is "split awareness"?

READING TIP

To quickly locate topic sentences in paragraphs, pay close attention to the relationships between sentences. If the author opens with a general sentence and then illustrates or further explains it in more specific language, that first sentence is the topic sentence summing up the main idea.

*detached: separate and disconnected.

◆ EXERCISE 6   Supplying the Topic Sentence

DIRECTIONS   Each item in this exercise gives you the topic and the supporting details. Your job is to come up with a topic sentence, a general sentence that ties them all together.

EXAMPLE

Topic   Abraham Lincoln

Topic Sentence   A great many myths surround the figure of Abraham Lincoln.

Supporting Details   One long-standing myth has persisted for years: the belief that Lincoln was a poor country lawyer. He wasn't. In the 1850s he successfully and profitably represented two huge companies, the Illinois Central Railroad and the Rock Island Bridge Company. Some gay rights activists have also insisted that Lincoln was homosexual. This claim seems to be flatly contradicted by the fact that Lincoln had four children and, prior to his marriage, occasionally visited prostitutes. Yet another story that doesn't hold up is the claim that Lincoln suffered for years from devastating depression. Given that untreated depression makes normal functioning all but impossible, it's difficult to believe that Lincoln was deeply depressed. He was, after all, a remarkably effective president, who carried out all the tasks of his office.

EXPLANATION   The topic sentence shown above does what it's supposed to do. It identifies the topic and tells readers, in general terms, what they need to know *about* the topic. Like a good topic sentence should, it can also sum up the more specific supporting details that follow it.

Topic   **1.** Long-term memories

Topic Sentence   _____

_____

Supporting Details   When researchers refer to a procedural memory, they are referring to long-term memories about basic habits and behaviors like how to drive a car or get dressed. Semantic memory, in contrast, refers to memories of more formal and more complex knowledge. Included in this category of long-term memories are word meanings, grammatical rules, and ideas or theories associated with people, places, and events. Episodic memories are those in which we ourselves play some kind of role. You might remember, for instance, that while you were growing up, everyone loved Madonna. You, however, couldn't stand her music or her style.

Topic 2. Roberta Walker's lawsuit

Topic Sentence _____

_____

Supporting Details In 1993, Roberta Walker filed a class action suit[†] against Pacific Gas & Electric Company. She and several other residents had discovered that the company was responsible for contaminating the ground water that came into their homes in the small town of Hinkley, California. To her surprise, Walker won her case, and the company paid her and others involved in the suit $333 million. Walker breathed a sigh of relief and assumed that the worst was over. But now the unthinkable has happened and chromium, the same substance that contaminated drinking water in 1993, is showing up in it again. This time it's supposedly at "safe" levels, but residents like Walker who stayed on in Hinckley after the suit was won—many of the others who filed the suit moved away—are not so sure. They feel like they are reliving a nightmare from which they can't wake up.

Explanatory Pattern 2: Opening with Introductory Sentences

| Introduction |
| Topic sentence |
| |
| Specific details |

It's certainly true that paragraphs starting with a topic sentence are popular in textbooks. However, that doesn't mean every paragraph will open with a statement of the main idea. In and out of textbooks, paragraphs often open with an introductory sentence. **Introductory sentences** are general sentences that provide background or context for the main idea. The topic sentence expressing the main idea then follows the introduction, as in this paragraph:

The introductory sentence suggests the writer is going to discuss abusive behavior toward children in public places.

[1]One need spend only an hour or so in a supermarket of a shopping mall to observe instances of children being physically or verbally abused. [2]*Unfortunately*, such public behavior is but the tip of the iceberg; the private reality is much worse. [3]A 2005 PNS survey found that

---

[†]This case was the basis for the 2000 movie *Erin Brockovich*.

Note how the word unfortunately has reversed the writer's train of thought, moving it away from "public behavior" and into the "private" sphere.

64 percent of American adults agree that "a good hard spanking" is sometimes necessary in disciplining a child. [4]This is despite accumulating evidence that children who get spanked regularly are more likely to cheat or lie or be disobedient at school, to bully others, and have less remorse for what they did wrong. [5]Sadly, child abuse, in private, goes far beyond unnecessary spanking. [6]Abuse may involve burning, scalding, beating, and smothering. [7]In 2006 alone, there were 905,000 reported cases of child maltreatment. (Adapted from Hughes and Kroehler. *Sociology, The Core*, p. 335.)

While not quite as common as paragraphs that open with a topic sentence, paragraphs like the sample above turn up frequently in textbooks and other kinds of writing. The introductory sentence usually alerts readers to the topic by providing some context or background about the main idea. The sentence itself, however, gets no further development. Instead, the topic sentence follows, putting into words the real point of the paragraph. The supporting details take over from there.

◆ **EXERCISE 7**   **Recognizing Topic and Introductory Sentences**

DIRECTIONS   Circle the correct letter to indicate if the topic sentence is the first or second sentence in the paragraph.

1. [1]A bad economy, reduced funds for animal control, and the persistent popularity of dog fighting have created a hidden epidemic in many of America's biggest cities, where stray and wild dogs have banded together to survive. [2]Generally the dogs congregate in areas where buildings have been abandoned, and they can go unnoticed. [3]Aware that they are often targets of human aggression, the dogs are smart enough to emerge only at night or during bad weather to hunt for food. [4]According to Randy Grim, who runs *Stray Rescue* in St. Louis, Missouri, the problem is huge and growing all the time. [5]Of specific concern is the fact that some of the unneutered strays are giving birth to pups, which then grow up without human contact. [6]Pups born into roaming dog packs are wild animals rather than former pets, which have been let loose or gotten lost. [7]Thus, they are a greater threat to humans and to other dogs. [8]Not surprisingly the group People for the Ethical Treatment of Animals (PETA) has issued a warning about the growing urban epidemic. [9]PETA has

even suggested that euthanizing, or putting the dogs down, is a better fate than their life on the streets. (Source of information: Will Doig, "The Secret Life of Feral Dogs," *Salon*, January 14, 2012.)

a. Sentence 1

b. Sentence 2

2. ¹For centuries, earthquakes were considered warnings from the gods. ²It is only in the twentieth century that a fully developed theory, called *plate tectonics*, seemed to adequately explain the cause of earthquakes. ³According to this theory, the earth's surface consists of about a dozen giant rock plates, each seventy miles thick. ⁴Propelled by unknown forces, the plates are continuously in motion. ⁵Sometimes they collide and temporarily lock together. ⁶The locking of the plates builds up stress at the plates' edges, causing the rock to fracture. ⁷The fracture causes the plates to resume their motion, but the sudden release of energy can also produce an earthquake. ⁸The brainchild of Alfred Wegener, the concept of plate tectonics[†] was initially ridiculed when Wegener first proposed it in 1905. ⁹Tragically, Wegener died in 1930 without ever knowing that his theory would one day gain the respect of the scientific world.

a. Sentence 1

b. Sentence 2

3. ¹Over the years, the food pyramid with its six different food groups was often criticized for being confusing to consumers interested in understanding the basics of good nutrition. ²The people at the U.S. Department of Agriculture seem to have heard the complaints because the food pyramid has disappeared; in its place sits a brand-new four-color image of sound nutrition, called MyPlate. ³MyPlate is divided into four sections: fruits, vegetables, grains, and proteins. ⁴Next to the brightly colored plate sits a little circle of dairy. ⁵Fats, in contrast to the disgraced and dismissed food pyramid, are nowhere to be seen on the current nutritional symbol. ⁶In contrast to the food pyramid, MyPlate's message is clear on sight. ⁷Fruits and vegetables should be major players in our daily diet and on an equal footing with proteins and grains.

[†] Wegener laid the groundwork for the theory of plate tectonics by introducing the idea of continental drift, which explained how one big super continent turned into seven individual ones.

Food Guide pyramid.   MyPlate graphic.

[8]No one who sees MyPlate can ever again think that a quarter-pound cheese burger is a nutritionally sound meal because it also happens to have a slice of lettuce and tomato sitting on top of the melted cheese.

a. Sentence 1

b. Sentence 2

WEB QUEST
How and where did Alfred Wegener die? Why is the exact day of his death unknown?

_____

_____

_____

_____

Explanatory Pattern 3: Ending with the Topic Sentence

Specific details

Topic sentence

Especially at the beginning of individual chapter sections, textbook writers often reverse the typical relationship between general and specific sentences. Instead of starting out with a general sentence, they end with one, after listing the specific supporting details that back it up. Here's an example:

Think of something funny. What is the expression on your face? Now think of something in your past that made you sad. Did your face change? Chances are it did. Undoubtedly, you are aware that certain facial expressions coincide with specific emotions. Now consider this. Could you be equally successful in determining someone's emotional state based on facial expression if that person is from a different culture—say Romania, Sumatra, or Mongolia? In other words, do you believe facial expressions of emotion are universal? Think of the multitude of cultural differences in styles of dress, gestures, personal space, rules of etiquette, religious beliefs, attitudes, and so on. <u>With all of these differences influencing behavior, it would be rather amazing if any human characteristics, including emotional expressions, were identical across cultures.</u> (Adapted from Hughes and Kroehler *Sociology: The Core*, p. 44.)

This paragraph opens a chapter section discussing a famous study on facial expressions and emotions. Although the specific supporting details in the opening lay the groundwork for the final topic sentence, it's the remaining paragraphs in the chapter section that would provide the real support.

While you are less likely to see this particular explanatory pattern in the middle of a chapter section, it's very likely to turn up at the beginning, particularly in history, sociology and psychology texts. The next time you start reading a chapter section and the first paragraph seems to consist largely of equally specific sentences, pay close attention to the last sentence. It might well be the topic sentence of the paragraph. However, by the time you are through reading the chapter section, it might well turn out to be the focus of the entire section. But we'll talk more about that in the chapters that follow.

From Reader to Writer Pick a person, an animal, or a location that you know well. Write down all the specific details about that person or place that make it meaningful to you. Then make the last sentence the general statement that expresses the meaning of the details, for instance, "He was a dog whose loyalty knew no limits" or "It was a room no child could resist."

SUMMING UP THE KEY POINTS

1. Because authors of textbooks know they have to supply readers with a lot of unfamiliar information, they are inclined to take a direct route. They frequently present the main idea in a general sentence that either opens the paragraph or arrives right on the heels of the first sentence. Then they follow that sentence with more specific supporting details.

2. A common variation on this pattern is to use specific sentences that build up to the main idea. This pattern of piling up specifics to make a general point is typically found at the beginning of chapter sections and appears in the paragraph that immediately follows the heading.

3. The **main idea** is the key point or message of a paragraph or reading.

4. The **topic** is the subject under discussion; the **topic sentence** conveys the key point about the topic that the author wants readers to understand.

5. **Introductory sentences** pave the way for the main idea by providing background or context. Often, they identify or refer to the topic in the process.

6. **Supporting details** further explain the main idea, often answering questions readers might have about the topic sentence.

7. Because their purpose is to inform, textbook writers usually get right to the point. They don't spend time building suspense or creating mood as they might when writing an essay or short story.

READING TIPS

1. If the second sentence in a paragraph explains the first, the opening sentence is probably the topic sentence expressing the main idea.

2. If the second sentence in the paragraph does not follow up on the idea introduced in the first sentence, check to see if the remaining sentences explain the second sentence. If they do, the second sentence is the topic sentence.

3. If the specific sentences in a paragraph seem to be piling up, look closely at the last sentence. It might well be the topic sentence.

◆ EXERCISE 8   Recognizing Common Explanatory Patterns

DIRECTIONS   Read each paragraph. Then circle the appropriate letter to indicate which sentence is the topic sentence.

EXAMPLE   ¹Families have become as diverse as the American population and reflect different traditions, beliefs, and values. ²Within African-American families, for instance, traditional gender roles are often reversed, with women serving as head of the household. ³Kinship bonds often unite several households, as does a strong religious commitment. ⁴In Chinese-American families, both spouses may work and see themselves as breadwinners, but the wife may not have an equal role in decision making. ⁵In Hispanic families, wives and mothers are acknowledged and respected as healers and dispensers of wisdom. ⁶At the same time, they are expected to defer to their husbands, who see themselves as the strong, protective, dominant head of the family. (Adapted from Hales, *An Invitation to Health*, 7th ed., p. 219.)

Topic Sentence   (a.) The first sentence is the topic sentence.

     b.   The second sentence is the topic sentence.

     c.   The last sentence is the topic sentence.

EXPLANATION   The general sentence opening the paragraph introduces the topic, diversity among American families. This is the subject repeatedly referred to throughout the passage. The first sentence also expresses the author's general point about the topic: Families are as diverse as America itself. The remaining supporting details then provide specific examples of that diversity.

1.   ¹The eye is made up of many different parts, each one playing a significant role in an individual's ability to see. ²The eyeball is surrounded by three layers of protective tissue. ³The outer layer, called the *sclera*, is made from firm, tough, connective tissue and is white in color. ⁴The middle layer, called the *choroid coat*, is a delicate network of connective tissue that contains many blood vessels. ⁵The inner layer, which is called the *retina*, contains the nerve receptors for vision and approximately ten different layers of nerve cells. ⁶Two kinds of nerve cells are contained within the retina: *cones*, which are used mainly for light vision, and *rods*, which are used when it is dark or dim. (Clover, *Sports Medicine Essentials*, p. 385.)

Topic Sentence

    a. The first sentence is the topic sentence.

    b. The second sentence is the topic sentence.

    c. The last sentence is the topic sentence.

2. [1]Most adults want their love relationships to result in marriage. [2]However, U.S. residents are in no hurry to achieve this goal, and the median age at first marriage has been rising for several decades. [3]Between 1970 and 2006, the median age for first marriage rose nearly four years for both men and women, from roughly 23 to 27.5 for men and from roughly 21 to 25.5 for women. [4]This trend is not bad. [5]Women under age 20 at the time they are first married are three times more likely to end up divorced than women who first marry in their 20s and six times more likely to end up divorced than first-time wives in their thirties. (Kail and Cavanaugh, *Human Development*, 5th ed., p. 410.)

Topic Sentence

    a. The first sentence is the topic sentence.

    b. The second sentence is the topic sentence.

    c. The last sentence is the topic sentence.

3. [1]Prior to the 1960s, the definitive works on the sexual behavior of humans were the large-scale surveys of Americans' sexual activities published by Alfred Kinsey in the late 1940s and early 1950s. [2]The famous Kinsey Reports, *Sexual Behavior in the Human Male* (1948) and *Sexual Behavior in the Human Female* (1953), asked thousands of men and women about their sexual behavior and attitudes. [3]The topics of the questions ranged from frequency of intercourse to masturbation habits to homosexual experiences. [4]With the publication of Kinsey's reports, humans suddenly had a measure against which to compare their own sexual lifestyles. [5]The Kinsey Reports are still cited today as a source of statistical information about sexual behavior. (Adapted from Hock, *Forty Studies that Changed Psychology*, p. 159.)

Topic Sentence

    a. The first sentence is the topic sentence.

    b. The second sentence is the topic sentence.

    c. The last sentence is the topic sentence.

4. [1]In some Arab countries, where women do not have equal rights, men routinely cut in front of women waiting in line. [2]They see no reason why a man should wait in back of a woman. [3]In Britain and the United

States, where men and women are at least officially considered equal, few men would dare cut ahead of a woman who was standing ahead of them in line. [4]In countries like Italy and Spain, where individuality is highly prized above social conformity, lines are little more than an annoyance to be ignored at will. [5]Men and women routinely jostle for the best position in line, and the poor soul who stands and waits his or her turn is thought to be lacking in spirit. [6]Culture clearly has an effect on the behavior of people waiting, or refusing to wait, in a line.

Topic Sentence

a. The first sentence is the topic sentence.

b. The second sentence is the topic sentence.

c. The last sentence is the topic sentence.

5. [1]Among traditional Chinese families, marriage is less a matter of a man getting a wife than of bringing a child-bearer into the household. [2]Because marriage has less to do with relations between husband and wife than with those between the husband's family and a daughter-in-law, marriages in traditional Chinese families are almost always arranged, often at an early age, and there is little if any courtship. [3]When a boy is six or seven years old, his parents might hire a matchmaker to find a girl who will eventually be an appropriate bride. [4]Because they believe that the time of a person's birth influences his or her personality and fate, the parents might also enlist the services of a fortune teller to make the appropriate match…. [5]If the fortune teller deems* the girl appropriate, the matchmaker tries to convince the girl's parents to accept the match. [6]If she is successful, the *bride wealth*, the marriage gifts of the husband's family to the wife's parents, is then negotiated. (Shaffer, *Social and Personality Development*, 6th ed., p. 122.)

Topic Sentence

a. The first sentence is the topic sentence.

b. The second sentence is the topic sentence.

c. The last sentence is the topic sentence.

---

*deems: considers, judges, evaluates.

✔ CHECK YOUR UNDERSTANDING

1. Name and describe the three common ways general and specific sentences are combined in textbook paragraphs.

   _____

   _____

   _____

   _____

   _____

   _____

2. What's the difference between the topic and the main idea of a paragraph?

   _____

   _____

3. What's the difference between the introductory sentence and the topic sentence?

   _____

   _____

4. What role do supporting details play in a paragraph?

   _____

   _____

5. What is the purpose of textbook writing? _____ How does that purpose affect the author's method of writing?

   _____

   _____

VOCABULARY ROUND UP 2

Below are five words introduced in pages 135–46. The words are accompanied by more detailed definitions, the page on which they originally appear, and additional sample sentences. Spend time reviewing the words and their meanings because you will see them again in review tests at the end of the chapter. Use the online dictionary Wordnik to find more sentences illustrating the words in context. (Note: If you know of another dictionary, online or in print, with as many examples of words in context feel free to use that one instead.)

1. **repressive** (p. 135): restraining or restricting the freedom of a person or group. "Robert Mugabe's *repressive* measures in Zimbabwe have been criticized by the rest of the world, but criticism has no effect on Mugabe's brutal rule."

2. **liberate** (p. 135): free, break away from, set free from bondage or foreign control. "When the soldiers arrived at the camps to *liberate* the prisoners, they were greeted as heroes by those still strong enough to stand or speak."

3. **mutilation** (p. 135): cutting or damaging of the body, destruction of body parts, to damage beyond recognition. "The chimp's attack left the woman's face horribly *mutilated*, but surgeons were able to reconstruct it."

4. **detached** (p. 137): separated and disconnected; objective, uninvolved, lacking in self-interest. (1) "Should the retina become *detached*, blindness can be the result." (2) "She called upon him for advice because she felt his attitude was *detached* enough to be trusted."

5. **deems** (p. 147): considers, judges, evaluates, regards. "When Alfred Wegener presented his theory of plate tectonics to his colleagues, most *deemed* Wegener's ideas ridiculous, which shows just how wrong even experts can be."

DIGGING DEEPER Defining Culture

Looking Ahead Some of the readings in this chapter focused on the way culture influences behavior. In the reading that follows, Julia T. Wood, author of the textbook *Interpersonal Communication*, makes the same point. Only she goes into greater detail. Wood also provides her readers with a definition of that much-used and often misunderstood term *culture*.

Getting Focused The title along with the introductory note above make it clear that this reading will define the word *culture*. As soon as you locate the definition, paraphrase it. Then, as you read, keep asking yourself (1) what does the author want to say about culture, and (2) how does what she says differ from or resemble the readings that came before?

1 A culture is [the totality of beliefs, values, understandings, practices, and ways of interpreting experience that are shared by a number of people.] Culture forms the pattern of our lives and guides how we think, feel, and communicate. The influence of culture is so pervasive that we don't always recognize how powerfully it shapes our perceptions.

2 Consider a few aspects of modern Western culture that influence our perceptions. Western culture emphasizes technology and its offspring, speed. Most Westerners expect things to happen fast, almost instantly. Whether it's instant photos, accessing websites, or 1-hour dry cleaning, we live at an accelerated pace. We send letters by express mail. We jet across the country and we microwave meals. In countries such as Nepal and Mexico, however, life often proceeds at a more leisurely pace, and people spend more time talking, relaxing, and engaging in low-key activity.

3 The United States is also a highly individualistic culture in which personal initiative is expected and rewarded. In more collectivist cultures, identity is defined in terms of membership in family rather than as an individual quality. Because families are more valued in collectivist cultures, elders are given greater respect and care than they often receive in the United States. More communal countries also have policies that reflect the value they place on families. In every developed country except the United States, new parents, including adoptive parents, are given at least 6 weeks of paid parental leave, and some countries provide nearly a year's paid leave.

4 Many doctors in the United States now are encouraged to attend workshops that teach them about the cultural practices and folk beliefs of immigrants from other countries. One doctor, Jeffrey Syme, found

immediate application for what he learned in a workshop. A number of his patients had emigrated from Cape Verde, a string of islands off West Africa. Many of those patients asked him for Valium but refused to discuss their problems with him. According to Syme's training as well as United States drug policy, Valium is a medication that should be prescribed only for specific conditions. In the workshop, Syme learned that in Cape Verde, Valium is an over-the-counter treatment people routinely take for everyday blues. Thus, they perceived Valium as a mild medication that they could take as casually as many Americans take aspirin.

5   In another case, ignorance of folk beliefs led a doctor to faulty perceptions of a patient. A folk belief among many Guatemalans is that giant worms in the stomach govern well-being. One doctor attending the workshop said, "I just had a patient like that." What had the doctor done when her patient complained that giant worms in his stomach were making him feel bad? She referred him to mental health specialists because she perceived his statement to indicate that he was mentally unbalanced. In both cases, the doctors misperceived patients by not taking into account the patients' cultural customs and beliefs. (Adapted from Wood, *Interpersonal Communication: Everyday Encounters*, 6th ed., p. 86.)

Sharpening Your Skills

DIRECTIONS   Answer the questions by circling the letter of the correct response or writing the answer on the blank lines.

1. In the opening paragraph, where is the topic sentence of the paragraph?

   a. first sentence

   b. second sentence

   c. last sentence

2. In paragraph 2, the references to instant photos, accessing websites, and 1-hour dry cleaning are all specific examples of what general point made in the paragraph?

   a. Western culture emphasizes technology.

   b. Western culture emphasizes speed.

   c. In countries such as Nepal and Mexico, life often proceeds at a more leisurely pace.

3. Which sentence is the topic sentence in paragraph 3?

   a. first sentence

   b. second sentence

   c. last sentence

4. The specific example of Dr. Syme is used to illustrate what general main idea?

   _____

   _____

5. Overall the reading develops

   a. the first sentence in the opening paragraph.

   b. the second sentence in the opening paragraph.

   c. the last sentence in the opening paragraph.

Using Context Clues In the opening paragraph, note how the author uses the words *pervasive* and *perceptions*.

Based on their context, how would you define these two words?

Pervasive means _____.

Perceptions means _____.

Share Your Thoughts The previous reading identified some characteristics of our culture. We are, the author claims, strikingly individualistic. Do you think that's true? Why or why not? What additional characteristics do you think describe American culture as you know it? Please give a specific example of how this characteristic makes itself felt in everyday life.

▶ TEST 1   Reviewing Key Concepts

DIRECTIONS   Answer the following questions by circling the letter of the correct response.

1. General sentences

   a. narrow the range of meanings a reader can apply to a word or phrase.
   b. sum up or comment on a number of different events, people, or ideas.
   c. are always at the very beginning of readings because they express the author's main idea.

2. Specific sentences

   a. are essential to general sentences because they help restrict the range of meanings a reader can apply to the author's words.
   b. are essential to writing because they provide the kind of colorful details that keep the reader interested in what the author has to say.
   c. always follow general sentences because they contain information that is less important.

3. The topic of a paragraph is

   a. the general point the writer wants to communicate to the reader.
   b. the subject most repeatedly referred to in the paragraph.
   c. the key thought introduced in the first sentence of the paragraph.

4. The main idea is

   a. the sentence that sums up the point of the paragraph.
   b. the central thought that the author wants to communicate to readers.
   c. the subject most often referred to in the paragraph.

5. The topic sentence

   a. mentions or refers to the topic without introducing the main idea.
   b. mentions or refers to the topic and makes a point about the topic.
   c. is always the first sentence of a textbook paragraph.

6. Supporting details

   a. restate the main idea in more specific language.

   b. provide examples and illustrations of the main idea.

   c. anticipate and answer questions readers might raise about the main idea.

7. Readers need to notice when the writer shifts between general and specific levels of language because

   a. they will forget the author's original point if they don't notice the specific examples accompanying it.

   b. it's impossible to understand general language without specific details.

   c. it will help them stay in touch with the author's train of thought.

8. Textbook authors usually come straight to the point because

   a. their purpose is to inform.

   b. they want their readers to take them seriously.

   c. they don't want their readers to be distracted by colorful details.

9. The most common location for paragraphs that introduce the topic sentence at the very end is

   a. at the beginning of a chapter section.

   b. in the middle of a chapter section.

   c. at the end of a chapter section.

10. The topic sentence is most likely to be the first sentence in which kind of textbook?

    a. sociology

    b. history

    c. business

TEST 2   **Recognizing the Most General Sentence**

DIRECTIONS   In each group of sentences, one is more general than the others. Circle the letter of the most general statement.

1. a. In the African country of Dahomey, music historians were carefully trained to preserve important records.

    b. There was a time when the music of Africa was also the history of the African people.

    c. In the African country of Burundi, singers followed soldiers to war and recorded great actions in song.

    d. Many African countries trained men and women to be living books who could record important events in song.

    e. If the songs contained important information, some African musicians had to learn them in secret.

    f. In the Sudan, singers recited the history of the nation at public gatherings and sang the deeds of great heroes.

2. a. Tornadoes are clouds shaped like funnels: they reach all the way to the ground, doing enormous damage.

    b. Although all storms have fearful aspects, tornadoes are the most frightening.

    c. Winds within the funnel of the tornado can reach speeds of more than several hundred miles per hour.

    d. Tornadoes strike without warning: they seem to come out of nowhere.

    e. Sometimes buildings actually blow up as the tornado passes over them.

    f. The heavy rain and hail that accompany a tornado also do much damage.

3. a. Because of the way he looked, Joseph Merrick (1862–1890) could not go into the street without being mobbed by curious strangers who stared at and ridiculed him.

    b. Before he came under a doctor's care, Joseph Merrick was exhibited in the circus, like an animal.

c. The victim of a terrible and deforming disease, Joseph Merrick could not sleep like other people; he had to sit up with his heavy head resting on his knees.

d. The head of the Elephant Man was enormous and misshapen.

e. Joseph Merrick, also known as the Elephant Man, had a brief and tortured life.

f. Joseph Merrick never forgot the brutal beatings and terrible humiliation of his life in the circus.

4. a. It took a while for L. Frank Baum, author of *The Wonderful Wizard of Oz*, to find just the right title for his masterpiece.

b. While the book was in production, Baum changed the title to *From Kansas to Fairyland*.

c. An author sometimes has great difficulty choosing the title of a book.

d. When Baum first submitted his manuscript in 1899, it was called *The Emerald City*.

e. Just before the book appeared in print, Baum changed the title again, this time to *The City of the Great Oz*.

f. In the end, the book was published in 1900 as *The Wonderful Wizard of Oz*.

5. a. During the American Revolution, British and American spies used a mixture of water and ferrous sulfate to create ink that was invisible until baking soda was brushed over the paper.

b. There are references to the use of invisible ink in the writing of Pliny the Elder, a Roman general, who, as a military man, had a reason to keep secrets.

c. Public interest groups have tried to get access to the formula for invisible ink developed in World War I, but the information remains classified.

d. Many people think that invisible ink is the stuff of fiction, but it's real and has been around for centuries.

e. In 2008 Habib Ahmed was given a ten-year sentence in Britain for bringing books written in invisible ink into the country.

▶ **TEST 3** **Clarifying General Sentences**

DIRECTIONS Read each general sentence. Then circle the letters of the three more specific sentences that support it.

General Sentence 1. The German psychologist Hermann Ebbinghaus was the first person to systematically study the process of forgetting.

Supporting Details
a. One theory of forgetting suggests that we forget when new information interferes with what's previously been learned.

b. Ebbinghaus spent thousands of hours memorizing nonsense syllables.

c. After learning the nonsense syllables, Ebbinghaus measured the time it took to forget them.

d. Another theory of forgetting stresses that we forget whenever we don't intend to remember.

e. As a result of his research, Ebbinghaus discovered that the greatest memory loss occurs right after learning.

f. Another memory researcher, A. P. Bumstead, discovered that several learning sessions stretched out over time actually decreased forgetting.

General Sentence 2. It's easy to understand why the threat of rabies inspires great fear.

Supporting Details
a. In its final stages, rabies produces hallucinations.

b. Few people recover from rabies once symptoms appear.

c. Rabies has been around a long time; there are references to it as early as 700 BCE.

d. Once the disease takes hold, the victim can neither stand nor lie down comfortably.

e. Recently, scientists have improved the treatment for rabies; the new treatment is much less painful than the old.

f. In the early stages of rabies, a dog is likely to appear tired and nervous; it will try to hide, even from its master.

General Sentence 3. Many people believe that mystery stories are a product of modern times, but the mystery story actually has a long history.

Supporting Details
a. Historians of the detective story claim to have found elements of the mystery story in the pages of the Bible.
b. Dorothy Sayers was for many years an enormously popular mystery writer.
c. Poe's "The Murders in the Rue Morgue," published in 1841, presented the classic mystery plot of a dead body found in a sealed room.
d. Mystery historians like to argue about which books may or may not be classified as true mystery stories.
e. Nineteenth-century authors Charles Dickens and Edgar Allan Poe are often cited as the fathers of the modern mystery.
f. Raymond Chandler wrote mystery stories so good that literary critics called his crime novels art.

General Sentence 4. People should be very careful about what they post on Facebook.

Supporting Details
a. Facebook is all too ready to decide for its users what news is important and what news is not.
b. When Dawnmarie Souza posted her thoughts on her employers at American Medical Response in Connecticut, she was fired.
c. Facebook has made Mark Zuckerberg one of the richest men in the United States.
d. When a high school supervisor in Cohasset, Massachusetts, complained about both her students and their parents, she lost her job.
e. Many employers regularly check out job applicants on Facebook and if the applicant has posted pictures suggesting he or she leads a wild social life, potential employers tend to think twice about hiring that person.
f. Facebook is more about marketing products than it is about keeping in touch with friends.

▶ TEST 4   Locating Topic Sentences

DIRECTIONS   Circle the appropriate letter to identify the location of the topic sentence that sums up the main idea.

1. ¹Textbooks have long taught that the seventeenth-century English settlement at Jamestown, Virginia, struggled and almost perished because the colonists didn't like hard work. ²However, when scientists analyzed the rings of Jamestown cypress trees during a 1998 climate study, they found that the trees' growth was significantly stunted between 1606 and 1612. ³Based on this information, the study's authors argued that when Jamestown was founded in 1607, a lack of rain caused fresh water supplies to dry up and parched corn to turn brown on the stalk. ⁴The subsequent food shortage would have aggravated relations between the colonists and the Powhatan Indians, who were also forced to compete for scarce resources. ⁵In 1608, Captain John Smith noted in his journal that the Indians would not trade corn for colonists' goods because that year's crop had been poor, and the Indians did not have enough for themselves. ⁶Based on current research, it now seems possible that a drought, rather than laziness or greed, was to blame for Jamestown's disappearance. (Source of information: Jeffery L. Sheler, "Rethinking Jamestown," *Smithsonian*, January 2005, pp. 48–56.)

Topic Sentence

a. first sentence

b. second sentence

c. last sentence

2. ¹Fraternities have been around practically since the first university was founded. ²Fraternity hazing, however, has never before been so brutal or so deadly; with good reason, schools are cracking down on the practice. ³After a nineteen-year-old student died during a hazing episode that included mock kidnapping, public humiliation, and forced drinking, Cornell University banned all fraternity pledging. ⁴New York State's Binghamton University halted all pledging in the spring of 2012 because of an "alarmingly high number of serious hazing complaints." ⁵In 2011, the parents of Michael Starks, a nineteen-year-old student who died during a hazing ceremony, sued Utah State University and won. ⁶But the parents' goal was not money. ⁷Their goal was to get the university to publicize

the dangers of hazing and the binge drinking that accompanies it. [8]The university has agreed to do so. [9]After a drum major at Florida's A&M University was found dead from a brutal beating endured during a hazing ritual, the school introduced stricter controls over fraternity hazing.

Topic Sentence

a. first sentence

b. second sentence

c. last sentence

3. [1]To persons living in the industrialized countries, measles is a minor childhood disease. [2]Yet among children in developing countries, measles is a major cause of death. [3]Measles accounts for 6.3 percent of deaths among children under age five in the developing nations. [4]Deaths due to measles occur when children, already weakened by malnutrition and poor living conditions, become further weakened by measles. [5]Their bodies' ability to fight disease diminishes, leaving them susceptible to other potentially deadly diseases. [6]However, rates of measles have declined almost by half since 1990, following a worldwide World Health Organization (WHO) measles vaccination campaign. [7]Vaccination campaigns, though, have had far less effect in Africa due to the continent's ongoing and severe economic problems. (Adapted from Weitz, *The Sociology of Health, Illness and Health Care*, 5th ed., p. 329.)

Topic Sentence

a. first sentence

b. second sentence

c. last sentence

4. [1]Men who are quick to express anger are more likely to develop heart disease than men who are calmer and more relaxed. [2]Hostility also appears to double the risk of recurrent heart attacks in men (but not in women). [3]Research has linked hostility to increased cardiac risk factors and to decreased survival in men with coronary artery disease if they are below the age of sixty-one. [4]Hostility has also been linked to an increased risk of heart attack and abnormal heart rhythms. [5]In a study that tracked more than 1,000 physicians for 36 years and took into account other physical and psychological risk factors, the angriest men were likely to suffer heart attacks by 55 and three times more likely to develop cardiovascular disease.

[6]At least where men are concerned, anger and hostility have both short- and long-term consequences for the heart. (Adapted from Hales, *An Invitation to Health*, p. 279.)

Topic Sentence

a. first sentence

b. second sentence

c. last sentence

5. [1]Only in modern times have most people married for love. [2]In the "good old days," most married for money and labor—marriage was an economic arrangement between families and love was not an issue. [3]The key questions were how much land or wealth did the man have? [4]How large a dowry would the bride bring to the spouse? [5]Emotional attachments were of no importance to parents in arranging marriages and neither the bride nor the groom expected emotional fulfillment from marriage. [6]The most common emotions couples expressed seem to have been resentment and anger. [7]Not only was wife beating commonplace but so was husband beating. [8]And when wives beat their husbands, it was the husband, not the wife, who was likely to be punished by the community because he had shamed the village by not controlling his wife properly. (Adapted from Stark, *Sociology*, 10th ed., pp. 370–71.)

Topic Sentence

a. first sentence

b. second sentence

c. last sentence

♦ **TEST 5**   **Reviewing Chapter 3 Vocabulary**

DIRECTIONS   Circle the letter of the sentence that uses the italicized vocabulary word correctly.

1. a. The director was a *compassionate* human being, whose temper tantrums were legendary.

   b. *Compassionate* by nature, she fell in love every other month but soon lost interest in the current great love of her life.

   c. The novelist Ayn Rand was not known for her *compassion*; she thought poor people lacked ambition and were personally responsible for their poverty.

2. a. As a long-time victim of *discrimination*, the singer Harry Belafonte became a passionate fighter for civil rights.

   b. The lobbyist's *discriminating* comments gave him away and the police arrested him shortly after hearing a tape of his conversation.

   c. The woman hurled angry *discriminations* at her ex-husband as they emerged from the courtroom.

3. a. The lawyer made it clear that there wasn't a *flotilla* of truth in the witness's statements.

   b. The farmer had to *flotilla* the ground before the vegetables could go into it, and the rocks kept on getting in the way.

   c. The "Freedom *Flotilla*" got a lot of publicity, both good and bad, after the ships set sail for the Middle East.

4. a. The nasty *creed* he wrote about his former superiors finished the general's career forever.

   b. Spending most of the day in complete silence was part of the monk's *creed*.

   c. The stepdaughter's *creedy* attitude was part of what made her so difficult to deal with when it came to deciding how to care for their ailing mother.

5. a. The chimps were *liberated* from the cages, and like their human counterparts they were joyous over their newfound freedom.

   b. The cat seemed fascinated by the *liberating* movement of the fan.

   c. He *liberated* for a long time over the contract, deciding in the end not to sign it.

6. a. The scholar *deemed* deeply into the book in order to better understand all of the historical details of the event under discussion at the conference.

    b. The president should select for the panel anyone he *deems* adequately knowledgable about climate change.

    c. The con man *deemed* and lied at every opportunity, but he was so charming no one could resist his pleas for help or money.

7. a. Even for a pie-eating contest, the teenager ate a *repressive* amount of pie, and the other participants were awestruck.

    b. In 2011, to protest the *repressive* government of Hosni Mubarak, thousands of Egyptians marched into Tahrir Square and refused to leave despite being surrounded by Mubarak's armed supporters.

    c. The curly-haired child had a wonderfully *repressive* face that mirrored her every emotion.

8. a. The second home was more expensive than the first because the garage was not *detached* from the house.

    b. The child is so *detached* to his mother, he will have a hard time entering school the first year.

    c. The snake's eyes had a focused and *detached* look that suggested it was about to strike.

9. a. When the Brazilian soccer team won the gold cup, there was *mutilation* in the streets at the victory.

    b. The ticket had been so *mutilated* by all of the feet stepping on it, it was impossible to tell if the winning number was on it as its owner claimed.

    c. The *mutilated* company had taken over the production of sugar throughout the country.

10. a. The *facilities* in the sand made it easy to follow the wolf's tracks.

    b. Although the general was known for being a tough task master, he did have a warm *facility* where his children were concerned.

    c. The dining *facilities* had to be spotless by early morning when the first of the guests arrived for coffee.

Getting to the Point of Paragraphs

4

> *"Understanding depends on mutual empathy, on reader and writer appreciating each other's task."*
>
> —Larry Wright, professor, philosopher, and author of *Critical Thinking: An Introduction to Analytical Reading and Reasoning*

Chapter 4 reviews and enlarges what you learned about paragraphs in Chapter 3 (pp. 135–47). It further describes and illustrates the kinds of explanatory patterns textbook writers use when combining general and specific sentences in paragraphs. The chapter also gives you an additional strategy for dealing with paragraphs where you can't quite get a handle on the author's meaning, despite your understanding of how general and specific sentences relate to one another.

How? Additional Ways Authors Introduce Topic Sentences

As you know from Chapter 3, authors sometimes introduce the topic sentence by offering background or context about the topic *before* presenting the main idea. But what you may not realize is that those introductions can be longer than a single sentence. In the following paragraph, for example, two sentences—rather than one—pave the way for the topic sentence expressing the main idea.

[1]For the past twenty years, it's been claimed that low self-esteem causes numerous social and psychological ills. [2]Think well of yourself and you will behave better was the reigning theory. [3]**Yet, as it turns out, exaggerated self-esteem seems to be more prevalent* and more problematic than low self-esteem.** [4]In a wide range of studies focused on self-esteem, participants consistently gave themselves higher ratings than they gave others. [5]They also overestimated their personal contribution to team efforts; exaggerated their ability to control life's events; and made unrealistic predictions about their future success. [6]Participants in the studies also tended to get angry when things did not turn out as expected. [7]Similar research on self-image also shows that many people overestimate their intellectual and social skills. [8]What was particularly interesting about this tendency was that those who had the poorest intellectual and social skills were the most likely to overrate their performance in both areas. [9]For instance, researchers Justin Kruger and David Dunning found that college students with the lowest scores on tests of logic and grammar generally assumed that their scores would be among the highest. [10]Interestingly enough, when these same students received training in grammar and logic, their self-assessments became less confident and more realistic. (Adapted from Brehm, Kassin, and Fein, *Social Psychology*, 5th ed., p. 138.)

"That Was Then, This Is Now" Introduction

The above sample paragraph illustrates a typical introduction authors use to pave the way for the main idea. The introductory sentences tell readers what has been thought in the past *before* introducing them to more current thinking on the topic. The description of the current thinking then becomes the true point of the paragraph.

You can confirm that the discussion of the current thinking is the true point of the paragraph by a quick glance at the supporting details. As you can see above, the details provide evidence for the current claim that exaggerated self-esteem causes more trouble than low self-esteem. If the more traditional concept, or idea, about self-esteem was the point of the paragraph, the supporting details would tell readers more about low self-esteem and its supposed effect on behavior and performance.

---

*prevalent: widespread.

When an opening sentence tells you what's been thought in the past *or* what most people are inclined or ready to believe, it's a strong signal that the opening sentence is *not* the topic sentence. Writers usually use these kinds of statements purely as introductions. They then follow up with more up-to-date or more evidence-based thinking that is the real point of the paragraph.

Moving Toward the Middle

Specific details

Topic sentence

Specific details

As you might expect, introductions in paragraphs aren't limited to two sentences either. In fact, introductions can get so long they push the topic sentence closer and closer to the middle of the paragraph. This is especially true when the author wants to give you some history or background related to the topic or main idea prior to introducing the main idea. Here's an example:

Dr. Frankenstein's monster.

[1]Most people know the gruesome story of Baron Victor Frankenstein, the arrogant doctor who created a living creature from the bodies of corpses, only to see his creation turn murderous. [2]The story has been told and retold. [3]It has also been the subject of numerous films, and most people are familiar with the tale, so much so that we use allusions, or references, to Frankenstein's monster to describe a good idea gone very wrong. [4]**What many people don't know, however, is that the chilling story of Dr. Frankenstein and his creature was written by a nineteen-year-old newlywed named Mary Shelley.** [5]As a young bride, Shelley liked to take part in storytelling competitions with her husband, the poet Percy Bysshe Shelley, and his friend and fellow poet George Gordon Byron. [6]On one particularly long evening in 1816, Byron suggested that everyone compose a ghost story. [7]In response to Byron's suggestion, Mary Shelley spent the night writing and was ready the next day with the story of Dr. Frankenstein, the man who constructed a creature from body parts and galvanized* it into action. [8]When she read it aloud, everyone agreed Shelley's story was the best by far, and by 1818 she had published it as a novel.

Topic sentences in the middle or close to the middle of a paragraph are not nearly as common as topic sentences at the beginning. But they do exist, Thus you should be prepared for this variation on the more standard

---

*galvanized: forced into action with electricity; caused to act, produced a strong reaction.

explanatory pattern of a one- or two-sentence introduction followed by the topic sentence.

If a paragraph opens with a series of general sentences, but only one general sentence gets the support of more specific details, the sentence getting the support is the topic sentence. In the above paragraph, sentence number 4 is the only one that gets additional clarification through more specific supporting details. That makes sentence 4 the topic sentence.

WEB QUEST

Mary Shelley called her novel *Frankenstein; or, The Modern Prometheus.* Why did she link her novel to Prometheus, a figure from Greek mythology? What's the connection?

Prometheus was

Doubling Up on Topic Sentences

Topic sentence
Specific details
Topic sentence

To make doubly sure that their readers get the main idea, writers sometimes use two topic sentences, making their point in the first *and* the last sentence of the paragraph. Here's an example:

The career of George Smith Patton Jr., the much-decorated four-star army general, stalled because he didn't know how to control his temper. During World War II, in August of 1943, Patton visited ailing and wounded soldiers in two separate army hospitals. On each visit he publicly slapped a soldier who complained about losing the nerve to fight. Patton viewed the men with contempt and insisted that "real" soldiers should not have to look at gutless cowards afraid of the battle field. Although Patton thought his behavior perfectly appropriate, his commanding officer, Dwight D. Eisenhower, did not. Eisenhower made Patton publicly apologize to the hospital staff and to the men themselves. Eisenhower also made sure that Patton never rose any higher on the ladder of military command. **Thanks to his uncontrollable temper, George S. Patton's brilliant military career stalled and never got re-started.**

If a paragraph says much the same thing in the first sentence and the last, you can be sure that the idea expressed in those two sentences is the main idea.

Reversal Transitions Are Clues to Topic Sentences

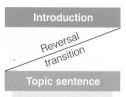

When main ideas start moving beyond the first sentence, the reader has to work harder to find them. Writers know this. For that reason they often use a **reversal or contrast transition** (see the list on p. 169) to tell readers, "I'm shifting gears now; here comes the real point of the paragraph."

In the sample paragraph on self-esteem (p. 165), for instance, the transition *yet* announced the arrival of the topic sentence. In the paragraph about Mary Shelley (p. 166), the reversal transition *however* indicated that the topic sentence was coming up.

Using what you know about introductory sentences and reversal transitions, read through the following paragraph. In the blank at the end of the paragraph, write the number of the topic sentence expressing the main idea.

[1]Most Americans are accustomed to thinking that lie detectors, because they are machines, can, without error, separate the guilty from the innocent. [2]But, in fact, lie detectors can and do make mistakes. [3]For one thing, those who administer the tests are not necessarily qualified experts. [4]Many states don't employ licensed examiners trained to read and interpret lie detector printouts. [5]In addition, many subjects react to taking a lie detector test by becoming anxious. [6]As a result, their bodies behave as if the subjects were lying even when they are telling the truth. [7]Unfortunately, some people are smart enough to use relaxation techniques or tranquilizers to remain calm when they are telling a pack of lies. _____

Since the paragraph as a whole does not focus on the accuracy of lie detectors, the first sentence can't be the topic sentence. Also, the first sentence tells us what "most Americans think." This opening phrase is the author's way of saying to readers, "I will tell you what we used to think before I tell you what's really true, correct, or current." In other words, it's a signal to the reader to be on the alert for more up-to-date information.

The signal that the more up-to-date information is coming right up appears at the opening of sentence 2, "But, in fact." That phrase tells readers to get ready for the real point of the paragraph: Lie detectors can make errors.

READING TIP

Any time you think you've found the topic sentence, you can confirm your guess by checking out how the remaining sentences relate to your presumed topic sentence. Do they explain it more precisely? Do they give reasons why it's true or provide examples to make it clearer? If the answer to questions like these is yes, then you've found the topic sentence. If the answer is consistently no, it's time to re-think your topic sentence.

You already know some reversal transitions from Chapter 2. What follows is a more extensive list:

Reversal and Contrast Transitions ♦		
Be that as it may	On the other hand	
But	Regardless	
Conversely	Still	
Despite that fact	That fact notwithstanding	
Even so	Tragically	
However	Unfortunately	
In contrast	When in fact	
In spite of	While that might be true, it's also true that	
Nevertheless		
Nonetheless	Yet	
On the contrary	Yet as it turns out	

Because transitions can sometimes be full sentences, be on the lookout for transitional sentences like the following:

Sample Transitional Sentences ♦
Things did not turn out as planned.
But it was not to be.
But that didn't happen.
Then something strange occurred.
The challenge wasn't long in coming.
However, one thing is clear.
Things did not stay that way, however.

◆ **EXERCISE 1**   **Recognizing Topic Sentences and Reversal Transitions**

DIRECTIONS   Some of the following paragraphs open with the topic sentence. Some don't. Identify the topic sentence by writing the number of the sentence in the blank. If you see a reversal transition, circle it.

1. ¹One of the most dramatic of sleep problems is narcolepsy (nar-koe-lep-see), or sudden irresistible sleep attacks. ²The attacks last anywhere from a few minutes to a half hour. ³Victims may fall asleep while standing, talking, or even driving. ⁴Emotional excitement, especially laughter, commonly triggers narcolepsy. ⁵Tell an especially good joke and a narcoleptic may fall asleep. ⁶More than half of all narcolepsy victims also suffer from something called cataplexy (cat-uh-plec-see), a sudden temporary paralysis of the muscles, leading to complete body collapse. (Adapted from Coon and Mitterer, *Introduction to Psychology*, 11th ed., p. 102.)

Topic Sentence   _____

2. ¹The debate continues to this day about how successful the Homestead Act of 1862 truly was. ²Estimates range from a partial success to a total failure. ³But one thing is clear. ⁴Many of those who expected to make a new life thanks to the Homestead Act were bitterly disappointed. ⁵Although the act gave five acres of publicly owned land to every person willing and able to farm it, estimates vary as to how many homesteaders were actually able to carry the land to "patent," i.e., finalize their claims of ownership. ⁶There is every indication that only about half of those claiming public lands were able or willing to hold on to them. ⁷Many of those homesteaders who went West determined to make a better life for themselves had no idea what they were getting into, and they were shocked by the level of hardship they were expected to endure. ⁸In response to the harsh weather, sandy soil, and intense loneliness, many of the early homesteaders gave up and went home.

Topic Sentence   _____

3. ¹When Anne Sullivan first arrived to teach her young pupil, six-year-old Helen Keller, she found a little girl who could not see, hear, or speak. ²Cut off from the world because she was deaf, mute, and blind, Keller reacted like a frightened animal. ³She would try to bite, scratch, and kick those who came too close. ⁴But Anne Sullivan changed all that. ⁵Playing the roles of teacher and friend, Sullivan transformed

Keller's life, revealing to the little girl the true scope of her talents. [6]It wasn't long before Keller, with Sullivan as her guide, could name the things and people she saw around her. [7]She could even use those names to communicate with others. [8]Over time, and with Sullivan's help, Keller learned to read Braille, the system of writing for the visually impaired. [9]She read Braille in English, then in Latin, Greek, French, and German. [10]With Sullivan's assistance, Keller also learned sign language. [11]In the end, she proved the truth of the first words she spoke with Anne Sullivan's help, "I'm not dumb."[1]

Topic Sentence _____

F. W. Murnau's film *Nosferatu*, a German take on the vampire legend, is a movie classic.

© Bettmann/Corbis.

4. [1]The history of horror films is almost as long as the history of movie-going. [2]The first movie theater opened in 1905. [3]But it didn't take long, only five years, for J. Searle Dawley, along with producer Thomas Edison, to shoot the 1910 movie *Frankenstein* about Mary Shelley's man-made monster. [4]Ten years later, German directors Carl Boese and Paul Wegener returned to the subject of man-made monsters in *The Golem*, a classic horror film highly regarded to this day. [5]*The Golem* tells the story of a rabbi who created and brought to life a giant creature made of clay. [6]The 1919 film *The Cabinet of Dr. Caligari*, sometimes referred to as "the granddaddy of all horror films," portrayed a sadistic* doctor and played in what was to become a classic horror setting, an asylum.* [7]By 1922, famed director F. W. Murnau filmed the horror masterpiece, *Nosferatu*, a brilliant

---

[1]You can see a video of Keller and Sullivan on YouTube.
*sadistic: enjoying the inflicting of pain.
*asylum: in this context, an institution for the mentally ill; also used in the context of "seeking asylum," or safety from harm.

interpretation of the Bram Stoker novel *Dracula*. [8]But if the Germans owned the horror film in the twenties, it was the Americans who took over the genre* in the thirties. [9]The thirties saw the arrival of films like *Dracula, The Mummy, Frankenstein, The Phantom,* and *Dr. Jekyll and Mr. Hyde*, all of them box office blockbusters, suggesting that movie-goers and horror films were made for one another. [10]Judging by the popularity of modern horror films like *Paranormal Activity, Saw,* and *Shutter Island*, they still are.

Topic Sentence _____

5. [1]Artists from Mark Twain to Norman Rockwell have used the image of kids swimming in a river to suggest the ease and joy of childhood. [2]That image certainly makes sense because kids, more than adults, do take to the river during summertime. [3]Particularly in areas where the income level is not high, swimming in the river—rather than the parent's swimming pool—is the only alternative to the sweltering heat. [4]But in some cases, the decision to jump into the river on a hot day can prove deadly. [5]Although health officials report only a few cases per year, children sometimes die after a river swim, because they have come into contact with *Naegleria fowleri*, a deadly amoeba that destroys the brain. [6]The amoeba enters the swimmer's body through the nose and finds its way to the brain, where it starts eating brain cells. [7]By the time it's through, the victim cannot function normally, showing symptoms like confusion, loss of balance, and hallucinations. [8]Most victims die within seven days after the symptoms start. [9]The primary treatment for an attack is an antifungal medication that is injected into the veins and the brain. [10]But so far, only one victim has survived the onset of symptoms thanks to the use of medication. [11]Although coming in contact with *Naegleria fowleri* is a rare occurrence, the results are so deadly, the Centers for Disease Control says that anyone swimming in freshwater ponds and rivers throughout the summer months should use nose clips.

Topic Sentence _____

---

*genre: a particular category of film or literature with specific characteristics that identify it.

READING TIPS

1. To check that you have truly identified the topic sentence of a paragraph, turn the topic sentence into a question, e.g., What mistakes do lie detectors make? If the supporting details provide an answer, you have correctly identified the topic sentence.

2. If a reversal transition opens the second or third sentence of a paragraph, there's a very good chance the sentence starting with the reversal transition is the topic sentence.

From Reader to Writer   Write a paragraph that starts off something like this: "There was a time when I thought that _____ ." (You can substitute any number of words for *thought*, e.g., *believed, argued, insisted*, etc.) Fill in the blank by describing your previous thinking about any topic you choose, i.e., friendship, pets, politics, astrology, religion.

Then use a reversal transition to introduce a sentence explaining how your thinking on the subject has changed. Follow that sentence with a specific description of the event or experience that changed your mind. Here's a sample opening: "I used to think that spending time on Facebook was a total waste of time with no effect on real life. But now I know that Facebook can have a huge impact on the real world."

SUMMING UP THE KEY POINTS

1. Writers don't necessarily limit themselves to one introductory sentence per paragraph. Often they want to provide their readers with more background and context, so they enlarge the introduction and push the topic sentence deeper into the paragraph.

2. Writers who do this are likely to introduce the topic sentence with a reversal transition like *however, but, yet,* or *unfortunately*.

3. Frequently, writers start paragraphs with introductions that identify past thinking about the topic. Or they identify what's traditionally assumed about the topic. Such introductions pave the way for the author to introduce a main idea that differs significantly from earlier thinking or traditional beliefs.

Introductory Questions Can Replace Introductory Sentences

Particularly in textbooks, writers are inclined to use introductory questions as much as introductory sentences. Like introductory sentences, **introductory questions** introduce the topic and pave the way for the main idea. In textbooks introductory questions can appear in the heading of a chapter section. However, they are even more likely to open the paragraph. This is especially true for psychology texts, for instance:

Topic Sentence [1]What determines our long-term satisfaction, and why are some of us happier than others? [2]**Seeking the roots of happiness, Ed Diener and his colleagues (1999) reviewed years of research and found that there are three key predictors of happiness.** [3]The first is social relationships: People with an active social life, close friends, and a happy marriage are more satisfied than those who lack these intimate connections. [4]The second is employment status. [5]Regardless of income, employed people are happier than those who are out of work. [6]Finally, people who are physically healthy are happier than those who are not. (Adapted from Brehm, Kassin, and Fein, *Social Psychology*, 5th ed., p. 536.)

This paragraph illustrates a common way writers use questions to point the way to the topic sentence. The question paves the way for the topic by pointing readers in the direction of "happiness," the actual subject of the paragraph. Then the topic sentence arrives to provide an answer.

The Answers Don't Always Arrive Right After the Question

When a question opens a paragraph, it's very common for the answer to come right after the question and for that answer to be the topic sentence. But textbook authors, who are especially fond of making a question either the heading or the first sentence, sometimes delay the answer to their question. Here's an example:

*Opening
Question*

*The second
sentence does
not provide the
answer.*

*The third
sentence,
however,
does answer
the opening
question.*

[1]What is the difference between civil and criminal law? [2]The distinction between civil and criminal actions is important to understanding the legal process. [3]**Civil actions** involve a conflict between private persons and/or organizations whereas **criminal law** applies to offenses against the public order and entails a specified range of punishments. [4]Typical of cases involving civil law are those involving disputes over contracts, claims for damages, and divorce cases. [5]In a civil case, the person bringing the suit is called the *plaintiff,* and the person being sued is the *defendant.* [6]Acts that are in violation of criminal law are specifically detailed in government statutes. [7]The party demanding legal action is called the *prosecution,* and the person being prosecuted is called the *defendant.* [8]Most of these cases arise in state courts, although there is a growing body of federal criminal law dealing with such issues as kidnapping, tax evasion, and the sale of narcotics. (Adapted from Gitelson, Dudley, and Dubnick, *American Government,* 10th ed., p. 352.)

If the sentence immediately following an opening question does not provide the answer to that question, keep looking. The answer might well be delayed by a sentence or two. If by the end of the paragraph, you still haven't identified the answer, then you might have to infer, or come up with, your own. But we will talk more about that in Chapter 8.

READING TIP

If the writer opens a paragraph with a question, chances are good that the answer is also the main idea. However, if the author provides an answer but doesn't develop it with more specific supporting details, then he or she has varied the pattern, making both question *and* answer part of the introduction. That means you need to be a flexible reader and keep looking for the main idea.

◆ EXERCISE 2   Recognizing Topic Sentences

DIRECTIONS   Write the number of the topic sentence in the blank following each paragraph.

1. [1]Why do we dream? [2]The truth is no one really knows for sure why we dream; all we currently have are different theories. [3]Some evidence suggests that dreaming may help us consolidate* old

---

*consolidate: to combine separate elements into a unified whole.

memories with the new learning that occurred during the day. [4]Yet research for these claims is inconsistent. [5]Dreams may have other functions as well. [6]Ernest Hartmann, a leading dream investigator, believes dreams help us sort through possible solutions to every day problems and concerns. [7]Yet another prominent theory holds that dreams are attempts by the brain to make sense of the random* discharges of electrical activity that occur during REM (Rapid Eye Movement) sleep. [8]The electrical activity arises from the brain stem, the part of the brain responsible for such basic functions as breathing and heart rate. [9]According to this hypothesis, the brain creates a story line to explain those random signals. (Adapted from Nevid, *Psychology: Concepts and Applications,* 3rd ed., p. 148.)

Topic Sentence _____

2. [1]The stage was set for the "Teapot Dome Scandal" in 1921 when the Department of the Interior was given permission to dispose of rich oil reserves. [2]Then in 1922 the Secretary of the Interior Albert B. Fall leased the Teapot Dome Reserve to the Mammoth Oil Company. [3]He also leased the Elk Hills Reserve to the Pan American Petroleum Company. [4]No competitive bidding occurred in the leasing of either reserve, and Fall was generously rewarded by the oil companies for his help. [5]After a long investigation, Fall was convicted of accepting a bribe and sentenced to a year in prison. [6]The oil leases were declared illegal by the Supreme Court. [7]Anyone who thinks political corruption is a consequence of modern day immorality needs to get an American history book and read up on the Teapot Dome scandal of the 1920s, which shows that political corruption is nothing new.

Topic Sentence _____

3. [1]Communal* movements are almost as old as America itself. [2]As early as the mid-1800s, writer and philosopher Ralph Waldo Emerson remarked that every other person seemed to carry in his pocket a plan for the "perfect society." [3]Indeed, although Emerson declined an invitation to be part of the group, several of his friends and acquaintances, among them Nathaniel Hawthorne, experimented

_____

*random: not based on a consistent pattern, happening by chance.
*communal: shared by a group or members of a community movement.

with group living at the much-written-about Brook Farm.[†] [4]Doing their part for the communal movement, city newspapers ran ads for those interested in forming or joining communal associations. [5]Historically, communal movements in America have been most prominent during times of social unrest. [6]Thus, the desire for communal living saw a swell of enthusiasm in the 1840s and 1850s, prior to the outbreak of the Civil War. [7]Following the war, the interest in communal movements persisted, and more than one hundred group-living communities sprang up around the country. [8]Most of them, however, survived only a few years. [9]It wasn't until the 1960s and the explosion of social unrest and political activism that communal movements once again became popular in parts of the United States. [10]In fact, a few communal living arrangements still probably persist from that era but not enough to be counted as part of a movement.

Topic Sentence _____

4. [1]What's the difference between a science and a pseudoscience? [2]Astronomers have low opinions of beliefs such as astrology because they are a form of pseudoscience, from the Greek *pseudo* meaning false. [3]A pseudoscience is a set of beliefs that appear to be based on scientific ideas but that fail to obey the most basic rule of real science: All scientific claims must be repeatedly tested and verified, or proved true, especially in the face of contradictory evidence. [4]For example, in the 1970s a claim was made that pyramid shapes focus cosmic forces and might even have healing properties. [5]Proponents of the pyramid theory claimed, for instance, that placing a pyramid made out of paper or plastic over a piece of fruit could preserve it from rotting. [6]What real science showed, though, was that any material shape, not just a pyramid, protects fruit from airborne spores and allows it to dry without rotting. [7]When experiments contradicted the claims about the power of pyramids, those making the claims did not respond with carefully controlled experiments of their own. [8]Instead, they just ignored the contradictory evidence, yet another indication that their belief was based on pseudoscience.

(Adapted from Seeds and Backman, *Foundations of Astronomy*, 11th ed., p. 25.)

Topic Sentence _____

[†]Brook Farm: an experiment in group living that lasted for six years and attracted some famous literary figures.

5. [1]Cognitive theorists believe that the way in which people interpret events contributes to emotional disorders such as depression. [2]One of the most influential cognitive theorists is the psychiatrist Aaron Beck, the developer of cognitive therapy. [3]Beck and his colleagues believe that people who adopt a negatively slanted way of thinking are prone to depression when they encounter disappointing or unfortunate life events. . . . [4]A minor disappointment is blown out of proportion— experienced more as a crushing blow than as a mild setback. [5]Along with his colleagues, Beck has identified a number of faulty thinking patterns, called *cognitive distortions*. [6]These cognitive distortions are believed to increase vulnerability to the onset of depression following negative life events. [7]The more distorted thinking patterns dominate a person's thoughts, the greater the vulnerability to depression. (Adapted from Nevid, *Psychology: Concepts and Applications*, 3rd ed., p. 538.)

Topic Sentence   _____

◆ **EXERCISE 3**   **Recognizing the Most Accurate Paraphrase**

DIRECTIONS   Read each paragraph. Write the number (or numbers) of the topic sentence in the blank. Then circle the letter of the most accurate paraphrase. If the topic sentence is introduced with a reversal transition, please circle the transition. *Paraphrasing Note*: A paraphrase that makes specific words more general does not qualify as a good paraphrase. The same is true for paraphrases that add information or points of view not present in the original.

1. [1]Cocaine became an outlawed substance in 1914. [2]But, for centuries before that, cocaine was considered a beneficial drug that served a variety of useful purposes. [3]Before the Spanish conquest of Peru, the coca plant was reserved for Incan[†] royalty, who used it in rituals and celebrations. [4]By the sixteenth century, when Spanish explorers first began arriving in South America, the native inhabitants had a 5,000-year history of chewing coca leaves to fight fatigue and hunger and increase endurance. [5]Then the Spanish explorers introduced coca leaves to Europe, where the leaves were smoked or consumed only occasionally. [6]In 1860, however, Germany's Albert Niemann isolated the plant's active ingredient and processed it into powder and liquid

---

[†]Incan: related to the Peruvian people who established an empire from Ecuador to central Chile.

forms. [7]Thanks to Niemann, doctors were able to dispense cocaine for a variety of ailments, from toothaches to hay fever. [8]They also used it as an anesthetic during surgery. [9]It didn't take long before cocaine was available over the counter and as an ingredient in cigarettes, chocolate, and wine. [10]In 1886, Atlanta surgeon and chemist John Pemberton introduced Coca-Cola, a drink that contained coca leaf extract and was advertised as a cure for nervous ailments, "offering the virtues of coca without the vices of alcohol." [11]Not until the early 1900s did the medical community begin to understand the drug's addictive nature, which led to its being banned. [12]Prior to being banned though, cocaine was legal and widely used. (Source of information: "In Search of the Big Bang," www.cocaine.org.)

Topic Sentence _____

Paraphrase

a. Cocaine is destructive and highly addictive; it should remain illegal.

b. Cocaine offers medical benefits, but the dangers outweigh any positive effects.

c. Cocaine should never have been made illegal.

d. Prior to the twentieth century, cocaine was freely used in any number of ways.

2. [1]Many of the young heroes and heroines in children's literature—including popular characters like J. K. Rowling's Harry Potter, Roald Dahl's James Henry Trotter of *James and the Giant Peach*, and Lucy Maud Montgomery's Anne of *Anne of Green Gables*—are orphans. [2]Although the presence of so many orphans in young adult fiction may seem to suggest a very sad worldview, literature experts say that orphaned characters actually serve a positive purpose. [3]According to English professor and children's literature specialist Philip Nel, an orphaned literary character expresses the powerlessness many young readers feel. [4]Still, says Nel, "many literary orphans are resilient characters who, despite their lack of power, find the emotional resources to beat the odds and make their way in the world." [5]Thus, orphaned characters make young readers believe it's possible to have some control over a world dominated by adults. [6]Nel also believes that literary orphans encourage children to think about growing up. [7]He says that a hero or heroine who has been prematurely separated from his or her parents encourages young readers to explore the idea of leaving and seeking independence. [8]By imagining a world

free of their parents, young readers prepare for the transition from child to adult. (Source of quotation: Deirdre Donahue, "Orphans in Literature Empower Children," *USA Today*, July 3, 2003, p. 7D.)

Topic Sentence _____

Paraphrase

a. The large number of orphans in children's fiction suggests kids don't want adults in their lives.

b. Some experts think orphaned literary characters help young readers feel more in control of their world.

c. The pessimism in children's literature is cause for concern.

d. Youthful readers need to express resentment toward parents; that may be why there are so many orphans in children's literature.

3. [1]*Munchausen syndrome* is a psychiatric disorder in which people fake illness in order to get attention and treatment. [2]People affected with Munchausen syndrome will, for instance, scratch and cut themselves or add blood to their urine specimens. [3]They may also inject a variety of substances into their blood or veins in order to cause illness. [4]Those afflicted with Munchausen syndrome usually have enough medical knowledge to appear convincingly sick. [5]They will present themselves at emergency rooms, reporting a variety of symptoms, and willingly undergo any number of tests. [6]If the test results do not match their symptoms, these individuals will turn around and report an entirely different set of symptoms. [7]If confronted, victims of Munchausen syndrome are inclined to get hostile and demand treatment at another facility. [8]Those afflicted with Munchausen syndrome will do just about anything to get the attention and treatment they crave. (Adapted from Neighbors and Tannehill-Jones, *Human Diseases*, 2nd ed., p. 420.)

Topic Sentence _____

Paraphrase

a. Munchausen syndrome is a serious mental illness that afflicts millions of people who don't even know they have it.

b. People with Munchausen syndrome take sadistic pleasure in hurting themselves because, on some level, they feel guilty.

c. People with Munchausen syndrome worry constantly about their health and will get numerous medical tests in the hopes of finding they have an illness.

d. Victims of Munchausen syndrome are so desperate for attention, they will fake an illness so they can get noticed and treated.

4. [1]What makes a friendship? [2]Although a number of factors influence friendship, one of the most important is *proximity*, or nearness. [3]If you live in a college dormitory, your friends are more likely to live down the hall than across campus. [4]Your earliest friends were probably children who lived next door or down the block from you. [5]It's simple. [6]Proximity increases the chances of interacting with others and getting to know them better, thus providing a basis for developing feelings of affection for them. [7]Another explanation for the positive effects of proximity on friendship is the tendency for people to have more in common with people who live nearby or attend the same classes. (Adapted from Nevid, *Psychology: Applications and Concepts*, 3rd ed., p. 604.)

Topic Sentence _____

Paraphrase

a. Although friendships are formed for many different reasons, proximity, or nearness, is the most important.

b. We are more likely to become friendly with people who live close by.

c. Friendships form for different reasons, but proximity is an especially powerful factor.

d. A shared childhood is probably the most important factor in the development of a lifelong friendship.

5. [1]Jury duty is an essential part of living in a democratic society. [2]But you'd never know it from the way some American citizens behave. [3]For many, jury duty is an inconvenience they try to avoid. [4]Some people simply throw away the summons to jury duty. [5]They know that if the state authorities come after them, it's easy enough to claim the notice never arrived. [6]Should the authorities pursue the issue—and they often don't—it's up to the state to prove that the notice actually got into the potential juror's hands, and that's not easy to do. [7]For those who lack the nerve to just chuck the notice into the wastebasket, there's a second choice. [8]During the interview stage of jury selection, jury dodgers can display their acting skills. [9]An agitated tone, much eyeball rolling, and excessive hand-wringing signal that the potential juror is overly biased or mentally unbalanced. [10]Both states of mind are reason for dismissal.

Topic Sentence _____

Paraphrase

a. Jury dodgers think nothing of lying in order to get out of jury duty.

b. Many people pay no attention to jury duty notices because they are convinced the authorities will not pursue them if they don't show up.

c. Many people treat jury duty as an annoyance and try to get out of it through any number of excuses.

d. Pretending to be mentally disturbed is a very effective way of avoiding jury duty, but most people don't have the acting skill to pull it off.

▶ **SHARE YOUR THOUGHTS**
Do you think people who try to get out of jury duty should be penalized for failing to do their duty as an American citizen? Or do you perfectly understand why some people don't want to do jury duty and think that jury dodgers should *not* be penalized if they throw the notice away and don't bother showing up? Can you explain *why* you feel as you do?

WEB QUEST
What tragic mistake did Sigmund Freud, the father of psychoanalysis—an influential theory of the mind and its ills—make about the use of cocaine?

_____

_____

_____

Working with the Writer to Construct the Topic and Main Idea

"A writer only begins a book. A reader finishes it."
—Writer and poet Samuel Johnson

When a paragraph opens with a general sentence followed by two or three specific illustrations, skilled readers immediately recognize this explanatory pattern. They correctly conclude that the first sentence is the topic sentence. However, not all paragraphs are so straightforward. As you already know, writers don't always introduce the main idea in the first sentence. Nor do they always use a reversal transition to announce the delayed topic sentence is about to arrive.

For paragraphs that vary from the standard, or familiar, patterns of explanation, you need to consider an additional strategy. You need to think, that is, about mentally tracking the chains of repetition and reference provided by the author.

Chains of repetition and reference are the words or phrases most frequently repeated, referred to, or suggested in a reading. They are the author's way of saying to readers, "These are the words central to the idea I am trying to communicate." They are the most significant or important words in the paragraph. It follows, then, that identifying the chains of repetition and reference in a paragraph will help you identify both the topic, or subject, under discussion and the main idea the author hopes to convey.

Tracking Repetition and Reference to Identify the Topic

For an illustration of how you can use chains of repetition and reference to identify the topic, read the following paragraph. As you do, pay close attention to the italicized words and phrases. They will lead you right to the topic.

[1]Prior to the nineteenth century, America was a largely agricultural country and daily life required so much effort that there was little time for leisure. [2]But as industry grew so did city life and leisure time. [3]With that dramatic change came an interest in *sports*, and in the cities, *one sport in particular dominated*. [4]By the nineteenth century, *baseball* had emerged as the most popular *new urban sport*. [5]*The game* first appeared in *its* modern form in the 1840s when a group of wealthy New Yorkers organized the Knickerbocker Club. [6]Then in 1862, in Brooklyn, William H. Cammeyer built the first enclosed *baseball field* in the country. [7]However, it was not until 1869 that *teams* began to *charge admission* and pay *players*. [8]In 1876, *eight teams*—New York, Philadelphia, Hartford, Boston, Chicago, Louisville, Cincinnati, and St. Louis—came together to form the National *League of Professional Baseball Clubs*. [9]By the late 1880s, annual attendance at *National League games* had reached eight million, and both men and boys in vacant lots and empty streets were emulating the *professional players they admired*.

(Adapted from Gillon and Matson, *The American Experiment*, 2nd ed., p. 747.)

Already in the nineteenth century, baseball was a popular sport.

Although the author sets the stage for the topic with the more general word *sports*, it's already clear by the middle of the paragraph that the topic of this passage is the more specific word *baseball*. No other person, object, event, or place in the paragraph gets quite the same amount of attention. As you can see, the more general word *sport* disappears as the authors take up their true subject—baseball.

Topics Are Implicit as Well as Explicit

This sample paragraph, with all of its italicized references to baseball, illustrates a key point about paragraph topics and, for that matter, writing in general: Writers don't rely solely on repetition to keep key words front and center in the reader's mind. Instead, they refer to or suggest key words **implicitly**, or indirectly, through a variety of methods. (See the chart on pages 187–89 for a more detailed list.)

Look, for instance, at sentence 5 of the sample paragraph. Because context eliminates any questions about which "game" the writers have in mind, the word *game* acts as a substitute, or stand-in, for "baseball." It reminds readers that the writers are still discussing the beginnings of baseball *before* adding a new piece of information about the topic.

In this case, the new information concerns when the Knickerbocker Club, the first organized association for baseball fans, was formed. Similarly, sentence 9 doesn't even mention the word *baseball*. But the phrases

National League games and *professional players* signal to readers that baseball is still the topic under discussion. The question now, of course, is what does the author want to say *about* that topic? What's the main idea?

> **READING TIPS**
>
> 1. Texts are made up of words. But some words are more important than others. Identifying chains of repetition and reference is a quick way to identify the most important words in a paragraph.
> 2. Sometimes topics are suggested even more than stated, so think on two levels while reading, What do the words mean and what do they suggest?

3 From Topic to Main Idea via Repetition and Reference

"All words are not equal. In any given sentence, some words provide basic content and meaning whereas others serve quieter support functions."
—James Pennebaker, author of *The Secret Life of Pronouns*

At this point, you may already know the main idea of the baseball paragraph. But for the sake of illustration, let's assume you don't and see how repetition and reference can lead you to it.

Take another look at the sample paragraph. This time different words are italicized. These words and phrases aren't repeated or referred to as often as the word *baseball*. Still they clearly get a lot of attention. In other words, they too form chains of repetition and reference. That means they play a role in the author's main idea. Combine them with the topic and you will know what that main idea is.

As you re-read the paragraph and check out the italicized words, ask yourself (1) What other chains of repetition and reference is the author developing? and (2) How could they combine with the topic of baseball to convey a general message or point?

> [1]*Prior to the nineteenth century*, America was a largely agricultural country and daily life required so much effort that there was little time for *leisure*. [2]But *as industry grew* so did *city life* and *leisure time*. [3]With that *dramatic change* came an interest in *sports*, and *in the cities, one sport in particular dominated*. [4]By the nineteenth century, baseball had *emerged* as the most popular *new urban sport*. [5]The game *first appeared* in *its modern form in the 1840s* when a group of wealthy New Yorkers *organized the Knickerbocker Club*. [6]Then *in 1862*, in Brooklyn, William H. Cammeyer built the *first* enclosed baseball field in the country. [7]However, it was not until *1869* that teams *began to charge* admission and pay players. [8]*In 1876, eight teams*—New York, Philadelphia, Hartford, Boston, Chicago,

Louisville, Cincinnati, and St. Louis—*came together* to form the National League of Professional Baseball Clubs. [9]*By the late 1880s*, annual attendance at National League games *had reached eight million*, while men and boys in *vacant lots* and *empty streets* were emulating professional players. (Adapted from Gillon and Matson, *The American Experiment*, 2nd ed., p. 747.)

What the italicized words and phrases in the sample paragraph show is the authors' emphasis on three threads of thought. Note first of all the repetition of **time order transitions** such as "Prior to the nineteenth century," "In 1876," and "By the late 1880s." The time order transitions in the sample paragraph help readers follow the course of events as they occurred in real time. But by their frequency, they also tell readers that change over time is critical to the main idea.

The arrival of something new and growing rapidly is another thread, suggested by the phrases *dramatic change, began to charge admission and pay players, first enclosed baseball field,* and *had reached eight million.* Important too is the chain of repetition and reference related to cities: *city life, in the cities, new urban sport, New Yorkers, vacant lots,* and *empty streets.*

Once you have the different chains of repetition and reference that tie a paragraph together, you need to think about how you can combine them into a sentence that sums up the author's point. In the case of the sample paragraph, you might well come up with something that reads like this: "During the nineteenth century, baseball got its start as a popular sport in the cities," or like this: "In the nineteenth century, baseball first became the game to play in the cities."

Either one is fine because they both rely on the chains of repetition and reference that thread their way through the paragraph. Both can also generally sum up the more specific details in the paragraph, which any self-respecting main idea needs to do.

The question now is this: Is there a topic sentence in the paragraph that matches either of these sentences? Certainly sentence 4 comes very close. The match between the author's topic sentence and our version of the main idea is a solid indication that we are following the same train of thought as the author, which is essential to being a skillful reader.

Different Texts Require Different Approaches

Sometimes the topic sentence of a paragraph practically leaps off the page. You'll see a general sentence followed by specific illustrations and know immediately that you are dealing with a basic explanatory pattern—general topic sentence followed by specific illustrations. But for paragraphs that are a little more difficult, not quite so straightforward, you should try the approach just described. As you work your way through a reading, use chains of repetition and reference to come up with a main idea. Then look for a topic sentence that confirms you are correct.

And even if the paragraph you are reading doesn't have a topic sentence (more on those in Chapter 8), you can still test your main idea for accuracy by seeing how well it summarizes the more specific sentences in the paragraph. Do the more specific sentences flesh out some of the words used to construct your main idea? Do they answer questions that a reader might have about the main idea you have come up with? If they do, then you and the author are following the same mental path, which, at this stage of reading, is precisely what you want to be doing.

Following the Chains of Repetition and Reference ♦

The Writer's Link: Word Repetition
The second sentence opens with a word that comes at the end of the previous sentence.

[1]Warren G. Harding could not be nominated today when, at the first mention of his name, a hundred reporters would be digging for <u>dirt</u> in his past. [2]The <u>dirt</u> was there. (Conlin, *The American Past*, p. 642.)

The Writer's Link: Transition Words
The sentence that comes after opens with a transition, which explicitly identifies its relationship to the previous sentence.

[1]Already as a young child, the writer knew that becoming fluent in English was separating him from his Spanish-speaking grandmother. [2]<u>Thus,</u> he tried to hide how well he had mastered the language of his new country and made a point of not speaking it at home, even when his parents, proud of his achievement, encouraged him to.

The Writer's Link: An Implied Example or Clarification
The following sentence supplies a specific illustration of some idea, attitude, theory, or opinion that has just been mentioned.

[1]Warren G. Harding could not be nominated today when, at the first mention of his name, a hundred reporters would be digging for dirt in his past. [2]The dirt was there. [3]<u>For fifteen years in Marion, Ohio, he carried on a sexual affair with a neighbor.</u>

The Writer's Link: Pronouns like *This* or *That* The next sentence opens with a pronoun that refers to a general idea or action described in the previous sentence.

[1]In 2000, <u>Dow Chemical fired 24 employees and disciplined 235 others</u> after an email investigation turned up hard-core pornography and violent subject matter. [2]<u>This</u> is the type of response companies need to make if we are to have a harassment-free workplace.

(Adapted from Kreitner, *Management*, p. 333.)

The Writer's Link: A General Category Word Used as a Stand-In for a More Specific Word The second sentence opens with a more general word that includes or covers a more specific event in the previous sentence.

[1]The <u>first electrocution of a criminal</u> was carried out in New York's Auburn Prison on August 6, 1890. [2]<u>The event</u> drew a group of curious doctors who positioned themselves in a circle around the chair as William Kemmler of Buffalo was strapped into the device.

The Writer's Link: An Associated Word or Phrase is Used as a Substitute The next sentence opens with a phrase commonly associated with what's just been mentioned.

[1]For pedigreed <u>dog</u> owners, the Westminster Dog Show is a major event that arouses much rivalry in pet owners, each of whom thinks his or her <u>dog</u> deserves the blue ribbon. [2]But given the <u>mutual sniffing and tail-wagging</u> that takes place among the participants, it's pretty clear they aren't especially concerned about who walks away with first prize.

The Writer's Link: Variation on a Word Already Mentioned The sentence that follows includes the same word or words but the endings are different.

[1]Freud's idea of <u>therapy</u> consisted of long sessions of free <u>association</u> with the sessions sometimes going on for years. [2]The <u>therapists</u> who have followed in his footsteps, however, are far less interested in having their patients <u>free associate</u> their way through their childhood memories.

The Writer's Link: An Implied Word or Phrase Echoes the Previous Sentence
The second sentence suggests a word or phrase from the previous sentence but doesn't explicitly state it because the writer assumes the reader will supply it.[†]

[1]When <u>the killer flu of 1918</u> finally came to an end, the public breathed a sigh of relief, convinced that something so deadly was a one-time occurrence. [2]But those in the scientific community were not convinced. *Note*: The suggested but unstated phrase at the end of sentence 2 is something like "that the flu was a one-time occurrence."

[†]The formal term for an implied but unstated word or phrase that the writer expects readers to supply is *ellipsis*.

SUMMING UP THE KEY POINTS

1. Readers can determine the topic and the main idea of a paragraph by tracking the chain (or chains) of repetition and reference that run through the paragraph.

2. Chains of repetition and reference are created through the author's use of pronouns, examples, substitutes, associated words, and ellipsis. (See the chart above for an example of ellipsis.)

3. Tracking chains of repetition is an additional reading strategy that should be used to identify the topic and main idea in combination with recognizing general and specific sentences.

◆ **EXERCISE 4** **Recognizing the Chains of Repetition and Reference**

DIRECTIONS Read each passage. Then answer the questions about how the sentences connect through repetition and reference.

EXAMPLE [1]If two people with sharply different spending styles commit to a relationship, problems usually arise. [2]This is particularly true in a marriage. [3]For example, the conflict of "his" and "her" money may come into play, and whoever earns the larger salary may want to tell the other how to spend. ⁴In disagreements over money, the larger earner may think or say, "I earned it and I'll spend it." (Adapted from Garman and Forgue, *Personal Finance*, 10th ed., p. 119.)

a. Sentence 2 uses what word to refer to the point made in sentence 1?

This

b. Sentences 2 and 3 both refer to and illustrate what key phrase in sentence 1?

different spending styles; problems

c. Sentences 3 and 4 do not say so explicitly, but they assume readers know that the example they describe takes place in the context of what personal relationship?

marriage

d. Which of the following main ideas fits the key words in the paragraph?

1. Marriages in which one person makes more money than the other are bound to have problems.

2. If two people marry and think of their money as his and hers, problems will arise.

3. When people with different spending styles marry, the chance of conflict increases.

EXPLANATION   References to these two topics—different spending styles and problems between married couples—reappear in the sample paragraph, making answer 3 correct. The other answers are self-explanatory.

1. ¹Most well-designed studies show that although children almost always find divorce stressful, the bulk of them survive divorces without much, if any, long-term psychological damage. ²By and large, these investigations show that 75 percent to 85 percent of children studied coped quite well in the wake of their parents' divorces. ³Moreover, the studies indicate that when parents experience severe conflict prior to the divorce, the apparent adverse* effects of divorce appear to be minimal. ⁴That's probably because children find the divorce to be a welcome escape from their parents' bitter arguing. (Adapted from Lilienfield et al., *50 Great Myths of Popular Psychology*, p. 170.)

*adverse: unpleasant, negative.

a. What word in sentence 2 is used as a stand-in for the word *studies* in sentence 1? _____

b. What general phrase from sentence 1 does sentence 2 make more specific? _____

c. What word in sentence 3 echoes the idea that children "survive divorces without much . . . long-term damage"? _____

d. The word *that's* in sentence 4 refers to what idea in sentence 3?

_____

_____

e. Which of the following main ideas fits the key words in the paragraph?

1. No matter how much parents may try to avoid it, children are bound to suffer during a divorce.

2. Studies generally show that divorce usually makes children anxious but does not cause long-term harm.

3. Studies show that children suffer no harm from their parents' divorcing.

2. ¹Brazil has the sixth largest economy in the world and is one of the richest countries on earth. ²But it is a rich country full of poor people. ³Brazil has the dubious distinction of having one of the most unequal distributions of wealth in the world. ⁴In 2002, the richest 20 percent of the population earned twenty-nine times as much as the poorest. ⁵Compare this to Mexico, where the richest 20 percent of the population earned sixteen times as much as the poorest, or the United States where the richest 20 percent of the population earned nine times as much as the poorest. (Adapted from Hirschberg and Hirschberg, *One World, Many Cultures,* p. 212.)

a. What point from sentence 1 is repeated in sentence 2? What new information does sentence 2 add?

_____

_____

b. What phrase in sentence 3 makes a connection to the word *poor* in sentence 2?

_____

c. Sentence 4 is a specific illustration of what general phrase in sentence 3?

_____

d. Which of the following main ideas generally fits the key words in the paragraph?

1. Brazil is an extremely wealthy country.
2. Despite the country's extreme wealth, much of Brazil's population is poor.
3. Brazilian society has no class mobility, and there is no chance for a poor person to even become rich.

3. [1]An ancient Chinese form of medicine, acupuncture is based on the philosophy that energy circulating through the body controls health. [2]Thus pain and disease are the result of a disturbance in the energy flow, which can be corrected by inserting long, thin needles at specific points, or meridians, in the body. [3]Each point controls a different corresponding part of the body. [4]Once inserted the needles are rotated gently back and forth or charged with a small electric current for a short time. [5]Research studies have found that acupuncture helps alleviate nausea in cancer patients undergoing chemotherapy. [6]It also helps in treating chronic lower back pain and may or may not be of value for irritable bowel syndrome. (Adapted from Hales, *An Invitation to Health*, 7th ed., p. 438.)

Acupuncture is believed to bring about healing through the insertion and manipulation of needles.

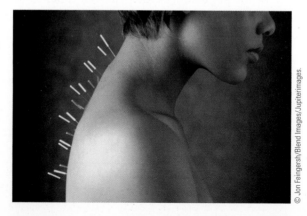

a. Where in sentence 2 is the first indication that the author is continuing the discussion of acupuncture philosophy begun in sentence 1? _____

b. The word *which* in sentence 2 refers to what phrase in the first part of the sentence? _____

c. In sentence 4, the author expects the reader to supply what phrase after the word *inserted*? _____

d. Sentence 6 offers another example of what phrase introduced in sentence 5? _____

e. Which of the following main ideas generally fits the key words in the paragraph?

   1. Practiced in ancient China, acupuncture is based on the idea that good health depends on how energy moves through the body.

   2. Research in the effectiveness of acupuncture, an ancient form of Chinese medicine, has shown mixed results.

   3. Acupuncturists heal the body by inserting needles in meridians that correspond to and control different body parts.

4. [1]Between the nineteenth and twentieth centuries, the huge area in America known as the Great Plains underwent startling changes. [2]At the beginning of the nineteenth century, there were few settlements, and one could walk for miles without seeing a house. [3]But by the end of the century, settlements were springing up all over, and growing numbers of men and women were seeking their fortunes in the region that had once been known as "The Great American Desert." [4]In 1800 the plains had been covered by herds of buffalo. [5]These huge, dumb animals were the natural cattle of the plains, and the Indian tribes living in the area hunted them for food and for the animals' hides, which could be turned into clothing and blankets. [6]Many of the pioneers who came west followed suit. [7]Still the herds managed to survive. [8]But as trains entered the region, shooting buffalo for sport became a popular practice, and passengers would open up a window and take aim. [9]By the turn of the century, the buffalo's numbers had sharply dwindled. [10]The Apache, Sioux, and Navajo who had hunted the buffalo also disappeared from the plains. [11]By 1900 they were enclosed on reservations.

a. Sentences 2 and 3 pick up on what word mentioned in sentence 1?

_____

b. In sentence 5, what word tells readers the writer is still talking about the buffalo introduced in sentence 4? _____

c. In sentence 6 the phrase "followed suit" refers to what activity described in sentence 5? _____

d. Sentence 9 describes the effect of what cause identified in sentence 8? _____

e. Which of the following main ideas generally fits the key words in the paragraph?

1. Although herds of buffalo have returned to the region once known as the Great Plains, the herds are markedly smaller than they were at the turn of the century.

2. The years between 1890 and 1910 were the most devastating decades for the Indian tribes that had once ridden freely over the region of America known as the "Great Plains."

3. Over the course of one century, between 1800 and 1900, the Great Plains underwent a huge transformation.

◆ **EXERCISE 5** **Using Repetition and Reference to Identify Main Ideas**

DIRECTIONS On the first line following the paragraph, write the words or phrases you think are consistently repeated, referred to, or suggested in the paragraph. On the next two lines write what you think is the main idea. Then write the number of the author's topic sentence in the blank. *Note*: This is the time to check if you and the author are following the same train of thought. The topic sentence and your version of the main idea should be similar.

EXAMPLE ¹In the nineteenth century, American and British fishermen nearly wiped out the seals of Antarctica. ²The Antarctic seals, however, after almost becoming extinct, have made an astonishing comeback. ³The population is now rapidly increasing. ⁴Although scientists admit that other factors may be responsible for the seal's rebound, they are convinced that the severe decrease in the baleen whale population is a major cause. ⁵The baleen whale and the Antarctic seal once competed for the same food source—a tiny shellfish called krill. ⁶With the baleen whale practically extinct now, the seals have inherited an almost unlimited food supply. ⁷That increase in the seals' food supply is considered a major reason for the seals' comeback.

Against all odds, the Antarctic seal is still in existence.

Volodymyr Goinyk/Shutterstock.com.

a. What words and phrases are consistently repeated, referred to, or suggested throughout the paragraph?

Antarctic seals, comeback, increase, decrease, baleen whale

b. In your own words, what's the main idea?

Now that the baleen whale is no longer competing with them for food, the

Antarctic seals are starting to multiply.

c. Where's the topic sentence that matches your main idea? _____2_____

EXPLANATION Every sentence in the paragraph mentions or refers to the seals of Antarctica so that's a dead giveaway to the topic. But almost every sentence mentions their comeback. Consequently, that has to be part of what the author wants to say *about* the topic. In other words, it's got to be part of the main idea.

The last oft-referred-to idea is how the "severe decrease" in the baleen whale population affected the Antarctic seal. Put all three elements together and you have the main idea. Look for the sentence closest to the main idea we inferred and you will find it expressed in sentence 2, which is the topic sentence of the paragraph.

1. ¹Throughout history, societies from all parts of the world have performed a ritual known as *couvade*, a ceremony in which the husband pretends he is suffering from labor pains while his wife actually gives birth. ²Although no one knows the exact origins of the couvade, there are several theories. ³According to one, the ritual of couvade began as a way of warding off evil spirits. ⁴Supporters of

this interpretation suggest that the husband enacts a pregnancy in order to attract the evil spirits to himself and away from his wife. [5]Yet another theory speculates* that the couvade is a way of publicly identifying the father so that his paternity is not in doubt. [6]Among those anthropologists who study the habits and practices of other cultures, this particular theory about the couvade's origins has the most support.

a. What words and phrases are consistently repeated, referred to, or suggested throughout the paragraph?

_____

_____

b. In your own words, what's the main idea?

_____

_____

c. Where's the topic sentence that matches your main idea? _____

2. [1]Sudden infant death syndrome (SIDS) is a mysterious and tragic disease in which a sleeping baby stops breathing and dies. [2]In the United States, SIDS strikes about two of every thousand infants, usually when they are two to four months old. [3]SIDS is less common in cultures where infants and parents sleep in the same bed, suggesting that sleeping position may be important. [4]Indeed, about half of apparent SIDS cases may be accidental suffocations caused when infants lie face down on soft surfaces. [5]Other SIDS cases may stem from problems with brain systems regulating breathing or from exposure to cigarette smoke. (Bernstein et al., *Psychology*, 8th ed., p. 173.)

a. What words and phrases are consistently repeated, referred to, or suggested throughout the paragraph?

_____

_____

b. In your own words, what's the main idea?

_____

_____

c. Where's the topic sentence that matches your main idea? _____

_____

*speculates: puts forth an as yet unproven theory, theorizes.

3. [1]Emergency medical technicians (EMTs) and paramedics are trained to respond quickly to medical emergencies. [2]Once the technicians and paramedics arrive at a scene, they determine the nature and extent of the patient's condition. [3]They also try to determine if the patient has any existing medical problem. [4]Following strict procedures, they give appropriate emergency care and then transport the patient to a medical facility. [5]Guidance for handling complicated problems is given by radio or phone from a physician. [6]EMTs and paramedics work both indoors and outdoors in all kinds of weather. [7]They are required to do considerable kneeling, bending, and heavy lifting. [8]Formal certification and training is needed in all states to become an EMT or paramedic. [9]Job outlook is good, as demand is expected to grow faster than average. (Adapted from Scott and Fong, *Body Structures and Functions,*11th ed., p. 274.)

   a. What words and phrases are consistently repeated, referred to, or suggested throughout the entire paragraph?

   _____

   _____

   b. In your own words, what's the main idea?

   _____

   _____

   c. Where's the topic sentence that matches your main idea? _____

4. [1]In the summer of 2010, an Army inspector general's investigation confirmed what had long been rumored: The U.S. Army has misidentified some of the grave sites at Arlington National Cemetery, the resting place for over 300,000 soldiers. [2]The inspector general's report led to congressional hearings and cries of outrage from veterans' organizations. [3]In response to the situation, Army Secretary John McHugh forced out the cemetery's superintendent and apologized to the families of those buried at Arlington. [4]McHugh also installed a new superintendent, Kathryn Condon, who has acknowledged that the problems at Arlington are far worse than the Army had previously admitted. [5]At least twelve grave sites were found to be empty and records did not match gravestones in more than 200 additional cases. [6]According to the inspector general's report, the problems with the graves seem to have stemmed from a long-standing feud between the cemetery's superintendent and his deputy.

a. What words and phrases are consistently repeated, referred to, or suggested throughout the entire paragraph?

_____

_____

b. In your own words, what's the main idea?

_____

_____

c. Where's the topic sentence that matches your main idea? _____

5. [1]In 1927, when Charles Lindbergh decided to fly nonstop over the Atlantic, everyone said it was impossible. [2]But Lindbergh didn't listen. [3]He flew anyway, becoming an international hero, as the first person to make the trip. [4]In 1933, when the public demanded that he return a medal given to him by the Nazis, Lindbergh refused. [5]No matter how unpopular his decision, he was not about to bend to the opinion of others. [6]True to character, Lindbergh also planned his own funeral. [7]Typically, he refused to leave such an important event in anyone else's hands. [8]In the end, Charles Lindbergh's independent character shaped every event of his extraordinary life.

a. What words and phrases are consistently repeated, referred to, or suggested throughout the entire paragraph?

_____

_____

b. In your own words, what's the main idea?

_____

_____

c. Where's the topic sentence that matches your main idea? _____

READING TIPS

1. If a passage is particularly hard to understand, re-read it to make sure you can match every pronoun to its antecedent.

2. Especially important in this context are pronouns such as *what*, *this*, and *that*. They often refer to entire ideas rather than single words. That's why misunderstanding, or misinterpreting, them can interfere with your comprehension. It pays to give them special attention.

✔ CHECK YOUR UNDERSTANDING

1. In writing, what is a chain of repetition and reference?

    _____

    _____

2. What methods do authors use to create chains of repetition and reference?

    _____

    _____

3. How should readers respond to chains of repetition and reference?

    _____

    _____

    _____

◆ **EXERCISE 6**   **Matching Your Main Idea to the Topic Sentence**

DIRECTIONS   Read each paragraph and write your version of the main idea in the blanks. Then underline the author's topic sentence. *Note:* If you can't find a topic sentence that matches your main idea, you need to re-think your main idea.

1. ¹Inhalant abuse, an addictive habit with dangerous and sometimes deadly consequences, is the intentional breathing of common household products in order to get high. ²This intentional breathing is commonly called "huffing," "snuffing," or "bagging." ³Bagging is the most dangerous as it entails placing a plastic bag over the head to get a longer effect. ⁴Using inhalants over a period of time may result in permanent brain, heart, kidney, and liver damage. ⁵Some products like paint and gasoline contain lead and may cause death from lead poisoning. ⁶Inhalant abuse is the third most common kind of substance abuse by individuals aged twelve to fourteen years, surpassed only by alcohol and tobacco. ⁷Symptoms of inhalant abuse include

spots or sores around the mouth, a glassy-eyed look, fumes on the breath or clothing, anxiety, and loss of appetite. (Adapted from Neighbors and Tannehill-Jones, *Human Diseases*, 2nd ed., p. 414.)

What's the main idea?

_____

_____

2. [1]The Federal Reserve of the United States has a very difficult job. [2]The Federal Reserve must strike a delicate balance in managing the economy. [3]If the economy grows more slowly than it is capable of, then we are wasting economic potential. [4]Plants that make PT Cruisers sit idle; the workers who might have jobs there are unemployed instead. [5]An economy that has the capacity to grow at 3 percent instead limps along at 1.5 percent, or even slips into recession. [6]Thus, the Fed must feed enough credit to the economy to create jobs and prosperity but not so much that the economy begins to overheat. [7]William McChesney Martin Jr., Federal Reserve chairman during the 1950s and 1960s, once noted that the Fed's job is to take away the punch bowl just as the party gets going. (Wheelan, *Naked Economics*, p. 222.)

What's the main idea?

_____

_____

3. [1]In 1947, builder William Levitt adapted Henry Ford's assembly-line methods to revolutionize home building. [2]By 1949, instead of four or five custom homes per year, Levitt's company built 180 houses a week. [3]They were very basic—four and a half rooms on a 60-by-100 foot lot, all with identical floor plans disguised by four different exteriors. [4]By rotating seven paint colors, Levitt guaranteed that only 1 in every seven houses would be identical. [5]The basic house sold for $7,900. [6]Other home builders quickly adopted Levitt's techniques. (Norton et al., *A People and a Nation*, 9th ed., p. 760.)

What's the main idea?

_____

_____

For many Americans, Levittown, Long Island, the first affordable housing development, was a dream come true.

4. [1]Which dream theory is most widely accepted? [2]Each theory has its strengths and weaknesses. [3]However, studies of dream content do support the neurocognitive† focus on the continuity between dreams and waking thought: Rather than being exotic or bizarre, most dreams reflect everyday events. [4]For example, athletes tend to dream about the previous day's athletic activities. [5]And in general, the favorite dream setting is a familiar room in a house. [6]Dream action usually takes place between the dreamer and two or three other emotionally important people—friends, enemies, loved ones, or employers. [7]Dream actions are also mostly familiar activities such as running, jumping, riding, sitting, talking, and watching a sports event. (Adapted from Coon and Mitterer, *Introduction to Psychology*, 11th ed., p. 193.)

What's the main idea?

_____

_____

---

†neurocognitive: focusing on how specific parts of the brain react during different kinds of thinking.

READING TIPS

1. Remember what you learned in Chapter 1. Good readers are flexible readers. When one strategy doesn't work, they try another.

2. Check your comprehension regularly when you read, right after you finish a difficult paragraph and at the end of chapter sections. If you can't paraphrase, you need to mark the passage for a second reading.

VOCABULARY ROUND UP

Below are ten words introduced in pages 165–96. The words are accompanied by more detailed definitions, the page on which they originally appeared, and additional sample sentences. Spend time reviewing the words and their meanings because you will see them again in review tests at the end of the chapter. Use the online dictionary *Wordnik* to find more sentences illustrating the words in context. (*Note*: If you know of another dictionary, online or in print, with as many examples of the words in context feel free to use that one instead.)

1. **prevalent** (p. 165): widespread, common, occurring in many different places. "In many African countries, malaria is *prevalent* and deadly."

2. **galvanized** (p. 166): forced into action, produced a strong reaction, stimulated or shocked into activity. "After standing in the rain for hours, the crowd was losing energy, but the sounds of the band *galvanized* the audience into action and people began shouting and clapping for the show to begin."

3. **sadistic** (p. 171): enjoying the inflicting of pain, cruel, taking pleasure in the misery of others. "People who like dog fights have a strong *sadistic* streak."

4. **asylum** (p. 171): institution for the mentally ill; place providing safety from harm. (1) "Much of the movie *Shutter Island* takes place in an *asylum* for the criminally insane." (2) "When Papa Doc Duvalier was in power in Haiti, many Haitians unsuccessfully tried to gain *asylum* in the United States."

5. **genre** (p. 172): a particular category of film or literature with specific characteristics that identify it. "Calvin Trillin is a writer who can write in almost any *genre*; he can write moving memoirs, clever poems, and hilarious restaurant reviews."

6. **consolidate** (p. 175): to combine separate efforts into a unified whole; also to strengthen or make internally strong. "If the members could *consolidate* their efforts, they might actually have a chance at making management address their growing list of complaints."

7. **random** (p. 176): not based on a consistent pattern, happening by chance, without any planned order. "The skier's death was a *random* accident that no one had ever expected could happen under such seemingly perfect skiing conditions."

8. **communal** (p. 176): shared by a group or members of a community. "The block party every year was a *communal* effort that had brought neighbors together."

9. **adverse** (p. 190): unpleasant, negative. "The *adverse* effects of the drug did not wear off for over twenty-four hours."

10. **speculates** (p. 196): puts forth an idea or theory that is yet to be proven, suggests a theory; engages in the buying and selling of goods. (1)"The politician was more comfortable in a situation where he could *speculate* without having to prove anything he said." (2) "If she *speculates* too often in the stock market, she's liable to lose her entire pension."

DIGGING   Making It in America: The Challenge
DEEPER   of Acculturative Stress

Looking Ahead   The excerpt on page 187 mentions how mastering the language of a new culture can undermine ties to the one you were born into. The following reading, excerpted from Jeffrey Nevid's textbook *Psychology: Concepts and Applications* talks more about crosscultural stress.

Getting Focused   Even a quick look at the reading that follows indicates that the term *acculturative stress* is essential to the author's explanation. As you read the selection, make sure you understand what each paragraph adds to your understanding of that term.

1   For immigrants, the demands of adjusting to a new culture can be a significant source of stress. Establishing a new life in one's adopted country can be a difficult adjustment, especially when there are differences in language and culture and few available jobs or training opportunities. One significant source of stress is pressure to become acculturated—to adopt the values, language preferences, and customs of the host culture.

2   How does acculturative stress, which results from this pressure, affect one's psychological health and adjustment? Evidence is accumulating that shows linkages between acculturative stress and poorer psychological adjustment. The life stress faced by poorly acculturated immigrants in trying to gain an economic foothold in the host country may contribute to emotional problems in the form of anxiety and depression.

3   Yet acculturating successfully may be something of a two-edged sword. Acculturation can lead to an erosion of traditional family networks and values, which in turn may increase vulnerability to psychological problems in the face of life stress. The erosion of traditional cultural values may also help explain findings of higher rates of sexual intercourse among more acculturated Hispanic teens.

4   The ability to manage acculturative stress effectively depends on many aspects of living in a new culture, including economic opportunities, ability to speak the language of the host culture, success in forming social connections with people with whom one can identify, and maintaining one's ethnic identity. However, withdrawal from mainstream society may prevent the individual from making the adjustments needed to function effectively in a multicultural society. For many groups, making a successful transition to life in America is a process of balancing participating in the mainstream culture while maintaining their ethnic identity or cultural heritage.

5   The leading theory of acculturative stress, generally called the *bicultural theory*, posits that immigrants fare better psychologically when they maintain their identity with their traditional values and beliefs while also making efforts to adapt to the host culture. That is, adaptability combined with a supportive cultural tradition and a sense of ethnic identification is linked to better psychological health in many groups, including Asian American adolescents and Navajo youth. (Nevid, *Psychology: Concepts and Applications*, 3rd ed., p. 452.)

Sharpening Your Skills

DIRECTIONS   Answer the following questions by circling the letter of the correct response or writing the answer on the blank lines.

1. Which explanatory pattern does the first paragraph fit?

   a. The topic sentence is the first sentence.

   b. The topic sentence follows an introductory sentence.

   c. The topic sentence is the last sentence.

2. What explanatory pattern introduced in Chapter 4 is used in paragraph 2?

   _____

3. Is the author speaking literally or figuratively when he talks about a "two-edged sword" in paragraph 3? _____

   How would you paraphrase the opening sentence of paragraph 3?

   _____

4. In paragraph 4, the following phrases are all references to what word in the first sentence of that paragraph: "economic opportunities, ability to speak the language of the host culture, success in forming social connections with people with whom one can identify, and maintaining one's ethnic identity"?

   _____

5. Which of the following statements best paraphrases the main idea of paragraph 5?

   a. The bicultural theory assumes that immigrants are most comfortable in their new country when they remain as close as possible to members of their own culture.

   b. The bicultural theory argues that successful acculturation only occurs when immigrants cut their ties to their birth country.

   c. The bicultural theory suggests that successful acculturation occurs when immigrants adapt to the ways of the new country without giving up all connections to the country of their birth.

Using Context Clues   In paragraph 5, based on the context clues, what do you think the word *posits* means in the first sentence?

_____

Share Your Thoughts   If you have ever had to get accustomed to life in a new country, can you describe what you think was the biggest challenge? And if you have never had to adjust to life in a new country, what do you imagine would be the biggest challenge?

▶ **TEST 1**   **Reviewing Key Concepts**

DIRECTIONS   Answer each question by filling in the blank or circling the letter of the correct response.

1. If the author uses an explanatory pattern that gets right to the point, what does the first sentence in a paragraph do?

    a. Paves the way for the topic sentence.

    b. Introduces the topic.

    c. Sums up the main idea.

2. When the second sentence of a paragraph opens with a reversal transition, what's very likely to follow?

    _____

3. Which one of the following is not a reversal transition?

    a. Yet unfortunately

    b. Still

    c. However

    d. Next

4. If the author wants to be absolutely sure you get the main idea of a paragraph, he or she is likely to _____

    _____ .

5. When the author opens a paragraph with a question, the answer is often the _____ .

6. When introductory sentences multiply, it's even possible for the topic sentence to appear _____ .

7. If you are reading a paragraph, and it's not clear to you which general sentence is the topic sentence, what's another reading strategy you can use?

    _____

8. What word or phrase in sentence 2 is a reference to "the boy" introduced in sentence 1?

   [1]The search party had been looking for the boy since the night before. [2]One moment he had been holding his mother's hand and the next he was seen entering the woods.

   _____

9. What word or phrase in sentence 2 is a reference to the pit bulls introduced in sentence 1?

   [1]Pit bulls have too often been misused by their owners. [2]The breed does not deserve its fearsome reputation.

   _____

10. What word or phrase in sentence 2 is a reference to the dance introduced in sentence 1?

   [1]The dance had attracted a huge number of people, none of whom wanted to go home. [2]It was three o'clock in the morning before the band stopped playing.

   _____

▶ **TEST 2**   **Identifying Topics and Main Ideas**

DIRECTIONS   Circle the letter of the topic and write the number of the topic sentence in the blank.

Gothic Novel - Sub

1. ¹For a period of about seventy-five years (1765–1840), the Gothic novel, an early relative of the modern horror story, was wildly popular throughout Europe. ²Many of the most popular Gothic novels—those written by Horace Walpole, Ann Radcliffe, and Matthew Lewis—sold in the thousands. ³They were quickly translated, and just as quickly plagiarized. ⁴Gothic novels were popular largely because they described a mysterious world where ghostly figures flitted through the dark passageways of ruined buildings, usually in the dead of night. ⁵Because Gothic novels were read and enjoyed by men and women of all classes, publishers, ever alert to a ready market, made sure that the books were available at bargain prices. ⁶Even the poorest members of the working class could afford to pay a penny to enter the Gothic world of terror, and they paid their pennies in astonishing numbers.

Topic

a. Horace Walpole

b. horror stories of the eighteenth century

c. Gothic novels

d. modern horror novels versus Gothic novels

Topic Sentence   *1*

2. ¹When we read or hear about the suffering of wild animals illegally caught, shipped, and sold, we are likely to sigh deeply for about fifteen seconds, then forget both the animals and their suffering. *Reversed* ²However, we should be concerned about the wild animal trade, particularly right now, with the threat of bird flu still hovering in the air. ³Imported animals don't come into the country alone. ⁴They carry with them germs and diseases. ⁵In 2005, for instance, British inspectors identified a parrot carrying the bird flu virus. ⁶Because the parrot was being imported legally, it was kept in isolation for several weeks. ⁷But many parrots sold in Britain come into the country illegally and are never checked for disease. ⁸One of those birds could also be infected with bird flu and spread the virus to its

human owner. [9]It wouldn't be long until the owner infected someone else, and cases of the disease would multiply.

Topic

a. exotic animals

(b.) illegal wild animal trade

c. the suffering of animals

d. the dangers of importing parrots

Topic Sentence ___2___

Texting & Driving Young people

3. [1]Texting and driving are a deadly combination. [2]Yet poll after poll shows that people, particularly those under thirty, continue to text and drive. [3]Thus the question has become, How do we get people, especially young people, to stop texting while driving? [4]A judge in Haverhill, Massachusetts, thinks he may have found a way to deter young people from texting while driving. [5]In June 2012, Judge Stephen Abany imposed a maximum sentence on teenager Aaron Deveau, who caused a fatal accident due to texting while he was at the wheel. [6]Deveau got two-and-a-half years for vehicular homicide and two years for negligent operation of a motor vehicle. [7]In imposing the sentence, Judge Abany made a point of saying that "deterrence was his primary concern." [8]Although most of the sentence was suspended, Deveau will spend one year in the Essex County House of Corrections. [9]He will also lose his driver's license for fifteen years.

Topic

(a.) deterring texting while driving

b. Judge Stephen Abany

c. vehicular homicide

d. texting

Topic Sentence ___4___

4. [1]Researchers use interviews, rating scales, and questionnaires to identify observable psychological traits. [2]However, when seeking to uncover hidden or unconscious wishes, psychologists are likely to turn to *projective tests.* [3]In some projective tests, the subject is asked to tell a story about a picture or an image. [4]With others, subjects are told to respond to a word by calling up other words they associate with it. [5]Perhaps the most famous projective test is the Rorschach Technique. [6]Developed by Swiss psychologist Hermann Rorschach,

the test consists of ten inkblots. ⁷Subjects look at the inkblots and then describe what they see in them. ⁸Yet another famous example of a projective test is the Thematic Apperception Test (TAT). ⁹During the TAT, subjects are shown pictures and asked to make up stories about the people depicted. ¹⁰Although projective tests like the Rorschach and the TAT have been popular for decades, many psychologists now question their reliability as diagnostic tools.

Topic

a. psychological testing

b. unconscious wishes

c. projective tests

d. the Thematic Apperception Test

Topic Sentence   ___2___

5. ¹As everyone knows, identity theft is on the rise. ²What's the latest scheme to get people to reveal personal information that identity thieves can use? ³Clever con artists are using jury duty to trick people into giving out personal information. ⁴The scheme works like this. ⁵The con artist calls his or her victim and tells the person that he or she has not appeared for jury duty despite a notice having been sent. ⁶As a result, a warrant has been issued for the alleged jury dodger's arrest. ⁷When the victim protests that he or she never got the notice, the identity thief asks for a birth date and Social Security number. ⁸This information will supposedly allow the phony official to check the records and verify that a mistake has been made. ⁹But, the con artist warns, the checking has to be done immediately in order to cancel the arrest warrant. ¹⁰Otherwise the police may arrive at the victim's door within twenty-four hours. ¹¹It's this threat that often makes people so terrified they give out the requested information, and at that point their fate is sealed. ¹²So far the jury duty scam has been reported in eleven different states.

Topic

a. jury duty scam

b. clever con artists

c. identity theft

d. the fear of police

Topic Sentence   ___3___

▶ **TEST 3**   **Constructing Main Ideas and Recognizing Topic Sentences**

DIRECTIONS   After identifying the words and phrases you think are repeated and referred to throughout the paragraph, write your version of the main idea in the blank lines. Then fill in the blank at the end with the number of the author's topic sentence.

1. [1]In the third century BCE, the Chinese were the first to sight Halley's comet. [2]In the fourteenth, the Florentine painter Giotto put the whirling ball of light into one of his paintings; in the sixteenth, William Shakespeare mentioned it in two of his plays. [3]But it took the eighteenth-century astronomer Edmund Halley (1656–1742) to recognize that the comet seen by the Chinese, the Italians, and the British was the same comet returning on a fixed schedule. [4]While studying what seemed to be the appearance of many different comets, Halley realized that there might be only one comet that regularly appeared every seventy-six years. [5]As a result of his studies, he predicted that the comet would return in 1758. [6]His prediction was proven correct when the comet showed up on schedule. [7]From that moment on, the comet bore his name. [8]Unfortunately, Halley died without knowing that his prediction had come true.

   1. What words or phrases are repeated, referred to, or suggested throughout the paragraph?

   _____

   2. In your own words, what's the main idea of the paragraph?

   _____

   _____

   3. What's the topic sentence that matches your main idea? _____

2. [1]In the 1920s, millions of Americans crowded into halls to watch boxers slug it out in the ring. [2]However, no boxer was more admired than the boxer Jack Dempsey, who embodied the nation's tough, frontier past. [3]Raised in Manassas, Colorado, he learned to fight in local bars against miners, cowboys, and anyone foolish enough to challenge him. [4]"Jack Dempsey hit like a sledgehammer and absorbed punishment like a sponge," wrote historian Michael Parrish. [5]"He was not a boxer but an earthquake that left blood, flesh, and

bone scattered in its wake." [6]During the twenties, his two grueling championship bouts with Gene Tunney proved enormously popular. [7]In 1926, Tunney defeated Dempsey in their first fight before a rain-soaked crowd in Philadelphia. [8]While as many as 150,000 people paid to see their rematch the following year in Chicago, some 50 million listened to it on radio. [9]The referee's famous "long count" may have cost Dempsey the second fight when he knocked Tunney to the canvas but failed to go immediately to a neutral corner.

(Adapted from Gillon and Matson, *The American Experiment*, 2nd ed., p. 936.)

1. What words or phrases are repeated, referred to, or suggested throughout the paragraph?

    _____

2. In your own words, what's the main idea of the paragraph?

    _____

    _____

3. What's the topic sentence that matches your main idea? _____

3. [1]Some people express their personal philosophies by tattooing themselves with phrases like "Live Hard" or "Love Thy Neighbor." [2]Others consider tattoos a way of displaying their taste in art. [3]They might tattoo a William Blake[†] drawing or a Georgia O'Keeffe[†] flower on some part of their bodies. [4]But in different cultures and eras, tattoos have also served religious purposes. [5]Mexico's Mayan people expressed their religious beliefs by tattooing themselves with images of jaguars, snakes, turtles, and toads. [6]From the 1700s until the present, many Muslims tattooed themselves to show their devotion to Allah. [7]Some Native-American tribes used tattooing for medicinal purposes, believing that tattoos would ward off illness. [8]The Cree, for instance, would tattoo a cross on each cheek to protect against toothaches, and members of the Ojibwa tribe tattooed small circles on their temples to prevent headaches. [9]Throughout history tattooing has been widely used as a means of identification. [10]Before 787 CE, early Christians used tattoos to identify members of their faith.

[†]William Blake was a famous eighteenth-century poet, whose drawings were as famous as his poems; Georgia O' Keeffe was an American painter famous for her paintings of boldly colored flowers.

[11]Similarly, members of the military or fraternities may have themselves tattooed to publicly show their commitment. [12]Some cultures have tattooed prisoners, the most sinister example being the Nazis, who tattooed numbers on the arms of concentration camp victims during World War II. [13]Throughout history, tattoos have served many different purposes.

1. What words or phrases are repeated, referred to, or suggested throughout the paragraph?

_____

2. In your own words, what's the main idea of the paragraph?

_____

_____

3. What's the topic sentence that matches your main idea? _____

4. [1]For hunters, fall is prime time. [2]It's deer season, the time to stock the freezer with venison. [3]Yet despite being enthusiastically hunted every fall, deer are not on the endangered list. [4]Actually, for a number of reasons, the wild deer population in the United States is skyrocketing. [5]Hunting regulations, including hunting bans and strict limits on the number of deer killed, have allowed the animals to thrive. [6]The rate of deer reproduction, too, has contributed to the growing population. [7]One doe usually gives birth to twins every year. [8]Furthermore, reduced numbers of natural predators such as wolves, along with a series of mild winters, have resulted in a lower mortality, or death, rate. [9]Deer have also successfully adapted to the destruction of their habitats[†] by humans. [10]Even when forests are cut down, deer manage to find enough food and shelter in the remaining vegetation. [11]They also boldly venture into suburbs to snack on tasty garden vegetables and flowers.

1. What words or phrases are repeated throughout the paragraph?

_____

_____

†habitats: living areas.

2. In your own words, what's the main idea of the paragraph?

_____

_____

3. What's the topic sentence that matches your main idea? _____

5. [1]The causes of depression in adolescents are complex. [2]The exact causes, in fact, are not completely understood by psychologists. [3]Researchers, though, have noticed a common link among depressed children. [4]While studies of family relationships suggest that depression can be inherited, they also suggest that certain family climates are typical among depressed children. [5]Children who witness or are victims of domestic violence seem to be particularly at risk for depression. [6]It may be that abusive parents, whose poor parenting skills may be caused by their own depressed state, weaken their children's ability to regulate their emotional highs and lows. [7]It might also be true that abusive parents encourage their children to develop negative ideas about social relationships and a depressed outlook on life. (Adapted from Bukatko and Daehler, _Child Development_, 5th ed., p. 396.)

1. What words or phrases are repeated, referred to, or suggested throughout the paragraph?

_____

_____

2. In your own words, what's the main idea of the paragraph?

_____

_____

3. What's the topic sentence that matches your main idea? _____

▶ **TEST 4**　　　　**Reviewing Chapter 4 Vocabulary**

DIRECTIONS　For each underlined word or phrase, pick the vocabulary word that would most effectively replace it. Write that word in the blank at the end.

adverse	genre	galvanized	communal	asylum
consolidate	random	sadistic	prevalent	speculate

1. The new city planner wanted to <u>combine</u> the three small towns into one. _____

2. The town council was <u>forced</u> into action by the daily protests. _____

3. The <u>mean</u> concentration camp guard enjoyed seeing his victims struggle under the loads they had to carry. _____

4. In the mystery and horror <u>category</u>, Stephen King still reigns supreme. _____

5. The introduction of neighborhood block watch had been a <u>shared</u> effort. _____

6. The farmers being hunted by the military police were hoping to find a <u>safe place</u> in the local church. _____

7. In this country, diabetes is all too <u>common</u> among those over forty. _____

8. The crimes were <u>without a pattern</u> and that made them even more frightening to the neighborhood under attack. _____

9. The comment had clearly had a <u>bad</u> effect on the manager's mood. _____

10. I like to <u>come up with theories</u> about global warming, but doing anything about it is too demanding and time-consuming. _____

Getting to the Point of Longer Readings

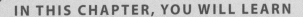

"Learning thrives on structure, and one way to increase reading comprehension is to teach students about text structures that they are certain to encounter when reading."

—Writer James Withers

Leaf through the pages of most college textbooks, and you'll see that the chapters break down into sections of various lengths. Some of those chapter sections are only a paragraph long. Occasionally as long as twelve or fifteen sentences, these single paragraphs still focus on one main idea.

However, as you can tell from even a brief survey, many textbook chapters are broken up into sections that extend beyond a single paragraph. Thus, in this chapter, we'll talk about how to apply what you know about explanatory patterns in single paragraphs to longer multi-paragraph reading.

Later on, we'll look more closely at longer reading selections. But for now we'll discuss how to think your way through readings that consist of no more than six paragraphs.

Pattern 1: Opening with the Main Idea

When background or context about the topic or main idea isn't a necessity, textbook authors are inclined to introduce the overall main idea of a chapter section in the very first paragraph. Actually, they are likely to introduce it in the very first sentence. Take, for example, the following reading. Note how, after the first sentence, the remaining paragraphs keep coming back to the idea it expresses: Heavy drinking in the old West was the norm.

Whiskey in the Old West

1 The men and women of the frontier days were heavy drinkers. They launched their days with an "eye opener" or "flem-cutter": raw, homemade whiskey. A jug sat on shop counters like a dish of mints today; general stores doubled as saloons. Westerners swigged whiskey like wine with their meals and like water when they worked. Preachers refreshed themselves with "the creature during their sermons. . . ."

2 **Whiskey Lightened the Misery**. Illness explains some of the drinking. Frontier settlers suffered chronically from the alternating chills and fevers of malaria. (They called it the "ague.") The medicine for which they reached was alcohol. Isolation also contributed. Travelers in the Ohio Valley invariably described conversations with men, and especially women, who commented mournfully on the lack of company. Whiskey was their companion.

3 **The Price Was Right**. Finally, whiskey was cheap. The corn and rye from which it was made were easy to grow. The technology was simple: Ferment[†] a mash of grain and water; boil it in an enclosed kettle; condense the steam that escaped and, presto, white lightning. Many family farmers kept a small still[†] percolating day and night. And on the frontier, whiskey was a cash crop. (Adapted from Conlin, *The American Past*, 9th ed., p. 191.)

No matter what you have seen in movies, the saloon, where men, and a few women, met to drink and forget the harshness of frontier life, was not a glamorous place.

iStockphoto.com/chechele.

[†]ferment: in this context, to cause a chemical change that turns sugar into alcohol; also to excite or stir up.
[†]still: apparatus for making whiskey.

This reading illustrates a textbook template you already know from paragraphs. The first sentence in the reading introduces a general idea that is explained in more specific detail by the two supporting paragraphs, making it the overall main idea of the reading. The only real difference is in the label for the opening sentence. It's called a "thesis statement" instead of a topic sentence. Different, too, is the length of the supporting details. Supporting details are now paragraphs rather than sentences.

Thesis statements do for longer readings what topic sentences do for paragraphs: They generally sum up the main idea. With thesis statements, however, the main idea governs or controls several paragraphs rather than one. And unlike topic sentences, thesis statements aren't restricted to single sentences. They can consist of one, two, or even three sentences, depending on the complexity of the idea addressed.

Supporting Details: Connecting the Familiar to the New

Notice, too, how the author weaves references to the words *whiskey*, *frontier* (a synonym for *Old West*), and *drinking* throughout the supporting paragraphs. These chains of repetition and reference are there to keep readers in touch with the main idea introduced in the opening paragraph, "The men and women of the frontier days were heavy drinkers," while at the same time adding some new information to that main idea. People drank a lot because (1) they didn't feel particularly good most of the time and (2) whiskey was a cheap pick-me-up.

Subheadings for Supporting Details Are a Bonus

Multi-paragraph textbook readings often introduce the supporting details with subheadings like the ones shown on page 218. In this case, the subheadings spell out the main ideas of the supporting paragraphs. Sometimes, though, they simply identify the topic. If that were the case with the reading above, then the headings would be only a word or phrase, for instance, "Loneliness" and "Low Cost of Whiskey."

READING TIPS

1. Whether they introduce the topic or the main idea, titles and subheadings in chapter sections are important clues. They help readers make the right connections between the overall main idea of the reading and the supporting details that serve to explain it.

2. If a heading is a complete sentence, then it very likely expresses the main idea of the chapter section or paragraph as well.

3. The title often provides a clue to the main idea. As you read, look for any references to words used in the title. References to the title are likely to be central to developing the overall main idea.

The Function of Supporting Details in Longer Readings
◆

As they do in paragraphs, supporting details in longer readings

1. **show** how the main idea expressed by the thesis statement applies in different contexts or settings.

2. **provide** examples of people, events, or theories that illustrate the main idea.

3. **identify** key terms that are necessary to understanding the main idea.

4. **describe** the consequences of some situation or event related to the main idea.

5. **offer** reasons, studies, or statistics meant to prove the main idea correct.

6. **divide** some larger group down into smaller subcategories, describing each one in more specific detail.

7. **trace** a sequence of events that led up to or followed the event or events mentioned in the main idea.

◆ **EXERCISE 1**   **Identifying the Thesis Statement**

DIRECTIONS   Each reading is complete except for the first sentence or two. The missing sentence or sentences comprise, or make up, the thesis statement. After reading the chapter section, circle the letter of the thesis statement that would fit the entire reading.

1. The Ethics of Product Placement

1   _____. The goal of product placement is to capture viewers' attention while they're caught up in the fun or drama of a movie, television program, or video game. While viewers note the brand names on everything from cell phones to coffee makers, marketers don't have to announce that the presence of their products is not an accident. In other words, money exchanged hands in order for it to happen.

2   Proponents of this practice say that consumers are sophisticated enough not to be misled. They argue that consumers recognize marketers usually pay to have their brands featured. Critics, however, say that paid product placement should be identified as such. One way to avoid any misunderstanding is to run a notice at the bottom of the screen when the product appears. Another idea is to insert a brief announcement at the beginning or end of the entertainment, the way television shows are required to disclose product plugs.

3   Product placement is even more controversial when news programs are involved. Not long ago, for instance, McDonald's paid to put iced coffee drinks on anchors' desks during television newscasts in Las Vegas. Although the European Union doesn't allow product placement within news shows, the United States has no such ban. There are critics, though, who think a similar ban is needed here. (Adapted from Pride, Hughes, and Kapoor, *Business*, 10th ed., p. 434.)

a. Product placement on news programs is inappropriate, and the United States should follow the Europeans in forbidding the practice of allowing advertising during a news program.

b. Companies routinely use product placement—the paid-for placement of branded products in videos, television, and movies—to lure consumers into buying their goods. While product placement is a profitable marketing strategy, not everyone approves of it.

c. Product placement—the paid-for appearance of brand names in videos, television, and movies—is not unethical as long as the viewer is aware that money has changed hands in order for the product to appear.

2. Encoding Strategies

1 _____. Failure to encode is one of the main reasons why new information does not make its way into long-term memory.

2 **Rehearsal**   The more you *rehearse* (mentally review) information as you read, the better you will remember it. But maintenance rehearsal alone is not very effective. *Elaborative encoding*, in which you look for connections to existing knowledge, is far more useful.

3 **Selection**   The Dutch scholar Erasmus said that a good memory should be like a fish net: It should keep all the big fish and let the little ones escape. If you boil down paragraphs in most textbooks to one or two important terms or ideas, your memory chores will be more manageable. Mark your texts selectively and use marginal notes to further summarize ideas.

4 **Create Chunks**   Assume that you must memorize the following list of words: north, man, red, spring, woman, east, autumn, yellow, summer, boy, blue, west, winter, girl, green, south. This rather difficult list could be reorganized into chunks as follows: (directions) north-south-east-west, (seasons) spring-summer-autumn-winter, (colors) red-yellow-green-blue, (genders) man-woman-boy-girl.

5 **Construct Cues and Make Connections**   The best memory cues (stimuli or triggers that call up the memory) are closely related to the information you want to remember and linked to something you already know. For instance, if you want to remember what the word *nebulous* means (cloudy or vague), you might link it to the phrase "cumulus cloud," which you know from science class. For extra insurance, match that cue to a visual image of a cumulus cloud. (Paragraphs 1–4 adapted from Coon and Mitterer, *Introduction to Psychology*, 11th ed., p. 277.)

To remember *nebulous*, think *cumulus*.

Tyler Olson/Shutterstock.com.

a. One way to improve your memory is to use techniques that make sure you fully *encode* information, organizing it into a usable or memorable form.

b. Creating chunks of information is an effective way of making sure that new information gets stored in long-term memory.

c. If you want to remember new information, make connections between the new information you want to remember and the already familiar information stored in your long-term memory.

Pattern 2: Ending with the Main Idea

When a chapter section consists of one long paragraph, it's not that common for the main idea to appear at the end of the paragraph. The same, however, is not true for multi-paragraph chapter sections.

With a multi-paragraph chapter section, the opening sentences of the first paragraph often provide background about the topic or the overall main idea. Then the last sentence introduces the thesis statement. That thesis statement focuses and unifies the entire reading while the remaining paragraphs provide the specifics.

Here's an illustration. The heading introduces the topic, "negative campaigning." But notice that the main idea developed throughout the reading doesn't appear until the end of the opening paragraph.

The title suggests the topic.

The last sentence picks up the title phrase, which is a signal that this sentence is the thesis statement.

Here is where the author connects the paragraph to the overall main idea about the states taking action.

Note how the author opens with a reference to the states enacting laws. This is a way of telling readers, I'm continuing with the same point

Negative Campaigning

1   The level of negativism in political campaigns, especially in advertising, has increased, even as the public registers its disapproval of mudslinging. The strident* tone projected in campaigns seems to have fueled mistrust of government and politics. It may also have the effect of reducing voter turnout. Tired of the unrelenting nastiness, states are exploring different ways of controlling negative campaigning.

2   Negative campaign advertising comes in three flavors: *fair*, *false*, and *deceptive*. A fair ad might emphasize some embarassing aspect of an opponent's voting record or some long-forgotten personal mistake. A false ad, as the label implies, contains untrue statements. More problematic are deceptive advertisements, which distort the truth about an opponent. The task for states is to regulate negative campaign advertising without violating the free-speech guarantees of the U.S. Constitution. False advertising that is done with actual malice can be prohibited by a state. However, deceptive ads, complete with accusations and innuendo* are more difficult to regulate.

3   States have enacted laws prohibiting false campaign statements; candidates who use false ads against their opponents can be fined. One of the problems with these laws is that the damage is done long before the remedy can be applied. Fining a candidate after the election is akin to latching the barn door after the horse has fled. Several states have

---

*strident: loud, angry.
*innuendo: a hint, usually about something unpleasant or damaging to someone else.

already under discussion. "States are looking for ways to eliminate or control negative campaigning."

adopted a fair campaign practices code. These codes typically contain broad guidelines such as "Do not misrepresent the facts" or "Do not make appeals to prejudice based on race or sex." The limitation of the codes is that following them is voluntary rather than mandatory. (Adapted from Bowman and Kearney, *State and Local Government*, 4th ed., p. 107.)

The fact that paragraphs 2 and 3 explain, in more specific terms, the last sentence in the first paragraph is significant. It means that the last sentence is more than the topic sentence of paragraph 1. It is also the thesis statement of the entire reading.

Overall, paragraphs with the topic sentence in last position are far less common than paragraphs with the topic sentence in first position. However, when it comes to the opening paragraph of chapter sections, writers frequently make the topic sentence appear at the end. That's because the topic sentence will, as the reading unfolds, turn into the thesis statement.

READING TIP

Sometimes textbook authors open a chapter section with an anecdote, or story, that illustrates the main idea. Then the last sentence of the paragraph sums up the point of the anecdote. The sentence expressing the point of the story is usually both topic sentence and thesis statement.

◆ **EXERCISE 2**   **Recognizing Thesis Statements**

DIRECTIONS   Read each chapter section and underline the thesis statement to indicate if it's the first or last sentence in the opening paragraph.

1. The Social Causes of Violence

1   One view of violent behavior holds that improper socialization* and upbringing are responsible for violent acts. Absent or deviant* parents, inconsistent discipline, physical abuse, and lack of supervision have all been linked to persistently violent offenders.

2   Although infants demonstrate individual temperaments, who they become may have a lot to do with how they are treated during their early years. Parents who fail to set adequate limits or to use consistent discipline reinforce a child's aggressive behavior. The effects of

---

*socialization: passing on or training in the customs and beliefs related to a particular society.
*deviant: not following normal standards of behavior.

inadequate parenting and early rejection may affect violent behavior throughout life. There is evidence that children who are maltreated and neglected in early childhood are the ones most likely to be initiated into criminality and thereafter continue or persist in a criminal career.

3   There are also indications that children who are subject to even minimal amounts of physical punishment may be more likely one day to use violence themselves. Sociologist Murray Straus reviewed the concept of discipline in a series of surveys and found a powerful relationship between exposure to physical punishment and later aggression. When kids experience physical punishment in the absence of parental involvement, they feel angry and unjustly treated and are more willing to defy their parents and engage in antisocial behavior.

(Adapted from Siegel, *Criminology*, 10th ed., pp. 303–4.)

2. Hate Crimes

1   In the fall of 1998, Matthew Shepard, a gay college student, was kidnapped and severely beaten. He died five days after he was found unconscious on a Wyoming ranch, where he had been left tied to a fence for eighteen hours in near-freezing temperatures. His two killers, Aaron J. McKinney and Russell A. Henderson, both twenty-two, were sentenced to life in prison after the Shepard family granted them mercy. *Hate* or *bias crimes* like the one committed against Matthew Shepard, are violent acts directed toward a particular person or members of a group merely because the targets share a discernible* racial, ethnic, religious, or gender characteristic.

2   Hate crimes can include the desecration* of a house of worship or cemetery, harassment of a minority group family that has moved into a previously all-white neighborhood, or a racially motivated murder. For example, on August 23, 1989, Yusef Hawkins, a black youth, was killed in the Bensonhurst section of Brooklyn, New York, because he had wandered into an all-white neighborhood.

3   Hate crimes usually involve convenient, vulnerable targets, who are incapable of fighting back. For example, there have been numerous reported incidents of teenagers attacking the homeless in an effort to rid their town or neighborhood of people they consider undesirable. Another group targeted for hate crimes is gay men and women: gay bashing has become common in some U.S. cities.

---

*discernible: capable of being seen, noticeable.
*desecration: act of destroying or showing disrespect for objects or places considered sacred by some group.

4 Racial and ethnic minorities have also been the targets of attack. In California, Mexican laborers have been attacked and killed. In New Jersey, Indian immigrants have been the targets of racial hatred. Although hate crimes are often mindless attacks directed toward "traditional" minority victims, political and economic trends may cause this form of violence to be redirected. For example, Asians have been attacked by groups who resent the growing economic power of Japan and Korea as well as the commercial success of Asian Americans. (Adapted from Siegel, *Criminology*, 10th ed., p. 322.)

VOCABULARY ROUND UP 1

Below are six words introduced in pages 223–25. The words are accompanied by more detailed definitions, the page on which they originally appeared, and additional sample sentences. Spend time reviewing the words and their meanings because you will see them again in review tests at the end of the chapter. Use the online dictionary Wordnik to find more sentences illustrating the words in context. (*Note*: If you know of another dictionary, online or in print, with as many examples of the words in context, feel free to use that one instead.)

1. **strident** (p. 223): loud, angry, harsh. "For some reason women who are outspoken are likely to be called *strident*, but men who speak their minds are labeled confident and forceful."

2. **innuendo** (p. 223): a hint, something that is not directly said but still suggests something unpleasant. "His opponent did not say it outright, but the *innuendo* was there; as a twice-married man, he was immoral and unfit for office."

3. **socialization** (p. 224): the conscious and unconscious passing on of a society's traditions, values, and beliefs. "In Japan, *socialization* focuses on what it means to be part of a group; in the United States being an individual is considered more important than being part of a group."

4. **deviant** (p. 224): not following normal standards of behavior; also a person who does not follow existing social or moral standards of behavior. "The definition of *deviant* behavior can change dramatically over time; in the nineteenth century, women who wanted to work for a living were considered social *deviants*."

5. **discernible** (p. 225): capable of being seen, noticeable. "When the medical examiner looked at the picture again, she noticed a small but *discernible* bruise on the victim's shoulder."

6. **desecration** (p. 225): act of destroying or showing disrespect for objects or places considered sacred by some group. "The Navajo Indians were furious at what they considered a *desecration* of their sacred mountains by the owners of a ski resort, who sprinkled the mountaintops with fake snow."

Pattern 3: Using Reversal Transitions to Introduce Thesis Statements

Textbook authors can set that stage for the thesis statement in any number of ways, from offering some history about the topic to recounting a news event related to the main idea. But whatever approach they take to the introduction, writers, particularly of textbooks, are likely to use reversal transitions to tell readers, "I've finished the introduction. Here comes the thesis statement."

In the reading below, for instance, the author introduces the thesis statement by first describing a common image of Thomas Jefferson. But that's not the overall main idea of the reading. In fact, the author's point is quite the opposite. Note how he prepares the reader for the shift from introduction to main idea by using the words *personally* and *however*.

Shop 'Til You Drop

The first two sentences offer the public image of Jefferson.

Note how the word personally *shifts the context from public to private while the word* however *paves the way for the thesis statement.*

1 Jefferson† is the patron saint*of economical government, an honor he deserves. He insisted that his secretary of the treasury count by the penny when he drafted federal budgets. Personally, *however,* Jefferson was a spendthrift. He spent as much as $2,800 a year on wine, up to $50 a day on groceries at a time when a turkey cost 50 cents. Twice when he had a new architectural idea, he had large parts of Monticello, his home, torn down and rebuilt.

2 In Paris, during the 1780s, he lived as extravagantly as the French nobles with whom he hobnobbed. When he visited John and Abigail Adams in London, the frenzy* of his shopping spree appalled the thrifty New Englanders.

---

†Thomas Jefferson: Jefferson was the country's third president and the author of the Declaration of Independence, which was a declaration of rebellion against British rule.
*patron saint: protecting and guiding spirit.
*frenzy: period of wild excitement and/or behavior.

In your own words, what's the main idea of the reading?

People who marry someone else immediately after getting dumped and enter into a

rebound marriage may well live to regret it.

EXPLANATION   Recognizing the topic of this reading is not especially difficult. Every paragraph returns to the subject of rebound marriages. What might be less clear is why the first two sentences are underlined as the thesis statement. Maybe you are thinking that the first sentence, which defines rebound marriage, expresses the overall main idea. But that's not really true.

Look at the other chain of repetition and reference that runs through the reading. The links in that chain focus on the "negative consequences" of marrying on the rebound. So if someone were to ask you what the reading was about, you couldn't just define the term *rebound marriage*. You would also have to mention that the reading outlines the drawbacks of rebound marriages. That's why you need to underline two sentences rather than one for the thesis statement.

1. Some Offbeat Candidates for Governor

1   Without question, the governorship of a state is a highly respected office. Yet, respected or not, the governor's office sometimes attracts true wackos as candidates. One such case was Jonathon "The Impaler" Sharkey. A self-proclaimed PhD and "Satanic Dark Priest, Sanguinarian[†] Vampyre and Hecate[†] Witch," Sharkey announced his candidacy for the 2006 governorship of Minnesota. A former pro-wrestler and co-owner of Kat's Underworld Coven,[†] the gubernatorial wannabe announced a unique plan for dealing with terrorists who might be tempted to infiltrate the Gopher State. Any such terrorist caught in Minnesota would "find out what the true meaning of my nickname, 'The Impaler' means." Literally, the unfortunate suspect would be impaled on the capitol grounds.

2   Another colorful candidate was Texas mystery writer, song writer, and performer Kinky Friedman. His country band in the 1970s, called Kinky Friedman and the Texas Jewboys, recorded various alternative* hits, including "They Ain't Making Jews Like Jesus Anymore," and "The Mail Don't Move Too Fast in Rapid City, South Dakota." While cracking jokes and one-liners, Friedman also campaigned on serious issues,

Former gubernatorial candidate Kinky Friedman.

[†]Sanguinarian: a person who drinks blood.
[†]Hecate: a Greek and Roman goddess associated with witchcraft.
[†]coven: a place where witches hang out together.
*alternative: in this context, not being part of the mainstream; also another choice or possibility.

including election reform and education improvement. Friedman again placed his name in the Democratic primary in 2009. (Adapted from Bowman and Kearney, *State and Local Government*, 8th ed., p. 173.)

In your own words, what's the main idea of the reading?

_____

_____

2. Protecting Children from Toxic Chemicals

1   In 2005, the Environmental Working Group analyzed umbilical cord blood from ten randomly* selected newborns in U.S. hospitals. Of the 287 chemicals detected, 180 cause cancers in humans or animals, 217 damage the brain and nervous system in test animals, and 208 cause birth defects or abnormal development in test animals. Scientists do not know what harm, if any, the very low concentrations of these chemicals found in the infants' blood might cause, but they are deeply concerned.

2   Infants and young children are more susceptible to the effects of toxic substances than are adults for three major reasons. First, children breathe more air, drink more water, and eat more food per unit of body weight than do adults. Second, they are exposed to toxins in dust or soil when they put their fingers, toys, or other objects in their mouths. Third, children usually have less well-developed immune systems and body detoxification processes than adults have.

3   In 2003, the U.S. Environmental Protection Agency (EPA) proposed that in determining risk, regulators should assume children have 10 times the exposure risk of adults to cancer-causing chemicals. Some health scientists contend that these guidelines are too weak. They suggest that, to be on the safe side, we should assume that the risk of harm from toxins for children is 100 times that of adults. Others support doing this on ethical grounds. They say it is wrong not to give children much greater protection from harmful chemicals in the environment. (Adapted from Miller, *Living in the Environment*, 15th ed., p. 432.)

In your own words, what's the main idea of the reading?

_____

_____

_____

*randomly: with no particular pattern. *Random* was introduced in Chapter 4.

Pattern 4: Answering a Question with the Thesis Statement

As they do with single paragraphs, writers—textbook writers in particular—like to use questions to focus readers' attention on the main idea. Similar to single paragraphs, the answer to the opening question of a chapter section is likely to be the thesis statement expressing the main idea. This textbook template appears in all disciplines, or subjects. But once again, it is particularly popular in psychology texts, for example:

The Function of REM Sleep

The opening question focuses readers' attention on the point of the reading to tell readers about the purpose of REM sleep.

The thesis statement provides an immediate answer.

Note how the opening phrase of paragraph 2 helps the reader shift the context to infants.

1 *What is the purpose of REM sleep?* REM[†] sleep appears to sharpen our memories of the previous day's most significant experiences. This is why daytime stress tends to increase REM sleep, which may rise dramatically when there is a death in the family, trouble at work, a marital* conflict, or other emotionally charged events. The value of more REM sleep is that it helps us sort and retain memories, especially memories about strategies for solving problems. This is why, after studying for a long period, you may remember more if you go to sleep, rather than pulling an all-nighter. (REMember to get some REM!)

2 Early in life, REM sleep may stimulate the developing brain. Newborn babies have lots of new experiences to process so they spend a hearty eight or nine hours a day in REM sleep. That's about 50 percent of their total sleep time. But infants may need that much REM sleep in order to take in all of the new experiences they encounter on a daily basis. (Adapted from Coon and Mitterer, *Introduction to Psychology*, 11th ed., p. 187.)

As it so often does, a question like the one opening this two-paragraph selection, points the way to what the author wants you to learn from the reading. Once you finish it, you should be able to answer the question: What is the purpose of REM sleep?

The answer to that question comes in the second sentence of paragraph 1. That sentence is not just the topic sentence of the opening paragraph. It is also the thesis statement of the two-paragraph selection: REM sleep intensifies our awareness of the day's significant events. The

---

*marital: related to marriage.
†REM is an acronym. That means it's made up of the first letter of each word in a term or phrase (in this case, Rapid Eye Movement) and used as a pronounceable word in its own right. This acronym was also defined, more briefly, in Chapter 4.

remainder of the paragraph tells us more about the type of memories REM sleep heightens.

Typically, when a chapter section opens with a question—particularly if the question is a separate heading—the answer to the question is also the thesis statement of the entire reading. It's rare for writers to start off a chapter section with a question and then not make the answer the overall main idea. However, it's not always true that the answer immediately follows the question. Sometimes the question will appear in one paragraph, the answer in another.

READING TIP   Writers don't *always* answer their opening questions immediately. Sometimes they give a traditional or commonsense answer only to reverse it before introducing the answer they really intend to address. Writers who take this approach will usually introduce the real answer to the question, i.e., the thesis statement, with a reversal transition, so it will be easy to spot.

♦ EXERCISE 4   Paraphrasing Thesis Statements in Multi-Paragraph Readings

DIRECTIONS   Underline the author's thesis statement. Then paraphrase it in the blanks that follow.

1. Are Cross-Pressures a Problem for Adolescents?

1   In years gone by, adolescence was often characterized as a stormy period when all youths experience *cross-pressures*—strong conflicts that stem from differences in the values or practices advocated by their parents and those favored by peers. How accurate is this life portrait of the teenage years? It may have some merit* for adolescents, particularly those "rejected" youths, who form deviant peer cliques that endorse and promote antisocial conduct. But there are reasons why the so-called cross-pressures "problem" is simply not a problem for most adolescents.

2   One reason that parent/peer conflicts are kept to a minimum is that parents and peers tend to exert their influence in different domains.* Hans Sebald, for example, asked adolescents whether they would seek the advice of their parents or the advice of their peers on a number of

*to have merit: to show accuracy or truth; to be convincing.
*domains: areas or spheres of influence.

different issues. Peers were likely to be more influential than parents on such issues as what styles to wear and which clubs, social events, hobbies, and other recreational activities to choose. By contrast, adolescents claimed that they would depend more on their parents when the issue involved school or work-related goals. Teenagers are unlikely to be torn between parent and peer pressure as long as parents and peers have different primary areas of influence.

3   A second more important reason why parent/peer warfare is typically kept to a minimum is parents, by virtue of their parenting styles, have a good deal of influence on the company their adolescents keep. Authoritative parents who are warm, neither too controlling nor too lax, and who are consistent in their discipline generally find that their adolescents are closely attached to them and have internalized their values. These adolescents have little need to rebel or to desperately seek acceptance from peers when they are so warmly received at home. (Adapted from Shaffer, *Social and Personality Development*, 6th ed., p. 487.)

In your own words, what's the overall main idea of this reading?

_____

_____

2. Whorf's Theory of Language

1   Does the language we speak affect how we think? Might French Canadians, Chinese, and Africans see the world differently because of the vocabulary and syntax, or word order, of their native languages? According to the **linguistic relativity hypothesis**, the answer is yes; the language we speak does affect how we think. This theory—also called the Whorfian hypothesis after Benjamin Whorf the amateur linguist who developed it—holds that the language we use determines how we think and how we perceive reality.

2   Whorf (1956) pointed out that some cultures have many different words for colors, whereas others have only a few. English has eleven words for basic colors: black, white, red, green, yellow, blue, brown, purple, pink, orange, and gray. At the other end of the spectrum is the Navajo language, which has no separate words for blue and green. Based on Whorf's theory, members of the culture with fewer words for colors would not see the same number of different colors as those coming from a culture that had more words. Research, however, on precisely this issue has not proven Whorf correct.

3   Overall, research evidence fails to support the strictest version of the Whorfian hypothesis, that language *determines* how we think and what we see. But a weaker version of the theory does have merit. This version proposes that our culture and the language we speak *influence* how we perceive, or understand, the world. This view is consistent with the experiences of many bilingual and multilingual people, who say they think differently when using each of their languages.

4   Language influences thinking in more than one way. Consider this sentence: "A person should always be respectful of his parents." If the very concept of personhood implies maleness, where does that leave females? As non-persons? Similarly, if we talk about arguments or disagreements in violent terms—"They fought bitterly," "She shot his argument down," "Point by point, he knocked down his opponent's argument"—we tend to think of arguing as negative activity rather than an energetic exploration of differences. (Adapted from Nevid, *Psychology: Concepts and Applications*, 4th ed., p. 266.)

In your own words, what's the overall main idea of this reading?

_____

_____

3. The Truth About ADHD

1   Many myths surround Attention Deficit/Hyperactivity Disorder (ADHD). One myth concerns causes. At one time or another, TV, food allergies, sugar, and poor home life have all been proposed as causes of ADHD. But heredity is actually a much more important factor.

2   Twin studies show that identical twins are often diagnosed with ADHD, but this is uncommon for fraternal twins.[†] Similarly, adoption studies show that children are more prone to ADHD when a biological parent has been diagnosed with ADHD than when an adoptive parent has. In addition, prenatal exposure to alcohol and other drugs can place children at risk for ADHD.

3   Another myth is that children "grow out of" ADHD in adolescence or young adulthood. More than half of the children diagnosed with ADHD will have problems related to overactivity, inattention, and impulsivity in adolescence and adulthood. Few of these young adults complete college, and some will have work- and family-related problems.

[†]fraternal twins: siblings born at the same time but who are not identical.

4   One final myth is that many healthy children are wrongly diagnosed with ADHD. The number of children diagnosed with ADHD increased substantially during the 1990s, but this was not because children were being routinely misdiagnosed. The increased numbers reflected growing awareness of ADHD and more frequent diagnoses of ADHD in girls and adolescents. (Adapted from Kail and Cavanaugh, *Human Development*, 5th ed., p. 230.)

In your own words, what's the overall main idea of this reading?

_____

_____

4. Increasing Requirements for a Marriage License

1   Should marriage licenses be obtained so easily? Should couples be required, or at least encouraged, to participate in premarital education before saying "I do"? Given the high rate of divorce today, policy makers are considering this issue. Although evidence of long-term effectiveness of premarital education remains elusive,* some believe that "mandatory* counseling will promote marital stability.". . .

2   Several states, for instance, have proposed legislation requiring premarital education. For example, an Oklahoma statute provides that parties who complete a premarital education program pay a reduced fee for their marriage license. Also in Lenawee County, Michigan, local civil servants and clergy have made a pact: They will not marry a couple unless that couple has attended marriage education classes. Other states that are considering policies to require or encourage premarital education include Arizona, Illinois, Maryland, Minnesota, Mississippi, Missouri, Oregon, and Washington.

3   Proposed policies include not only mandating premarital education and lowering marriage license fees for those who attend courses but also imposing delays on issuing marriage licenses for those who refuse premarital education. However, "no state mandates premarital counseling as a prerequisite to obtaining a license." (Adapted from Knox and Schacht, *Choices in Relationships*, 10th ed., p. 196.)

In your own words, what's the overall main idea of this reading?

_____

_____

_____

*elusive: hard to prove or catch, or understand.
*mandatory: required or commanded by authority.

▶ **SHARE YOUR THOUGHTS**

What's your opinion on the idea of linking a marriage license to mandatory marital counseling? Are you for or against that idea, and, equally important, what are your reasons for holding the opinion that you do?

SUMMING UP THE KEY POINTS

1. In multi-paragraph readings, the stated main idea is called the *thesis statement*.

2. Like paragraphs, multi-paragraph readings in textbooks rely heavily on some basic explanatory patterns or textbook templates.

   • The thesis statement starts the reading and the remaining paragraphs function as the supporting details.

   • The reading opens with an introduction followed by a reversal transition that announces the arrival of the thesis statement.

   • The first paragraph introduces the main idea at the end and that main idea is further developed by the supporting paragraphs, making the topic sentence of one paragraph the thesis statement for the entire reading.

   • The reading opens with a question and the thesis statement provides the answer.

3. Just as with single paragraphs, chains of repetition and reference are clues to the meaning of longer, multi-paragraph readings. As you move from paragraph to paragraph, note the words and phrases that come up repeatedly. Try to determine how they combine into a main idea that governs the entire reading.

VOCABULARY ROUND UP 2

Below are the seven words and two phrases introduced in pages 227–36. The words are accompanied by more detailed definitions, the page on which they originally appeared, and additional sample sentences. Spend time reviewing the words and their meanings because you will see them again in review tests at the end of the chapter. Use the online dictionary Wordnik to find more sentences illustrating the words in context.

(*Note*: If you know of another dictionary, online or in print, with as many examples of the words in context feel free to use that one instead.)

1. **patron saint** (p. 227): guiding and protecting spirit of some group; a person who represents or embodies all the values of a group or nation. "Saint Nicholas is the *patron saint* of sailors."

2. **frenzy** (p. 227): state of wild excitement, temporary madness. "Wherever he goes, the disgraced politician causes a media *frenzy*."

3. **alternative** (p. 230): not being part of the mainstream; the choice between two possibilities. (1) "Poets of the Fall is an *alternative* rock band with a significant following." (2) "Getting old can be tough, but the *alternative* is even worse."

4. **randomly** (p. 231): lacking in any consistent pattern, having no particular pattern, purpose, or goal. "The criminal acts occurring *randomly* in the area were doubly frightening because there was no pattern to them and no way to predict when they would occur."

5. **marital** (p. 232): related to marriage. "Falling in love is easy, maintaining *marital* happiness is much harder."

6. **to have merit** (p. 233): to be worthy of consideration or respect. "The plan for removing the island residents prior to the hurricane definitely *had merit*. However, it wasn't clear that the residents would cooperate."

7. **domains** (p. 233): areas or spheres of influence, control, mastery or emphasis. "I'd like to say I could identify the artist, but art history is not my *domain*."

8. **elusive** (p. 236): hard to catch, understand, remember or make happen. "The team played hard, but victory remained elusive."

9. **mandatory** (p. 236): required or commanded by authority or rule, not a matter of choice. "The evaluation was *mandatory*; without it, she could not rise to the next job category."

CHECK YOUR UNDERSTANDING

1. Describe four common ways that textbook authors introduce the main ideas of chapter sections.

    _____

    _____

    _____

    _____

2. How does a thesis statement differ from a topic sentence?

    _____

3. Why is it important to look for words from the title while you read?

    _____

DIGGING DEEPER Jury Dodgers Beware!

Looking Ahead As the paragraph on page 181 explained, some citizens take jury duty very seriously, while others throw away their jury notices. As the following reading suggests, those who shirk jury duty might want to re-think their attitude.

Getting Focused The title and "Looking Ahead" preview for this reading both suggest that jury dodgers might have something to fear. Read to discover what that might be.

1 Recently, in Passaic County, New Jersey, fourteen citizens were collected by the sheriff's department and brought before a judge at the county courthouse. Their offense? Refusing to respond to multiple notices to report for service as jurors. Their punishment? Fines up to $500 and assignment to jury duty. Although the keystone of the U.S. justice system is the right to a trial by a jury of one's peers, Passaic County's problem is not an isolated case; many courts have experienced serious problems in getting people to perform their civic duty. In fact, jury avoidance is at an all-time high, and it is not uncommon for trials to be delayed because too few jurors are available. As a result, the courts are taking actions designed to discourage jury dodging.

2 Most juries continue to number twelve individuals, although six are sometimes used. Most jury decisions must be unanimous—anything short of that leads to a hung jury and either retrial or dismissal. Potential jurors are summoned by the court for assignment to a jury pool. Jurors usually must be U.S. citizens eighteen years of age or older. Questioning by the judge, prosecuting attorney, and defense attorney—known as *voir dire*—disqualifies individuals with potential conflicts of interest, bias, or other factors germane to the case. Once selected, the juror may be required to give a day or two of service, or months for the occasional long, complex trial. Remuneration is minimal, ranging from $15 a day in California and New Jersey to $40 in South Dakota and New York.

3 Why has jury-dodging become a problem? First, some individuals suffer a loss of income from not being able to work. Employers may be required to keep employee-jurors on their payroll and are prohibited from firing them for serving jury duty, but abuses occur. For the self-employed, jury duty can be a serious hardship, as it can be for potential jurors with small children and no day care arrangement. Other burdens of jury duty include

time spent away from one's job, family, or leisure activities. Jurors in tough criminal cases can suffer psychological disturbances. A relatively minor— but annoying—problem is the uninviting, uncomfortable surroundings of many jury waiting rooms.

4   All states have provisions for excusing or postponing service for people selected for duty (such as old age, disability, undue hardship, extreme inconvenience, military duty). For those who ignore their summons, judges may respond with a stick, like the Passaic County judge. In Grant County, Washington, two randomly picked jury scofflaws are regularly brought to answer before the judge. In North Dakota, New Jersey, and other states, they are reported in the local newspaper. A judge in Baltimore once placed non-reporting jurors in jail for several hours. A kinder approach is to improve the quality of jury duty by, for instance, installing computer work stations, libraries, and other amenities in the jury lounges. Arizona's 2003 jury reform bill imposed a filing fee on civil cases that significantly hiked juror pay and promised jurors they would only serve one day every two years unless picked for a trial.

5   Gradually, courts are incorporating information technology to cre- ate a cyberjuror. Basic touch-tone telephone systems inform members of the jury pool whether they are going to be needed the next day. Online, twenty-four-hour interactive systems that qualify potential jurors by ad- ministering an electronic *voir dire* make specific assignments and process excuse and postponement requests. Postage savings alone can be sub- stantial, and the new cyberjurors appreciate the convenience. (Adapted from Bowman and Kearney, *State and Local Government*, 7th ed., p. 247.)

In 1957, *Twelve Angry Men* was a famous and successful film about the importance of jury duty, but it's doubtful that it would have the same appeal today.

© CinemaPhoto/Corbis.

Sharpening Your Skills

DIRECTIONS   Answer the questions by filling in the blanks or circling the letters of the correct response.

1. The topic of this reading is ___JURY DODGING___.

2. Which of the following is the thesis statement for the entire reading?

   a. Recently, in Passaic County, New Jersey, fourteen citizens were collected by the sheriff's department and brought before a judge at the county courthouse.

   b. In fact, jury avoidance is at an all-time high, and it is not uncommon for trials to be delayed because too few jurors are available. As a result, the courts are taking actions designed to discourage jury dodging.

   c. Most juries continue to number twelve individuals, although six are sometimes used. Most jury decisions must be unanimous— anything short of that leads to a hung jury and either retrial or dismissal. Potential jurors are summoned by the court for assignment to a jury pool.

3. How would you paraphrase the thesis statement?

   _____

   _____

4. Several methods of introducing the thesis statement are described on pages 217–37. Which one did the authors use? _____

   _____

5. Which one of the following questions do the supporting paragraphs not answer?

   a. What happens during jury duty?

   b. How successful have the attempts to stop jury dodgers actually been?

   c. What are the courts doing to try and stop people from dodging jury duty?

6. Which of the following is the best paraphrase for the term *voir dire*?

   a. the process of interviewing jurors to determine any factors that might disqualify them as members of the jury

    b. the process of interviewing potential jurors to see if they might be sympathetic to the person on trial

    c. the process in which a judge talks to the juror and decides if he or she should serve on the jury

7. Paragraph 3 opens with a question. What does the word *first* following the question tell you about the answer?

    _____

8. In paragraph 4, the authors say this: "For those who ignore their summons, judges may respond with a stick, like the Passaic County judge." Is the word *stick* in this sentence used literally or figuratively? _____

9. What's another way of saying the same thing?

    a. For the people who ignore a summons to jury duty, judges may respond by using some form of punishment.

    b. Those who ignore their summons to jury duty can expect judges to give them jail time.

    c. Those who pay no attention to their duty as jurors can expect to be replaced by an alternate juror.

10. The randomly picked up "scofflaws" referred to in paragraph 4 are another example of judges doing what? _get a stick_

Using Context Clues Based on the context, how would you define the words *germane* and *remuneration* in paragraph 2?

Germane means _relevent to the case_.

Remuneration means _REWARD_.

Share Your Thoughts What does the photo from the film *Twelve Angry Men* suggest to you about society in 1957? Could this film be made today?

From Reader to Writer Use a question-and-answer format to organize a paragraph or two that answers a question like this one: Why is it that so many people do not take jury duty seriously?

▶ **TEST 1**   **Reviewing Key Concepts**

DIRECTIONS   Answer the following questions by filling in the blanks.

1. What is the function of a thesis statement?

   _____

   How does it differ from a topic sentence?

   _____

   _____

2. When a textbook author gets right to the point, how does he or she start a chapter section?

   _____

3. With a multi-paragraph chapter section, the opening sentences of the first paragraph often provide background about the topic and the overall main idea. Then the last sentence introduces

   _____ of the paragraph, which also functions

   as the _____ .

4. If the author opens a chapter section with a question, what will be the function of the thesis statement?

   _____

5. When an author opens a chapter section by telling you what was traditionally thought or said about a topic or main idea, you

   should be on the lookout for a _____ that signals

   _____ .

▶ **TEST 2**   **Recognizing Thesis Statements**

DIRECTIONS   Underline the thesis statement in each reading.

1. Is Joint Custody Becoming the Norm?

1   As men have become more involved in the nurturing of children, the courts no longer assume that "parent" means "mother." Instead, a new family relations model is emerging. It suggests that even nonbiological parents may be awarded joint custody or visitation rights as long as they have been economically and emotionally involved in the life of the child.

2   Given that fathers are no longer routinely excluded from custody considerations, over half of the states have enacted legislation authorizing joint custody. About 16 percent of separated and divorced couples actually have a joint custody arrangement. In a typical joint physical custody arrangement, the parents continue to live near one another. The children may spend part of each week with each parent or may spend alternating weeks with each parent. New terminology is even being introduced in the lives of divorcing spouses and in the courts. The term "joint custody," which implies ownership, is being replaced with "shared parenting," which implies cooperation in taking care of children.

3   There are several advantages to joint custody or shared parenting. Ex-spouses may fight less if they have joint custody because there is no inequality in terms of involvement in their children's lives. Children will benefit from the resulting decrease in hostility between parents who have both "won" them.

4   Unlike sole-parent custody, in which one parent wins (usually the mother) and the other parent loses, joint custody allows children to continue to benefit from the love and attention of both parents. Children in homes where joint custody has been awarded might also have greater financial resources available to them than children in sole-custody homes.

5   Joint physical custody may also be advantageous in that the stress of parenting does not fall on one parent but rather is shared. One mother who has a joint custody arrangement with her ex-husband said, "When my kids are with their dad, I get a break from the parenting role, and I have a chance to do things for myself. I love my kids but I also love having time away from them." Another joint-parenting

father said, "When you live with your kids every day, you can get very frustrated and are not always happy to be with them. But after you haven't seen them for three days, it feels good to see them again."

(Adapted from Knox and Schacht, *Choices in Relationships*, 10th ed., p. 510.)

2. Lost in the Fog of War

1   Decimated by war, first with France in the 1950s, then with the United States, the South East Asian country of Vietnam appears to be booming again, with many of the country's citizens enjoying a sense of peace and well-being. That's true at least for those citizens who don't have freckles, white skin, or blue eyes. In Vietnam, freckles are a source of shame. They announce American parentage and make their owners despised because they are Vietnamese Amerasians, the children of mothers who slept with American soldiers during the country's war with the United States. Considered offspring of a once-hated enemy, Vietnam's Amerasians are despised by the people they live with and rejected by the country to which they believe they rightly belong: the United States.

2   Initially, though, the United States did make attempts to reach a hand out to the children U.S. soldiers had left behind after the Vietnam war ended in 1975. The 1987 Congressional "Homecoming Act" even funded a city center for Vietnamese Amerasians. At the same time, the government also offered visas to the offspring of American soldiers. At that point, the only thing needed to qualify for a visa was an obviously mixed-race appearance. That alone could guarantee resettlement in the United States. But these good intentions on the part of the Americans quickly fell apart as con artists began picking kids up off the streets and attaching them to fake relatives, who also wanted a new life in the United States.

3   The easy visas, however, dried up as officials began demanding hard evidence—documents, letters, and pictures—as proof of an American father. The problem was that any such evidence had been quickly destroyed after the war with the United States ended and the Viet Cong took over Vietnam. No woman who had been involved with the enemy wanted visible proof of the relationship. In addition, a country in wartime doesn't usually excel at filing documents.

4   Thus, Vietnam's Amerasians, most of whom desperately want to leave a country that despises them because of their parents, are left to search for their fathers on the Internet, using what little they know

about their past to search out a father who may not even care to know they exist. For a number of years, they have had an ally in a Danish furniture painter named Brian Hjort, who created a website called FatherFounded.com. Backpacking through Vietnam in the 1990s, Hjort became friendly with some Amerasian war orphans, and was impressed by their generosity and warmth. He became determined to aid their cause, even though he knew most of the fathers he was searching for could probably never be found.

5   Hjort's website has brought about a few successful reunions. But he depends on donations for continuing his work, and it's not clear how long he can carry on. Still, for now at least, the site remains in existence, and Hjort does his best to reunite American fathers with the children they fathered during war time, because as he says on his website, "Amerasians are paying the price for past events in Vietnam." In his mind, at least, someone needs to take responsibility for their plight.

(Source of information: Patrick Winn, "Vietnam War Babies: Grown Up and Low on Luck," September 2, 2011, Salon.com.)

▶ **TEST 3**   **Recognizing and Paraphrasing Thesis Statements**

DIRECTIONS   Underline the thesis statement. Then paraphrase it in the blanks that follow.

1. **Dreams and Creativity**

1   History is full of cases where dreams have been a pathway to creativity and discovery. A striking example is provided by Dr. Otto Loewi, a pharmacologist and winner of a Nobel Prize. Loewi had spent years studying the chemical transmission of nerve impulses. A tremendous breakthrough in his research came when he dreamed of an experiment three nights in a row. The first two nights he woke up and scribbled the experiment on a pad. But the next morning, he couldn't tell what the notes meant. On the third night, he got up after having the dream. This time, instead of making notes he went straight to his laboratory and performed the crucial experiment. Loewi said later that if the experiment had occurred to him while awake, he would have rejected it.

2   Loewi's experience gives some insight into using dreams to produce creative solutions. Inhibitions are reduced during dreaming, which may be especially useful in solving problems that require a fresh point of view. Even unimaginative people may create amazing worlds each night in their dreams. For many of us, this rich ability to create is lost in the daily rush of everyday life when we are pulled in so many different directions.

3   The ability to take advantage of dreams for problem solving is improved if you "set" yourself before retiring. Before you go to bed, try to visualize or think intently about a problem you wish to solve. Steep yourself in the problem by stating it clearly and reviewing all relevant information.

4   Although this method is not guaranteed to produce a novel solution or a new insight, it is certain to be an adventure. In one study, at least half of the subjects, all of them college students, recalled a dream that helped them solve a personal problem. (Adapted from Coon and Mitterer, *Introduction to Psychology*, 11th ed., p. 214.)

Paraphrase   _____

_____

2. Mind Reading Endangers Communication

1   Mind readers claim to understand what other people think, feel, or perceive. Now in a carnival setting, this might have some appeal. But in everyday life, acting as if you know what is in someone else's mind can interfere with effective communication.

2   Consider a few examples. One person says to her partner, "I know you didn't plan anything for our anniversary because it's not important to you." In fact, the partner has planned a surprise party. A supervisor notices that an employee is late for work several days in a row and just assumes the employee isn't committed to the job. The truth is the employee has been taking a route where road work is being done and there have been repeated traffic jams. Gina is late meeting Alex, who assumes she's late because Gina's still mad about an argument they had the day before. The reality is that Gina has forgotten what she and Alex argued about. She's late because she got lost.

3   Mind reading also occurs when we make statements like, "I know why you're upset" or "It's obvious that you don't care about me anymore." No matter how perceptive we think we are, we don't really know what's going on in someone else's mind. We can only guess what other people think or feel.

4   The problem with mind reading is this: When we mind read, we impose our perspectives on others instead of allowing them to say what they think. This can lead not just to misunderstandings but also to resentment. Most of us prefer to speak for ourselves. If someone tells us what we think or feel *before* we express our thoughts or feelings, we are likely to become annoyed. That's hardly the way to lay the groundwork for successful communication. (Adapted from Wood, *Interpersonal Communication*, 5th ed., p. 91.)

Paraphrase _____

_____

▶ TEST 4   Recognizing and Paraphrasing Thesis Statements

DIRECTIONS   Underline the thesis statement. Then paraphrase it in the blanks that follow.

1. Debt and the Federal Government

1   Like most Americans, you probably think about the way the government spends its money the same way you think about how you ought to spend yours. If you spend more than you earn, you will have to borrow money and pay it back to the bank. If you want to buy a car or a house, you will have to get a loan and make monthly payments on it. If you run up so many charges on your credit card that it is maxed out, you won't be able to charge anything more on it. Surely the government ought to work the same way: spend no more than it earns and pay back its loans.

2   But it doesn't. And there are two basic reasons why the government can, on a regular basis, spend more than it earns. One reason is that a debt is important or worrisome only insofar as the government cannot make the payments on its bonds in a currency that people regard as stable and valuable. As long as people believe that the American dollar is stable and valuable, they line up to buy Treasury bonds. As a result, the government in Washington, like the owners of Wal-Mart, can pay for whatever they want.

3   The government can also run up debt because it can afford to pay the interest. The total federal debt is a very large number (in 2010 it was already over thirteen trillion dollars) But the number, while huge, does not mean much when taken alone. Currently interest rates have remained low and the economy can afford the interest payments. Federal interest payments take up about 1.7 percent of the total value of all of the goods and services the nation produces, called the *Gross Domestic Product* or *GDP*. If interest rates stay low, the government may be able to continue to do what consumers can't do, which is spend more than it earns. But if interest rates start climbing, the government might have to look more closely at spending versus debt.

(Adapted from Wilson and Dilulio, *American Government*, 10th ed., p. 486; source of updated debt figure www.cbo.gov/doc.cfm?index=11999.)

Paraphrase   _____

_____

2. **On the Trail of Typhoid Mary**

1　November 11, 1938, a woman called Mary Mallon died of a stroke. She was seventy years old at the time, and at her death, at least three deaths and fifty-three cases of typhoid had been attributed to her. Due to her deadly history, the press had dubbed Mary Mallon "Typhoid Mary," a nickname she richly deserved because everywhere she went, the disease called "typhoid" was not far behind, until, that is, one man decided to stop her.

2　In 1906, while working as a cook for New York City banker Charles Henry Warren, Mallon prepared a delicious dinner—cold cucumber soup, lobster, wild rice, and strawberry ice cream with peaches. Warren and his guests ate heartily. But less than ten days later, several guests ended up in the hospital. All of them were eventually diagnosed with typhoid fever.

3　Careful research and some clever detective work by Dr. George Soper, a sanitary engineer employed by the New York Department of Health, traced the disease to Mary Mallon. Unfortunately, by the time Soper had identified Mallon as the source of infection, she was gone, on to yet another job as a cook or housekeeper. Hot on Mallon's trail, Dr. Soper discovered that the woman changed jobs frequently; wherever she worked, someone developed typhoid fever.

4　When Soper finally caught up with Mallon in 1907, she was hardly apologetic. On the contrary, she chased him away with a carving knife. Mallon only submitted to testing when Soper returned with three police officers. Tests done over her objections showed Mallon carried the bacteria that caused typhoid. But, for some reason, she herself showed no symptoms of the disease. Told to have her gall bladder removed—the gall bladder was believed to be the site of the infection—Mallon refused and began a lengthy court battle to gain her freedom from hospital isolation.

5　In 1910, Mary Mallon was released. However, she had to promise never to work as a cook again. She also had to report to the New York Department of Health every ninety days, allowing officials to keep her under a watchful eye. But by now, the newspapers all knew who Mallon was. Hounded by reporters, Mallon disappeared again only to resurface in 1915 when an outbreak of typhoid was reported at the Sloane Hospital for Women. As George Soper had suspected, Mary Mallon had been working in the hospital kitchen shortly before the outbreak. This time, when police caught up with Mallon, they arrested her. By court mandate, she was confined to Riverside Hospital in New York, where she spent the rest of her life.

Paraphrase _____

_____

▶ **TEST 5**   **Recognizing and Paraphrasing Thesis Statements**

DIRECTIONS   Underline the thesis statement. Then paraphrase it in the blanks that follow.

1. Communicating with Waiters: A Test of Character

1   Office Depot CEO Steve Odland remembers like it was yesterday working in an upscale French restaurant in Denver. The purple sorbet in cut glass he was serving tumbled onto the expensive white gown of an obviously rich and important woman. "I watched it in slow motion ruining her dress for the evening," Odland says. "I thought I would be shot on sight."

2   Thirty years have passed, but Odland can't get the scene out of his mind, nor the woman's kind reaction. She was startled, regained composure, and, in a reassuring voice, told the teenage Odland, "It's OK. It wasn't your fault." When she left the restaurant, she also left the future Fortune 500 CEO with a life lesson: You can tell a lot about a potential employee by the way he or she treats the waiter.

3   Odland isn't the only CEO to have made this discovery. Rather it seems to be one of those rare laws of the land that every CEO learns on the way up. How others treat the CEO says nothing, they say. But how others treat the waiter is like a magical window into the soul.

4   The Waiter Rule also applies to the way people treat hotel maids, mailroom clerks, bellmen, and security guards. Au Bon Pain cofounder Ron Shaich, now CEO of Panera Bread, says he was interviewing a candidate for general counsel in St. Louis. She was "sweet" to Shaich but turned amazingly rude to someone cleaning the tables; as a result, she didn't get the job. Any time candidates are being considered for executive positions at Panera Bread, Shaich asks his assistant, Laura Parisi, how they treated her, because some applicants are "pushy, self-absorbed and rude" before she transfers the call to him.

5   People view waiters as their temporary personal employees. Therefore, how executives treat waiters probably demonstrates how they treat their actual employees, says Sara Lee CEO Brenda Barnes, a former waitress and postal clerk, who says she is a demanding boss but never shouts at or demeans an employee. "Sitting in the chair of CEO makes me no better person that the forklift operator in our plant," she said. "If you treat the waiter, or a subordinate, like garbage, guess what? Are they going to give it their all? I don't think so." ("CEOs Vouch for Waiter Rule: Watch How People Treat Staff" from *USA Today*, April 14, 2006. Copyright © 2006 Gannett. All rights reserved. Used by permission and protected by the Copyright Laws of the United States.)

Paraphrase _____

_____

2. Why Should We Be Concerned About a Warmer Earth?

1   So what is the big deal? Why should we worry about a possible rise of only a few degrees in the earth's average surface temperature? We often have that much change between May and July, or even between yesterday and today. So why should we care about a few degrees change in temperature?

2   Climate scientists warn that the concern is not only how much the temperature changes but how rapidly it occurs. Most past changes in the temperature took place over thousands to a hundred thousand years. The problem we face now is a significant increase in temperature *during this century*. Such rapid climate change could have dramatic and drastic effects on the earth's environment.

3   A 2003 U.S. National Academy of Sciences report laid out a nightmarish worst-case-scenario in which human activities or combination of human activities and natural climate changes succeed in triggering a new and abrupt climate change. At this point, the global climate system reaches a tipping point, when it will be too late to reverse catastrophic change for tens of thousands of years.

4   The report describes whole environments in complete collapse, low-lying cities being flooded, forests consumed in vast fires, while grasslands dry out and turn into dustbowls. It also calls up the threat of wildlife disappearing, more frequent and intensified coastal storms, and hurricanes with tropical waterborne and insect-transmitted infectious disease spreading rapidly beyond their current ranges.

5   The possibilities outlined in the National Academy report were supported by a 2004 analysis carried out by Peter Schwartz and Doug Randall for the U.S. Department of Defense. The authors concluded that global warming "must be viewed as a serious threat to global stability and should be elevated beyond a scientific debate to a U.S. national security concern." In 2004, the United Kingdom's chief science adviser David A. King wrote, "In my view, climate change is the most severe problem we are facing today—more serious than the threat of terrorism." (Adapted from Miller, *Living in the Environment*, 15th ed., p. 471.)

Paraphrase _____

_____

▶ **TEST 6**   **Reviewing Chapter 5 Vocabulary**

DIRECTIONS   For each sentence, fill in the blank with the appropriate vocabulary word.

> desecrated   discernible   domains   deviant   socialization
> merit   frenzy   elusive   patron saint innuendo
> strident   marital   mandatory   random   alternatives

1. Butterflies, true love, and a thief with a thousand disguises are all likely to be described as _____.

2. Going to school until the age of sixteen, stopping at red lights, and paying taxes are all considered _____.

3. Playing with others, listening to our parents, and going to school are all methods of _____.

4. Politics, religion, and sports are three topics that are liable to make people become _____ during a discussion.

5. Home schooling, private schools, and charter schools are some possible _____ to the public school system.

6. Marrying your cousin, going to a party in your underwear, and hitting people you don't like are all examples of _____ behavior.

7. Churches, mosques, synagogues, cemeteries, and burial grounds are all places that can be _____.

8. Losing something precious, getting lost in a strange place, and becoming seriously ill are all times when people are likely to call on a(n) _____ for assistance.

9. Anger, dancing, madness, and love can all induce a(n) _____ in people.

10. _____ thrives in political campaigns, divorce proceedings, and *The National Enquirer*.

11. Unlike viruses, bacteria, and cells, grass, dust bunnies, and dandelions are _____ with the naked eye.

12. Physics, automotive mechanics, and veterinary science are all _____ that require long training to be understood.

13. Wedding gowns, vows, couples, and guests are part of most _____ ceremonies.

14. Being loyal to your friends, planning for the future, and not letting infatuation become the basis for marriage are all ideas that have

_____.

15. Giving a couple of dollars to a stranger who can't quite come up with enough cash for groceries, offering your seat on the bus to someone elderly, and asking a foreign student who is alone for the holidays home for dinner all qualify as _____ acts of kindness.

Focusing on Supporting Details in Paragraphs

"God is in the details."

—Architect Ludwig Mies van der Rohe

"The devil is in the details."

—Anonymous

Chapter 6 returns to the paragraph to look more closely at supporting details and how they combine with topic sentences to explain the author's main idea. You'll learn how major supporting details directly support the main idea while minor details reinforce major ones, sometimes in very important ways that should not be ignored despite the label "minor."

You'll also learn how concluding sentences in paragraphs can get slightly off the track of the main idea yet still need to be accounted for in your notes. As before, your work with this chapter will lay the groundwork for the next, where you will look at supporting details in longer readings drawn primarily from textbooks.

The Function of Supporting Details

Paul: I thought June's behavior at that meeting was extraordinary.

Marisa: I thought the same thing. I couldn't believe how rude she was. She's too outspoken for my taste.

Paul: That's not what I meant at all. I thought she was great. When she believes in something, she's not afraid to speak her mind.

READING

◆ EXERCIS

Topic Se

Supporting

Topic Se

When the conversation between Paul and Marisa stays on a general level, both speakers are inclined to agree. It's only when Marisa moves to a more specific level that the speakers realize they actually disagree. This is a good example of how important supporting details are to the exchange of ideas. They make general statements more specific and place restrictions on how the listener or speaker can interpret, or understand, what's been said. Supporting details help both speakers and writers avoid a communication breakdown.

Supporting Details and Main Ideas

Supporting details in paragraphs are the specific sentences that clarify, prove, or suggest the author's main idea. Supporting details can provide reasons, examples, studies, definitions, etc., that are essential to getting a clear understanding of the author's central point. The form they take depends on the main idea expressed in the topic sentence or implied by the author's selection of details (more about implied main ideas in Chapter 8).

But whatever their form, the function of supporting details remains the same: They are there to make sure readers understand the main idea. To see how topic sentences and supporting details work together in a paragraph, read the following statement:

> Prolonged unemployment can create serious psychological problems that, in the long run, actually contribute to continued joblessness.

By itself, the sentence tells us that long-term unemployment can do psychological damage. But what does the author mean by that general phrase "prolonged unemployment"? Is she talking about six months or six years? Exactly what kind of psychological problems does she have in mind? After all, that phrase is fairly general and covers a lot of ground. Also, how do psychological problems contribute to or help cause continued joblessness?

Left on its own, the sentence raises several questions. Those questions get answered when the sentence is followed by specific supporting details:

> [1]Prolonged unemployment can create serious psychological problems that, in the long run, actually contribute to continued joblessness. [2]In a society that stresses the relationship between productive

The polio epidemic introduced the iron lung breathing machine into hospitals, where children stricken with polio were struggling for breath.

Top

◆ **EXERCISE 2**   **Identifying Irrelevant or Unrelated Supporting Details**

DIRECTIONS   Read each paragraph. Write the number of the topic sentence in the first blank. Each paragraph includes a supporting detail that does not relate to the topic sentence. Write the number of that sentence in the second blank.

EXAMPLE   [1]Orthorexia nervosa is a new eating disorder that occurs when health-conscious individuals become obsessed with the quality of the food they eat. [2]People who suffer from this disorder base their self-esteem on their ability to maintain a diet of only healthy foods. [3]They decide, for example, that beans and rice are healthy and restrict themselves to eating only those two foods. [4]Should they go off their restricted diet, they feel intensely guilty and depressed. [5]Bulimics overeat and then feel guilty about the amount of food they have consumed. [6]Victims of orthorexia nervosa don't seem to realize that excessive reliance on a few select foods can deprive their bodies of critical nutrients.*

Topic Sentence   ___1___

Irrelevant Detail   ___5___

EXPLANATION   With the exception of sentence 5, the supporting details in the sample paragraph all describe the eating disorder orthorexia nervosa. Sentence 5, however, talks about the eating disorder bulimia and never relates it to orthorexia, making the detail in sentence 5 irrelevant to the rest of the paragraph.

――――――――――――

*nutrients: substances the body needs for good health.

1. [1]In 1894, Japan and China waged war chiefly for the control of Korea; the Chinese, however, were no match for their opponents. [2]Within one year, the war was over, and the Japanese had almost completely destroyed the Chinese naval forces. [3]As a result of the war, China had to pay large sums of money to Japan and recognize the full independence of Korea; it also had to give up the resource-rich island of Taiwan. [4]Although the war was brief, it proved without a doubt that Japan was a military power to be reckoned with. [5]During World War II, Japan invaded China.

Topic Sentence   1

Irrelevant Detail   5

2. [1]Child abuse can take several forms. [2]Sometimes the child is injured physically and may suffer from an odd or a disturbing combination of cuts, burns, bruises, or broken bones. [3]Usually the parents or guardians claim that the child "had an accident," even though no normal accident could cause such injuries. [4]Abused children have a greater chance of becoming abusive parents. [5]But child abuse may also take the form of emotional neglect; the parents will simply ignore the child and refuse to respond to bids for attention. [6]Children suffering from this kind of abuse often show symptoms of the *failure to thrive* syndrome*, in which physical growth is delayed. [7]In still other cases of maltreatment, the child may be emotionally abused. [8]One or both parents may ridicule or belittle the child. [9]In this case, physical problems may be absent, but the child's self-esteem will be seriously undermined.

Topic Sentence   1

Irrelevant Detail   4

3. [1]Do you need to memorize a list of items in a particular order? [2]If you do, you should take the *serial position effect* into account. [3]The serial position effect refers to the tendency of many people to make the most errors when trying to remember the middle of a list or series. [4]If, for example, you are introduced to a long line of people, you are most likely to forget the names of those in the middle of the line. [5]Many people refuse to believe that the ability to remember is

---

*thrive: grow or develop well.

a skill that can be improved with training. ⁶Anytime you need to learn a long poem or speech, be sure that you take the serial position effect into account.

Topic Sentence _____

Irrelevant Detail _____

4. ¹Most people run or scream in terror when they see a snake. ²Yet if snakes are examined without prejudice, they prove to be fascinating and relatively harmless members of the reptile family. ³Like other reptiles, they are cold-blooded, and their temperatures change with the environment. ⁴Although most people think that snakes are slimy and wet, the opposite is true. ⁵Their skins are cool and dry, even pleasant to the touch. ⁶The Hopi Indians perform ritual dances with live rattlesnakes in their mouths. ⁷Despite their reputation, most snakes do more good than harm by helping to control the rodent population.

Topic Sentence _____

Irrelevant Detail _____

Major and Minor Supporting Details

To understand how a supporting detail can be labeled major or minor, consider the following paragraph. The major supporting details appear in **boldface**, the minor ones in *italics*.

Psychologists have identified three basic styles of parenting. **Controlling parents think their children have few rights and many responsibilities.** *They tend to demand strict obedience to rigid standards of behavior and expect their children to obey their commands unquestioningly.* **Permissive parents, in contrast, require little responsible behavior from their children.** *Rules are not enforced, and the child usually gets his or her own way.* **Effective parents find a balance between their rights and their children's rights.** *They control their children's behavior without being harsh or rigid.*

In this paragraph, the topic sentence announces that psychologists have identified three different parenting styles. The natural response of most readers would be to say: "What are the three styles of parenting?" Notice how all the major details (printed in boldface) speak directly to that question.

Based on this illustration, we can say then that **major details** further define key words or phrases essential to understanding the main idea expressed in the topic sentence. Major details anticipate the questions readers might raise about the main idea and start to supply answers. Sometimes they supply answers that are complete and need no further support. However, sometimes major details need the help of minor details. **Minor details** are more specific sentences that follow major ones. They further explain, illustrate, or emphasize a term or point introduced by the major details.

♦ EXERCISE 3   Diagramming Major and Minor Details

DIRECTIONS   Read each paragraph. Then fill in the boxes with brief paraphrases of the major and minor details.

EXAMPLE   ¹It seems impossible that large prehistoric creatures are alive today. ²Yet huge creatures from the dinosaur age may still exist beneath the sea. ³After all, as fossil remains show, dinosaurs had relatives called plesiosaurs, who lived in the sea. ⁴They were huge and had long necks and snakelike heads. ⁵People who maintain that plesiosaurs still live point to recent accounts of strange sea creatures that fit the description of ancient sea monsters. ⁶According to reports, the modern-day sea creatures also have long necks and snakelike heads.

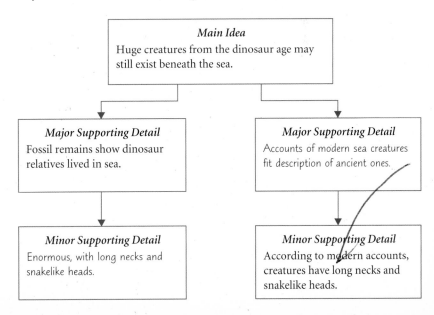

Main Idea
Huge creatures from the dinosaur age may still exist beneath the sea.

Major Supporting Detail
Fossil remains show dinosaur relatives lived in sea.

Major Supporting Detail
Accounts of modern sea creatures fit description of ancient ones.

Minor Supporting Detail
Enormous, with long necks and snakelike heads.

Minor Supporting Detail
According to modern accounts, creatures have long necks and snakelike heads.

EXPLANATION   The topic sentence claims that huge creatures from the dinosaur age might still exist beneath the sea. Two major supporting details help make that statement more convincing. Each major detail is followed by a minor one that adds more information.

1. [1]To the ordinary observer, the earth appears to be a solid mass. [2]Scientists, however, know that the earth is composed of several distinct layers. [3]Called the *crust*, the layer closest to the surface consists of lightweight rock that extends for about twenty miles beneath the earth's surface. [4]Just underneath the crust is a second layer, about two thousand miles thick, known as the *mantle*. [5]Portions of the mantle are extremely hot. [6]The third layer, or the *core* of the earth, is made up primarily of nickel and iron, and it too reaches extremely high temperatures. [7]The temperatures are hot enough to melt both metals, but the fifty pounds of pressure borne by each square inch keeps them solid.

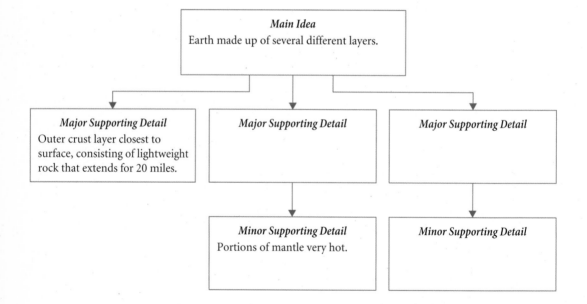

2. [1]Between 1959 and 1975, the American psychologist Harry Harlow conducted a series of experiments with rhesus monkeys. [2]The goal of the experiments was to determine the effects of maternal deprivation and social isolation. [3]Then and now, Harlow's experiments have been harshly criticized on ethical grounds because of the intense suffering they caused the monkeys under observation.

[4]In 1959, Harlow and fellow researcher Robert Zimmerman placed one group of infant monkeys in a cage with both a terrycloth figure designed for physical contact and a wire figure that dispensed food. [5]A second group of monkey subjects only had contact with a wire food dispenser. [6]When the study was completed, the monkeys that had been given food and a chance to cuddle with the terrycloth figure were much better adjusted than those who had had food but no experience of physical contact. [7]In 1962, Harlow and his wife, Margaret, raised one group of monkeys with a cloth figure for comfort and another group in complete isolation. [8]At the end of the experiment, the monkeys raised in isolation would bite their arms and legs and attack others who approached them. [9]By the 1970s Harlow was engaging in experiments that called for infant monkeys to be housed in steel chambers that were appropriately nicknamed "the pits of despair." [10]Not surprisingly the monkeys who spent time in the chambers were devastated by the experience.

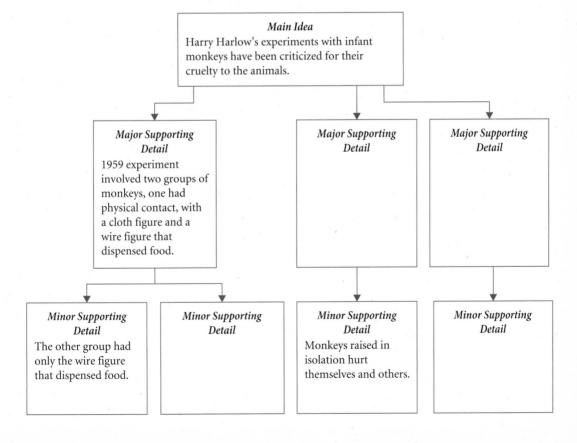

Main Idea
Harry Harlow's experiments with infant monkeys have been criticized for their cruelty to the animals.

Major Supporting Detail
1959 experiment involved two groups of monkeys, one had physical contact, with a cloth figure and a wire figure that dispensed food.

Major Supporting Detail

Major Supporting Detail

Minor Supporting Detail
The other group had only the wire figure that dispensed food.

Minor Supporting Detail

Minor Supporting Detail
Monkeys raised in isolation hurt themselves and others.

Minor Supporting Detail

Harry Harlow's monkey subjects craved affection almost as much as they craved food.

Evaluating the Contribution of Minor Details

From looking at the paragraph on styles of parenting, you might assume that minor details aren't important. Within the sample paragraph, the major details do the work of defining "the three basic styles of parenting." The minor details then add some very specific and very obvious examples of the three behaviors described. Thus you could safely say that you understood the paragraph without reference to the minor details. After all, they only repeat, with greater specificity, the point of the major details.

However, that's not always the case. Could you, for instance, react the same way to the minor details italicized in this next paragraph? They follow the major details. They are more specific than the major details, which they serve to explain. But are they unimportant?

Topic Sentence ¹The human ear is a complicated structure that can be divided into three main parts. ²The external part is the outer ear. ³*It collects sound waves and directs them to the auditory canal, which ends at a membrane called the tympanum or eardrum.* ⁴The middle part of the ear contains three small bones. ⁵*These are called the hammer, anvil, and stirrup.* ⁶*These three small bones channel the vibrations collected from the eardrum into the inner ear.* ⁷The inner ear contains the actual hearing apparatus,* a small, shell-like organ filled with fluid and nerve endings. [8]*It is called the cochlea.* [9]*When the nerve endings receive vibrations from the fluid in the cochlea, they transmit them directly to the hearing portion of the brain.*

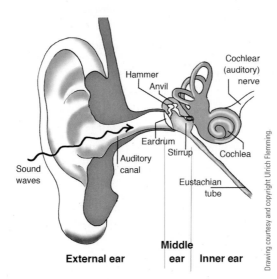

The human ear consists of three main parts: the outer ear, middle ear, and inner ear.

In this case, the topic sentence tells you that the human ear has three main parts. The first major detail identifies one of those parts as the "outer ear." But look closely at the minor detail modifying the first major one. It's the minor detail that explains the function of the outer ear. Ignore that piece of information and all you know about the outer ear is what it's called. You don't know what it does.

The same is true for the next new major detail in the sample paragraph (sentence 4), which introduces another one of the three parts of the ear. Here again it's the two minor details that provide the real meat of the explanation.

When Minor Details Double Up, the Reader Needs to Think Twice

And what about this next paragraph? In this case, here again there are two minor details following one major one. Would you say that both of the minor details are irrelevant, or unnecessary, for your understanding of the underlined topic sentence?

---

*apparatus: a part or device that performs a specific function.

Topic Sentence

[1]Vision is the slowest of the senses to develop in infants. [2]Infants have blurry vision at birth, but their visual world is not a complete blur. [3]They can see closer objects more clearly and can discern meaningful patterns. [4]For example, newborns show preferences for looking at facelike patterns over nonfacelike patterns. [5]They can recognize their own mother's face and even show a preference for looking at her face over other faces. (Nevid, *Psychology*, 3rd ed., p. 336.)

In this case, the major detail further explains the topic sentence's claim that the "visual world is not a complete blur" for infants. Then sentence 4, a minor detail, gives us an example of a "meaningful pattern," the human face. That minor detail is followed by another minor detail, sentence 5, which makes the previous sentence even more specific. The face of the infant's mother is a particularly meaningful pattern.

Because the phrase "meaningful patterns" is so general, we definitely need the first minor detail to clarify the phrase, making that detail essential to our understanding of the paragraph's message. The second minor detail describes a specific face that is meaningful to infants. But while it's interesting to learn that babies can tell the difference between their mom's face and the faces of others, it's not a detail we need in order to understand the point of the paragraph.

The moral of both previous examples is this: Don't equate the label "minor" with a lack of importance. Minor details flesh out, or further develop, some part or point of the major detail. Sometimes they are critical to your understanding of a paragraph. Sometimes they are not.

WEB QUEST
Use the Web to write brief answers to this question: What controversy is related to the part of the ear called the "cochlea"?

_____

_____

_____

SUMMING UP THE KEY POINTS

Major Details

- are less general than topic or introductory sentences.
- provide the examples, reasons, statistics, and studies that help make the main idea clear and convincing.
- anticipate readers' questions about the main idea.
- are essential to your understanding of the paragraph.

Minor Details

- are the most specific sentences in the paragraph.
- follow and further explain major details.
- must be evaluated because they may or may not be important enough to include in reading notes.

◆ **EXERCISE 4**   **Recognizing Major and Minor Details**

DIRECTIONS   Use the underlined topic sentence to determine if the sentences that follow are major or minor details. Then answer the accompanying questions.

EXAMPLE

Topic sentence provokes the question, "What were those attempts?"

Sentence 2 introduces the first of those attempts.

Sentences 3–7 add more specific information about the fight to gain political power.

¹Over the last fifty years, Native Americans have made numerous attempts to gain more political power. ²In late 1969, a group of Native Americans publicized their grievances by occupying Alcatraz, the abandoned prison in San Francisco Bay, for nineteen months. ³In 1963, tribes in the Northwest waged a campaign to have their fishing rights recognized in parts of Washington State. ⁴These were eventually granted by the Supreme Court in 1968. ⁵In 1972, a group of Native Americans marched on Washington, D.C., to dramatize what they called a "trail of broken treaties" and present the government with a series of demands. ⁶In 1973, members of AIM, the American Indian Movement, took over Wounded Knee, South Dakota, for seventy-two days to protest the government's treatment of Native Americans. ⁷Since the early 1980s, several tribes have filed lawsuits to win back lands and mineral rights illegally taken from their ancestors. (Adapted from Thio, *Sociology*, 4th ed., p. 255.)

1. How many major details appear in this paragraph? __5__

2. Which sentence or sentences provide major details? _2, 3, 5, 6, 7_

3. What question or questions do the major details answer about the topic sentence?

   How did Native Americans try to go about gaining more political power?

   What were the attempts that the author referred to in the topic sentence?

4. How many minor details appear in the paragraph? __1__ Which sentence or sentences are minor details? __4__

5. How essential is/are the minor detail(s)? Please explain your answer.

   In this case, the minor detail doesn't add information essential to understanding

   the main idea. It just tells the reader more about the success of one specific

   attempt to gain more political power.

EXPLANATION   Sentences 2, 3, 5, 6, and 7 are all major details that answer the obvious questions raised by the topic sentence. How have Native Americans gone about demanding more political power? What are some of those "attempts"? The exception is sentence 4, which further explains sentence 3. It's a minor detail that tells us how Native Americans triumphed in one particular court case. While it certainly adds information to the preceding sentence, it doesn't add much to your understanding of the topic sentence, so it's not an essential detail.

1. ¹A sole proprietorship is a business that is owned and usually operated by one person. ²Although a few sole proprietorships are large and have many employees, most are small. ³Sole proprietorship is the simplest form of business ownership and the easiest to start. ⁴In most instances, the owner (the sole proprietor) simply decides that he or she is in business and begins operations. ⁵Some of today's largest corporations including Ford Motor Company, H. J. Heinz Company, and Procter and Gamble, started out as tiny—and in many cases struggling—sole proprietorships. (Pride, Hughes, and Kapoor, *Business*, 10th ed., p. 108.)

   1. How many major details appear in this paragraph? _____

   2. Which sentence or sentences provide major details? _____

3. What question or questions do the major details answer about the topic sentence?

_____

4. How many minor details appear in the paragraph? _____ Which sentence or sentences are minor details? _____

5. How essential is/are the minor detail(s)? Please explain your answer.

_____

_____

_____

2. [1]It's not exactly news that men and women tend to use speech in different ways. [2]In conversation, men interrupt more than women and are far more likely to assert strong opinions without indicating that another point of view might exist, for instance, "Bank fees are a form of highway robbery." [3]Women, however, are more likely to express opinions as questions, e.g., "I think bank fees are excessive, don't you?" [4]The assumption has been that the differences in speech were a result of cultural training. [5]But a book published in 2011, _Duels and Duets_ offers an alternative point of view; it suggests that the difference in speech patterns is a result of evolutionary* history rather than social inequality. [6]According to the author, John L. Locke, a professor of linguistics† at Lehman College, women tend to be less assertive in conversation because, historically, they were the physically weaker sex. [7]As the weaker sex, they needed to create social or group bonds as a form of protection. [8]They had to find strength as part of a group because they could not rely on brawn and muscle. [9]But for men the evolutionary story was very different. [10]Men who publicly displayed their assertiveness,* in conversation and in combat, often gained in status, particularly if the man was physically strong enough to beat his rivals. [11]In the early stages of human development, men were encouraged to duel, or fight, in conversation while women, for safety's sake, were more given to duets, to pairing up for safety's sake. [12]If the author of _Duels and Duets_ is correct, it appears that old habits die hard.

---

*evolutionary: related to gradual change or development over the course of time.
†linguistics: the study of language and its structure.
*assertiveness: boldness, having confidence in one's ideas or actions.

1. How many major details appear in this paragraph? _____

2. Which sentence or sentences provide major details? _____

3. What question or questions do the major details answer about the topic sentence?

_____

_____

4. How many minor details appear in the paragraph? _____ Which sentence or sentences provide minor details? _____

5. How essential is/are the minor detail(s)? Please explain your answer.

_____

_____

_____

WEB QUEST
Why was Alcatraz chosen as the site of AIM's protest?

_____

_____

_____

_____

✔ CHECK YOUR UNDERSTANDING

1. In the context of a paragraph, what's the purpose of major supporting details?

_____

_____

2. What do minor supporting details do?

_____

_____

3. Why do minor details need to be evaluated?

_____

_____

Category Words in Topic Sentences Signal Major Details

Especially in textbooks, topic sentences are likely to include broad category words. **Category words** sum up and generally refer to a variety of more specific activities, events, and behaviors. They usually appear as part of a larger phrase, for instance:

1. Child abuse can take several different *forms*.

2. Psychologists have identified three *styles* of parenting.

3. Even when identical twins are reared in different homes, they often show many *similarities* in taste and behavior.

Using Category Words to Keep Readers on Track

Topic sentences like the three shown above tell readers to be alert to each sentence introducing another member of the larger category or group. Based on the topic sentence, readers know immediately that every new *form*, *style*, or *similarity* is a major detail.

For an illustration, read the following paragraph. Note the circled phrase in the underlined topic sentence. That phrase tells you that each myth described will be a major detail. It also tells you that there are *three* major details in the paragraph. Guided by the topic sentence, skilled readers look for references, both explicit and implicit, to the word *myth* to sort out the three major details. (This paragraph, by the way, is another illustration of how important minor details can often be).

"One classic" is an elliptical phrase that expects the reader to supply the word myth.

"Another myth" signals another major detail.

The introduction of another long-held belief in sentence 7 suggests another myth and another major detail.

[1]Education is one of those much-discussed topics that seem to attract misinformation like a magnet attracts iron. [2]Thus it's not surprising that there are at least three common myths about education that have almost no factual basis. [3]One classic is the belief that IQ scores don't change when in fact they can and do. [4]Especially among children, IQ shifts of five to ten points can occur over the course of a few months. [5]According to another myth of long standing, grouping students by ability improves their performance. [6]But, in fact, very little research supports this claim. [7]For at least two decades, many in education have also insisted that "discovery learning," in which students master scientific principles through problem solving rather than direct instruction, was the best way to teach science. [8]Yet a review of research indicates that direct instruction is often superior to discovery learning in the context of teaching science. (Source of information: Lillienfeld et al., *Fifty Common Myths*, p. 114.)

The sample paragraph illustrates how useful category words in topic sentences can be when it comes to identifying major and minor details. In the above example, each reference to a new myth is a major detail.

Similarly, if you were reading a paragraph where the topic sentence said something like "Three different kinds of behavior separate alcoholism from social drinking," you would know immediately that each sentence introducing one of those "three kinds of behavior" was a major detail.

Commonly Used Category Words ◆

Behaviors	Goals	Stages
Categories	Incidents	Steps
Causes	Kinds	Strategies
Characteristics	Materials	Studies
Classes	Methods	Stages
Components	Mores	Standards
Consequences	Motives	Symptoms
Differences	Objectives	Tactics
Disparities	Offices	Talents
Distinctions	Pointers	Techniques
Effects	Precautions	Traditions
Elements	Problems	Traits
Examples	Reasons	Ways
Factors	Rules	Values
Functions	Similarities	Virtues
Groups	Skills	

◆ **EXERCISE 5**   **Using Category Words to Identify Major Details**

DIRECTIONS   Underline the topic sentence and circle the category word or phrase that guides your search for major details. Then label the sentences that follow as *M* (for major) or *m* (for minor).

1. Parents typically discipline children in one of three ways. *Power assertion* refers to physical punishment or a show of force, such as taking away toys or privileges. _____ Another alternative is for parents to use *withdrawal of love* or the withholding of affection. _____ They can, for instance, refuse to speak to the child, threaten to leave, or act as if the child were temporarily unlovable. _____ *Management techniques* combine praise, approval, rules, reasoning, and the like to encourage desirable behavior. _____ (Adapted from Coon, *Essentials of Psychology*, 9th ed., p. 101.)

2. At one time, lotteries were illegal. But that time has clearly passed as more than forty states now allow and regulate lotteries. Several factors account for the birth of what some have called the lottery or "bettor government." Obviously, lotteries can bring in meaningful sums of money—some $23 billion in "profits" in 2008 alone. _____ That's a huge portion of state revenue. _____ Lotteries are also popular and entertaining. _____ What's more, they are voluntary. _____ No one can force you to participate in a lottery. _____ In addition, lotteries help relieve the pressure to increase taxes. _____ In some states, net lottery earnings have taken the place of a one-cent increase in the sales tax. _____ By taking control of lotteries, states offer a legal and fair alternative to illegal gambling operations, such as neighborhood numbers games. _____ (Adapted from Bowman and Kearney, *State and Local Government*, 8th ed., p. 364.)

Outside the Topic Sentence, Category Words Can Turn into Transitions

If a broad category word appears in a topic sentence, you can usually expect to see that same word repeated or referred to within the paragraph. The author will use it, at least once, probably more, as a transition introducing a major detail.

For instance, in this next paragraph, the second sentence is the topic sentence. It tells us that honeybees can only survive in a community where they all have "a number of special functions." If you think that the phrase "a number of special functions" is a clue to the major details, you are correct. But note as well how new major details are integrated, or blended, into the paragraph by the repetition of or reference to the word *function*.

In sentence 3, for example is a reference to the number of special functions.

In sentence 5, the word functions is used in connection to worker bees to indicate a new function is being introduced.

In sentence 8, the word function is attached to another member of the colony, drones, as a way of indicating to readers that yet another function is being addressed.

¹The honeybee is a highly social insect that can survive only when it is part of a community. ²Within the honeybee community, the members have a *number of special functions* that help ensure survival. ³The queen, for example, is the only sexually productive female; she gives birth to all of the drones, workers, and future queens. ⁴Her capacity for laying eggs is enormous, and her daily output exceeds 1,500 eggs. ⁵Although they lack the ability to mate or reproduce, worker bees also perform important functions. ⁶They secrete wax, construct the honeycomb, gather food, turn nectar into honey, guard the hive against intruders, and regulate the hive's temperature. ⁷If, for instance, the hive becomes too hot, worker bees cool the air by fanning their wings. ⁸In contrast to worker bees, drones have only one function—to mate with the queen. ⁹After the mating, which takes place in flight, a drone immediately dies; he has served his sole function. ¹⁰He is no longer necessary to the community.

Honeybees work together to keep their colonies safe and productive.

◆ EXERCISE 6   Using Category Words in Paragraphs

DIRECTIONS   Use one of the category words listed below to fill in the blanks in the topic sentences. Then use the same word in its singular form to create a transition to the first major detail.

EXAMPLE   Halloween is one of those holidays that has a lot of <u>traditions</u> associated with it. Perhaps the most famous <u>tradition</u> is trick or treating.

EXPLANATION   Note how the category word in the topic sentence gets repeated in order to create a transition from the topic sentence to the first supporting detail, in this case "trick or treating."

> advantages   traditions   symptoms
> studies   techniques   objectives

1. Journalists need a number of good _____ to make their subjects speak freely during an interview. The most important _____ is the ability to draw a person out and encourage him or her to talk freely.

2. The disease Dengue fever has several horrifying _____. The most obvious _____ is a red rash that spreads over the entire body, causing it to swell.

3. The high school reading program has four _____. One _____ is to encourage students to look closely at the connections between sentences.

4. There are several _____ to keeping music and art education part of the elementary and high school curriculum. The most essential _____ is the effect of music and art on the human spirit.

5. Numerous _____ suggest that multitasking is a bad idea. In one _____, subjects who were heavy multitaskers made more mistakes completing a simple sorting task than did those who did not multitask or who engaged in it infrequently.

From Reader to Writer   Start your paragraph with a topic sentence like this one, "All of my friends have several qualities in common," or maybe this one, "The person I marry has to have three key characteristics." Then use the category word you chose for your topic sentence as a transition to help your reader follow your description of the characteristics, attitudes, behaviors, etc., you expect to find in a friend, mate, teacher, or co-worker.

Addition Transitions Are Clues to Major Details

Topic sentences that include category words often appear in combination with addition transitions like *first*, *second*, *third*, *furthermore*, *moreover*, and *also*. (A more complete list appears on page 281.) However, even if addition transitions don't turn up in the company of category words, they still provide excellent clues to major details.

Addition transitions are the author's way of saying to readers, "With this sentence I am adding something new to the train of thought I started previously." When linked to category words, addition transitions are even more specific: They tell the reader, "Here's another major reason, illustration, advantage, or consequence to consider."

Look, for example, at the following passage and notice how the italicized transitions help readers sort out the subgroups included under the larger category word *reasons*, which appears in the topic sentence.

The transition first of all tells readers to be on the lookout for the first reason why children should not watch wrestling.

The transition furthermore announces the second reason.

The transition in addition tells readers that yet another reason is on its way.

[1]There are a number of reasons why parents should not allow young, impressionable children to watch wrestling. [2]*First of all*, wrestling suggests to children that physical violence causes no real harm. [3]In a wrestling match, no one seems to get hurt and most of the wrestlers come back the following week. [4]*Furthermore*, wrestling suggests that people are valued according to the damage they can do since the superstars of wrestling are those men and women who most effectively hurt and humiliate their opponents. [5]This is not an especially good message to be giving children. [6]*In addition*, wrestling celebrates crude and loutish behavior. [7]Watching a wrestling match on television or on YouTube, it's hard to say whose behavior is more despicable.* [8]It's a toss-up between the wrestlers shouting at the top of their lungs that they are going to demolish their opponent and the scantily clad women who parade around exhibiting score cards and occasionally jump in the ring to join the fray.*

*despicable: unworthy of respect, disgraceful.
*fray: fight, intense activity; to wear down or unravel.

In this paragraph, the author says there are several reasons why young children should not be allowed to watch wrestling matches. The transitions then help the reader recognize each of the reasons presented.

Transitions That Signal Addition or Continuation ◆		
	After all	In addition
	Also	Last
	And	Lastly
	As a matter of fact	Last of all
	Finally	Moreover
	First	Next
	First and foremost	One point, example, kind, etc.
	First of all	Second, Third, Fourth
	For example	Similarly
	For instance	Then
	For one thing	Therefore
	For this reason	Too
	Furthermore	

◆ **EXERCISE 7**   **Using Category Words**

DIRECTIONS   Read each paragraph. Circle the category word or phrase used in the underlined topic sentence. Circle as well the addition transitions. When you finish, answer the questions that follow.

EXAMPLE   ¹Human activities are disrupting and degrading many of the world's freshwater rivers, lakes, and wetlands. ²These activities affect freshwater systems in four major ways. ³First, dams and canals fragment up to 40 percent of the world's 237 rivers, thereby altering or destroying wildlife habitats, or living spaces, both on land and in the water. ⁴Second, flood control levees and dikes built along rivers disconnect the rivers from their flood plains, destroy habitats, and alter or reduce the functions of nearby wetlands. ⁵Third, cities and farms add pollutants and excess plant nutrients to streams, rivers, and lakes. ⁶And fourth, many inland wetlands have been drained or filled to grow crops or have been covered with concrete, asphalt, and buildings. (Adapted from Miller and Spoolman, *Sustaining the Earth,* 9th ed., p. 65.)

1. What does the topic sentence signal you to look for as you read the rest of the passage?

   <u>the four major ways human activities are affecting the world's freshwater systems</u>

2. Which sentence introduces the first major detail? ___3___

3. How many major details are there? ___4___

4. How many minor details are there? ___0___

EXPLANATION   As it was meant to, the topic sentence sends the reader in search of the four major ways human activities affect our freshwater systems. Note, then, how the author introduces each of the four ways with an addition transition. No minor details follow the major details because the major details communicate their point all by themselves.

1. [1]One approach to minimizing the limitations of both computers and humans is to have them work together in ways that create a better outcome than either could achieve alone. [2]In medical diagnosis, for example, the human's role is to establish the presence and nature of a patient's symptoms. [3]The computer then combines this information in a completely unbiased way to identify the most likely diagnosis. [4]Similarly, laboratory technologists who examine blood samples for the causes of disease are assisted by computer programs that serve to reduce errors and memory lapses by (1) keeping track of findings from previous tests, (2) listing possible tests that remain to be tried, and (3) indicating either that certain tests have been left undone or that a new sequence of tests should be done. [5]This kind of human-machine teamwork can also help with the assessment of psychological problems. (Bernstein et al., *Psychology*, 8th ed., p. 300.)

   1. What does the topic sentence signal you to look for as you read the rest of the passage?

      _____

      _____

   2. Which sentence introduces the first major detail? _____

   3. How many major details are there? _____

   4. How many minor details are there? _____

2. [1]Mixed martial arts (MMA) is a full-contact combat sport that, as the name suggests, combines a mix of martial arts, ranging from jujitsu to kickboxing and wrestling. [2]For a while, the sport was confined to grown men and women, but it has gotten a toehold among kids, who are training to learn the various moves, holds, and blows that may one day permit them to participate in the Ultimate Fighting Championship (UFC), which is wildly popular on cable television. [3]<u>While many are horrified by the idea of children learning mixed martial arts, some parents argue that real benefits are derived from children training for this sport.</u> [4]Supporters of MMA for children claim that the training teaches them discipline. [5]To participate, they have to follow regimented* routines that do not allow for laziness or a careless attitude toward instructions. [6]Supporters also argue that in the United States where childhood obesity* is steadily growing, the physical activity demanded by MMA is a blessing, rather than a curse. [7]Moreover, proponents insist that mixed martial arts will encourage children to work hard and compete to win, teaching them, at the same time, how to learn from defeat.

1. What does the topic sentence signal you to look for as you read the rest of the passage?

_____

2. Which sentence introduces the first major detail? _____

3. How many major details are there? _____

4. How many minor details are there? _____

▶**SHARE YOUR THOUGHTS**

Some of the reasons for letting children participate in mixed martial arts events came from blogger Matt Seen, whose post can be found here: www.mmatraining.com/featured/why-i-want-my-children-to-be-mma-fighters/.

If you have kids, or plan on having kids, would you encourage them to participate in UFC events? Why or why not? Would you permit your child to watch them? Please explain your reasoning.

---

*regimented: strictly controlled and ordered.
*obesity: a condition in which the body has begun to store a large amount of excess fat.

From Reader to Writer Write a paragraph expressing your point of view on children engaging in competitive sports of any kind. Is competition a character builder or an ego destroyer? Give at least two reasons that support your point of view.

When Addition Transitions Are Used More Sparingly

Sometimes writers mark every new major detail with an addition transition. But the emphasis here is on the word *sometimes*. Despite the example shown on page 280, you can't assume that every major detail will have a transitional marker. Look, for example, at this next paragraph.

Topic Sentence

Sentence 2 introduces the first "way" Houdini exposed fakery.

The opening transition more-over tells readers another "way" is coming up.

In addition an-nounces the third and final "way".

[1]Although the famed magician Harry Houdini could have benefited from his audience's belief in the world of spirits, he tried in a number of ways to expose the fakery behind supposed supernatural* happenings. [2]Throughout his career, Houdini carefully investigated and proved false hundreds of claims by people who said they could communicate with the spirit world. [3]*Moreover*, he kept a file of fake mediums† and he instructed that, after his death, the file be made public. [4]To ensure that his wishes were carried out, Houdini entrusted a key to the file to his friend and fellow magician Joseph Dunninger. [5]*In addition*, Houdini purposely eliminated the "magic" behind his tricks by explaining how they were performed. [6]This was his way of proving to people that miracles could actually be faked.

In the sample paragraph, the writer doesn't use a transition to introduce the first "way" Houdini tried to expose fakes. Based on the location of the topic sentence, the writer expects readers to infer that sentence 2 describes the first of the "ways" Houdini exposed the fakery behind supernatural events.

Because it is further away from the topic sentence, sentence 3 opens with the addition transition *moreover*. The transition signals to readers that this sentence describes a new and different way that Houdini tried to outwit the fakes. Sentence 4 is a minor detail modifying sentence 3; it includes no addition transition. To do so would confuse the relationship between the sentences. In sentence 5, however, the author uses the transitional phrase *in addition* to highlight another "way" Houdini tried to expose fakery. Once again the transition serves to keep the reader in touch with the writer's train of thought.

---

*supernatural: other worldly, magical.
†mediums: people who claim that they are in touch with the world of spirits.

Although witnesses tested the locks, Houdini could still escape from his chains in a matter of minutes.

© Corbis.

A Note on Two Common Addition Transitions

Addition transitions like *for instance* or *for example* are common in all kinds of writing. But they are particularly common in textbooks. Writers use them to tell readers, "Here's an illustration of the general statement you just read."

Experienced readers respond based on their understanding of the material. If they think they already understand the point of the general sentence, they skim the example. If they find the general sentence confusing, they read the example slowly. They might even read it twice.

◆ **EXERCISE 8** **Using Addition Transitions**

DIRECTIONS Fill in the blanks in each paragraph with one of the addition transitions listed below.

> also   first   finally   moreover   second

1. Polls sponsored by the American Automobile Association and other highway safety organizations consistently suggest that many Americans are bad drivers who don't want to improve. Because most states do not require motorists to periodically refresh their skills, adult drivers have generally not taken a test on road rules, road signs, or driving skills since they first got their driver's license as teenagers. _____, the majority of drivers polled admit to speeding while one-third say they frequently run yellow or even red lights. Many drivers _____ engage in distracting behaviors while behind the wheel. In a 2008 poll by Vlingo, a mobile application company, one in four adults said that they text while driving. As the age of the driver decreased, the amount of texting increased. According to the pollsters at Vlingo, 66 percent of "the *least experienced* drivers, those sixteen to nineteen," admitted to texting while driving." (Source of the Vlingo study: Breitbart.com.)

2. People who engage in "extreme couponing," i.e., who make coupon clipping practically a full-time job in the name of saving money, need to put down the scissors and consider whether what they are doing is a good idea. If you are into extreme couponing, consider _____ the basis for your shopping list. Is it based on what you like to eat or on what's good for your health? Or are you basing your shopping list on what bargain some fast food corporation has decided to offer for that week? If you are, there's no guarantee that good nutrition or enjoyable meals come with a coupon attached. _____, coupons usually accompany processed food, and processed food is likely to have a great many chemical ingredients. Given the number of chemicals in processed foods, you might want to think twice before you stock up on frozen pizza and corn fritters, even if you do have a coupon that lets you buy two packages and get one free. _____, cooking your own food from scratch is probably cheaper than using coupons. It takes less than a dollar and a half to buy a package of dried black beans or lentils, and those beans and lentils can be turned into a soup, which will last you for two or three meals.

> ▶ **SHARE YOUR THOUGHTS**
> Thirty-eight states ban texting while driving. Do you think such bans should be eliminated or extended to all fifty states? Please explain the basis for your answer.

Concluding Sentences versus Supporting Details

Most of the time, the last sentence in a paragraph does exactly what you would expect it to do. Directly, as a major detail, or indirectly, as a minor one, it supports the main idea. Sometimes, however, the last sentence of a paragraph does not play the role of supporting detail. Instead it functions as a **concluding sentence** that tells you how a situation described in the paragraph was or should be resolved.

Take, for example, the following paragraph. The underlined topic sentence tells us that between 1692 and 1693, Salem, Massachusetts, was the scene of witchcraft trials. Except for the last one, all the remaining sentences in the paragraph, tell us more about what happened in Salem during those trials.

> ¹<u>From 1692 through 1693, Salem, Massachusetts, was the scene of a series of witchcraft trials.</u> ²The trials began when four young girls, Betty Parris, Abigail Williams, Elizabeth Hubbard, and Ann Putnam Jr., appeared to be suffering fits of madness during which they threw themselves on the floor screaming in terror or whimpered and hid under the bed. ³During these bouts, the girls accused several men and women in the town of dealings with the devil. ⁴The girls' accusations were believed and before the townspeople came to their senses, nineteen men and women had been hanged. ⁵Many others were cruelly tortured, tormented, and imprisoned, until it became clear that the girls had been lying all along and there were no witches in Salem. ⁶Following the events in Salem, witchcraft trials practically disappeared from the colonies.

In this illustration, sentences 2–5 talk about the Salem trials, how they got started, and what went on as a result. The last sentence moves away from the main idea of the paragraph. Instead it tells us what happened in the colonies *after* the Salem experience. Writers frequently use the last sentence of a paragraph in this way, to say to readers, "OK this is how things stand now" or "This is where the subject or situation is headed."

Such concluding sentences are not unrelated to the main idea of the paragraph, even if they do not directly explain it. Concluding sentences like the one in the paragraph on witchcraft trials almost always help you understand more about the topic or issue under discussion. Don't ignore them. Evaluate them and decide how important they are to your understanding of the material and your purpose in learning it.

Concluding Sentences Look Ahead to the Next Paragraph

It's also true that concluding sentences frequently signal to readers what's coming up next. For instance, based on the last sentence of the previous paragraph, readers might rightly expect the next paragraph to explain why witchcraft trials disappeared from the colonies. That expectation would be correct as the following paragraph illustrates.

> [1]From the very beginning, many colonists had been appalled by the Salem trials but were too frightened to speak out against them. [2]After all, the girls could easily accuse them next. [3]However, when the wife of the governor of Massachusetts was also named as a witch, the trials had run their course. [4]Paris, Putnam, Hubbard, and Williams had gone too far with their wild accusations. [5]They had attacked a respected woman, whose husband was in a position of power. [6]As a result, people began speaking out against the Salem trials and their awful accomplishments. [7]Increase Mather, the influential president of Harvard, expressed the new anti-witch hunting mood of Salem and the rest of the colonies when he said, "It were better that ten suspected witches should escape than one innocent person should be condemned."

Evaluating the Final Sentences

Whenever you come to the end of a paragraph, make sure you are clear on the function of the last sentence. Is it a supporting detail that develops the main idea? If so, what does it add to your understanding of that main idea? If the last sentence is a concluding sentence, make sure you understand how it sums up an event or situation described in the paragraph. Use it as well to shape your expectations about the direction the author's thought will take in the next paragraph.

WEB QUEST
Use the Web to discover the meaning of "spectral evidence" and the role it played in the Salem witchcraft trials.

_____

_____

_____

SUMMING UP THE KEY POINTS

1. Be alert to category words appearing in topic sentences. When words like *rules*, *laws*, *differences*, and *varieties* appear, you can use them to identify major details. Each new *rule*, *law*, *difference*, or *variety* described will usually be a major detail.

2. To provide a transition for a major detail, writers frequently repeat the category word used in the topic sentence.

3. *Addition transitions* such as *moreover*, *similarly*, *first*, and *second* can also signal that a major detail is on its way.

4. *Concluding sentences* describe how a situation or event described in the paragraph turned out. That information is relevant to your understanding of the topic or issue addressed in the paragraph.

5. Concluding sentences also frequently point to the direction the next paragraph will take. Thus they can help shape your expectations as you move from paragraph to paragraph.

♦ **EXERCISE 9**   **Recognizing the Function of the Last Sentence**

DIRECTIONS   Read each paragraph and notice the underlined topic sentence. Circle the letter of the answer that best describes the function of the last detail in the paragraph.

EXAMPLE   ¹In 1856, Henry Bessemer developed a new method for manufacturing steel, one that consisted of three basic steps. ²First, a blast of cold air was forced through the mass of hot melting iron. ³The enormous heat created then burned out the impurities in the iron and left it ready for the final step. ⁴During the last step, carbon, manganese, and other substances were added in order to make the steel stronger. [5]The introduction of the Bessemer process revolutionized the steel industry, making steel a profitable American export.

   a. The last sentence in the paragraph provides a supporting detail that develops the main idea.

   b. The last sentence in the paragraph is a concluding sentence that explains how someone or something mentioned in the paragraph turned out or might develop over the course of time.

EXPLANATION   The last sentence does not describe one of the three basic steps in the Bessemer process. That eliminates answer *a*, making answer *b* the correct choice.

1. [1]In 1886, French chemist Louis Pasteur believed that he had found a vaccine to combat the dreaded disease called rabies. [2]Pasteur, however, was fearful of using the rabies vaccine on human beings and did not use it on humans until the decision to do so was forced on him. [3]On July 6, 1885, a young boy named Joseph Meister was brought to Pasteur for treatment. [4]The boy had been bitten on the arms and legs by a rabid dog. [5]Pasteur consulted with several physicians who assured him that the boy was going to die. [6]It was only then that Pasteur decided to use his rabies vaccine. [7]Meister lived to become gatekeeper of the Pasteur Institute and committed suicide fifty-five years later.

   a. The last sentence in the paragraph provides a supporting detail that develops the main idea.

   b. The last sentence in the paragraph is a concluding sentence that explains how someone or something turned out or might develop over the course of time.

2. [1]Can robot authors write books that people want to read? The answer to that question depends on whom you to talk to. [2]There are some who believe that robot authors—software programs that collect information about a topic and organize it into book form—are the wave of the future, while others consider such books to be of limited value at best. [3]The inventor and economist Philip Parker, for instance, sees a rosy future for computer-generated books. [4]More than a decade ago, Parker began using automatic text-generating software to "write" books, and he has written or published over

100,000 of them. [5]Parker claims that his books and others like them are the perfect solution for people who speak languages that are not widely shared, like Chichewa, the African language of Malawi. [6]Thanks to robot-authored books, the farmer who needs to understand the latest planting techniques can, indeed, find a book on the subject and written in his or her own language no less. [7]Talk to Chris Csikszentmihalyi, of the Massachusetts Institute of Technology, however, and you will hear a different story. [8]Csikszentmihalyi points out that disaster can occur if the software makes an error in, for instance, dispensing medical advice. [9]As he puts it, "Would you really want to bet your life on text generated by a robot?" (Source of quotation: Pagan Kennedy, "I-Robot Book," *The New York Times Book Review*, October 16, 2011, p. 15.)

a. The last sentence in the paragraph provides a supporting detail that develops the main idea.

b. The last sentence in the paragraph is a concluding sentence that explains how someone or something turned out or might develop over the course of time.

3. [1]In 2005, Cyndy Bizon thought her husband, Joel, was dying. [2]Anguished at the thought of losing him, she watched her spouse being wheeled into the operating room. [3]Shortly after, she collapsed from a condition known as "broken heart syndrome," a physical response that mimics a heart attack without really being one. [4]Broken heart syndrome, like the attack that afflicted Cyndy Bizon, occurs when the body absorbs a huge shock, even one with positive associations like winning the lottery. [5]In most cases it strikes not men but women over the age of fifty-five. [6]Out of the 6,229 cases reported, only 671 involved men. [7]Using a government database that gathered information from 1,000 hospitals, Dr. Abhishek Deshmukh of the University of Arkansas has tried to pinpoint why women outnumber men as victims. [8]But as of yet, he has found no answer. [9]Theories abound. [10]It might be hormonal differences. [11]It might be that men are more used to handling stress and, as a result, their bodies have adapted to it better. [12]But so far, no one knows for sure what causes the syndrome. [13]The good news is that most people recover from an attack of broken heart syndrome with little or no signs of permanent damage. (Source of statistics: http://news.yahoo.com/women-more-likely-broken-heart-syndrome-184939504.html.)

a. The last sentence in the paragraph provides a supporting detail that develops the main idea.

b. The last sentence in the paragraph is a concluding sentence that explains how someone or something turned out or might develop over the course of time.

4. [1]In the nineteenth century, opium was brought into China by British merchants, who profited handsomely from the opium trade and fought hard to maintain their money-making export. [2]Thanks to British merchants, use of the drug became so widespread in China that the Chinese government banned the importation of opium altogether. [3]Despite the ban, the British smuggled the drug in, and the attempt to eliminate its use was unsuccessful. [4]Confiscation of large quantities of opium by the Chinese government led to the Opium War of 1839, in which the Chinese battled the British for control of the opium trade. [5]The Chinese lost the war, and the British were able to force the Chinese government to legalize opium use. [6]Eventually China drove the British out, and the country became the main source of opium for the rest of the world. (Adapted from Waughfield, *Mental Health Concepts,* 5th ed., p. 354.)

a. The last sentence in the paragraph provides a supporting detail that develops the main idea.

b. The last sentence in the paragraph provides a detail that explains how someone or something turned out or will develop over the course of time.

VOCABULARY ROUND UP

Below are ten words introduced in pages 262–84. The words are accompanied by more detailed definitions, the page on which they originally appeared, and additional sample sentences. Spend time reviewing the words and their meanings because you will see them again in review tests at the end of the chapter. Use the online dictionary Wordnik to find additional sentences illustrating the words in context. *Note*: If you know of another dictionary with as many examples of words in context feel free to use that one instead.

1. **nutrients** (p. 262): substances the body needs for good health, sources of nourishment. "Seaweed is filled with *nutrients*."

2. **thrive** (p. 263): grow, develop well; prosper. (1) "Children don't *thrive* in homes where they are neglected." (2) "Their newly opened market is *thriving*."

3. **apparatus** (p. 269): a part or device that performs a specific function; machines and materials devoted to a specific function or task. "The *apparatus* going into the building suggested the new tenant was a dentist."

4. **evolutionary** (p. 273): concerned with development or change over the course of time. "The older members of the group favored slow, *evolutionary* change, but the younger ones wanted the revolution now!"

5. **assertiveness** (p. 273): boldness, having confidence in one's ideas or actions. "Public companies that manage prisons have come in for some harsh criticism about both their methods and their motives, but that has not diminished the *assertiveness* of their claims."

6. **despicable** (p. 280): unworthy of respect, disgraceful. "Although John Edwards's behavior toward his cancer-stricken wife was *despicable*, the government's case against him was without merit."

7. **fray** (p. 280): confusion, brawl, fight, intense activity; to wear down or unravel. (1) "Looking at the fight on the football field, those in the bleachers didn't think that anyone would emerge from the *fray* unharmed." (2) "His nerves had been badly *frayed* by the repeated false alarms."

8. **regimented** (p. 283): strictly controlled and ordered. "The factories in China have a very *regimented* system, with workers spending long hours on the job and having little time for relaxation or pleasure."

9. **obesity** (p. 283): a condition in which the body has stored a large amount of excess fat. "*Obesity* is linked to a number of diseases such as diabetes and cancer."

10. **supernatural** (p. 284): otherworldly, magical, miraculous. "In fairy tales, animals with *supernatural* powers are common figures."

✔ CHECK YOUR UNDERSTANDING

1. Why are category words in topic sentences important?

   _____

   _____

2. What are some examples of addition transitions?

   _____

3. Why do authors frequently repeat the category word used in a topic sentence?

   _____

   _____

4. The last sentence in a paragraph may not directly support the main idea, but if it doesn't, what two other functions might it fulfill?

   a. _____

   _____

   b. _____

   _____

DIGGING DEEPER Debating Private Prisons

Looking Ahead The privatization of prisons is a controversial issue, with harsh critics and vocal supporters. The authors of the following article outline some of the pros and cons.

Getting Focused Any time you see the word *debate* in the title, you know that by the end of the reading, you should be able to paraphrase the positions taken by each side of that debate.

1   Despite the rapid growth of private prisons throughout the 1980s and 1990s, prison privatization is a controversial idea. Those who support it claim that prisons built and operated by the private sector will save the taxpayers money. Because of less red tape, facilities can be constructed and operated more economically. Most importantly, advocates claim that private prisons reduce overcrowding.

2   Opponents of privatization, however, question whether firms can build and operate correctional facilities significantly less expensively than state or local governments can. They believe that the profit motive is misplaced in a prison setting, where firms may skimp on nutritious food, health care, or skilled personnel to cut operating costs. A company whose business benefits from filling up cell space as soon as it is built might foster a lock-'em-up-and-throw-away-the-key approach. Such a firm might also lobby for and contribute campaign dollars to legislators in favor of stricter sentencing requirements and additional prisons.

3   Evidence on the economics of prison privatization is mixed. Most of the experimentation has involved juveniles, illegal aliens, and minimum- and medium-security offenders. The majority of studies indicate that operating-cost savings have been marginal or nonexistent. Corrections Corporation of America and other private prison firms have reported significant financial losses in recent years. And although overcrowded conditions may be relieved more promptly through privatization, the burden on the taxpayers appears to be about the same.

4   One of the basic questions to be addressed is whether the delegation of the corrections function to a private firm is constitutionally permissible. The U.S. Supreme Court and state courts will have to determine not only whether incarceration, punishment, deterrence, and rehabilitation can properly be delegated, but also who is legally responsible for a private facility. The Supreme Court spoke on one such issue by declaring

that private prison guards who violate inmates' rights are not entitled to qualified immunity—unlike public-sector guards.

5   Another set of legal considerations concerns practical accountability for the day-to-day operation of jails and prisons. Consider, for example, this case. In Texas, two men escaped from a private prison near Houston. They nearly made it to Dallas before they were caught. But Texas authorities couldn't prosecute them for their escape because by breaking out of a private facility, the men had not committed an offense under Texas law. The men, who had been sent to the Houston facility from Oregon, could not be prosecuted in Oregon because the escape happened in Texas.

6   Economic and legal issues aside, perhaps the most important question is, Who should operate our jails and prisons? Legal scholar Ira Robbins suggests that we should remember the words of the novelist Fyodor Dostoevsky: "The degree of civilization in a society can be measured by entering its prisons." (Adapted from Bowman and Kearney, *State and Local Government*, p. 453.)

Sharpening Your Skills

DIRECTIONS   Answer the following questions by filling in the blanks or circling the letters of the correct response.

1. Which statement best expresses the overall main idea of the reading?

    a. Private prisons have not been as successful as supporters claim.

    b. Currently, the jury is still out on the effectiveness of privatizing prisons.

    c. Private prisons have been a complete failure.

    d. Privatizing prisons can solve the twin problems of overcrowding and prison violence against both guards and inmates.

2. In paragraph 3, Corrections Corporation of America is mentioned in a minor detail that clarifies a major detail. What is the point of the major detail?

    _____

3. "Evidence on the economics of prison privatization is mixed" is the topic sentence of paragraph 3. What word or words in this topic sentence need to be clarified in the supporting details?

    _____

4. What question do the supporting details in paragraph 4 need to answer?

_____

_____

5. Here are four definitions for *rehabilitate*: (1) To restore to good health or useful life, as through therapy and education; (2) to reinstate the good name of; (3) to restore the former rank, privileges, or rights of; (4) to return to good health after illness. Which of those definitions would best fit the use of *rehabilitation* in paragraph 4? _____

6. In paragraph 5, the supporting details recount the escape of two men from a privately owned Texas prison. That example suggests that "practical accountability for the day-to-day operation of jails and prisons" is

   a. the responsibility of the state where the prison is located.

   b. the responsibility of the company running the prison.

   c. unclear.

7. In your own words, what reasons do supporters of privatization give?

   a. _____

   b. _____

8. What do the opponents of private prisons say?

   a. _____

   _____

   b. _____

   _____

   c. _____

   _____

   d. _____

   _____

9. The last paragraph opens with a question. What is the answer to that question?

_____

_____

10. The reading comes from a textbook, where authors try hard not to reveal their personal feelings about a topic. Did the authors of this textbook excerpt succeed in eliminating all evidence of bias for or against privatization? _____ Please explain. _____

_____

_____

_____

Using Context Clues Based on the context, what is a good approximate definition for the word *facilities* in paragraph 1? _____

Based on the context, what is a good approximate definition for *marginal* in paragraph 3? _____

Share Your Thoughts Where do you stand on the subject of private prisons? Is putting prisons under the control of private companies a good or a bad idea?

From Reader to Writer Write a paper explaining your position on private prisons. Don't worry about the introduction until you have a first draft. Then think about a paragraph that could guide your reader into the thesis statement.

♦ **TEST 1**   **Reviewing Key Concepts**

DIRECTIONS   Answer the following questions by filling in the blanks.

1. The form supporting details take _____

_____ .

2. What are some of the different forms supporting details can take in order to support the main idea?

_____

3. Explain the difference between major and minor details.

_____

_____

_____

_____

_____

4. How should the reader treat minor details?

_____

_____

5. What kinds of words in topic sentences are clues to major details?

_____

6. What are some examples of these words?

_____

7. What kinds of transitions are clues to major details?

_____

8. What are some examples of these transitions?

   _____

9. Concluding sentences fulfill two functions. What are those two functions?

   _____

   _____

   _____

10. When taking notes, are you free to just ignore the information in concluding sentences? _____ Please explain.

    _____

    _____

▶ **TEST 2**   **Recognizing Supporting Details**

DIRECTIONS   The first sentence in each group of sentences is the topic sentence. That topic sentence is followed by five supporting details. Circle the letters of the three sentences that help make the topic sentence clear and convincing.

Topic Sentence   **1.** Over the years, salamanders—small, lizardlike creatures that walk on four legs—have been the focus of numerous legends.

Supporting Details

a. In England, a salamander is also the name of a portable stove.

b. The philosopher Aristotle claimed that salamanders could put out fires simply by walking through them.

c. The word *salamander* comes from the Greek word *salamandra*.

d. It was once believed that twining a salamander around a tree would kill the tree and poison its fruit.

e. According to legend, 4,000 soldiers died when they drank from a stream into which a salamander had fallen.

Topic Sentence   **2.** The Walt Disney film *Pinocchio* is based on a novel by nineteenth-century Italian writer Carlo Collodi, but the novel was far more violent than the film.

Supporting Details

a. In both the novel and the film, Pinocchio is transformed into a donkey.

b. Disney's *Pinocchio* did not achieve the popularity of the fabulously successful *Snow White.*

c. In Collodi's novel, when Pinocchio is attacked by a cat, he bites off the cat's paw.

d. In the Italian version, Pinocchio kills a talking cricket when the insect tries to keep him from getting into trouble.

e. In the novel, when Pinocchio falls asleep by the fire, he wakes up with his wooden feet burned off.

Topic Sentence   **3.** Until a cure was discovered in the nineteenth century, scurvy, a disease caused by a lack of vitamin C, plagued sailors on long sea voyages.

Supporting Details

a. In the late 1490s, the explorer Vasco da Gama lost more than half of his crew to scurvy.

b. In his autobiography, *Two Years Before the Mast*, nineteenth-century writer Richard Henry Dana described the sufferings of a fellow sailor who had contracted scurvy: "His legs swelled…his flesh lost its elasticity… and his gums swelled until he could not open his mouth."

c. Scurvy no longer plagues sailors who spend long periods of time at sea.

d. During the Napoleonic wars (1803–1814), French soldiers, who did not have daily doses of vitamin C, suffered from scurvy, but British soldiers, who drank daily doses of lime juice, escaped the disease.

e. British sailors became so associated with the drinking of lime juice that they were nicknamed "limeys."

Topic Sentence   4. For centuries, dogs have held a very special place in the hearts of humans.

Supporting Details   a. In the fifteenth and sixteenth centuries, no high-born lady was complete without her lap dog, and many fine ladies took their pets to church.

b. Unlike most dogs, border collies would rather work than play.

c. Rudyard Kipling (1865–1936), one of the most popular writers of his time, celebrated the British military but he also found time to write a poem in praise of dogs, titled "Four Feet."

d. The French Emperor Napoleon (1769–1821) claimed that his beloved Josephine preferred her dog Fortune to him.

e. Some people do not understand the bond that can develop between human beings and their pets.

▶ **TEST 3**   **Identifying Topic Sentences and Supporting Details**

DIRECTIONS   Circle the appropriate letter to identify the one sentence in each group that could function as the topic sentence.

1. a. The digestive system performs several important functions from which the body benefits.
    b. During digestion, food is broken down into smaller pieces.
    c. The digestive juices turn the food we eat into fat, carbohydrates, and protein, all of which are needed by the body.
    d. During the digestive process, nutrients are absorbed into the bloodstream.
    e. At the end of digestion, waste products are eliminated from the body.

2. a. The California Department of Fish and Game uses GIS to track and monitor endangered species of plants and animals.
    b. The fire department in Greenville, South Carolina, uses GIS to map the best routes to a fire.
    c. Chicago uses GIS for parking violations and meter repair.
    d. Police in Denver use GIS to track crime trends throughout the city.
    e. The technology known as geographic information systems (GIS) is transforming the policies and operations of state and local governments. (Adapted from Bowman and Kearney, *State and Local Government,* p. 238.)

3. a. According to Gordon Allport, mature adults are interested in others and consider the welfare of others as important as their own.
    b. Gordon Allport believed that mature adults are problem solvers, who have developed the necessary skills to complete current and future tasks.
    c. The psychologist Gordon Allport developed several criteria, or standards, for what he considered to be the "mature" personality.
    d. The ability to relate emotionally to other people was yet another of Gordon Allport's criteria.
    e. Self-insight was another character trait Gordon Allport associated with maturity.

4. a. People suffering from test anxiety worry they will perform poorly and be considered stupid as a result.

   b. Test anxiety is a very common problem with profound consequences.

   c. Test takers who suffer from test anxiety often know the right answers, but their minds go blank due to high anxiety.

   d. Some children who suffer from test anxiety refuse to go to school.

   e. Boys and girls seem to suffer equally from test anxiety.

5. a. With the passage of the North American Free Trade Agreement (NAFTA) in 1994, it became easier for U.S. companies to move their plants to locations where labor was much cheaper than in the United States.

   b. Rulings by the World Trade Organization made it easier for foreign products to be imported into the United States.

   c. American workers are no longer competing with one another; they are competing with workers around the world.

   d. In India and Russia, wages for computer programmers average less than 10 percent of the wages for programmers in the United States.

   e. During the recession of 2001–2003, more than 15 percent of the American jobs lost were outsourced to workers from other countries where the labor was cheap.

▶ **TEST 4**   **Distinguishing Between Major and Minor Details**

DIRECTIONS   Read each paragraph. Circle any addition transitions. Then fill in the boxes using the numbers of the sentences to identify the major and minor details.

1. ¹Biologically, chimpanzees and humans differ by little more than 1 percent of their DNA, which means that chimpanzees are actually more closely related to humans than they are to gorillas. ²The anatomy of a chimpanzee's brain and central nervous system is amazingly like that of humans. ³And like humans, chimpanzees can also create and use tools, make decisions, and cooperate in groups. ⁴Chimpanzees also demonstrate many human communication skills. ⁵They use sign languages and gestures to indicate what they want. ⁶They use nonverbal behaviors such as kissing, hugging, back patting, and fist shaking in the same ways humans do. ⁷Furthermore, chimpanzees feel and express human emotions such as happiness, sorrow, fear, and despair. ⁸These animals are like us in many of their behaviors, too. ⁹For example, mother chimpanzees care for their offspring during their long childhood, and chimps also divide into groups that go to war against one another.

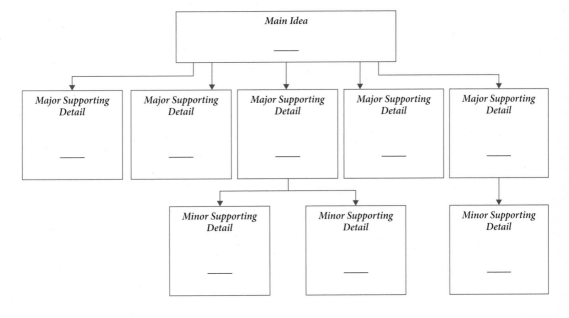

2. [1]Defined in general terms, monarchies are systems of government ruled, or appearing to be ruled, by one person, and four types of monarchies are still in existence throughout the world. [2]The first type includes monarchies in which the king (or queen) is both head of the government and head of state, and the monarch is directly involved in ruling the country. [3]This kind of monarchy, found mostly in the Middle East, includes Jordan, Saudi Arabia, and Morocco. [4]The second type of monarchy is one based on religious authority. [5]In Japan, Thailand, Nepal, and Bhutan, for example, monarchs are actually above the government, and they remain remote from politics and the public while observing formal rituals of conduct. [6]Monarchs in the third category, which includes democracies of Northern Europe and the Scandinavian states, have no political or religious role, serving instead as symbols of national unity. [7]The Netherlands, Denmark, and Luxembourg all have this type of monarch. [8]The fourth and final type of monarchy is the hybrid type illustrated by Britain, where the queen has some political authority, serves a religious role as head of the Anglican Church, and also functions as a symbol of her nation's identity.

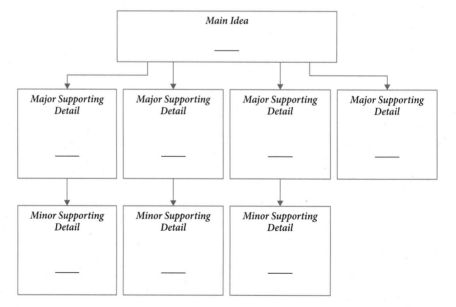

▶ **TEST 5**   **Using Category Words as Clues to Major Details**

DIRECTIONS   Read each paragraph. Then underline the topic sentence and answer the questions that follow the reading.

1. ¹Many of us use recitation as a memory aid. ²Having finished reading an essay, for instance, we mentally repeat the key points. ³But even those of us who use recitation to remember don't realize that there are two different methods: active and passive. ⁴When we use *active* recitation, we paraphrase the material, repeating key points in our own words. ⁵When we use *passive* recitation, we simply repeat what we see before us in the text. ⁶We don't even attempt to replace the author's words with our own. ⁷Over the years, numerous studies have shown that active recitation, especially when combined with visualization, is a much better device for remembering than passive recitation.

   a. Based on the topic sentence, what category word or phrase will help you locate major details? _____

   b. Which sentence introduces the first major detail? _____

   c. How many major details are in the paragraph? _____

   d. How many minor ones are there? _____

   e. How would you label the last sentence? Is it a concluding sentence or a supporting detail? _____

2. ¹Most middle-class Americans generally maintain four principal zones of distance in their personal and professional relationships. ²*Intimate distance* covers a space varying from direct physical contact with another person to a distance of six to eighteen inches. ³This is the distance considered appropriate for close friends, romantic partners, and family members. ⁴It's the one used for intimate situations. ⁵*Personal distance*—eighteen inches to four feet—is the distance married couples use in public; it's also the distance used for conversation about things not considered especially private. ⁶*Social or business distance* covers a four-to-twelve-foot zone that is used for casual social exchanges and business negotiations. ⁷Eye contact is almost always maintained at this distance, because the lack of

it suggests that someone's attention is wandering. [8]*Public speaking distance* can be a separation of only twelve feet, but usually it's not more than twenty-five. [9]The goal of public speaking distance is to put a barrier between one's self and one's audience while making sure that listeners stay within the speaker's field of vision. (Source of information: www.linus-geisler.de/dp/dpo3_distance.html.)

   a. Based on the topic sentence, what category word or phrase will help you locate major details? _____

   b. Which sentence introduces the first major detail? _____

   c. How many major details are in the paragraph? _____

   d. How many minor ones are there? _____

   e. How would you label the last sentence? Is it a concluding sentence or a supporting detail? _____

3. [1]Many people have superstitions, beliefs about good or bad things that will or will not happen in response to totally unrelated actions or events. [2]But professional sports, fueled by the fear of failure in front of a crowd, seems to be an especially fertile ground for superstitious beliefs, and some of the most famous athletes have also been the most superstitious. [3]Baseball Hall of Famer Wade Boggs wouldn't eat anything but chicken the night before a game, and before every turn at bat, he would write the Hebrew word *Chai*, meaning "life," into the dirt. [4]If tennis player Goran Ivanisevic won a match, the next time he played, he would make sure to follow the exact same routine he had used on the winning day. [5]He would wear the same clothes, eat the same meal at the same restaurant, and, if possible, talk to the same people. [6]Tennis great Serena Williams says that closely following a specific routine contributes to her victories on the court. [7]For that reason she always brings her shower sandals courtside, bounces the ball exactly five times before her first serve and only twice before the second. [8]Patrick Roy, perhaps the greatest goaltender in hockey history, believed he had a spiritual relationship with the goal posts, whom he called his friends. [9]When a puck hit the posts, Roy always made it a point to say thank you to the goal posts he tended.

   a. Based on the topic sentence, what category word or phrase will help you locate major details? _____

b. Which sentence introduces the first major detail? _____

c. How many major details are in the paragraph? _____

d. How many minor ones are there? _____

e. How would you label the last sentence? Is it a concluding sentence or a supporting detail? _____

4. [1]What everyday rules for behavior guide parents' efforts to socialize their children? [2]To answer that question, Heidi Gralinski and Claire Kopp (1993) observed and interviewed mothers with their children. [3]The research by Gralinski and Kopp suggests that maternal rules vary with the child's age. [4]They found that for fifteen-month-olds, mothers' rules and requests centered on ensuring the children's safety, respecting basic social niceties ("Don't bite"; "No kicking"), and learning to accept delays. [5]As children's ages and thinking abilities increased, the numbers and kinds of prohibitions and requests expanded. [6]The focus now was on family routines, self-care, and other concerns regarding the child's independence. [7]By the time children were three, new kinds of rules emerged: "Do not scream in a restaurant, run around naked in front of company, pretend to kill your sister, hang up the phone when someone is using it, fight with children in school, play with guns, or pick your nose." (Adapted from Seifert, Hofnung, and Hofnung, *Lifespan Development*, p. 179.)

a. Based on the topic sentence, what category word or phrase will help you locate major details? _____

b. Which sentence introduces the first major detail? _____

c. How many major details are in the paragraph? _____

d. How many minor ones are there? _____

e. How would you label the last sentence? Is it a concluding sentence or a supporting detail? _____

▶ **TEST 6**   **Recognizing Supporting Details and Concluding Sentences**

DIRECTIONS   Read each paragraph. The topic sentence in each paragraph is underlined. Label each of the sentences that follow the topic sentence as a major (*M*) or minor (*m*) detail. If you think the paragraph ends with a concluding sentence, write a *c* in the final blank.

1. [1]Although we associate penguins with the Antarctic, only two of approximately twenty species live on the continent of Antarctica. [2]These are the two largest, the emperor and the king penguins. _____ [3]Both of them stand about four feet high. _____ [4]Most other species are found on the islands in the Antarctic region, but a few breed as far north as Australia, New Zealand, South Africa, and South America. _____

2. [1]Leadership and management are in some ways similar forms of influence, but in one very crucial way they are quite different. [2]Managers can direct the efforts of others because of their status or power within an organization. _____ [3]Simply put, employees follow the directions of a manager largely because they know that not to do so would endanger their jobs. _____ [4]Leaders, in contrast, don't have to rely on their position or rank; often it is the power of their personality that makes them an influence to be reckoned with. _____ [5]At the Marriott Corporation, for example, employees often go beyond their normal duties largely because they respect and admire Bill Marriott. _____

3. [1]Surprising as it may seem to those of us who grew up with him, Santa Claus was not always pictured as a roly-poly figure with chubby cheeks, a big belly, and a long white beard. [2]The Santa Claus we know today was created in the mid-nineteenth century by the cartoonist Thomas Nast. [3]The European ancestor of our Santa Claus, Saint Nicholas, was always pictured as a tall, lean, and bearded bishop who bore no trace of extra fat. _____ [4]However, during the years 1863 to 1885, Nast was commissioned by *Harper's Weekly* to do a series of Christmas drawings; during that twenty-two-year period, he created the pudgy figure so beloved by children today. _____ [5]It was Nast who decided that Santa should wear

a fur-trimmed red suit and hat. _____ [6]Nast's cartoons also showed the world how Santa spent his entire year—making toys, checking on children's behavior, and reading their letters. _____ [7]Ultimately, however, Nast's fame rests not on his Santa Claus drawings but on his cartoons attacking political dishonesty and wrongdoing. _____

4. [1]The first American comic strip appeared at the end of the nineteenth century. [2]Comic books, however, arrived after the turn of the century, and it wasn't until the 1930s that comic books successfully became part of American culture. [3]The first comic book, published by Dell Publishing Company, was a huge failure, but the second one, also published by Dell, succeeded. _____ [4]Called "Famous Funnies," the comic book cost ten cents, and all thirty-five thousand copies quickly sold out. _____ [5]Not surprisingly, many more comic books followed, most of them featuring cartoon characters, such as Popeye and Flash Gordon, that had originally appeared in newspapers. _____ [6]The biggest comic book breakthrough, however, came in 1938 with the introduction of a red-caped, blue-suited figure called Superman. _____ [7]Appearing in the first issue of *Action Comics*, Superman was an immediate sensation. _____ [8]Today, that first issue of *Action Comics* can fetch its owner around $100,000. _____

▶ **TEST 7**   **Reviewing Chapter 6 Vocabulary**

DIRECTIONS   Circle the letter of the sentence that correctly uses the underlined vocabulary word.

1. a. He carried the fray in his suitcase and hoped it didn't get inspected.
   b. She tried to fray the costs of the car by getting a second job.
   c. The players ignored the coaches warning and jumped into the fray.

2. a. The thrive of fish were moving slowly upstream.
   b. Those plants are sun-loving; they will not thrive in shade.
   c. After the stock market crash, thriving on the market was forbidden.

3. a. She had several lovely nutrients that made him fall in love with her.
   b. Acai berries are said to have all the nutrients necessary for good health.
   c. He had a nutrient interest in books about death and disease.

4. a. The Duchess of Windsor looked so glamorous and despicable, the photographers could not stop snapping her photo.
   b. The volcano is probably still despicable despite its not having erupted for fifty years.
   c. The lawyer's bullying treatment of the paralegal was utterly despicable.

5. a. The roasting apparatus was smack in the middle of the restaurant's kitchen.
   b. The new television comedy went on apparatus in mid-season.
   c. After a lengthy exam, the doctor diagnosed a severe brain apparatus.

6. a. After working for years in a competitive industry, the engineer was looking forward to a relaxing and tightly regimented period of rest.
   b. Regimented by alphabetical order, the books were easier for scholars to scan and store.
   c. Because her father had been in the military, her upbringing had been extremely regimented, and her strong sense of self-discipline served her well as an adult.

7. a. Groups need obesity; the members should not all reflect the same point of view.

b. The obesity that developed at adolescence had made his life a misery: People snickered when he walked into a room, clothes were hard to find, and romance seemed out of the question.

c. The issue of censoring the Internet was plagued by obesity.

8. a. Realistic novels have to have supernatural settings.

b. The car was old, supernatural even.

c. Latin-American writers are famous for blending realistic settings with supernatural effects like sparrows that talk.

9. a. Her shyness showed in her assertiveness.

b. In the nineteenth century, assertiveness in middle class women was not considered a desirable trait; nice women did what men told them to do.

c. The car's assertiveness was a big reason for its high price tag.

10. a. In the nineteenth century, Charles Darwin's evolutionary theory, which suggested that humans had started out as a more primitive species of animal, upset many who believed that humans had been created by god.

b. Having a positive, evolutionary attitude toward life is good for your health.

c. The Chinese leader Mao Tse-tung[†] was a true evolutionary, who believed that the old economic system had to be completely destroyed before a new economic system could be born.

[†]Mao Tse-tung: the leader of the Chinese Communist Party from 1935 until his death in 1971.

Focusing on Supporting Details in Longer Readings

7

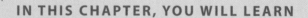

IN THIS CHAPTER, YOU WILL LEARN

- how to adapt what you know about supporting details in paragraphs to longer readings.

- how to recognize connections between paragraphs.

- how to use informal outlines for taking notes.

"Beware of the person who can't be bothered by details."

—Writer and publisher William Feather

Chapter 7 shows you how experienced readers think their way through a longer, multi-paragraph reading. In particular, the chapter focuses on how supporting detail paragraphs clarify and support the main idea of an extended reading. Equally important, the chapter illustrates how writers help readers make connections between paragraphs.

By the end of Chapter 7, everything you know about supporting details in paragraphs and in longer readings will come together when you learn how to make an *informal outline* for note-taking. Informal outlines are a great way to sort out complicated information by reducing it to a bare bones blueprint of the main idea and the major and minor details.

Responding to Supporting Details in Longer Readings

Supporting details in paragraphs are single sentences. But in longer readings, one major detail might get an entire paragraph of explanation. It might even get two paragraphs.

But you can relax. That's not a major obstacle. When you are working with supporting details in longer readings, you don't have to do anything you haven't already done within the context of a paragraph. Once again, you need to (1) look for familiar patterns of general and specific sentences and (2) note any chains of repetition and reference. If anything, with longer, multi-paragraph readings, you get a little more help from the author. That help comes in the form of major and minor headings, which point the way to the author's train of thought.

Once you think you have a handle on the main idea of the entire reading, then you need to determine if there is a thesis statement[†] that sums up that main idea. If there is, you know you are on the right track, and you can start consciously figuring out what each supporting detail paragraph contributes to the main idea expressed in the thesis statement.

As with paragraphs, supporting details in multi-paragraph readings can fulfill a variety of functions depending on the needs of the main idea. They can be examples, reasons, studies, statistics, exceptions, and definitions. The role they fill depends on the questions raised by the main idea expressed in the thesis statement.

READING TIP

If you can't find a thesis statement that matches the main idea you came up with *and* none of the paragraphs in the reading support the main idea you were considering, then you know you have to re-think your first guess about the overall or controlling main idea.

Thesis Statement Locations

The location of the thesis statement in a chapter section should affect your expectations about and search for major details. If you think the author starts right off with the thesis statement summing up the main idea of the reading, some of the major details might well appear in the opening paragraph. But if the thesis statement concludes the first paragraph, then you can expect the next paragraph to introduce the first major detail.

When It Comes to Reading, There Are No Rigid Rules

Remember, though, there's no rule saying the author has to open or close the first paragraph of a chapter section with the thesis statement. These

---

[†]At this point, depending on the chapters that you have covered, you might want to review the meaning of the term *thesis statement* introduced in Chapter 5. You can turn to pages 218–19 in Chapter 5 or check the glossary of key terms on the inside cover.

are just typical locations, particularly in textbooks, where authors use thesis statements just like they use topic sentences—to get their general point across as quickly as possible. Even in textbooks, though, thesis statements can move around, and the textbook templates, or explanatory patterns, you learned about in the previous chapter will not always apply.

The following reading, for example, comes from a sociology text. In this instance, the opening paragraph does *not* introduce the thesis statement of the reading. The thesis statement is neither the first sentence nor the last. There is no opening question guiding you to the thesis statement and no reversal transition telling you, "Forget that introduction; here comes the real main idea."

The question now is what do you do since none of the previous explanatory patterns fit the reading? Well, you'll do what you did with paragraphs when they became more complicated. You'll look for patterns of general and specific sentences, and you'll follow chains of repetition and reference. In addition, you'll have the heading to help guide your thoughts and make sure they match up with the author's.

Becoming Human

What does the heading suggest to you? What question does it raise?

1   Several years ago a Seattle judge gave permanent custody of a six-year-old boy to the county welfare department. The judge asked that efforts be made to have the child adopted, despite protests from the child's father and mother. The judge based his decision on the fact that the child could not speak intelligibly, crawled rather than walked, and barked like a dog when people approached him. . . . This little boy's tragic condition was the result of isolation and almost total neglect. From infancy he had spent most of his days and nights alone in a filthy one-room house. His father was in prison and his mother was rarely home, stopping by now and then only to feed him.

All of the sentences in paragraph 1 are equally specific. What does that suggest to you?

2   There have been countless cases like this, of children whose parents so neglected them and so isolated them from all human contact that when they were discovered, they acted more like wild animals than human beings. In fact, children like this are often called feral children (the word *feral* means "untamed"), and some people had mistakenly assumed that such children had been reared in the wild by an animal.

What words or phrases are repeated in paragraphs 1 and 2?

3   Human children cannot be raised by mother wolves, dogs, or other animals—such stories are fantasies. Unfortunately, cruel and unfit parents can raise their children like animals. Sometimes children thought to be feral are actually victims of mental retardation or severe mental illness, not

How could stories of feral children help you understand how we become human?

neglect. But others, like the little boy in Seattle, are born with normal capacities, for they make rapid progress once they are rescued from isolation.

4   Feral children demonstrate an important principle: Our biological heritage alone cannot make us into adequate human beings. Only through social relations—constant intimate interaction—can the rich cultural legacy that sets humans apart from other animals be transmitted to humans. An infant is born without culture. Reared in isolation, a human being will not even learn to talk or walk, let alone sing or read. . . .

What general word in the first sentence of paragraph 4 suggests the writer might be zeroing in on the main idea?

5   The learning process by which infants are made into normal human beings possessed of culture and able to participate in social relations is called *socialization*. This process, which literally means to be "made social," begins at birth and continues until death. We never cease to be shaped by our interactions with others. (Adapted from Stark, *Sociology*, 10th ed., p. 148.)

In this case, the main idea doesn't appear until the fourth paragraph. That means the paragraphs that precede it fulfill a dual function. They act as an introduction to the controlling main idea —"We need interaction with others in order to learn human, as opposed to animal, behavior." But at the same time, they function as supporting details. They tell readers what happens when we don't have the "intimate interaction" with others referred to in paragraph 4. The examples of feral children are proof that we need others in our efforts to become human.

When the thesis statement turns up in the middle or the end of a reading, it is not unusual for the opening paragraphs to serve a dual function, as introduction and support.

READING TIPS

1. If a chapter section does not fit an explanatory pattern you are familiar with, start thinking about the relationship between general and specific sentences, and be on the lookout for chains of repetition and reference.

2. Use the heading of a chapter section to guide your search for the main idea and the supporting details that explain it.

3. When you start to get answers to your questions about the heading, you are also zeroing in on the main idea of the entire reading.

Major and Minor Details Revisited

Sometimes writers can't fully explain a major supporting detail in one paragraph. They need a second paragraph for further clarification. That makes the second paragraph a minor detail.

As they do in single paragraphs, minor details in longer readings vary in their significance. If they simply repeat the same point for emphasis or provide an additional or obvious example, they can be skimmed and forgotten.

But here again *minor details need to be evaluated.* If a writer takes two paragraphs to develop the same point and the second paragraph is needed to fully explain the first, then the minor detail paragraph needs close attention. The information it contains probably also needs to appear in your notes.

READING TIP

To determine the relationship between major and minor details, *look carefully at the opening sentences of each paragraph.* The sentence openings are where writers usually link what came before to what's coming next. They will give you the best clues to how paragraphs relate to one another.

SUMMING UP THE KEY POINTS

1. Understanding the function of supporting details in longer readings calls upon the same skills you used to understand them in paragraphs. Once you have a sense of the main idea, start looking for a thesis statement that confirms you are on the right track.

2. The relationship between general and specific sentences and the chains of repetition and reference in the reading will help you determine both the main idea and the function of the supporting details.

3. The heading of a chapter section will also help you understand the function of the supporting details. The heading will raise questions and the supporting details will help answer those questions.

4. Major details in longer readings answer questions about the heading and the main idea. Minor details further clarify major ones and must be evaluated for importance with each new reading.

5. As they do in paragraphs, major and minor supporting details can fulfill any number of functions depending on the needs of the main idea. They can be examples, reasons, studies, statistics, definitions, exceptions, etc. Whatever form they take, they answer the questions readers might have about the main idea of the chapter section or reading.

◆ **EXERCISE 1**   **Recognizing Main Idea and Supporting Detail Paragraphs**

DIRECTIONS   When correctly assembled, the six paragraphs labeled a–f make up a complete, multi-paragraph reading about hiking a famous trail in the rain. One paragraph is pure introduction. One paragraph introduces the thesis statement. There are three major detail paragraphs and one minor one. On the blanks following the reading, use the paragraph letters to indicate how the paragraphs should be arranged in order to make sense to the reader.

The Half Dome peak in Yosemite National Park is a gorgeous sight, but some have died trying to reach it.

Half Dome in the Rain Turns Deadly

a. Yet many hikers don't fear the rain's effect on Half Dome. Thinking, as most people do, that tragedy won't strike them, they charge ahead, despite the posted signs and warnings of park officials that rainy weather and Half Dome's trail are a dangerous mix. In the fall of 2011, the problem of hiking Half Dome in bad weather came to a head because the rains were unusually heavy. Although the heavy rains were making the Half Dome trail treacherous, even deadly, some hikers kept on trying to beat the odds, with disastrous, even deadly results.

b. The Half Dome trail is the most demanding day hike in California's Yosemite National Park. Hikers with the strength and stamina to walk to the top of Half Dome go straight up a mountain of rock, climbing a total of 4,800 feet.[†] At the top, the view is glorious. It's certainly worth the effort. But if it's raining, the demanding day hike can turn deadly because the rock becomes slippery and treacherous.

c. Twenty-six-year-old Hayley LaFlamme did not have Castillo's luck with her the day she set out to climb Half Dome along with her sister and two friends. It had rained in the morning and rain and lightning were still threatening when the small group set out. Despite the slippery conditions, though, LaFlamme made it to the top of Half Dome. It was on the descent that tragedy struck. Making her way down the cable ladder that threads its way along Half Dome's trail, LaFlamme lost her grip and fell 600 feet to her death.

d. While Castillo may have lacked common sense, he didn't lack nerve. An experienced salsa dancer, he convinced himself that he was in good physical condition and could successfully make the trip back to safety. When the rain stopped, he started out on foot. But after a fall, he sat down and scooted the rest of the way down the mountain. It wasn't a particularly dignified trip. But he made it and lived to tell his story. In fact, he says he is going back to complete the hike under better weather conditions.

e. For Armando Castillo, hiking Half Dome in the rain proved dangerous and terrifying, but in the end he made it back alive. About three-quarters of the way up Half Dome, Castillo and some other hikers were confronted by a hailstorm. When the storm cleared, the other hikers

---

[†]Half Dome is more than 8,800 feet high, but hikers don't usually start at the very bottom.

turned back, unwilling to trust their luck. Castillo decided to trust his and kept going, feeling he had come too far to turn back. When a freezing thunderstorm hit, he was trapped at the 8,842 foot summit. He called 911 to get rescued, but rangers don't fly in weather that might kill them along with the stranded hikers. His only alternative was to find shelter under a rocky ledge and try to figure out how to make it back alive.

f. In addition to LaFlamme, at least twenty people have died attempting to scale or return from Half Dome. According to park officials, in most of those deaths rain was a factor, and there is a growing worry that if unseasonably heavy rains continue due to climate change, the number of tragic deaths might multiply as hikers continue to tempt fate. Park officials are currently mulling over alternatives for how to best prevent hikers from attempting Half Dome in the rain. But they are pessimistic since so many people in the past have assumed that warnings about rain on Half Dome being deadly didn't apply to them.

1. Introductory Paragraph: ⎯⎯

2. Thesis Statement Paragraph: ⎯⎯

3. Major Detail Paragraph: ⎯⎯

4. Minor Detail Paragraph: ⎯⎯

5. Major Detail Paragraph: ⎯⎯

6. Major Detail Paragraph: ⎯⎯

READING TIP

Even more than in single paragraphs, category words like *circumstances*, *reasons*, and *consequences* at the beginning of a reading are a clue to the major details.

◆ **EXERCISE 2**   **Understanding the Function of Supporting Details**

DIRECTIONS   Read through each selection. Note the underlined thesis statement. Then answer the questions that follow.

EXAMPLE

Is Romance Essential to Marriage?

1 The majority of Americans and Europeans believe that couples should first fall in love and then get married. Yet in many other countries, including India and China, the reverse is much more common. First, an individual marries someone chosen by family members; *then* the couple finds love. Anthropologists say that the arranged marriage is actually common throughout history, with even colonial* Americans approaching matrimony in this way. Today, in fact, as many as 60 percent of the world's marriages are still arranged. There appear to be two main reasons why arranged marriages have never gone out of fashion.

2 First, in many cultures, marriage is viewed as the union of two families, rather than just two people. Because marriage is a valuable tool for creating alliances* that benefit both parties, the selection of a mate is considered too important to be left up to the young and inexperienced. Often with the help of professional matchmakers, parents search for someone who possesses the specific temperament, interests, and background that will suit both their child *and* their family.

3 Unlike Western relationships, which usually begin from chance encounters between two people who may or may not have much in common, the arranged marriage involves a focused search that ends by matching up two very compatible* people. Thus, children are raised with the expectation that their parents will help them find the best possible husband or wife so that the blending of the two families will be permanent.

4 The other reason why the tradition of arranged marriage remains strong is the belief that romantic love can hinder the establishment of a lasting partnership. Proponents* of arranged marriage believe that in a union based on romance, serious problems can arise when the excitement of courtship begins to fade and the partners' flaws and differences become more apparent. Because arranged marriages are not based on love to begin with, they are not usually dissolved, as many Western marriages are, once passion dies. Thus, while about half of romantic marriages end in divorce, only about 5 percent of arranged marriages fail.

---

*colonial: relating to the period of time in which America was a colony under British control.
*alliances: unions of two or more people who share a legal or informal connection or relationship, a union, or an association that benefits both sides.
*compatible: fitting together well, sharing a common background and interests.
*proponents: supporters.

5   Still, arranged marriages are not necessarily loveless. On the contrary, in societies that arrange marriages, couples often become loving life partners. Because the spouses were matched based on compatible characteristics, they usually possess the necessary foundation* for building mutual respect, affection, and even love. In Western marriages, passionate love is often damaged by the intrusion of everyday life. In arranged marriages, however, couples begin their courtship *after* the wedding as they blend gradually blossoming affection with the realities of day-to-day existence.

1. Based on the underlined thesis statement, what question or questions do you think the supporting detail paragraphs will answer for the reader?

    What are the two reasons why arranged marriages have remained popular?

2. Which of the supporting detail paragraphs answer that question?

    2 and 4

3. Are there any minor supporting detail paragraphs in this reading? ____yes____ If your answer was yes, which paragraphs introduce minor details? ___3 and 5___

EXPLANATION   "Two main reasons" is the key phrase in the thesis statement, which appears at the very end of the first paragraph, a typical location of main ideas in longer readings (see pages 223–24 in Chapter 5). Having used this phrase, the writer who wants to communicate with readers has to start the next paragraph with the first of the two reasons.

Paragraph 3 doesn't introduce another reason but describes the focused search for a partner, continuing the theme of the previous paragraph—that marriage is an alliance, or a union, between families. Paragraph 4 does introduce the second reason, as the opening transition signals it will.

---

*foundation: basis; body or ground on which other parts rest.

In addition to being plump, Fiji islanders like the look of body paint.

1. No Diet Books on the Fiji Islands

why?

1   On the Fiji Islands of the South Pacific, diet books would never be the big sellers they are in the United States. Although Fiji Islanders have definite ideas about how a person should look, they don't much care about being overweight. On the contrary, Fijians like sturdy muscles and a generally well-fed look in both men and women. To a large degree, the preference for plumpness among Fijians stems from their culture's emphasis on community rather than appearance. *explain.*

2   Unlike Americans, who prize individualism, the Fijians care more about the good of the community than they do about themselves as individuals. For them, standing out in a crowd is never as important as showing a caring attitude toward friends. And what is the main vehicle for showing your friends you care? It's serving them food, of course. For the Fijians, offering food to friends and family shows you're concerned about their physical and emotional well-being. At dinnertime, Fijians routinely open their windows and doors so that the aroma of the meal will waft outside and attract passersby. Extra food is always prepared so that anyone attracted by the smell of dinner can stop by for a snack. It is, in fact, a social disgrace not to have enough food for drop-in guests.

3   Because they believe that sharing food encourages a sense of community, Fijians consider dieting socially unacceptable. Dieting prevents a person invited to dine with friends from accepting the invitation. In addition, what dieter would willingly prepare huge, tempting meals for friends and family? Suspicious of diets, parents watch their children carefully for signs that they might be losing weight. They do so not because they want their children to achieve and maintain a certain weight but because they want to make sure their children are fully participating in the community through the sharing of food.

4   As a result of the Fijians' attitude toward food, children in particular are spared the painful experience so common to Americans of all ages—the failed diet. Children aren't obsessed by their personal appearance, and they don't constantly compare themselves to those a bit trimmer or thinner. If anything, they pity others for failing to be appropriately plump. However, the Fijian emphasis on food and the celebration of body fat does have one drawback. Children who need to limit their intake of calories for reasons of health—say, a child with diabetes—can become anxious or depressed because they are unable to fully participate in the community's common feasting. (Source of information: Seifert, Hoffnung, and Hoffnung, *Lifespan Development,* pp. 264–65.)

1. Based on the underlined thesis statement, what question or questions do you think the supporting details answer for the reader?

   _____

   _____

2. Which of the supporting detail paragraphs answer that question?

   _____

3. Are there any minor supporting detail paragraphs in this reading? _____ If your answer was yes, which paragraphs introduce minor details? _____

2. Remembering Ebbinghaus

1 At the end of the nineteenth century, a German psychologist named Hermann Ebbinghaus became interested in the carefully controlled laboratory experiments being used to do scientific research. He decided to introduce similar methods into the study of human memory.

2 Using only himself as a subject, Ebbinghaus devoted six years of research to his experiments. In one of them, he memorized lists of nonsense syllables, put them aside for specified amounts of time, and then relearned them. By comparing the time taken to learn the lists with the time taken to relearn them, Ebbinghaus was able to reach several important conclusions about the role of memory in learning. After more than a century of research, these conclusions have been repeatedly confirmed.

Rates of Forgetting

3 As a result of his research, Ebbinghaus maintained that the rate of forgetting becomes progressively slower over time. A list of nonsense syllables that he had memorized and put aside for an hour required more than half the original study time to relearn. But a list that had been put aside for nine hours was not, as one would expect, totally forgotten. The rate of forgetting had slowed down, and only two-thirds of the original study time was required to relearn the nonsense syllables.

4 Since 1885, when Ebbinghaus first published his work, investigators have continued to study the rate of forgetting. They have used not only nonsense syllables but also passages of prose, lists of facts, and excerpts from poetry. Like Ebbinghaus, they have discovered that the rate of forgetting slows down over time. It is rapid at first. But it becomes

slower as the amount of time between learning and relearning increases. This was the first of Ebbinghaus's conclusions to be confirmed.

Overlearning

5 Another of Ebbinghaus's conclusions confirmed by modern research is that overlearning during the initial learning period makes relearning at a later time easier. Based on his experiments, Ebbinghaus maintained that the more repetitions involved in the original learning experience, the fewer repetitions needed for relearning. Later investigators have come to a similar conclusion. However, they have also concluded that each repetition will not produce an equal return in time saved during the relearning period. After a point, the repetition of material already memorized does not produce a sufficient reward.

Distributed Learning

6 Research that followed Ebbinghaus's experiments by more than half a century also confirmed his belief that learning sessions devoted to memorizing are more effective if they are distributed over time. In 1940, an American psychologist, A. P. Bumstead, conducted a series of experiments to determine whether it was better to have several short learning sessions spaced out over a period of time or one long, unbroken learning session. Using only himself as a subject, Bumstead memorized several different poetry selections, spacing his learning sessions at intervals that varied from one hour to eight days. After finishing the experiment, Bumstead concluded that increasing the time between learning sessions actually decreased the amount of time needed to memorize the material.

1. Based on the underlined thesis statement, what question or questions do you think the supporting details answer for the reader?

   _____

   _____

2. Which of the supporting detail paragraphs answer that question or those questions? _____

3. Are there any minor supporting detail paragraphs in this reading? _____ If your answer was yes, which paragraphs introduce minor details? _____

WEB QUEST
One issue that Ebbinghaus did not research is context-specific or context-dependent remembering. What does that term mean and how might you apply it to learning?

_____

_____

_____

From Reader to Writer Write at least three or four paragraphs explaining why you think romance is (or is not) a necessary ingredient for marriage. Use a brief discussion of arranged marriages as an introduction to your main idea. Start your paper by saying that countries where arranged marriages are common have the right (or the wrong) idea.

✔ CHECK YOUR UNDERSTANDING

1. If the chapter section you are reading does not fit a common explanatory pattern, what should you do?

_____

_____

2. What should you do once you think you have a sense of the overall main idea of the reading?

_____

_____

3. What's the relationship between the heading of a chapter section and the supporting details?

_____

_____

4. What dictates the function of supporting details in longer readings?

_____

5. Do readers need to pay attention to minor supporting details in longer readings? Explain.

_____

_____

_____

▶**SHARE YOUR THOUGHTS**
Do the Fijians have the right idea? How is their attitude similar to or different from the way Americans view the consumption of food? Please explain.

From Reader to Writer Write a few paragraphs describing the different relationships people have to food. Make your thesis statement sum up the different connections to food that you've noticed among friends and family. (You can also focus on one friend or family member.) Then use concrete examples for supporting details. For instance, if your thesis statement refers to people who use food to calm anxiety, try to describe, as concretely as possible, someone you know who won't confront a problem without a Snickers in one hand and a bag of Moose Munch in the other.

Outlining (Informally) Multi-Paragraph Readings

In some of your courses, you may find that taking notes in the margins of your text would be enough for you to understand and remember what you have read. But when the material is detailed and difficult, informal outlining is a great way to sort and record information.

With an informal outline, you know exactly what you need to remember and what you can safely forget. An informal outline is also a terrific tool for figuring out relationships between ideas. It forces you to determine which ideas are central to a reading and which are not.

Making an Informal Outline

As you know from Chapter 1, informal outlines have no fixed format. You can mix phrases with sentences and leave an *a* without a *b*. The only test of an informal outline is how well it works for you. If your outline (1) records the main idea of the entire reading, (2) identifies and paraphrases the supporting details essential to understanding that main idea, and (3) shows the relationship between them, then it's perfect. Here, as another illustration, is a brief reading followed by an informal outline.

Each Species Plays a Unique Role in Its Ecosystem

1   An important principle of ecology* is that each species has a distinct role to play in the ecosystems where it is found, which is called an *ecological niche*, or simply **niche** (pronounced "nitch"). A species niche includes everything that affects its survival and reproduction, such as how much water and sunlight it needs, how much space it requires, and the temperatures it can tolerate. A species niche should not be confused with its habitat, which is the place where it lives.

2   Scientists use niches to classify species broadly as *generalists* or *specialists*. Generalist species have broad niches. They can live in many different places, eat a variety of foods and often tolerate a wide range of environmental conditions. Flies, cockroaches, mice, rats, white-tailed deer, raccoons, and humans are generalist species.

3   Specialist species, on the other hand, occupy narrow niches. For example, tiger salamanders are specialists because they can breed only in fishless ponds where their larvae will not be eaten. Another specialist is the red-cockaded woodpecker, which carves nest holes almost exclusively in longleaf pines that are at least 75 years old. China's highly endangered giant pandas are also specialists. They feed almost exclusively on various types of bamboo.

4   Is it better to be a generalist than a specialist? It depends. When environmental conditions are fairly constant, as in a tropical rain forest, specialists have an advantage because they have fewer competitors. But under rapidly changing environmental conditions, the generalist usually is better off than the specialist. (Miller and Spoolman, *Sustaining the Earth*, 9th ed., p. 69.)

---

*ecology: branch of biology dealing with living things in nature and how they interact.

Look now at the informal outline used to take notes on the reading:

Title: Each Species Plays a Unique Role in Its Ecosystem (p. 69)

Main Idea: Each species has its own ecological niche.

Supporting Details:
1. Ecological niche refers to everything that sustains the species from drinking water to space and temperature.

2. Based on their ecological niche, scientists classify species as generalists or specialists.

3. Generalists survive almost anywhere.

    Ex. flies, roaches, raccoons, and humans

4. Specialists need "special" conditions.

    Ex. tiger salamanders thrive only in fishless ponds, red-cockaded woodpecker needs old pines and pandas have to have bamboo.

5. If there are rapid changes in the environment, generalists fare better than specialists.

To a large degree, how you organize an informal outline is up to you. Still, there are some definite guidelines to follow if you want to take notes that are brief, complete, and well organized.

Guidelines for Informal Outlining ◆	1. **Indent to show relationships.** Even with a quick glance, your outline should clearly identify the main idea of the entire reading. Always start off by writing the main idea close to the left-hand margin. Underneath and indented, list the supporting details used to explain it.
	2. **Condense and abbreviate.** Whenever you can, use phrases instead of sentences. If possible, make up your own shorthand for common words and use it consistently. If a name appears several times, spell it out once, and then use initials. For example, if you are reading about President Lyndon Baines Johnson's[†] role in creating the Great Society, start using the initials L.B.J. and G.S. to refer to the man and his most famous project.
	3. **Paraphrase the author's words.** If you just copy the author's words into your outline, you can't be sure you've understood them.
	4. **Leave plenty of space.** As you gather additional information from lectures or outside reading, you may want to add to it, so leave plenty of space in your initial outline both in the margins and between sentences.
	5. **Reorder the material if it helps you remember it.** There's no law saying you have to re-create the author's original order. If you think combining facts or ideas that appeared in separate paragraphs will help you remember them more easily, then, by all means, do it.

◆ **EXERCISE 3**   **Outlining Longer Readings**

DIRECTIONS   Read and outline each selection. Make sure to paraphrase rather than copy sentences from the original. *Paraphrasing note*: If you have trouble paraphrasing a sentence, start by paraphrasing any words or phrases set off by commas. Often that will make it easier for you to find the language you need for the rest of the sentence.

EXAMPLE

Harriet Tubman and the Underground Railroad[†]

1   Even though the famed abolitionist[†] Harriet Tubman (1820?–1913) gave several interviews about her early life, the facts are hard to

---

[†]Johnson, the thirty-sixth president (1963–1969), put together an ambitious plan to eliminate poverty in the United States. The plan was called the "Great Society."
[†]Underground Railroad: The nineteenth-century organization dedicated to helping slaves gain their freedom.
[†]abolitionist: person who fought to eliminate slavery in the nineteenth century.

verify* There are, for example, no exact records of her birth, although most history books cite 1820 as the year she was born. However, one item in Harriet Tubman's biography needs no verification: Because of her efforts, hundreds of slaves found their way to freedom.

2   According to Tubman's own account, she decided on her life's work when she was only thirteen years old. Badly beaten and wounded in the head by her owner, she prayed that guilt would make him repent and see the light. But when he came to visit her, intent only on seeing if she was well enough to sell, the girl realized that prayers were not enough. From that moment on, she knew that she had no choice but to escape to the North and wage a battle against slavery.

3   Although Tubman married in 1844, she did not forget her vow to fight. Quiet as she seemed to those around her, she was only biding her time until she could escape with her two brothers, and, in 1849, the three set out together. Although her brothers eventually gave up, Tubman did not. Hunger and exhaustion could not deter her. From her point of view, death was a better alternative than slavery. Spending long nights alone in the woods, Tubman traveled hundreds of miles until she arrived in Philadelphia, a free woman. The year was 1850, and Tubman was just thirty years old.

4   Before long, Tubman made contact with members of the Underground Railroad, an organization dedicated to helping slaves make an escape to freedom. Tubman made it a point to learn all the names of people and places that could guarantee safety for fleeing slaves. With her knowledge of the secret network, Tubman returned to the South for her sister and her sister's children. One year later, in 1851, she returned again for her brothers. That same year, she returned for her husband, only to find that he had a new family and was content to stay where he was.

5   During the next ten years, Tubman traveled back and forth between the free and slave states, making about twenty secret journeys in all. Ultimately, she was personally responsible for the escape of more than 300 men, women, and children.

6   Because some of the escapes were extraordinary and because she was subject to strange seizures, some people thought Harriet Tubman had magical powers. But those who traveled with her knew otherwise. To them, Tubman's success was not mysterious. It was the result of brains, daring, and ingenuity.* Magic had nothing to do with it.

---

*verify: prove true or accurate.
*ingenuity: imagination, originality.

7   Tubman planned her rescues with enormous attention to detail and flatly refused to take any chances that might endanger her charges. If, for example, wanted notices were posted describing the number and appearance of her group, she would change the group's makeup. If the description said one man and two women, she would dress one of the women in men's clothes to outwit her pursuers. If any member of her party aroused her suspicions, she would refuse to take that person. It was this attention to minute detail that made her rescue attempts so successful and earned her the nickname "Moses."

8   Yet another black American to escape slavery and become an influential abolitionist was Frederick Douglass, whose contributions are outlined in the section that follows.

Main Idea   Harriet Tubman enabled hundreds of slaves to gain freedom.

Supporting Details   1.   After being badly beaten, she decided to escape slavery and take action against it.

2.   1844; got married but did not forget her determination to fight.

   a.   1849; escaped.

   b.   1850; arrived in Philadelphia a free woman at the age of thirty.

3.   Made contact with the Underground Railroad to learn who could guarantee safety.

   a.   Made twenty secret journeys.

   b.   She was so successful, people thought she had magical powers.

4.   Planned her rescues with great attention to detail.

   a.   If wanted notices described her party, she would change the group's appearance.

   b.   If she had doubts about a person, she wouldn't take that person.

   c.   Earned the nickname "Moses."

EXPLANATION   Because most of the reading deals with Tubman's efforts to free other enslaved people, the last sentence in paragraph 1 is the thesis statement. It effectively sums up the reading. Although there are eight paragraphs, only four of them contain major details that are essential to explaining the main idea. Note, too, the transitional sentence that ends the reading.

This kind of transition could help you focus your reading of the next section, but it need not appear in your notes.

1. Parents as Victims

1 Most of us find it difficult to imagine children attacking their parents because it so profoundly violates our image of parent-child relations. Parents possess the authority and power in the family hierarchy.* Furthermore, there is greater social disapproval of a child striking a parent than of a parent striking a child; it is the parent who has the right to hit. Although we know fairly little about adolescent violence against parents, scattered studies indicate that it is almost as prevalent as spousal violence.

2 Most children who attack parents are between the ages of thirteen and twenty-four, but incidence* of abuse differs according to gender. Sons are slightly more likely to be abusive than daughters. The rate of severe male violence tends to increase with age, whereas that of females decreases. Boys apparently take advantage of their increasing size and the cultural expectation of male aggression. Girls, in contrast, may become less violent because society views female aggression more negatively. Most researchers believe that mothers are the primary targets of violence and abuse because they may lack physical strength or social resources to defend themselves (Gelles and Cornell, 1985).

3 **Abuse of Elderly Parents** Of all the forms of hidden family violence, only the abuse of elderly parents by their grown children (or in some cases, by their grandchildren), has received considerable public attention. Elder mistreatment may be an act of commission (abuse) or omission (neglect) (Wolf 1995).

4 It is estimated that approximately 500,000 elderly people are physically abused annually. An additional 2 million are thought to be emotionally abused or neglected. Although mandatory reporting of suspected cases of elder abuse is the law in forty-two states and the District of Columbia, much abuse of the elderly goes unnoticed, unrecognized, and unreported (Wolf 1995)…. Although some research indicates that the abused elder may have been an abusing parent, more knowledge must be gained before we can draw firm conclusions about the causes of elder abuse. (Adapted from Strong, Devault, and Cohen, *The Marriage and Family Experience*, pp. 476–77.)

---

*hierarchy: order of importance or power, ranking.
*incidence: frequency of occurrence.

Main Idea

_____

_____

Supporting Details

_____

_____

_____

_____

_____

_____

_____

_____

_____

_____

2. The Positive and Negative Effect of First Impressions

1 Labeling people according to our first impressions is an inevitable part of the perception process. These labels are a way of making interpretations. "She seems cheerful." "He seems sincere." "They sound awfully conceited."

2 The problem is that first impressions have a lasting effect and sometimes that works in our favor, sometimes not. If first impressions are accurate, they can be useful ways of deciding how to respond best to people in the future. Problems arise, however, when the labels we attach based on a first impression are inaccurate.

3 Maintaining an opinion formed on the basis of a first impression is most clearly illustrated in what sociologists call the **halo effect**, a term that describes the tendency to form an overall positive impression of a person on the basis of one positive characteristic. Most typically, the positive impression comes from physical attractiveness, which can lead people to attribute all sorts of other virtues to the good-looking person.

4 For example, employment interviewers tend to rate mediocre but attractive job applicants higher than their less attractive candidates. And once employers form a positive impression, they often ask questions that confirm the image of the applicant. An interviewer might,

for instance, ask leading questions aimed at supporting her positive views, such as "What lessons did you learn from that setback?" The interviewer might also be inclined to interpret any answer given in a positive light, "Ah, taking time away from school to travel was a good idea, makes you a more well-rounded human being!"

5   The opposite of the halo effect is "the devil effect." When this effect is in play, the first impression formed is negative. From that point on, no positive information gets processed by the person holding the negative opinion. "So you were a straight-A student, don't you think school should be about more than grades?" (Adapted from Adler and Proctor, *Looking Out, Looking In*, 12th ed., p. 104.)

Main Idea

_____

_____

Supporting Details

_____

_____

_____

_____

_____

_____

_____

VOCABULARY ROUND UP

Below are ten words introduced in pages 322–34. The words are accompanied by more detailed definitions, the page on which they originally appear, and additional sample sentences. Spend time reviewing the words and their meanings because you will see them again in review tests at the end of the chapter. Use the online dictionary Wordnik to find additional sentences illustrating the words in context. (Note: If you know of another dictionary, online or in print, with as many examples of words in context feel free to use that one instead.)

1. **colonial** (p. 322): relating to the period of time in which America was a colony under British control; have the status of a dependent under the control of another. "During *colonial* times, British officials thought nothing of overruling local laws that did not favor British interests."

2. **alliances** (p. 322): unions of two or more people who share a legal or informal connection or relationship, a union or association that benefits both sides, a connection based on common interest. "For a brief period, Russia and the United States formed an *alliance* that ended as soon as World War II was over."

3. **compatible** (p. 322): similar in nature or attitude, fitting together well. "The police were suspicious because the husband's and the wife's accounts of events were not *compatible*."

4. **proponents** (p. 322): supporters, people in favor. "*Proponents* of the new leash law were determined to make the fines high so that people would not just ignore the law and let the dogs run through the park."

5. **foundation** (p. 323): basis, body or ground on which other parts or ideas are based; an institution that does not work for profit. (1) "The heated political situation was hardly a solid *foundation* for peace negotiations." (2) "The Bill and Melinda Gates *Foundation* has spent millions of dollars promoting privately owned charter schools."

6. **ecology** (p. 329): branch of biology dealing with living things in nature and how they interact with one another. "The *ecology* of the Gulf stream has been badly damaged by the oil spill."

7. **verify** (p. 332): to prove true or accurate, to prove true by providing evidence. "Once she was able to *verify* her whereabouts for the evening in question, the police had to let her go."

8. **ingenuity** (p. 332): originality, imagination, cleverness. "Benjamin Franklin, the writer, inventor, and statesman, believed that *ingenuity* was more valuable than genius."

9. **hierarchy** (p. 334): order of importance or power, a group of things or people organized according to increasing rank or importance. "According to Abraham Maslow's *hierarchy* of human needs, physical needs like food and drink are the most basic; once these are satisfied, needs like intimacy and affection become more important."

10. **incidence** (p. 334): frequency of occurrence. "The *incidence* of domestic violence tends to increase when unemployment rises."

DIGGING DEEPER   Is Risk-Taking in Our Genes?

Looking Ahead   The reading about hiking the Half Dome in Yosemite National Park (p. 320) pointed out that people sometimes take risks that common sense tells them could cost them their lives. The more timid among us probably wonder how anyone could think the thrill of the risk was worth the loss. The reading below from *Psychology Today* suggests that how willing we are to take or avoid risks may actually be in our genes.

Getting Focused   Use the question in the title to focus your reading. When you finish, you should be able to answer with more than a *yes* or *no*. You should also be able to generally explain how the author, journalist Paul Roberts, supports his claim.

1   In the land of seatbelts and safety helmets, the leisure pursuit of danger is a growth industry. Some experts say that courting uncertainty is the only way to protect the inner force America was founded on. Or to define the self. Whatever the reason, RISKY BUSINESS HAS NEVER BEEN MORE POPULAR. Mountain climbing is among the fastest growing sports....Extreme skiing—in which skiers descend cliff-like runs by dropping from ledge to snow-covered ledge—is drawing wider interest. Sports like paragliding and cliff-parachuting are marching into the recreational mainstream while the adventurer-travel business, which often mixes activities like climbing or river rafting with wildlife safaris, has grown into a multimillion-dollar industry. "Forget the beach," declared *Newsweek* last year. "We're hot for mountain biking, river running, ice climbing, and bungee jumping."

2   Thirty-six-year-old Derek Hersey knew a thing or two about life on the edge. Where most rock climbers used ropes and other safety gear, the wiry, wise-cracking Brit usually climbed "free solo"—alone, using nothing but climbing shoes, finger chalk, and his wits. As one climbing buddy put it, Hersey went "for the adrenaline and risk," and on May 28, 1993, he got a dose of both. High on the face of Yosemite's Sentinel Rock, Hersey met with rain and, apparently a slick rock. Friends who found the battered body reckon he fell several hundred feet. In the not-too-distant past, students of human behavior might have explained Hersey's fall as death-wish fulfillment. Under conventional personality theories, normal individuals do everything possible to avoid tension and risk.

3   In fact, as researchers are discovering, the psychology of risk involves far more than a simple "death wish." Studies now indicate that the inclination to

take high risks may be hardwired into the brain, intimately linked to arousal and pleasure mechanisms, and may offer such a thrill that it functions like an addiction for some. The tendency probably affects one in five people, mostly young males, and declines with age. It may ensure our survival, even spur our evolution as individuals and as a species. Risk-taking probably bestowed a crucial evolutionary advantage, inciting the fighting and foraging of the hunter-gatherer.

4   In mapping out the mechanisms of risk, psychologists hope to do more than explain why people climb mountains. Risk-taking, which one researcher defines as "engaging in any activity with an uncertain outcome," arises in nearly all walks of life. Asking someone on a date, accepting a challenging work assignment, raising a sensitive issue with a spouse or a friend, confronting an abusive boss—all involve uncertain outcomes, and present some level of risk. Understanding the psychology of risk, understanding why some individuals will take chances and others won't, could have important consequences in everything from career counseling to programs for juvenile delinquents.

5   Researchers don't yet know precisely how a risk-taking impulse arises from within or what role is played by environmental factors, from upbringing to the culture at large. And, while some level of risk-taking is clearly necessary for survival (try crossing a busy street without it), scientists are

Risk-takers are not inclined to play it safe.

divided as to whether, in a modern society, a "high-risk gene" is still advantageous. Some scientists, like Frank Farley, Ph.D., a University of Wisconsin psychologist and past president of the American Psychological Association, see a willingness to take big risks as essential for success. The same inner force that pushed Derek Hersey, Farley argues, may also explain why some dare to run for office, launch a corporate raid, or lead a civil-rights demonstration.

6   Yet research has also revealed the darker side of risk-taking. High-risk-takers are easily bored and may suffer low job satisfaction. Their craving for stimulation can make them more likely to abuse drugs, gamble, commit crimes, and be promiscuous. As psychologist Salvadore Maddi, Ph.D., of the University of California-Davis warns, high-risk-takers may "have a hard time deriving meaning and purpose from everyday life."

7   Indeed, this peculiar form of dissatisfaction could help explain the explosion of high-risk sports in America and other postindustrial Western nations. In unstable cultures, such as those at war or suffering poverty, people rarely seek out additional thrills. But in a rich and safety-obsessed country like America, land of guardrails, seat belts, and personal-injury lawsuits, everyday life may have become too safe, predictable, and boring for those programmed for risk-taking. ("Risk" by Paul Roberts from *Psychology Today*, November/December 1994. Reprinted with permission from Psychology Today Magazine. Copyright © 1986 Sussex Publishers, LLC.)

Sharpening Your Skills

DIRECTIONS   Answer the following questions by filling in the blanks or circling the letter of the correct response.

1. Based on the repetition and reference in the first two paragraphs, what's the likely topic for this reading?

   a. Derek Hersey

   b. mountain climbing

   c. risk-taking

   d. extreme skiing

2. Which paragraph introduces the thesis statement?

   a. paragraph 1

   b. paragraph 2

   c. paragraph 3

3. Based on your view about the overall main idea expressed in the thesis statement, how would you classify paragraph 4, as a major or a minor detail? _____

   Please explain the reasoning behind your answer.

   _____

   _____

4. How would you classify paragraph 5, as a major or minor detail? _____

   Please explain the reasoning behind your answer.

   _____

   _____

5. How would you classify paragraph 6, as a major or minor detail? _____

   Please explain the reasoning behind your answer.

   _____

   _____

6. Why does the author open paragraph 6 with the reversal transition "yet."

   _____

   _____

7. How would you classify paragraph 7, as a major or minor detail? _____

   Please explain the reasoning behind your answer.

   _____

   _____

   _____

8. In your own words, what two views do researchers hold about the value of risk-taking?

_____

_____

_____

_____

9. According to the article, have researchers clearly identified the source of risk-taking? _____ Please cite statements in the reading that support your answer.

_____

_____

_____

_____

10. In paragraph 7, the opening phrase, "this peculiar form of dissatisfaction," refers to what in the previous paragraph?

_____

Using Context Clues At the end of paragraph 2, the author talks about "conventional personality theories." Based on the context, how would you define the word *conventional*?

_____

Share Your Thoughts The reading you just finished focuses on physical risks. What are some other kinds of risk people take in life? Would you call yourself a risk-taker? Why or why not?

TEST 1　　　　**Reviewing Key Concepts**

DIRECTIONS　　Answer the following questions by filling in the blanks.

1. Once you think you know the overall main idea of a reading, what two things do you need to do to see if you are on the right track?

   _____

   _____

   _____

   _____

2. If you think the first sentence or two of the opening paragraph is the thesis statement, where should you look for the first major supporting detail?

   _____

3. If you think the last sentence in the first paragraph of a chapter section introduces the thesis statement, where should you look for the first major supporting detail?

   _____

4. If the chapter section you are reading doesn't seem to fit any of the familiar explanatory patterns you know about, what should you do?

   _____

   _____

5. If the thesis statement turns up close to the end of the reading, what two functions will the paragraphs that precede it serve?

   _____

   _____

6. What's the main difference between major and minor supporting details in paragraphs and in longer, multi-paragraph readings?

_____

7. What's an essential similarity between minor details in paragraphs and minor details in longer, multi-paragraph readings?

_____

_____

8. In longer readings, where is the author most likely to tell you how the paragraph you are reading connects to the one that came before?

_____

9. In both paragraphs and longer readings, what kinds of words offer solid clues to the major details?

_____

10. Why is it important to indent when making an informal outline?

_____

▶ **TEST 2** **Recognizing Thesis Statements and Supporting Details in Longer Readings**

DIRECTIONS After reading each selection, answer the questions by circling the appropriate letter and filling in the blanks.

1. The Debate Over Legalizing Marijuana

1 Controversy exists over whether marijuana should be legalized for the limited use of pain relief and nausea control for seriously ill individuals, including cancer patients and those individuals suffering from AIDS. Many medical professionals have testified in state and federal hearings that they believe that marijuana is more effective and has fewer side effects than other forms of legal pain relief. Others dispute the findings. There has been a move recently in several states to pass medical marijuana laws that allow for limited use of small amounts of marijuana if it's medically prescribed.

Laws

2 The federal government's drug laws do not make an exception for the medical use of marijuana. California passed a law allowing medical uses of marijuana to be regulated but decriminalized. The Supreme Court held that the federal laws "trumped" California law. As of 2010, there are ten states that have passed some version of a medical marijuana law, allowing for some limited prescription of marijuana, but federal laws against any use still remain.

Policy

3 Federal drug officials under President George W. Bush made it clear that they would enforce the federal laws against doctors and medical co-ops that distribute marijuana. In a new development, after President Obama took office, the Justice Department has indicated that they will not pursue these types of cases in states that have laws allowing for the use of medically prescribed marijuana. This is a major change in policy for the Justice Department. (Adapted from Pollock, *Ethical Dilemmas and Decisions in Criminal Justice*, 7th ed., p. 15.)

1. Which of the following sentences is most likely to be the thesis statement of this reading?

   a. "Controversy exists over whether marijuana should be legalized for the limited use of pain relief and nausea control for seriously ill individuals, including cancer patients and those individuals suffering from AIDS."

b. "Many medical professionals have testified in state and federal hearings that they believe that marijuana is more effective and has fewer side effects than other forms of legal pain relief."

c. "The federal government's drug laws do not make an exception for the medical use of marijuana."

2. In paragraph 2, the description of the California law and the Supreme Court decision is there to illustrate what word in the thesis statement? _____

3. In paragraph 3, the description of how the federal law against marijuana for medical purposes has been pursued by different administrations is present to illustrate what word in the thesis statement? _____

4. In this reading, what question about the main idea is answered by the supporting details?

_____

_____

2. Anorexia Nervosa: The Starvation Disease

1 When their children begin talking about dieting, most parents don't worry. In weight-conscious America, everyone wants to be a size smaller than they are. However, for some teenagers, dieting is no laughing matter. For them, dieting is not a momentary whim to be pursued and forgotten; instead, it is the symptom of a serious emotional disorder called *anorexia nervosa*, a disease that can have terrible, even fatal, consequences.

2   The disease usually strikes adolescent and preadolescent girls who have no reason to diet. They are not overweight, nor have they been told to diet by their doctors. They are not preparing to take part in specialized sports activities requiring a slender figure. These girls stop eating because, despite all evidence to the contrary, they believe they are fat. Determined to lose the imaginary excess poundage, they

refuse to eat more than a few morsels of food per day. Usually, weight loss is rapid, sometimes over fifty pounds in a matter of months.[†]

3   Some teenagers who are obsessed with the need to diet seek treatment because they or, more typically, their parents realize that the diet is leading to starvation. Others do not seek treatment but simply begin eating normally again on their own. However, because the disease comes in waves, or bouts, a few victims manage to keep it a secret and so avoid both exposure and treatment.

4   Unfortunately, members of this group are in the most serious danger. Although they may be able to keep their secret into adulthood, the disease, if untreated, almost always goes out of control, with tragic results. In fact, some victims—like gymnast Christy Henrich, pop singer Karen Carpenter, and model Ana Carolina Reston—die from the physical effects of prolonged starvation. Mortality rates are high: Between 5 and 10 percent of all anorexics will die within ten years of the disease being diagnosed; 18 to 20 percent will die after twenty years. Current statistics indicate that only 30–40 percent of anorexics will fully recover.

5   To date, the actual cause of the starvation disease has not been determined. According to one theory, teenagers may be starving themselves in order to rebel against parental authority. Traditionally, the refusal to eat has been a young child's weapon against parental discipline. The parent may plead and even demand that the child eat, but, by refusing, the child demonstrates his or her power over the situation. Unconsciously, teenagers who diet to the point of starvation may be attempting to teach their parents the same lesson: Control is not in the hands of the parents.

6   According to another theory, anorexia may indicate a young girl's deep-rooted fear of growing up. From this perspective, starving the body can be viewed as a way of maintaining its childish contours and rejecting adult femininity. Yet another hypothesis views the disease as a form of self-punishment. The victims may have extraordinarily high standards of perfection and punish themselves for failing to meet their goals.

[†]According to the South Carolina Department of Mental Health, one in two hundred American women suffers from anorexia, and around 90 percent of those suffering from eating disorders are female. All statistics for this reading come from this source.

1. Which of the following sentences is most likely to be the thesis statement of this reading?

   a. "When their children begin talking about dieting, most parents don't worry. In weight-conscious America, everyone wants to be a size smaller than they are."

   b. "However, for some teenagers, dieting is no laughing matter. For them, dieting is not a momentary whim to be pursued and forgotten; instead, it is the symptom of a serious emotional disorder called *anorexia nervosa*, a disease that can have terrible, even fatal, consequences."

   c. "The disease usually strikes adolescent and preadolescent girls who have no reason to diet. They are not overweight, nor have they been told to diet by their doctors."

2. In paragraph 2, the description of the girls' refusal to eat and resulting rapid weight loss is there to illustrate what word in the thesis statement? _____

3. Does paragraph 3 illustrate the same word in the thesis statement? _____ Please explain.

   _____

   _____

4. What do the opening words in paragraph 4 signal about its relationship to paragraph 3?

   _____

   _____

▶ **TEST 3**   **Recognizing Thesis Statements and Supporting Details in Longer Readings**

DIRECTIONS   After reading each selection, answer the questions by circling the appropriate letter and filling in the blanks.

1. Henry Ford's Model T

1   Long before he invented the car known as the Model T, Henry Ford made the American public a promise: "I will build a car for the great multitude." Ford kept his promise and forever changed the life of working Americans. Using an assembly-line method of production, which he refined for maximum efficiency, Henry Ford produced a car that ordinary working people could afford. The first Model T appeared in 1908. By the following year, close to 10,000 Model Ts were putt-putting their way across America's frequently bumpy roadways. Unlike in earlier years, the drivers were no longer wealthy businessmen but farmers and factory workers.

2   Light in weight, the Model T was still strong enough to be driven on rough country roads that had never known pavement. At a price of less than $900, even farmers could afford to save up and buy one. And buy them they did, using their cars for everything from carting eggs to making Sunday calls. As one farmer's wife delightedly wrote to Ford, "Your car has lifted us out of the mud."

3   To be sure, the Model T was not restricted to rural areas. As cities continued to spring up across the nation, more and more people began using cars to drive to and from work. When the weekend rolled around, what could be cheaper than piling the family into the Model T for an excursion? By the time production stopped in 1927, more than 15 million Model Ts had been sold, and the price had been reduced, making the cars even more affordable for the masses of people who wanted to buy them.

4   What made the Model T so cheap to produce for a mass audience—and ultimately such a gold mine—was the interchangeability of its parts. Every Model T was like the previous one. That meant the Model T could be mass produced on assembly lines, whereas other cars had to be put together one by one. But Ford didn't stop there. Always looking to cut production costs, he introduced the *moving* assembly line, making it easier and quicker for factories to turn out Model Ts, again at a cheaper price.

5   An astute businessman, Ford was also willing to pass on his savings to consumers because he knew full well that lowering the price of the Model T would increase its sales, which is exactly what happened. The decrease in price boosted sales and broadened the spectrum of ordinary working people who could afford to buy a car. By 1923, the price of a Model T, which had started out selling for $850, was at an all-time low of $290, a price not beyond the range of average working people. Thus, between 1908 and 1927, Ford sold a whopping 15.8 million Model Ts. He also established a production record that was not shattered until the arrival of the Volkswagen Beetle during World War II.

1. Which of the following sentences is most likely to be the thesis statement of this reading?

    a. "Ford kept his promise and forever changed the life of working Americans. Using an assembly-line method of production, which he refined for maximum efficiency, Henry Ford produced a car that ordinary working people could afford."

    b. "The first Model T appeared in 1908. By the following year, close to 10,000 Model Ts were putt-putting their way across America's frequently bumpy roadways."

    c. "Light in weight, the Model T was still strong enough to be driven on rough country roads that had never known pavement. At a price of less than $900, even farmers could afford to save up and buy one."

2. Which of the following statements accurately describes the quote from the farmer's wife in paragraph 2?

    a. The quotation is a major detail in both the paragraph and in the reading as a whole.

    b. The quotation is a major detail in the paragraph but a minor detail in the reading as a whole.

    c. The quotation is a minor detail in both the paragraph and in the reading as a whole.

    Please explain the reasoning behind your answer.

    _____

    _____

3. Which sentence best expresses the main idea of paragraph 4?

a. Henry Ford invented the assembly line.

b. Henry Ford may have developed ways to cheapen the price of the Model T, but he also turned factory life into a workers' nightmare.

c. The Model T's ability to be mass produced on an assembly line made the car both cheap and profitable.

d. Henry Ford revolutionized factory production in America.

In relation to the main idea of the entire reading, the main idea of paragraph 4 is a

a. major detail.

b. minor detail.

Please explain the reasoning behind your answer.

_____

_____

4. Which sentence best expresses the main idea of paragraph 5?

a. Ford boosted sales by passing his savings on to consumers in the form of lower prices.

b. When it came to passing on his savings to consumers, Ford was an exception to the general rule of millionaire business-men who never cut prices no matter how cheap the labor costs.

c. Ford's production record was not challenged until the arrival of the Volkswagen Beetle.

d. Like Ford's Model T, the Volkswagen Beetle was very much a "people's car."

In relation to the main idea of the entire reading, the main idea of paragraph 5 is a

a. major detail.

b. minor detail.

Please explain the reasoning behind your answer.

_____

_____

2. Medical Remedies: Leeches, Maggots, and Dirt

1   If a patient became ill with a fever in the eighteenth century, a surgeon might prescribe leeches. Several of these glossy black worms would be placed on the patient's body, where they would puncture the skin and draw small amounts of blood. If the doctor thought that the patient should be drained of more blood than leeches could drink, he would next turn to bloodletting, which involved cutting a vein and allowing ounces or even whole pints of blood to flow from the body, often until the patient fainted.

2   During the Civil War, physicians sometimes treated a soldier's open wound by putting maggots, the wormlike larvae of flies, directly onto the patient's damaged flesh. If a patient complained of intestinal problems, the physician might order him to eat dirt.

3   Do you shudder when you think of such revolting remedies? Are you relieved that advances in medical knowledge have put a stop to these kinds of treatments? You may be surprised to know that scientists have discovered that many of these old cures work; in some cases, they are actually more effective than other, more modern techniques. As a result, a number of disgusting medical remedies are making a comeback in today's hospitals.

4   **Leeches to the Rescue**   For instance, doctors are once again using leeches for bloodletting. The crawly creatures are proving to be particularly useful after surgeries involving the reattachment of severed body parts. When areas swell with congested blood, leeches are applied to relieve the pressure by sucking up the blood. Leech saliva contains a natural anesthetic, so the bite is pain free. The saliva also contains substances that prevent bacteria from infecting the wound area and cause blood vessels to open wider. Therefore, the worms promote the circulation of blood necessary for healing. Leech saliva also contains a chemical that keeps blood from clotting. Thus the creatures also have been used to unclog blood vessels during heart surgery.

5   **Maggots Make a Comeback**   Another creepy-crawly making a comeback in doctors' offices is the wormlike maggot. In the nineteenth

and early twentieth centuries, battlefield physicians noticed that maggot-infested wounds healed better than those injuries that were bug free. It turned out that maggots eat dead flesh and kill harmful bacteria that cause infection, which make them highly beneficial as healing agents. Today's laboratories grow the larvae and put them into special bandages that keep the creatures in a wound. Then they ship the bug-filled bandages to the more than 200 hospitals in the United States and Europe that have prescribed maggots for patients with bedsores, leg ulcers, stab wounds, or any other injury that won't heal. The practice is even referred to now as *biosurgery.*

6 **The Healing Power of Dirt**   One more disgusting treatment that actually works is *geophagy*, or dirt eating. For thousands of years, people suffering from intestinal disorders have eaten a little soil to settle their stomachs. As a matter of fact, geophagy has always been relatively common in central Africa and in the southern United States. Scientific research has confirmed that some forms of clay and earth neutralize acid, which is why the antidiarrhea product Kaopectate when first manufactured contained a white clay called kaolin, and the laxative-antacid milk of magnesia contained the same ingredients as soil found around Magnesia in Greece. Dirt also contains phosphorus, potassium, copper, zinc, manganese, and iron—minerals that are essential to the body's functions—so doctors may even prescribe geophagy for patients suffering from deficiencies of these nutrients.

7   They may not have known *why* these therapies worked, but doctors of days gone by knew their remedies were effective. Today, of course, modern scientific research has revealed the reasons for the success of these treatments. The next time you're in one of our modern, sterile hospitals, don't be surprised if you see a few bugs and a little dirt.

1. Which of the following sentences is most likely to be the thesis statement of this reading?

    a. "During the Civil War, physicians sometimes treated a soldier's open wound by putting maggots, the wormlike larvae of flies, directly onto the patient's damaged flesh. If a patient complained of intestinal problems, the physician might order him to eat dirt."

    b. "You may be surprised to know that scientists have discovered that many of these old cures actually work; in some cases, they are actually more effective than other, more modern techniques. As a result, a number of disgusting medical remedies are making a comeback in today's hospitals."

c. "Another creepy-crawly making a comeback in doctors' offices is the wormlike maggot."

2. Which sentence best expresses the main idea of paragraph 4?

   a. Leeches are particularly helpful to people undergoing surgery for the reattachment of body parts.
   b. Leeches may one day make surgery unnecessary.
   c. Leeches are again being used to draw off the build-up of blood.
   d. Leeches are now a required element of all microsurgeries.

   In relation to the main idea of the entire reading, the main idea of paragraph 4 is a

   a. major detail.
   b. minor detail.

   Please explain the reasoning behind your answer.

   _____

   _____

3. Which sentence best expresses the main idea of paragraph 5?

   a. Maggots are also experiencing a medical revival.
   b. Already in the nineteenth century physicians were using maggots to treat wounds.
   c. Maggots eat flesh and the bacteria it contains.
   d. Today, entire laboratories are devoted to the production of maggots.

   In relation to the main idea of the entire reading, the main idea of paragraph 5 is a

   a. major detail.
   b. minor detail.

   Please explain the reasoning behind your answer.

   _____

   _____

4. Which sentence best expresses the main idea of paragraph 6?

   a. Over-the-counter remedies like Kaopectate are actually not very safe.
   b. Geophagy is an age-old treatment for stomach problems.
   c. As it turns out, eating dirt actually has health benefits.
   d. Dirt-eating is common the world over.

   In relation to the main idea of the entire reading, the main idea of paragraph 6 is a

   a. major detail.
   b. minor detail.

   Please explain the reasoning behind your answer.

   _____

   _____

▶ **TEST 4**   **Reviewing Chapter 7 Vocabulary**

DIRECTIONS   Fill in the blanks with one of the following words.

proponents	hierarchy	ecology	ingenuity	alliance
compatibility	verify	colonial	incidence	foundation

1. Pure democracy, which in theory gives every person an equal say in how the government is organized, would be the opposite of a(n) _____.

2. If you were trying to cross the border of a foreign country, you would be expected to _____ your identity.

3. If someone were to invent a computer program that could understand and respond to natural language (i.e., the responses would be spontaneous and vary with the question or statement rather than being fixed responses that don't change with the comment made or question posed), you would probably say that the inventor of that program had a lot of _____.

4. The person in charge of a group studying how a decrease in wetlands will affect existing plant and animal life should probably have a background in _____.

5. People who believe in the expression "You can't fight City Hall" probably don't understand the power of a(n) _____.

6. A high degree of _____ is something you probably want in a marriage.

7. People who do not seek medical help when ill but instead rely on the power of faith and prayer are _____ of Christian Science.

8. The student who takes biology and health courses in order to become a physician's assistant and the builder who pours the concrete structure on which a house will one day stand are both building a(n) _____.

9. If you are going to study early American history, at some point, you will have to learn about America's _____ past.

10. Cancer researchers insist that the high _____ of skin cancer is linked to an increase in outdoor summer activity.

Focusing on Inferences in Paragraphs

IN THIS CHAPTER, YOU WILL LEARN

- about the different kinds of inferences essential to reading.
- how to tell the difference between logical inferences and illogical inferences.
- about the importance of linking pronouns and antecedents in topic sentences.
- how to combine information from two or more sentences to create a main idea statement that sums up the paragraph.
- how to infer implied main ideas.
- when and how to add information and connections to supporting details.

"An inference is a statement about the unknown made on the basis of the known."

—S. I. Hayakawa, *Language in Thought and Action*

Words like *imply*, *infer*, and *inference* have been turning up regularly in the previous chapters. There's a reason for that. To some degree, all writers expect readers to infer, or create, some of the text they read. Experienced writers know they don't have the time, energy, or space to put every single word necessary to their message on the page or screen. Instead, they rely on readers to fill in gaps by adding the words, ideas, or relationships essential to completing their written message.

If you think about it for a moment, you will realize that this is no different from what we do in speech, where more is implied than what's actually said. After all, if the person bagging your groceries at the supermarket says to you, "Paper or plastic," you know immediately that he or she is asking you, "Do you want a *paper* or a *plastic* bag?" Language almost always says more than the spoken or written words. That's why drawing inferences is so essential to understanding what you hear and read.

How Inferences Work

As you move through this chapter, you will see that different kinds of inferences are required for different aspects, or parts, of a text. You'll also get a solid understanding of the difference between logical inferences that help readers get the author's message and illogical inferences that lead them astray.

Logical inferences are evidence-based guesses that rely on the author's words, subject matter, and context to determine what the author has implied, or suggested, but not directly stated. **Illogical inferences** over-rely on the reader's personal experience and are not firmly grounded in the author's actual language. For the most part, they lack supporting evidence and don't fit the writer's context. Sometimes they even contradict the author's actual words or give too much emphasis to one sentence while ignoring others.

We'll talk more about logical and illogical inferences in paragraphs later on. But for now, you'll get a general understanding of the difference by looking at the drawing below and deciding which of the three captions that follow fits the details of the drawing.

If you had to identify the caption for this drawing, what would it be?

1. "I wish I was as fabulous as my dog thinks I am."[†]

2. "Dogs define the word *loyalty*."

3. "Dream big! Dare the impossible!"

4. "Dogs are a source of unconditional love."

Most people who look at this drawing correctly pick number 3 as the caption. They arrive at the right caption by looking at the clues in the drawing and figuring out which caption fits or follows from the details shown. What are those clues and how do they add up? See the list below.

1. The dog is wearing a tutu; in the real world, dogs don't dress up as ballet dancers.

2. Dogs also don't dance; in particular they don't do ballet, but this dog seems to be not only dancing but trying out for a part in the famous ballet *Swan Lake*.

3. The ability of a dog to stand *en pointe*[†] is a seemingly impossible feat. Yet the drawing shows a dog doing just that, which fits the words "Dare the impossible."

4. The drawing makes the impossible—a dog auditioning for a part in the famous ballet *Swan Lake*—look possible.

When Inferences Go Astray and Become Illogical

Now imagine that you picked caption 2, "Dogs define the word *loyalty*." If you are a dog lover, this caption might well express your point of view. Most people who know anything about dogs would probably feel the same way. But your personal feelings about dogs can't—and shouldn't—make up for the fact that nothing in the drawing suggests loyalty, either to humans or other dogs. After all, the only one in the drawing is the dancing dog, so there is no one for her to be loyal to. In short, caption number 2 would be an illogical inference because it doesn't match the clues provided.

[†]This is actually a popular saying on bumper stickers.
[†]*En pointe* is a dance term meaning to be raised up on the tip of your toe.

That, in a nutshell, is the key to drawing logical inferences. The idea or conclusion you come up with has to fit the information explicitly given. If it doesn't, it's illogical and will probably lead you away from the author's meaning rather than toward it.

◆ **EXERCISE 1**   **Matching Your Inferences to the Visual and Verbal Clues**

DIRECTIONS   Look at the following cartoon. Read the clues provided in each frame. Then on the blanks that follow, explain the inference the reader is supposed to supply to make sense of the cartoon.

1. What does the first frame tell you about Calvin's state of mind?

_____

_____

2. Why does the second frame show Calvin smiling with an exclamation point over his head?

_____

_____

3. What does the third frame show Calvin doing, and how do his actions relate to the first frame?

_____

_____

4. Why does Calvin say he loves loopholes and what does the last frame have to do with the first?

_____

_____

_____

◆ EXERCISE 2   Drawing Inferences from Quotations

DIRECTIONS   The following statements or claims require inferences to make sense. Rewrite each one to make the meaning more explicit than implicit.

EXAMPLE   "My lyrics are pretty straightforward; I don't Shakespeare 'em up." —Singer Bruno Mars in an interview with *Rolling Stone*

What does Mars imply when he says, "I don't Shakespeare 'em up"?

The language of my lyrics is not elaborate or unfamiliar like Shakespeare's language.

It's easy to understand.

EXPLANATION   No matter how beautiful the language of Shakespeare might be, it's not easy to read. It takes some time to understand. Mars compares his language to Shakespeare's to say that the language of his songs is the exact opposite. In the song "Grenade," for instance, he sings about giving his love "all he had" only to have her toss it "in the trash." The lyric is clearly not open to multiple interpretations. Note that to make sense of what Mars says, it's the reader who has to *infer* the connection between the opening statement and the allusion, or reference, to Shakespeare.

1. "Friendship and money; oil and water." —Mario Puzo, author of *The Godfather*

What does Puzo imply about connecting friendship to money?

_____

_____

2. "If men were angels, no government would be necessary." —James Madison, Federalist Paper #51[†]

What does Madison suggest about human character with this quote?

_____

_____

3. "It is the mind that makes the body." —Sojourner Truth, ex-slave and abolitionist

What does Sojourner Truth imply about the relationship between mind and body?

_____

4. "It infuriates me to be wrong when I know I'm right." —Molière, French playwright

What does Molière imply about his response to being told he is wrong?

_____

_____

5. "Our errors are surely not such awfully solemn things." —William James, philosopher and psychologist

_____

WEB QUEST

Sojourner Truth made a convention speech that became famous. What is it called? When was it delivered and to whom?

_____

_____

_____

[†]James Madison, John Jay, and Alexander Hamilton wrote a series of articles in 1787–1788 that came to be known as "The Federalist Papers." The purpose of the papers was to convince New Yorkers that the country needed to be united under the laws laid out by the Constitution.

From Reader to Writer Write a sentence or two describing someone famous. But don't say who the person is. Instead, select details that will make your audience recognize the person without being named, for instance, "Married to the King of Hip Hop, she's a star in her own right, a true Destiny's Child, whose talent propelled her to fame and fortune."

Connecting Topic Sentence Pronouns to Their Antecedents

Connecting pronouns to antecedents is one of the most basic inferences readers draw while reading. Consider, for instance, these two sentences below, excerpted from a history text:

> In the early nineteenth century, as reformers launched changes in many cities and considered ways to improve society, Robert M. LaFollette pushed Wisconsin to the forefront of reform. A Republican, he entered politics soon after graduating from the University of Wisconsin. (Adapted from Berkin et al., *Making America*, 6th ed., p. 535.)

You are so used to connecting pronouns like *he* and *she* to their antecedents, or the nouns to which they refer, you probably didn't even think about it when you connected the pronoun *he* to its antecedent, Robert LaFollette. Still, it's you, the reader, who infers the connection. The author doesn't connect pronoun and antecedent for you.

Similarly, the underlined topic sentence in the paragraph that follows doesn't state the topic. Instead, it uses a pronoun. The author's expectation is that the reader will infer the correct antecedent.

> [1]At one time, the right side of the brain was regarded as the minor hemisphere, or half. [2]We now know, however, that it has its own special set of talents and isn't "minor" at all. [3]The right hemisphere is superior at recognizing patterns, faces, and melodies. [4]It's also involved in detecting and expressing emotions. [5]The right brain is actually better than the left at visualization skills, such as arranging blocks to match a pattern, putting together a puzzle, or drawing pictures.

The first sentence in the sample paragraph is an introductory sentence. As introductory sentences so often do, this one tells you what people *used to think* about the right side of the brain, the topic under discussion. If you doubt that's the topic, notice how many times the phrase is repeated and referred to. Keep in mind, too, that *hemisphere* is a synonym for *side*. That means every sentence has something to say about this topic.

Based on that kind of opening, you'd be correct to expect the topic sentence to arrive soon. And, indeed, it does. It's also accompanied by another dead giveaway, the reversal transition, *however*.

But suppose you wanted to take notes on the topic sentence. How would you paraphrase it? (1) *It* isn't a minor hemisphere but has its own talents or (2) *The right brain* isn't the minor hemisphere; it has its own talents? If you wanted to understand your notes two or three weeks after you read the paragraph, you'd definitely opt for sentence 2. That means you'd make sure to infer the correct antecedent and include it in your paraphrase of the original.

Whenever a topic sentence uses a pronoun to refer to the topic, be sure to mentally connect the pronoun to its antecedent. Include the antecedent, rather than the pronoun, in your notes.

◆ **EXERCISE 3** **Filling in the Gaps in Topic Sentences**

DIRECTIONS Underline the partially complete topic sentence in each paragraph. Then in the blanks at the end of the paragraph, write a topic sentence that includes any necessary information missing from the original. *Note*: Sometimes the completed topic sentence will only need a noun. However, be prepared to add more information when necessary.

EXAMPLE ¹Who was Will Rogers? ²He was the cowboy-philosopher who won America's heart in the 1920s. ³Born in Oklahoma, Rogers began his career onstage playing a rope-twirling cowboy-comedian and in 1915 joined the Ziegfeld Follies.† ⁴Soon his widely quoted wisecracks about the American political scene made him famous nationwide. ⁵The public loved the way he ridiculed politicians. ⁶"I am not a member of any organized party—I am a Democrat." ⁷By the time he died in a plane crash in 1935, Rogers had made more than twenty films, and quotes from his newspaper column had appeared on the front page of the *New York Times*.

Will Rogers was the cowboy-philosopher who won America's heart in the 1920s.

---

†Ziegfeld Follies: Flo Ziegfeld was famous for his stage shows, which bore his name. Follies are stage shows with very elaborate costumes and special effects

EXPLANATION   In this case the completed topic sentence required only the addition of Will Rogers's name.

1. [1]As a relatively young man, the actor Bela Lugosi became rich and famous. [2]Taken by his 1931 performance as the blood-drinking Count Dracula, movie audiences willingly paid to see Lugosi's special brand of elegant evil. [3]But all that changed as Bela Lugosi grew older. [4]When he died, he had nothing left of the fame and fortune playing Dracula had brought him. [5]Because Lugosi had become so closely identified with the figure of the count, producers were hesitant to cast him in other roles. [6]In addition, his thick Hungarian accent, so effective in *Dracula*, was a handicap for other parts. [7]As a result, Lugosi was reduced to making ridiculous, low-grade thrillers like *Bela Lugosi Meets a Brooklyn Gorilla* and *Mother Riley Meets the Vampire*. [8]By the mid-1950s, Lugosi was all but forgotten by Hollywood and his fans. [9]By 1956, he was dead, a victim of drugs and alcohol.

_____

_____

2. [1]Throughout the 1800s, explorers had dreamed of reaching the North Pole. [2]But it wasn't until 1909 that anyone claimed to have arrived at the North Pole. [3]Who did it first, though, is still the subject of argument. [4]Dr. Frederick Cook claimed that he had reached the Pole on April 21, 1908, spending two days there until drifting ice forced him to move westward. [5]The world press celebrated Cook's achievement until cables began arriving from Robert Peary, who insisted that he had been the first man to reach the Pole. [6]The controversy continued even after the two men had died. [7]In fact, some historians insist that both claims lacked the appropriate proof and therefore cannot be honored. [8]They propose instead that Richard Byrd was the first man to really arrive at the North Pole, flying over it in 1926. [9]Some Russian historians, for their part, dispute any such claims. [10]They insist that in 1937 the Russian scientist Otto Schmidt was the first person to ever set foot at the North Pole.

_____

_____

3. [1]When baseball was still ruled by the strict segregation, or separation, of players into white or black teams, Satchel Paige was the highest paid player in the Negro Leagues. [2]And without a doubt, he was worth every penny of his $40,000 salary; he was the most talented pitcher baseball has ever seen, now or then. [3]Batters who came up against him could expect to strike out. [4]In 1932, he pitched sixty-two straight scoreless innings. [5]To get a hit off him, you had to be at the top of your game, and not many were up to the challenge. [6]Joe DiMaggio, considered by many to be one of the greatest players of all time, said Paige was "the best I ever faced, and the fastest." [7]People came from all over to watch Paige play, and even all-stars were in awe of his legendary bag of pitches, each with its own Paige-bestowed nickname. [8]There was the bee ball, the trouble ball, the Long Tom, the two-hump blooper, and, perhaps the most famous of them all, the hesitation pitch.

_____

_____

WEB QUEST

When forty-one-year-old Satchel Paige was signed to play in the American league, some complained that he was too old to play. How did Paige respond?

_____

Piecing Together Main Idea Statements

Topic sentences, those single sentences that sum up a paragraph's main idea, are very popular in textbook writing. They're popular because they provide a quick and efficient way for writers to tell readers, "Here's my point."

Still, topic sentences are not the only way textbook authors communicate the main idea of a paragraph. While authors of business texts rely on them almost exclusively, the same is not true for authors of history and psychology texts. Authors in these disciplines certainly use topic sentences. But they also vary their introduction of the main idea by presenting parts of it in two or occasionally three different sentences. Then they leave it up to the reader to knit the parts together into a main idea statement. This method of introducing the main idea is particularly popular with paragraphs that rely on a question-and-answer format, for example:

> [1]In 2008, the tanker *Sirius Star* was hijacked by pirates; carrying two million barrels of oil, it was the largest tanker ever taken at sea. [2]Boarded in waters off the coast of Somalia, where the majority of pirate attacks occur, the seizure of the *Sirius Star* raised, yet again, the question haunting shipping companies, sailors, and maritime security organizations: How can ships at sea be kept safe from pirate attacks? [3]Vahan Simidian, the chief executive officer of HPV Technologies, believes his company's magnetic acoustic device (MAD), which functions as both alarm and weapon, provides the answer. [4]If the ship's captain is concerned about an approaching vessel, he can use MAD to produce a siren-like sound that tells pirates they have been sighted. [5]If the pirates keep coming, MAD can be notched up to another level of piercing sound. [6]At this point, the sound the device produces is so loud it's painful to the ears and can disorient and confuse those who hear it. [7]As Mr. Simidian says, when asked if MAD can do serious harm, "Absolutely." (Source of information: Daniel Emery, "Technology Sets Sights on Piracy," BBC News.)

In this example, sentence 2 poses a question. Sentence 3 provides the answer. Left on its own, though, neither sentence provides a clear statement of the main idea. To arrive at that, you need to combine the two sentences, taking a piece from each one: "Vahan Simidian thinks his company's magnetic acoustic device, which functions as both alarm and weapon, can keep ships safe from pirate attacks."

Paragraphs that rely on readers to weave together parts of different sentences don't have to focus on answering a question. Look, for example, at the following:

> [1]Unlike most minorities, Native Americans directly benefited from the New Deal.[†] [2]They had a strong supporter in Secretary of the Interior Harold Ickes and an even stronger one in the Commissioner of Indian Affairs, John Collier. [3]Both opposed existing Indian policies that since 1887 had sought to destroy the reservation system and eradicate* Indian cultures. [4]But it was Collier who really maintained the momentum for change. [5]At Collier's urging, Congress passed the Indian Reorganization Act in 1934. [6]The act returned land and

John Collier truly appreciated Native-American culture, and he worked hard to make the public share his respect.

[†]New Deal: When Franklin D. Roosevelt became president in 1932, he announced a program of economic reforms called the New Deal. The goal of the program was to kick-start the country out of a terrible economic depression.
*eradicate: eliminate, wipe out.

community control to tribal organizations. [7]It provided Indian self-rule on the reservations and prevented individual ownership on tribal lands. [8]To improve the squalid* conditions found on most reservations and provide jobs, Collier organized an agency for Indians and ensured that other New Deal agencies played a part in improving Indian lands and providing jobs. [9]He also promoted Native-American culture. [10]Working with tribal leaders, Collier took measures to protect, preserve, and encourage Indian customs, languages, religions, and folkways. (Adapted from Berkin et al., *Making America*, 6th ed., p. 744.)

In this case, the main idea statement has to be pieced together from sentences 1 and 2: "Unlike most minorities, Native Americans directly benefited from the New Deal, largely *because* they had a strong supporter in Secretary of the Interior Harold Ickes and an even stronger one in the Commissioner of Indian Affairs, John Collier." In principle, this main idea statement was produced by precisely the same method as the previous example. To come up with a statement of the main idea, the reader had to combine the information from two different sentences.

There is, however, an additional piece of information that the writers of the second paragraph expected readers to infer: the relationship between sentences 1 and 2. That relationship is expressed in the word *because*. *Because* is a **conjunction**, or linking word, that says one event (the effect) was the result of another (the cause).

As you can see, the sample main idea statement makes explicit what the authors only implied—that Native Americans benefited from the New Deal *as a result* of some effort put forth by Harold Ickes and the even greater efforts of John Collier.

The more conscious you become of the role inferences play in reading, the more you'll realize that writers constantly expect readers to infer connections between sentences. They expect them to make what language researchers call **bridging inferences**. These are inferences that clarify relationships between sentences and paragraphs.

Although there are other relationships beyond cause and effect that you will have to infer when you read (more in Chapters 10 and 11), cause and effect is probably the most common. Writers of all kinds, from textbook authors to novelists, expect their readers to bridge the gap between sentences by inferring that one event led to or produced another. Keep that in mind while you complete the next exercise.

*squalid: poverty-stricken.

♦ **EXERCISE 4**   **Constructing Main Idea Statements**

DIRECTIONS   Combine different parts of sentences to create a main idea statement that sums up the paragraph in the same way a topic sentence would. *Note*: If you need to change the wording to make the sentences combine more smoothly, feel free to do so. Just don't alter the meanings of the sentences.

EXAMPLE   [1]For more than twenty years, Billy Tipton was a popular jazz musician, who played both the saxophone and the piano. [2]Tipton, however, had a secret. [3]He was a woman who had decided to live her life as a man. [4]Although Tipton has been dead for over two decades, it's still not clear what his motive was. [5]The general consensus is that Tipton was desperate to pursue a career in jazz and assumed that being a female would inhibit his chances. [6]Jazz was and is a largely male club. [7]How Tipton kept his secret for so long is unclear. [8]He married three times and adopted three sons, claiming that an old injury prevented him from having sexual relations. [9]With age, Tipton's health deteriorated. [10]But he refused medical care, probably fearing his secret would come out. [11]He died of a bleeding ulcer in 1989. [12]He could have survived the condition if he had sought care. [13]But getting medical attention meant he would have had to reveal his true sex. [14]That was apparently a secret he wanted to take to his grave.

Main Idea
Statement

Billy Tipton was a popular jazz musician who kept a secret for years: He was a woman who had decided to live life as a man.

EXPLANATION   Sentence 1 introduces the topic Billy Tipton. It tells the reader who he was and what he did. Sentence 2 announces that Tipton had a secret without saying what it was. That piece of information is left for sentence 3. Since the remaining supporting details describe the lengths Tipton went to keep his secret, we need to combine all three sentences to come up with a main idea statement those supporting details could develop.

1.   [1]In 1871, the *New York Herald* sent Henry Morton Stanley to Africa in search of David Livingstone, the English missionary.* [2]Stanley faced sickness, unfriendly natives, and starvation to find the missionary and win himself a reputation as one of the bravest men in the world. [3]Since that time, history books have celebrated Stanley as a hero. [4]But Henry

---

*missionary: a person who goes to foreign countries to do religious or charitable work.

Morton Stanley had another side, one not so prominently* displayed in the history books. [5]His cruelty toward his men was legendary. [6]Like many men who have led a hard life, he considered the world a hard and brutal place. [7]His response to his vision of the world was to eliminate all trace of humanity from his personality. [8]Underlings who didn't obey his orders were severely beaten. [9]Subordinates who challenged his authority were shot. [10]Ashley Jackson, a professor of military history, has written: "Stanley had one of the biggest kill rates of all the great African explorers in terms of the number of people who died during his journeys, and you can't gloss over the fact."

Main Idea Statement _____

_____

2. [1]In the early nineteenth century, many runaway slaves sought refuge among Florida's Seminole Indians. [2]As a result, the U.S. government ordered the Seminoles to leave Florida, but they refused. [3]They were encouraged to rebel by their much-respected leader, Osceola. [4]Osceola's response to the order was to spear the announcement with a dagger and proclaim, "There, this is the only treaty I will make with the whites." [5]His words weren't empty boasting. [6]When government troops arrived to subdue the Seminole rebellion, they were killed. [7]The war between the Seminoles and the United States government had officially begun. [8]Even after Osceola was captured and died in prison, the war continued as Osceola's Seminole followers fought in his name. [9]In 1842, however, the tribe was finally defeated and force-marched to the state of Oklahoma.

Main Idea Statement _____

_____

_____

Inferring the Main Idea from Start to Finish

Sometimes writers don't supply even parts of the topic sentences. Instead, they provide a series of specific statements designed to lead readers to the implied main idea of the paragraph. The statements can't be

*prominently: obviously, openly, overtly.

combined into a main idea statement. But they do add up to an **implied main idea**, an idea that is strongly suggested by the author without ever being directly stated. For an illustration, read the following paragraph:

T. E. Lawrence, nicknamed Lawrence of Arabia, dreamed of an independent Middle East that he did not live to see.

¹As a young man, the British soldier and writer T. E. Lawrence took part in an archaeological* expedition in the Middle East. ²The work fascinated him, as did the land, and he became possessed by a dream: The Arabs would one day overthrow Turkish rule and take control of their own country. ³Lawrence sought to make his dream become reality during World War I when the British, at war with the Turks, seemed ready to help the Arabs revolt. ⁴Seeing a chance for Arab independence, Lawrence arranged a meeting between British and Arab leaders. ⁵Supplied with British arms and aided by Lawrence's military strategy, the Arabs rose up and captured several major Turkish strongholds, helping the British cause in the process. ⁶By 1919, when the war ended, the Turks had been defeated. ⁷Thrilled by what he saw as an Arab victory, Lawrence was now convinced that his dream of Arab self-rule would become a reality. ⁸But when he was called to the Paris Peace Conference that formally ended the war, he was stunned to discover that the British had no intention of giving up their newly won control of the Middle East.

The author hasn't included a topic sentence in this paragraph. Instead, she leaves a trail of clues and expects readers to infer the implied main idea: "Although T. E. Lawrence believed helping the British during World War I would win independence for the Arab countries, the British betrayed him and replaced the Turks as the Arabs' new rulers." The basis for that inference is found in the following statements:

1. According to the author, Lawrence was "possessed" by the dream of Arab independence. The word *possessed* suggests Lawrence was passionately committed to the idea of Arab autonomy.

2. The author says Lawrence tried to turn "his dream" into a reality during World War I.

3. Believing the British were going to help the Arabs if they could beat the Turks, he arranged a meeting between the British and Arab leaders.

4. Guided in part by Lawrence's military strategy, the Arabs did help the British defeat the Turks.

*archaeological: related to discovering the remains of lost civilizations.

5. Lawrence went to the Paris Peace Conference believing the British were going to reward the Arabs for their help.

6. The author uses the word *stunned* to describe the shock Lawrence felt about learning that the British were not giving up control of the Middle East.

7. Instead, they were taking over the countries the Turks had lost, thanks to the Arab revolts.

Given both the language and the content of the paragraph, it would be hard not to infer that Lawrence was betrayed by the British refusal to give the Arabs self-rule. The clues also suggest that the British led Lawrence to believe they were backing his attempts to gain Arab independence. Instead, as soon as the Arabs helped them beat the Turks, the British took control of the countries once ruled by the Turks.

WEB QUEST

In 2011, what Arab country was profoundly altered by events in a place called Tahrir Square? _____

In your own words, briefly describe the change that occurred.

_____

_____

When Should You Think About Inferring the Main Idea?

Any time you read a passage and can't find a general sentence that even partially sums up the main idea, look at all the specific statements supplied by the author and ask yourself what they suggest about the topic.

Look, for instance, at the following paragraph. The chains of repetition and reference running through the paragraph suggest the topic is "fear of spiders." Look over all the specific details related to that topic. Then at the end write what you think is the implied main idea of the paragraph.

[1]Ms. B, a twenty-three-year-old woman, complained of a phobia, or fear, of spiders that she had had for as long as she could remember.

[2]She had no history of any other psychiatric symptoms. [3]In treatment, when first approached with a closed glass jar containing spiders, she breathed heavily, wept, and rated her distress as extremely high. [4]Suddenly she began scratching the back of her hand, stating she felt as though spiders were crawling under her skin, although she knew this was not really the case. [5]The sensation lasted only a few seconds and did not recur. [6]Her total treatment consisted of four one-hour sessions distributed over the span of a month. [7]At completion, she had lost all fear of spiders and was able to let them crawl freely about her arms, legs, and face, as well as inside her clothing, with no distress. [8]She remained free of fear at a one-year follow-up exam and expressed disbelief that she had allowed such a "silly fear" to dominate her life for so long (Curtis, 1981, p. 1095). (Adapted from Sue et al., *Understanding Abnormal Behavior*, 8th ed., p. 136.)

If your implied main idea goes something like, "Ms. B's treatment helped her overcome her fear of spiders," you drew a logical inference. It's logical because it is solidly based on the following details:

1. Ms. B arrived for treatment unable to even look at spiders without having a violent reaction.

2. She then had four one-hour treatments.

3. After the treatments, she did not have a violent reaction and was actually able to let spiders crawl on her body.

Now, of course, you could claim that Ms. B's new response was a miracle. But that wouldn't be a logical inference. It wouldn't be based on or fit what's actually said in the paragraph, which explicitly describes the actions Ms. B took to combat her fear. The paragraph doesn't just say that Ms. B. suddenly and miraculously stopped being afraid of spiders. If it did, then calling her response a miracle would make more sense.

To be logical, reading inferences have to derive, or come from, what's actually said in the paragraph. You must, that is, be able to say: This is the implied main idea *because* of these words and statements. If you cannot point to anything in the paragraph that supports your version of the implied main idea, you and the author are no longer thinking along the same lines.

READING TIPS

1. Paragraphs that open with a question along with paragraphs that compare and contrast two topics often imply rather than state the main idea.

2. In paragraphs that imply the main idea, many of the sentences are likely to be equally specific.

SUMMING UP THE KEY POINTS

1. If the topic sentence uses a pronoun in place of the topic, make sure to mentally link the pronoun to the correct antecedent.

2. When two or three sentences in the paragraph almost but not quite sum up the main idea about the paragraph's topic, consider combining them into a main idea statement that would function just like a topic sentence.

3. If no general sentence seems to sum up a main idea about the topic, and you can't find any sentences that even come close, then you need to look at all the specific statements in the paragraph and consider what idea they suggest when taken together.

4. Inferring implied main ideas is a two-step process. First, you need to understand what each sentence contributes to your knowledge of the topic. Next, you need to ask yourself what all the sentences combine to suggest about the topic. The answer to that question is the implied main idea of the paragraph.

VOCABULARY ROUND UP 1

Below are five words introduced in pages 368–72. The words are accompanied by more detailed definitions, the page on which they originally appeared, and additional sample sentences. Spend time reviewing the words and their meanings because you will see them again in review tests at the end of the chapter. Use the online dictionary Wordnik to find additional sentences illustrating the words in context. (*Note:* If you know of another dictionary, online or in print, with as many examples of words in context feel free to use that one instead.)

1. **eradicate** (p. 368): eliminate, wipe out, remove all traces of. "The new ruler tried to *eradicate* all traces of the previous leader."

2. **squalid** (p. 369): poverty-stricken, having a poor or wretched appearance. "*Vanity Fair* is a famous novel in which a young woman rises above her *squalid* surroundings and climbs up the social ladder."

3. **missionary** (p. 370): a person who goes to foreign countries to do religious or charitable work. "The *missionaries* who tried to turn Native Americans into good Christians had no respect for the customs and language of the people they were determined to save."

4. **prominently** (p. 371): obviously, openly, overtly, immediately noticeable. "The jewelry was *prominently* displayed in the store window; the price tags, however, were nowhere to be seen."

5. **archaeological** (p. 372): related to discovering the remains of lost civilizations. "It was rumored that everyone who had been on the *archaeological* expedition had died a sudden death, but, like many such rumors, this one turned out to be nonsense."

◆ **EXERCISE 5**   **Recognizing the Implied Main Idea**

DIRECTIONS   Each item in this exercise contains four sentences that combine to imply a main idea. Circle the letter of that implied main idea.

EXAMPLE

a. During the nineteenth century, factory owners hired young orphans, whom they could force to work fifteen hours a day.

b. Many factory owners preferred hiring women, who could move quickly among the machinery and were easily frightened by threats of dismissal.

c. Whenever possible, the employers increased their profits by reducing the workers' wages.

d. Workers who complained about the hours or poor working conditions were promptly fired; whenever possible, employers saw to it that rebellious workers were thrown into jail.

Implied Main Idea   (a.) Nineteenth-century factory owners cruelly exploited the men, women, and children who worked for them.

b. In the nineteenth century, factory owners were quick to hire women because they were too timid to make any demands.

c. In the nineteenth century, children were expected to work rather than play.

EXPLANATION   The first four sentences give examples of the way nineteenth-century employers abused *all* their employees, not just women and children. Thus, *a* is the only implied main idea that follows from all the specific statements given. It's certainly the only sentence that could summarize the first four.

1. a. On October 15, 1917, the famed Dutch dancer Mata Hari was brought before a French firing squad and executed as a spy.

   b. Although Mata Hari had agreed to spy for the Germans, there is no evidence that she ever gave them any information.

   c. Information about a new British tank, said to have been given to the Germans by Mata Hari, was actually provided by a British prisoner of war.

   d. The case against Mata Hari was based largely on telegrams supplied by the head of France's espionage agency, who had tampered with them before the trial.

Implied Main Idea
   a. Mata Hari was executed not because she was a spy but because she was hated by the head of France's espionage bureau.

   b. Mata Hari may not have been guilty of the crimes that earned her a death sentence.

   c. There is no evidence Mata Hari agreed to spy for the Germans.

2. a. Thanks to Henry Ford's invention of a cheap automobile—called the first "people's car"—farmers from small rural towns were able to sell their products to larger markets located some distance away.

   b. Ford's Model T was introduced in 1908 and priced at $850; by 1923 it cost only $290, and people from all walks of life had the chance to own a car.

   c. Ford's Model T was so famous, popular songs and jokes alluded to it.

   d. In the early part of the twentieth century, almost half the American population lived in the country, but Ford's Model T made access to city life much easier, and the rural population began to diminish.

Implied Main Idea

    a. The invention of the Model T had a profound effect on American life.

    b. Henry Ford was determined to make a car that even working people could afford.

    c. Henry Ford was a genius when it came to making money.

3. a. The month of January got its name from Janus, the Roman god of beginnings.

    b. Saturday was named after Saturn, the Roman god of agriculture.

    c. The sporting goods company Nike took its name from the Greek goddess of victory.

    d. The planet Neptune was named after the Roman god of the sea.

Implied Main Idea

    a. The gods and goddesses of Greek and Roman mythology had exotic and colorful names.

    b. The names of the ancient gods and goddesses live on in our language.

    c. Our calendar is a constant reminder of Greek mythology's long-lasting influence.

READING TIP

The main idea you infer from the specific details should sum up the paragraph in the same way a topic sentence does.

◆ **EXERCISE 6**   **Matching Details to Implied Main Ideas**

DIRECTIONS   Read each paragraph. The implied main idea is written in the blank above the partially completed passage. One detail supporting that implied main idea is missing, however. Circle the letter of the detail that would make the most sense in relation to the implied main idea.

EXAMPLE

Implied Main Idea   The figure of the wolf is a common one in American idioms.*

_____

*idioms: expressions that develop from usage in a specific language and can't easily be translated word for word, a fact that confuses new speakers of the language. "*Don't burn your bridges*" before quitting" is an example.

Perhaps because wolves over the years have menaced farmers' livestock, we are likely to call a smiling enemy "a wolf in sheep's clothing." The implication of the idiom is that the person pretending to be our friend is actually a threat and not to be trusted. We also use the idiom "wolfing down" food as a way of indicating that the person doing the eating is gobbling food like a hungry animal. Then there's the idiom to "cry wolf," meaning that a person's calls for help are no longer thought trustworthy. The person sounding the alarm is considered untrustworthy because he or she has too often called out for help when no real danger was present.

a. And let's not forget the big bad wolf in "Little Red Riding Hood"; he's a fairy-tale figure that has been around for centuries.

(b.) Then, too, we frequently call a person who likes to be alone a good deal, "a lone wolf."

c. And finally, we have to consider how wolves have been hunted almost to extinction.

EXPLANATION The correct answer is *b*. It's the only sentence relevant to the implied main idea, which focuses on idioms. Answer *a* discusses wolves in fairy tales, not idioms. Answer *c* picks up on the image of the wolf being part of the landscape, introduced in sentence 1. However, here again the topic of the paragraph is idioms that use the figure of the wolf. The paragraph is not focused on wolves in the natural world.

Implied Main Idea **1.** Warren G. Harding wasn't exactly presidential material.

Those who claim that U.S. presidents must be exceptionally smart to be elected president might want to consider the career of our twenty-ninth president, Warren G. Harding (1921–1923). Harding was considered none too bright by most of the people he worked with. An incurious man, he mainly liked to play poker, golf, drink, and chase women. Thought by many historians to be one of the worst presidents in history, Harding never really wanted the job. But his wife, Florence, did, and Harding let Florence stage manage most of his political career. Prodded by Florence, Harding rose from one office to another, managing to never distinguish* himself. Elected to the U.S. Senate in 1914, he was absent for two of the most important political debates—on women's suffrage, or right to vote, and

*distinguish: to make one's self respected or famous; also to recognize a difference.

Prohibition. What Harding had going for him were his magnificent looks. As his admirers as well as his critics liked to point out, Harding *looked* presidential. He also had a magnificent speaking voice, even if he had little to say.

a. Harding gave few speeches during his campaign for the presidency, which was conducted mainly from his front porch, but his reluctance to campaign across the nation did not keep him from winning the office he sought.

b. Still, Harding defeated his opponent by a landslide and was remarkably popular throughout the two years of his presidency, which ended when he unexpectedly died of a stroke.

c. According to a former Secretary of the Treasury, William McAdoo, Harding had mastered the art of making flowery speeches that consisted of "pompous phrases moving over the landscape in search of an idea."

Implied Main Idea **2.** The consumption of alcohol and worries about its use have been

with us for a very long time.

It's generally believed that during the Stone Age, humans chewed berries or grapes in order to make themselves giddy and lightheaded, similar to the way we now feel after consuming a couple of glasses of wine or beer. By 3000 BCE, the Egyptians had perfected the art of manufacturing beer and wine. By the first century CE, the process of distillation† had been invented and was being used to make more potent* alcoholic beverages. In the Middle Ages, even monks in monasteries were perfecting the manufacture of fine wines. Although some of those wines were used in religious ceremonies, many of the finer wines were sold to wealthy wine lovers. In America at least, the early nineteenth century witnessed increasing anxiety over liquor consumption. The Temperance† movement emerged with women, in particular, insisting on the need for a reduction in the consumption of alcohol.

---

†distillation: the process of heating a liquid until it separates into its individual components or parts.
*potent: strong, powerful.
*Temperance movement: movement to reduce alcohol consumption.

a. By the early twentieth century, worries about alcohol consumption had grown even greater, and in 1919 the Constitution was amended to prohibit the sale of alcohol throughout the United States.

b. The Eighteenth Amendment to the Constitution, prohibiting the sale of alcohol, is the only amendment ever to have been repealed, or revoked.

c. In a unique historical moment, the Twenty-First Amendment to the Constitution was introduced with the sole purpose of repealing the Eighteenth Amendment.

Questions for Evaluating Inferences
◆

1. **Is your inference solidly based on statements in the paragraph?** If asked to defend the main idea you inferred, you should be able to point to specific words and sentences that support it.

2. **Are you relying more on the author's words than on your own personal point of view?** Don't draw an inference based mainly on what you think or feel about the subject. When drawing inferences, it's the writer's mind you have to read, not your own.

3. **Are you sure that none of the author's statements contradict your inference?** If any of the sentences in a passage contradict the idea you've inferred, you probably haven't hit upon the main idea the author intended.

4. **Do the sentences in the paragraph connect to the main idea you inferred?** If you jot your inference in the margins, you should immediately see how the supporting details help develop it.

◆ **EXERCISE 7**   **Recognizing Implied Main Ideas**

DIRECTIONS   Read each paragraph. Then circle the letter of the implied main idea.

1. In the past, many men and women decided to become flight attendants because they were attracted to the glamorous, fun, jet-setting lifestyle that came with the job. Now, however, flight attendants are spending most of their workdays dealing with rude, disgruntled passengers who are frustrated by delays, crowded flights, and the disappearance of perks like free food. These cranky travelers often leave their manners in the airport terminal and bombard flight attendants with complaints. Flight attendants must also worry about the

possibility of terrorism. Since the terrorist hijackings of four airliners on September 11, 2001, flight attendants have to carefully scrutinize passengers' behavior, check suspicious baggage, and take additional security measures. What's more, the crew must endure the stress and anxiety of working in an environment that is a terrorist target. Working in an industry that is struggling financially, flight attendants also now worry constantly about layoffs and wage or benefit cuts.

Implied Main Idea

a. The airline industry is in a state of massive confusion.

b. The job of flight attendant has lost much of its glamour.

c. The September 11, 2001, terrorist attacks have significantly affected the airline industry.

2. Adolescent yearnings for independence often lead to some withdrawal from family members and to arguments with parents over issues of autonomy and decision making. Some distancing from parents may be healthy during adolescence, as young people form meaningful relationships outside the family and develop a sense of independence and social competence. As it turns out, and despite popular misconceptions to the contrary, most adolescents and their parents express love and respect for each other and agree on many of the principal issues in life. Though disagreements with parents are common, serious and prolonged conflict is neither normal nor helpful for adolescents. (Adapted from Nevid, *Psychology*, 3rd ed., p. 374.)

Implied Main Idea

a. While there is some benefit to adolescents withdrawing somewhat from their parents, a major break is neither typical nor beneficial.

b. Adolescents need to learn how to live on their own, and it's healthy for them to pull away from their parents.

c. Adolescents who withdraw from their parents are the exception; in general, adolescents feel affection and respect for their parents.

3. Already in 1967, a study done at Harvard Medical School showed that during meditation, people use 17 percent less oxygen, lower their heart rates by three beats per minute, and increase the type of brain waves that occur during the state of relaxation preceding sleep. More recent studies of the brain have confirmed that meditation shifts activity from the right hemisphere of the prefrontal cortex[†] to the left

---

[†]prefrontal cortex: Part of the brain that is highly developed in humans, the prefrontal cortex plays a large role in regulating thought, emotion, and behavior.

hemisphere. As a result, the brain switches to a calmer, more content state. For this reason, meditation can eliminate the need for medication to treat anxiety, tension, and even pain. In fact, many individuals are managing the pain of chronic diseases or injuries not with painkillers but with meditation, which helps people learn to accept their discomfort rather than struggle against it. Other patients suffering from diseases like cancer are meditating to actually boost their immune systems. Studies show that people who meditate have higher levels of disease-fighting antibodies in their blood.

Implied Main Idea

    a. Meditation offers some significant health benefits.

    b. Meditation is growing in popularity.

    c. Meditation can sharpen one's ability to think.

4. Was the 5,300-year-old, mummified body discovered in 1991 and now known as the "Iceman" killed, or did he freeze to death after being caught in a storm? One of the hikers who discovered the body in the Italian Alps said that before the Iceman was freed from a melting glacier, he had been clutching a knife in one hand. In 2001, an Italian radiologist discovered an arrowhead embedded in the shoulder of the Iceman; its position indicated that he had been hit from behind. Medical examiners have found a deep gash in one of the corpse's hands, in addition to a cut on his other hand and bruises on his body. Furthermore, DNA specialists have analyzed blood found on the arrows the Iceman was carrying. They have also found blood on the back of his cloak and his knife. They say that this blood came from four different people. The blood of two people was found on the same arrow in the Iceman's quiver, suggesting that this arrow had struck two different individuals and then been pulled free.

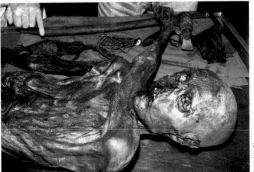

A well-preserved corpse, now known as the "Iceman," was found in the Italian Alps in 1991.

Europics/Newscom.

Implied Main Idea

a. Scientists cannot decide if the Iceman froze to death or was murdered.

b. Evidence suggests that the Iceman was probably killed in a fight.

c. DNA testing has finally proven that the Iceman died after being shot in the back with an arrow.

5. Dogs trained by the military are remarkably effective at locating improvised explosive devices (IEDs). IEDs are composed of chemicals, not metals, making them especially hard to detect via electronic monitoring systems. Dogs, however, can sniff the explosives out and that talent has made them a common sight on the fields of war. In addition to bomb detection, dogs in the military are widely used to help treat soldiers with post-traumatic stress disorder, or PTSD, both at home and in the field of war. But their service comes with a price. Military veterinarians have noted that dogs who spend many months on the battlefield often start exhibiting behavior that is similar to some of their human companions. The sound of gunfire, for instance, can suddenly begin to elicit wild barking, even if in the past the dog seemed to tolerate it without anxiety. Other battle-weary dogs will start refusing to go into buildings or enter cars. Giving the dogs more time off from the job seems to help. The anti-anxiety drug Xanax also seems to help.

Implied Main Idea

a. Dogs trained in the military are a huge help to soldiers on the ground.

b. Dogs trained in the military usually end up completely broken by the horrors of war.

c. Some military dogs seem to be suffering their own version of PTSD.

CHECK YOUR UNDERSTANDING

1. When writers put parts of the main idea into different sentences, what should readers do?

_____

2. When writers don't give readers even parts of topic sentences, how should readers respond?

_____

_____

Reviewing Logical and Illogical Inferences

You've already looked closely at logical and illogical inferences in relation to visual material. Now, it's worth your while to consider this concept in relation to written paragraphs as well.

To see the difference between logical and illogical inferences, read the following passage about Joan of Arc. Then look carefully at the two possible implied main ideas or inferences that follow. One is a logical inference that follows from, or is based on, the paragraph. The other is an illogical inference. It reflects the reader's point of view more than the author's. Your job is to decide which is which.

> Joan of Arc, the national heroine and patron saint of France, was born in 1412 to a family of poor peasants. In 1425, at the age of thirteen, Joan claimed to hear voices that she believed belonged to the early Christian saints and martyrs.* Four years later, in 1429, those same voices told her to help the young king of France Charles VII fight the British, who were trying to take control of France in the Hundred Years War.† When the king believed her story and gave her troops to command, Joan put on a suit of armor and led her soldiers to victory. Yet when the British captured Joan in 1430 and tried her for heresy* and wearing masculine dress, Charles refused to help her, allowing her to be condemned to death. On May 30, 1431, Joan was burned at the stake, still swearing loyalty to the king of France.

---

*martyrs: people willing to die for their faith or to save the lives of others.
†Hundred Years War (1337–1453): an episodic struggle on land that lasted a century and varied from times of peace to periods of intense violence.
*heresy: challenging church law.

Which of the following implied main ideas effectively sums up the above paragraph?

Implied Main Idea 1 Even though Joan of Arc sacrificed her life to save his throne, the king of France failed to return her loyalty.

Implied Main Idea 2 Although she died swearing her loyalty to the king of France, Joan of Arc must have hated him for his betrayal.

Did you decide that the first implied main idea was a more logical inference than the second? If you did, you are absolutely correct. The paragraph definitely implies that Joan sacrificed everything for a king who did not return her loyalty

Statement 2, in contrast, is an illogical inference. It could easily lead the reader away from the writer's real point. There is simply no evidence in the paragraph to support the notion that Joan hated the king for his betrayal. On the contrary, the last sentence of the paragraph contradicts the idea that Joan hated the king.

SUMMING UP THE KEY POINTS

1. Logical inferences
   - follow from or are based on what's said in the paragraph.
   - do not favor the reader's experience or knowledge over the author's words.
   - are not contradicted by any statements appearing in the paragraph.
   - do not divert the reader from the author's intended meaning.
   - could function as the topic sentence

2. Illogical inferences
   - give more weight to the reader's thoughts than they do the author's words.
   - are based on a few stray words or one or two sentences rather than most of the sentences in the paragraph.
   - are likely to be contradicted by one or more statements appearing in the paragraph.
   - couldn't effectively function as topic sentences.
   - are likely to lead readers away from the author's intended meaning.

VOCABULARY ROUND UP 2

Below are five words introduced in pages 378–85. The words are accompanied by more detailed definitions, the page on which they originally appeared, and additional sample sentences. Spend time reviewing the words and their meanings because you will see them again in review tests at the end of the chapter. Use the online dictionary Wordnik to find additional sentences illustrating the words in context. (*Note*: If you know of another dictionary, online or in print, with as many examples of words in context feel free to use that one instead.)

1. **idioms** (p. 378): expressions that develop from usage in a specific language and can't easily be translated word for word, a fact that confuses new speakers of the language. "When the student from Chile heard one friend tell another that he shouldn't burn his bridges, the Chilean student didn't understand the *idiom* and was worried that he had become friends with an arsonist."

2. **distinguish** (p. 379): make one's self respected or famous; to recognize a difference. (1) "As a young man, Chicago mayor Rahm Emanuel hoped to *distinguish* himself as a ballet dancer, but he ended up making a career in politics instead." (2) "You can *distinguish* African elephants from European ones by looking at their ears."

3. **potent** (p. 380): strong, powerful. "Margaritas look like lemonade, but they are actually extremely *potent* and after two of them, you will feel the room start to spin."

4. **martyrs** (p. 385): people willing to die for their faith or to save the lives of others. "Many people consider Archbishop Oscar Romero to be a *martyr*, who died in an effort to improve the lives of El Salvador's poor."

5. **heresy** (p. 385): challenging church law or traditional thinking. "When the fifteenth-century scientist Galileo[†] thought he might be burned at the stake for *heresy*, he quickly took back his claim that the earth revolved around the sun and reverted to the church's belief—that the sun revolved around earth."

[†]Galileo: an Italian scientist (1564–1642) who constructed a telescope that allowed him to get an accurate sense of how the planets related to the sun.

◆ EXERCISE 8   Identifying Implied Main Ideas That Follow from the Text

DIRECTIONS   Read each paragraph. Then circle the letter of the implied main idea. *Note:* Be sure the answer you choose fits the description of a logical inference.

1. The drug called cocaine was formally identified in 1855. By the 1870s, surgeons used it as an anesthetic for minor surgery. In the 1880s, it was used to treat opium addiction, alcoholism, and depression. The drug came to the notice of the young Sigmund Freud when he read reports of how small doses could restore the spirits of soldiers exhausted by war. Freud was so enthusiastic about the beneficial uses to which cocaine could be put he prescribed it for a young colleague who was addicted to morphine. The drug, however, did not cure the addiction. Instead, the young man began hallucinating wildly. Believing that snakes were crawling under his skin, he committed suicide, leaving Freud devastated by what he had done.

Implied Main Idea
    a. Sigmund Freud believed the reports of cocaine's beneficial effects and prescribed it for his patients.

    b. Sigmund Freud never got over the mistake he made when he prescribed cocaine for a colleague who then killed himself.

    c. Sigmund Freud was sadly mistaken in his early enthusiasm for cocaine.

    d. Sigmund Freud's own drug addiction was the source of a tragic mistake concerning his young colleague.

2. Entrants in the "Little Miss of America" beauty pageant—girls between the ages of three and six—are not asked to pay a fee. Their indulgent* parents, however, willingly pay hundreds of dollars just to have their children's photographs included in the pageant catalog. They also must pay for the singing and dancing lessons that will allow their child to participate in the talent section of the contest. But perhaps even more costly than the lessons are the extensive* wardrobes of party dresses and costumes that the girls must have in order to participate in the contest and its related functions. Furthermore, traveling expenses for the children and the relatives who accompany them can easily run into thousands of dollars.

*indulgent: ready to spoil, overly fond.
*extensive: wide-ranging, large, covering a lot of territory.

Implied Main Idea

a. It costs a lot of money to enter the Little Miss of America beauty contest.

b. Little girls should not be encouraged to participate in beauty pageants.

c. When parents enter their little girls into beauty pageants, they have no idea of the costs associated with being in the pageant.

d. Parents who enter their children in beauty contests are doing their children great harm, whether or not they know it.

3. On January 30, 1889, young Crown Prince Rudolf of Austria was found shot to death in his hunting lodge on the outskirts of Vienna. Lying next to him was the body of his lover, seventeen-year-old Baroness Marie Vetsera. She, too, had been shot. In the years since that tragic event, some have claimed that Rudolf ended his life because he was depressed over a terminal* illness. According to this theory, when Marie found him, she decided to take her life. Others insist, however, that Rudolf was murdered by members of the court who feared his progressive* beliefs would become public policy when Rudolf reached the throne. According to another theory, Marie and Rudolf entered into a suicide pact when their parents forbade the couple to marry.

Implied Main Idea

a. Although there are many theories about how Crown Prince Rudolf and Marie Vetsera died, the theory that they were murdered makes the most sense.

b. No one really knows for sure how Crown Prince Rudolf and Marie Vetsera died.

c. Love drove Crown Prince Rudolf of Austria to suicide.

d. In despair at their inability to wed, Crown Prince Rudolf and Marie Vetsera decided to die together.

4. Can babies inside the womb hear what's going on outside of the mother's body? Although earlobes start to form in the eighth week of pregnancy, it takes three months for the ears to become fully functional. At that point, the baby can hear the mother's heartbeat or her growling stomach. Moms-to-be report that babies also respond to voices outside the womb, particularly the mother's. Although infants in the

*terminal: ending in death, having a limit or boundary.
*progressive: forward-thinking, open-to-change.

womb respond to voices in general, their heartbeat is more likely to slow at the sound of the mother's voice. This suggests that, to some degree, infants can not only hear but also distinguish between voices. Sonograms have also revealed that babies in the womb turn their heads in response to noises. They also jerk or kick at the sound of loud and unexpected noises like a car backfiring or a door slamming.

Implied Main Idea

a. There is evidence that babies do hear what's going on outside the womb.

b. Without question, babies remember everything they experience in the womb.

c. Babies inside the womb can hear the sounds of the mother's body very clearly but they hear sounds outside the womb just faintly.

d. Already in the womb, babies seem to have highly developed tastes for what they like to hear.

From Reader to Writer Using paragraph 4 as a model, write a paragraph that opens with a question about little girls participating in beauty pageants, e.g., What's wrong with little girls participating in beauty pageants? Why are some people opposed to preteen girls participating in beauty pageants? Answer the question with a topic sentence and supporting details, or let a series of specific sentences imply or suggest your answer to the reader.

◆ EXERCISE 9   Inferring the Implied Main Idea

DIRECTIONS   Read each paragraph. Then, in the blanks that follow, write the implied main idea of the paragraph.

EXAMPLE   The plow was invented during the Middle Ages. Thanks to its invention, farmers could dig more deeply into the soil and do it with much greater ease. That meant they could farm more land, using less labor. Another important innovation* in the Middle Ages was the collar harness. The old yoke harness had worked well with oxen, but tended to choke horses. With the collar harness, farmers could exchange oxen for horses. Horses had more staying power and worked faster than oxen. Thus farmers could work fewer hours while still covering the same amount of ground. The Middle Ages also saw the invention of the water mill. With water-powered mills, farmers could grind more corn with less effort.

—————————
*innovation: introduction of something new.

Implied Main Idea   *During the Middle Ages, several important inventions made farming easier and more*

productive.

> **EXPLANATION**   The paragraph describes three specific inventions that appeared in the Middle Ages. Each of those inventions helped farmers do more work with less effort. Because this inference is general enough to include all three inventions, it effectively sums up the implied main idea of the paragraph.

1. Anyone who orders a milk shake in Rhode Island and expects a drink made with ice cream is in for a surprise. In Rhode Island, a "milk shake" contains no ice cream. It's made only of milk and flavored syrup. If you want ice cream in your drink, you'd better call it a "cabinet." The name comes from the wooden cabinet encasing the mixer that shakes up the milk. Similarly, anyone in search of a long sandwich made with layers of meat and cheese should ask for a "sub" or a "hero" in the North. But in the South, you had better request a "poor boy," or the waiter will be confused. If you want a soda in Boston, you should probably ask for a "tonic." However, if you are in Minneapolis, you'd better ask for a "pop," or else you're likely to get a glass of flavored seltzer water.

Implied Main Idea   _____

_____

2. Body modification, the altering of the body for non-medical reasons, may seem odd to those not given to the practice. But there are those who believe that consciously modifying, or changing, the body is a way of taking control of one's life and identity. To that end, no risk or expense is too much. Corneal tattooing, for instance, used to be done to improve the appearance of an eye that had some injury or defect. But now it is more frequently done by a tattoo artist, who, upon request, can put a heart, a star, or a patch of blue in the corner of a person's eye. Can the procedure go wrong and end in blindness? It certainly can. But to the committed believer in body modification, the risk is worth it. For some young women, corset piercings have become a desirable body modification. To achieve the right look, the women have their back pierced in two vertical columns. That way a ribbon can be laced through eyelet closures tacked into the skin, giving the naked back the appearance of an old-fashioned

find additional sentences illustrating the words in context. (*Note*: If you know of another dictionary, online or in print, with as many examples of words in context feel free to use that one instead.)

1. **indulgent** (p. 388): overly fond, lenient; inclined to spoil. "Steve Jobs's parents were such *indulgent* parents, they couldn't say no to their gifted and determined son."

2. **extensive** (p. 388): having a wide range, covering a lot of territory, varied. "In the eighteenth century, Japan had *extensive* trade relationships with the Dutch."

3. **terminal** (p. 389): ending in death; having a limit or boundary; a place where trains, buses, or planes arrive and depart. (1) "After the disease was diagnosed as *terminal* cancer, she made a list of things to do before she died." (2) "They stopped looking for the boy because the swamp was the *terminal* point for the search."

4. **progressive** (p. 389): forward-thinking, open to change. "Said, the son of Moammar Gadhafi, was considered the most *progressive* member of the Gadhafi family, but when his father's bloody rule was challenged, Said showed his true colors."

5. **innovation** (p. 390): introduction or creation of something new, the newly created product or process. "*Innovation* usually relies heavily on trial and error; in other words, originality tends to be inefficient."

Inferring Supporting Details

Main ideas are not the only text element readers need to infer. Inferences also play a big role in making supporting details meaningful. For an illustration, read the following example. As you do, consider what information you have to infer in order to fully understand what the supporting details contribute to the main idea.

Topic Sentence

Notice how the reader has to supply the meaning

[1]According to social exchange theory, the development and continuation of intimate relationships are associated with the rewards and costs involved. [2]Research has shown that dating couples who experience an increase in rewards as their relationship progresses are likely to stay

appropriate to the context. These are not financial rewards and costs.

The reader also has to figure out how the comparison level contributes to expectations.

together. ³In contrast, dating couples who experience fewer reward increases are less likely to stay together. ⁴Rewards and costs, however, do not arise on their own and in isolation. ⁵People bring to their relationships certain expectations. ⁶John Thibaut and Harold Kelley coined the term "comparison level" (CL) to refer to the expected outcome in relationships. ⁷A person with a high CL expects his or her relationships to be rewarding. ⁸Someone with a low CL does not. ⁹Even a bad relationship can look pretty good to someone who has a low CL. (Adapted from Brehm, Kassin, and Fein, *Social Psychology*, 5th ed., p. 208.)

Inferring the Meanings Appropriate to the Context

Note that the writers of the paragraph on social exchange theory do not specifically define the meanings of the two key words, *rewards* and *costs*, even though both words need to be understood in a particular way: as emotional rather than financial rewards and costs. If those two words aren't defined in this way, the social exchange theory wouldn't make much sense when applied to intimate relationships. Yet the writers don't supply those specific meanings. They just supply the context for the two words. It's up to readers to draw the right inferences.

Inferring Relationships and Adding Information

The need for reader-supplied supporting details, however, does not end with the definitions of these two words. Sentences 2 and 3 can only develop the topic sentence if readers draw a bridging inference. They have to infer a cause-and-effect relationship in which one event produces another. Dating couples who get an increased number of rewards stay together *because* they like the rewards. Similarly, couples who experience fewer rewards are less likely to stay together *because* there aren't enough rewards in the relationship.

Even sentence 4, which looks so simple, requires readers to infer two implied phrases shown here in brackets: "Rewards and costs [*within couple relationships*] do not arise on their own or in isolation [*from all other influences*]." In short, this entire paragraph only makes sense if the reader is willing to work with the author and supply the necessary content and connections.

READING TIP

Writers don't always identify relationships with specific transitions like *however* and *for example*. It's up to you, the reader, to keep asking yourself, What does the sentence I am currently reading have to do with the one that came before?

SUMMING UP THE KEY POINTS

1. The need to draw inferences in reading does not apply solely to main ideas. It also applies to supporting details, where readers sometimes need to supply part of the content.

2. In addition to information, readers may also need to infer the connections between sentences, figuring out for themselves why one sentence follows another.

◆ EXERCISE 10   Drawing Inferences About Supporting Details

DIRECTIONS   Read each paragraph and underline the topic sentence. Then circle the appropriate letter to identify the inference readers need to add to the supporting details.

EXAMPLE   ¹Knowledge about emotions is learned, at least in part, from parents. ²Children who display knowledge about emotions—who can label emotional expressions on faces, describe the feelings of another person in an emotional situation, and talk about the causes of emotions—typically have mothers willing to discuss and explain the power of emotions. ³In the context of learning about emotions, these mothers are good "coaches." ⁴However, when parents react negatively to children expressing emotion (e.g., "You're overreacting!"), children's understanding of emotions is poorer and, as a result, the children are less socially competent. ⁵Parents who engage in such negative behaviors are missing opportunities to explain to their children the key elements of emotional responses. ⁶The extreme case is represented by children who are physically abused or neglected by their parents. ⁷These children lack the ability to call up the emotional expressions appropriate to particular situations, such as going to the zoo and getting a balloon or losing a pet to disease. (Adapted from Bukatko and Daehler, *Child Development*, 5th ed., p. 393.)

1. To make sentences 2 and 3 fit together in a meaningful way, which inference does the reader need to add to the supporting details?

   a. Mothers who criticize their children for not expressing how they feel create adults who are emotionally cold.

   (b.) Mothers open to talking about their own emotions provide role models that help their children deal with their own emotional life.

   c. Some mothers who are open to discussing emotions are likely to do so only when their children express negative emotions.

2. To make sentences 6 and 7 fit together in a meaningful way, which inference do readers need to add to the supporting details?

   a. Parents who discourage their children from showing emotion do so because they themselves don't know how to express their feelings.

   b. When parents discourage their children from showing emotion, they do so because they equate showing emotion with weakness.

   (c.) Abused children, whose emotional responses often don't fit the social situation, probably don't have parents who coach them on how to express feelings of happiness or sadness.

EXPLANATION   Sentence 2 tells us that children who know how to handle their emotions typically have a mother willing to discuss her own emotions. But the authors don't tell us exactly how the mother's ability is handed on to her offspring. Instead, in sentence 3, the authors use the word *coaches* to imply that some mothers teach their children about emotions in the same way coaches teach kids about sports. However, it's up to readers to draw that inference, which is answer *b*.

Although the authors don't say it explicitly, it's very unlikely that abusive or neglectful parents would spend much time coaching their children in how to go about handling their emotions. This is the inference readers have to draw for the second question, making answer *c* correct.

1. [1]What would become one of the most dramatic symbols of the civil rights movement occurred in Mississippi in 1955. [2]In September, Emmett Till, a fourteen-year-old black youth from Chicago, visited relatives near Greenwood, Mississippi. [3]After buying some candy at a local store, Till supposedly said "Bye, baby" to the white female clerk. [4]Three days later, after midnight, the girl's husband and

brother dragged Till from his relatives' home, shot him through the head, brutally beat him, and dumped his body in the Tallahatchie River. [5]After her son's death, Till's mother insisted on an open casket at the funeral so that, in her words, "All the world can see what they did to my boy." [6]The image of Till's mutilated body, captured on television, seared itself into the consciousness of a generation of black leaders. [7]Yet despite overwhelming evidence of guilt, an all-white, all-male jury found the two white suspects innocent of kidnapping.

(Adapted from Gillon and Matson, *The American Experiment*, 2nd ed., p. 1123.)

1. To make sentences 3 and 4 fit together in a meaningful way, which inference do readers need to add to the supporting details?

   a. The husband and brother of the female clerk were outraged that a black man would speak in such a familiar way to a white woman.

   b. Emmett Till was dragged from his relatives' home by people who were ready to make trouble with the first person who crossed their path.

   c. The people who kidnapped Emmett Till were trying to avenge a similar crime that had been committed against another teenage boy who was white.

2. To make sentences 5–7 fit together in a meaningful way, which inference do readers need to add to the supporting details?

   a. Till's mother never really cared about her son, and she showed her feelings by leaving the casket of her son open for all to view.

   b. The mother's attempt to make others experience her grief succeeded with a generation of black leaders but seemed not to have affected the white jurors sitting in judgment on the men who kidnapped and killed Till.

   c. Till's mother was so distraught from grief, she could not think straight.

2. [1]The turning point of the 1960 presidential campaign came in a series of four televised debates between September 26 and October 24. [2]Facing off against Richard M. Nixon, John F. Kennedy used the debates—the first-ever televised debates between presidential contenders—to demolish the Republican charge that he was inexperienced and poorly informed. [3]And he succeeded far better than his opponent in communicating the qualities of

boldness, imagination, and poise. [4]Kennedy appeared alert, aggressive, and cool. [5]Nixon, who perspired profusely, looked nervous and uncomfortable. [6]Not surprisingly, radio listeners divided evenly on who won the debate. [7]However, television viewers, the overwhelming majority, gave Kennedy a decisive edge. [8]The performance energized Kennedy's campaign, and the debates institutionalized television's role as a major force in American politics. (Adapted from Gillon and Matson, *The American Experiment*, 2nd ed., p. 1130.)

1. To make sentences 1–5 fit together in a meaningful way, which inference do readers need to add to the supporting details?

   a. Kennedy was also perspiring, but he knew how to stand in front of the camera so that his perspiration did not show.

   b. Kennedy was just as uncomfortable as Nixon was on television, but he didn't show it while Nixon did.

   c. The contrasting image of a cool Kennedy and a sweating Nixon made the 1960 debate a major turning point in the campaign.

2. To make sentences 6 and 7 fit together in a meaningful way, which inference do readers need to add to the supporting details?

   a. Because the reception was not good, people who listened to the debate on radio couldn't hear what the candidates said with the same clarity as those watching it on television.

   b. Kennedy had spent a good deal of time being coached on how to debate, whereas Nixon had not.

   c. People who saw the debate on television were heavily influenced by the appearance and manner of the two men, whereas people listening on radio were not.

CHECK YOUR UNDERSTANDING

What two kinds of inferences do readers need to add to supporting details?

_____

_____

_____

▶ **TEST 1**   **Reviewing Key Concepts**

DIRECTIONS   Answer the following questions by filling in the blanks or circling the letter of the correct response.

1. Readers who draw logical inferences base them heavily on _____
   _____.

2. Readers who draw illogical inferences are inclined to ignore ____
   _____ in favor of _____
   _____.

3. Readers need to avoid illogical inferences because they can have what effect?

   _____

4. If the topic sentence identifies the topic through a pronoun, the reader needs to be clear about the pronoun's _____.

5. When parts of the main idea appear in different sentences, it's the reader's job to _____.

6. If you have to infer the main idea of a paragraph, the main idea you infer should _____.

7. Inferences about relationships between sentences are called _____
   _____.

8. When it comes to supporting details, reader-supplied inferences

   a. are not as important as they are for main ideas.
   b. are seldom necessary.
   c. are as central to supporting details as they are to main ideas.

♦ **TEST 2**   **Linking Pronouns to Antecedents in Topic Sentences**

DIRECTIONS   Underline the topic sentence. Then rewrite it in the blanks, making sure to replace the pronoun with its antecedent. *Note*: If you need to, add any other necessary information that is implied but not stated in the topic sentence.

1. [1]Because of research indicating that drinking coffee contributes to diseases ranging from cancer to heart attacks, coffee has long been a guilty pleasure for many. [2]New research, however, suggests that it may actually offer significant health benefits. [3]For instance, researchers at the National Institute of Diabetes and Digestive Diseases found that coffee significantly reduces the risk of chronic liver disease. [4]Turning old research on its head, two studies of American nurses have shown that the biggest coffee drinkers actually have a lower risk for developing high blood pressure. [5]Drinking too much sometimes causes the heart to race, but the effect is apparently harmless. [6]Similarly, coffee's connections to breast cancer, osteoporosis, and dehydration have been exposed as weak and unproven. [7]What coffee does do is improve athletic ability by triggering a release of adrenaline that strengthens muscle contractions while improving speed and endurance. [8]And coffee's benefits aren't just physical. [9]Caffeine, functioning as a mild antidepressant, also helps to chase away the blues.

    _____

    _____

    _____

2. [1]Like the famed Titanic, the British cruise ship *Lusitania* was another "floating palace" that sank. [2]The target of a German torpedo, it plummeted into the depths of the ocean a little more than three years after the *Titanic*, on May 7, 1915, with similar tragic results. [3]The death toll for the *Lusitania* was a devastating 1,198 people (or 61 percent of those aboard). [4]Those victims, too, died from injuries, drowning, and cold exposure. [5]Images of the sinking ship still horrify to this day. [6]Because the ship sank in less water than the length of the ship, it ended up with the bow on the ocean floor and the stern facing the sky. [7]The tragedy also had significant international impact. [8]The ship had been carrying over one hundred Americans, and the public

outcry against the Germans was huge. [9]The United States government had, up to that point, been reluctant to enter World War I. [10]But the sinking of the *Lusitania* put an end to that reluctance.

———————————————————————————

———————————————————————————

———————————————————————————

3. [1]Wilbur and Orville Wright are usually credited with being the first to fly an airplane. [2]However, some people argue that New Zealand farmer Richard Pearse and aviation pioneer Gustave A. Whitehead were the first to do it. [3]Pearse designed his own engine-powered flying machine. [4]On March 31, 1903, his aircraft rose fifty yards into the air. [5]That was eight months before the first Wrights' flight. [6]But the only accounts of the flight are from eyewitnesses so Pearse has not generally been given credit for his achievement. [7]Whitehead built his first airplane with flapping wings in 1897 but failed to get it into the air. [8]He didn't give up, however. [9]He kept experimenting and flew his aircraft for the first time in Bridgeport, Connecticut, on August 14, 1901, more than two years before the Wrights' aircraft took flight. [10]Like Pearse, Whitehead's flight has been documented by witnesses, not photographs, and his accomplishment remains in dispute.

———————————————————————————

———————————————————————————

———————————————————————————

4. [1]In 2003, researchers at the Harvard University School of Public Health wanted to find out if it's healthier for men to express their anger or to keep angry feelings to themselves. [2]They conducted a study of 23,522 male health professionals, aged fifty to eight-five, and concluded that it's healthier for men to express anger than to keep it in under wraps. [3]Relying on questionnaires, researchers asked the subjects to identify how they behaved when they got angry. [4]The subjects were asked to choose among options such as "I argue with others" and "I do things like slam doors." [5]The study went on for two years and revealed that men who expressed their anger in moderate ways were half as likely to suffer from a non-fatal heart attack as men who almost never showed

their anger. [6]The study also showed that the risk of stroke decreased as the levels of anger expression increased.

_____

_____

_____

▶ **TEST 3**   **Constructing Main Idea Statements**

DIRECTIONS   Read each paragraph and look for sentences that sum up parts of what you think is the main idea. Combine those sentences and write the main idea statement on the blanks.

1. ¹The white-tailed deer was one of the first animals to be protected by legislation. ²But as it turns out, they don't need protection. ³The white-tailed deer has proven to be a highly adaptable creature. ⁴They have actually flourished and their population has not diminished despite the loss of wooded areas. ⁵In most cases, the wooded areas that have been demolished have been given over to suburban developments. ⁶Fortunately for the deer, suburban landscaping has provided quite a bit of vegetation to munch on, and they haven't minded adding, say, holly bushes to their diet. ⁷It's also true that suburbia is not welcoming to hunters. ⁸Thus the deer have generally been able to roam the suburban landscape without fear. ⁹Suburbanites also like gardens and, once again, woodland deer have been happy to expand their diet to include garden-grown produce.

Main Idea
Statement

_____

_____

_____

2. ¹Melvin L. Kohn was for many years chief of the Laboratory of Socioenvironmental Studies of the National Institute of Mental Health in Washington D.C. ²In 1956, he conducted a study of the values guiding child-rearing practices among American parents. ³The results revealed some notable class differences. ⁴For example, working-class parents (manual laborers and blue-collar workers) placed greater stress on such values as obedience, neatness, and cleanliness than did middle-class parents. ⁵Middle-class parents thought such values as curiosity, happiness, consideration for others, and especially self-control were more important. ⁶Both groups gave equally high importance to honesty. (Adapted from Stark, *Sociology,* 10th ed., p. 163.)

Main Idea
Statement

_____

_____

_____

3. [1]Bill collection agencies aren't known for caring much about the people behind the debts they collect. [2]Their position is if you can't pay your debts, we will harass you until you do. [3]But in a time when debts and unemployment are particularly high, the agencies are even going a step further. [4]They are employing—some say abusing—old state laws that are still on the books. [5]These ancient laws make failure to pay a debt a crime and some collection agencies are using them to put people with unpaid debts into jail. [6]Although around one-third of U.S. states have such laws, Illinois has been singled out as a state where the practice is particularly popular among collection agencies. [7]As a result, the state's attorney general Lisa Madigan is fighting to get state judges to throw debtor cases out of the courts. [8]Getting into a debt is not a crime according to the federal government, and debtor prisons have not been legal since the 1850s. [9]But if a person does not show up after a collection agency has filed a charge against him or her in the courts, judges have been known to find in favor of the agency.

Main Idea Statement

_____

_____

_____

4. [1]Following the 2011 nuclear crisis in Japan in the wake of a towering tsunami, long-suppressed fears about nuclear power resurfaced. [2]This was true at least in some countries around the world. [3]But it wasn't true for all. [4]In the wake of Japan's nuclear disaster, Switzerland froze plans to build any new nuclear plants. [5]The Germans did the same, while Austria's minister of the environment proposed a stress test for plants all across the European Union. [6]Public opposition to nuclear plants broke out in places as far apart as Turkey and South Africa. [7]The Spanish government, however, did not follow suit. [8]Nor did the governments of Russia, Poland, China, and Chile. [9]Their official stance is that no hasty decisions should be made on the basis of the Japanese experience. [10]The United States appears to be on the side of the Russians and the Chinese. [11]Government officials say, however, that safety lessons need to be learned from the Japanese experience.

Main Idea Statement

_____

_____

_____

▶ **TEST 4**   **Recognizing the Implied Main Idea**

DIRECTIONS   Read each paragraph. Then circle the letter of the implied main idea.

1. The word *natural* in advertisements clearly sells products. Juices and foods filled with "natural" goodness along with "natural" vitamins and herbs are big money makers. Consumers seem to believe that anything coming straight from nature has to be good for you. Yet if you're one of those consumers, you might want to reconsider your trust in Mother Nature. Aflatoxin, one of the most potent cancer-causing substances that exists, is a natural product of mold. Ricin, one of the deadliest poisons on earth, comes from nature's own castor beans. Take just one bite of the naturally growing mushroom *Amanita phalloides*, and you won't be around long enough to discuss its bitter aftertaste. Next time you're thinking of buying an herbal supplement because it's "natural"—and therefore has to be good for you—just remember, bee stings and poison ivy are also "natural."

Implied Main Idea   a. Synthetic products are better for you than natural ones are.

b. We shouldn't just assume that "natural" products are safe.

c. The word *natural* is a big selling point for all kinds of products.

2. In 1995, gray wolves, listed as an endangered species, were reintroduced into Yellowstone National Park, where they had once roamed freely. To the surprise of biologists, the wolves multiplied faster than expected, so much so that their status is now listed as "threatened" rather than endangered. Perhaps because of the population spurt, the wolves have begun to stray outside the park's boundaries. In a few cases, they have ventured onto bordering ranch lands and killed domestic livestock. The U.S. Fish and Wildlife Service responded quickly by shooting or capturing the wolves believed to be preying on livestock. But some ranchers have taken the law into their own hands and shot the wolves themselves. The ranchers want the legal right to shoot any wolf that ventures onto their property.

Implied Main Idea   a. The reintroduction of gray wolves was a bad idea from the beginning.

b. The reintroduction of gray wolves into Yellowstone National Park proves that endangered animals can be saved by human intervention.

c. The 1995 reintroduction of gray wolves into Yellowstone National Park has saved them from extinction; however, it has also caused some serious problems.

3. Currently, children in the United States receive more vaccinations than ever before. On average, they get approximately twenty-four inoculations for fourteen different diseases. As a result, potential killers such as polio and diphtheria are all but unknown in the United States. One would think that would be cause for gratitude among parents anxious to protect their children from illness. But some parents are not so thrilled. Instead, they worry about the possible adverse effects of so many vaccinations. Wary about the possibility that vaccines might do their children harm, a growing number of parents are limiting the number of vaccinations their children can receive, a practice known as "shot limiting." In some cases, they are refusing to let their children be vaccinated at all. According to a 2011 study reported in the journal *Pediatrics*, one in ten parents has decided to delay vaccinations, refused to grant permission for all the standard vaccinations, or refused to vaccinate altogether. Public health officials worry that parental reluctance concerning vaccinations will have dangerous consequences. Diseases once considered threats of the past, thanks to vaccinations, may make a comeback. In 2010 and 2012, for instance, outbreaks of whooping cough occurred for the first time in decades.

Implied Main Idea

a. Although vaccinating America's children has had obvious benefits, some parents still worry about possible adverse reactions and are limiting or refusing inoculations.

b. Parents who delay, limit, or refuse vaccinations for their children are doing them more harm than good.

c. Anxious about their children's health, some parents have launched a very public fight against unnecessary vaccinations.

4. It's common knowledge that bullying is a problem both in elementary and high school. When we think of bullying, we think of it as a kid-on-kid issue. Donald Brian Wood, however, might not agree. Wood is an algebra teacher who had a meltdown in front of his students after he could not get them to quiet down. When the students kept on goading him, Wood threw a chair out the window. One of Wood's students filmed the teacher's emotional collapse and put

it on YouTube. Wood was placed on administrative leave, since it was clear from the video that he had lost control of himself and his classroom. Kathy Klein, a 68-year-old bus monitor, did keep control of herself, limiting her reaction to the elementary school students taunting her by saying quietly, "If you can't say something nice, don't say it." But her mild reprimand didn't help. Surrounded by jeering students shouting insults, Klein, too, ended up on You-Tube because someone on the bus filmed her humiliation. According to Elizabeth Englander, executive director of the Massachusetts Aggression Reduction Center, this kind of behavior among students occurs when students feel themselves part of a pack and individual responsibility evaporates. Englander argues that students need to learn "digital citizenship." Let's hope they learn it soon since according to a 2012[†] report, one in five teachers claims to have been the victim of what's come to be known as *cyberbaiting*, incidents in which students goad a teacher or an aide into breaking down, film the emotional collapse, and then post it on YouTube.

Implied Main Idea

a. Cyberbaiting may or may not be a real issue of concern, since so far there has been only one major attempt to verify its existence.

b. Cyberbaiting is a new term, coined to identify a troubling phenomenon in which students goad a teacher or an aide into a public meltdown so they can film it and post it on the Web.

c. Cyberbaiting is another indication that technology in the classroom is not having the beneficial effect many expected.

[†]The report was conducted by Symantec, the maker of anti-virus software.

▶ **TEST 5**   **Recognizing the Implied Main Idea**

DIRECTIONS   Read each paragraph. Then circle the letter of the implied main idea.

1. According to the rules of their order, Carmelite nuns begin their days at the crack of dawn. Rising at 5:00 a.m., they sing hymns and eat breakfast. Breakfast, like the rest of their meals, is simple. The nuns are not allowed to eat meat. In addition, they have taken a vow of poverty, so rich food is out of the question. Once breakfast is over, the Carmelites spend their days doing chores or saying prayers. Conversation of any sort is forbidden, as are visitors. If the nuns speak at all to outsiders, it is through an iron grill that symbolizes their separation from the world. As one might expect, radio, television, and computers are not usually found among the Carmelites.

Implied Main Idea
     a. In time, the rules of the Carmelite order are bound to become less strict.

     b. Most Carmelite nuns enter the order because they have been wounded by the world.

     c. The Carmelites will never change the strict rules of their order.

     d. The rules of the Carmelite order ensure that the nuns lead a life of solitude and simplicity.

2. History books have long insisted that the Spanish explorer Hernando Cortés defeated the Aztec Empire after Montezuma, the empire's too-trusting king, welcomed Cortés into Tenochtitlan (now Mexico City) and extended him his hospitality. Cortés returned the courtesy by throwing Montezuma into jail. Then with the help of a few hundred men and the arrival of European diseases like typhus and smallpox, he turned the Aztec Empire into a Spanish colony. That, in any case, is the conventional version of events. But now researchers at an archaeological dig about 100 miles east of modern Mexico City have unearthed hundreds of skeletons, bones, and ancient objects that tell another story. The remains found are from a 1520 caravan of Spanish conquistadors, their families, and servants, all of whom were on their way to Tenochtitlan, probably to help put the finishing touches on Cortés's defeat of the Aztecs. According to Enrique Martinez, director of the dig, the newfound evidence strongly suggests that the travelers were set upon and captured by

Aztec warriors. The captors then apparently kept their victims in cages for an extended period of time, perhaps up to six months. During that time, Aztec priests made regular selections of those who were to be used as human sacrifices in religious rituals. Close examination also suggests that the caravan's captors engaged in cannibalism, eating the bodies of those who had been sacrificed. This seems to explain why Cortés named the town where it all happened "Tecuaque," which means "where people were eaten."

Implied Main Idea

a. Historians have long underestimated the courage of Montezuma's warriors.

b. Enrique Martinez has found conclusive evidence that cannibalism was part of Aztec society.

c. A new archaeological discovery disputes the notion that the Aztecs let themselves be conquered without fighting back.

d. In at least one instance, Cortés's followers got exactly what they deserved for plundering the great Aztec Empire.

3. Spectacled cobras—six-foot-long brown snakes that can kill with a single bite—are everywhere in the country of Sri Lanka. It's not surprising, therefore, that thousands of people are bitten yearly. Many victims are children, and some of them die. What's surprising is that most Sri Lankans will not harm a cobra that happens to venture into a nearby woodpile or rice field. The majority of Sri Lankans are Buddhists. According to their religion, the spectacled cobra once gave shelter to Buddha by opening the hood at the back of its neck. To show that the cobra was under his protection, Buddha is said to have given the snake the spectacles-like red mark that appears on the back of its head.

Implied Main Idea

a. Given the number of people who die from snake bites, the people of Sri Lanka should stop worshipping cobras.

b. The people of Sri Lanka should do something about the threat of cobra bites to their children.

c. The people of Sri Lanka do not kill cobras because they believe the snakes are under the protection of Buddha.

d. Should the number of victims suffering from cobra bites continue to rise, the people of Sri Lanka are bound to change their attitudes toward cobras.

4. Listeria is a food-borne bacterium that has been found in hot dogs, deli meats, soft cheeses, undercooked meat, poultry, and seafood. On a yearly basis, listeria sickens about 2,500 Americans. One serious outbreak of listeria poisoning, in 1998, was traced to meat processed at a Sara Lee Corporation plant in Michigan. The company had to recall fifteen million pounds of hot dogs and luncheon meats. In 2002, seven people died after eating Wampler brand turkey tainted by listeria. In 2011, thirteen people died and seventy-two were sickened after eating cantaloupe contaminated by listeria. In the healthy, listeria is an unpleasant nuisance, causing flu-like symptoms that last several days. But if the elderly are stricken by listeria poisoning, they can die from it. If a pregnant woman ingests the bacterium, a miscarriage or a stillbirth often results, even if the mother herself experiences no symptoms.

Implied Main Idea

a. Processed meats have long been the source of food poisoning.

b. Given the high incidence of listeria poisoning, it is surprising that meatpacking plants are not required to test for it.

c. Outbreaks of listeria poisoning are bound to increase.

d. Depending on who is stricken, listeria poisoning can be an unpleasant nuisance or a deadly tragedy.

▶ **TEST 6**　　　　**Inferring the Implied Main Idea**

DIRECTIONS　　Read each paragraph. Then write the implied main idea in the blanks that follow.

1. Some people claim that declawing a cat does no real harm, but for reasons of their own, they are denying the obvious. Cats remove old skin and dry hair by scratching themselves. A cat without claws can't groom itself properly. Cats also need their claws to jump. A cat's claws are like landing gear. They help cats maintain their balance. If deprived of claws, the animals find it hard to jump from place to place. Worst of all, if a declawed house cat escapes its home, it could quickly die of starvation. Grabbing for a mouse or bird would be an empty gesture, leaving the cat to starve. An even more horrible fate awaits the declawed cat who gets into a fight with another animal.

Implied Main Idea
_____

_____

2. On December 18, 1912, an amateur archaeologist named Charles Dawson and his friend Arthur Smith Woodward presented what they claimed were extraordinary findings to the Geological Society of London. Woodward and Dawson presented the skeleton of a creature alleged to be half-man and half-ape. The two men claimed they had discovered what was believed to be the missing link between humans and apes. With relatively little investigation, Piltdown man—as the skeleton came to be called—was accepted as genuine. As time went by, however, doubts began to surface, and researchers examined and reexamined the skeleton. In 1953, close analysis of the skeleton revealed that someone had created it by fusing together the bones of a human being and an orangutan.

Implied Main Idea
_____

_____

3. Why do so few women pursue careers in science and engineering?[†] A common answer has been that these are socially defined as male occupations, and women are discouraged from entering them,

_____

[†]It should be noted here that the percentage of women in engineering and science has been steadily increasing.

either by negative attitudes or by actual discrimination. Even more popular is the idea that childhood socialization gives women negative feelings about these careers. Some even have proposed that biological differences are involved, that women excel at relational thinking, while men excel at linear thinking, which is better suited for doing science. Ironically, some feminists have, perhaps unwittingly, encouraged this biological view by claiming that women do think differently and that a feminist approach would lead to better science. (Adapted from Stark. *Sociology*, 10th ed., p. 169.)

Implied Main Idea _____

_____

4. Vitamin A helps with vision, bone growth, and healthy skin. A deficiency in vitamin A can produce eye diseases. Dairy products, nuts, and yellow vegetables all contain vitamin A. Vitamin C helps fight colds and is essential to healthy teeth. Oranges, lemons, tomatoes, and strawberries all contain this important vitamin. Vitamin D, the sunshine vitamin, helps keep bones and teeth strong; a lack of this vitamin can contribute to arthritis. Fish and eggs are the best sources of vitamin D. The vitamin B complex—B_1, B_2, B_6, and B_{12}—is also extremely important. It keeps the skin healthy and develops muscle tone. Vitamin B may even help reduce stress and tension. Green, leafy vegetables, milk, and grains help supply this important group of vitamins.

Implied Main Idea _____

_____

▶ **TEST 7**   **Inferring the Implied Main Idea**

DIRECTIONS   Read each paragraph. Then write the implied main idea in the blanks that follow.

1. During the Civil War, the first war to be covered by newspaper journalists, some reporters considered it their duty to rally the troops. During the famous battle of Bull Run, for example, Edmund Clarence Stedmen of the *New York World* would wave the regiment flag whenever he thought the troops he was covering were losing their will to fight. Junius Browne from the *New York Tribune* went a step further. If he thought a rebel sniper was in the surrounding area, he would pick up a gun and start firing. Aware that Union[†] leader Ulysses S. Grant liked to drink, Sylvanus Cadwallader of the *Chicago Times* did his part to win the war: He locked himself and Grant in the bathroom to keep the general from hitting the bottle. Even more than his colleagues, Samuel Wilkeson of the *New York Times* participated in the war he covered. After the bloody battle of Gettysburg, Wilkeson wrote his report standing beside the grave of his oldest son.

Implied Main Idea   _____

    _____

2. In the stable and moist conditions of the tropical rain forests, plants and animals are more varied and diverse than anywhere else on earth. The variety and diversity of the rain forest makes it a treasure trove for all kinds of riches, from exotic perfumes to cures for deadly diseases. Yet every year, a rain-forest region the size of Belgium is cut down to make way for agriculture. The cutting occurs despite the fact that the soil in the rain forest is not particularly suitable for either growing or grazing. The soil is sandy. Lacking nutrients from the trees, it quickly becomes too dry to be useful for farming or herding. Still, the cutting continues, although no one knows what miraculous cure for disease has been lost in the process.

Implied Main Idea   _____

    _____

[†]Union: loyal to the U.S. government during the Civil War.

3. Lasers, devices that produce an intense, focused beam of light, have been around since 1960, when Theodore H. Maiman put the first one together. At the time, however, no one quite knew what to do with the laser. In fact, in the 1960s and early 1970s, the laser was often described as a solution looking for a good problem. But today, no one makes that little joke any more. Laser technology is being used to correct vision problems. Many who undergo laser surgery no longer need glasses to see. Lasers are also now commonly used to remove cataracts and gallstones. Heart surgeons also use them to remove blood clots from coronary arteries. In addition to medical uses, lasers are important tools of the military. They are central to all kinds of weaponry, including the so-called "smart" bombs. Moreover, traveling at the speed of light, lasers can burn a hole in missiles or their warheads and thereby render them ineffective. They are also a central part of military warning and detecting systems. In addition, lasers have found their place in industry. They play a key role in machine-tool operations, communication systems, tunnel construction, and welding.

Implied Main Idea _____

_____

4. The first successful blood transfusion was performed in the seventeenth century, but the practice was outlawed because of the dangers it posed to the patient. The practice was revived in the nineteenth century, but it was accompanied by terrible risks, like blood clots and kidney failure. Austrian-born Karl Landsteiner (1868–1943), however, had a theory. He argued that the blood of humans had inborn differences and similarities. The key, from Landsteiner's perspective, was to understand both the differences and the similarities. Once they were understood, Landsteiner thought the risks of blood transfusion might be eliminated. To that end, he analyzed numerous blood samples. By 1901, he had classified blood donors into three different categories called A, B, and O (AB was added in 1902). Following that discovery, the transfusion of blood became a relatively safe procedure.

Implied Main Idea _____

_____

5. In 1789 the French Revolution exploded in France with far-reaching consequences. The revolution even reached across the ocean to the tiny island of Saint Dominique, which was under French control. A slave on the island named Toussaint Bréda heard and took to heart the revolution's passionate slogans about extending rights and independence to all men, not just those wearing royal cloth and not just those with white skin. When slave owners on Saint Dominique rebelled against the new revolutionary government's demand to end slavery on the island, France's revolutionaries backtracked, unwilling to live up to the promise of their early slogans. Bréda, however, had taken the promise of freedom for all seriously, and he wasn't backing down. Calling himself Toussaint L'Ouverture ("the one who finds an opening"), the now ex-slave successfully fought the French soldiers who came to support not the rights of man but the rights of slaveholders. The war to end slavery on the island continued for fourteen years with Toussaint L'Ouverture outwitting all those who came up against him. The situation looked so hopeless for the French that France's new leader, Napoleon Bonaparte, invited L'Ouverture to negotiate terms of peace with the promise of safe conduct. When L'Ouverture arrived for the meeting, Napoleon had him thrown in jail, where he died of cold, hunger, and neglect. His soldiers fought on despite his loss until 1803 when Napoleon granted the island its independence and it assumed the name it had always been called by its black inhabitants, Haiti, meaning "land of mountains."

Implied Main Idea _____

_____

▶ **TEST 8**   **Reviewing Chapter 8 Vocabulary**

DIRECTIONS   Circle the letter of the sentence that correctly uses the underlined vocabulary word.

1. a. They tried to eradicate the seal by teaching him a series of special drills.
   b. How closely can you eradicate the length of the floor?
   c. Painful childhood memories are hard to eradicate.

2. a. He was an indulgent parent who expected his children to snap to attention.
   b. She was an indulgent mother who had a particularly hard time saying no to her firstborn.
   c. The indulgent lamp lit up the room.

3. a. The fabulous innovation ended early even though everyone seemed to be having a great time.
   b. The laboratory wanted to foster innovation among its scientists and offered bonuses to those who came up with new ideas.
   c. The innovation of the insect's offspring showed some strange changes at the cell level.

4. a. Martyrs like to have a good time and can always be counted on for a party.
   b. The rebellion had produced many martyrs who were determined to gain independence at any cost.
   c. After he martyrs the basement walls, he will probably work on the chimney.

5. a. The higher the alcohol content the more potent the drink.
   b. The appearance of the bat in the sky was an evil potent.
   c. The student leader tried to potent a strike but no one was interested in missing finals.

6. a. The <u>terminal</u> presence of the school's president was a surprise to everyone.
   b. Faced with a <u>terminal</u> illness, the athlete had to give up her place on the team; she simply did not know if she would be alive at the time of the competition.
   c. The <u>terminal</u> question in the middle of the speaker's list was left unanswered.

7. a. The <u>progressive</u> candidate disliked the very idea of change.
   b. The dog was extremely <u>progressive</u>, and its owners were worried that he might attack without warning.
   c. Senator Bernie Sanders of Vermont is considered to be very <u>progressive</u>, and for some that's a virtue; for others it's a failing.

8. a. He used a strong spray against the <u>idioms</u> to make sure he got rid of all of them.
   b. Most at home in conversation, <u>idioms</u> do also make their way into academic writing.
   c. Because she was in a rage, her speech was filled with <u>idioms</u>.

9. a. He tried to <u>distinguish</u> the fire but there simply wasn't enough water, and it came blazing back.
   b. Runner Wilma Rudolph overcame polio to <u>distinguish</u> herself at the 1960 Olympics by winning three gold medals.
   c. The talk show host was <u>distinguished</u> from her job after she joked about the tragedy in Japan.

10. a. The house's <u>squalid</u> surroundings further increased its market price.
    b. Moving at a <u>squalid</u> pace, the horse looked as if it had forgotten how to run.
    c. Born in <u>squalid</u> surroundings, the blues singer Billie Holiday tried to escape her poverty-stricken past, but couldn't beat her addiction to drugs despite her enormous talent.

11. a. In an effort to escape the police, the thief hid <u>prominently</u> behind the house.

    b. Behind the curtains, the children breathed <u>prominently</u> so their presence would not be detected.

    c. <u>Prominently</u> among the mourners at the wake was the deceased's ex-wife, who greeted those who came to pay their respects as if she were the man's grieving widow.

12. a. Amy Carmichael was an Irish <u>missionary</u>, who left her homeland and spent fifty-six years in India in an effort to spread Christianity.

    b. The <u>missionary</u> was closed for the afternoon and the prisoners were out of luck.

    c. For ten dollars, the <u>missionary</u> claimed she could tell the future.

13. a. He had had <u>archaeological</u> problems prior to arriving at school, but the new surroundings made them worse, and he started acting strangely.

    b. Bit by bit, the diggers on the <u>archaeological</u> expedition had uncovered an ancient town that had been covered over by the eruption of a volcano.

    c. The <u>archaeological</u> firm had signed on to construct the new building that would house the city orchestra.

14. a. The woman had an <u>extensive</u> vocabulary of insults at her disposal.

    b. He finished his <u>extensive</u> one-page essay in less than an hour.

    c. Limited to only three feet by five, the garden was still <u>extensive</u>.

15. a. The cow was suffering from <u>heresy</u> and was foaming at the mouth.

    b. The defendant claimed that too much <u>heresy</u> had made him lose control and hit the other patron in the bar.

    c. In 1896, the Reverend W. T. Brown was tried for <u>heresy</u> because he publicly insisted that certain teachings in the Bible were not true.

Understanding the Role of Inferences in Longer Readings

IN THIS CHAPTER, YOU WILL LEARN

- how to adapt what you know about inferring main ideas in paragraphs to longer readings.

- about the importance of inferring *connections* between paragraphs.

- the basics of summary writing.

> *"Much of what we understand—whether when listening or reading—we understand indirectly, by inference."*
>
> —Writer Dan Kurland

You already know how to infer the main ideas of paragraphs. But as you might have guessed, implied main ideas aren't limited to paragraphs. They also turn up in longer, multi-paragraph readings. This chapter will give you some examples of readings unified by an implied, rather than a stated, main idea. It will also show you how to use the writer's clues to come up with your inferred version of a thesis statement.

Chapter 9 will also talk more about another kind of inference essential to reading longer selections. It will extend the discussion begun in Chapter 8 and show you how readers supply the inferences that link paragraphs together in support of an overall meaning or main idea. And finally, it will look at a skill essential for just about every college course, summary writing.

Implied Main Ideas Can Sum Up Longer Readings

In longer readings, the controlling main idea is usually expressed in a thesis statement. Although the length of the reading plays a key role in the location of that thesis statement, somewhere within the first three or four paragraphs is the most likely location. This is particularly true of chapter sections within textbooks, because textbook writers are not concerned with creating a mood or heightening suspense. They want to make sure their readers absorb a lot of new information as quickly as possible. With that goal in mind, they are likely to introduce the thesis statement fairly quickly so readers don't miss it. Only occasionally does it appear at the very end.

That doesn't mean, however, that every chapter section will have a thesis statement. Writers of all kinds, and that includes writers of text-books, do sometimes expect readers to infer the implied main idea that unifies an entire reading. Here's an example:

The Gorilla's Two Faces

1   Even many die-hard wrestling fans don't remember his name anymore, but in the mid-sixties, the wrestler Gorilla Monsoon was a major star. At 6 feet and 5 inches, Monsoon was a towering figure. He weighed more than four hundred pounds and fought some eight thousand bouts. When announcers said his name, their voices tended to quaver a little, for Gorilla was wrestling's first real "bad guy." He was the wrestler audiences loved to hate because he was tougher and meaner than anyone else around.

2   Wearing a body suit with one strap draped over a massive shoulder, Gorilla would enter the ring looking as if he could, in a hungry moment, chew and digest rusty nails. After toying with his opponent for a while, he

One of the stars of wrestling in the sixties and seventies, Gorilla Monsoon, a.k.a. Robert Marella, went on to become a play-by-play announcer for the World Wrestling Entertainment company.

© Bettmann/Corbis.

428 ◆ **Chapter 9** Understanding the Role of Inferences in Longer Readings

usually liked to end the bout with the "airplane spin," the wrestling hold that made him famous. Knocking his opponent to the floor, he would wrap the man's feet around his enormous waist. Seemingly without effort, he would then lift and twirl his opponent round and round, keeping him at waist level for at least thirty seconds. To further embroider his image of pure evil, Gorilla would cackle with laughter the entire time. Staged or not, it was a terrifying display, and the audience couldn't get enough of it.

3   Out of the ring, however, Gorilla Monsoon was Robert Marella. Quiet and soft-spoken, Mr. Marella, as he liked to be called, was college educated. Prior to becoming a professional wrestler, he had thought about becoming an English teacher. But teaching wasn't particularly lucrative. Wrestling paid better, and so "Gorilla Monsoon" was born.

4   Despite his brutal appearance in the ring, Marella had a way with words. When asked why anyone would ever pay to see grown men throw one another around in a ring, he paused for a moment and then paraphrased St. Augustine:[†] "For those who believe in our sport, no explanation is necessary."

5   He was equally articulate* when interviewed, long past his heyday, about the current state of wrestling. Asked about the new and more profitable face of wrestling, he shrugged it off as little more than people from the pages of "comic books." From Marella's perspective, wrestling in the old days was a more serious sport, and wrestlers were treated with both respect and fear. As he put it, "People really thought I was the Devil." (Source of quotations: David Hadju, "When Wrestling Was Noir,"[†] *New York Times Magazine*, January 2, 2000, p. 43.)

Drawing the Logical Inference

The sample reading breaks into two sections. The first section, paragraphs 1 and 2, deals with the man in the ring. Here is where we learn about Gorilla Monsoon's public image. He was the wrestler everyone loved to hate. But in the second section of the reading—paragraphs 3–5—a new and different image emerges, along with Gorilla's real name, Robert Marella. We are told that, out of the ring, Marella was anything but the hulking bully he portrayed in it. He was soft-spoken, well-read, and an intellectual.

[†]St. Augustine (354–430): Catholic saint who, when questioned about his faith, responded, "For those who believe, no explanation is necessary."
*articulate: well-spoken, good with words.
[†]noir: a term usually applied to books or movies about characters who were dangerous and living outside the mainstream.

Yet if we look for a thesis statement that sums up both sides of Gorilla's personality, we won't find it. Almost all the sentences in the reading are equally specific. No general statement sums them up. Instead, readers are left to infer one like the following: "Sixties wrestler Gorilla Monsoon may have been a brute in the ring, but out of it, he was a smart, thoughtful man who took his profession seriously." As it should, that inference functions like a thesis statement. It sums up the main idea of the entire reading.

Like paragraphs with topic sentences, longer readings usually express the main idea in a thesis statement. But that's not always the case. If you read an article, an essay, or a chapter section and don't find any general statements that summarize the meaning of the more specific ones, you need to infer one.

READING TIPS

1. Readings that break apart in the middle with the author moving on to a point different from the one developed by the opening paragraphs are very likely to imply rather than state the main idea of the reading.

2. Writing that (1) compares and contrasts two topics, (2) talks about the difference between the past and present, and (3) opens with a question but doesn't follow with an immediate answer is very likely to imply the main idea of the reading.

Checking Your Inference Against the Author's Words

As with paragraphs, you need to make sure that the main idea you infer fits the information provided by the author. Once you infer the main idea, go through each paragraph and check to see what it adds to your understanding of the main idea you inferred. If the individual paragraph main ideas and the overall main idea you inferred don't seem to have any relationship, you need to re-think your initial inference.

SUMMING UP THE KEY POINTS

1. Like individual paragraphs, longer multi-paragraph readings don't always state the main idea directly. Sometimes they leave out the thesis statement and provide enough clues for readers to infer the overall or controlling main idea of the reading.

2. Inferring the implied main idea of a reading is only part of the reader's job. The next step is to check the implied main idea against the author's actual words. There has to be a connection between them. If the supporting paragraphs don't match the main idea the reader has inferred, then there is something wrong with the reader's inference.

◆ **EXERCISE 1**   **Recognizing Implied Main Ideas**

DIRECTIONS   Read each selection. Then circle the letter of the statement implied by the reading.

1. **The Future of Genetic Testing**

1   In August 2000, a test-tube baby named Adam Nash was born in Denver, Colorado. After cutting Adam's umbilical cord, doctors collected some cells from that cord. A month later, they infused those same cells into the body of Adam's six-year-old sister, Molly. The procedure saved Molly's life.

2   Afflicted with a rare bone marrow disease called Fanconi anemia, Molly's only hope was a cell transplant from a sibling. Because both parents carried the Fanconi gene, which gave them a 25 percent chance of giving birth to a child carrying the same disease as Molly, doctors needed to select an embryo not affected by the disease-carrying gene. That selection process could only be carried out in an in vitro[†]-produced pregnancy followed by sophisticated gene testing. Doctors would test embryo cells to discover which of them did not carry the diseased gene and then impregnate the mother with only those cells that tested normal.

3   In part at least, the Nash case[†] resembles a similar one from 1989, which involved sixteen-year-old Anissa Ayala, a young girl diagnosed with a lethal form of leukemia. In an effort to save her life, the girl's father, Abe Ayala, had his vasectomy reversed so that he and his wife, Mary, could have a third child who would be a bone marrow donor for Anissa. Although the Ayalas had a one-in-four chance of having a child with the right cells to be a donor, luck was on their side. Genetic testing showed that Anissa's newborn sister, Marissa, had inherited all the right genes, and she did, in fact, prove to be an ideal donor. Thanks to Marissa, Anissa got a new lease on life.

[†]in vitro: taking place in a test tube.
[†]As of 2010, both Adam and Molly Nash were doing fine.

4   In situations like these where a child's suffering can be cured, genetic testing does indeed seem like a godsend. Certainly, this position is promoted by Charles Strom, director of the Illinois Masonic Medical Center, which was heavily involved in both cases. Thanks to genetic testing, lives can be saved and tragedy avoided. As long as the children born to be donors are loved, says Strom, that's all that matters; and in both cases, the children born to save their siblings are very much cherished.

5   Yet both cases have raised a central question: Are the increasing sophistication and use of genetic testing where reproduction is involved always a cause for jubilation?* If you ask Leon Kass, former chief of the President's Council on Bioethics,† the answer is no. Like other bioethicists before him, Mr. Kass takes issue with the idea of children coming into the world to be donors. He fears that eventually the children will feel exploited by their parents and angry at the siblings they helped save. Other bioethicists like Jeffrey Kahn, director of the University of Minnesota's Center for Bioethics, don't take issue with parents bringing a child into the world in order to be a donor. Instead, Kahn fears a future in which reproductive technology allows some parents—primarily those who can afford it—to choose their children's physical and mental makeup.

6   Kahn, who is as pessimistic as Strom is hopeful, claims that having a child "is quickly becoming like buying a new car." Parents can choose the options they do or do not want. He believes that as genetic tests become more available to the public, there will be more and more parents attempting to create "designer babies, and parents will be asking for "embryos without a predisposition* to homosexuality or for kids who will grow to more than six feet tall." (Sources of information: "Abigail Trafford, "Miracle Babies Draw Us into an Ethical Swamp," *Washington Post*, November 14, 2000, p. 28; Dan Vergano, "Embryo Genetic Screening Controversial—and Successful," *USA Today* 1/10/2010, available on the Web.)

Implied Main Idea

a. The negative consequences of genetic testing far outweigh its positive uses.

b. Genetic testing should not be allowed to play a role in human reproduction.

---

*jubilation: joy, triumph, celebration.
†bioethics: the study of moral and ethical implications caused by new scientific discoveries. The Council on Bioethics was a group appointed by then president George W. Bush, and it met between 2002 and 2009.
*predisposition: leaning, inclination, or tendency toward a particular condition or behavior.

c. Thanks to genetic testing, children like Molly Nash now have a chance to lead a normal life.

d. Genetic testing as the basis for human reproduction has become the center of an ethical controversy.

2. The Pros and Cons of Tort Reform

1 In Houston, a woman who scalded herself with hot coffee sued McDonald's and won $2.9 million (later reduced to a "mere" $480,000). In Maine, a woman golfer hit a shot that bounced off an obstacle and struck her in the face. She sued the country club and won $40,000. In Connecticut, a twelve-year-old Little League baseball player uncorked a wild throw that conked a woman in the stands. The woman promptly sued the player and the local government. In New York City, several prison inmates somehow shot themselves in the feet and then sued the city for negligence.

2 Such stories seem to be increasingly common, as 800,000 lawyers in the United States seek to justify their existence and citizens look for an easy dollar instead of for a sense of personal responsibility. The results are a reduction in the gross national product of an estimated $2.5 million per attorney, personal and corporate financial tragedies, and local governments that must hike taxes to cover legal fees and liability settlements.

3 The biggest problem is that of *torts*, damage suits over product liability,* personal injury, medical malpractice, and related claims. Throughout the twentieth century, state courts gradually eliminated restrictions on tort liability and substituted legal doctrines favoring plaintiffs* over defendants. For example, nearly all states have a strict liability rule for product safety. This means that manufacturers of defective products (or even very hot coffee) may be held fully liable for damages caused by their product, regardless of whether the manufacturer was negligent.

4 Today, state legislatures are actively engaged in tort reform that shifts the advantage more toward defendants. Punitive damage awards have been capped in Alabama, New Jersey, Illinois, Texas, and other states. Laws protecting local governments and their employees from exorbitant* liability awards have been adopted in several states. There has been a surge of business interest in judicial* elections in

---

*liability: responsibility for a mistake or malfunction.
*plaintiffs: people who bring suit to court in order to win damages.
*exorbitant: excessive, especially in the sense of price or demands.
*judicial: related to the courts and judges.

California and other states, as judges known for generous tort decisions have come under electoral* attack and, in some cases, gone down to defeat.

5   Aligned against tort reform are powerful trial lawyers; litigation,* product liability, and personal injury suits are their bread and butter. Also against tort reform are certain consumer groups, who see unlimited tort liability as a fundamental right for injured citizens and a means to hold individuals and firms accountable for shoddy and dangerous practices and merchandise. These opponents of tort reform are fighting against insurance companies, manufacturers, and others in courtrooms and in state capitols. Recently, the supreme courts of several states (e.g., Indiana, Ohio, and Oregon) have overturned tort reforms. (Adapted from Bowman and Kearney, *State and Local Government*, 7th ed., p. 268.)

Implied Main Idea

a. Tort reform has been a long time coming, but the public, fed up with lawsuits, has decided to take the plunge and reduce the rewards of litigation.

b. While many states are actively engaged in tort reform, both lawyers and consumers fear that the reforms will go too far.

c. Lawsuits over product liability are a menace to the economy and to citizens' sense of personal liability; they are fueled more by the lure of easy money than by any real harm done by a product.

d. Although state legislators are working hard to protect companies from lawsuits over product liability, consumers do not support their efforts.

► **SHARE YOUR THOUGHTS**

Do you think there should be legal limits placed on an individual's right to sue a company for damages if the company's product malfunctions or causes injuries?

READING TIP

Look to the beginning of paragraphs for help answering two questions that should *always* be on a reader's mind: Why does this paragraph follow the previous one? What connects them to one another?

---

*electoral: related to voting in elections.
*litigation: legal proceeding in a courtroom, lawsuit to win damages.

◆ EXERCISE 2   Inferring Implied Main Ideas

DIRECTIONS   Read each selection and infer the implied main idea. Then write your inference in the blank lines that follow.

EXAMPLE

Are You Sure You Want to Be a Leader?

1   The word *leader* has positive connotations for most people. Thus, most of us, if asked whether we would like to be in a position of leadership, will say yes. To be sure, being a leader has its satisfactions. Leadership brings with it power and prestige. Often it brings status, respect, and opportunities for professional advancement and financial gain. Yet those of us intent on pursuing leadership roles in our professional lives don't always take into account the fact that leaders are usually expected to work longer hours than other employees are. Actually, people in organizational leadership positions typically spend about fifty-five hours per week working. During periods of peak demand, this figure can rise to eighty hours per week.

2   Being a leader is also a good way to discover the validity of Murphy's law: "If anything can go wrong, it will." A leader is constantly required to solve numerous problems involving both people and things. Because of those problems and the difficulties attendant* on solving them, many people find leadership positions enormously stressful. As a result, many managers experience burnout and abandon their positions.

3   In addition, people in managerial positions complain repeatedly that they are held responsible for things over which they have little control. As a leader, for example, you might be expected to work with an ill-performing team member, yet you might not have the power to fire him or her. You might also be called on to produce a high-quality service or product but not be given the staff or the funds to get the job done effectively.

4   In a sense, the higher you rise as a leader, the more lonely you are likely to be. After all, leadership limits the number of people in whom you can confide. It is awkward, not to mention unprofessional, to complain about one of your employees to another employee. Then, too, you need to be wary about voicing complaints against your superiors to the people who work for you. Such complaints are bad for morale. Even worse, they can threaten your job security. Not surprisingly, people in leadership positions complain that they miss being "one of the gang."

---

*attendant: related to, connected to

5   People at all levels of an organization, from the office assistant to the chairperson of the board, must be aware of political factors. Yet you can avoid politics more easily as an individual contributor than you can as a leader. As a leader you have to engage in political byplay from three directions: below, sideways, and upward. Political tactics such as forming alliances and coalitions are a necessary part of a leader's role. (Adapted from Dubrin, *Leadership*, 6th ed., pp. 16–17.)

Implied Main Idea Although being a leader has some very positive consequences, it also has some negative ones that need to be carefully considered.

EXPLANATION The first paragraph opens by describing the positive consequences of being a leader. The remaining paragraphs describe the negative effects of assuming a leadership role. Yet if you look for a general statement that sums up both the positive and the negative consequences of leadership, you won't find it. What this means is that the reader has to draw an inference like the one shown above.

1. The Reality of Prison Life

1   Many Americans firmly believe that prison inmates spend their days lifting weights, watching television, or playing basketball while hard-working taxpayers pay for prisoners' food, clothing, shelter, education, and health care. However, in a minimum-security prison, the day typically begins with a wake-up call at 6:00 a.m. Prisoners then head for the community bathrooms. Because hundreds of men often share a bathroom, they usually wait in line to use the facilities. Inmates are also expected to make their beds and clean their cells.

2   Prisons are noisy. Arguments, fistfights, and robberies among convicts are common. Many prisons, even those in sweltering southern states, are not air-conditioned. In spite of regular cleaning, they often smell of urine and body odor because fresh air cannot enter the sealed buildings.

3   At many institutions, prisoners might attend psychological counseling or educational programs for part of the day, the goal of which is to provide personal improvement. But everyone who is able usually works between four and eight hours daily. At some of this country's penal institutions, inmates labor in prison factories where they are paid between $0.10 and $1.35 per hour. Others are assigned to food service, laundry, maintenance, or janitorial service. A typical workday lasts from 7:30 a.m. to 3:30 p.m., with a break for lunch. Yet the majority

of prisoners earn less than $25 a month, out of which they must buy their snacks, sodas, aspirins, and toiletries.

4   At 4:00 p.m. every day, prisoners must be in their cells and on their feet while guards count heads and make sure everyone is present. From 4:30 p.m. until the evening meal and then again until about 9:30 p.m., prisoners read mail, watch one of three available television channels, exercise, play cards and board games, or receive visitors. After these visits, prisoners are strip-searched before going back to their cell blocks, where they can watch television, wait in long lines to use the telephone, or visit with other inmates until lights out at 11:30.

(Source of information: http://people.howstuffworks.com/prison1.htm.)

Implied Main Idea

_____

_____

2. Is Local News Really News?

1   Do you consider yourself an informed citizen because you're in the habit of watching the local news? If you do, you might want to consider how you are defining the word *informed*. Think about it. While watching your local news, it's unlikely that you will see or hear many reports about significant events concerning politics, culture, business, and government. Instead, you're probably learning about violent crimes, major accidents, deadly disasters, and celebrity breakups.

2   In a half-hour local news broadcast, only about fifteen minutes are left once the time for commercials, weather, sports, traffic, and bantering by news anchors is subtracted. This is not much time to relate all of the news of the day. Therefore, each individual news story is, by necessity, quite short. In fact, studies have shown that 70 percent of all news stories are no more than a minute long. Forty-three percent are less than thirty seconds long. Only about 16 percent of stories are longer than two minutes; in the television news industry, any story more than a minute and a half long is billed as an "in-depth" report.

3   Typically, the television news anchors who introduce or read these stories are not experts in any of the fields—such as education, the environment, business, government, and health—that are covered. Most are hired not for their understanding of the news but for their ability to read a story well while conveying the appropriate emotion (anger, fear, sympathy, admiration, disgust, etc.). The reporters who gather the news are not experts either. They are hired primarily for their ability to communicate well on camera, as well as for their writing skill and general common sense.

4   Local news reporters are under tremendous pressure to produce a story. They usually get their assignments about mid-morning. That leaves them only a few hours to gather the facts and write the story so that it can be ready for a 5:00 or 6:00 p.m. broadcast. As a result, reporters have little time for research, making their sources rather thin: Only 25 percent of TV news stories have more than one source. Not surprisingly, news directors avoid assigning hundreds of important stories that would require some real research.

5   The truth is that television news broadcasts feature stories that readily lend themselves to videotape footage and pictures. For that reason, there's little coverage of events that are important but difficult to illustrate, such as political speeches, school board meetings, or city council sessions. One survey revealed that only about 7 percent of news stories cover economic issues. Another study of six thousand news stories showed that only 9 percent of them concerned poverty or welfare. Instead, TV news focuses on events that are relatively trivial but also very visual, and it tends to sensationalize those events by making them look even more dramatic than they actually were.

6   In addition to avoiding non-visual news stories, TV newscasts seldom include negative stories about their advertisers or about police officers and firefighters. According to one survey, more than half of news directors interviewed said that they had been pressured by advertisers to either kill critical stories or promote favorable ones. The largest number of consumer complaints concern new car dealerships, but because car dealers buy a lot of commercial airtime, they are rarely subjected to a news station's scrutiny.

7   Neither will viewers see many critical stories about grocery and clothing stores, shopping malls, banks, insurance and health care providers, soda manufacturers, or fast food restaurants, all of which buy a significant amount of commercial airtime. Police and firefighters are also rarely cast in a negative light on local TV news stations because reporters need the cooperation of law enforcement and public safety officials to get the crime stories that are their lifeblood. That's why viewers see few, if any, stories about issues like radar traps, brutality, and/or police or firefighter mistakes. (For source of statistics: Amy Mitchell, "The Big Picture," in the online archives of the *Columbia Journalism Review*, January/February 1999; see also Greg Byron, "TV News: What Local Stations Don't Want You to Know," http://jerz.setonhill.edu/EL227/2009/08/31/.)

Implied Main Idea

_____

_____

From Reader to Writer Write two or three paragraphs that contrast how you think about a person, place, or event now as opposed to when you were a child. Start by explaining how you felt as a kid, e.g., "When I was little, I thought my dad was much too strict." Make sure to give a specific example or two that illustrates what you mean, for instance, "We were in serious trouble if we came home even five minutes after curfew." When you finish the section on childhood, use a reversal or time transition to take your reader with you as you describe how your feelings have changed. "Now that I have kids of my own, I realize that my dad was trying..." Again be specific about how your thinking has changed. Overall, let the contrast between then and now tell your readers what they need to know. Don't provide a thesis statement to sum up the difference between you as a kid and you as an adult. Let your examples speak for themselves.

VOCABULARY ROUND UP 1

Below are ten words introduced in pages 428–33. The words are accompanied by more detailed definitions, the page on which they originally appeared, and additional sample sentences. Spend time reviewing the words and their meanings because you will see them again in review tests at the end of the chapter. Use the online dictionary Wordnik to find additional sentences illustrating the words in context. (*Note*: If you know of another dictionary with as many examples of words in context feel free to use that one instead.)

1. **articulate** (p. 428): well-spoken, good with words. "The scientist was not especially good at casual conversation, but when he talked about his work, he became remarkably *articulate*."

2. **jubilation** (p. 431): great joy, triumph, or celebration. "There was *jubilation* throughout Chile after thirty-three miners trapped underground for sixty-nine days were finally rescued."

3. **predisposition** (p. 431): leaning, inclination, or tendency toward a particular kind of behavior or condition. "He had a *predisposition* toward acting first and thinking afterward."

4. **liability** (p. 432): responsibility for a mistake or malfunction. "The court determined that the makers of the toy had no *liability* if the toy was purchased for a child younger than the age stated on both the directions and the packaging."

5. **plaintiffs** (p. 432): people who bring suits to court in order to win damages. "The *plaintiff* in the consumer fraud case won a huge settlement."

6. **exorbitant** (p. 432): excessive, extremely expensive, overpriced. "Some banks charge *exorbitant* fees despite the fact that computers have decreased the amount of work they actually have to pay people for."

7. **judicial** (p. 432): related to the courts, judges, laws, or the handing out of justice. "Not every country has the same kind of *judicial* system as we do."

8. **electoral** (p. 433): related to voting in elections. "Because she is running as an outsider to Washington, her *electoral* prospects are looking promising; outsiders are in demand in the current political climate."

9. **litigation** (p. 433): lawsuit, the act of bringing legal action in a court. "The inventor believed that the company had stolen her work, and she was threatening *litigation* unless she got both credit and payment."

10. **attendant** (p. 434): related to, connected to. "The brothers wanted to dissolve the company, but were worried about the *attendant* tax problems that might result."

✔ CHECK YOUR UNDERSTANDING

1. What should you do if you are reading a chapter section and don't find a general sentence or two that sums up the point of the reading?

   _____

2. If the author hasn't put the main idea of the reading into a thesis statement, how can you know that your inference is correct?

   _____

   _____

3. Which three methods of organizing information are very likely to imply rather than state the main idea?

   _____

Inferring Connections Between Paragraphs

Although we've looked at the way sentences relate to one another, we've talked a good deal less about how paragraphs connect to one another in longer readings. Yet this is a critical part of reading multi-paragraph chapter sections, essays, and articles. Not surprisingly, inferences play an important role here, too.

For an illustration, look at the following pair of paragraphs and ask yourself, What's the connection between paragraphs 1 and 2?

New Technology in Police Work

1 While police still use common sense, hands-on community policing, new advances in technology have given law enforcement new and increasingly imaginative approaches to locking up the bad guys.

2 San Diego's bait-and-switch-off operation nabs car thieves who try to steal specially equipped vehicles. Once the thief breaks into the vehicle, police are notified electronically. Via remote control, police officers can lock the doors, close the windows, and turn off the engine. Audio monitors have the added benefit of recording the criminal's sometimes humorous—and abundantly profane—verbal reactions to his plight.

(Adapted from Bowman and Kearney, *State and Local Government*, 8th ed., p. 445.)

Because you spotted the category word *approaches* at the end of the first sentence, you probably drew the correct inference. The "bait-and-switch-off operation" in San Diego is an example of the "increasingly imaginative approaches" to locking up the bad guys mentioned in the opening paragraph. Note, though, that there is no transitional phrase like "for example" or "for instance" linking paragraph 1 with paragraph 2. Instead, the writer leaves it up to the reader to draw the logical inference: Paragraph 2 provides specific examples of the general point in paragraph 1.

Here now is the third paragraph of that same reading. What's the connection between this paragraph and the two that came before?

3 Technological applications for crime fighting are developing rapidly and show much promise. Computer based fingerprint identification systems and other data-sharing systems track criminals across multiple jurisdictions.* CSI-type labs perform forensic† work to identify criminals

---

*jurisdictions: areas of control or authority.
†forensic: related to the use of science and technology to investigate criminal activity.

and victims. Twenty states now require police to take DNA swabs of any individual charged with a felony. Computer mapping by New York City's COMPSTAT approach facilitates police planning and response by linking crime statistics to geographic information systems. Commercial cell phone translation services help police break through language barriers almost instantly.

Notice how the third paragraph provides a more specific version of the point made in the opening paragraph: Police are employing new technology to pursue new "approaches" to crime stopping. The third paragraph offers some very specific "technological applications" that further illustrate that opening claim. Here again, though, the reader has to infer the right connection.

Note, too, that at this point, we can be pretty sure that the opening sentence is also the thesis statement. Anytime one train of thought is continued for three paragraphs, it's likely to be the controlling idea of the entire reading, unless, of course, the reading goes on for several pages. But that's not the case here. The entire excerpt is only four paragraphs. And the fourth paragraph, shown below, fully confirms our guess that the first sentence of the reading is also thesis statement. Read the paragraph and see if you can explain why.

4 Closed-circuit TVs are deployed in Baltimore and other major cities to keep a 24-7 eye on crime-prone areas. Retired cops or officers assigned to light duty may then notify officers when something threatening or suspicious occurs. A senior citizen walking alone at night with youths clustered nearby bears watching, as does an apparent drug handoff or weapon display. The cameras produce a constant stream of police intelligence data and are believed to reduce crime rates. In San Francisco, gunfire sensors have been installed around the city to detect instances in which a firearm is discharged. Police can proceed immediately to the location to investigate.

Police monitor high-crime areas with closed-circuit televisions.

Why does this paragraph confirm that the opening sentence of paragraph 1 is the thesis statement?

_____

_____

_____

Making Paragraph Connections

"What goes on at the beginning strongly determines how readers will understand what follows."
—Writer and researcher Joseph Williams, from *Style: Ten Lessons in Clarity and Grace*

Writers often use the openings of paragraphs to tell readers the direction they are taking. Consequently, you need to pay especially close attention to the beginnings of paragraphs. This is where you will get your strongest sense of what connects the previous paragraph to the one you are about to read.

But remember, too, what you learned in Chapter 6. Sentences at the end of paragraphs frequently diverge from the main idea in order to point the way to what's coming up next. This means that, particularly in textbooks, both beginnings and endings of paragraphs deserve special attention.

Your understanding of longer readings would also benefit from a willingness to take note of what writers do when they explain or argue a point. As you move from paragraph to paragraph, keep asking yourself questions like these:

1. Why is this paragraph here?

2. What does this paragraph have to do with the one that came before?

3. What connection does the author want me to make between the previous paragraph and the one I am reading now?

Over time, you'll get a good sense of the different kinds of clues to connections writers leave in order to guide readers along the path of their thinking.

Common Paragraph Relationships
♦

When one paragraph follows another, the new paragraph might do any of the following:

1. show how the personal experience previously described has wider or general significance.
2. offer a more specific illustration of what's just been said.
3. add to the example or examples previously introduced.
4. explain how the traditional thinking described in a previous paragraph has been changed, reversed, or modified.
5. describe what happened as a result of the events related in a previous paragraph.
6. provide evidence for a point previously introduced.
7. identify the cause of the situation described in the previous paragraph.
8. offer a solution to the problem just introduced.
9. give a reason for the claim just made.
10. outline a point of view that opposes the one just cited in the previous paragraph.

SUMMING UP THE KEY POINTS

1. Writers often use opening phrases in new paragraphs to tell readers the direction they are taking. Pay attention to those sentence openings. Let them help you follow the writer's train of thought.
2. Whenever possible, use the concluding sentences of paragraphs to determine the direction the next paragraph will take.
3. For each new paragraph, ask yourself, "Why is this paragraph here?" "What is the relationship of this paragraph to the one that came before?"

◆ **EXERCISE 3**   **Making Connections Between Paragraphs**

DIRECTIONS   As you finish each paragraph of the extended reading starting on page 448, answer the questions that follow.

EXAMPLE

Guided by the title, read to find out what mystery the author is referring to.

The phrase "a much bigger problem" signals that the writer isn't going to spend more time on ordinary sailors or the poor.

An Arctic Mystery

1   When the Napoleonic Wars[†] ended in 1815, the British victors were faced with the problem of a returning navy that was no longer needed to wage war. It was easy enough to ignore the homecoming of ordinary sailors. They could be left to starve on the streets like most of Britain's poor. A much bigger problem was how to employ returning naval officers, who were socially well-connected and couldn't be so easily discarded or ignored. As it turned out, the solution to officer unemployment was naval exploration, and thus began a series of British expeditions into the unexplored and frigid landscapes of the Arctic and Antarctica.

1. At this point, based on the title and first paragraph, what's your prediction about the topic of this reading?

> British naval exploration in the Arctic seems a likely topic.

Which sentences look like they might serve as the thesis statement?

> The last two sentences of the paragraph seem general enough to require more
>
> explanation and appear at the end of the first paragraph, a typical thesis state-
>
> ment location.

Here's the second paragraph. Try to determine if the author's train of thought is becoming more general or more specific. Ask yourself if this paragraph continues,

2   By 1818, the "Heroic Age" of Britain's Arctic exploration had begun. Sir John Ross, an officer in the British Royal Navy was sent by the British Admiralty to explore Baffin Bay, which he did successfully. Sir William Edward Parry, Ross's second in command, quickly followed on a voyage of his own in 1821 and again in 1827, becoming the first man to overwinter in the Arctic. However, it was the 1845 Arctic voyage of Sir John Franklin that truly caught the public's attention in both Europe and America. Franklin had made three Arctic voyages prior to this, his last one, and he had explored more of the Arctic than any one before

[†]Napoleonic Wars: wars fought between France during the French emperor Napoleon Bonaparte's reign and other European nations, among them England.

modifies, or discards an idea from the previous paragraph.

him. Yet it was the mysterious disappearance of Franklin, his two ships, *Erebus* and *Terror*, and his entire 129-man crew that brought him posthumous* fame and inadvertently* stimulated even greater exploration of the Arctic's frozen terrain.

2. Does paragraph 2 continue to develop the topic you selected or is it focusing on a new topic? At this point, what do you think might be the main idea?

The topic is still Britain's naval exploration in the Arctic, but the author appears

to be zeroing in on a particular explorer, making the "1845 voyage of Sir John

Franklin," a more likely topic. The main idea might focus on how the "mysterious

disappearance" of Franklin's ships and crew caught the public's attention.

Now see if you can figure out what paragraph 3 adds to the story of Franklin and his men.

All the references to Crozier should suggest that he plays a key role in the reading.

3   The British Admiralty had sent Sir John sailing into the Arctic North in the hopes of discovering the legendary Northwest Passage, a narrow channel connecting the Pacific and Atlantic Oceans. However, the Admiralty probably would have done better to assign Franklin's second-in-command, Francis Moira Crozier, to head the expedition. While Franklin had great experience with Arctic trekking,* Crozier was much more experienced at sailing through ice. Then, too, Crozier was recently returned from the Arctic while Franklin had not sailed through ice-packed waters for over a quarter of a century. In a personal letter, Crozier had openly acknowledged misgivings about Franklin's judgment. Yet he had no choice but to obey his commander.

3. What's the point of focusing on the differences between Franklin and Crozier? How do the two men fit into the overall idea that you think is being developed?

The differences between the two men helps explain the "mysterious disappearance"

of the Franklin expedition introduced in paragraph 2. The paragraph tries to

explain why the ships did not make it home safely, with one reason being Franklin's

possible incompetence.

---

*posthumous: after death.
*inadvertently: unintentionally, by chance.
*trekking: walking on rough terrain or land.

Here's paragraph 4. It moves away from Franklin's drawbacks to discuss what new thread or theme? And how does that theme relate to what came before?

4   But whatever Franklin's shortcomings may or may not have been—and Franklin's competence is the subject of argument to this day—the expedition he commanded was probably doomed from the start. Both *Terror* and *Erebus* were heavily stocked with something new on the market—canned food. There was enough of it, in fact, to last five years if necessary. But as later analysis of the cans showed, many of them were not properly constructed, and the food in them quickly became loaded with bacteria. In addition, the lead used in the tin casing seems to have poisoned crew members. It's also true that during the years of the expedition, 1845 to 1850,[†] Arctic winters were especially severe. As if that weren't enough, the huge, steel-tipped, icebreaker ships the British were so proud of needed deep water to sail and deep water froze early, leaving the *Terror* and the *Erebus* stuck in ice.

4. The author has moved away from Franklin to focus on what? And how does this change in focus fit in with what came before?

This paragraph continues to describe the causes of the "mysterious disappearance" already introduced in paragraph 1. Only now the focus is on the problems facing the expedition in general, no matter who was at the helm.

Consider what paragraph 5 contributes to the story of the Franklin expedition.

5   Franklin himself died in 1847 when the ships he commanded must have been already stranded in the ice. By that time, hunger had set in and officers and crew were coming down with scurvy.[†] Command of the two ships then passed to Captain Crozier, who, at some point, ordered his men to abandon both ships. Crozier proceeded to lead the crew in a doomed trek across the ice in the hopes of finding food, being rescued, or at the very least, getting help from the local Inuit[†] natives. It is thanks to the natives, who encountered members of the crew up until 1850, that anything at all is known about the crew's final days. And what is known is almost too horrible to consider. Freezing, sick, and starved, the men who had sailed forth to find the Northwest Passage began, according to several Inuit accounts, feeding on one another. Bones found during later rescue efforts seem to confirm the Inuits' claims.

[†]1850 was the last year that any members of the crew were seen, although they might have survived somewhat longer.
[†]scurvy: a disease caused by lack of vitamin C. It causes severe bleeding that eventually produces anemia.
[†]*Inuit* is the term that has replaced *Eskimo*.

5. What connection does the author want readers to make between this paragraph and the paragraphs that came before? At this point, can you say for sure what the main idea of the entire reading is?

Paragraph 5 explains what happened after the ships got stuck in the ice. It also tells us more about the "mysterious disappearance," which just about confirms the last sentence of paragraph 2 as the thesis statement.

Here's the final paragraph of the reading. Like concluding sentences, the final paragraph of an extended reading sometimes goes off in a slightly different direction from the main idea to explain how a problem was solved or describe the outcome of an experience. Do you think that's happening in this paragraph?

6   Meanwhile back at home, it was Lady Jane Franklin who would not give up the search for her husband. Famous for her determined will, Lady Jane browbeat her highborn friends into publicly insisting to anyone who would listen that Franklin or, at the very least, his body, be brought home. By the time she was through, more than thirty expeditions had been launched in an effort to find out what had happened to the doomed ships under Franklin's command. The story of the Franklin expedition was by now so famous even American ships joined in the search, motivated, to some degree, by the huge reward Lady Jane and the Admiralty had united to create. But, in part, searchers were also motivated by the desire to solve the mystery of the crew and ships' disappearance. Together, the money and the mystery kept the searchers going. In the process, larger and larger regions of the Arctic were explored until, in 1855, on yet another mission to rescue Franklin and his men, Captain Robert McClure located the fabled Northwest Passage. The actual fate of Franklin, Crozier, and the rest of the crew, however, remains an unsolved mystery to this day.

This is the frozen landscape that surrounded Crozier and the ships he commanded.

Courtesy and copyright Ulrich Flemming.

6. What does the opening transition of paragraph 6 help the reader do? Paragraph 6 then further develops what point introduced early on in the reading?

The transition helps the reader switch locations. The paragraph then returns to the

point made in paragraph 1: Inadvertently, the search for Franklin led to greater

exploration of the Arctic.

EXPLANATION   Please note that throughout this reading, it's the reader who figures out how the ideas in the individual paragraphs relate to one another. The author doesn't say, "Here are several examples of naval exploration, but I'm really only interested in one in particular." That connection is left up to readers to make.

When You're Haunted by a Past That Isn't Yours

1   The Data Protection Act of 1998 went into force in 2000. It was meant to ensure that companies or organizations that provided personal data, or information, about individuals got their facts right. As a result of the Data Protection Act, individuals could get access to their personal information and, if necessary, challenge its accuracy. The thinking was that if people could get access to background information and discover it was wrong, they might sue the data provider. Thus, fear of litigation would keep personal data providers on their toes and ensure that the information they gave out was accurate. That was the assumption anyway.

1. What does the last sentence of paragraph 1 suggest about how the reading will develop?

_____

Based on the first paragraph what might be the main idea?

_____

2   Dennis Teague might have his doubts that things worked out as planned. When Teague was rejected for a job at the Wisconsin State Fair, he pushed to find out why. He was astonished to learn that he had a long criminal record. Or at least that's what his background check showed. According to the Wisconsin Department of Justice, Teague had a lengthy criminal history.

2. Does paragraph 2 continue the train of thought begun by the last sentence of paragraph 1? Please explain your answer.

_____

_____

3   As it turned out, though, the record wasn't Teague's. His second cousin had used his name when he was arrested. Although the fake name had eventually been discovered and the real culprit identified, Teague's name was still attached to a long list of crimes he didn't commit. Teague sued the Wisconsin Department of Justice claiming that the system used to perform background checks is flawed, generating information about the person being checked as well as about people who might have used the person's name as an alias.

3. How does Dennis Teague's story help explain the meaning of the title?

_____

4   Kathleen Ann Casey probably shares Dennis Teague's skepticism. Casey applied for a job as a pharmacy assistant. But she didn't get the job. Her background check had turned up a criminal past that showed Casey repeatedly being charged with forgery. Casey not only didn't get the job, she also ended up losing her apartment because she couldn't pay her rent. Yet Kathleen Ann Casey had never done anything illegal. The same could not be said, though, for Kathleen A. Casey, a much younger woman who lived in another town and didn't have her namesake's scruples about forging other people's names onto checks and credit card slips.

4. Why has Kathleen Ann Casey been introduced by the author? What role does she play in developing the main idea?

_____

_____

What does the author imply about Kathleen A. Casey?

_____

5   The arrival of computers and the Web was supposed to make doing background checks easier. After all, if someone wanted to do a background check, that person no longer needed to go to a courthouse and thumb through records. All he or she had to do was pay a fee to a company or an institution that had gathered the information electronically, often from public records available online. Unfortunately, many of the companies that now routinely collect and sell information so easily don't necessarily double-check for accuracy or even update their files regularly as Gina Marie Haynes learned to her dismay.

5. How does this paragraph help explain the title of the reading?

_____

_____

What does the last sentence in paragraph 5 suggest you are going to learn about Gina Marie Haynes?

_____

_____

6   Haynes refused to pay for a used car that broke down as soon as she drove off the lot. The used car company filed fraud charges, which were eventually dismissed. To her shock, Haynes discovered through a background check that companies collecting information from public records on the Web had noted the fraud charge but neglected to remove it from the records. She has spent the last year trying to get the fraud accusation off the records of the many different companies and organizations that now freely sell her data, accurate or not, to anyone who asks for it. (Source of information about Dennis Teague: Bruce Vielmetti, "Wisconsin Sued Over Criminal Reports," www.thebackgroundinvestigator.com/current_issue/index .asp?id=1479; about Kathleen Ann Casey and Gina Marie Haynes, http://finance.yahoo .com/news/ap-impact-criminal-past-isnt-182335059.html.)

6. What would you say is the implied main idea of this reading?

_____

_____

_____

CHECK YOUR UNDERSTANDING

1. Where are you most likely to find clues to the relationships between paragraphs?

_____

2. Each time you start a new paragraph, what kinds of questions should you be asking?

_____

Writing Summaries

"Summarization is a scholarly skill, but it's not for scholars alone. . . ."
—Teacher and writer Rick Wormelli from *Summarization in any Subject*

At this point you are familiar with the way writers, particularly writers of textbooks, state or imply main ideas in both paragraphs and longer readings. That means you are ready to think about a skill that is absolutely central to college success—the ability to write summaries.

Except for mathematics, instructors in just about every discipline assign written summaries for homework. In preparation for these assignments, you need a clear understanding of what a summary is and how to go about writing one.

Summarizing: Paraphrasing with a Difference

A **summary** is a condensed version of a writer's original thoughts. However, it doesn't use the writer's original language except, perhaps, to introduce a name or key term. This is, as you might have guessed, another instance where knowing how to paraphrase is crucial.

However, unlike paraphrasing for a paper where you try to reproduce in your own words the entire original text, *paraphrasing for a summary requires you to exclude some of the original.* A good summary should include the author's main idea and only those supporting details essential to understanding that main idea. Introductory sentences, extra examples, concluding sentences, and obvious or repetitive details can and should be left out.

Let's say, for instance, that you were summarizing the following paragraph. Which supporting details would you need to keep in your summary and which ones do you think you could leave out?

[1]To the inexperienced listener, *narcocorridos* are ballads that sound like pumped up polkas. [2]But unlike polkas with their harmless, often trivial, lyrics, *narcocorridos* are no laughing matter. [3]Those who write and sing the ballads are putting their lives on the line, and some have, literally, died for a song. [4]*Narcocorridos* tell the story of Mexican drug lords and the lengths they go to maintain control of drug trafficking to and from the United States. [5]Although a *narcocorrido* singer can make a fortune if he is commissioned by a gang who wants to be celebrated in song, the singer is then linked to that gang. [6]That link makes him an enemy of opposing gangs. [7]This is the likely reason why Sergio Vega known as "El Shaka" was shot and killed. [8]It's also why Sergio Gómez was kidnapped right after a concert, tortured, and strangled. [9]Valentín Elizalde's *narcocorrido* "To My Enemies" put his name on a hit list, and Elizalde ended up being gunned down in front of witnesses right after performing at a concert in Texas. [10]The name of *narcocorrido* singer Gerardo Ortiz was almost added to that list when his car was attacked after a concert. [11]Two people in the vehicle were killed, but the singer escaped and went into hiding.

Read the paragraph through and you'll see that the main chain of repetition and reference describes the danger associated with singing a *narcocorrido*. The general statement of that point is sentence 3, which, with the addition of the antecedent "narcocorrido singers" forms the main idea statement, "Narcocorrido singers are putting their lives on the line, and some have, literally, died for a song."

Start with the Main Idea

As you might suspect, a good place to start your summary is with a paraphrased statement of that main idea. So here's one possibility: "Narcocorrido singers pen lyrics that sometimes get them killed."

Consider Your Purpose and Audience

The next sentence you add to your summary depends on two things: (1) your purpose in writing and (2) your audience. If you are summarizing in order to take notes for a paper you are writing, then you'll want to make it clear why *narcocorrido* singers come under fire. You'll also want to add some names to your summary to illustrate your point. That means your summary would look like this:

Summary 1

Narcocorrido singers pen lyrics that sometimes get them killed because the lyrics angered a rival gang. Among those who have died because their songs glorified one gang and infuriated another are Sergio Vega, Sergio Gómez, and Valentín Elizalde.

But if you're writing a summary for an instructor's assignment, then you can't take for granted that your instructor knows what *narcocorrido* music is. Therefore, you'll need to paraphrase the definition and add that to the summary. You'll also need to provide the author and source of the original article. For instance,

Summary 2

As Ellis Ward points out in his *New York Times* article "Balladeers for the Drug Cartels," *narcocorrido* singers put their lives on the line when they sing, and more than one has died for a song. *Narcocorrido* ballads make drug lords sound like heroes, but in glorifying one drug kingpin, the singer infuriates a rival gang and makes enemies. Sergio Vega, Sergio Gómez, and Valentín Elizalde are among those *narcocorrido* singers whose songs led to their being killed by rival gangs.

Narcocorrido singers celebrate the bravery and daring of drug cartels, and some have lost their lives for their songs.

WEB QUEST
What war popularized the singing of corridos?

_____

While the word *corridos* is currently linked in the press to the drug wars, historically, what was the subject of the early corridos?

_____

_____

◆ EXERCISE 4   Evaluating Summaries

DIRECTIONS   Read each paragraph. Then circle the letter of the better summary. On the blank lines explain why one summary is better than the other.

EXAMPLE

Original: Between 300,000 and 600,000 U.S. citizens a year survive a suicide attempt, and about 19,000 of those survivors are permanently disabled. Suicide is the eighth leading cause of death in the United States.

Young people between the ages of fifteen and twenty-four constitute* the largest increase in suicides during the past thirty years. Men kill themselves at approximately four times the rate for women. The highest risk for many years has been Caucasian men over thirty-five, but the suicide rate among teenagers and young black males has been dramatically increasing since the middle of the twentieth century. Native Americans kill themselves at about one and one-half the times the national U.S. rate. Even though the elderly make up roughly 10 percent of the total population, 25 percent of all suicides occur in the over-sixty-five population, and suicide rates increase after age seventy. (Adapted from James, *Crisis Intervention Strategies*, 6th ed., pp. 180–81.)

Which of the following summaries used to take notes on the paragraph is better?

a. Suicide is a major problem in the United States. It is the eighth leading cause of death, with young people, men over thirty-five, African Americans, Native Americans, and the elderly being the populations hardest hit.

b. Between 300,000 and 600,000 U.S. citizens a year survive their attempt to commit suicide. But many who try do succeed, making suicide the eighth leading cause of death. More and more young people are killing themselves, although, for the most part, it is the elderly who are most likely to commit suicide.

Please explain the reasoning behind your choice.

Summary *b* doesn't infer any main idea from all of the statistics, even though, taken together, the figures suggest a serious social problem. Summary *b* also leaves out entirely some of the populations in which suicides are high.

1. *Original*: To believe that only women who are partners in a conjugal* relationship are victims of violence is to be badly mistaken. Studies on courtship violence estimate that it occurs in anywhere from 22 to 67 percent of courtship relationships and cuts across college, high school, and nonschool dating populations. A conservative estimate is that violence occurs in approximately 25 percent of courtship relationships. As simplistic as the following may sound as a predictor of violence, one study found that the number of dating

---

*constitute: make up, comprise, consist of.
*conjugal: related to marriage.

partners and dating frequency had the highest positive correlation*
and that grade point average had the highest negative correlation.
(Adapted from James, *Crisis Intervention Strategies*, 6th ed., p. 284.)

Which of the following summaries used to take notes on the paragraph is better?

a. To think that only women who are partners in a conjugal relationship are victims of violence is to make a mistake. Studies on courtship violence in romantic relationships estimate that violence also occurs in courtship relationships, with different studies suggesting figures that range from 22 to 67 percent. At a conservative estimate, around one-quarter of all dating relationships include some degree of violence. As for predicting which relationships will tend to include violence and which ones will not, one study found a high correlation between violence in a relationship and numerous dating partners. The study also found that people with high grades had the least chance of being in a relationship that was violent.

b. It's not only married women who can be the victims of violence. Violence can be part of courtship as well as marriage. Even with a conservative estimate, at least 25 percent of all romantic relationships are marred by violence.

Please explain the reasoning behind your choice.

_____

_____

_____

2. *Original*: Marxists[†] and anarchists* have been trying to claim Emiliano Zapata (1879–1919) as one of their own ever since his assassination in 1910. But Zapata was never motivated by political ideology, or theory. He fought for economic justice. When the price of sugar went up and produced huge profits, Mexican *hacienderos*, or plantation owners, began forcing small farmers off their

_____

*correlation: a mutual connection or relationship between two events, parts or things that seem to influence one another.
[†]Marxists: people who believe in the economic theories of Karl Marx.
*anarchists: people who believe that government is a source of evil.

Emiliano Zapata was a horse trainer by profession but ended up becoming a heroic leader of the Mexican revolution.

land in order to grow more sugarcane. Zapata tried first by peaceful, political means to convince the big landowners to give back the land they had taken illegally. When those attempts failed, he founded a guerilla movement known as the Zapatistas and focused on his now famous slogan *Tierra y Libertad* or Land and Liberty. Zapata was so successful at taking back land from the wealthy, Mexico's new political leader Venustiano Carranza, who was opposed to land reform and feared Zapata's influence and success, laid a trap for his opponent. On April 10, 1919, Zapata arrived for what he thought was a meeting with a colonel defecting from Carranza's forces and was shot to death by federal soldiers.

Which of the following summaries used to take notes on the paragraph is better?

a. Emiliano Zapata (1879–1919) fought to bring justice to Mexico's small landowners. Using guerilla tactics, he and his supporters forced the large plantation owners to give up the land they had taken from small farmers. Under his leadership, the Zapatistas were so successful fighting for "Tierra y Libertad," or Land and Liberty, that Mexico's leader Venustiano Carranza, who was on the landowners' side, had Zapata killed.

b. Marxists and anarchists have always tried to claim Emiliano Zapata as a political supporter of their theories, but Zapata was his own man and that's what made him an enemy of Mexican leader Venustiano Carranza, who had Zapata assassinated.

Please explain the reasoning behind your choice.

_____

_____

_____

WEB QUEST
Emiliano Zapata was a major figure in the Mexican revolution that took place between 1910 and 1920. Who was the other major revolutionary figure who fought in the North while Zapata did battle in the South?

_____

Summarizing Longer Readings

Everything that applies to summarizing paragraphs applies to longer readings as well. The main difference is in the amount of information that has to be evaluated as essential or nonessential.

Let Your Purpose and Audience Determine the Details

Summaries of longer readings should start off just like paragraph summaries do—with the main idea. But then you also have to determine (1) which main ideas from the supporting detail paragraphs you need to include and (2) how much additional description or explanation the supporting details need in order to be clear. Once again, both of those decisions depend on the purpose and audience for your summary.

Say that you were writing a summary of the reading on page 444 about the doomed Arctic journey of the two ships *Terror* and *Erebus*. But, because your purpose was to describe the fate of the expedition in preparation for writing a paper about changes in the Arctic due to global warming, your audience consisted of only you. In other words, you wanted to have the gist of the reading clear in your mind but knew it wasn't going to play a major role in your paper. It would merely be part of the introduction. In that context, the following summary would work just fine.

Summary 1

Even though John Franklin's expedition to the Arctic (1845–1850) ended with the disappearance of the ships and crew, the trip made Franklin posthumously famous and encouraged the exploration of the Arctic. When Franklin's ships *Terror* and *Erebus* froze in the ice and did not return, the public was fascinated and wanted to know what happened to Franklin and his men. In addition, his determined and influential wife Lady Jane Franklin kept the Navy looking for her husband and thereby furthered the exploration of the Arctic.

Here again, the summary of a longer reading starts off with the overall main idea. But the supporting details about what went wrong on the expedition are kept to a bare minimum.

If the Purpose Changes, So Can the Details

Here's another summary. Only in this case, the purpose of the summary has changed. The summary is included to help make a larger point—that the British are willing to celebrate as heroes those who fail at what they set out to do. Notice how the change in purpose changes the details selected.

Summary 2

As many admirers and critics have pointed out, the British are just as likely to celebrate those who fail as those who succeed.[†] Take, for instance, the last voyage of Sir John Franklin, who set out in 1845 to find the Northwest Passage but ended up with his ships, *Terror* and *Erebus*, stranded in ice and his men reduced to cannibalism. Franklin may not have been suited for the job to begin with since he had not sailed through ice in over twenty years. But even had he been well-prepared, he faced several obstacles that all but guaranteed his failure. The winters of his journey were especially cold, his ships were too large to stay out of freezing water, and his food supply was tainted. Yet, despite his failure to achieve his goal, Franklin achieved great posthumous fame, and efforts to locate both him and the men under his command furthered Arctic exploration.

If the purpose were changed again, say to fulfill an assignment asking you to summarize the gist or essential elements of the reading, there would be yet another shift in the details included. Then the summary would touch on all the supporting main ideas in the reading: (1) Franklin's lack of expertise, (2) the obstacles the expedition faced, (3) the horror Franklin's crew underwent after his death, and (4) the Arctic exploration that came out of the many searches instigated by his wife.

Pointers for Summary Writing ♦	**1.** Summaries are *paraphrased* and *abbreviated* versions of original text. Thus, your summary should never be as long as the original article, essay, or chapter section. Summaries, however, don't have a fixed length. How long or short they are depends on the audience and the purpose of the summary

---

[†]For a discussion of Britain's fondness of heroic failures, see this website: www.screenonline.org.uk/tours/heroes/tour5.html.

2. In a summary, the language and length of the original changes; the meaning does not.

3. The number of major or minor details you include in a summary will vary with the purpose and audience.

4. If the reading you are summarizing implies but doesn't state the main idea, your summary should express the implied main idea directly in a thesis statement.

5. If you are writing a summary for someone other than yourself, always assume that person hasn't read the original. Then decide what major and minor details are essential to making the main idea of the reading clear to the reader.

6. While a summary should not change the meaning of the original, it can change the order in which ideas are presented. Notice in the sample summary on page 459 that the detail about Franklin's men resorting to cannibalism comes earlier in the summary than it does in the original.

7. When you are considering what can be eliminated, look closely at illustrations or examples. Often one example will do for a summary and you can eliminate the rest. Quotations, for the most part, can usually be left out of the summary. Quotations almost always provide emphasis, and in a summary you don't need to say things in different ways. Once is enough.

8. Unlike examples, reasons for a particular idea or action should not be cut although they can be trimmed down. Reasons are there to prove a point in the original text and should always make their way into a summary.

9. Authors sometimes use repetition for emphasis. But repetition has no place in a summary. Eliminate any sentences that serve that purpose.

10. If you are summarizing an article for an assignment, make sure to include the author and source of the article somewhere in the opening lines.

11. While you may use a date or a bit of background from the original introduction, most introductory material should not find its way into your summary.

12. Leave your personal opinion out of the summary unless, of course, you are instructed to include it.

SUMMING UP THE KEY POINTS

1. Summaries are abbreviated versions of longer texts. Never let the summary match the original in length.

2. Unlike a paraphrase for a term paper, a summary requires you to eliminate some of the original material

3. A good summary should include the author's main idea and only those supporting details essential to understanding the main idea.

4. A good summary should exclude introductory sentences, extra examples, concluding sentences, obvious or repetitive details.

5. The form and content of a summary varies with the purpose and audience.

♦ **EXERCISE 5**   **Writing Summaries**

DIRECTIONS   Read and summarize the following article. Include the author and title of the article at the beginning of your summary.

EXAMPLE

Drop Dead Ads Banned in UK†

1   Gorgeous, yes. A little too thin for British tastes? Apparently so. British fashion line Drop Dead Clothing is the most recent company to come under fire by the UK's† Advertising Standards Authority—this time for featuring an overly thin model in its ads. The model, who dons a colorful two-piece in the controversial advertisements, is "underweight and looked anorexic," according to the ASA assessment.

2   Furthermore, the ASA said in a statement: "In the bikini images her hip, rib and collar bones were highly visible. We also noted that in the bikini and denim shorts images, hollows in her thighs were noticeable and she had prominent thigh bones. We considered that in combination with the stretched out pose and heavy eye makeup, the model looked underweight in the pictures."

3   The ASA also pointed to the fact that the clothing company targets a young audience, meaning that the ads could possibly warp* young girls' perceptions of a healthy body image. The same model appears in various ads for the clothing company.

---

†UK: United Kingdom: consists of Great Britain and Northern Ireland.
*warp: distort, bend in the wrong way.

4   In its defense, Drop Dead responded that its model "was a standard size eight…[and] while many people in the UK may find a size eight too slim, a size eight was a normal UK clothing size." The company also called the ASA's accusations "unreasonable." But Drop Dead is just the latest in a slew of fashion and beauty brands that have recently been criticized by the ASA. ("Drop Dead Ads Banned in UK Over Super Skinny Model" by Joyce Chen from *New York Daily News*, November 10, 2011. Used by permission.)

Summary   As Joyce Chen reported in the New York Daily News, another company, Drop Dead Clothing, has been cited by Britain's Advertising Standards Authority for inappropriate ads. This time the ad showed an anorexic young model. The ASA believes the ad would encourage young girls to think they have to be really thin to be attractive. Drop Dead Clothing said the ASA was being "unreasonable." They also said the model was a size 8, which was a normal clothing size.

EXPLANATION   The summary includes the main idea of the article. It includes only enough supporting detail to indicate (1) why the ad was banned and (2) how the company that created the ad responded to the ban.

Children in Alcoholic Families

1   Children raised in homes where open communication is practiced and consistency of lifestyle is the norm* usually have the ability to adopt a wide variety of roles. Children growing up in alcoholic homes seldom learn the combination of roles that mold healthy personalities. They become locked into roles based on their perception of what they need to do to survive and bring some stability into their chaotic lives. The following roles of children in alcoholic families have been identified.

2   **The Scapegoat**   The scapegoat is the typical troubled child in the alcoholic family. This acting-out child is the one who comes to the attention of school administrators, police, and social services. These children have extremely poor self-images and attempt to enhance themselves by rebellious, attention-seeking behavior. Scapegoat children use unacceptable forms of behavior to say, "Care about me," or "I can't cope."

---

*norm: standard or typical pattern, the usual way things happen.

3　**The Hero**　The oldest child is most likely to be a very sophisticated child or family hero. This is the little adult who takes care of the alcoholic, the spouse, and the other children. In attempting to care for the family, the responsible child enables the alcoholic by giving her or him more time to drink. Not only are such children highly responsible to the family, they are also highly responsible in their academic and extracurricular activities.

4　**The Lost Child**　This is usually the middle or younger child. The lost child follows directions, handles whatever has to be handled and adjusts to the circumstances, however horrible they may be. The lost child outwardly appears to be more flexible, spontaneous, and somewhat more selfish than others in the home. These children don't feel, question, get upset, or act in any way to draw attention to themselves. They enable the alcoholic by not being a "bother."

5　**The Family Mascot**　The family mascot is usually the youngest child, who placates and comforts everybody in the family and makes them feel better. This child thinks that by making family members feel better, he or she can divert attention from the problem, and it will go away. The mascot may also assume a role of sympathetic counselor to the rest of the family. The mascot abets the alcoholic by distracting the family from the constant conflict alcoholism causes in a family setting. (James, *Crisis Intervention Strategies*, p. 318.)

Summary

_____

_____

_____

_____

_____

_____

_____

_____

_____

_____

_____

_____

_____

✔ CHECK YOUR UNDERSTANDING

1. How does writing a summary differ from paraphrasing for a term paper?

   _____

   _____

2. A summary should never _____.

3. A summary should always include _____

   and only those _____.

4. What should a good summary exclude?

   _____

5. The form and content of a summary varies according to _____ and

   _____.

VOCABULARY ROUND UP 2

Below are ten words introduced in pages 440–62. The words are accompanied by more detailed definitions, the page on which they originally appeared, and additional sample sentences. Spend time reviewing the words and their meanings because you will see them again in review tests at the end of the chapter. Use the online dictionary Wordnik to find additional sentences illustrating the words in context. (*Note*: If you know of another dictionary with as many examples of words in context feel free to use that one instead.)

1. **jurisdiction** (p. 440): area of authority or control, the right and power to apply the law. "If he entered the court's *jurisdiction*, he could expect to be thrown in jail."

2. **posthumous** (p. 445): after death. "The actor's *posthumous* fame came too late for him to enjoy it."

3. **inadvertently** (p. 445): unintentionally, not on purpose. "She *inadvertently* picked up the belt when she grabbed for her purse, and it was dangling over her shoulder, along with the purse strap, during the entire bus ride."

4. **trekking** (p. 445): walking or hiking over rough terrain or landscape. "Even after *trekking* across the desert for miles, the guide never seemed to show fatigue."

5. **constitute** (p. 455): make up, consist of, comprise. "Probable cause is necessary for police to get a search warrant, but what *constitutes* probable cause is open to interpretation."

6. **conjugal** (p. 455): related to or dealing with marriage. "After the fight, the prisoners lost all rights to *conjugal* visits."

7. **correlation** (p. 456): a mutual connection or relationship between two events, parts, or things that tend to be associated with one another in a way not based on chance alone. "As a person who would be lost without spell-check, she was happy to hear that there was no *correlation* between spelling ability and intelligence."

8. **anarchists** (p. 456): people who believe that state or federal governments are an unnecessary evil. "Emma Goldman was probably America's most famous *anarchist*."

9. **warp** (p. 461): distort, twist, bend in the wrong direction. "His mind had been *warped* by years of loneliness and isolation."

10. **norm** (p. 462): standard pattern or typical model, common way of thinking or behaving generally accepted by the culture or society. "The American novelist Kate Chopin lived at a time when it was the *norm* for women to be dutiful wives, but her novel *The Awakening* openly challenged that traditional notion."

DIGGING DEEPER Winning Legal Rights for Animals

Looking Ahead The reading on tort reform (pages 432–33) suggested that there might be too many lawyers at work in the United States. This reading suggests that their number might well increase due to a growing number of cases involving the legal rights of animals.

Getting Focused Read to get a more specific sense of what the author means with the phrase "legal rights for animals."

1 A little more than two decades ago, something called "animal law" started gaining public notice. There were several pet custody and wrongful death cases mentioned in the press that immediately became fodder for late-night comedians. Except for those involved, almost everyone seemed to think that talking about the legal rights of animals was a huge joke. In addition to the comic monologues, there were numerous cartoons showing a dog or cat sitting in the witness chair of a courtroom with paw raised in preparation for taking an oath. These were often accompanied by editorials with titles like "It Really Is a Kangaroo Court."[†]

No Joke Anymore

2 But make no mistake; these days, no one is laughing. Animal law, once unheard of both in and out of law school, is now being taught at more than a dozen law schools. Among them are some of the most prestigious: Georgetown, Harvard, and the University of California at Los Angeles. According to Stephen Wise, a Boston lawyer who teaches animal law at Harvard, the number of animal law classes is "sky-rocketing." Wise himself, the former president of the Animal Legal Defense Fund, wrote one of the first books on animal law, *Rattling the Cage: Toward Legal Rights for Animals* (2001). But numerous others have followed his lead and explored the position of animals in the legal system in books like *Animal Law: Cases and Materials* (2009), *An Introduction to Animals and the Law* (2010), and *A World View of Animal Law* (2011).

3 A widespread interest in animal law was ignited in 1999 when an appellate court of appeals in New York reversed a trial court decision and awarded custody of Lovey, a ten-year-old cat, on the basis of the

---

[†]kangaroo court: a court that's dishonest or illegal.

cat's "best interests." This was in direct contrast to what had been the basis for awarding pet ownership: the animal would go to whoever came up with the bill of sale or certificate of adoption. Simply put, the animal was a piece of property. The New York decision, however, challenged the long-held assumption that, like jewelry or furniture, animals are property, devoid of interests or rights.

4   In 2000, Tennessee became the first state in the nation to approve emotional-distress damages for a pet's loss, and according to Michigan State's Animal Legal & Historical Center, other states followed Tennessee's lead. Attorneys specializing in animal law are intent on making the legal system recognize and respond to the human suffering caused by the loss of a beloved pet.

5   The noticeable toughening of anticruelty laws is further evidence that animal law is being taken seriously. In 1994, all but six states considered cruelty to animals a misdemeanor and punished it with small fines or short jail sentences. At the present time, "aggravated cruelty" to animals has been elevated from a misdemeanor to a felony in forty-six out of fifty states. In short, if someone intentionally kills or causes serious physical injury to a pet or other animal, that person can end up paying a large fine and spending time in prison. Such tough sentencing is a far cry from the days when hurting or killing an animal was punished with a fifty-dollar fine. It is also a further indication of the justice system's changing attitude toward animals.

6   The much-publicized 2007 case of Atlanta Falcon quarterback Michael Vick is a perfect illustration of how much the law has revised its stance on cruelty to animals. Indicted by a grand jury in July 2007, Vick was sentenced to twenty-three months in prison. Although many people thought the sentence too short given the deadly abuse Vick and his co-conspirators had meted out to the dogs they had used as fighters or, even worse, as bait, there was a time when imprisonment would not have been part of the penalty. After all, Vick's dog fighting ring had harmed only animals, not people, and it was once generally assumed that laws were designed to protect only the latter, not the former.

7   In a country of devoted pet owners, though, that assumption has been re-examined and found wanting. Witness the fact that there now exist a variety of textbooks devoted to animal law. There are also websites focusing on the same subject and many of the sites link to a "Bibliography of Animal Law Resources." There are also student chapters of the Animal Legal Defense Fund across the country, and law schools routinely host discussions and debates dedicated to the subject of

animal law. Although some of the groups involved in monitoring and changing the laws governing relationships between humans and animals sport amusing names like "Pawtropolis" and "Kitty Crusaders," their intent is serious—to make the general public aware that animals can no longer be neglected, hurt, or, in the worst cases, killed with impunity. If the toughening stance vis-à-vis animal cruelty wasn't evidence enough, the number of lawyers registered with the Animal Legal Defense Fund continues to rise, and no one thinks that number has anywhere to go but up.

Sharpening Your Skills

DIRECTIONS   Answer the questions by circling the letter of the correct response or by writing out the answer.

1. Based on the context in which the words *misdemeanor* and *felony* appear in paragraph 5, "At the present time, 'aggravated cruelty' to animals has been elevated from a misdemeanor to a felony in forty-six out of fifty states," which makes more sense to you?

   a. A misdemeanor is the more serious crime.

   b. A felony is the more serious crime.

2. Based on the context in which *vis-à-vis* is used in paragraph 7, "If the toughening stance *vis-à-vis* animal cruelty wasn't evidence enough, the number of lawyers registered with the Animal Legal Defense Fund continues to rise, and no one thinks that number has anywhere to go but up," which definition makes the most sense?

   a. in contrast to

   b. in relation to

   c. up against

   d. as a way out of

3. Which statement best expresses the main idea of the entire reading?

   a. Animal law is better known than it once was, but it is still not being taken seriously by legal scholars.

   b. The penalties for the abuse of animals need to be harsher.

c. If animal law gains serious recognition, all experiments involving animals will result in lawsuits.

d. Animal law is no longer the subject of jokes; it is taken seriously by both the legal system and the general public.

4. The main idea is

a. stated.

b. implied.

5. What does the pronoun *this* refer to in sentence 2 of paragraph 3?

a. a court in New York

b. Lovey's custody being awarded on the basis of her "best interests"

c. August 1999

d. conflict over a cat in a divorce case

6. What does the phrase "simply put" (paragraph 3) signal about the sentence that follows?

a. The author is going to reverse the previous point.

b. The author is going to introduce a new point.

c. The author is going to restate the previous point.

7. Which sentence best paraphrases the topic sentence of paragraph 3?

a. The 1999 appellate court decision awarded Lovey to the person who had the cat's best interests at heart.

b. The 1999 appellate court decision undermined the notion that pets are property.

c. In the past, pets involved in divorce cases were treated as property.

d. Thanks to the 1999 appellate court decision involving Lovey the cat, animals involved in divorce cases will never again be treated like property.

8. Which statement best paraphrases the topic sentence of paragraph 5?

a. Although a few states have made cruelty to animals a felony, the majority have not followed suit.

b. Anyone who purposely injures an animal deserves to serve time in prison.

   c. The growing tendency to make animal cruelty a serious crime is another indication that animals are winning legal rights.

   d. There was a time when people who purposely injured animals would be punished with nothing more than a small fine.

9. Here's the last sentence in paragraph 5: "It is also a further indication of the justice system's changing attitude toward animals." What's the connection between this sentence and the description of the Michael Vick case that follows in paragraph 6?

_____

_____

10. In paragraph 7, the phrase "that assumption" refers to what idea summed up at the end of paragraph 6?

_____

Share Your Thoughts It's been argued that people who harm animals when they are small children are inclined to be violent adults when they grow up. Does that make sense to you? Why or why not?

From Reader to Writer Use the Web to read up on why Michael Vick went to jail. Then write a few paragraphs explaining why you think his punishment did or did not fit the crime. It's up to you if you write an introduction, but do make sure that you take a stand one way or another and give reasons for your position.

▶ **TEST 1**   **Reviewing Key Concepts**

DIRECTIONS   Answer the following questions by filling in the blanks.

1. After you infer the main idea of a longer reading, what should you do?

   _____

   _____

2. If the supporting paragraphs don't match the main idea the reader has inferred, what should the reader do?

   _____

   _____

3. What three kinds of texts are likely to imply rather than state the controlling main idea?

   _____

   _____

   _____

4. Where are you most likely to find clues to the relationships between paragraphs?

   _____

   _____

5. Each time you start a new paragraph, what kinds of questions should you be asking?

   _____

   _____

6. A summary is _____.

7. Unlike a paraphrase for a term paper, a summary requires you to _____.

8. A good summary should include _____ and _____.

   It should exclude _____

   _____.

9. What two key elements affect the contents of a summary?

   _____

10. A summary should never be as long as _____.

▶ **TEST 2**   **Recognizing the Implied Main Idea**

DIRECTIONS   Answer the following questions by circling the letter of the correct response.

1. Victimless Crime

1   Prostitution, pornography, illegal drug use, music and movie pirating, and ignoring car seatbelt and motor cycle helmet laws are all examples of victimless crimes....Victimless crimes are voluntary acts that violate the law but are perceived by some to present little or no threat to individuals or society. Up to 50 percent of all arrests in urban areas are estimated to be on charges of victimless crimes.

2   Some people argue that such crimes should be wiped off the books because those who engage in these activities suffer willingly (if at all). A strong case can be made for legalizing, regulating, and taxing prostitution and recreational drugs. People will pursue these activities any way, the argument goes, so why criminalize a large portion of the population unnecessarily. Instead, why not get a little piece of the action for the public purse? State regulation of gambling helps diminish the role of organized crime in gambling. Similarly, regulation of prostitution could help prevent the spread of sexually transmitted disease by requiring regular medical checkups for prostitutes.

3   In states where criminal behavior includes victimless crimes, there are extra burdens on the criminal justice system. Prosecutors and law enforcement authorities find much of their time consumed by relatively minor and non-threatening activities when they could be concentrating on more serious crimes. The courts must also spend a great deal of time processing these cases. The legalization of victimless crimes would immediately shorten the dockets† of prosecutors, police, and judges. For example, a growing number of states and localities have decriminalized possession of small amounts of marijuana. Even more have legalized the use of marijuana for medical purposes.

4   Opponents of decriminalizing victimless crimes say that "victimless" is the wrong word to describe actions that fall under this category. For example, with the selling of sex, prostitutes and their clients can become infected with the virus that causes AIDs and other communicable diseases. It is not uncommon for prostitutes to commit other types of crime and endure serious emotional and physical costs. Opponents

---

†dockets: a calendar or list of cases to be heard in a courtroom.

also insist that legalization of drugs such as methamphetamines, heroin, or crack cocaine might lead to a significant rise in addiction and require higher taxes for treatment and health care. And if legalization were selective (say, only marijuana, cocaine, and ecstasy were made available legally), then new, more powerful designer drugs would likely debut on the market. (Adapted from Bowman and Kearney, *State and Local Government*, 8th ed., p. 450.)

Which sentence best expresses the implied main idea of the reading?

a. Victimless crimes do no one any harm, and the activities that fall under this category should be made legal.

b. There is strong disagreement about whether or not victimless crimes should be legalized.

c. The idea that victimless crimes should be wiped off the books because no one suffers from them is misguided.

d. Making victimless crimes legal activities will have a host of unexpected and extremely negative consequences.

2. America Cools Off

1 In 1902, mechanical engineer Willis Carrier needed to solve a problem for one of his employer's clients, a printing company that was having trouble with its paper, which expanded and contracted in the heat and humidity. As Carrier pondered the problem, he figured out the relationship between temperature, humidity, and dew point. Then he went ahead and invented the air conditioner, which cooled the printing plant for the first time on July 17, 1902, solving the paper problem. Carrier's system was the first one that chilled, cleaned, and dried the air, resulting in an indoor climate that could remain a comfortable 72 degrees even on the hottest of summer days.

2   But the printing industry was not the only one that benefited from the invention of air conditioning. This new control over interior climates resulted in increased efficiency and productivity for a variety of industries, including textiles, cigars, chocolate, pasta, and celluloid film, among many others. As a result, air conditioning was in common use in commercial buildings by the 1940s. The technology also had a significant economic impact on the retail and entertainment industries. Department stores, movie theaters, sports arenas, and shopping malls have grown and prospered thanks in part to their ability to entice customers into their comfortably cool buildings. Air conditioning

allowed businesses—such as movie theaters—that were once forced to close during the sweltering summer months to stay open year-round. And air conditioning itself has grown to a huge $32-billion-a-year industry.

3   The technological impact of air conditioning, too, has been profound. It not only opened up many new areas of medical and scientific research, but it made space travel possible as well. Without air conditioning, astronauts could never have explored the moon.

4   Air conditioning affected where Americans lived. It opened up the steamy South and the desert Southwest for settlement. As a result, migration from southern states reversed in the 1960s, and cities such as Phoenix, Houston, Las Vegas, and Miami grew in size. Without air conditioning, these booming cities would probably still be small towns.

5   All over the country, air conditioning caused significant changes in architecture. Thanks to climate control, skyscraper windows could be sealed, allowing buildings to rise higher and higher. Residential architecture was transformed, too. Windows that were once placed in order to provide cross-ventilation were rearranged and reduced in size, the overhanging eaves and large porches that once helped cool a house were eliminated, and two-story Victorian homes with high ceilings were replaced by suburban, single-story ranch homes.

6   These architectural changes went on to produce profound social changes. People who once sought relief from the heat out on their front porches, where neighbors could interact regularly with one another, began staying inside their cooler, air-conditioned houses. As the streets emptied, social interaction outside the home diminished. America became a much more private place.

Which sentence best expresses the main idea of the entire reading?

a. The invention of air conditioning caused a number of dramatic changes in the way Americans lived and worked.

b. Willis Carrier was a technological genius, who single-handedly figured out how to protect paper from the effects of heat and humidity, thereby saving the printing industry from bankruptcy.

c. Thanks to Willis Carrier, the printing industry was saved from complete financial ruin.

d. The invention of air conditioning gave birth to the great American symbol—the skyscraper.

▶ **TEST 3**   **Inferring the Implied Main Idea**

DIRECTIONS Write the implied main idea on the blank lines.

1. The Jury Deliberation Process

1   During a courtroom trial, the jury listens as both the defense and the prosecution present their witnesses and their evidence. Both sides finish presenting their cases by making closing arguments to the jury. Then, the judge sends the jury to the jury room to deliberate, i.e., decide on a verdict of "guilty" or "not guilty."

2   The first stage in making that decision is a relaxed period of *orientation*. The jury members select a group leader (the foreperson), set an agenda, and discuss the judge's instructions. Next, jurors begin to explore what they have heard in the courtroom. They talk about the evidence the lawyers have presented and raise questions. This initial discussion ends with a vote, and each jury member reveals his or her opinion about the verdict.

3   If the necessary consensus, or agreement, is not reached, the jury shifts into a period of *open conflict*. During this phase, the discussion becomes more argumentative. The two opposing groups go over the evidence and try to construct stories to explain it. If some members disagree, the majority group tries to convince those in disagreement by presenting information to support its argument. The majority group may also try to pressure the minority group to conform to the majority's opinion.

4   When a consensus is finally reached, the group enters a *reconciliation* phase. During this period, group members smooth over the conflicts between them. They express their satisfaction with their decision. On some juries, however, the majority is not able to persuade the holdouts to change their minds. In that case, the jury is "hung." A hung jury causes a mistrial, and the case must be retried with a new jury.

(Source of information: Brehm, Kassin, and Fein, *Social Psychology*, 5th ed., p. 460.)

Implied Main Idea   _____

                             _____

2. Texting and Driving

1   We all know that drinking and driving don't mix. Usually the people who do mix the two have already drunk too much to realize that they are doing something dangerous and stupid. But when it comes to texting, even people who are completely sober seem to think that texting

while driving is not a real problem. In any case, it's not as dangerous as drinking and driving. Or is it?

2   As it turns out, some skeptics at *Car and Driver* magazine did some research in order to find out which is a bigger threat, drinking while driving or texting while driving. They rigged a car so a red light would go off when the driver had to brake suddenly. Then they tested driver reactions under four different conditions: (1) unimpaired, (2) legally drunk at .08, (3) reading an email, and (4) texting. Texting while driving produced the slowest reaction time while emailing came in second.

3   If that doesn't make you think about turning off your cell phone while you drive, consider the tragic chain of events set off when a 19-year-old Missouri driver was texting his friend about a visit to the country fair. The teenager was driving around fifty-five miles per hour and looking at his cell phone. Thus he didn't notice that the pickup truck in front of him had slowed down for a construction site. By the time he slammed on his brakes, it was too late. The boy crashed into the truck at 55 mph. Then two buses coming up behind the crumpled vehicles couldn't stop fast enough to avoid the crash site. The result was a pileup that left two people dead and many others injured.

4   The incident in Missouri is not an isolated one. The University of North Texas Health Science Center looked at traffic data from the Fatality Accident Reporting System and came to an alarming conclusion: Between 2001 and 2007, texting while driving was responsible for 16,141 deaths. Because cell phone use and texting has only increased since that study was done, it's doubtful that this number has declined. A 2011 study by the National Highway Traffic Safety Administration places the number of drivers likely to be holding a cell phone to their ears at any given moment at 660,000. This means that there are over half a million drivers on the road who, at some point, are looking at the screens on their cell phone, not at the road, all the while assuming that they aren't doing something incredibly dangerous. Like the person who drinks four beers and picks up his or her car keys to get on the road, those who are texting and driving need to consider the potentially lethal consequences of their actions. (Source of statistics and accident description: http://techcrunch.com/2010/09/24/study-texting-while-driving-r; Jim Suhr and Jim Slater, "Texting While Driving Ban Isn't Academic for Missouri Students," *Huffington Post*, December 17, 2011.)

Implied Main Idea   _____

_____

▶ TEST 4 — Inferring Connections Between Sentences and Paragraphs

DIRECTIONS Read the selection through once. Then re-read it and answer the questions following each selection.

1. The Birth of Vaccines

1 **Immunization** refers to the processes designed to induce immunity, or protection, from disease. In active immunization, a vaccine that contains an antigen (a substance that triggers an immune response from the body) is given by mouth or by injection. The first immunization elicits a primary immune response, just as an infection would. A second immunization, or booster, elicits a secondary immune response and increases immunity to disease. In passive immunization, a person receives antibodies purified from the blood of another individual. The treatment offers immediate benefit for someone who has been exposed to a potentially deadly agent or disease such as tetanus or rabies.

2   The first vaccine was the result of desperate attempts to survive smallpox epidemics that repeatedly occurred all over the world. Smallpox is a severe disease that kills up to one-third of the people it infects. Before 1880, no one knew what caused infectious diseases or how to protect anyone from getting them. But there were clues. In the case of smallpox, survivors seldom contracted the disease a second time. They were immune, or protected from infection.

3   The idea of acquiring immunity to smallpox was so appealing that people had been risking their lives on it for two thousand years. For example, many people poked into their skin bits of scabs or threads soaked in pus. Some survived the crude practices and became immune to smallpox, but many others did not.

4   By the late 1700s, it was known that dairymaids did not get smallpox if they had already recovered from cowpox, a mild disease that affects cattle as well as humans. To better understand the mysterious connection, Edward Jenner, an English physician, injected liquid from a cowpox sore into the arm of a healthy boy. Six weeks later, Jenner injected the boy with liquid from a smallpox sore. The boy did not get smallpox. Thus Jenner's experiment showed directly that the agent of smallpox confers, or gives, immunity to smallpox.

5   Jenner named his procedure "vaccination" after the Latin word for cowpox (vaccinia). The use of Jenner's vaccine spread quickly through Europe, then to the rest of the world. The last known case of naturally

occurring smallpox was in 1977, in Somalia. The vaccine had eradicated the disease. (Adapted from Starr et al. *Biology: The Unity and Diversity of Life,* 12th ed., p. 674.)

1. What does the topic of paragraph 1, immunization, have to do with the "vaccines" introduced in the title?

   _____

2. What do the opening words of paragraph 2—"The first vaccine was the result of"— suggest about how the author's train of thought will continue?

   a. The author will continue to discuss immunization and the benefits of each type.

   b. The author will describe some of the diseases that can be controlled through the use of vaccines.

   c. The author will tell readers how vaccines came to be discovered.

3. In paragraph 3, why do the authors tell readers what people had been doing for two thousand years? What does this contribute to the main idea of the reading?

   _____

   _____

   _____

4. What connection does the writer expect readers to make between the title of the reading and paragraph 4?

   _____

5. If the main idea of the reading is expressed in a thesis statement, write the thesis statement here:

   _____

   _____

If you had to infer the main idea, write your inference here:

_____

_____

_____

_____

2. China's Adoption Problem

1   For at least a decade, couples desperate to adopt a child and tired of the paperwork and long waits required in the United States have turned to China. As a consequence of the government's population control policy, Chinese orphanages had a ready supply of healthy little girls available for adoption. China's one-child-per-family policy had resulted in many parents abandoning their first child if it was a girl rather than a boy. The hope was that the second child, or if need be, the third, would be a boy child because a boy could contribute more money to the household and take care of the parents in their old age.

2   Once the consequences of China's one-child-per-family policy became public knowledge in the United States, China became a haven for parents who wanted to adopt. According to the State Department, between 1999 and 2010, American parents adopted 64,043 Chinese children. Most of the children adopted were girls.

3   For the adoptive parents, there was an added bonus to adopting from a Chinese orphanage. They could adopt with a clear conscience. Unlike other countries, such as Ecuador, Vietnam, and Romania, there were no rumors about Chinese babies being stolen from their parents and sold on the black market.

4   New reports coming out of China since 2009, however, have altered that initially positive picture. At least one orphanage in the province of Hunan has been publicly accused of selling children for the explicit purpose of adoption by foreign parents. There are rumors of other orphanages doing the same. Since orphanages that arrange international adoptions get hefty fees of around $5,000 or more from the couples seeking to adopt, it's clear that international adoptions are a profitable venture.

5   But the profitability of arranging adoptions is not what's come into question currently. What's being discussed in China and in the

international press is the question of how the orphanages got the children in the first place. There was a time when the standard of living was so poor and the attitude toward girls so negative that orphanages had a steady supply of girl babies to put up for adoption. However, as living standards rose and families began practicing selective abortion,[†] fewer children became available for adoption. That's when stories about government officials searching homes for a second child began to surface. If one were found, the parents would be forced to give it up for adoption. Even twins were separated, with population control officials insisting that there were no exceptions to the one-child-per-family rule. The confiscated children would then be sent to an orphanage that specialized in arranging international adoptions.

6   Some U.S parents with Chinese adoptive children have been devastated by the news of China's underground adoption policies. One mother interviewed by the *New York Times* said she was "haunted" by the idea that her child might have been taken away from her birth mother by threats or force. Other parents insist that their children could not have been forcibly removed from their families. They argue that their adoption agency would never have allowed such a thing to happen.

7   This position infuriates Karen Moline, a New York writer and board member of the group "Parents for Ethical Adoption Reform." She insists that the amount of money that changes hands in an international adoption and the difficulty accounting for that money (many of the payments are made in cash) makes the situation ripe for corruption.

8   Moline's belief that China's adoption process has been tainted by greed has some backing from a mother who reports bringing home two adopted girls from two different Chinese provinces. One of the daughters, from an orphanage in Guangxi province, was adopted with eleven other children, who came to the states at the same time. When the parents of the children discussed their experiences, they discovered that the twelve adopted children from Guangxi province had, almost word for word, recounted the exact same stories about their lives in the orphanage. As the mother of the two newly adopted girls explained, it was "all too specific to be believable." (Source of information: John Leland, "For Adoptive Parents, Questions Without Answers," *New York Times*, Sunday September 18, 2011, pp. C-1 and C-6.)

[†]selective abortion: When the parents find out the sex of the child, if it's a girl, the wife will get an abortion.

1. How does the reading define the word *problem* in the title?

   _____

   _____

2. What is the relationship between paragraphs 1 and 2?

   a. then and now

   b. comparison and contrast

   c. cause and effect

3. What key category word at the beginning of paragraph 2 helps readers grasp the relationship between the two paragraphs?

   _____

4. In paragraph 7, what position does the opening phrase of the paragraph refer to?

   _____

   _____

   _____

5. If the main idea of the reading is expressed in a thesis statement, write the thesis statement here:

   _____

   _____

   If you had to infer the main idea, write your inference here:

   _____

   _____

   _____

   _____

▶ **TEST 5**   **Writing a Summary**

DIRECTIONS   Read the following selection. Then write a summary that is six to twelve sentences long. Consider the purpose of the summary to be notes for your own use. Thus, you don't need to include the source of information.

Celebrating Singlehood

1   A quick question: Do you know what the third week of September is? Not Labor Day, that's weeks earlier. Give up? According to a report by the U.S. Census Bureau, the third week of September is "Unmarried and Single Americans Week," a week in which we are supposed to acknowledge the contributions single people make to society.

2   First started as "National Singles Week" in 1982 in Ohio by the Buckeye Singles Council and taken over by the American Association for Single People in 2001, the weeklong "celebration" was renamed in recognition that many unmarried people are in relationships or are widowed and don't see themselves as "single."

3   Although the week dedicated to singles has been around for more than a quarter century, and is recognized by mayors, city councils, and governors in some thirty-three states, it has yet to be legitimized and incorporated into mainstream American culture, as indicated by both the absence of greeting cards for the occasion and the number of people (including millions of unmarried people) unaware that the weeklong recognition of singlehood exists.

4   Yet even a casual inspection of demographics[†] in this country illustrates the increasing phenomenon of singlehood. The trend, which has taken root and grown substantially since 1960, includes divorced, widowed, and never married individuals. Each year more adult Americans are single.

5   According to the U.S. Census Bureau, the percentage of unmarried Americans varies by race and ethnicity. Among non-Hispanic whites, 20.6 percent have never married. Among African Americans, that figure is 39.4 percent. Among Hispanics, 28 percent have never tied the knot. In the Asian population, 28.5 percent have never married. Altogether the population of singles is quite large.

[†]demographics: statistical data, or information, describing the various groups in a larger population of people.

6   The varieties of unmarried lifestyles in the United States are too numerous to fit under one "umbrella" and too complex to be understood with any one category. They include: never married, divorced, young, old single parents, gay men, lesbians, widows, widowers, and so on. In research on the unmarried, however, those generally regarded as "single" are young or middle age, heterosexual, not living with someone, and working rather than attending school or college. Although there are numerous single lesbians and gay men, they have not traditionally been included as singles in such research. (Adapted from Strong, Devault, and Cohen, *The Marriage and Family Experience*, 10th ed., p. 303.)

Summary

_____

_____

_____

_____

_____

_____

_____

_____

_____

_____

⬧ **TEST 6**   **Reviewing Chapter 9 Vocabulary**

DIRECTIONS   Fill in the blanks with one of the words listed below.

> anarchists litigation posthumously conjugal jurisdiction
> constitutes correlation trekking inadvertently warped

1. Locking yourself out of the car, making a slip of the tongue, revealing a secret you swore not to tell are all things you are likely to do _____.

2. When you are talking about things related to marriage, you can use the word *marital,* but in certain contexts, you can also use the word _____.

3. Both minds and woods can end up _____ by bad circumstances.

4. Sturdy boots, good arches, and thick socks are all things you will need if you ever go _____.

5. External rules, rigid regulations, and, above all, the idea of a federal or state government are detested by _____ everywhere.

6. Several studies have found a high _____ between being self-employed and being happy.

7. Most of us want fame while we can still enjoy it, so becoming famous _____ isn't worth much.

8. Sheriffs, judges, and courts are people and institutions that have limited but still powerful _____ over our lives.

9. In casual conversation, we might talk about what "makes" for a good legal decision, but in a more formal and scholarly setting, we would probably use the word _____.

10. Courts, lawyers, judges, claims, and counter claims are all part of

_____.

▶ **TEST 7**   **Reviewing Chapter 9 Vocabulary**

DIRECTIONS Fill in the blanks with one of the words listed below.

jubilation	plaintiffs	judicial	exorbitant	attendant
electoral	liability	norm	articulate	predisposition

1. If you are going to bill yourself as a public speaker, it pays to be

    _____.

2. Outside the confines of a hospital, some doctors and nurses are fearful of coming to the aid of people who have been seriously hurt; they are wary of assuming _____ should their treatment not save the patient.

3. Graduation, the birth of a child, a wedding, and winning at lotto are all events likely to inspire _____.

4. Having a(n) _____ to diabetes does not mean you will automatically develop the disease.

5. Even if they win, most people aren't happy about being _____ in a lawsuit.

6. Health risks, job loss, and loss of brain cells are all consequences _____ on the habit of drinking to excess.

7. It generally takes a lot of self-confidence to deviate from the _____ and not feel guilty about it.

8. Fees, price tags, and taxes are all things that are likely to be labeled

    _____.

9. During presidential elections, the _____ college almost always comes under fire, but then it's forgotten until the next election.

10. The long-running TV series *Law and Order* told stories that described the crime in the first half of the program and how the criminal fared in our _____ system in the second half.

Learning from Organizational Patterns in Paragraphs

10

IN THIS CHAPTER, YOU WILL LEARN

- how to identify six organizational patterns commonly used to highlight or emphasize relationships between general and specific sentences.

- about common clues to those six patterns.

- how to determine the primary pattern of organization.

- how to make your notes reflect the patterns.

"To understand is to perceive patterns."

—Historian Isaiah Berlin

"What we call chaos is just patterns we haven't recognized."

—Novelist Chuck Palahniuk

Chapter 10 continues the discussion of explanatory patterns begun in the previous chapters. But the focus here is on explanatory patterns that convey a specific type of content and, therefore, rely on a particular type of organization. The organizational patterns covered in this chapter are the following: *definition, time order, simple listing, comparison and contrast, cause and effect*, and *classification*.

The ability to recognize these six organizational patterns will help you (1) identify key points, (2) grasp relationships between ideas, (3) decide how best to take notes, and (4) provide a mental framework for remembering individual details.

It's the Thought That Counts

The organizational patterns introduced in the following pages (see the table on page 490) describe the ways writers, particularly writers of textbooks, organize information in order to communicate their thoughts.

Organizational patterns are the verbal frameworks that writers frequently turn to when they want to do any of the following:

Type of Thinking	Organizational Pattern
1. Give readers the meaning or meanings associated with a word or term.	Definition
2. Trace a fixed sequence of steps that produce an outcome or a product.	Time Order: Process
Help readers follow a chain of events that happened in real time and are central to understanding a significant period in history or the achievements of a person's career.	Time Order: Sequence of Dates and Events
3. Describe the characteristics associated with a typical event or experience.	Simple Listing
4. Show readers how two people, events, or experiences do or do not resemble one another.	Comparison and Contrast
5. Help readers see how one event made another event happen.	Cause and Effect
6. Describe the various smaller groups that comprise, or make up, some larger group or whole.	Classification

The organizational patterns described individually in this chapter occur frequently in your textbooks and will serve you well as you attempt to understand your assignments. The characteristics of these patterns, though, are not fixed in stone. You can't assume that every time an author wants to compare and contrast two people or events, he or she will always use the typical transitions associated with the comparison and contrast pattern, such as *in contrast* and *similarly*. By the same token, a writer may describe a cause-and-effect relationship implicitly without ever saying directly that one event *caused* or was the *result* of another.

Thus, your job as a reader is to be alert to the thought relationships that connect the writer's ideas. As you read, keep asking yourself, what's the author trying to do here? Is he showing me how this event caused the one described in the next sentence? Is she telling me that despite some superficial similarities, two events normally linked together are really quite different?

In other words, it's the relationships between the ideas that should be your focus. The *characteristics associated with the patterns will help you spot those relationships*. But even if all the characteristics are not present, you need to be on the lookout for the kind of thinking the patterns are meant to communicate. Those relationships are central to the way we think about the world, whether in school or out.

Pattern 1: Definition

Although the definition pattern of development appears in all kinds of texts, this pattern in its purest form is found in business, sociology, science, and government texts.[†] When writing about these subjects, authors make a point of using whole paragraphs to define specialized vocabulary central to the discussion of their subject matter.

It's rare, however, for the definition pattern to govern an entire paragraph in a history text. Often, where history is concerned, definitions of key terms are included as part of larger explanations, and the most authors do is highlight the term they want you to remember. Sometimes they don't even do that, and you'll only recognize a key term by the amount of attention the author pays to its explanation.

Particularly in business and psychology texts, the **definition pattern** starts off with a general topic sentence identifying and defining the key word or term under discussion. That definition is followed by more specific sentences, which might do any of the following: (1) add to the definition by offering specific examples; (2) provide information about history, location, context, or usage; (3) explain how the term differs from a similar word or phrase; and (4) further define the key term by introducing its antonym, or term opposite in meaning.

In the illustration that follows, the definition for *puberty* starts out quite general but quickly becomes more specific.

[†]The definition pattern is also common in science and health texts, but, in these contexts, it's usually combined with the cause and effect pattern, as you will see in Chapter 11.

Puberty is a difficult time for both boys and girls.

The topic sentence highlights and generally defines the key term puberty.

Supporting details zero in on the physical changes referred to in the topic sentence.

Puberty *denotes two general types of physical changes that mark the transition from childhood to young adulthood.* The first set of changes that define puberty concern physical appearance. These usually include a dramatic increase in height and weight, as well as changes in the body's fat and muscle content. The second defining change concerns sexual maturation, including change in the reproductive organs and the appearance of secondary sexual characteristics, such as facial and body hair and the growth of breasts. (Adapted from Kail and Cavanaugh, *Human Development*, 5th ed., p. 294.)

Typically for this pattern, the topic sentence provides the broadest definition of the word *puberty*, and the reader learns that it refers to "two general types of physical changes." The supporting details then further define the types of physical changes. Note that the authors have also used boldface to highlight the term they are defining and put the definition itself into italic.

Pattern Variations

Although much of the time, the definition pattern will follow the sequence described above, you will encounter variations, particularly when you are reading sociology texts. Within sociology texts, it's just as likely for the author to start off with a specific description of how the term being defined came into being or is applied. Then, somewhere in the middle of the paragraph, the author will introduce and formally define the term central to the paragraph, for instance:

An early view of female crime focused on the supposed dynamics* of sexual relationships. Female criminals were viewed as either sexually controlling or sexually naïve. They either manipulated men for profit or were manipulated by men. Thus, the female's criminality was often masked because criminal justice authorities were reluctant to take action against a woman. This perspective is known as the **chivalry hypothesis**, which holds that much female criminality is hidden because of the culture's generally protective and forgiving attitude toward women. In other words, police are less likely to arrest, juries are less likely to convict, and judges are less likely to put female offenders into prison. (Adapted from Siegel, *Criminology*, 10th ed., p. 54.)

Despite the variation in structure, the key element of this paragraph is the definition of the term *chivalry hypothesis*. That definition should be the focus of both your attention and your notes.

Typical Topic Sentences

When topic sentences like the following open a paragraph, it's extremely likely that the supporting details will all be devoted to further explaining the term mentioned in the topic sentence.

1. Nineteenth-century America was guided by the concept of **Manifest Destiny**, the belief that the United States was on a mission from God to occupy North America from coast to coast.

2. The *greenhouse effect* is the name for what happens when excessive carbon dioxide and other gases build up in earth's atmosphere.

3. A *flashbulb memory* is an especially vivid image that seems to be frozen in memory at the time of a personal tragedy, an accident, or other emotionally significant events. (Adapted from Coon and Mitterer, *Introduction to Psychology*, 12th ed., p. 271.)

4. A *database* is a collection of information arranged for easy access and retrieval. (Pride, Hughes, and Kapoor, *Busin*ess, 10th ed., p. 354.)

---

*dynamics: psychological interaction in relationships.

Taking Notes on Definition Patterns

Notes on the definition pattern should include three elements:

1. the term being defined

2. a complete definition

3. any other more specific details that might help clarify the definition—e.g., examples, contrasting words, origins

To illustrate, here are notes on the definition paragraph from page 492:

Main Idea   The term *puberty* refers to two major changes that mark the transition from being a child to being considered an adult.

Supporting Details   1. Bodily changes like increases in height and weight.

2. Arrival of sexual maturity with changes in reproductive organs and secondary sexual characteristics like breasts and facial hair.

When authors include background material about how a word came into being, or they define a key term by telling you what it is *not*, this information is not always essential. Read it through carefully. Then decide if you need it to understand and apply the definition.

NOTE-TAKING TIP

When taking notes in the margins of your textbook, it's a good idea to make the word or words being defined stand out by circling, boxing, underlining, or highlighting them. This way, during review, you'll be sure to study important key terms.

If you are a fan of diagramming, you'll be happy to learn that definition passages readily lend themselves to mapping, for instance:

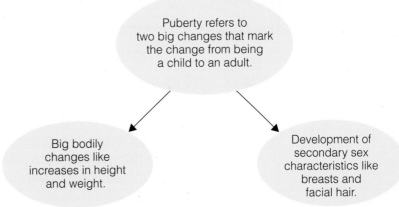

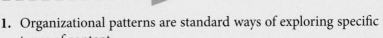

SUMMING UP THE KEY POINTS

1. Organizational patterns are standard ways of exploring specific types of content.

2. Recognizing standard organizational patterns can tell you what you should pay attention to as you read. But since all the elements of the pattern are not always on the page, it's your job to look for the thought relationships underlying the authors' words. *It's the thought that counts and the pattern follows.*

3. In business, psychology, and science texts, paragraphs relying on the definition pattern frequently open with a topic sentence that defines a key term. That term is typically highlighted in some way, through boldface, italic, colored ink, or marginal notation. However, in sociology texts, authors sometimes build up to the definition that is central to the paragraph rather than starting out with it. In history texts, key terms are usually presented as part of a larger explanation and may or may not be highlighted in bold or italic.

4. Topic sentences in the definition pattern often use phrases such as "refers to," "is the name for," "is said to be," and "is defined as."

5. Notes on the definition pattern should include (1) the term defined, (2) a clearly stated definition, and (3) examples or explanations of origins that clarify the word's meaning.

◆ EXERCISE 1   Understanding Definition Patterns

DIRECTIONS   Read and take notes on each paragraph, making sure to paraphrase and abbreviate in your notes.

*The word **psychodrama** in bold is the first major clue to the definition pattern. The phrase "refers to" is an additional clue.*

The rest of the paragraph explains the word's origin.

EXAMPLE   The psychiatric term **psychodrama** refers to a particular kind of group therapy created and developed by therapist Jacob Moreno in the early 1950s. In a psychodrama, individuals act out disturbing incidents from their lives, often playing multiple roles. The purpose of a psychodrama is to help patients better understand the troubling situations that may have contributed to their psychological problems. Moreno believed that the insights gained during a psychodrama could then be transferred to real life. For example, a teenager jealous of and in conflict with a twin might better understand both his own feelings and the feelings of his brother by acting out one of their quarrels.

Main Idea   In the 1950s, Jacob Moreno developed a special kind of group therapy called psychodrama.

Supporting Details   1. During psychodrama, individuals act out disturbing real-life situations.

2. Objective is to better understand situations that may contribute to psychological disturbance.

3. Moreno thought insights gained during a psychodrama could be applied to real life.

a. A teenager in conflict with his twin might gain understanding by acting out a typical quarrel.

EXPLANATION   Here, the key term is *psychodrama* and our notes define it. They also include some essential background about the word—the name of Jacob Moreno and the approximate time when the term came into being. Note, too, that an example clarifying the key term has been included.

1. A **self-concept** is a person's perception, or view, of his or her personality and character traits. It consists of all your ideas and feelings about how you define yourself. To discover your self-concept, you might ask yourself, "What kind of person am I? Am I compassionate?* Selfish? Stubborn?" Self-concepts are built out of daily experiences and our reactions to those experiences. For example, let's say

———————

*compassionate: caring of others.

that you consistently do well in sports but find it hard to be part of a team. You might then begin to describe your self-concept in the following terms: "I'm a good athlete, but I'm not much of a team player." Self-concepts, however, can—and sometimes should—be revised, particularly if they are overly negative.

Main Idea

_____

_____

Supporting Details

_____

_____

_____

_____

_____

_____

_____

2. In neighborhoods where people know one another and feel mutual trust, children are less likely to become involved with deviant peers. They are also less likely to engage in problem behaviors. In these neighborhoods, kids are able to use their wits to avoid violent confrontations and to feel safe in their own neighborhood. They have what's known as **street efficacy**, the ability to navigate their world without resorting to violence. In contrast, kids who don't live in such neighborhoods lose confidence in their ability to avoid violence. As research by sociologist Patrick Sharkey has shown, kids with a high level of street efficacy are less likely to resort to violence or to associate with delinquent peers. (Adapted from Siegel, _Criminology_, 10th ed., pp. 189–90.)

Main Idea

_____

_____

Supporting Details

_____

_____

_____

_____

_____

_____

✔ CHECK YOUR UNDERSTANDING

1. How do paragraphs based on the definition pattern generally begin in a business text?

    _____

2. What variation might you expect in a sociology text?

    _____

    _____

3. What variation can you expect in a history text?

    _____

    _____

4. Topic sentences signaling the definition pattern often include what phrases?

    _____

5. Notes on the definition pattern should include what?

    _____

    _____

Pattern 2: Time Order

The central characteristic of the time order pattern is its reliance on order in real time. Writers use it when they want to describe a process that produces an outcome or a product. They also use it when they want to chart someone's career, explain what made a span of time noteworthy, or describe a sequence of events that led up to a larger, more significant event.

Time Order: Process

Writers use the **process pattern** to tell their readers how something works, happens, or develops. Because explaining how a product, process, being, or phenomenon develops over the course of time is crucial to writing about both science and business, these are the two contexts in which you will see this pattern most often. For an illustration, look at the following paragraph, where the author describes the three stages of growth in identical twins.

Identical twins can be hard to tell apart.

Kenneth Sponsler/Shutterstock.com.

The word stages in the underlined topic sentence signals that the process pattern is coming up.

There are three basic stages involved in the development of identical twins. Their growth begins when the father's sperm pierces the egg of the mother. The fertilized egg then splits and divides into equal halves, each half receiving exactly the same number of chromosomes* and

---

*chromosomes: bodies within a cell that consist of hundreds of clear, jellylike particles strung together like beads. They carry the genes.

The supporting details describe each stage.

genes.* The halves of the egg then develop into two babies who are of the same sex and who are identical in all hereditary traits, such as hair and eye color.

Because the author wants to tell readers how identical twins develop in the womb, she uses a process pattern of development. Typically for this pattern, the topic sentence tells us there are three specific stages. The supporting details then describe each of the stages.

Transitional Signals

An author who wants readers to understand the steps or stages in a process is likely to use transitions like the following.

Transitions That Describe a Process ◆	After	In	Over time
	At the onset	In the beginning	Right after
	At this point	In the early stages	Shortly after
	Before	In the end	Soon
	By	Last	Then
	During	Later	Today
	Eventually	Meanwhile	When
	Finally	Next	Within hours (or days)
	First, second, third	Now	
	Following	Once	

Typical Topic Sentences

Any time a topic sentence uses words and phrases like *process, sequence of steps,* or *series of stages,* you are probably dealing with a paragraph that employs the process pattern of explanation. Note, however, that this pattern does not always employ a topic sentence that includes one of these words or phrases.

1. The process of photosynthesis is essential to plant life.

2. Storing information in long-term memory involves several distinct steps.

---

*genes: the elements responsible for hereditary characteristics, such as hair and eye color.

3. The barn owl follows an intricate courting ritual.

4. Learning gender roles begins immediately after birth. <small>(Coon and Mitterer, *Introduction to Psychology*, 12th ed., p. 366.)</small>

You should also know that authors sometimes just describe the steps or stages and let them imply a main idea such as "Elizabeth Kübler Ross's model of the grief process includes five stages."

Telltale Visual Aids

Flow charts are a dead giveaway to the process pattern. If you see a paragraph or chapter section accompanied by a flow chart like on the one shown on page 502, it's likely that the process pattern organizes the selection.

Taking Notes on Process Patterns

Notes on paragraphs describing a process should include the following:

1. the larger process being described

2. the specific steps in the process

3. the order in which they are presented

4. any specialized vocabulary used to describe the steps or stages

Notes based on an outline format would look something like this:

Main Idea There are three stages in the development of identical twins.

Supporting Details
1. Father's sperm pierces mother's egg.

2. Fertilized egg splits and divides into equal halves; each half receives same number of chromosomes and genes.

3. Halves of eggs develop into two babies of same sex, identical in all hereditary traits, such as hair and eye color.

However, some readers prefer setting off the steps or stages in a process with a flow chart. A **flow chart** uses circles or boxes and arrows to make the individual steps or stages in a process visually memorable. If the author doesn't include one in the text, you might consider making a flow chart to take notes. The result would look something like this:

Three stages in development of identical twins.

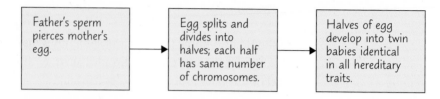

| Father's sperm pierces mother's egg. | → | Egg splits and divides into halves; each half has same number of chromosomes. | → | Halves of egg develop into twin babies identical in all hereditary traits. |

NOTE-TAKING TIP

When you are taking notes on the process pattern, don't get so caught up in describing the individual steps and fail to identify the overall process. By the same token, make sure to note anything the author says about the importance or complexity of the larger process being described.

SUMMING UP THE KEY POINTS

1. The goal of the process pattern is to explain how something works, functions, or develops by outlining the crucial steps in real-time order. The process pattern is particularly common in science and business texts.

2. In the process pattern, transitions that introduce each new step in the larger sequence are especially important. The presence of words and phrases such as "in the first step," "then," "next," and "finally" are all signals to the underlying process pattern.

3. Flow charts frequently accompany the process pattern. Writers use them to make the individual steps clear to readers.

4. Notes on the process pattern need to clearly identify the overall process being described. They should also list and describe, *in the correct order*, the individual steps that make up the larger whole.

5. When specialized vocabulary is included in the pattern, it should appear in your notes.

6. Flow charts are a good note-taking strategy for recording information organized by the process pattern.

◆ **EXERCISE 2** **Understanding Process Patterns**

> **DIRECTIONS** Read and take notes on each paragraph. Circle the time-order transitions.

Notice how transitional phrases help mark off the steps or stages in the courtship ritual.

EXAMPLE In spring, the stickleback, a small fish found in both fresh and salt water, goes through a strange courtship ritual. With the coming of the spring months, the male stickleback begins to look for a place where he can build his nest. Once he has found it, he grows aggressive and fights off all invaders. After finishing the nest, he searches for a female. When he finds one, he leads her to the nest, and she enters it. The male then hits the tail of the female, forcing her to deposit her eggs. Once she lays the eggs, the female swims off, and the male enters the nest.

Main Idea In spring, the stickleback goes through an odd courtship ritual.

Supporting Details
1. Male stickleback looks for place to build nest.
2. Finding one, he grows aggressive.
3. After finishing nest, he looks for female.
4. Leads her to nest, which she enters.
5. Male hits female's tail, forcing her to deposit eggs.
6. Once eggs are laid, she swims off and male enters nest.

EXPLANATION Because the notes contain the main idea and all the steps described in the paragraph, we have everything of importance.

1. The first act of a newly hatched queen bee is to seek a mate. Three to five days after hatching, she attempts her first flight, flying far from the hive to avoid inbreeding. When she is far enough, the queen produces a scent that attracts drones from distant hives. Once a drone arrives, mating takes place at an altitude of about fifty feet. Following the mating, the queen flies home to lay her eggs. A queen who does not mate by the time she is two weeks old will never mate and will remain barren.

Main Idea

_____

_____

Supporting Details

_____

_____

_____

_____

_____

_____

2. The psychological disorder known as paranoia develops in four basic stages. At the illness's onset, victims begin to distrust the motives of others. The paranoid are constantly alert for ulterior, or secret, motives in the actions of others. If suspicion marks the first stage, self-protection is central to the second. At this point, any personal failure is seen as the fault of others, and victims no longer take responsibility for their actions. In the third stage, paranoia sufferers become hostile; they are openly angry at their supposed ill treatment at the hands of other people. This period of anger usually leads to a moment of paranoid illumination.* In this final stage, everything falls into place, and the truly paranoid wholeheartedly believe that a plot or conspiracy is being directed against them. Seeing enemies everywhere, they are now convinced that someone, often a whole group, is trying to do them bodily harm and perhaps even kill them.

Main Idea

_____

_____

Supporting Details

_____

_____

_____

_____

_____

*illumination: understanding.

_____

_____

_____

_____

Time Order: Sequence of Dates and Events

Textbook authors in all fields—except perhaps in mathematics—frequently use a **sequence of dates and events** to (1) describe what made a particular span of time eventful or memorable; (2) chart the career of an important figure; or (3) explain how some theory, invention, or activity came to be part of culture or history. Here, for example, is a time order paragraph that traces a sequence of dates and events according to the order in which they occurred. The purpose or goal of the reading is to help readers see how the Internet developed over time and became part of daily life.

Notice how many sentences start with dates.

Putting dates at the beginning of sentences is purely intentional on the author's part. The dates make it easier for the reader to follow the sequence of events.

What we now call the Internet began in 1969 when the U.S. Defense Department linked up computers at four universities to create ARPANET (Advanced Research Projects Agency Network). By 1972, thirty-seven universities were connected over ARPANET. In 1983, ARPANET interlinked with other computer networks to create the Internet. Between 1983 and 1990, the Internet was used mainly to transmit messages known as electronic mail, or e-mail, among researchers. In 1991, a group of European physicists devised a system for transmitting a wide range of materials, including graphics and photographs, over the Internet. By 1994, households all over the world were logging on to the Internet's World Wide Web. By 2011, worldwide Internet usage was a staggering 2,267,233,742. (Adapted from Janda et al., *The Challenge of Democracy*, 5th ed., p. 181; statistic from www.internetworldstats.com/stats.htm.)

The main idea of this paragraph is implied. Taken together the dates, and the events attached to them, suggest a thought like the following: "Although the Internet did not start out as a technological tool for ordinary people, in a little over thirty years it became an essential way to communicate for people around the world."

Notice how the dates and events in the paragraph all contribute to this implied main idea. The first dates mark events that show how the early

Internet was really very specialized in its goals. Then, as researchers expanded the Internet's capabilities, the dates indicate when it started to become important to ordinary people.

Transitional Signals

The sample paragraph above includes some typical time order transitions that appear when a paragraph is organized to present a sequence of dates and events. They are the authors' way of saying, "We've finished describing the previous event; get ready for the next one." Here are more transitions likely to appear in a paragraph tracing a sequence of dates and events.

Transitions Commonly Used to Organize Dates and Events ◆	After that
	At that time or point
	Before
	Between _____ and _____
	By the end of the year
	By the year _____
	During _____
	During that time, period
	Finally
	From _____ to _____
	In January (etc.) _____
	In the days (weeks, months, years, century) following
	In the spring (summer, fall, winter) of
	In the following year
	In the next year
	In the years since
	In the year _____
	On the day (afternoon, evening) of _____
	Until
	When
	While
	Years later

Typical Topic Sentences

The sequence of dates and events organizational pattern often has a main idea that is implied rather than stated. However, when a topic sentence is included, it's likely to make some reference to a period of time, as do all of the topic sentences listed below.

1. The years leading up to the Great Depression were filled with a sense of optimism that was destroyed almost overnight.

2. Between 1939 and 1944, most of Europe descended into a nightmare world of terror, violence, and death.

3. In their youth, the inventors of the airplane, Wilbur and Orville Wright, seemed destined for failure.

4. Between 1872 and 1889, soldiers, railroad workers, and trophy hunters almost managed to complete the wholesale destruction of the American bison.

Taking Notes on Dates and Events Patterns

When you take notes on paragraphs devoted to dates and events, include the following information:

1. the main idea

2. the dates and events used to develop the main idea

3. any other supporting details that lack dates but still seem essential to developing the main idea

Here, to illustrate, are notes on the paragraph about the Internet.

Main Idea Although the Internet started out as a tool for researchers, it only took three decades to enter regular households.

Supporting Details 1. 1969: The first step toward developing the Internet came when the Defense Department linked computers at four universities to form ARPANET (Advanced Research Projects Agency Network).

2. 1972: Thirty-seven universities were connected over ARPANET.

3. 1983–1990: ARPANET interlinks with other computers to create Internet, used

   primarily for e-mail among researchers.

4. 1991: European physicists created a standardized system for encoding and

   transmitting graphics.

5. Early 90s: Ordinary citizens start exploring the Net.

6. By 2011, billions of people making use of the Internet.

NOTE-TAKING TIP

The supporting details in the sample notes all start off with the dates mentioned in the paragraph. This is a good format to use when taking notes on dates and events.

READING TIPS

1. Readings accompanied by timelines are likely to include paragraphs tracing a sequence of dates and events.

2. Although paragraphs can rely on the dates and events pattern, it's in longer multi-paragraph readings that this pattern really makes its presence felt. This is particularly true of history texts.

SUMMING UP THE KEY POINTS

1. In the sequence of dates and events pattern, the *order* of events as they happened in real time plays an essential role.

2. Paragraphs using this pattern often describe how a series of separate events made some time period special or significant. The pattern is also used to chart the career of famous people or explain how some institution, activity, or invention became part of the culture.

3. Transitional phrases like "in 1999," "before 2001," and "after the election of 2008" are clues to this pattern. So, too, are topic sentences that emphasize a particular span of time; for instance, "*During the 1950s*, America underwent some startling changes in lifestyle."

4. Notes on this pattern should include the dates and events used to explain the main idea, along with any other undated details that seem relevant to the main idea.

◆ **EXERCISE 3**   **Understanding Dates and Events Patterns**

DIRECTIONS   Read and take notes on each paragraph. Circle the time-order transitions.

This is a case where the underlined topic sentence needs an antecedent to be complete. Note too how the topic sentence refers to a span of time.

The supporting details following the topic sentence open with dates to give a precise meaning to the phrase "every few years."

EXAMPLE   In the mid-nineteenth century, after the California mines played out, prospectors looking to strike it rich fanned out over the mountains and deserts of the West. For more than a generation, they discovered new deposits almost annually and very rich ones every few years. (In 1859,) there were two great strikes. A find in the Pike's Peak area of Colorado led to a frantic rush. (About the same time,) gold miners in northern Nevada discovered that the "blue mud" stalling their machinery contained one of the richest silver ores ever discovered. (In 1862,) Tombstone, Arizona, was founded on the site of a gold mine. (In 1864,) Helena, Montana, rose atop another. (In 1876,) rich deposits were discovered in the Black Hills of South Dakota. Whites were forbidden by a treaty with the Sioux from entering the Black Hills, but they went anyway and, as usual, the government defended them. (Conlin, *The American Past*, 9th ed., p. 511.)

Main Idea   When miners went West in search of gold and silver, they found rich deposits every few years.

Supporting Details
1. In 1859, two big strikes, one in Colorado and another in Nevada.

2. 1862, city of Tombstone, Arizona, marks the site of a gold mine.

3. 1864, city of Helena, Montana, marks another gold mine.

4. 1876, gold discovered in the Black Hills — Treaty with the Sioux forbid prospecting in the Black Hills, but prospectors moved in anyway and the government backed them.

EXPLANATION   Because the author wants to give specific examples of his claim that "every few years," prospectors found rich veins of gold and silver, he uses the sequence of dates and events pattern. Those dates and events are then repeated in the notes.

1. Born in 1912, future German rocket scientist Wernher von Braun demonstrated his interests early on. As a boy, he tried to make his wagon fly by attaching rockets to its sides. By 1932, von Braun had already earned an engineering degree and was heading a newly created rocket program in Kummersdorf, Germany. By 1934, von Braun had received a doctorate in physics and his work was being funded by the new German leader, Adolf Hitler, who was enthusiastic about the potential of rocket science. It was only four years later that von Braun's team had developed the deadly V-2 missile, which could carry explosives almost two hundred miles. The V-2, in fact, was instrumental in Germany's deadly bombing raids on London. However, by 1945, the Nazi regime was collapsing. Von Braun, always careful to advance his own interests, decided to get on the winning side and surrendered to American troops. Initially skeptical of von Braun's motives, the Americans quickly realized how valuable he was to their own rocket program and decided to overlook his past. The Cold War was heating up, and von Braun was a gold mine of information. By 1960, von Braun was the head of NASA's George C. Marshall Flight Center. He was jubilant when his agency landed a man on the moon in 1969, and the country celebrated with him In 1975, he was awarded the National Medal of Science. Wernher von Braun's story is worth remembering the next time anyone tells you with great certainty that "what goes around, comes around."

Main Idea

_____

_____

Supporting Details

_____

_____

_____

_____

_____

_____

_____

_____

_____

_____

2. Although the idea of constructing a canal across Panama dates back to the sixteenth century, the canal did not become a reality until the twentieth century. As early as 1534 Holy Roman Emperor Charles V suggested that building a waterway across the narrowest part of central America would allow ships to travel more easily to Peru and Ecuador. His idea was revived now and then as the years went by, but construction was not actually attempted until 1880, when the French broke ground on January 1. Thirteen years later, in 1893, they abandoned the project as too difficult. In 1903, the United States, under President Theodore Roosevelt, gained control of the unfinished Panama Canal, and in 1904 construction resumed. Over the next ten years, workers built the canal's foundation and system of locks. On August 15, 1914, the canal formally opened when the cargo ship *Ancon* became the first to use it. After World War II, controversy swirled around the canal over who the rightful owners were, the Americans or the Panamanians. In 1977, U.S. President Jimmy Carter signed a treaty returning control of the canal zone to Panama.

Main Idea _____

_____

Supporting Details _____

_____

_____

_____

_____

_____

_____

_____

_____

✔ CHECK YOUR UNDERSTANDING

1. In the sequence of dates and events pattern, how does the author organize the events covered in the reading?

_____

2. Paragraphs organized in a sequence of dates and events pattern are likely to fulfill what three purposes?

_____

_____

_____

3. Give three examples of transitions likely to be used in this pattern of organization.

_____

4. What should notes on this organizational pattern include?

_____

VOCABULARY ROUND UP 1

Below are five words introduced in pages 493–504. The words are accompanied by more detailed definitions, the page on which they originally appeared, and additional sample sentences. Spend time reviewing the words and their meanings because you will see them again in review tests at the end of the chapter. Use the online dictionary Wordnik to find additional sentences illustrating the words in context. (*Note*: If you know of another dictionary with as many examples of words in context feel free to use that one instead.)

1. **dynamics** (p. 493): the psychological interaction that takes place in relationships; the physical or moral forces that bring about movement and change. (1) "Family *dynamics* are central to the creation of personality." (2) "The *dynamics* of international trade were a mystery to the young stockbroker, but that didn't stop him from investing his clients' money in funds devoted to international trading."

2. **compassionate** (p. 496): caring and thoughtful about others, sympathetic, aware of the suffering of others. "A nurse for over twenty years, he was adored by his patients, who were grateful for his *compassionate* care."

3. **chromosomes** (p. 499): bodies within a cell that consist of hundreds of clear, jellylike particles strung together like beads. Chromosomes carry the body's genes. "*Chromosomes* occur in pairs; half of each pair comes from the mother, the other half from the father."

4. **genes** (p. 500): the elements responsible for hereditary characteristics, such as hair and eye color; units of hereditary characteristics that are carried on chromosomes. "*Genes* play a role in achievement, but a willingness to work hard is probably more important than heredity."

5. **illumination** (p. 504): understanding, comprehension; the coming of light. (1) "Listening to the long-winded speech, she kept on hoping for a moment of *illumination*, but it never came." (2) "The *illumination* of the street lights was a welcome relief from the pitch black darkness they had previously encountered during the walk home."

Pattern 3: Simple Listing

In time order explanations of events, the dates and events or the steps in a process have to be presented according to how they occur (or occurred) in real time. The same is not true, however, for the **simple listing pattern**. With this pattern, the order of the details can vary with the writer. That's because the content does not rely on any specific order. Look, for example, at the following paragraph:

If you ask several American citizens who the country's greatest presidents were, don't expect complete agreement. For each person, greatness in a president depends on an individual's sense of what presidents should accomplish for the country. Those who believe it's the government's job to create social equality are likely to name Abraham Lincoln, Franklin Delano Roosevelt, maybe even Lyndon Johnson, all of whom proudly announced their determination to use the power of government for the creation of social justice. For those convinced, though, that the best president is one who governs least, Ronald Reagan is likely to be named the greatest president of all time. It was Reagan who repeatedly proclaimed that each individual was responsible for his or her own destiny. The government could not and would not step in to help those who had failed to adequately advance on society's economic ladder. For those who argue, however, that the Constitution is what makes the country both strong and special, the greatest presidents will be men like Thomas Jefferson, James Madison, and John Adams, all of whom helped frame the Constitution that guides our lives to this very day.

According to the above paragraph, Americans decide who is the best president based on their personal ideas of how government should function. The writer then expands on that general point by giving examples. Those examples, however, do not have to be presented in any particular order. In fact, after adding some transitional links, the details could reappear with a totally different order:

If you ask several American citizens who the country's greatest presidents were, don't expect complete agreement. For each person, greatness in a president depends on the individual's sense of what presidents should accomplish for the country. Those who believe that what makes our country great is its Constitution would be likely to choose presidents like Thomas Jefferson, John Adams, and James Madison, men who played central roles in framing the Constitution. However, for those convinced that the best president is the one who governs least, Ronald Reagan is likely to be named the greatest president of them all. It was Reagan who repeatedly proclaimed that each individual was responsible for his or her own destiny. The government could not and would not step in to help those who had failed to adequately advance on society's economic ladder. But for those citizens passionately convinced that it's the government's job to help create social equality, the greatest presidents would be men like Abraham Lincoln, Franklin Delano Roosevelt, maybe even Lyndon Johnson, all of whom proudly announced their determination to use the power of government for the creation of social justice.

As this paragraph shows, the simple listing pattern does not rely on the order of events or steps to make a point.

Typical Topic Sentences

Topic sentences that signal the listing pattern often contain some general category word that needs to be illustrated to be meaningful—for example, "African honeybees have a number of *characteristics* that make them especially dangerous." But again, category words are *typical* in these sentences. That doesn't mean, however, that they always appear. Neither of the sample paragraphs on how we choose our favorite president, for instance, includes a category word.

The following are all topic sentences that suggest a listing pattern.

1. Unlike the previous generation who relied on letters and phone calls to keep in touch, people today have many different ways to stay connected to friends and family.

2. More than ever before, there is wide range of digital games expressly created for educational purposes.

3. Abused children tend to exhibit similar behavior patterns.

4. Diseases of the bronchi and lungs are usually severe and can be life threatening. (Adapted from Neighbors and Tannenhill-Jones, *Human Disease*, 2nd ed., p. 159.)

READING TIP   In the listing pattern, the topic sentence is most likely to appear at the beginning or end of the paragraph.

Transitional Signals

Transitions like *for instance* and *for example* are likely to appear in the listing pattern. So, too, are transitions such as *first, second, third, next,* and *finally.*

Taking Notes on the Simple Listing Pattern

Notes on the simple listing pattern should include the following:

1. the main idea

2. any supporting details necessary to itemize and explain the plural word or phrase included in the topic sentence—for example, *ways*, *digital games*, *patterns*, and *diseases*.

Because order does not play a significant role in this pattern, you might consider using a diagram to take notes.

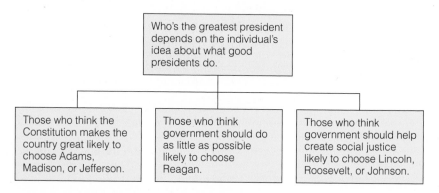

Who's the greatest president depends on the individual's idea about what good presidents do.

Those who think the Constitution makes the country great likely to choose Adams, Madison, or Jefferson.

Those who think government should do as little as possible likely to choose Reagan.

Those who think government should help create social justice likely to choose Lincoln, Roosevelt, or Johnson.

SUMMING UP THE KEY POINTS

1. In the simple listing pattern, the order of the supporting details can vary dramatically, depending on how the writer chooses to arrange the details.

2. Because the order of information is not a significant factor in this pattern, your notes can present the details in any way that makes them easy to remember.

3. Topic sentences in this pattern will appear at the very beginning or at the very end.

4. Topic sentences in the simple listing pattern are also likely to include some general category word that needs more specific examples to be meaningful, for instance, *characteristics*, *indications*, and *strategies*.

5. Typical transitions are *for instance* and *for example*, along with transitions like *first*, *second*, and *third*. These transitions help readers identify the individual items being listed.

◆ **EXERCISE 4**   **Understanding Simple Listing**

DIRECTIONS   Read each passage. Then take notes using the space provided to create an outline or a diagram.

The phrase "signs and symptoms" in the topic sentence suggests the simple listing pattern.

Supporting details requiring no particular order confirm the simple listing pattern.

EXAMPLE   There are many common signs and symptoms of respiratory disease. One typical symptom is difficulty breathing in a prone position. This symptom is especially significant if breathing becomes easier when the person sits or stands up straight. Coughing is another common symptom, and it's caused by irritation of the airways or a buildup of fluid in the lung tissue. Coughing up blood is called *hemoptysis* and can be a sign of serious respiratory disease. Nasal discharge is another symptom of respiratory problems and is present in both inflammation and allergic respiratory reactions. Most frequently, nasal discharge is a symptom of the common cold, but it can also be a symptom of other more serious respiratory disorders. Surprisingly, hiccups, at least if they are persistent, can be a sign of respiratory disease. A barrel-chested appearance and enlarged fingertips can also be signs that a respiratory disease is present.

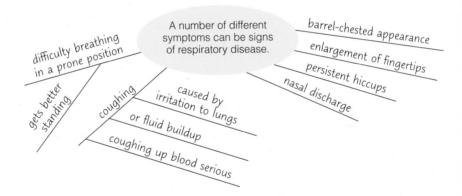

EXPLANATION   As is typical of this pattern, the topic sentence appears at the beginning and includes a phrase, "signs and symptoms," that needs to be narrowed if it is to convey any information to the reader. The symptoms are then listed in a way the writer finds effective. However, another writer might just as easily choose to start with the most severe symptoms followed by those that are less severe because the material requires no fixed order of presentation.

1. Offering an apology would seem to be a simple act. All you have to do is say, "I'm sorry." Right? Well, not exactly. For some people

apologizing is easy. They just admit they made a mistake. But for others, it's more difficult. The different ways people view making an apology may be the reason there are, at the very least, three different kinds. For example, there's the "I'm sorry you feel that way" apology. This is an irritating apology to those on the receiving end. It suggests that the person apologizing didn't do anything wrong and is only sorry that the person who was hurt is such a super-sensitive creature, thin-skinned enough to interpret harmless actions in the wrong way. A more satisfying apology for the person being apologized to goes something like this, "I'm sorry. That was a mistake on my part. I won't do it again." But this is one of the toughest apologies to make and many people just can't bring the words across their lips. Easier, perhaps because it suggests an exchange principle that levels the playing ground and eliminates guilt, is an apology like this one. "I'm sorry that what I did hurt you. How can I make it up to you?"

2. There are three learning strategies students should use to make sure they understand and remember new information. One strategy is *rehearsal*, or repetition, of what's just been read or heard. Thus, students who repeat the main idea of a paragraph right after they finish reading it are more likely to understand and remember the paragraph's point. *Synthesizing** is another key learning strategy. For instance, students reading a chapter that compares the press's

---

*synthesizing: the combining of separate thoughts to create a new idea.

role during the first and second Gulf War will have a better understanding of the material if they can link the chapter sections with a synthesis statement. A synthesis statement makes connections between different chapter sections (or even different readings), for example: "During the first Gulf War, the government and the military, worried about a possibly adversarial* press, imposed blanket censorship. But in the second, they used embedding† to keep the press informed and cooperative." The third strategy, *elaboration*, requires the learner to relate new information to prior knowledge by, for instance, comparing the author's point of view to another writer who disagrees or shares the same opinion, for example: "Robert Caro despises Johnson as a man and president, but Robert Dallek is a more sympathetic critic on both counts."

✔ CHECK YOUR UNDERSTANDING

1. How does the simple listing pattern differ from the time order pattern?

_____

_____

_____

2. In the simple listing pattern, where is the topic sentence most likely to occur?

_____

_____

---

*adversarial: challenging, ready to criticize.
†embedding: journalists were assigned to military units engaged in armed conflicts.

3. What kind of word is likely to appear in a topic sentence that introduces the simple listing pattern?

_____

_____

4. What are some transitions that are likely to accompany this pattern?

_____

_____

From Reader to Writer Pick a topic like friendship, marriage, pets, studying, debt, etc., and write a paragraph that organizes the details in the simple listing pattern. The paragraph should open or close with a topic sentence like "There are three things you should never do if you want to make a good impression on a date." The supporting details should then further explain each of those things to be avoided.

Pattern 4: Comparison and Contrast

Paragraphs based on **comparison and contrast** describe the similarities and/or differences between two people, events, animals, or objects. Take, for example, the following paragraph:

Emphasis on differences in the introductory sentence and topic sentence suggest comparison and contrast.

Supporting details emphasize differences between the two topics discussed, Japanese and American management.

Much attention, perhaps too much, has been paid to the differences between Japanese and American workers. *But* perhaps we should examine more carefully the differences between Japanese and American management at the highest levels of decision making. In Japan, the heads of companies are discouraged from earning more than sixteen times the salary of their highest-paid workers. In America, *in contrast*, the company's chief officer can be expected to earn as much as 300 to 500 times more than the highest-salaried worker. In Japan, if someone in top management makes a serious blunder, he is in disgrace and will publicly acknowledge it. *However*, if the same thing happens in America, the company may suffer bankruptcy. But the person who erred is unlikely to publicly take responsibility. On the contrary, past experience suggests he or she, although statistically it's usually he, will often depart from the company with a hefty financial package.

While the introductory sentence suggests a paragraph that will focus on the differences between Japanese and American workers, the transition *but* reverses the opening train of thought and paves the way for the topic sentence—"But perhaps we should examine more carefully the differences between Japanese and American management at the highest levels of decision making." That topic sentence makes it clear that the paragraph will concentrate on differences between Japanese and American management rather than workers. The major supporting details then describe the specific differences.

In some cases, however, paragraphs do both: They compare *and* contrast two topics. Here's an example:

The topic sentence suggests the paragraph discusses similarities and differences between two kinds of bees.

Italicized verbs and comparative adjectives also signal the comparison and contrast pattern.

The African or so-called killer bees have entered the United States, and their arrival has, for good reason, aroused intense fear. *While in some ways* African honeybees *resemble* harmless American honeybees, they are different in a significant and dangerous way. *When it comes to similarities*, the African honeybee's venom is *no more poisonous* than the American honeybee's. It's *also* true that the African bee is *not much more aggressive* than the honeybee. What *distinguishes* the African honeybee from the American honeybee is its determined defense of territory. If African honeybees are disturbed in their nest, they mount a furious attack and pursue intruders for miles. American honeybees, *in contrast*, quickly get bored and give up the chase.

In this paragraph, the topic sentence moves away from the focus of the introductory sentence, which talks about African killer bees. The topic sentence tells readers to expect a discussion of the similarities and differences between African *and* American honeybees: "While in some ways the African honeybees resemble harmless American honeybees, they are different in a significant and dangerous way." The supporting details fulfill the promise of that sentence, specifically identifying two similarities and one dangerous difference.

Transitional Signals

Notice the italicized transitions in the sample paragraphs. They are typical of transitions that signal the comparison and contrast pattern, as are the transitions that follow.

Transitions That Signal Similarity ♦		
Along the same lines	In like fashion (manner)	Just as
Also	In much the same way (manner)	Just like
By the same token		Like
Comparatively	In terms of similarities	Likewise
In comparison	In the same vein	Similarly

Transitions That Signal Difference ♦		
Actually	In reality	Opposing that position
Although	Instead	
And yet	Ironically	Rather
But	Just the opposite	Still
Conversely	Nevertheless	Though
Despite that fact	Nonetheless	Unfortunately
Even though	On the contrary	Unlike
However	On the one hand	Whereas
In contrast	On the other hand	While
In opposition		Yet

Typical Topic Sentences

Transitions like those listed above are clues to the comparison and contrast pattern. So, too, are topic sentences like the following:

1. In contrast to African Americans, Mexican Americans were not forced into segregated military units during World War II.

2. Researcher Susan Harter found that some children view achievement tasks as a means of satisfying personal needs (**intrinsic motivation**),

whereas others strive to do well primarily to earn external rewards such as grades, prizes, or social approval (**extrinsic motivation**). (Adapted from Shaffer, *Social and Personality Development*, 6th ed., p. 210.)

3. Rodrigo Díaz de Vivar, also known as El Cid, and Agustina de Aragón, called the Spanish Joan of Arc, were alike in their complete and unselfish devotion to their country's independence from foreign rule.

4. One of the oldest controversies among education theorists is the nature versus nurture issue. (Adapted from Shaffer, *Social and Personality Development*, 6th ed., p. 210.)

Topic sentences that identify two topics and refer to a similarity and/or difference between the two, are almost sure to be indicators of the comparison and contrast pattern. However, it's also true that authors frequently identify the similarities and differences between two topics and let the details imply the overall point.

Taking Notes on Comparison and Contrast Patterns

Notes on a paragraph using a comparison and contrast pattern should clearly identify three essential elements:

1. the two topics being compared and/or contrasted

2. the similarities and/or differences between the two

3. the main idea they explain or support

Here, to illustrate, are notes on the paragraph on page 521.

Main Idea Although there are some similarities between American honeybees and African honeybees, there is an important and dangerous difference.

Supporting Details 1. African bees' venom no more poisonous than honeybees'.

2. The two bees about equally aggressive.

3. What makes African bees different and dangerous is determined defense of territory.

   a. Attack in a group and pursue for miles.

   b. Honeybees quickly give up the chase.

When taking notes on the comparison and contrast pattern, consider as well making a diagram that looks something like this:

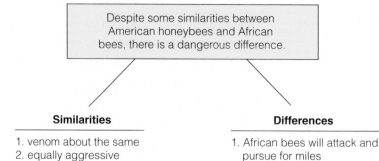

Similarities	Differences
1. venom about the same 2. equally aggressive	1. African bees will attack and pursue for miles 2. honeybees quickly give up

Linking Pattern to Purpose

In Chapter 12, we will talk at some length about persuasion in writing. But at this point, you need to know a key detail about the comparison and contrast pattern of organization. Within textbooks, readings with this pattern are likely to have a primarily informative purpose. But outside of textbooks, writers frequently compare and contrast to persuade. They try, that is, to prove, or at least make convincing a point, that others might disagree with. When the writer's intent is to persuade, the similarities and differences cited are usually in the text in order to make a value judgment convincing and encourage readers to share it.

Topic sentences like these two, for instance, suggest a persuasive purpose and practically demand a discussion of similarities and differences. "The remake of the movie classic *King Kong* was far inferior to the original" or "These vastly different pay scales suggest that women are still not getting a fair shake in the world of high finance."

READING TIP

Don't get so caught up identifying similarities and differences that you forget about the idea they illustrate. Make sure you always know what main idea is developed by the author's description of differences and similarities.

SUMMING UP THE KEY POINTS

1. Paragraphs based on the comparison and contrast pattern of organization always present the reader with two different topics. Based on the needs of the main idea, the supporting details then highlight similarities and differences between the two. Some paragraphs using this pattern describe both similarities and differences.

2. Transitions such as *likewise, similarly, but*, and *however* are clues to this pattern. However, the real clues are the presence of the two topics and the references to similarities and/or differences.

3. Topic sentences that explain how two things, people, ideas, or events do or do not resemble one another are also a clue to this pattern. It's also true that in the comparison and contrast pattern, the main idea is frequently implied rather than stated. In this case, the author lets the similarities and differences speak for themselves.

4. Notes on the comparison and contrast pattern need to include the two topics being compared and/or contrasted. They also need to include the central similarities and differences between the two, along with the implied or stated main idea that the details develop.

5. Crucial to notes on the comparison and contrast pattern is the presence of the main idea. Sometimes readers get caught up in the similarities and differences and forget to indicate why they are present in the paragraph.

6. In textbooks, writers compare and contrast in order to communicate information about two topics. In editorials and essays, however, writers usually compare and contrast in order to convey a point of view they want you to share.

◆ **EXERCISE 5**   **Understanding Comparison and Contrast Patterns**

DIRECTIONS   Read each paragraph. Then circle the appropriate letter to indicate whether the author has (1) compared two topics, (2) contrasted two topics, or (3) compared *and* contrasted two topics. Circle all comparison and contrast transitions, and use the blank lines to take notes on the paragraph. *Paraphrasing note*: Don't worry if you can't find new language to refer to the topics. That may not be possible. Focus more on finding different words to discuss similarities or differences.

After arrival in the United States, new immigrants had to pass through inspection by customs officials, who often changed the arrivals' names because their foreign names were hard to pronounce.

As is typical of this pattern, the main idea is implied based on the contrasts identified in the supporting details.

The transitions but *and* instead *emphasize the focus on contrast.*

EXAMPLE Between 1890 and 1910, millions of people from southern and eastern Europe left their homes in search of the American dream. The new immigrants hoped to find a comfortable place where they could settle and live out their lives. (But) the cities to which they came were not prepared for the influx of immigrants, and many immigrant families ended up in ugly apartments that were poorly supplied with light, heat, and water. The new arrivals had dreamed of finding work that could make them independent, even rich. (Instead,) they found that jobs were scarce. Immigrants often had to take jobs for which they were unsuited, and the work left them exhausted and depressed. Moreover, many found that they were treated as outsiders, and their accents were subject to insults or ridicule.

In this paragraph, the author

    a. compares two topics.

    (b.) contrasts two topics.

    c. compares and contrasts two topics.

Main Idea Immigrants who came in search of the American dream between 1890 and 1910 were
terribly disappointed.

Supporting Details 1. Instead of comfortable place to live, had to settle for cold, ugly, and poorly lit
apartments.

2. Instead of suitable jobs, found unemployment or hard, tedious work.

3. Instead of warm welcome, ridiculed as outsiders with odd customs and funny way
of speaking.

EXPLANATION   The paragraph contrasts what immigrants hoped to find in their new country with what they actually found. Each difference reinforces the implied main idea: "Immigrants who came in search of the American dream between 1890 and 1910 were terribly disappointed."

1. Mary Shelley's *Frankenstein* (1818) and Bram Stoker's *Dracula* (1897) are the grandparents of the modern day horror story. Both novels are over a century old, yet they are still read and enjoyed today. Much of their staying power comes from the monsters who inhabit them. Similar in their ability to compel fear and allegedly based on real historical figures,[†] they also differ in several important respects. Shelley's nameless monster, constructed out of stolen body parts, suggests that scientific knowledge, used without ethical guidance or a moral conscience, can wreak havoc* on the world. Stoker's *Dracula*, in contrast, is a reminder that there are things in the world that science can neither explain nor control. Stoker's Dracula, for all his paleness and red eyes, is a sexy presence, a fact that movies based on the novel have emphasized. Women, in particular, are drawn to him and fall readily under his spell. The monster in *Frankenstein* is so far from sexy that a blind man is the only one who doesn't scream at the sight of him. If anything, it's the monster's repulsiveness that separates him from Stoker's Count Dracula. Smart and articulate,

---

[†]Stoker is believed to have based Count Dracula on a nobleman called Vlad the Impaler, who had a taste for spilling and drinking the blood of his victims. Shelley is said to have visited Castle Frankenstein, where a man named Johann Konrad Dippel was believed to have carried out experiments that involved stitching together human bodies.
*havoc: confusion, chaos.

Shelley's monster would like to be part of society but is an outcast because of his gruesome appearance. Count Dracula, on the other hand, has no desire to be part of a community except when he is in need of fresh blood. The count doesn't long to be normal in the way Shelley's desperate monster does.

In this paragraph, the author

a. compares two topics.

b. contrasts two topics.

c. compares and contrasts two topics.

Main Idea

_____

_____

Supporting Details

_____

_____

_____

_____

_____

_____

_____

2. To some degree, all societies are altered by time. But for Nigerian society, the changes between life in early-nineteenth-century Nigeria and now are especially striking. Most notable is the shift in economic and political power, which was originally in the hands of local leaders who governed Nigeria's twenty-three individual states. Currently, power is concentrated in the hands of a small group of business and military leaders. While local leaders in the early nineteenth century often waged war in pursuit of expanding the territory they controlled, modern tribal leaders exert influence through behind-the-scenes political wheeling and dealing rather

than military conquest. Although the power and influence of local leaders has been dramatically curtailed by the arrival of democratic traditions, one thing has not altered. Community leaders are still regarded as the custodians of past tradition and as the final word on questions about what it means to be a Nigerian in moral or ethical terms. Another area where dramatic change has occurred is in the conduct of courtship. In the past, there was no such thing as dating. If a couple was seen together in public, they were expected to marry. City couples, at least, are now free to date without expectations of marriage. In the countryside, however, courtship rules are somewhat stricter, and dating as we know it is not encouraged.

In this paragraph, the author

a. compares two topics.

b. contrasts two topics.

c. compares and contrasts two topics.

Main Idea
_____

_____

Supporting Details
_____

_____

_____

_____

_____

From Reader to Writer You just read a paragraph that compared Mary Shelley's monster in *Frankenstein* to Count Dracula in Bram Stoker's *Dracula*. Write a paragraph in which you compare and contrast two heroes, villains, or monsters from a movie or comic series. Contrast, for instance, Freddy Krueger from the *Nightmare on Elm Street* series with the creepy Michael Myers of the *Halloween* series. Are they more similar than different? Or are they strikingly different in the way they embody evil? Remember the similarities and differences have to add up to some larger point such as "While some movie monsters are meant to inspire sympathy because of their isolation, Freddy and Michael embody pure evil."

✔ **CHECK YOUR UNDERSTANDING**

1. What are the essential characteristics of the comparison and contrast pattern?

_____

_____

2. Name four transitions that are typical of this pattern.

_____

3. What kind of topic sentence is likely to appear in this pattern?

_____

_____

4. What should notes on this pattern include?

_____

_____

5. What mistake do readers sometimes make when taking notes on this pattern?

_____

_____

Pattern 5: Cause and Effect

"Life is a perpetual instruction in cause and effect."
— American writer and philosopher Ralph Waldo Emerson

Whatever type of reading you do, you are bound to run across passages that explain how one event—the **cause**—leads to or produces another event—the **effect**. Look, for example, at the following paragraph:

Fear has a profound effect on the human body. When you become frightened, you breathe more deeply, thereby sending your muscles more oxygen and energy. *Consequently*, your heart beats faster, making your blood circulate more quickly and thereby rushing oxygen to all parts of your body. *In response* to fear, your stomach and intestines stop contracting and all digestive activity ceases. Your saliva also stops flowing, causing your mouth to become dry. Fear also causes the body's blood vessels to shrink, making your face lose its natural color.

For her portrayal of a woman in the grip of all-consuming fear in the movie classic *Psycho*, actress Janet Leigh was nominated for an Oscar.

In the above paragraph, the topic sentence identifies the cause and effect relationship under discussion: Fear has a profound effect on the human body. The supporting details then describe those effects more specifically. Note, too, that some details also describe *cycles of causes and effects* in which one effect turns into the cause of another. Fear, for example, causes your blood vessels to shrink, which, in turn, produces another effect—your face loses color. If diagrammed, the relationships among these statements would look like this:

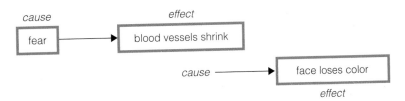

Transitional Signals

As the italicized transitions in the paragraph above suggest, transitions are often clues to the cause and effect pattern. Should you see any of the

The topic sentence covers all of the ways that voting can take place in the House of Representatives.

The supporting details then further describe those ways, giving each one a name and a brief description.

Members of the House of Representatives may vote in four different ways. The most common method is the *voice vote*. Members in favor of a bill say "yea," while those opposed say "nay." The Speaker of the House then judges, largely by volume, which side has the most voice votes and announces the result. If any member feels that the Speaker is mistaken, the Speaker can be forced to call for a *division* or *standing vote* in which the members stand to be counted for or against. A third method is the *yea or nay vote*. If one-fifth of the members present demand, all the members of the House present must be recorded as saying *yea* or *nay* to the measure being proposed. The *recorded vote* is taken when at least twenty-five members of the House request it, and the results are tallied electronically. (Adapted from Shick and Pfister, *American Government: Continuity and Change*, p. 29.)

Typically for the classification pattern, the authors open by telling their readers two things: (1) the larger group to be subdivided, voting in the House of Representatives, and (2) the number of categories produced by classification, four. They then proceed to describe each category in more specific detail.

Typical Topic Sentences

Topic sentences like those listed here practically guarantee that a classification pattern organizes the paragraph.

1. Psychologists have identified four key determinants of attraction.
   (Adapted from Nevid, *Psychology: Concepts and Applications*, 4th ed., p. 528.)

2. There are three different kinds of lies.

3. Researchers in interpersonal communication have identified four types of conversation.

4. The Indian caste system once assigned human beings to four different groups, with Brahmins at the top of the heap and the untouchables at the bottom.

Frequently Used Words in Classification Topic Sentences ◆	Categories	Groups
	Classes	Kinds
	Components	Parts
	Elements	Problems
	Factors	Ranks
	Features	Types
	Fields	

Telltale Visual Aids

Tables like the following frequently signal the presence of the classification pattern. Keep in mind, though, that you can also use tables to review (just cover the right-hand side and see what you can remember about each classification category) or as a model for note-taking.

Table 10.1: The Four Basic Components of a Strategy

Scope	• Identifies the markets or industries in which firm will compete
Resource Deployment	• Indicates how company will allocate or use resources
Competitive Advantage	• Specifies what advantages a firm has relative to competitors
Synergy	• Reflects extent to which businesses inside the firm can draw upon one another

Source of information: Van Fleet and Peterson, *Contemporary Management*, 2nd ed., pp. 73–74.

Taking Notes on the Classification Pattern

To be complete, notes on the classification pattern require the following information:

1. the name of the larger group being broken down into subgroups

2. the names of the categories if they are supplied

3. a brief description of each category

Here to illustrate are notes on the paragraph on page 538.

Main Idea   Members of the House have four different ways to vote.

Supporting Details
1. "Voice vote." Members voting in favor say "yea," those opposed say "nay," and the Speaker judges which side is louder.

2. "Standing or division vote." If someone thinks the Speaker is mistaken, then members must stand to be counted.

3. "Yea or Nay." If one-fifth of all present members demand, members' "yea" or "nay" response must be counted individually.

4. "Recorded Vote." Twenty-five members need to ask for this method and responses are electronically recorded.

NOTE-TAKING TIP

If names of categories do appear in the classification paragraph, put those names first in your notes. This note-taking format highlights the individual categories. Keep in mind, though, that the subgroups in this pattern are not always named.

SUMMING UP THE KEY POINTS

1. Like simple listing, the classification pattern does not require that supporting details be presented in a particular order. However, the classification pattern, unlike simple listing, always makes the same point: It explains how some larger group can be broken down into smaller subgroups. Then the supporting details describe each subgroup in detail.

2. The topic sentence of the classification pattern usually names the number of subgroups that make up the larger whole—for example, "Currently, there are three different kinds of medication that deal with anxiety."

3. Categories in the classification pattern are not always identified by name. However, if they are identified by name, the names should be included in your notes. Include as well the characteristics that describe each subgroup.

◆ **EXERCISE 7**   **Recognizing and Understanding Classification Patterns**

DIRECTIONS   Read and take notes on each paragraph. *Paraphrasing Note*: If the categories have names, those should not change. Concentrate on paraphrasing the descriptive details used to differentiate between or among the categories.

The words classified and categories in the topic sentence give the pattern away.

The supporting details then describe each subgroup of the larger category.

EXAMPLE   Psychological problems are generally classified into two categories: externalizing disorders and internalizing disorders. The **externalizing disorders** are characterized by aggression turned out-ward, such as striking out at other people or the environment. People suffering from these kinds of disorders exhibit behaviors such as lying, stealing, disobedience, and delinquency. Other common symptoms of externalizing disorders include fighting, cruelty to animals, property destruction, temper tantrums, hostility toward authority figures, and violating the rights of others. The **internalizing disorders** are directed inward. These affect the individual rather than other people or the environment. These disorders are characterized by anxiety, depression, worrying, withdrawal, phobias, and panic attacks. (Source of information: Kaplan, *Adolescence*, pp. 463–64.)

Main Idea Psychological problems are generally divided into two groups: externalizing disorders and internalizing disorders.

Supporting Details 1. Externalizing disorders are directed toward others or the environment.

    a. Include not telling the truth, theft, refusing to obey rules, and delinquency.

    b. Also include violence, fighting, animal cruelty, property damage, temper blowups, hostility, and ignoring the rights of others.

2. Internalizing disorders are directed inward, toward self.

    a. Include worry, depression, self-isolation, irrational fears, and panic attacks.

EXPLANATION   The notes contain the essential elements of the classification pattern. The larger group is divided into two smaller categories, and the names and characteristics of each group are listed.

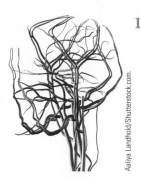

Arteries carry blood away from the heart; veins carry it back.

1. In the human body, blood circulates through elastic, tube-like canals called *blood vessels*. Consisting of three different types, blood vessels are well adapted to their functions. The vessels called *arteries* carry blood away from the heart to all parts of the body. The largest artery in the human body is the *aorta*. Arterial blood appears bright red because it is filled with oxygen. In contrast, blood in the *veins*, another type of blood vessel, appears purplish because it is no longer carrying a supply of oxygen. Veins, which carry blood back to the heart, contain small valves that prevent the blood from flowing backward. This is important in the lower parts of the body where the blood has to move against the pull of gravity. The third type of blood vessel is the *capillary*. Capillaries are tiny vessels connecting arteries and veins. Capillary walls are extremely thin. They have to be thin so that digested food can pass through them to the cells of the body.

Main Idea

_____

_____

Supporting Details

_____

_____

_____

_____

_____

_____

_____

_____

_____

2. Researcher John Lee has identified what he calls six different styles of love. The **erotic lover** focuses on the physical aspects of being in love. He or she is not especially jealous or possessive, and although emotions are intense, this lover is not likely to undergo much self-sacrifice in an effort to obtain love. The **ludic lover** sees love as a

game played for fun. This individual avoids deep relationships and may juggle a number of partners at the same time. Just the right degree of emotionality is maintained so that personal commitment never becomes too demanding. The **storgic lover** sees love as a slow, steady climb toward commitment. Neither intense emotions nor sexual encounters are central to the relationship. Instead of seeking the ups and downs of a passionate relationship, the storgic lover approaches love as a relationship mostly based on shared activities and interests. The **manic lover** contrasts with the storge. The manic lover is obsessed with his or her partner. Jealous and possessive, he or she is filled with anxiety that something will ruin the relationship. The **pragmatic lover** knows what he or she wants and "shops" to find a partner with the desired interests and goals. The relationship that ensues is not a highly passionate or intense one; rather it is one that fits into a well-defined pattern. The **agapic lover** is patient, kind, altruistic, and compassionate. Love is given without any conditions and may involve self-sacrifice. Lee found no examples of pure agapic love in his research but did find some aspects of agape in a number of relationships. (Adapted from Kaplan, *Adolesence*, pp. 348–49.)

Main Idea

_____

_____

Supporting Details

_____

_____

_____

_____

_____

_____

_____

_____

_____

_____

_____

_____

_____

_____

_____

✔ CHECK YOUR UNDERSTANDING

1. What's the major difference between the simple listing pattern and the classification pattern?

   _____

   _____

   _____

2. What does the topic sentence in the classification pattern usually do?

   _____

3. When taking notes on the classification pattern, what should you include in your notes?

   _____

▶ **SHARE YOUR THOUGHTS**
Do you think that the six categories of lovers accurately reflect what you know about people in love? Why or why not? Of the six, which one do you think is most likely to find happiness in love? Which one is the least likely?

Identifying the Primary Pattern

Until now, you've been working with one organizational pattern at a time. But in the next exercise, you'll be asked to select one particular pattern among several possibilities. That means it's time to introduce the notion of the primary pattern.

When writers rely on a particular organizational pattern, that doesn't mean every sentence will reflect the **primary pattern**, or overall pattern. There may be a sentence or two that doesn't. Consider, for instance, sentences 6 and 8 in the following paragraph:

Sentences 1 and 2 make up a main idea statement that describes a change or shift in the original cause and effect relationship introduced.

The supporting details provide the causes behind the shift. Note how the phrases "one reason" and "another cause" suggest the cause and effect pattern.

[1]Mention the word *outsourcing* to most American workers and you are not likely to put a smile on their face. [2]The practice of sending jobs out of the country in order to increase corporate profits by using cheap labor has left many workers in the United States scrambling to earn a living. [3]But that situation might be changing as more and more companies once again think about turning out made-in-America products. [4]One reason for the shift in thinking is the rising cost of labor among big suppliers. [5]In some sections of China, for instance, the price of labor has gone up by 15 percent. [6]Another cause for the shift from outsourcing to *insourcing*— the newly coined term that perfectly describes the corporate world's change of heart—is the rising price of shipping costs around the world. [7]As shipping costs rise, profits decrease and directly undermine one of the main reasons for outsourcing in the first place. [8]Companies considering producing their wares in the United States also know that American workers are, with the exception of workers in Ireland and Norway, among the world's most productive. (Source of productivity statistic: http://www.csoonline.com/article/221017/is-insourcing-the-new-outsourcing.)

If you trace the chains of repetition and reference, you'll see that practically every sentence tries to help explain *why* more companies are thinking about producing goods at home rather than out of the country. That makes the primary pattern of organization cause and effect, even though sentence 6 introduces a definition and sentence 8 makes a comparison. It would be a mistake to say that the primary pattern of this paragraph is either definition or comparison and contrast. One or two sentences do not a pattern make.

There will be times when patterns balance each other out so equally we can talk about mixed paragraph patterns. We'll discuss those in the next chapter. But much of the time, and certainly within this chapter, you'll be working solely with primary, rather than mixed, patterns.

◆ EXERCISE 8   Recognizing Primary Patterns of Organization

DIRECTIONS   Read each paragraph. Then circle the appropriate letter to identify the primary pattern of organization.

1. A **generic product**, sometimes called a **generic brand**, is a product with no brand name at all. Its plain package carries only the name of the product—applesauce, peanut butter, potato chips, or whatever—in black type. Generic products, available in supermarkets since 1977, usually are made by the major producers that manufacture name brands. They appeal mainly to consumers who are willing to sacrifice consistency in size or quality for a lower price. However, generic products are not necessarily lower in quality. Even though generic brands may have accounted for as much as 10 percent of all grocery sales several years ago, they currently represent less than 1 percent. (Pride, Hughes, and Kapoor, *Business*, 10th ed., p. 403.)

   a. definition

   b. comparison and contrast

   c. cause and effect

   d. classification

2. Child psychologists are inclined to label aggressive behavior as *overt* or *relational*. *Overt aggression* harms others through actual physical damage or the threat of physical harm. Children who engage in overt aggression are likely to push, hit, or kick a peer. At the very least, those who are overtly aggressive will make explicit threats to do some kind of physical harm in the future. Unlike overt aggression, relational aggression is more psychological than physical, and it revolves around threats to or criticism of peer relations. Children who use relational aggression don't physically hurt their victims. Instead, they may taunt a peer by saying that he or she is unlikable and has no friends. At one time, parents and educators focused on strategies to avoid overt aggression among children, because this kind of aggression seemed the more harmful of the two. But research has shown that children also suffer from being the target of

relational aggression. Although there are other kinds of aggression among children, these two forms tend to be the most common.

a. time order: process

b. simple listing

c. cause and effect

d. comparison and contrast

3. The painting known as the *Mona Lisa* has fascinated art lovers for centuries. But it wasn't until the twentieth century that one man fell so in love with the *Mona Lisa* that he decided to steal her from the Louvre.[†] In 1909, Italian-born Vincenzo Peruggia was employed by the Louvre to do some painting; it was at this point that Peruggia first got a look at the masterpiece that was to get him into so much trouble. On August 21, 1911, Peruggia returned to the Louvre as a visitor and headed straight for the *Mona Lisa*. Twenty minutes later, he left the museum with the painting tucked inside his jacket. For more than two years, investigators hunted unsuccessfully for the painting. Then, on November 29, 1913, a wealthy Italian art dealer received a letter saying the *Mona Lisa* would be returned for a price. On December 10, 1913, the art dealer arranged to meet with the painting's new owner. After Peruggia produced the painting, police took him into custody. At his trial in 1914, Peruggia explained that he had stolen the *Mona Lisa* because he couldn't forget her smile. The unsympathetic judge sentenced the would-be art collector to three years in jail.

a. time order: dates and events

b. comparison and contrast

c. cause and effect

d. simple listing

4. Certain attitudes toward life help make us successful. However, if those same attitudes are strictly maintained and never deviate, or change, they often prove to be an obstacle to happiness. The behavior of a problem-solver, someone who immediately tries to find solutions to difficult situations, perfectly illustrates how a positive attitude can turn negative. There simply are problems and questions in life with

---

[†]Louvre: a famous museum in Paris, France.

no solutions or answers. Why is it, for example, that some perfectly wonderful people die young while some evil ones survive and thrive? Unfortunately, people who insist on coming up with the right solution for every difficulty are inclined to get frustrated with such situations and they search for answers that can't be found. Relying relentlessly on logic is another attitude that can become harmful when pushed to extremes. There are situations in life where sympathy and empathy are more crucial than logic. But the person who has made reliance on logic a religion never figures that out. Yet another attitude that can have a down side is fear of failure. If we try hard to succeed because we fear failure, that's a good thing. But if we are overly terrified of failing, we are unlikely to engage in the original thinking creativity requires.

a. comparison and contrast

b. simple listing

c. classification

d. time order: process

5. The human brain has two hemispheres—the right and the left. Although the hemispheres cooperate for many functions, research suggests that they control highly different activities. Thanks to the left side of our brain, we are able to master and manipulate language, using it to communicate our thoughts. The left side of our brain helps us make sense by giving order and logic to our utterances.* The right hemisphere is less crucial to language production and appears to be more concerned with the creation of images. Research suggests that the right brain dominates during infancy. Babies make sense of the world by visualizing, rather than naming, and visualization is controlled by the right side of the brain.

a. time order: dates and events

b. comparison and contrast

c. cause and effect

d. simple listing

6. The tendency is to think of rape as an act of a stranger. But close to 80 percent of rape victims know their attacker. In fact, over one million women a year are sexually assaulted by a current or former

---

*utterances: verbal statements.

partner. Victims of partner rape are likely to be raped repeatedly over an extended period of time and are often afraid of leaving the partner who has raped them. The overwhelming majority of these women suffer a range of subsequent* symptoms that are both physical and psychological. Depression, sleeplessness, suicidal thoughts, anxiety, and panic attacks are some of the immediate psychological effects with eating disorders, difficulty concentrating, and self-hatred developing long term. (Source of statistic: National Coalition Against Domestic Violence.)

a. time order: process
b. comparison and contrast
c. cause and effect
d. classification

7. An attacker has put you in a wristlock to force you to submit. He has grabbed your wrist, pressing hard on the bones and nerves to cause you pain. If you try to pull away, you cause yourself more pain, and you could actually break your own wrist in an attempt to escape. However, if you remember a simple self-defense technique, you can free yourself. First, fight your instinct to tighten the muscles in your hands and arms. Doing so will actually cause you more pain because the tension will exert more pressure. If you are in pain, you cannot strike out to free yourself from your opponent. Second, let your hand and wrist relax and go limp. This will lessen the pain you're experiencing long enough for you to punch, kick, or bite your attacker as a way of forcing him to let you go. Relaxing your hand may also surprise him, causing him to loosen his grip for a moment. Third, the thumb is the weakest link in a person's grip, so rotate your arm and pull your hand toward your attacker's thumb for the best chance of breaking free.

a. definition
b. time order: process
c. comparison and contrast
d. classification

*subsequent: following in time, succeeding, coming after.

8. There are four common types of vegetarians, each of whom follows a different set of rules. Lacto-ovo vegetarians don't eat meat, but they do eat eggs and dairy products. Lacto vegetarians consume dairy products but won't touch eggs, whereas ovo vegetarians eat eggs but avoid dairy products. For members of the fourth category, vegans, eggs and dairy products are completely off the menu. So, too, are all animal by-products. Some vegans won't even touch honey. The restriction on animal by-products can extend to other aspects of life: Some vegans refuse to wear leather, silk, or wool.

a. comparison and contrast

b. classification

c. cause and effect

d. time order: process

9. Although Venus is Earth's twin in size, its atmosphere is truly unearthly. The composition, temperature, and density* of Venus's atmosphere make the planet's surface entirely inhospitable* to human life. About 96 percent of the atmosphere is carbon dioxide, and 3.5 percent is nitrogen. The thick clouds that hide the surface of Venus are composed of sulfuric acid droplets and microscopic sulfur crystals. Soviet and U.S. spacecraft dropped probes into the atmosphere of Venus, and those probes radioed information back to Earth. These studies show that Venus's cloud layers are much higher and more stable than those on Earth. The highest layer of clouds surrounding Venus extends about forty to forty-five miles above the planet's surface. By comparison, the clouds on Earth normally do not extend higher than about ten miles. (Adapted from Seeds and Backman, *Foundations of Astronomy*, 11th ed., p. 466.)

a. comparison and contrast

b. classification

c. cause and effect

d. time order: process

---

*density: thickness or consistency.
*inhospitable: unfriendly.

10. In the world of corporate America, there seems to be no penalty for incompetence. When Pacific Gas and Electric filed for bankruptcy, it paid all of its top executives big bonuses as rewards for their splendid work. Coca Cola's CEO, after supervising the loss of $4 billion, was given a check for $18 million. American Telephone and Telegraph fired CEO John Walther after nine months because he "lacked intellectual leadership." Nevertheless, AT&T wrote him a final check for $26 million. Under the management of Jill Barron, a toy manufacturer, Mattel, lost $2.5 billion. She joined the line at the unemployment office with $40 million in pay and bonuses in her purse. (Adapted from Conlin, *The American Past*, 9th ed., p. 846.)

    a. comparison and contrast

    b. classification

    c. simple listing

    d. time order: process

VOCABULARY ROUND UP 2

Below are ten words introduced in pages 518–50. The words are accompanied by a more detailed definition, the page on which they originally appeared and another sample sentence. Spend time reviewing the words and their meanings because you will see them again in review tests at the end of the chapter. Use the online dictionary Wordnik to find additional sentences illustrating the words in context. (*Note*: If you know of another dictionary with as many examples of words in context feel free to use that one instead.)

1. synthesizing (p. 518): the combining of separate thoughts in order to create a new idea; uniting separate parts into one whole. "The artist Willem de Kooning was a genius at *synthesizing* different styles into works of art that were uniquely his own."

2. adversarial (p. 519): challenging, ready to criticize or fight, antagonistic. "Many journalists are proud of their close ties to political figures, claiming that such ties give them access to information, but perhaps it would be better for all of us if the press were in a more *adversarial* relationship with people in power."

3. **havoc** (p. 527): confusion, chaos, disorder, and devastation. "The discovery of gold in the hills should have been a good thing for the little town of Deadwood, but it brought with it nothing but *havoc*."

4. **coercive** (p. 535): forcing someone to do something against his or her will, bullying. "The police were accused of using *coercive* techniques in order to get a confession from the suspect."

5. **stench** (p. 536): stink or smell. "The *stench* of garbage was like perfume to the band of homeless dogs that had been left to wander the streets after their owners were forced to leave their homes."

6. **range** (p. 536): move about, travel; extent of coverage or movement; a large area of open land where livestock roam. (1) "Like a lot of romantics, he had *ranged* over the world in pursuit of the perfect love, and at the age of sixty, he was still looking." (2) "Benjamin Franklin was famous for his wide *range* of political and practical knowledge."

7. **utterances** (p. 548): verbal statements, statements said aloud. "When Marie Antoinette arrived in France, every *utterance* of the young French queen was criticized and ridiculed."

8. **subsequent** (p. 549): following in time, succeeding, coming after. "The young tennis player made numerous mistakes in his first match, but he learned quickly and in *subsequent* games, he made very few unforced errors."

9. **density** (p. 550): thickness or consistency; complexity of structure or content. (1) "The *density* of the clouds interfered with the pilot's visibility." (2) "The *density* of the writing made reading the novel a long and unrewarding process."

10. **inhospitable** (p. 550): unfavorable to life; unfriendly, ungracious. (1) "On his expedition to the Antarctic, Robert Falcon Scott used ponies to haul supplies, but the freezing climate was *inhospitable* to the creatures, and they died, along with the rest of Scott's party." (2) "The museum director made it a point to be *inhospitable* to the scientists questioning the authenticity of the statues."

DIGGING DEEPER Hormones and Behavior

Looking Ahead A 1985 study of Vietnam veterans came to some surprising conclusions about the hormone testosterone.

Getting Focused Any time you see a reading that spends time discussing a study, you need to make sure you understand (1) what the researchers were looking for, (2) who their subjects were,[†] and (3) what conclusions the researchers came to after completing the study.

1   In 1985, researchers at the U.S. Centers for Disease Control in Atlanta were assigned to study the "health status" of Vietnam veterans. To do so, they first selected a random sample of men (selected from military records) who had served in Vietnam during the period of 1965–1971—officers were not included. Efforts were made to locate each man drawn in the sample and to recruit him to participate in a very comprehensive study that included elaborate interviews covering an immense array of topics, such as educational and work histories, family and marital histories, drug and alcohol abuse, childhood delinquency, adult criminality, and sexual behavior.

2   In 1988 the centers' report on the veterans was released. It was long, highly technical, and not very stimulating. But amid the blizzard of facts about veterans was the amazing revelation that the data included a measure of testosterone level for every one of these veterans. Suddenly researchers who had struggled along with tiny numbers of cases could base their research on this huge sample, and because data collected by the government are in the public domain, any scholar could obtain the complete database for free.

3   Subsequent to the release of this huge study, more research has come out. And the results are clearer and more extensive and powerful than had been anticipated. The higher their level of testosterone, the more likely men[†] are

- to get divorced

- to physically abuse their wives

[†]If possible, you should also know how the subjects were selected, but that's not information the reader is always given.
[†]Women also produce testosterone but not as much as men do. Studies of testosterone level in women have shown similar results as the 1985 study of veterans.

- to engage in extramarital sex
- to have many sexual partners
- to have problems with alcoholism
- to use drugs
- to have been punished while in military service
- to have been a juvenile delinquent
- to get in trouble with the law as an adult
- to be unemployed

As it turned out, none of these effects proved spurious when the study results were analyzed by other researchers. So, now we know that hormones strongly intrude into domains social scientists have long been accustomed to regard as theirs alone. (Adapted from Stark, *Sociology*, 10th ed., p. 136.)

Sharpening Your Skills

DIRECTIONS　Answer the following questions by filling in the blanks or circling the letter of the correct response.

1. When the researchers described in this reading first started out, what was their objective or goal?

   _____

2. What did they end up discovering?

   _____

   _____

3. What patterns organize the information in the first and second paragraphs?

   a. time order: process
   b. comparison and contrast
   c. definition
   d. cause and effect

4. What kinds of transitions dominate the paragraph openings in this reading?

   a. time order

   b. cause and effect

   c. addition

   d. contrast

5. What pattern of organization ties together the information in the third paragraph?

   a. time order: process

   b. comparison and contrast

   c. definition

   d. cause and effect

6. What's the primary pattern of the reading?

   a. time order: dates and events

   b. comparison and contrast

   c. definition

   d. classification

   e. cause and effect

7. In paragraph 2, the author uses the phrase "blizzard of facts." That language is meant to be taken

   a. literally.

   b. figuratively.

8. What does the phrase suggest about the number of facts available to the researchers?

   _____

9. In the second sentence of paragraph 3, what phrase does the reader need to supply to connect the second sentence to the first: "Subsequent to the release of this huge study, more research has come out. And the results are clearer and more extensive and powerful than had been anticipated."

_____

10. Is the main idea of this reading stated or implied? _____

Which statement best sums up the main idea of the entire reading?

a. A 1985 study of Vietnam veterans turned up some interesting results about the testosterone levels of veterans; it suggests that soldiers have high testosterone levels.

b. A 1985 study of Vietnam veterans suggests that high levels of testosterone are linked to antisocial behavior, a conclusion that has been confirmed by other studies as well.

c. A 1985 study of Vietnam veterans was published in 1988, but beyond its conclusions about testosterone, the study revealed nothing of interest.

Using Context Clues Based on the context, what do you think *spurious* means in the following sentence? "As it turned out, none of these effects proved *spurious* when the study results were analyzed by other researchers."

_____

▶ **TEST 1**   **Reviewing Key Concepts**

DIRECTIONS   Answer the following questions by filling in the blanks.

1. Paragraphs relying on the definition pattern frequently open ____ _____.

2. In the time order pattern of organization, the goal is to explain steps or events according to _____.

3. _____ are a good alternative to informal outlines when it comes to taking notes on the process pattern of development.

4. When a writer uses the simple listing pattern of organization, the topic sentence is likely to include a _____ word.

5. Paragraphs organized by the comparison and contrast pattern absolutely must have _____.

6. When readers take notes on the comparison and contrast pattern, they should not get so caught up in listing the _____ ____ that they forget about _____.

7. Paragraphs organized around _____ always explain how one or more events _____ another event or set of events.

8. Transitions such as _____ are likely to appear in the cause and effect pattern as are the verbs _____.

9. Some paragraphs explain how one effect becomes a cause of another and that cause, in turn, produces a new effect. This is called a

_____.

10. Paragraphs that use the classification pattern usually open with a

_____

_____.

▶ **TEST 2**   **Recognizing Primary Patterns**

DIRECTIONS   Identify the primary pattern of organization by circling the letter of the correct response.

1. The meaning of silence can vary with one's culture. Americans, for example, often view silence as negative. At business meetings, participants frequently force themselves to speak. They fear that being silent will make it appear as if they had nothing to say. On a personal level, silence is often interpreted as a sign that things are not going well. In a group, for example, members frequently mistrust the person who remains silent. It's assumed that he or she is bored or disinterested in the group's activities. In Japan, however, silence is viewed in an altogether different light. Silence, in a personal or a professional context, is often interpreted as positive. People who are silent at meetings are thought to reflect more deeply on the issues under discussion. During personal conversations, remaining silent so that the other person has a chance to speak is considered the height of politeness and courtesy. The Japanese, in general, prefer silence to speech.

   a. definition

   b. time order: process

   c. comparison and contrast

2. As a result of the tsunami disaster that struck Japan in 2011, hundreds of thousands of men, women, and children were left homeless. In response to the tragedy, many people began suffering from the signs and symptoms of severe depression. While efforts are being made to reunite families and rebuild lost housing, all of these efforts to return to normal will take time. In this period of intense sorrow and heartache, though, one small, quick fix has emerged in the shape of a fluffy, robot seal called Paro. Paro is programmed to respond to human touch and is being used to combat depression among those who have lost everything but their lives. The seal robots are housed in community shelters, where people can come to pet and play with them. In response to being stroked, the seals emit gurgling sounds of pleasure and wiggle their flippers. Although it remains to be seen how many people can actually be helped by the robot pets, there are some signs that the seals are doing some good.

One woman reported that she and her friends liked visiting the seals because they had lost their pets in the Tsunami-caused flooding. Those who had lost their pets didn't want to get new ones until they knew where they would eventually be living. The robot seals helped fill the gap left by the animals' loss.

a. time order: process

b. cause and effect

c. comparison and contrast

3. During the Middle Ages (600–1500) in Europe, most ordinary people could not read. They had to rely on village gossip and on tales relayed by bands of storytellers. During this period, four main types of storytellers developed, each specializing in particular themes and characters. In northern Europe, *bards* recited poems about heavenly gods and earthly heroes. The poem *Beowulf*, for example, was probably first recited by an English bard. In France and Spain, *minstrels* related the great deeds performed by King Charlemagne's knights in stories like the *Song of Roland.* In France and Italy, *troubadours* spun tales of courtly romance that placed women on a pedestal with men under their command. In Germany, poet-musicians called *minne-singers* performed stories of passion and romance.

a. comparison and contrast

b. time order: dates and events

c. classification

4. New York City's size and layout changed greatly between 1728 and 1890. A flourishing center of trade, New York grew in the early and mid-1700s without a definite plan. Farmers sold land for buildings plot by plot, as need demanded, and this stop-and-start development is reflected in lower Manhattan's irregular streets. After the Revolutionary War, the 1782 Act of Confiscation took land away from anyone who had sided with the British, leaving many areas of New York available for organization and urban planning. A commission was set up in 1807 to create a street layout that would keep New York orderly, no matter how much trade or industry boomed. In 1811, the commission revealed its plan: a simple pattern of horizontal and vertical lines that didn't follow the natural landscape. A piece of wasteland purchased in 1853 was eventually turned into

the 843-acre Central Park. Otherwise, little open land remained for games or sports. By 1890, the island of Manhattan had grown into a thriving checkerboard of streets and buildings.

a. definition

b. time order: dates and events

c. simple listing

5. In Northern India, a wasp known as *Rogas indiscretus* kills the gypsy moths that harm trees in the foothills of the Himalayas.[†] Scientists say the wasp's methods are simple yet quite efficient. The female wasp stings a gypsy moth caterpillar and deposits an egg inside it. After hatching, the wormlike baby wasp eats the moth's insides. The infant wasp then spins a cocoon inside the moth's dead body; the cocoon is protected by the mummified husk, or shell. Within a few weeks, the infant wasp grows into an adult—which, if female, is ready to lay at least two hundred eggs in other gypsy moth caterpillars. (Information from *U.S. News & World Report*, April 7, 1997, pp. 70–71.)

a. time order: process

b. comparison and contrast

c. classification

[†]Himalayas: mountains in south central Asia.

▶ **TEST 3**   **Recognizing Primary Patterns**

DIRECTIONS   Identify the primary pattern of organization by circling the letter of the correct response.

1. If you are thinking about leaving your job either by choice or at the request of your employer, here are some things you should and should *not* do when you leave. Don't tell off either your co-workers or your superiors, even if you feel that you have been badly treated. You never know when you might meet them again in a professional setting. Unless you have been fired for some truly horrible offense in which you have been caught red-handed, do ask for a reference. In looking for your next job, you will have to indicate where you have worked before, and even if it's bad, you want to know what your previous employer will say if asked for a recommendation. Plus, many employers who might have written a bad evaluation if they thought you weren't going to see it might well write a more neutral one if they know you are going to be reading what they've written. If a replacement has already been hired, don't tell him or her anything bad about the company. Your problems may have been a matter of personal chemistry, and your replacement might not share your difficulties. By the same token, when you interview for a new job, don't criticize your previous employer. Your criticism may be justified, but your potential new employer doesn't know you and is likely to assume you are a complainer or a troublemaker.

   a. definition

   b. time order: process

   c. simple listing

   d. comparison and contrast

2. The body's response to fresh wounds is remarkably quick and efficient. The first stage in the body's response occurs when the blood begins to clot. Next, tiny bodies in the bloodstream called **platelets** rush to the wound site and disintegrate, or dissolve. Fibrous proteins begin to form, and the blood that has already escaped hardens into a scab. Once the bleeding stops, the body releases chemicals called **pyrogens**. These chemicals cause the area surrounding the wound to grow warm. In turn, blood vessels grow wider, allowing nutrients, oxygen, and white blood cells to feed the wounded area and start the formation of new tissue.

a. definition

b. time order: process

c. simple listing

d. comparison and contrast

3. Few events are more bizarre or unbelievable than sudden death said to be caused by "voodoo" or "magic." Nevertheless, death caused by voodoo does, indeed, seem to occur. In his influential and still cited article on the subject,[†] the researcher Walter Cannon believed he had found an answer to why some people really did sicken and die when exposed to what others would consider harmless voodoo charms like bones, dead animals, and stuffed dolls. Cannon, a well-known medical researcher, argued that there was a physiological basis for death by voodoo. He claimed that the victims, who had to be believers in voodoo magic, were literally scared to death. Their bodies, that is, were overwhelmed by the physical changes that took place in response to intense fear. Cannon argued that profound fear and its effects on the body are what caused believers in voodoo to die if they considered themselves cursed.

a. cause and effect

b. time order: dates and events

c. simple listing

d. comparison and contrast

4. **Genetic screening** is the widespread routine testing for alleles[†] associated with genetic disorders. Genetic screening provides information on reproductive risks and helps families that are already affected by a genetic disorder. If a genetic disorder is detected early enough, treatments can sometimes minimize the effects of the disease. Hospitals routinely screen newborns for genetic diseases. Besides helping individuals, genetic screening can help us estimate the prevalence and distribution of harmful alleles in populations.

(Adapted from Starr, Taggart, Evers, and Starr, *Biology*, 12th ed., p. 199.)

a. definition

b. time order: process

c. simple listing

d. comparison and contrast

[†]Cannon's article originally appeared in the *American Journal of Public Health*, and it was titled "Voodoo Death."

[†]alleles: a pair of genes that occupy a specific position on a chromosome.

▶ **TEST 4**   **Recognizing Primary Patterns**

> **DIRECTIONS**   Identify the primary pattern of organization by circling the letter of the correct response.

1. Though the U.S. president, unlike a prime minister, cannot command an automatic majority in the legislature, he does have some impressive powers. Simply by virtue of the office, the president is the official commander-in-chief of the armed forces. He can also grant reprieves and pardons for federal offenses, call Congress into special sessions, receive visiting dignitaries, and commission officers of the armed forces. Along with the Senate, the president has the power to make treaties with foreign countries, appoint judges to the Supreme Court, and place other high officials, like the Secretary of State, in office. The president also has the right to veto legislation and the power to ensure that legislation, once passed, is properly enforced. (Adapted from Wilson and DiIulio, *American Government*, 11th ed., p. 373.)

    a. time order: process

    b. simple listing

    c. comparison and contrast

    d. cause and effect

    e. classification

2. If you are not a snake lover, you probably won't understand the lengths some people go to in order to procure an exotic snake. But snake lovers do exist. Just type the phrase "people who love snakes" into a search engine, and you will be amazed at how many sites come up. People who love and want to own exotic snakes will pay huge amounts of money to get their hands on, say, a gold-colored tree boa, a deadly black mamba, or a rare Boelen's python. And therein, of course, is the source of a lot of misery for snakes who get ripped out of their native habitats and stored in places snakes were never meant to be, like inside suitcases, handbags, briefcases, even strapped to the human body. Although there are some fairly stiff restrictions against trading in exotic reptiles, greed consistently overcomes fear of the law, and snake traders run risks most people would never dream of. They will, for instance, anesthetize deadly reptiles and put them inside their clothing, all the while praying that the snakes don't wake up. All too often, snake traders get caught or

bitten. But then the traders knew what they were in for. The snakes didn't. Yet as Jennie Erin Smith writes in *Stolen World: A Tale of Reptiles, Smugglers, and Skullduggery,* far too many snakes never make it to their would-be owners. They die in transit, sometimes frozen in a plane's baggage compartment or infected with disease. Most typically, they die through suffocation, after being stuffed into a too tight container by an inexperienced snake trader who forgot that snakes need air to survive.

a. definition

b. time order: process

c. comparison and contrast

d. cause and effect

e. classification

3. Firms with an eye on the market often sponsor contests and sweepstakes to introduce new goods and services and to attract additional customers. Contests require entrants to complete a task such as solving a puzzle or answering questions in a trivia quiz, and they may also require proof of purchase. Sweepstakes, on the other hand, choose winners by chance, so no product purchase is necessary. Sweepstakes are more popular with consumers than contests because they do not take as much effort for consumers to enter. Marketers like them, too, because they are inexpensive to run and the number of winners is predetermined. With some contests, the sponsors cannot predict the number of people who will correctly complete the puzzles or gather the right number of symbols from scratched off cards. (Boone and Kurtz, *Contemporary Marketing,* 15th ed., p. 591.)

a. definition

b. time order: dates and events

c. comparison and contrast

d. cause and effect

e. classification

4. Spanish poet Federico García Lorca was born near the city of Granada, Spain, in 1898. His creative genius showed itself early on. As a teenager, he was already writing poems and reciting them in neighborhood cafes. Although Lorca started out studying philosophy and law, by 1919, he had abandoned both in favor of

writing poetry and plays. His first play, *The Butterfly's Evil Spell*, was staged in 1920. It closed in one night, but that did not discourage its creator. A year later, Lorca published a book of poems and seven years later, another volume called *The Gypsy Ballads.* This one made the thirty-year-old Lorca famous, earning him the nickname the "Gypsy Poet." Annoyed by what he saw as the public's attempt to pigeonhole his work, Lorca moved to New York to study English at Columbia University. He returned to Spain in 1931 and by 1933, he had another play staged, *Blood Wedding,* the story of a woman who runs off with her lover on her wedding night. This play was a success, and Lorca followed it with *Yerma,* the tale of a woman who murders her husband because he cannot give her a child. It was at this point that the poet caught the eye of the conservative political party that seized power in Spain in 1936. The group's leader, Francisco Franco, disapproved of plays that did not celebrate family values. Even worse in Franco's eyes, Lorca had made it clear that his sympathies lay with working people, not the wealthy industrialists who supported Franco. On the morning of August 19, 1936, Franco had Lorca shot and buried in an unmarked grave. The poet's writings were burned in Granada's central square.

a. time order: dates and events

b. simple listing

c. comparison and contrast

d. cause and effect

e. classification

▶ **TEST 5**   **Reviewing Chapter 10 Vocabulary**

DIRECTIONS   Fill in the blanks with one of the following words.

density	utterance	compassion	illumination	coercive
chromosomes	adversarial	genes	inhospitable	havoc
stench	subsequent	range	synthesize	dynamics

1. If you wanted to make it really clear that the smell in the room was bad, you could say _____ instead of "smell."

2. As movies like *Savages* (2012), *Alexander* (2004), *Wall Street* (1987), and *Salvador* (1986) illustrate, the director Oliver Stone is fascinated by the _____ of power.

3. Usually every person has one pair of sex _____ in each cell of the body, but they don't all carry the same number of _____.

4. Every word you say counts as a(n) _____.

5. _____ events are the opposite of preceding events.

6. The word _____ can be used in the context of travel, livestock, and complete coverage.

7. To write a term paper, you have to read several different sources on the same subject and then _____ the ideas to come up with an original thesis statement.

8. If you are not paying attention while you read, the best light in the world won't bring you _____, figuratively speaking, that is.

9. When two people get married, one expects their relationship to be friendly rather than _____.

10. When the war in Bosnia broke out, neighbors who had once cared for one another became enemies and seldom showed each other

    _____ or mercy.

11. The climate in the desert is _____ to humans but perfect for cactus.

12. When a substitute teacher steps into a classroom, a once orderly learning environment usually turns into _____.

13. The _____ measures taken against the protestors were caught on video.

14. The _____ of the landscape made it hard for the trackers to follow the wounded lion's trail.

Combining Patterns in Paragraphs and Longer Readings

11

IN THIS CHAPTER, YOU WILL LEARN

- why writers sometimes combine organizational patterns in paragraphs and longer readings.

- how skillful readers respond to combined patterns in paragraphs and extended readings.

- how to decide which patterns are central to the main idea and which ones are not.

- how to take complete notes on mixed patterns.

> *"The brain tries to make sense of information by reducing it to familiar patterns."*
>
> —From The Talking Page Literacy Organization

Until now, you've worked with paragraphs based primarily on one organizational pattern. But writers often use more than one pattern if explaining their main ideas requires it. This is particularly true of longer readings, where authors frequently combine two, three, sometimes even four patterns, in order to explain a complex idea.

Thus, it's important for you to learn how to (1) identify the different organizational patterns used in a longer reading, and (2) figure out which pattern or patterns are essential to developing the controlling main idea. Then you can use the underlying structure of the patterns to decide what's important and figure out how to best store the new information in your long-term memory.

Combining Patterns in Paragraphs

When the main idea calls for it, writers combine patterns rather than just relying on one. You can see that in the following paragraph, where two organizational patterns are necessary to develop the underlined topic sentence. The question for you is, Which two? Read the paragraph and answer the questions in the margin.

What pattern is suggested by the topic sentence?

¹Increased spells of warm weather and decreased use of pesticides have *resulted* in a plague of fire ants. ²Indeed, pleasant weather and an absence of pesticides have *encouraged* whole armies of ants to make their homes in farmers' fields, where they can leisurely munch on potato and okra crops. ³Should a tractor overturn one of their nests, the furious ants swarm over the machine and attack the driver. ⁴Using their jaws to hold the victim's skin, they thrust their stingers into the flesh, maintaining the same position for up to twenty-five seconds. ⁵The sting *produces* a sharp burning sensation and frequently *causes* painful infections that can last weeks and even months. ⁶Some victims who were especially allergic to the ants' poison have not survived a fire-ant attack.

What pattern does the author need to describe the ant's attack?

Trace the chains of repetition and reference that weave their way through this paragraph and you'll see that the author wants to talk about fire-ant attacks. That's the topic. Every sentence addresses this subject.

What does the author want to say about that topic? She wants to tell readers that due to pesticides being used less, fire-ant attacks are on the rise. That's the main idea, and it's based on a cause and effect relationship that looks like this:

| Decreased use of pesticides | → | Increase in fire-ant attacks |

But now look what happens in sentence 3. At this point, the writer wants to tell readers what the fire-ant attack feels like. To that end, the writer explains step by step what happens when fire ants get aggressive. Thus, we can rightly say that the paragraph is organized according to two different patterns, cause and effect *and* process. The two patterns are just about equal in importance because the author wants to communicate two kinds of information: (1) why the attacks are on the rise and (2) what an attack feels like.

Taking Notes on Mixed Pattern Paragraphs

Because the paragraph on fire ants describes a cause and effect relationship and outlines the steps in a process, you should first identify the key elements in each pattern. Then decide if all of those elements are essential to the main idea.

Since the cause and effect relationship is what structures the main idea of the paragraph, we definitely have to (1) identify and link both cause and effect in our notes and (2) provide any details about specific causes and effects. We should also include, as the author does, the steps or stages of an attack, because the author's purpose in describing the steps is to say to readers, "Here's why this main idea is worth talking about in the first place; fire-ant attacks can be scary, painful, even deadly."

But where the steps are concerned, there's some leeway in terms of what we can put in or leave out. Because the writer wants readers to understand how intense and awful the attack is, we don't necessarily have to include in our notes the fact that the ants eat potatoes and okra. We can also abbreviate or even eliminate any details that don't directly fulfill the author's purpose of telling readers why fire ants can be dangerous.

Notes on the fire-ant paragraph, then, would look something like this:

Main Idea More warm weather and decreased use of pesticides have produced a big increase in fire ants.

Supporting Details

1. Armies of ants have moved into farmers' fields.

2. If tractor overturns nest, ants swarm the machine and attack driver.

3. The ants thrust stingers into flesh, holding the same position for up to twenty-five seconds.

4. Sting produces painful burning sensation and can cause infections.

5. Some people with allergies have died following fire-ant attacks.

Not All Patterns Are Equal

In the paragraph on fire ants, both organizational paragraphs were equally essential to explaining the main idea. However, when taking notes on a paragraph with two or more organizational patterns, don't assume all the patterns included are always equal in importance. Instead, decide which pattern or patterns are most important based on two questions: (1) Which pattern or patterns are central to explaining the main idea? (2) Which pattern or patterns organize the most sentences? The answers to those two questions will tell you which patterns are essential to developing the main idea. Then some or all of the *key elements* of those patterns should appear in your notes.

Pattern Details Aren't All Equal Either. The phrase "key elements" in the previous sentence is italicized for a reason. Even after you decide what patterns are central to a reading, that doesn't mean every detail covered by the organizational pattern is significant.

For instance, in the reading on page 570, it is hardly necessary to mention that armies of fire ants were moving into farmers' fields *in order to eat potatoes and okra.* Thus, that detail from the process pattern did not make its way into the sample notes. As with so much else in learning, be selective about how you make use of organizational patterns. Decide what aspects of each pattern you need to include and which aspects you don't.

This is definitely the time to decide how central to the whole discussion the minor details in the paragraph might be. A minor detail might be absolutely essential, and then again it might add little except emphasis or human interest. It's up to you to decide what function it serves.

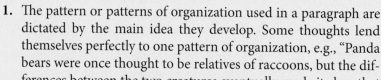

SUMMING UP THE KEY POINTS

1. The pattern or patterns of organization used in a paragraph are dictated by the main idea they develop. Some thoughts lend themselves perfectly to one pattern of organization, e.g., "Panda bears were once thought to be relatives of raccoons, but the differences between the two creatures eventually made it clear that they were not related."

2. Other ideas, however, clearly require more than one organizational pattern in order to be fully explained: "According to researchers Raymond Cattell and John Horn, there are two types of intelligence, fluid and crystallized, and each one follows a unique developmental course." In this case, the topic sentence demands two patterns of organization, comparison and contrast *and* process. In response, the reader would look for the details included in both patterns.

3. Because an author combines patterns in a paragraph, it doesn't mean that all the patterns present are equally important. Only

those essential to developing the main idea are really significant. The elements of the patterns that develop the main idea are the ones that should go into your notes.

4. Even if a paragraph or reading does include two or more patterns, don't assume that every detail associated with the pattern is essential and needs to be recorded. Be selective and focus only on those pattern elements that enhance your understanding of the main idea.

◆ EXERCISE 1   **Recognizing Mixed Patterns**

DIRECTIONS   Read each paragraph and write the main idea in the blanks that follow. Then circle the appropriate letter or letters to identify the organizational pattern or patterns used to explain the main idea.

Note the boldface and italic signaling the presence of a definition.

There's an implicit cause and effect relationship developing in sentence 2.

The category word efforts suggests simple listing.

EXAMPLE   ¹One type of drinking that is particularly troublesome among young adults, especially college students, is **binge drinking**, *defined for men as consuming five or more drinks—and for women as consuming four or more drinks—within two hours.* ²Binge drinking has been identified as a major health problem in the United States since the 1990s and is the focus of several efforts to reduce the number of college students who binge. ³These efforts include establishing low tolerance levels for the antisocial behaviors associated with binge drinking. ⁴They also include working with athletes, fraternities, and sororities, changing the expectations of incoming freshmen, and increasing the number of activities that don't include the presence of alcoholic beverages. ⁵These efforts come at a time when national and international attention is directed at the problem of binge drinking. (Adapted from Kail and Cavanaugh, *Human Development*, 5th ed., pp. 365–66.)

In your own words, what's the main idea of this paragraph?

Many different efforts are being made to control binge drinking among college students.

What pattern or patterns are needed to develop the main idea?

(a.) definition

b. time order

(c.) simple listing

d. comparison and contrast

(e.) cause and effect

f. classification

If you were taking notes on this paragraph, would you include information from the last sentence? __No__ Please explain your reasoning. The main idea of the reading is that binge drinking is a problem among college students. My notes need to define the problem and explain what's being done to combat it. That information is central to the main idea. The last sentence doesn't do anything to clarify that point or resolve some situation described in the paragraph.

EXPLANATION   The two main chains of repetition and reference that run through the passage refer to "binge drinking among students" and "efforts to prevent it." Thus the main idea has to include and connect some form of these two phrases. As you can see, it does precisely that.

The organizational patterns necessary to explaining that main idea are definition for the reader who might ask "What exactly is binge drinking?" and cause and effect to clarify the potential health problems produced by binge drinking. Lastly, the category word *efforts* brings into play the simple listing pattern because the reader needs to know what those efforts are.

1. In a **longitudinal study**, *the same individuals are observed or tested repeatedly at different points in their lives.* As the name implies, the longitudinal approach studies development over time and is the most direct way to watch it occur. More important, it is the only way to answer certain questions about the stability or instability of behavior: Will characteristics such as aggression, dependency, or mistrust observed in infancy or early childhood persist into adulthood? Will a regular exercise program begun in middle age have benefits in later life? Does people's satisfaction with their lives remain the same or change across adulthood? Such questions can only be explored by testing people at one point in their development and retesting them later. (Kail and Cavanaugh, *Human Development*, 5th ed., p. 28.)

In your own words, what's the main idea of this paragraph?

_____

_____

_____

What pattern or patterns are needed to develop this main idea?

a. definition

b. time order

c. simple listing

d. comparison and contrast

e. cause and effect

f. classification

If you were taking notes on this paragraph, would you record all three questions mentioned in the text? _____ Please explain your reasoning. _____

_____

_____

2. In a classic study begun in 1939, H. M. Skeels and H. B. Dye conducted research in an orphanage on infants whose intellectual development at nineteen months was judged so poor that they were considered unfit for adoption. These infants were transferred to an institution for the mentally handicapped, where Skeels and Dye arranged for each child to be put under the personal care of an adolescent girl who herself had limited intellectual ability. However, for the purpose of the study, the girls had been instructed at length in how to "mother" the children by giving them attention, affection, and mental stimulation. A control group stayed at the orphanage and received medical care but little personal attention. Twenty-seven years later, Skeels did a follow-up study of these same subjects. Most of the orphans who had been raised by the older, developmentally challenged young women had graduated from high school and one-third had gone to college. Nearly all of them were self-supporting and rated as normal. However, most of those who had been in the control group and remained in the orphanage had not progressed beyond the third grade. They had either remained in institutions or were not self-supporting. (Adapted from Stark, *Sociology*, 10th ed., p. 168.)

In your own words, what's the main idea of this paragraph?

_____

_____

_____

What pattern or patterns are needed to develop this main idea?

a. definition

b. time order

c. simple listing

d. comparison and contrast

e. cause and effect

f. classification

If you were taking notes on this paragraph, would you record information about the follow-up study twenty-seven years later? _____

Please explain your reasoning. _____

_____

_____

3. Who are the Democrats and the Republicans? These parties tend to attract different groups of supporters. Democrats maintain their greatest strength among African Americans and Hispanics, Catholics, and Jews, women, and individuals between the ages of eighteen and twenty-nine and those over age fifty. White southerners were once a critical part of the Democratic coalition, but a majority of them have voted for the Republicans over the past three decades. Democrats, though, still maintain a foothold in the South through the support of African Americans. Republicans are scattered across the country. They tend to be white, Protestant, and middle to upper class, and their views are comparatively conservative. (Gittelson, Dudley, and Dubnick, *American Government*, 10th ed., p. 161.)

In your own words, what's the main idea of this paragraph?

_____

What pattern or patterns are needed to develop this main idea?

a. definition

b. time order

c. simple listing

d. comparison and contrast

e. cause and effect

f. classification

If you were taking notes on this paragraph, would you record the information in these two sentences? "White southerners were once a critical part of the Democratic coalition, but a majority of them have voted for the Republicans over the past three decades. Democrats, though, still maintain a foothold in the South through the support of African Americans." _____ Please explain your reasoning.

_____

_____

4. Although the most beautiful actress of her day, Elizabeth Taylor, played Cleopatra on film, the Egyptian queen was not especially beautiful. Images of her show a woman who was not unattractive, but not movie star gorgeous either. Yet she managed to mesmerize two of the most powerful men of her time. In 48 BCE when Julius Caesar, famed Roman general and statesman, arrived in Egypt, his mission was to make the Egyptians pay their debts to Rome. Julius Caesar, however, quickly got distracted. Married at the time, he began an affair with the twenty-two-year-old Cleopatra, who bore his child in 47 BCE. But when Caesar was assassinated in 44 BCE, Cleopatra lost both her lover and her protector. That loss set the stage for the arrival of the Roman general Mark Antony in 43 BCE, who also came to Egypt on political matters but quickly turned his attentions elsewhere. Like Caesar, Antony became Cleopatra's lover, and for twelve years, they ruled Egypt together. But when the Romans and Egyptians went to war, Mark Antony made the mistake of taking Cleopatra's military advice. Antony wanted to fight on land. Cleopatra insisted on the sea. The result was the disastrous Battle of Actium (31 BCE), which destroyed the Egyptian fleet. Humiliated by the crushing defeat, Antony and Cleopatra vowed to take their lives. Cleopatra, however, only pretended to kill herself while Antony actually did. It was only when Egypt's Roman conqueror, Octavian, swore he would take Cleopatra back to Rome in chains that Cleopatra took her life on August 12, 30 BCE.[†]

In your own words, what's the main idea of this paragraph?

_____

_____

_____

[†]The date of Cleopatra's death varies from source to source by as much as two weeks. The date given here turns up most frequently in various reference works on the Web.

What pattern or patterns are needed to develop this main idea?

a. definition

b. time order

c. simple listing

d. comparison and contrast

e. cause and effect

f. classification

If you were taking notes on this paragraph, would you include the information about the Battle of Actium? _____ Please explain your reasoning. _____

_____

WEB QUEST
To this day, historians debate the reason behind Antony's mysterious behavior in the Battle of Actium. What did Antony do that, to this day, scholars puzzle over?

_____

_____

✔ CHECK YOUR UNDERSTANDING

1. What decides the pattern (or patterns) of organization a writer uses?

_____

2. Should you assume that every pattern present in a paragraph is equally important? Please explain your answer.

_____

_____

_____

3. Once you identify an organizational pattern that's central to the main idea, should you assume that every element of that pattern is essential for your notes? Please explain your answer.

_____

_____

From Pure to Mixed Patterns in Longer Readings

Longer, multi-paragraph readings do occasionally rely on a single pattern of organization. Look, for example, at the following selection, which relies almost exclusively on the comparison and contrast pattern of development. As you read, note the italicized transitions that are clues to that pattern.

In their search for the perfect mate, men and women differ a good deal.

© Heide Benser/Fancy/Jupiterimages.

Mating Strategies Differ Between the Sexes

1   In selecting a mate, both men and women seek out those who are attractive, kind, honest, and good-natured. In addition to wanting the same basic qualities in a potential mate, both sexes avoid certain characteristics such as insensitivity, bad manners, loudness or shrillness, and the tendency to brag about sexual conquests.

2   *Despite these similarities,* though, males and females differ in the emphasis they place on physical appearance and social status, at least for long-term relationships. Men are more concerned with appearance and women are more concerned with status. *How do we explain those differences?* Women's preference for status over attractiveness depends on several factors, such as whether the relationship is short or long term (looks are more important in the short term) and whether the woman perceives herself as attractive. Women who consider themselves very attractive appear to want it all—status and good looks (Buss and Shackelford, 2008).

3   In one study, men and women reported kindness and intelligence as necessary in their selection of mates. *But* their views of status and attractiveness differed. For the average woman seeking a long-term mate, status was a necessity. Good looks were a luxury. *In contrast,* men viewed physical attractiveness as a necessity rather than a luxury in mate selections—looks matter most when men are searching for mates (Le, Bailey, Kenrick, and Linsenmeier, 2002).

4   In another study, a researcher [Buss] asked ninety-two married couples which characteristics they valued most in their spouses. Women generally preferred men who were… good earners, ambitious, career oriented, from a good family, and fairly tall. Men tended to value good looks, cooking skills, and sexual faithfulness. Across some thirty-seven cultures studied, females valued a good financial prospect more than did men (Buss, 1989). In addition, women in all thirty-seven cultures tended to marry older men, who often are more settled and financially stable. (Adapted from Michael Gazzaniga, Todd Heatherton, and Diane Halpern, *Psychological Science.* New York: W. W. Norton and Company, 2010, p. 400.)

As long as the vocabulary and subject matter are familiar, readings like this one are fairly easy to interpret because the pattern is obvious. You know immediately that you have to understand the similarities and differences and link them to an overall point, which in this case appears in paragraph 2: When it comes to long-term relationships, men and women differ in how they view the importance of physical appearance and social status.

From Reader to Writer Write three to four paragraphs explaining what you think are some basic differences between male and female behavior at the start of a romantic relationship. Or, if you prefer, point out how similar the sexes are when it comes to romance.

> ▶ **SHARE YOUR THOUGHTS**
> Why do you think men and women seem to look for such different characteristics in a long-term mate?

When Patterns Combine in Longer Readings

In general, textbook readings are more likely to combine organizational patterns rather than relying solely on one. In this next example, three different patterns intermingle. Thus the reader has to figure out (1) what each one contributes to an explanation of the main idea and (2) which ones are most critical to understanding the material.

Read the following selection. After you finish each paragraph, answer the questions posed in the margins. When you complete the reading, write the main idea and the organizational patterns that develop it on the blank lines that follow:

Instincts: Behavior Programmed by Nature

The presence of dashes after a term in boldface suggests what pattern?

1   Birds build nests, and salmon return upstream to their birthplaces to spawn. They do not acquire these behaviors through experience or by attending nest-building or spawning schools. These are **instinctive behaviors**—fixed, inborn patterns of response that are specific to members of a particular species. **Instinct theory** holds that behavior is motivated by instincts.

How does the author answer the question that opens paragraph 2?

2   Does instinct theory explain the motives for human behavior? One man who thought so was William James, the father of American psychology. In his 1890 *The Principles of Psychology*, James listed thirty-seven instincts that he believed could explain most of human behavior. In 1908, in his very influential textbook, *An Introduction to Social Psychology*, the psychologist William McDougall, added to James's list. From that point on, the list kept growing and growing until, by the 1920s, it had ballooned to ten thousand instincts covering a wide range of human behavior.

Why does the author mention specific dates in the last sentence of paragraph 2 and the first

3   By the 1930s, however, the instinct theory was beginning to fall out of favor. One reason for its decline was that the lists of instincts had simply

sentence of paragraph 3?

grown too large to be useful. Another was that explaining behavior on the basis of instincts was merely a way of describing it, not explaining it. For example, saying a person is lazy because of a laziness instinct or stingy because of a stinginess instinct doesn't really explain the person's behavior. It merely attaches a label to it.

What's the big difference between paragraph 2 and paragraph 4?

4 Psychologists today recognize that human behavior is much more variable and flexible than would be the case if it were determined by instinct. Moreover, instinct theory fails to account for the important roles of culture and learning in determining human behavior. Though instincts account for some behavior in other animals, most psychologists reject the view that instincts motivate complex human behavior. They argue instead that human behavior is the result of the interplay between heredity and the social and cultural environment. (Adapted from Nevid, *Psychology*, 4th ed., pp. 288–89.)

What's the main idea?

_____

_____

_____

What organizational patterns explain that main idea?

_____

Evaluating the Organizational Patterns

The first thing to notice here is the role the sequence of dates and events pattern plays in the reading. Each reference to a year or time period is connected to a key point about the topic, which could be expressed as "psychologists' belief in instincts" or "theories of behavior," or even "psychologists' changing theories of behavior."

What main idea *about* that topic did the author want to convey? There's no thesis statement to point to in the reading. But an implied main idea does emerge based on the opening question and how the reading begins and ends. That main idea can be expressed as something like this: "Although at one time, psychologists were convinced that instinct determined behavior, that attitude changed dramatically over time. Today they believe that heredity and environment are the twin sources of behavior."

Implicit in that main idea is the need for the time order, sequence of dates and events pattern. A writer can't show readers how ideas changed over time without bringing the sequence of dates and events pattern into the reading. For those readers who might not be completely sure how to define instinct, the definition pattern is also essential to the mix.

But guiding the reading overall is the cause and effect pattern of organization. Some aspects of that pattern have to be present in notes because the author begins by explaining what psychologists used to think motivated behavior, and it ends with a more up-to-date view of why we do what we do. At the same time, paragraph 3 explicitly outlines a specific cause and effect relationship that, if diagrammed, would look like this:

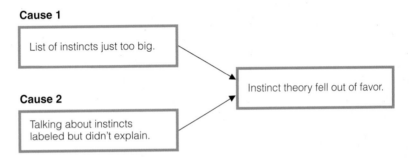

There were two reasons why instinct theory fell out of favor.

Taking Notes on Combined Patterns

While definition and sequence of dates play key roles in the instinct theory reading, it's the cause and effect pattern that requires the most attention. And it's cause and effect that dominates the selection of details for complete notes:

Main Idea The idea that instincts determine behavior was very popular in the late nineteenth and early twentieth century, but psychologists now believe that biology and environment are the sources of human behavior.

Supporting Details 1. William James (*The Principles of Psychology*) and William McDougall (*An Introduction to Social Psychology*) were among those who believed that instincts were what motivated behavior.

—By the 1920s, over ten thousand different instincts had been identified.

2. By the 1930s, the theory fell out of favor for two reasons:

   a. too many instincts

   b. didn't explain behavior, just called it an instinct, e.g., lazy people had the lazy instinct

3. Today's psychologists believe that our environment and our genetic inheritance are what influence behavior.

READING TIP

As soon as you see that a reading has numerous references to dates and periods of time, make sure you understand what events or shifts in thought occurred during the times identified.

SUMMING UP THE KEY POINTS

1. Multi-paragraph readings can and do rely on one organizational pattern. However, like paragraphs they often need more than one pattern to communicate their overall main idea to readers. That's because the content of the main idea frequently calls for different organizational patterns.

2. In response to readings that combine elements of different patterns, readers need to consider the main idea and ask this key question: Which pattern elements are essential to explaining the overall main idea and which ones are not?

3. The basic rule of note-taking is simple: The main idea is always essential to your notes. But you can pick and choose the number of pattern details you include based on what they add to your understanding of the main idea.

◆ **EXERCISE 2**   **Identifying Patterns in Longer Readings**

DIRECTIONS   Answer the following questions by filling in the blank lines and circling the letters of the correct response. *Paraphrasing Note*: If you are struggling to paraphrase a thesis statement or an implied main idea, ask questions about the stated or implied main idea, for instance: What action was taken? Who or what was the source of the action?

What were the consequences? Use your answers to those questions to put the main idea into words of your own.

EXAMPLE

Scott Joplin: The King of Ragtime

1   Born in 1868 in Texarkana on the Texas-Arkansas border, musician and composer Scott Joplin began his career playing piano in the saloons of St. Louis, Missouri, at the age of seventeen. During the next ten years, he perfected the jazz style that came to be known as ragtime. Then, from 1896 to 1900, Joplin studied at George R. Smith College in Sedalia, Missouri, so that he could write down the music he played so naturally.

2   In 1899, Joplin published his first piece of music, "Maple Leaf Rag." Less than a year later, ragtime—a unique American blend of African and European musical forms—took the country by storm. Suddenly, everyone wanted to hear "Maple Leaf Rag," and Scott Joplin became the first composer in the world to sell more than one million copies of a single tune.

3   But the King of Ragtime didn't want to devote his life to writing popular music. A serious artist, he resented white America's tendency to dismiss his music as trivial* because it grew out of African-American culture. To prove the value and beauty of ragtime, Joplin decided to compose an opera that would have ragtime rhythms at its core. By creating an opera, Joplin was demanding direct comparison with the greatest European composers and trying to prove to Americans that his music should be taken seriously. In the end, Joplin's opera would get him the acclaim* he dreamed of. Unfortunately, it would be too late for him to care.

4   The opera, titled *Treemonisha*, is the story of a poor black girl, Treemonisha,† who grows up to battle ignorant superstition and become a leader in her community. The opera combines new forms of ragtime, created specifically to accompany different kinds of dance including ballet. It also includes black work songs and soaring gospel music. When Joplin published it at his own expense in 1911—no one else was willing to take the job on—he called it "an entirely new form of operatic art." Yet despite Joplin's intense efforts to make the opera a success, the timing was wrong. The composer had invested all his money, energy, and hope in a work that

---

*trivial: insignificant, not serious.
*acclaim: enthusiastic and public praise.
†The girl's name combines her mother's name with the fact that the girl liked to play under a supposedly sacred tree.

displayed a strong social conscience at exactly the moment when the pay-ing public was clamoring for more frivolous* entertainment. Even worse for the play's prospects, the ragtime beat, which was threaded throughout the opera's music, was declining in popularity.

5   The one performance in New York City in 1915 was a disaster, with members of the audience leaving in mid-performance. Joplin had financed the production himself. It left him both bankrupt and humiliated. Two years later he was dead.

6   Had he lived to see it, Joplin would have been overjoyed to read the review of *Treemonisha* that appeared in the *New York Times* when the opera was staged again fifty-seven years later in 1972. The *Times* music reviewer Harold Schonberg called the opera "harmonically enchanting"* and said "it refuses to leave the mind." According to Schonberg, the audience at the performance "went out of its mind." *Treemonisha* was then successfully staged in Houston, Seattle, Washington, and New York City. Ironically,* the modern audiences wildly applauded the very same opera that, for Scott Joplin, had symbolized nothing but financial ruin and critical failure. (Source of quotation: From Argyle, *Scott Joplin and the Age of Ragtime*, p. 146.)

Scott Joplin would have been thrilled to know that his face would one day appear on a stamp.

1. In your own words, what's the main idea of this reading?

    In an attempt to make Americans take ragtime seriously, Scott Joplin wrote and

    produced an opera, but it failed miserably and it was only after his death that it

    got the admiration and praise he dreamed of.

2. What organizational patterns help develop that main idea?

    a. definition

    ⓑ time order: sequence of dates

    c. time order: process

    d. simple listing

    e. comparison and contrast

    ⓕ cause and effect

    g. classification

———————————

*frivolous: unserious, light.
*enchanting: delightful, engaging.
*ironically: contradicting what one might expect to be the case.

EXPLANATION   In this reading, the author makes the main idea convincing by explaining (1) how Scott Joplin tried to have his music taken seriously over the course of his career and (2) how his dream came true. To fulfill those goals, she uses two patterns: the sequence of dates pattern to trace the composer's career, and a cause and effect pattern to explain how the opera *Treemonisha* eventually made his dream a reality. Only it was too late for him to know it.

1. Ancient Beliefs About Mental Illness

1   Some half a million years ago, ancient societies apparently did not recognize any difference between mental and physical disorders. Abnormal behaviors, from simple headaches to convulsions,* were believed to be caused by evil spirits that lived in the victim's body. According to this system of belief—called *demonology*—those suffering from disease were considered responsible for their misfortune.

2   For this reason, some Stone Age cave dwellers appear to have treated behavior disorders by a surgical method called *trephining*. During this procedure, part of the skull was chipped away to make an opening. Once the skull was opened, the evil spirits could escape. It was believed that when the evil spirit left, the person would return to his or her normal state. Surprisingly, several trephined skulls that healed over have been found. This indicates that some patients survived what had to be an extremely crude operation. (Adapted from Sue et al., *Understanding Abnormal Behavior*, 5th ed., p. 16.)

1.   In your own words, what's the main idea of this reading?

_____

_____

2.   What organizational patterns help develop that main idea?

a.   definition

b.   time order: sequence of dates and events

c.   time order: process

d.   simple listing

e.   comparison and contrast

f.   cause and effect

g.   classification

---

*convulsions: uncontrolled fits in which the muscles contract wildly.

2. Capital Punishment

1   What sets capital punishment apart from all other punishments is its quality of irrevocability.* This type of punishment leaves no way to correct a mistake. For this reason, some believe that no mortal should have the power to inflict capital punishment because there is no way to guarantee that mistakes won't be made. The growing number of innocent men and women who came perilously close to being executed indicates that we have an imperfect system.

2   Public support for capital punishment has swung up and down. Public opinion polls reveal that public support for the death penalty declined gradually through the 1960s, reaching a low of 44 percent in 1966, but has increased over the past 30 years. In the late 1990s, 75 to 80 percent supported the death penalty. Public support seems to be declining in more recent years. In a poll in 2008, only 63 percent of Americans supported capital punishment.

3   Research indicates that certain groups are more likely to favor the use of capital punishment; for instance, support is higher by 20 to 25 percentage points among whites as compared to blacks. Membership in fundamentalist Protestant churches predicts higher support for the death penalty as well. Political conservatism* also predicts higher support. Interestingly, church activity negatively predicts support (the more active one is in one's church, the less likely one is to support the death penalty).

4   *Retentionists* (who believe that we should continue to utilize capital punishment) argue that capital punishment is just because it deters, or inhibits, others from committing murder and it definitely deters the individual who is executed. This is a utilitarian† argument. They also argue that capital punishment is just because murder deserves an equal punishment. They also say that the Bible dictates an "eye for an eye." This is, of course, a Judeo-Christian religious justification for capital punishment.

5   *Abolitionists* argue that capital punishment has never been shown to be effective in deterring others from committing murder, and,

---

*irrevocability: incapable of being changed or altered.
*conservatism: a political or social philosophy that emphasizes maintaining existing traditions and promoting individual responsibility over help from the government or other members of society
†utilitarian: having a useful function that benefits the greatest number of people. Derived from the work of philosophers John Stuart Mill and Jeremy Bentham, who called their philosophy "utilitarianism."

therefore, the evil of capital punishment far outweighs any potential benefits for society because there is no proof that it actually deters. Abolitionists also point to the religious command to "turn the other cheek," as an argument against any Christian justification for capital punishment. (Pollock, *Ethical Dilemmas and Decisions in Criminal Justice,* 5th ed., p. 332.)

1. In your own words, what's the main idea of this reading?

    _____

    _____

2. What organizational patterns help develop that main idea?

    a. definition
    b. time order: sequence of dates and events
    c. time order: process
    d. simple listing
    e. comparison and contrast
    f. cause and effect
    g. classification

3. **The Donner Party Goes West**

    1   Some time during 1845, brothers Jacob and George Donner caught the emigration fever and decided to head west to California. They sold their land, houses, farm equipment, and most of their belongings. They also talked their friend James Reed into moving his family west with theirs. Together they bought oxen, cattle, bagged and barreled food, and heavy Murphy wagons.

    2   Their plan was daring but not unusual. Already thousands of Americans had left behind land, jobs, and culture to move west. But from the start, the Donner party, as the group came to be called, met with more than its share of disappointments, failures, and, in the end, deadly disasters.

    3   The disappointments started already upon arrival at Independence, Missouri, in 1846 when members of Donner and Reed's group learned that most of the twelve hundred wagons going west had already departed. They took heart, though, after catching up with fifty other

California-bound wagons. Still being surrounded by other migrants*
during the days and weeks that followed didn't help as much as those
traveling west under Donner and Reed's leadership had thought
it would. Instead, fear and anxiety mounted as the homesteaders
trekked across the inhospitable land that seemed unfit for cultivation.*
Dust storms, thunderstorms, muddy roads, stubborn mules, and bad
water further strained tempers.

4   Desperate to speed up the pace, Donner and Reed began talking
about a "shortcut" around the southern edge of a settlement in Salt
Lake City. A couple of California trappers who overheard them warned
about the dangers of taking a large number of wagons, animals, and
people through the shorter route, saying that it had never been attempted by wagon trains. But knowing that they had to reach the far
side of the mountains before snow began to fall, the tired travelers
decided to take the risk.

5   By September 30 the Donner party was facing the Sierra Nevada
Mountain range, and the weather was worsening. Seasoned "mountain
men" had predicted a late snowfall for the winter of 1847. But they
were wrong. The exhausted travelers were hit with a blizzard already in
November. Not sure what to do, the group split in two with one group
waiting out the storm while another, headed by Donner and Reed,
moved on.

6   As hunger gnawed, the fifteen members who had followed Donner
and Reed managed to catch a scrawny coyote, an owl, and a squirrel.
Then they ate their dogs, oxen, and horses. After nine days and nights
in the cold, two men and two children had died. Their corpses became
food for the starving survivors. Four more of the party died over the
next twenty-three days, and their bodies, too, were used as food.

7   Back at the second encampment, thirty-seven of those who had
hoped to wait out the storm perished in the grueling struggle for life.
When the blizzard broke in February of 1847, seven of the Donner-
Reed group made it to safety. Then they organized a rescue party to
bring back more of the stranded survivors.

8   At the start, the Donner party had included eighty-one† people.
In the end, there were forty-five survivors. George Donner, the man
whose idea it was to move west, was not among them. He had already

---

*migrants: people on the move from one place to another.
*cultivation: farming, soil preparation.
†This number varies from account to account, largely because, in the beginning at least,
the Donner party gained and lost members as people decided to join up or leave.

died on March 17, 1847. His wife died a little more than a day later. George's brother, Jacob, and his wife, Elizabeth, met the same fate. The third leader of the party, James Reed, survived and made it to California, where he built up a fortune in real estate and ended up becoming the sheriff of San Jose. (Source of information: Gillon and Matson, *The American Experiment*, 2nd ed., pp. 494–95; www.donnerpartydiary.com/survivor.htm.)

This route has been named the Donner Pass in memory of the ill-fated Donner party.

1. In your own words, what's the main idea of this reading?

   _____

   _____

   _____

2. What organizational patterns help develop that main idea?

   a. definition

   b. time order: sequence of dates and events

   c. time order: process

   d. simple listing

   e. comparison and contrast

   f. cause and effect

   g. classification

4. Personality and Body Type

1   In the 1940s, some researchers tried to revive a much-debated theory of human behavior called *constitutional typology*. According to this theory, body type determines personality. Although critics point to the theory's lack of scientific evidence, constitutional typology still has some believers who argue that human beings fall into three basic categories of physique, or body type, with each one producing a particular set of character traits.

2   According to constitutional typologists, *endomorphs* tend to be round and soft, with protruding abdomens. They love gracious living and good food. They have gentle, relaxed temperaments and prefer to keep life uncomplicated. Said to embody the cliché about fat people being friendly, endomorphs like to be surrounded by their friends and are not comfortable being alone for any length of time.

3   The exact opposite of the endomorph, the *ectomorph* is described as all skin and bones, with a flat belly and long legs. Much less social than the fun-loving endomorph, the ectomorph prefers intellectual pursuits, especially if they can be carried on in relative isolation from people. Less good-natured than the endomorph, ectomorphs are nervous and high strung. Given to quick reactions and high-intensity relationships, they suffer from the aftermath of tension and have difficulty relaxing and falling asleep.

Even today, there are those who claim that body type can predict personality.

	Endomorphic	Mesomorphic	Ectomorphic
Body Type	Round, soft	Rugged, muscular	Fragile, thin
Temperament	Gentle, relaxed, sociable, and fond of food	Energetic, daring, domineering, assertive	Brainy, nervous, withdrawn

4   The *mesomorph* is neither fat nor thin but broad and muscular, with a strong, rugged physique. People in this category are said to love physical activity—the more daring and fast paced, the better. They also

enjoy games of risk or chance. Domineering by nature, mesomorphs like to be around people but prefer to be in situations they can control.

1. In your own words, what's the main idea of this reading?

   _____

   _____

   _____

2. What organizational patterns help develop that main idea?

   a. definition

   b. time order: process

   c. time order: sequence of dates and events

   d. simple listing

   e. comparison and contrast

   f. cause and effect

   g. classification

WEB QUEST

1. **Who was Keseberg the Cannibal?**

   _____

   _____

   _____

   _____

2. **Is everyone convinced that the members of the Donner party committed cannibalism?**

   _____

   _____

✔ CHECK YOUR UNDERSTANDING

1. Why do writers sometimes combine organizational patterns?

   _____

2. Do multi-paragraph readings always combine organizational patterns? _____
   Please explain.

   _____

   _____

3. When it comes to taking notes, what should readers do in response to readings that combine more than one pattern?

   _____

   _____

◆ Evaluating the Patterns

Whether you are dealing with one paragraph or several, the principle remains the same: When more than one organizational pattern is present, focus on the pattern or patterns most central to explaining the main idea. For instance, to get the most out of the following reading, start by determining the main idea. Next figure out which organizational patterns support that idea. Then decide if the patterns are equally important or if one is more central to explaining the main idea.

Barbie

1 Barbie, the all-American doll, is—like many Americans—an immigrant. Although introduced in 1959 by the American toy company Mattel, Barbie's origins lie in Germany where she was called Lilli. The German Lilli doll was a novelty toy for adult men (as evidenced by her proportions, equivalent to 39-21-31 in human terms). She was based on a

character that cartoonist Reinhard Beuthin drew for the German tabloid[†] newspaper *Das Bild* in 1952. Lilli was so popular that she became a regular feature, later made three dimensional as Bild Lilli, an eleven-and-a-half-inch-tall blonde doll with the figure Barbie would make famous.

2 Lilli came to America with Ruth Handler, one of the founders and co-directors of the Mattel toy company. While vacationing in Europe, she got a glimpse of Barbie in a store window. Handler bought three of the dolls and gave one to her daughter Barbara, after whom Lilli would be re-named. Mattel bought the rights to Lilli and unveiled her as Barbie in March 1959. Despite mothers' hesitations about buying a doll that looked like Barbie, within the first year of the doll's debut Mattel had sold 351,000 Barbies at $3 each (or about $17 in 2000 dollars). By 1997, over one billion Barbies had been sold.

3 Within the United States, Barbie has been controversial—at least among adults. Some have worried that Barbie's wildly unrealistic figure fosters girls' dissatisfaction with their own body—a serious problem in a culture plagued by eating disorders. Others claim that, despite Barbie's 1980s "Girls Can Do Anything" makeover, Barbie represents empty-headed femininity, focused on endless consumption. And many have noted that blonde, blue-eyed Barbie failed to represent the diversity of America's people.

4 In 2002, international labor-rights groups called for a boycott of Barbie. They cited studies showing that half of all Barbies are made by exploited young women in mainland China: Of the $10 retail price, Chinese factories receive only 35 cents per doll to cover their costs, including labor. Saudi Arabia banned Barbie in 2003, arguing that her skimpy outfits and the values she represents are not suitable for a Muslim nation. Still, the eleven-and-half-inch doll remains popular worldwide, selling in more than 150 countries. Today, the average American girl has ten Barbies—and the typical German girl owns five. For better or worse, Barbie continues to link the United States and the rest of the world. (Norton et al., *A People and a Nation*, Brief 9th ed., p. 777.)

If you look for a thesis statement that sums up the details included in this reading, you won't find it. The main idea of this reading is implied.

[†]tabloid: Technically, the word describes a newspaper of a particular size — 11 × 17 inches, with shorter articles and more pictures. Many tabloids peddle scandals, so the word has taken on negative connotations. However, there are some respectable tabloids that report hard news.

Perhaps because of their sex toy origins, Barbie dolls have always had a highly sexualized image.

Inferring the Main Idea

Look closely at the reading about Barbie, and you'll see it breaks into two parts. Up until paragraph 3, the reading is concerned with Barbie's history. It follows then that the first part of the reading relies heavily on the sequence of dates pattern.

By paragraph 3, though, the authors move away from Barbie's history to discuss how she causes the "controversy" mentioned in the topic sentence of the third paragraph. At this point, the underlying pattern becomes cause and effect with the authors identifying some of Barbie's alleged negative effects.

Put the two ideas together—(1) Barbie started in Germany and immigrated to the United States and (2) once she arrived in the U.S. she was both popular and controversial—and you will come up with an implied main idea that might be worded something like this: "Barbie got her start in Germany, but made her debut in the United States in 1959, proving to be extraordinarily successful. She has, however, also proved controversial."

In this case, there is nothing to suggest that the authors want readers to consider one pattern more important than the other. The title does not lean in one direction or the other. Nor does the accompanying picture. In addition, each pattern governs two paragraphs, so there's no difference in coverage.

The only other factor that might influence how you handle the elements of each pattern in your notes is outside the context of the reading. If, for instance, your instructor had already emphasized the cultural consequences of Barbie's popularity with young girls, then the cause and effect pattern underlying the reading might well be the emphasis in your notes. For that matter, if you yourself are interested in Barbie's European past, then you might decide for your own purposes to take more detailed notes on her history.

Sifting and Sorting Pattern Elements

The sample notes that follow assume that both patterns are of equal significance for the main idea. They don't, however, assume that every element of each pattern needs to be recorded:

Main Idea Barbie got her start in Germany, but made her debut in the United States in 1959, proving to be extraordinarily successful. She has, however, also proved controversial.

Supporting Details

1. Barbie started out as the German Lilli.

2. She was based on a 1952 cartoon by Reinhard Beuthin.

3. Mattel executive Ruth Handler brought Lilli to America and Mattel bought the rights to Lilli, unveiling her as Barbie in 1959.

   a. Within a year Mattel had sold thousands of Barbies.
   b. By 1997, a billion Barbies had been sold.

4. But Barbie has provoked controversy.

   a. Some people think her figure encourages girls to have a very unrealistic body image.
   b. Others think she encourages the notion of empty-headed femininity.
   c. She doesn't represent America's diversity.
   d. 2002 international labor rights groups protested how Barbies are produced, i.e., in sweatshops employing young girls.
   e. Saudi Arabia banned Barbie because her skimpy clothes didn't represent Muslim values.

As they should, the notes record the key dates and the events that accompanied them. But as with the notes on the fire ants on page 571, some details have been left out. The fact that Lilli became a regular figure in *Das Bild* doesn't add anything important to the main idea, so it doesn't appear. Nor does it seem crucial to remember that Ruth Handler was on vacation when she spotted Barbie.

READING TIP

When organizational patterns combine to develop the main idea, look for the elements typical of each pattern. Then decide which of those elements are essential to explaining the main idea. Those are the ones you need to take notes on.

▶ **SHARE YOUR THOUGHTS**

Since the mid-nineties, Mattel has been the subject of criticism for producing Barbie dolls in China, Thailand, and Indonesia and paying their teenage female workers sub-standard wages without maintaining adequate working conditions. If this is true—and you should check the Web to find out—would you buy a Barbie for your daughter? (And if you don't have a daughter, think hypothetically.)

From Reader to Writer One of the complaints about Barbie has always been that the dolls teach little girls to focus too much on looking pretty and being thin. Write three or four paragraphs in which you explain why Barbie is or is not a bad influence.

◆ **EXERCISE 3**   **Identifying Main Ideas and Evaluating Pattern Elements**

DIRECTIONS   Identify the main idea of each reading along with the pattern or patterns used to develop it. Then evaluate the significance of those patterns to decide if they are equal in importance or one is more important than the other.

EXAMPLE

The Dual Nature of Curare

1   *Curare* is a blackish, powder-like substance made from the roots and bark of a woody vine that grows in South America. Although many

people know that curare is a deadly poison, they do not know that it can save life as well as take it. Once known only as the "flying death," curare has become one of medicine's most trusted weapons in the fight against disease.

2   Rumors of curare's deadly powers began to circulate as early as the sixteenth century, when explorers came back from journeys to the Amazon. Upon their return, they described Indian hunters who could bring down prey with a single blow from a dart gun. According to eyewitness accounts, hunters boiled the roots and bark of a woody vine into a heavy syrup. Then they dipped darts into the thick liquid. Expert hunters, capable of finding a target more than a hundred yards away, would blow the darts through hollow reeds, killing their prey almost instantly. Birds died in less than five seconds, and human beings in less than five minutes.

3   Because the jungles were all but unreachable to everyone but the Indians, no one really understood how curare worked until the mid-nineteenth century, when experimenters began to uncover its secrets. It was found that curare, if swallowed, is fairly harmless. But if it penetrates the skin, curare is lethal. Because it relaxes all the muscles in the body—including those that control breathing—the victim quickly suffocates and dies.

4   Once researchers knew how curare worked, they were in a better position to figure out how it might be used to more beneficial ends. However, researchers were reluctant to experiment with curare imported from South America. Its strength varied, and one could never be sure how strong a dosage to use.

5   During World War II, Daniel Bovet, an Italian pharmacologist, developed the first synthetic, or artificial, form of curare, and the stage was set to discover curare's benefits to humans. In 1942, Dr. Harold Griffith successfully used it as an anesthetic during surgery. From that time on, a synthetic form of curare was used in many operations because it relaxed the patient's muscles and made the surgeon's work easier. Eventually, it was also used to treat rabies and tetanus, diseases that produce severe muscle cramps.

1.   What is the main idea of the entire reading?

    a. Curare is an incredibly dangerous poison that can kill in seconds.

    b. A deadly poison, curare can also save lives.

    c. Curare has a long and ancient history.

    d. The jungle kept curare a secret for centuries.

2. Which pattern or patterns does the author use to develop that main idea?

(a.) definition

(b.) time order: sequence of dates and events

(c.) time order: process

d. simple listing

e. comparison and contrast

(f.) cause and effect

g. classification

3. If more than one pattern organizes the reading, identify the most important.

cause and effect; definition; sequence of dates and events

Please explain.

Without definition and the cause and effect pattern, the writer couldn't tell readers what curare is or how it kills and cures. Without the sequence of dates and events, the writer couldn't explain how scientists unraveled the poison's secrets with the passage of time.

EXPLANATION Everything in the reading, including the title, points to answer *b* as the overall main idea: Curare has a double nature: It can kill *and* it can heal. To explain that main idea, the author needs the definition pattern to tell readers what curare is. The cause and effect organizational pattern is central to explaining curare's dual nature as killer and healer. The sequence of dates and events pattern plays a key role in organizing the description of how curare's other, more beneficial, uses came to light. Process, probably the least important pattern, helps explain how hunters turned curare into a poison so that they could dip their arrows into it.

1. Schizophrenia, the Mind in Two

1 The term *schizophrenia* was coined in 1911 by the Swiss psychiatrist Eugen Bleuler. Literally, the word means "split mind." Bleuler thought the term effectively expressed one of the disease's central symptoms—a split between the patient's internal world and the external world of social reality.

2 Since Bleuler's time, researchers still have not figured out what causes this mysterious and devastating disease. However, they have been able to identify and name three distinct types.

3   *Disorganized schizophrenia* expresses itself through bizarre and childlike behavior. Victims pay little attention to personal grooming. Sometimes they remain unwashed for days. Behaving like children, they are prone to making faces and spouting nonsense.

4   Those suffering from a second form of the disease, called *catatonic schizophrenia*, can remain immobile for hours. Mentally withdrawing from their environment, patients adopt rigid postures and fall silent for days, even months. Sometimes, without reason, sufferers will suddenly grow violent and attack anyone who comes near.

5   In *paranoid schizophrenia*, the most marked symptom is the presence of delusions or fantasies that bear no relation to reality. Patients suffering from this form fear that a person or group is trying to harm them. They often think they are surrounded by enemies and may, in response, become violent.

6   As research continues, it's becoming more and more likely that schizophrenia is not a single disease but a family of diseases that may arise from a variety of causes. By learning more about each type of schizophrenia, researchers hope to find more effective treatments.

1. What is the main idea of the entire reading?

    a. The term *schizophrenia* means "split mind," and was coined by Eugen Bleuler.

    b. Schizophrenia may well be a family of diseases.

    c. Although no one knows the cause of schizophrenia, researchers have identified three distinct types.

    d. Paranoid schizophrenia is perhaps the worst and most debilitating form of the disease.

2. Which pattern or patterns does the author use to develop that main idea?

    a. definition

    b. time order: sequence of dates and events

    c. time order: process

    d. simple listing

    e. comparison and contrast

    f. cause and effect

    g. classification

3. If more than one pattern organizes the reading, identify the most important.

_____

Please explain.

_____

_____

_____

_____

_____

2. The Johari Window

1   The Johari Window, named after its inventors, Joseph Luft and Harry Ingham, is a useful model for describing the complex process of human interaction. The window, or box, is divided into four panes, or areas, with each area labeled to indicate the kind of information that can be revealed or concealed when we communicate or interact with others: (1) open, (2) blind, (3) hidden, and (4) unknown. Because each person's window reflects his or her psychological makeup, the size of each pane varies with the individual.

2   The **open area** of the Johari Window represents your "public" or "awareness" area. This section symbolizes the information about yourself that both you and others recognize. It includes the information that you are willing to admit or make public. For example, you and everyone you know may be aware that you are a competitive person who doesn't like losing an argument or that your temper is easy to trigger when the subject is politics.

3   The **blind area** in the Johari Window represents the information about yourself that others may know, or think they know, but that you are not aware of. For instance, you may think that you have a tendency to be shy and a bit withdrawn, whereas others may see you as open, relaxed, and friendly. Over time, information in the blind area can shift to the open area if other people are willing to mention their view of your behavior.

4   The **hidden area** in the Johari Window shows information that you know but that others do not. This area reflects the private thoughts and feelings you prefer to keep to yourself. For example, you may not

want people to know that you are terrified of public speaking despite the fact that you do it frequently. Unlike the open and blind areas, the hidden area may not change over time. In other words, you may always choose to keep certain things about your life a secret.

5   The **unknown area** of the Johari Window is made up of things unknown both to you and to others. This area is reserved for those feelings, talents, and motives that are below the surface of awareness and have never been acknowledged or displayed. For example, you may have a talent for verbal expression, but if you are shy and avoid speaking a lot, you may never know that you have the ability. To offer another example, you may know that you get angry when talking to authority figures but have no idea that your anger stems from an unhappy relationship with your older brother. Obviously, if you don't recognize the cause and effect relationship between your childhood and your adult behavior, no one else is likely to either.

The Johari Window is used primarily with groups on the assumption that self-disclosure and feedback improve communication among group members.

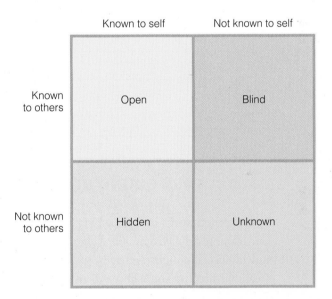

1. What is the main idea of the entire reading?

    a. The Johari Window is the creation of Joseph Luft.

    b. The Johari Window consists of four separate panes, or sections.

    c. The Johari Window offers an effective way to describe interactions with others.

    d. The size of the panes in the Johari Window varies with the individual.

2. Which pattern or patterns does the author use to develop that main idea?

   a. definition

   b. time order: sequence of dates and events

   c. time order: process

   d. simple listing

   e. comparison and contrast

   f. cause and effect

   g. classification

3. If more than one pattern organizes the reading, identify the most important.

   _____

   Please explain.

   _____

   _____

   _____

   _____

VOCABULARY ROUND UP

Below are ten words introduced in pages 585–90. The words are accompanied by more detailed definitions, the page on which they originally appeared, and additional sample sentences. Spend time reviewing the words and their meanings because you will see them again in review tests at the end of the chapter. Use the online dictionary Wordnik to find additional sentences illustrating the words in context. (*Note*: If you know of another dictionary with as many examples of the words in context feel free to use that one instead.)

1. **trivial** (p. 585): insignificant, not serious, of little value. "It would be a mistake to assume that blogs only discuss *trivial* issues."

2. **acclaim** (p. 585): enthusiastic and public praise, to salute or praise with great approval. "A book's arrival on the bestseller list is a sign of the public's *acclaim*."

3. **frivolous** (p. 586): unserious, light, unworthy of attention, trivial. "When Sarah Palin resigned as governor of Alaska, she said she was sick and tired of responding to *frivolous* accusations."

4. **enchanting** (p. 586): delightful, engaging, fascinating, charming. "The chief financial officer had an *enchanting* presence, which made her perfect for delivering bad news."

5. **ironically** (p. 586): contradicting what one might expect to be the case. "*Ironically*, they spent six months going through a messy divorce only to re-marry six months later because they missed one another intensely."

6. **convulsions** (p. 587): uncontrolled fits in which the muscles contract wildly, any violent and irregular motion; also often used figuratively to refer to upheaval. (1) "*Convulsions* can sometimes signal the presence of a brain tumor." (2) "In the spring of 2011, the Middle East was the setting for a bloody, political *convulsion*."

7. **irrevocability** (p. 588): incapable of being changed, altered, or revoked. "The *irrevocability* of death is what makes losing someone you love such a horrific emotional experience."

8. **conservatism** (p. 588): a political philosophy that opposes government aid and promotes individual responsibility for one's life. "When he was alive, Senator Barry Goldwater of Arizona was known for his political *conservatism*, but today, he would be considered a flaming liberal."

9. **migrants** (p. 590): people or animals that are constantly on the move from place to place; people with no firm employment, who travel from place to place in search of work. (1) "The scientists were trying to study the social relationships of African *migrants*, but it was difficult because the birds never stayed in one place for very long." (2) "Throughout the state, the regulations for farm workers were widely ignored and nearly all the local *migrants* live in camps located on the farms by which they are employed."

10. **cultivation** (p. 590): farming, the act of preparing soil for growing fruits and vegetables; also having a high degree of education and sophistication. (1) "According to one theory of ancient history, it was women who kept the early family alive through the *cultivation* of crops while men were hunters, whose supply of food was somewhat irregular." (2) "The young woman was working in a run-down bar in New York's Hell's Kitchen, but her manner of speaking suggested a high degree of *cultivation*."

DIGGING Can Whales Be Saved?
DEEPER

Looking Ahead Over-harvesting practically brought some species of whales to extinction. But regulation helped the whales make a comeback. That does not mean, however, that they aren't still under threat.

Getting Focused Both the title and the preview of the reading tell you that whales are in danger. Read to understand the nature of the threat and to see if you can answer the question posed in the title.

1 Whales are fairly easy to kill because of their size and their need to come to the surface to breathe. Mass slaughter became efficient with the use of radar and airplanes to locate the whales. Fast ships, harpoon guns, and inflation lances that pump dead whales full of air and make them float also aided in the harvesting of the huge creatures.

2 Whale harvesting, mostly in international waters, has followed a classic pattern with whalers killing an estimated 1.5 million whales between 1925 and 1975. Such over-harvesting reduced the population of eight of the eleven major species to commercial extinction, i.e., whales were so hard to find it no longer paid to hunt and kill them. It also drove some commercially prized species such as the giant blue whale to the brink of biological extinction. (Despite the whales being classified as endangered, which gives them some protection, biologists are not sure that the species can recover.)

3 In 1946, the International Convention for the Regulation of Whaling established the International Whaling Commission (IWC). Its mission was to regulate the whaling industry by setting annual quotas to prevent over-harvesting and commercial extinction.

4 This did not work well for two reasons. First, IWC quotas often were based on inadequate data or ignored by whaling countries. Second, without any powers of enforcement, the IWC was not able to stop the decline of most commercially hunted whale species.

5 In 1970, the United States stopped all commercial whaling and banned all imports of whale products. Under pressure from conservationists, the U.S. government, and the governments of many non-whaling countries, the IWC has imposed a moratorium on commercial whaling since 1986. It worked. The estimated number of whales killed commercially worldwide dropped from 41,480 in 1970 to about 1,300 in 2005.

6 Despite the ban, Japan, Norway, and Iceland kill about 1,300 whales of certain species each year for scientific purposes. Critics see these whale

hunts as poorly disguised commercial whaling because the whale meat is sold to restaurants with each whale worth up to $30,000 wholesale. In 2005, Japan more than doubled its whaling catch, allegedly for scientific purposes, from 440 minke whales to 850 minke whales and 10 fin whales, and began harvesting humpback whales in 2006.

7   Japan, Norway, Iceland, Russia, and a growing number of small tropical island countries—which Japan brought into the IWC to support its position—hope to overthrow the IWC ban on commercial whaling and reverse the international ban on buying and selling whale products. They argue that commercial whaling should be allowed because it has been a traditional part of the economics and culture of their countries. They also contend that the ban is based on emotion, not on updated scientific estimates of whale populations.

8   The moratorium on commercial whaling has led to a sharp rebound in the estimated populations of sperm, pilot, and minke whales. Proponents of whaling, therefore, see no scientific reason for not resuming controlled and sustainable hunting of these and other whale species with populations of at least 1 million. They argue that proposed hunting levels are too low to deplete stocks again.

9   Most conservationists disagree. Some argue that whales are peaceful, intelligent, sensitive, and highly social mammals that pose no threat to humans. Therefore, they should be protected for ethical reasons. Others question IWC estimates of the allegedly "recovered" whale species, noting the inaccuracy of past estimates of whale populations. Also, many conservationists fear that opening the door to any commercial whaling may eventually lead to widespread harvest of most whale species by weakening current international disapproval along with legal sanctions[†] against commercial whaling.

10   Proponents of resuming whaling say that people in other countries have no right to tell Japanese, Norwegians, and people in other whaling countries not to eat whales, just because some people like whales. This would be the same as people in India who consider cows sacred telling Americans and Europeans that they should not be allowed to eat beef.

(Adapted from Miller, *Living in the Environment*, 15th ed., pp. 257–58.)

[†]sanctions: penalties for doing something that is unapproved or illegal.

Sharpening Your Skills

DIRECTIONS   Answer the questions by filling in the blanks or circling the letters of the correct response.

1. The cause and effect pattern organizes the explanation in paragraph 1. The cause described is _____. The effect is _____.

2. What pattern organizes the explanation in paragraph 2?
    a. simple listing
    b. cause and effect
    c. comparison and contrast
    d. time order: process

3. In paragraph 4, what does the opening pronoun "this" refer to?

    _____

4. What key category word appears in paragraph 4?

    _____

5. In addition to the category word, what other clues to the major supporting details do the authors provide?

    _____

6. What organizational pattern ties paragraphs 3, 4 and 5 together?

    _____

7. What is the primary pattern organizing the entire reading?

    _____

8. Which of the following statements best sums up the main idea of the entire reading?

   a. The moratorium on whaling was not as successful as some would like to think. Many critics of whaling argue that the figures showing whale populations rebounding have been faked in order to roll back the ban on whaling.

   b. Efforts to save whales from biological extinction have been persistently undermined by Japanese whalers, who are determined to maintain a tradition that goes back hundreds of years.

   c. A moratorium on whale hunting saved many species of whales from extinction, but the increase in the whale populations has re-ignited the old controversy between supporters and critics of whaling.

   d. The most convincing argument for maintaining the moratorium on commercial whaling comes from those who make their living taking tourists whale watching. They argue correctly that whales are worth more alive than dead because whale watching is a $1 billion-dollar-a-year business.

9. Paragraph 9 identifies the reasons why opponents of commercial whaling oppose the practice. In your own words, what are the reasons they offer for maintaining the moratorium?

   _____

   _____

   _____

   _____

   _____

10. The authors' purpose in this reading is to

   a. outline for readers the controversy surrounding the killing of whales.

   b. convince readers that the moratorium on killing whales must remain in place.

   c. show readers that those who want to lift the moratorium on killing whales have legitimate reasons for doing so.

Share Your Thoughts What's your reaction to the point made in the last paragraph? Is it correct to say that telling people not to eat whale meat is the same as people from India telling people not to eat beef because cows are sacred?

From Reader to Writer Write a brief paper in which you argue that a moratorium on commercial whaling must be maintained or eliminated. Give at least two reasons why you take this position. You can use the reasons from the reading if they make sense to you. However, you can also provide different reasons if the ones mentioned don't reflect what you think.

▶ **TEST 1**   **Reviewing Key Concepts**

DIRECTIONS   Answer the following questions by filling in the blanks.

1. Why do writers sometimes combine organizational patterns? ___

_____

2. Do multi-paragraph readings always combine organizational patterns? _____ Please explain. _____

_____

_____

3. When a writer combines different organizational patterns, should the reader assume the patterns are all equally important? _____ Please explain. _____

_____

4. When readings combine different organizational patterns, how does the reader decide which elements of the patterns to include as notes?

_____

_____

_____

_____

5. What elements of a reading are always essential to your notes?

_____

_____

▶ **TEST 2** **Identifying Main Ideas and Patterns of Organization**

DIRECTIONS Read each selection. Write the main idea in the blanks that follow. Then circle the appropriate letters to identify the patterns organizing the reading.

1. Adopting New Products

1 Acceptance of new products—especially new-to-the-world products— usually doesn't happen overnight. In fact, acceptance of new products can actually take a very long time. People are sometimes cautious or even skeptical about new products. Those customers who do adopt new products usually go through an adoption process that has five stages.

2   The first stage is simple awareness, when the would-be consumer becomes conscious of the product's existence. Next, is the interest stage, when the individual seeks information about the product's price and comparative value. During the evaluation stage, potential buyers consider whether the product satisfies specific criteria, or standards, that are crucial to meeting their personal needs. In the trial stage, the people considering purchase find a way to experience the product without buying it. The individual may take advantage of free samples, purchase a small quantity, or borrow the product from someone else. In the final adoption stage, the decision is made to adopt the product because it appears to fulfill some specific need or needs.

3   Then, too, when an organization introduces a new product, people do not begin buying it all at the same time. Nor do they move through the process at the same speed. Some enter the adoption process quickly. Others wait. For most products, there is also a group of non-adopters who never even begin the adoption process. Because not everyone reacts to new products in the same way, people in marketing spend a good deal of time trying to understand what makes consumers buy or reject a new product.

4   Depending on the length of time it takes potential buyers to adopt a new product, marketers classify buyers into one of five major adopter categories: *innovators*, *early adopters*, *early majority*, *late majority*, and *laggards*. *Innovators* are the first to adopt a new product. They enjoy trying new products, tend to be adventurous, and like to be one of the first to own a new product. *Early adopters* choose new products carefully and are viewed as "the people to ask" by those in the other

categories. People in the *early majority* adopt a new product just prior to the average person. They are deliberate and cautious in trying new products. Individuals in the *late majority* are quite skeptical of new products but eventually adopt them because of economic necessity or social pressure. *Laggards*, the last to adopt a new product, are oriented toward the past. They are suspicious of new products. When they finally decide to adopt one, it may be in the process of being replaced by a newer product that the innovators and early adopters already possess. (Adapted from Pride and Ferrell, *Marketing*, 15th ed., p. 296.)

1. What's the main idea of the entire reading?

    _____

    _____

    _____

2. Which patterns does the author use to develop that main idea?

    a. definition

    b. time order

    c. simple listing

    d. comparison and contrast

    e. cause and effect

    f. classification

2. The Rise of Public Relations

1   You may think today's cash rebate programs from car manufacturers are relatively new. But in 1914, Henry Ford announced that if he sold 300,000 Model Ts that year, each customer would receive a rebate. When the company reached its goal, Ford returned $50 to each buyer. This was good business. It was also good public relations. *Public relations* involves creating an understanding for, or goodwill toward, a company, a person, or a product. Ford did precisely that with his fifty-dollar rebate.

2   There are three ways to encourage people to do what you want them to do: power, patronage, and persuasion. *Power* can be ruling by law or might. But it can also mean ruling by peer pressure—someone does something because his or her friends do. *Patronage* is a polite

term for bribery—paying someone to do what you want. The third method, persuasion, is the approach of public relations. *Persuasion* is the act of using argument or reasoning to induce someone to do something.

3   One of the first political leaders to realize the importance of public relations was Augustus Caesar, who in the first century commissioned statues of himself to be erected throughout the Roman Empire. The purpose of the statues was to enhance his image. Since then, many political leaders have ordered heroic images of themselves printed on coins and stamps.

4   The current public relations approach in the United States, however, can be traced not to the Romans but to journalists writing at the beginning of the twentieth century. Journalists were an important reason for the eventual emergence of public relations as a profession.

5   Before 1900, many businesspeople believed they could work alongside the press, or even ignore it. In general, stories that appeared in newspapers simply promoted companies that bought advertising. But after the Industrial Revolution† arrived in the United States at the end of the eighteenth century, and a new breed of industrialists began exploiting workers in pursuit of profits, the press's attitude toward industry began to change.

6   In response to what they saw as a great injustice, journalists like Lincoln Steffens (1866–1933) and Ida Tarbell (1857–1944) wrote stories that exposed corruption, with Tarbell taking on the oil industry and Steffens going after men who were manipulating the stock market. Thanks to the activities of these journalists, known as "muckrakers," the heads of big companies knew they could no longer just ignore the press. They had to get the press and the public on their side. Thus 1900 saw the appearance of the first publicity firm. It was called The Publicity Bureau, and it was based in Boston. The Publicity Bureau signaled that public relations had become a formal profession that wasn't going to disappear any time soon. (Adapted from Biagi, *Media/Impact*, 10th ed., p, 236.)

---

†Industrial Revolution: The Industrial Revolution began in England in the mid-eighteenth century, arriving later in the United States. Processes and products once done by hand were now being completed at high speed by machines.

1. What is the main idea of the entire reading?

   _____

   _____

   _____

2. Which patterns does the author use to develop that main idea?

   a. definition
   b. time order
   c. simple listing
   d. comparison and contrast
   e. cause and effect
   f. classification

♦ **TEST 3**   **Reviewing Chapter 11 Vocabulary**

DIRECTIONS   Fill in the blanks with the word that fits the sentence.

> frivolous   irrevocable   convulsions   ironically   trivial
> migrant   conservatives   cultivation   enchanting   acclaim

1. Brain tumors, epilepsy, and loss of fluids can all be the source of _____.

2. If you want to get your point across without being misunderstood, speaking _____ may not be the best way to do it.

3. Making _____ decisions on short notice is rarely a good idea.

4. Deciding whom you want to spend the rest of your life with is hardly a(n) _____ decision.

5. If you have lost your job, you are unlikely to make many unplanned and _____ purchases.

6. Successful artists, actors, and athletes are all the object of public _____.

7. If you have a bad cold that leaves you sneezing and coughing, being _____ on a date becomes difficult.

8. Political _____ are inclined to look to the past for their ideas about society.

9. Community gardens are popular because people share in the _____ of the soil and make the work of gardening easier.

10. For at least part of the year, _____ workers have no permanent home.

Responding to Persuasive Writing

IN THIS CHAPTER, YOU WILL LEARN

- how informative and persuasive writing differ.
- how informative and persuasive writing sometimes overlap.
- how fact and opinion are central to identifying purpose.
- about the role of tone in informative and persuasive writing.
- how to evaluate arguments in persuasive writing.

"The better shall my purpose work on him."

—Iago in Shakespeare's *Othello*

Most of the readings you have encountered in previous chapters have been from textbooks with an informative purpose. For that reason, we've concentrated mainly on how to determine the author's message or meaning. But before you leave the pages of this book, we need to look more closely at the characteristics that accompany persuasive writing. Persuasive writing differs from informative writing in a number of ways, and you should know when your textbooks have, with or without the author's conscious intention, combined informative and persuasive purposes.

Chapter 12 will also serve you well when you are assigned persuasive essays or editorials to read. Persuasion relies heavily on the writer or speaker's ability to make an argument. Thus, Chapter 12 shows you the elements of a convincing argument. It also illustrates some of the ways arguments can fail to meet the reader's expectations for relevant and adequate evidence.

Recognizing the Primary Purpose

Like organizational patterns, purposes can mix together in one piece of writing. But one pattern is almost always **primary**, or more central to the author's intention than the other. In textbooks, the primary purpose is generally informative. However, passages of persuasion can make their way into textbooks without the authors even realizing they have revealed their personal point of view.

When that happens, you need to notice how and where informative writing has veered toward persuasion. If you do, you can be more conscious about deciding whether you actually agree with what's being said or need to know more before you do. What you don't want to do is absorb someone else's point of view without considering it first, and that can happen when you are not clear on how persuasive and informative writing can intermingle.

How does the reader know when the two purposes have begun to merge? In textbook writing, the balance of verifiable fact and non-verifiable opinion is a key indicator of whether or not the writer has maintained a strictly informative purpose. So let's start there.

Facts and Opinions Are Clues to Purpose

The heavier the text is on facts, the more likely it is that the purpose of the writing is strictly informative. As you might expect, the more opinions that are present, the greater the chance that the author has taken on a persuasive purpose. However, in order to decide in which direction the author is leaning, you need to be absolutely certain about the difference between fact and opinion.

Facts

Facts are agreed upon pieces of information that can be verified or checked by turning to reference works, original documents, and knowledgeable experts. Look up, for instance, the dates of the American Civil War anywhere in the world, and they will be the same: 1861 to 1865. Similarly, you can check the date Nancy Pelosi was first elected speaker of the U.S.

House of Representatives anywhere in the world. It will always be January 4, 2007, whether you look the date up today or ten years from now.

In addition to being verifiable, facts are usually expressed in language that is more denotative than connotative. In other words, the language packs little or no emotional punch. Take, for instance, the following sentence:

> Chunking—the grouping of bits of information into meaningful and manageable clusters—aids the retention* and retrieval of information. (Matsumoto, *People: Psychology from a Cultural Perspective*, p. 55.)

Could you check if there are studies showing that chunking really does help people recall different bits of information? Yes, you could. That's what makes the statement a fact. Reinforcing the factual nature of the statement is the author's denotative language. Nothing in the sentence encourages the reader to feel anything about the situation described. The author conveys no judgment about the content. Nor does he encourage readers to see the information on chunking in a positive or a negative light.

To see the difference, compare the previous statement to this one:

> Probably the most effective aid to remembering is chunking—the grouping of bits of information into meaningful and manageable clusters—no other memory technique can match it.

With language like *effective* and *no other memory technique can match it*, we are getting into the area of opinions, or personal value judgments. After all, some people think visualizing is the key to remembering. Because there could be a difference of opinion about the best technique for remembering, the thoughtful reader would expect this statement to be followed by some proof that chunking really is the best strategy for remembering new information. Lacking any proof, the reader might well hold off before deciding that chunking is, indeed, the best technique.

Facts

1. can be verified for accuracy through online and print reference works, personal interviews, original documents, and news sources.

---

*retention: keeping something in one's memory.

2. rely on denotative language that doesn't express a point of view toward the topic under discussion.

3. are not shaped or affected by a writer's personality, background, or training and, therefore, do not vary from person to person or place to place.

4. frequently use numbers, statistics, dates, and measurements.

5. name and describe but do not evaluate.

Opinions

In contrast to facts, **statements of opinion** cannot be verified. Opinions are shaped by a person's background, personality, and training. They cannot be proven true or false. There is no way, for example, to prove to cat lovers that dogs make better pets. Nor can you convince a city lover that country life is really superior. Which pet a person favors or where best to live one's life are matters of opinion.

While opinions can't be verified, that doesn't mean they can't be evaluated. On the contrary, people speak all the time about *sound, valid,* or *informed* opinions. These are the terms used to refer to opinions based on solid evidence and logical reasoning. *Unsound, invalid,* or *uninformed* opinions lack evidence and rely on reasons not relevant, or related, to the opinion stated. While everyone has the right to an opinion, not every opinion is worthy of your attention or respect. Those lacking any supporting evidence definitely fall into this category.

In contrast to facts, opinions are likely to be laced with highly connotative language that carries with it some association or feeling. Look, for instance, at this statement drawn from a history textbook:

> *A ruthless land grab,* the Cherokee removal exposed the *prejudiced and greedy* side of Jacksonian democracy. (Divine et al., *America Past and Present,* vol. 1, p. 285.)

The two italicized phrases in this sentence have strong negative associations, which reveal that this statement—despite coming from a textbook—is more opinion than fact. There's nothing wrong with that. It happens all the time in textbooks because textbook authors are human. They have their personal likes and dislikes just like you do. And despite their best intentions to convey information to readers without making value judgments, their ideas or beliefs about their subject matter will occasionally emerge in a text.

That's only a problem if you don't pay attention and fail to notice that you are absorbing an opinion along with a statement of fact.

Opinions

1. cannot be verified for accuracy.

2. can only be labeled *valid* or *invalid*, *sound* or *unsound*, *informed* or *uninformed*, depending on the amount and type of support offered.

3. rely on connotative language that conveys a judgment or feeling.

4. are affected by a writer's personality, background, and training.

5. frequently express comparisons using words such as *more*, *better*, *most*, and *least*.

6. often make value judgments suggesting that some action or event has a positive or negative effect.

7. are likely to be introduced by verbs and adverbs that suggest doubt or possibility, such as *appears*, *seems*, *apparently*, *probably*, *potentially*, and *possibly*.

♦ **EXERCISE 1**   **Labeling Facts and Opinions**

DIRECTIONS   Label each statement *F* (for fact) or *O* (for opinion).

EXAMPLE   Microsoft has already invested more than five billion dollars trying to build an online business that can make money, and its online service is still losing millions of dollars. (Boone and Kurtz, *Contemporary Marketing*, 15th ed., p. 336.)   F

EXPLANATION   This statement is a clear-cut fact. You can check against any number of sources.

1. Harvard student Mark Zuckerberg first launched a version of Facebook in 2003. _____

2. If money is, indeed, the mother's milk of politics, efforts to make the money go away are not likely to work. (Wilson and DiIulio, *American Government*, p. 246.) _____

3. Social scientists have coined the term *halo effect* to describe the tendency to form an overall positive impression of a person on the basis of one positive characteristic. (Adler and Proctor, *Looking Out/Looking In*, 12th ed., p. 104.) _____

4. During the Seven Years' War,[†] the Cuban city of Havana was captured by the British. _____

5. In the general election for president, money does not make much difference, because both major-party candidates have the same amount, contributed by the federal government. (Wilson and DiIulio, *American Government*, p. 246.) _____

6. The 1973 U.S. Supreme Court case *Miller v. California* resulted in a method for testing obscenity. _____

7. The pop singer Beyoncé first became famous as a member of the girl group Destiny's Child. _____

8. Campaign contributions should not be considered a form of free speech. _____

9. The movie *Frida* does a poor job of illuminating the life of the brilliant artist Frida Kahlo. _____

10. One study (Begler 2010) revealed that women are more likely than men to regard expressions of love as genuine statements rather than attribute them to some other cause. (Adler and Proctor, *Looking Out/ Looking In*, 12th ed., p. 104.) _____

[†]Seven Years' War (1756–1763): the last great European conflict before the French Revolution (1787–1799). Havana was occupied because European interests overseas pulled the Americas into the war.

Combining Opinions with Facts

Up to this point, you have worked with statements that were either fact or opinion. But the truth is that writers don't always keep fact and opinion so neatly separated. Often, without realizing it, writers primarily intent on informing their readers include a word or phrase that expresses their personal point of view.

For an illustration, read the following sentence in search of words that evaluate Sigmund Freud's discussion of dreams:

> Sigmund Freud's revolutionary text *The Interpretation of Dreams* was published in 1900 and its impact is still relevant today. (Rubin et al., *Psychology: Being Human,* p. 52.)

Did you decide that the words *revolutionary* and *relevant* expressed an evaluation? If you did, good for you. Those are precisely the words that push an otherwise factual statement into the realm of opinion. The statement is, to be sure, *primarily* factual. But it definitely puts a personal opinion into the mix. In this context, *revolutionary* carries with it positive associations that suggest Freud's theories were original and groundbreaking enough to survive until the present day.

Now consider this sentence:

> Sigmund Freud's *The Interpretation of Dreams* was published in 1900, and the theories of dreaming it introduced are still used by some therapists despite the fact that Freud's theories have not been supported by scientific research on dreams and sleep.

Well now, there's another way to look at Freud's theories, which is not to say that this less positive view is the correct one. All it shows is that evaluations of Freud's book vary from person to person, making both of the above statements of opinion.

What the second sentence does suggest, though, is this: Before you assume *The Interpretation of Dreams* was so groundbreaking that its influence remains powerful over a century later, you might want to know a bit more about the current research on dreaming.

READING TIPS

1. An author's word choice counts a great deal when it comes to separating fact and opinion. A single word or phrase can inject a personal opinion into a statement that, at first glance at least, seems like hard fact.

2. Be wary of an author (or speaker) who starts a statement with the phrase, "It's a well-known fact . . ." Often the claim made in the statement isn't well known. Much of the time, it isn't even a fact.

SUMMING UP THE KEY POINTS

1. Like organizational patterns, the author's purpose does not always neatly fall into one category or the other. Sometimes a piece of writing is both informative and persuasive and the reader has to determine which purpose is *primary*, or major.

2. Even when the purpose of writing is primarily informative, as it usually is in textbooks, the reader should be on the lookout for passages where the author has slipped into persuasion.

3. Statements of fact offer descriptions of topics or issues. They do not evaluate them.

4. Factual statements can be verified, or checked, against outside sources. They don't vary from place to place or person to person.

5. Factual statements employ a cool, neutral tone, using words that do not call up strong emotional associations.

6. Unlike facts, opinions can't be verified. They can't be proven right or wrong, true or false. That doesn't mean, however, that opinions can't be evaluated. They can.

7. Opinions backed by sound evidence and reasoning are termed *sound*, *informed*, or *valid*. Those that aren't backed by relevant evidence are labeled *unsound*, *uninformed*, or *invalid*.

8. Without realizing it, writers sometimes add a word or phrase with positive or negative associations. That word or phrase then mixes an opinion in with facts.

◆ EXERCISE 2   Recognizing When Fact and Opinion Blend

DIRECTIONS   Label each statement *F* (for fact), *O* (for opinion), or *M* (for a mix of both).

EXAMPLE   The stuffed toy business is going to the dogs—and cats, cows, and avatars. Just ask Ganz, the company that sold two million Webkinz in the product line's first two years. The plush animals are cute and cuddly, but they also have an interactive element that children find irresistible. (Pride and Ferrell, *Marketing*, 15th ed., p. 290.)

_____M_____

EXPLANATION   Webkinz, Ganz's interactive stuffed animals, may well be *irresistible* to some children. But it's unlikely that all kids would find them *cute*, *cuddly*, and *irresistible*. Thus, there are value judgments included in this description of the company's success.

1. In 1963, in a decision that was typical of the Supreme Court ruled by Chief Justice Earl Warren, the Court prohibited the Lord's Prayer and Bible reading in schools.

_____

2. University students have a positive view of marriage therapy. (Knox and Schacht, *Choices in Relationships*, 10th ed., p. 479.)

_____

3. The heart is a hollow, muscular organ with four chambers that serve as two pumps. It is about the size of a clenched fist. (Hales, *An Invitation to Health*, 7th ed., p. 277.)

_____

4. Responding to increasing Republican accusations—including those from the House Un-American Activities Committee (HUAC)— that his administration let Communists into the government, Truman moved to beef up the existing loyalty program.... But Truman's loyalty program intensified rather than calmed fears about an "enemy within." (Adapted from Berkin et al., *Making America*, 5th ed., p. 803.)

_____

5. Government regulation and public awareness are external forces that have increased the social responsibility of business. (Pride, Hughes, and Kapoor, *Business*, 10th ed., p. 51.)

   _____

6. Cross-cultural studies…consistently indicate that some societies and subcultures are more violent and aggressive than others. (Shaffer, *Social and Personality Development*, 6th ed., p. 308.)

   _____

7. [Following the Mexican-American War], Mexico was dismembered like a carcass of beef. One-third of Mexican territory—an area larger than France and Spain combined—was detached because the Polk administration wanted it and the United States was strong enough to take it. (Conlin, *The American Past*, 9th ed., p. 393.)

   _____

8. On February 2, 1848, Trist [the American representative] signed the Treaty of Guadalupe Hidalgo, granting the United States all the territory between the Nueces River and the Rio Grande and between there and the Pacific. In exchange, Trist agreed that the United States would pay Mexico $15 million and any war reparations* owed to Americans. (Berkin et al., *Making America*, 6th ed., p. 325.)

   _____

9. Our friends who have children influence us to do likewise. (Knox and Schacht, *Choices in Relationships*, 10th ed., p. 311.)

   _____

10. These two great popular heroes of the revolution [Pancho Villa and Emiliano Zapata] could not have been more different in temperament. Zapata was reserved and cautious but determined, steadfast and fair in carrying out his promises, while the more physically dominant and temperamental Villa embodied a frontier code of

_____

*reparations: payments to help make up for a wrong that's been done.

fearlessness, honor, violence, and vengeance in pursuing his objectives. (Adapted from Meyer et al., *The Course of American History*, Oxford University Press, 9th ed., 2010, p. 400.)

_____

✔ CHECK YOUR UNDERSTANDING

1. Is it true or false that all writing can be divided into two kinds, informative or persuasive? _____ Please explain. _____

_____

2. The key difference between a fact and an opinion is that statements of fact can be

_____.

3. The language of facts is _____ rather than _____.

4. Unlike facts, opinions can't be _____. That doesn't mean, however, that opinions can't be _____. They can be labeled _____

_____.

5. Is it true or false that all statements can be labeled a fact or an opinion? _____ Please explain. _____

_____

6. If the statement is a fact, put an *F* in the blank. Put an *O* in the blank if it's an opinion.
   a. China is home to the world's largest Web population. _____
   b. The Chinese government has been remarkably unsuccessful in its efforts to control what its citizens view on the Web. _____

Recognizing When Persuasion Is Primary

We started this chapter by talking about the way informative writing in textbooks can cross over into persuasion. But, like informative writing, persuasion can be a writer's sole purpose in writing. The question is, How do you know when persuasion *is* the author's primary purpose? In general, persuasion is the author's main purpose when he or she offers an opinion and strongly suggests that you share it.

The Title Often Takes Sides

Writers determined to persuade often introduce an abbreviated version of their opinion in titles like "Lady Gaga Is No Madonna," "Say No to Higher Taxes," or "Stop Factory Farming." Thus, if you are trying to determine if the author's purpose is persuasive, start with the title. Does it simply identify the issue as it does here: "The Arrival of America's Railroads"? Or does the title already define a position: "Government Fraud and the Union Pacific"?

◆ **EXERCISE 3**   **Evaluating Titles**

DIRECTIONS   Look at each title. Then write an *I* or a *P* in the blank to indicate if the title suggests an informative or a persuasive purpose.

1. A Controversial Supreme Court Decision Makes Headlines _____

2. Corporations Don't Have Civil Rights _____

3. Are Bullies Getting Younger and Younger? _____

4. Viagra Is No Medical Necessity _____

5. Education in Denmark _____

6. Standardized Testing Deserves a Failing Grade _____

7. New Standards for New York Teachers _____

8. The Status of Greenland's Glaciers _____

9. Daring Mother Nature to Strike Back _____

10. Skinny Scarecrows Aren't Sexy _____

The Author Takes a Stand

"Almost everything worth writing about is worth arguing over."
—Writer and teacher Mina Shaughnessy

In purely informative writing, authors try not to take a stand on an issue. They supply readers with information while keeping their **personal perspective**, or point of view, out of the discussion. However, when writing becomes primarily persuasive, the writer's point of view becomes central to the discussion. It becomes the controlling main idea.

Writers motivated by a persuasive purpose see an issue in a certain light. Convinced of their correctness, they have decided it is important for readers to see things in the same way, or at least to seriously consider siding with the author. It's no surprise, then, that writing with a persuasive purpose includes statements like these, which express a definite point of view in language that is more connotative than denotative.

1. Instead of being treated as heroes, whistle-blowers are unfairly made the subject of criminal investigations, which are purposely designed to intimidate others from speaking out.

2. Beauty contests for children may serve the vanity of the parents, but they are enormously stressful for the anxious children put on display.

3. At the heart of factory farming is the belief that the suffering of animals just does not count. What counts is profit.

Persuasive writing puts forth an opinion, an idea, a belief, or an attitude that some readers might disagree with. It does not put forth ideas that no one disputes. This sentence would not be the thesis statement for a persuasive piece of writing: "Thomas Jefferson was the third president of the United States." This one, however, might well turn up as the focus of a persuasive article or essay: "Publicly Thomas Jefferson seemed to stand against the extension of slavery, but his behind-the-scenes position was a good deal more complicated."

◆ **EXERCISE 4** **Distinguishing Between Informative and Persuasive Thesis Statements**

DIRECTIONS Each of the following statements could provide the basis for either informative or persuasive writing. In the blank that follows each one, write *I* to indicate that the thesis appears to be primarily informative or *P* to indicate the opposite.

1. New reproductive technology has made it increasingly possible for parents over fifty to have children. _____

2. While reproductive technology has made it increasingly possible for parents over fifty to have children, the question those parents need to be asking is, Should parents in their sixties really be raising teenagers? _____

3. A growing number of companies are blocking their employees from accessing social media sites. _____

4. Companies that are blocking their employees from social media sites are damaging employee morale and decreasing, rather than encouraging, productivity. _____

5. The Obama administration passed health care legislation that strikes at the heart of individual freedom and responsibility. _____

6. If nothing else, the Obama administration's health care plan has eliminated a long-standing obstacle to health care in America— the ability of insurance companies to deny coverage for preexisting conditions. _____

7. In the spring of 2011, the protests in Egypt's Tahrir Square gave new and courageous meaning to the title of an old song, "Walk Like an Egyptian." _____

8. In the spring of 2011, Cairo's Tahrir Square was the scene of protests against the Egyptian dictator Hosni Mubarak. _____

9. For decades, Pakistani husbands who threw acid into the faces of the wives they wanted to replace received minimal punishment, but the legal system in Pakistan has begun to take action and men found guilty now get fourteen years to life in prison. _____

10. Filmmaker Sharmeen Obaid-Chinoy's documentary about acid attacks on women in Pakistan, called *Saving Face*, is a tribute to the activists and victims who have courageously spoken out against this barbaric practice. _____

The Supporting Details Provide the Evidence

"Without evidence, an argument is a windy, flimsy statement of one person's opinion."
—Professors Alison Pease and Livia Katz[†]

Authors looking to persuade their readers know that they have to give them more than the title and point of view. Persuasion requires an **argument**. In addition to stating their position, writers have to supply evidence that makes readers say, "I see your point" or, even better, "Based on that evidence, I'm inclined to agree with you."

The evidence supplied in an argument can take different forms. It can take the form of reasons, examples, studies, events, personal experiences, statistics, etc. Like all supporting details, evidence for an argument depends on the opinion, i.e., the thesis statement being proposed for readers' acceptance.

Here, for instance, the author argues that a writer who wrote a fake memoir* called *The Education of Little Tree* did so to cover up his violent racist past. Note how the evidence focuses on events from the subject's life. For the author of the argument, this is proof that the subject's past was both violent and racist. Therefore, it needed to be disguised as the country changed and racism was no longer tolerated.

The title offers a clue to the author's intention.

Asa Carter's Secret Past

1 Although Asa Earl Carter originally claimed that his book *The Education of Little Tree* was autobiographical, there is very little evidence to prove his claim of Native American heritage, and the book is now generally accepted as fiction rather than the autobiography Carter suggested it was. Unlike the main character of his book, Carter was not orphaned

---

[†]You can find the context for this quotation along with a brief but very good discussion of evidence here: www.jjay.cuny.edu/departments/english/Using_Evidence_to_Strengthen_Your_Arguments.pdf.
*memoir: life story.

at five years of age, and his Cherokee grandparents didn't raise him because he didn't have any Cherokee grandparents. Many of Carter's descriptions of Cherokee life have been widely disputed by those who are really Cherokee by birth. For the most part, the story of Carter's Indian past appears to have been invented to cover up the period of his life he wanted to keep hidden from the world—his years as a violent racist.

2   Born in Anniston, Alabama, in 1925, Carter started his career as a radio announcer. He specialized in attacking Jews, blacks, Yankees, and any of what he termed the "lesser breeds." He was especially hard on those who dared challenge the superiority of the white race. When he wasn't assaulting minorities over the radio waves, Carter was managing the Anniston chapter of the Ku Klux Klan, which he himself had founded. Under Carter's leadership, the Anniston Klan had several vile* accomplishments: They threw stones at black students trying to integrate the University of Alabama campus, savagely beat the civil rights activist Reverend Fred Shuttlesworth, and castrated a mentally handicapped black handyman.

3   Given Carter's credentials as a racist and a bigot, he was the natural choice of the 1962 gubernatorial candidate George Wallace, who thought he needed to show a more racist profile to make it into the governor's office. Anxious to escape the more liberal image of his mentor, Big Jim Folsom, Wallace tapped Carter as his speechwriter. After Wallace was elected, he again turned to Carter, who penned for Wallace his infamous inaugural slogan, "segregation now, segregation tomorrow, segregation forever."

4   The times were changing, though, and, after a while, even Carter figured out that spewing racist hatred was not the foundation for a successful career. After running, unsuccessfully, against his old friend Wallace for not being racist enough, Carter moved to Texas and started writing under the pseudonym Forrest Carter. His first novel, *The Rebel Outlaw: Josie Wales*, became a movie starring Clint Eastwood, But Carter really hit pay dirt when he penned his fake memoir, *The Education of Little Tree*. Although there were those suspicious of the book's authenticity from the beginning, most accepted Carter's claims about his Cherokee past as fact, and the book eventually became a huge best seller.

5   Ironically, *The Education of Little Tree* was celebrated as a symbol of the country's growing acceptance of a multicultural history in which minorities played a key role. Unfortunately, Carter wasn't alive to be

---

*vile: disgusting.

publicly shamed—if such a man could be shamed—when his literary sleight of hand was exposed in 1991 by a distant relative and Wallace biographer who described Carter's life as a Klansman in the pages of *The New York Times*. Asa Carter had died in 1979, while still being acclaimed for Forrest Carter's contribution to a growing body of literature written by people of color, precisely the people of color Carter had once insulted for being the "lesser breeds," who should know their place or suffer the consequences.[†]

The author uses both first names to emphasize that Carter tried to keep the two parts of his life separate.

As you can see, it's not hard to determine the author's position or point. Carter wrote *The Education of Little Tree* to cover his tracks. He knew the times had changed and figured it would be a wise move to get on the winning side. Most of the evidence provided for the author's claim has to do with proving that Carter was a violent racist, and on that score the author does well.

What's less grounded in hard fact is Carter's reason for writing *The Education of Little Tree*. Yes, he did write it at a time when the country was changing. Carter's brand of blind and vicious racism was coming under attack. Thus he may have wanted to hide the person he had been before moving to Texas.

Asa Carter was a Ku Klux Klan member who, when it became profitable, transformed himself into a champion of Native American rights.

© Jim McDonald/Corbis.

[†]The information for this reading comes from Dan T. Carter's *The Politics of Rage*, a biography of George Wallace. Carter is also the "distant relative," who wrote the *New York Times* article "The Transformation of a Klansman" exposing Forrest Carter's true identity.

But then again, he might also have simply been an opportunist. Realizing that works about minorities were being celebrated, he might have thought to himself, I can make some money by pretending to be a part-Cherokee writer who tells the story of his life. The claim about Carter's motives is simply harder to prove, and, for that reason, this part of the author's argument is less well substantiated, or backed up, than the claim about his past as a violent racist. That part of the author's argument is solid.

Choosing a Tone

"We often refuse to accept an idea merely because the tone of voice in which it has been expressed is unsympathetic to us."
—Philosopher Friedrich Nietzsche

In addition to offering an opinion and providing evidence, the reading on Asa/Forrest Carter reveals its persuasive purpose through the author's tone. **Tone** in writing resembles tone of voice in speaking. It's the feeling or attitude evoked, or called up, by the author's words.

Unlike informative writing, which usually mutes the author's tone, writing designed to persuade uses tone as a way of encouraging readers' agreement. In the reading on Carter, the tone—a mixture of sarcasm and contempt—encourages readers to feel equally appalled and disgusted by Carter's behavior.

But tone varies with the opinion proposed and the audience addressed. (See the box on pages 635–36 for a range of tones.) Writers with a persuasive purpose might use a friendly and highly personal tone to make readers feel sympathetic to the idea, attitude, situation, or action they propose. Then too, they might employ a furious tone to make readers share their anger and demand some change advocated by the author.

In the following excerpt, the author has learned from intimate experience that organ donation can be a complicated and extraordinarily difficult affair. This is an opinion she wants her readers to share. Notice how she creates an earnest yet casual tone that encourages readers to take her situation seriously. The casualness of her tone is important, because she doesn't want to lapse into self-pity. That might make her readers less responsive to her situation:

Despite the seriousness of the situation, the author's use of the word

Whaddya Have to Do to Get a Kidney Around Here?

It was almost a year ago that I found out my kidneys were slowly but ineluctably* failing. I'd been diagnosed with kidney disease a few years earlier, but the beans had been stable at 50 percent. Then a consult at Mass

---

*ineluctably: inescapably.

beans helps keep the tone light.

The statement "I am an odd duck" diminishes the distance between reader and writer and affirms the author's refusal to be miserable.

General concluded with the news that it could be as early as a year before I would need what was euphemistically* called "renal replacement therapy." Doctors are often discreet* in the way they describe things, but the message was clear. I would face three choices: death, dialysis, or transplant.

I am an odd duck, but I was energized by what was now to be a great adventure. I was going to have the opportunity to face my own mortality. At sixty-five, I had a wonderful life, a public voice, and made a modest contribution to a better world.…I loved my life and would enjoy more if it were available, but death was OK. I would take it as the last wonderful journey. I'd also do what needed to be done to continue to live a long and fruitful life, free of infirmity.* That meant finding a person who would donate his or her spare kidney to me before mine failed. It was not, the doctors said, too soon to begin the search. (Frances Kissling, "Whaddya Have to Do to Get a Kidney Around Here?" Salon.com Archive.)

Right from the title, the author uses tone to say to readers, "If you are looking for a sob story, don't look here." The person she presents to her readers through her choice of tone is serious about her condition. However, she is neither miserable nor despairing. One way or another, she will manage the situation and face whatever happens.

The Power of Tone

Tone may just be the most powerful device in the persuasive writer's toolbox. It's the voice readers "hear" on the page, and if they like the voice, they are all the more ready to listen to what the author has to say.

Because tone can be so inviting and encourage an emotional response that leaves logic behind, it pays to be aware of its effect on you. That means knowing how an author is using language, imagery, and detail to create it.

Some Words to Describe Tone ◆		
Admiring	Arrogant	Contemptuous
Amazed	Breezy	Critical
Angry	Cautious	Cynical
Anxious	Comical	Determined
Appalled	Confident	Disapproving

---

*euphemistically: expressed positively despite having negative connotations.
*discreet: careful, tactful, careful about what's said or revealed.
*infirmity: weakness, illness.

Disbelieving	Mistrustful	Regretful
Disgusted	Neutral	Respectful
Doubtful	Nostalgic (longing for a past time)	Rude
Enthusiastic		Sarcastic
Friendly	Objective	Shocked
Horrified	Outraged	Skeptical
Insulting	Passionate	Solemn
Ironic (saying the opposite of what is intended)	Patriotic	Sympathetic
	Proud	Worried
	Puzzled	

◆ **EXERCISE 5**   **Hearing the Author's Tone**

DIRECTIONS   Read each excerpt. Then circle the appropriate letter to identify the author's tone.

1. **The Medium Is the Message**

   The Wall Street Journal's L. Gordon Crovitz has suggested that easy-to-use networked readers like the Kindle "can help return to us our attention spans and extend what makes books great: words and their meaning." That's a sentiment most literary-minded folks would be eager to share. But it's wishful thinking. Crovitz has fallen victim to the blindness that [Marshall] McLuhan[†] warned against: the inability to see how a change in a medium's form is also a change in its content. (Nicholas Carr, *The Shallows*, W. W. Norton, 2011, p. 102.)

   The author's tone is

   a. neutral.

   b. admiring.

   c. irritated.

   d. disbelieving.

   _____

   [†]Influential during his lifetime, Canadian writer Marshall McLuhan (1911–1980) is probably even more so now. In books like *Understanding Media*, he argued that how we learn transforms how we think. Probably his most famous quote is "The medium is the message."

2. Where Have All the Tools Gone?

The disappearance of tools from our common education is the first step toward a wider ignorance of the world of artifacts[†] we inhabit. And, in fact, an engineering culture has developed in recent years in which the object is to "hide the works," rendering many of the devices we depend on every day unintelligible to direct inspection.... A decline in tool use would seem to betoken a shift in our relationship to our own stuff: more passive and more dependent. And, indeed, there are fewer occasions for the kind of spiritedness that is called forth when we take things in hand for ourselves, whether to fix them or to make them. What ordinary people once made, they buy; and what they once fixed for themselves, they replace entirely or hire an expert to repair, whose expert fix often involves replacing an entire system because some minute component has failed. (Mathew B. Crawford, *Shop Class as Soulcraft*, Penguin Books, 2010, p. 1.)

The author's tone is

a. neutral.

b. warning.

c. curious.

d. discouraged.

3. Joe Hill Was No Hero

Americans seem always to have lusted for rags-to-riches heroes. Failing to find them, we are too often inclined to invent them. This certainly seems to be the case when it comes to the man born Joel Hägglund who later came to be known as Joe Hill.[†] A poet and songwriter, Hill first came to public attention when he wrote a series of songs that were adopted by the early American labor movement. His name, however, did not become notorious until he was arrested for armed robbery and murder. According to the legend, Hill never committed the murder; he was executed in an attempt to destroy the labor movement. Although it is true that Hill

---

[†]artifacts: Objects made by human beings that are of historical interest.
[†]Two of Hill's most famous songs were "The Preacher and the Slave" and "Casey Jones—the Union Scab." Hill's life was also the subject of a song titled "Joe Hill," which singer Joan Baez made widely known at a famous concert in Woodstock, New York.

was tried and convicted on circumstantial evidence, it is equally true that his story contained numerous distortions and loopholes. At his best, he was a man unfairly tried and convicted; at his worst, he was a criminal who boldly proclaimed himself innocent. But in neither case was he a legendary hero, and the ridiculous tendency to call him heroic is a misguided attempt to make a hero out of a man totally unworthy of the name.

The author's tone is

a. neutral.

b. ironic.

c. mystified.

d. disgusted.

4. **Sympathy for the Candidate**

If you dislike campaign oratory* put yourself in the candidate's shoes for a moment. Every word you say will be scrutinized, especially for slips of the tongue. Interest group leaders and party activists will react sharply to any phrase that departs from their preferred policies. Your opponent stands ready to pounce on any error of fact or judgment. You must give countless speeches every day. The rational reaction to this state of affairs is to avoid controversy, stick to prepared texts and tested phrases, and shun anything that sounds original (and hence untested).... Voters may *say* that they admire a blunt, outspoken person, but in a tough political campaign, they would probably find such bluntness a little unnerving. (Wilson and DiIulio, *American Government*, 10th ed., p. 243.)

The author's tone is

a. neutral.

b. ironic.

c. puzzled.

d. sympathetic.

---

*oratory: speech making.

In Persuasive Writing, Both Sides Rarely Get Equal Time

Writers whose intention is to inform will present both sides of an argument just about equally so that readers can draw their own conclusion, for example:

Drug Use and Pregnancy

Notice that the title does not take a stand. All it tells you is the topic.

1 Court cases with policy implications for whether a woman can or should be arrested if she exposes a fetus to illegal drugs are continuing to be debated at the highest judicial levels, including the Supreme Court in the United States. Is this an effective way to reduce the likelihood of drug use and any of its accompanying risks for the fetus? That depends on your point of view.

The authors consistently use a question and answer format to make it clear that they are not endorsing any one point of view.

What Are the Opposing Arguments?

2 Some say a concerned society should impose criminal or other charges on a pregnant woman who uses a drug that may be dangerous to the fetus. A number of jurisdictions in the United States and provinces in Canada have implemented laws permitting a newborn to be removed from a parent on the grounds of child abuse or neglect because of drug exposure during pregnancy. In some cases, the woman has been ordered to be confined to a drug-treatment facility during pregnancy. After all, anyone found to provide such illegal substances to child would certainly expect to face criminal or other charges. Are the circumstances that much different in the case of a pregnant woman and her fetus?

To avoid taking a stand themselves, the authors pose a question without providing an answer.

Paragraph 3 offers the opposing point of view. And again the authors don't take a stand, suggesting both sides have merit.

3 Others believe the situation is vastly different and further claim that criminal charges, imprisonment, or mandatory treatment are counterproductive (Beckett, 1995; Farr, 1995). Legislation specifically targeted to pregnant drug users might actually drive prospective mothers, out of fear of being prosecuted, away from the care and treatment needed for both themselves and their fetuses. Moreover, the tendency to rely on criminal procedures could limit the resources available for the implementation of innovative, well-funded public health efforts for treating addiction and its consequences for the fetus (Chavkin, 2001). (Adapted from Bukatko and Daehler, *Child Development,* 5th ed., pp. 123–24.)

To see the difference between pure informative and pure persuasive writing, compare this reading to the one about Asa Carter (p. 631). The reading on Carter never even suggests that a different point of view exists. Yet it's sometimes argued that Carter wrote *The Education of Little Tree* to atone, or make up, for[†] his despicable past, after realizing late in life how wrong he had been.

In the author's mind, this point of view isn't even worthy of your consideration. Thus you, the reader, don't hear about it. For a writer with persuasive intentions, that's not unusual. And even when a writer with a persuasive purpose mentions an opposing point of view, it's usually to tell readers precisely how that opposing point of view is in error.

Ten Signs of Informative Writing ♦	
	1. Opens with a neutral title that does not judge or evaluate: "Latino Rock Pioneers of the 50s"; "World War II Propaganda."
	2. Describes a subject, an event, or an issue without offering a personal opinion, or making a value judgment: "In 2005, surgeons successfully performed a face transplant for the first time in medical history."
	3. Relies mainly on denotative language, which makes the author sound cool and personally uninvolved: "On the first day of the riots, one hundred people died."
	4. Leans heavily on factual evidence that can be verified, or checked, in other sources: "In May of 1968, approximately nine million workers went on strike in France."
	5. Describes the opinions of others without revealing if the author agrees or disagrees: "In a recent *New York Times* editorial, William Baude argued that states might 'use custody laws to curtail the movements of pregnant women.'"
	6. Avoids using the first-person singular (*I*) or plural (*we*): "It has been argued by some" as opposed to "I would argue here."
	7. Often gives both sides of an issue: "Judge William Rehnquist, who died in 2005 at the age of eighty, was considered by many to be an arch-conservative who helped divide the country. Others saw him as a consensus builder."

[†]Interestingly enough, Carter's former friend and boss Governor George Wallace did try to atone for his racist past, apologizing publicly and privately for his past behavior.

8. Expresses only value judgments that are attributed to others: "Some hold the opinion that both Republicans and Democrats failed to adequately help victims of Hurricane Katrina. Critics cite failures among Democrats at the local level and Republicans at the federal level."

9. Emphasizes the role of research that illustrates or supports the main idea: "The leading medical researcher at Harvard Medical School disputes the notion that eight glasses of water a day are essential for good health. His claim is supported by a number of studies done on athletes."

10. Commonly appears in reference works, textbooks, manuals, newspapers, and institutional reports.

Ten Signs of Persuasive Writing
◆

1. Opens with a title that suggests a point of view: "Voting Matters" or "Turkey Haunted by the Nightmare of Armenia."[†]

2. Expresses a personal opinion about a subject, an event, or an issue: "From my perspective, the best thing about the Winter Olympics is that they are over."

3. Frequently uses language that reveals strong feelings: "How many stories about desperate, terrified, and homeless people do we need to hear before we seriously commit to rebuilding New Orleans?"

4. Mentions an opposing point of view mainly to contradict it: "The notion that alcoholics can learn to drink moderately is wishful thinking."

5. Uses more facts that favor the writer's point of view. For instance, a writer who does not want readers to support the use of animals in research might include statistics about the number of mice killed in pursuit of a cancer treatment, while leaving out any statistic about the number of people living longer now that the drug is available.

6. Gives reasons why the author's opinion should be held by others: "There are several reasons why censorship during wartime is absolutely necessary."

[†]Although many of his fellow citizens disagree with Turkish writer Orhan Pamuk, others share his point of view. Pamuk insists his country carried out genocide, or planned mass slaughter, against the Armenians in 1915.

7. Often uses the first-person pronoun (*I*) or addresses the audience: "I know that you too must cringe when politicians claim to speak for America."

8. Refers to the audience as if agreement had already been established between the writer and the audience: "We all know that elections are not won by merit; they are won by money."

9. Uses rhetorical questions that neither expect nor want an answer: "Except to undermine parental authority, what other reason could there be for telling a small child to question authority?"

10. Commonly appears in essays, editorials, biographies, and books written to make readers aware of an issue or revise a long-held opinion.

READING TIP

Any time an author gives both sides of an issue an equal amount of space, pointing out the pluses and minuses of each position, you are dealing with writing meant to inform rather than persuade.

♦ **EXERCISE 6**   **Recognizing Main Idea, Purpose, and Tone**

DIRECTIONS   Read each of the following selections. Then in the blank lines that follow identify the author's main idea, purpose, and tone.

The title doesn't really make a judgment. It gives us the topic but not the purpose. However, the opening sentence has a definite "That was then this is now" feel to it.

The tone is fairly neutral, but the thesis statement comes close to taking a

EXAMPLE

Fingerprints on Trial

1 Fingerprints have long been considered an essential part of crime solving. If a trained expert said in a courtroom that fingerprints found at the scene of a crime matched those of the accused, the expert's testimony usually decided the case. The defendant was found guilty, case closed. But fingerprint evidence may no longer be considered unassailable proof of guilt. While fingerprints might not lie, the experts who analyze them can and do make mistakes. Sometimes poorly trained, they are not always subject to regular review by outside experts. Consequently, the use of fingerprint evidence is currently on trial, and the jury is still out as to whether fingerprint analysis makes for reliable evidence.

stand: Where fingerprints are concerned, mistakes have been made, making the tone somewhere between neutral and critical.

The use of the term sacred cows—*ideas held sacred more out of tradition than for merit— suggests the author's point of view that fingerprint evidence might be another sacred cow.*

The last paragraph is really the clincher. There are definitely two sides to this issue, but the author presents only the side that questions the value of fingerprint evidence.

This sentence moves the tone from neutral to critical.

2   Fingerprint evidence was first admitted into a U.S. courtroom in 1902 and went unchallenged for so long, in part, because no one really knew what standards should be applied to what was considered scientific evidence. However, all that changed with a 1993 case called *Daubert v. Merrell Dow Pharmaceuticals*. The case involved a child whose mother had taken a drug made by Merrell Dow Pharmaceuticals. The child suffered from serious birth defects, and lawyers representing the child's family argued that the drug had caused the defects. The pharmaceutical company insisted that there was no valid proof that the drug was at fault and raised the issue of what constituted scientific proof. The judge ruled in favor of the pharmaceutical company and laid down a set of standards for what could qualify as proof. Chief among them was the criterion that an evidence-gathering technique with a high error rate could no longer be accepted as solid evidence.

3   As a consequence of the *Daubert* ruling, judges were now required to take a more active role evaluating and deciding the "quality of evidence." It was at this point that the sacred cows of forensic* science came under attack. Handwriting evidence was no longer considered scientific, use of lie detector results as evidence was severely limited, and even ballistic tests claiming to match bullets to specific guns came into question.

4   Suddenly, questions were being asked that had rarely been posed in pre-1993 courtrooms: Has fingerprint identification been adequately tested? What's the error rate? What are the standards and controls for evaluating fingerprint experts? People like lawyer Robert Epstein, who has repeatedly challenged the validity of fingerprint evidence, would say that none of these questions has been adequately answered. And even when they have been answered, the result does not bode well for the survival of fingerprint analysis. Epstein is not alone in his opinion. Professor David Faigman of the University of California, Hastings College of Law, predicts "that…some judge somewhere in the country will write an opinion excluding fingerprinting. It's inevitable. The research is just too thin to let it in." (Source of statistics: Malcolm Ritter, "Fingerprint Evidence Faces Hurdles," April 7, 2001, www.scafo.org/Library/PDF/FP%20Evidence%20 Faces%Hurdlespdt.)

*forensic: related to courts of law and criminal investigations.

Given standards of proof introduced by the courts, some people say that fingerprints might not be a reliable source of evidence.

What is the main idea or point of the reading?

Fingerprint evidence is being attacked as not scientific enough to decide guilt or innocence.

The author's purpose is persuasive.

The tone is neutral but leaning toward critical.

EXPLANATION   In this case, the author argues that fingerprint evidence may not measure up to current standards of proof. Although the author uses a mostly neutral tone, the lack of a balance between those who still believe in fingerprint evidence and those who don't makes the purpose persuasive. In addition, phrases like "sacred cows" and "the result does not bode well" suggest a critical tone.

1. Congratulations, Dad! Are You Nuts, Mom?

1   Usually when a woman announces she is ready to give birth, most people, be they friends, relatives, or complete strangers, clap for joy. Impending motherhood is a miracle, after all, worthy of celebration. But that's hardly the response that British mother-to-be Elizabeth Adeney received when it was discovered in May 2009 that she was about to give birth.

2   Elizabeth Adeney, you see, was sixty-six years old and pregnant thanks to modern fertility treatments, which allow women long past childbearing age to bear children. As it was with sixty-six-year-old Adriana Iliescu, a Romanian woman who gave birth to a child in 2006, the public's view of Elizabeth Adeney was hotly critical. Her decision evoked numerous public attacks.

3   Among the nicer reactions was one from a blogger who said that much could be forgiven if Adeney, like some other older moms, had had a younger partner. Then the partner could presumably care for the child if anything happened to Adeney. But Adeney was divorced with no partner. She also didn't have brothers and sisters to step in if something happened to her.

4   Few took the position of one writer, who insisted that the whole affair was no one's business except the mother's. That mind-your-own-business take on the subject was, in fact, very much in line with what Adeney herself had said: that her pregnancy was no one's business except her own. As newspapers, blogs, and tweets around the world

confirmed, very few agreed. Adeney's situation was fodder for the tabloids, and everyone seemed ready and willing to take potshots at Adeney's decision to become an elderly mom.

5   Far fewer people asked the question posed by journalist Gail Parker of the *Belfast Telegraph*, who wondered in print why old moms, but not old dads, are the subject of scorn and abuse. As Parker wrote, "If Adeney had been a 66-year-old man, it would have been cigars all around and to hell with the actuary tables."[†] And she's right; no one batted an eyelash when Warren Beatty became a dad at fifty-five, Bruce Willis at fifty-seven, and even the stodgiest art critics can't restrain a smile at the mention of artist Pablo Picasso's fathering a child at sixty-eight.

6   Although there are probably legitimate reasons for thinking that having a child after the age of fifty is not the best idea in the world, it's clear that those reasons aren't applied equally. We seem to think old dads are a triumph over nature's limitations whereas old moms should have their heads examined. (Sources of quotations: www.anorak.co.uk/media/210798.html; www.belfasttelegraph.co.uk/opinion/columnists/gail-walker/why-are-the-old-mums-so-disliked-but-not-old-dads-14306592.html.)

What is the main idea or point of the reading?

_____

_____

_____

The author's purpose is _____.

The tone is _____.

2. The Long Road to Informed Consent

1   During the 1947 Nuremberg Trials following World War II, it was revealed that physicians in concentration camps had performed horrific medical research experiments on prisoners in the camps. That doctors, whose historic mission it was to heal, subjected their patients to painful and often deadly experiments—doctors would force feed patients poison to determine what dosage would kill them—shocked the

[†]actuary tables: tables indicating the average length of life given specific circumstances.

world and resulted in the Nuremberg Code, which set up guidelines for experiments that involved human beings:

> The voluntary consent of the human subject is absolutely essential. This means that the person involved should have legal capacity to give consent; should be so situated as to be able to exercise free power of choice, without the intervention of any element of force, fraud, deceit, duress, over-reaching, or other ulterior form of constraint or coercion; and should have sufficient knowledge and comprehension of the elements of the subject matter involved as to enable him to make an understanding and enlightened decision.[†]

2   The need for such a code became even more apparent in 1972 when the public learned of the Tuskegee Syphilis Project, carried on by the U.S. Public Health Service. During the course of the experiment, which lasted forty years, researchers had allowed syphilis to progress unchecked through the bodies of hundreds of black male sharecroppers, none of whom were told the real cause of their symptoms. The subjects of the experiment were also steered away from seeking outside treatment so that the disease's effects, among them blindness, madness, and death, could be carefully tracked. Even after it was discovered that penicillin could cure syphilis, the subjects of the experiment were kept ignorant of the cure.

3   When Peter Buxton, one of the physicians involved in the research, told a reporter what was happening in Tuskegee, the research was halted in response to the cries of public outrage. In 1997, in acknowledgment of the wrong that had been done, President Clinton publicly apologized for the government's actions. The victims of the experiment were also awarded ten million dollars as a result of a class action suit.

4   Immediately following Buxton's disclosure of the Tuskegee experiment's goals, the National Commission for the Protection of Human Subjects of Biomedical and Behavioral Research was established. Its expressed goal was to introduce legislation that would further ensure a patient's right to be informed about the details of any research in which he or she participated. Although the Public Health Service has admitted that mistakes were made in the Tuskegee research, no one has ever publicly acknowledged the similarities between the doctors tried at Nuremberg and the doctors working in Tuskegee.

[†]The complete Nuremberg Code can be found on the National Institutes of Health (NIH) website.

What is the main idea or point of the reading?

_____

_____

_____

The author's purpose is _____.

The tone is _____.

WEB QUEST
Who was Eunice Rivers, and what was her role in the Tuskegee Syphilis Project? How is she viewed as a result of that role?

_____

_____

_____

_____

_____

_____

Sound Arguments Need Sound Reasoning

"At the end of reasons comes persuasion."
—Philosopher Ludwig Wittgenstein

To be persuasive, writers need to put forth a sound argument. They need to (1) clearly identify the opinion or point of view they would like you to share or consider and (2) provide evidence for their position. You have already seen several examples of authors who do precisely that, but looking at one more won't hurt, for example:

Facebook Doesn't Belong on the Mountaintop

The title announces the author's point of view.

At this point, the author is providing

1   In December of 2011, legendary rock climber Tommy Caldwell spent sixteen days trying to reach the summit of El Capitan, the huge mountain of granite that towers over Yosemite National Park. Caldwell didn't complete his free climb up the daunting face of El Capitan. The icy weather

background through an introductory paragraph.

The author acknowledges that bringing Facebook up the mountain is an individual choice.

Note how the reversal transition yet moves away from seeming acceptance to introduce the opinion that matches the title.

The author uses quotations from experts on the subject as support for the point of view expressed. The first expert supplies one reason why social media should not be on the mountaintop: It takes away from the experience.

The experts refer to the danger of being too conscious that others are watching.

and the difficulty level of the climb forced him to give up his solitary quest to make it to the top. But then perhaps *solitary* isn't exactly the right word, because even after his wife left, ten days into the climb, Caldwell wasn't really alone. He had four thousand friends from all over the world along with him. They cheered him on as Caldwell chronicled his climb via his Facebook page.

2 Charging his cell phone through portable solar panels, Caldwell did what many climbers do these days. He allowed people to follow him in real time as they received a running commentary from the man doing the climbing. The fans loved it, so did Caldwell's sponsors, and certainly Caldwell is perfectly within his right to bring his "friends" with him as he risks life and limb. Yet for those who see the sport of mountain climbing as a test of the climber's individual self-sufficiency, courage, and determination, there's something a little depressing about the arrival of social media on the once lonely mountaintop. It sets the stage for the climber to start thinking about the perfect Kodak moment, instead of the next crevice to grab.

3 This certainly seems to be the worry Katie Ives, the editor of *Alpinist* magazine, has expressed in saying that the "representation of the experience" might become the important part of the climber's experience. Therefore, something crucial about the feeling of the adventure would get lost. This sentiment has also been echoed by David Roberts, a writer and climber, who says that social media could introduce a "fatal self-consciousness." Caldwell himself has said that chronicling the experience on his Facebook page changed the experience: "It felt like there were a lot of people watching our progress like a football game."

4 But isn't that precisely the problem with bringing Facebook up the mountain? If you are conscious people are watching, you start playing to the crowd, and that can be a fatal mistake. Zack Smith, a world-class climber put it best when he said, "Climbing mountains is a dangerous pursuit. When you mix in the potential desire to impress people, that's a very dangerous thing." (Source of quotations: Alex Lowther, "On Ledge and On Line: A Solitary Sport Turns Social," *New York Times*, December 9, 2011, p. 1.)

This example illustrates the core elements of an argument: (1) it offers an explicit statement of the author's perspective (although the perspective can also be implied), and (2) it provides relevant support for that perspective. The argument about mountain climbing and social media also includes a third common element, *recognition of an opposing point of view.* But as is typical for persuasion, that opposing point of view is quickly contradicted.

From Reader to Writer Do some research on Eunice Rivers and her role in the Tuskegee Experiment (p. 647). Write a paper that evaluates her behavior. Was she duped by the people she worked with? Was she just desperate for a job and willing to do anything to stay employed? Or was she just plain evil? Whatever position you take, be sure to supply evidence for your opinion.

Recognizing Shaky Support

Supporting evidence for a writer's point of view can vary enormously. It can take the form of facts, examples, expert opinion, statistics, reasons, studies, etc. However, there are times when writers let their **bias**, or personal prejudice in favor of or against an idea or person, get in the way of their ability to think carefully and logically. At times like these, the support for their opinions may get off track, and they may provide evidence that only appears convincing at first glance.

Here are some common errors writers sometimes make when they provide support for an opinion. If you see any one of them in a piece of writing, think twice before making the writer's point of view your own, at least until you know more about the topic.

Hasty Generalizations

One example or, for that matter, a few examples, are never enough to prove a broad generalization about huge numbers of people. Yet, writers who want to persuade are sometimes guilty of offering readers precisely this kind of **hasty generalization**. Here's an example:

Generalization

Without a doubt, the 1.5 to 2 million American children who are being homeschooled are learning more and learning it faster than children who are attending public or private schools. According to a study conducted in 2004 by the Home School Advocates organization, which examined the progress of 102 homeschooled children in fifty families, students who are taught at home by their parents consistently score in the eightieth percentile or above on standardized achievement tests. This same study also revealed that 75 percent of these 102 homeschooled children are enrolled in one or more grades higher than their public- and private-school counterparts of the same age. Clearly, a homeschool education is far superior to that of an education in any institutional setting.

Generalization

Don't be fooled by the presence of a study supporting the idea that children who are homeschooled do better than children who are not. One small study seldom proves anything. And, in this case, readers are being asked to accept a generalization about more than a million children based on a single study of 102 kids.

Where broad generalizations are concerned, writers need to give readers lots of examples. *The broader the generalization the more examples required.* Look, for instance, at the following paragraph to see an illustration of a generalization that is not hasty.

Falling Victim to the Forer Effect

Generalization —→ What has come to be known as the Forer effect may well explain why some people, despite all evidence showing that astrologers don't know any more than the rest of us, continue to read the astrology columns of their local newspapers: They do so because they, like most people, are ready to believe any statement that is positive and vague enough to apply to just about anyone. In 1948, psychology instructor Bertram R. Forer gave his students a personality test, ignored their answers, and gave them all the same evaluation. The evaluation read as follows:[†] "You have a need for other people to like and admire you, and yet you tend to be critical of yourself. While you have some personality weaknesses you are generally able to compensate for them. You have considerable unused capacity that you have not turned to your advantage. Disciplined and self-controlled on the outside, you tend to be worrisome and insecure on the inside…." Almost everyone in the class agreed with their "personality assessment," despite the fact that everyone received the same one.

This statement tells you that the author's point is not backed by one lonely example. The first such experiment was done in 1948 but has been repeated *hundreds of times* since. On every occasion at least 80 percent of the people tested have rated the descriptions of themselves as accurate.

The generalization in this paragraph is based on numerous studies conducted over a long period of time. That's the kind of support you want to see when an author generalizes about a large group.

Irrelevant Evidence

When you analyze a piece of persuasive writing, always be on the lookout for **irrelevant**, or **unrelated**, **evidence**. Authors in the grip of excessive bias will sometimes supply you with a fact or reason that fills up

---

[†]The evaluation is too long to quote in its entirety here.

space but has no particular bearing on the subject at hand. Look, for example, at the following paragraph, where the writer argues that John F. Kennedy does not deserve his high ranking on surveys of best presidents. Can you find a piece of irrelevant evidence?

When surveyed for its opinion about America's best presidents, the public consistently and mistakenly ranks John F. Kennedy either first or second. In reality, Kennedy was not a particularly effective president. No doubt, much of his appeal rests upon his image. He was seen as a dynamic leader reigning over a new "Camelot."[†] Kennedy's quick wit, excellent speaking skills, and good looks helped make him the media's darling, and his charm and charisma played well on television. Yet while the press portrayed him as a devoted family man, Kennedy actually was a womanizer who had a number of extramarital affairs, including one with a nineteen-year-old White House intern. He suffered from chronic health problems and took many drugs, including painkillers, to relieve colitis, back pain, and Addison's disease. His precarious physical state made him ill-suited to the nation's highest office, yet he irresponsibly duped the American people into believing that he was capable and fit. In truth, Kennedy was living on borrowed time; had he lived to be reelected to a second term, his failings eventually would have been exposed, and his house of cards would have come tumbling down.

The author of this passage argues that John F. Kennedy was not a particularly good president. To support that opinion, she offers two reasons: Kennedy was a womanizer, and he had serious health problems that he kept hidden.

John F. Kennedy may well have been a womanizer. However, unless the author can explain how that interfered with Kennedy's performance of his duties as president, the author has not supplied you with evidence relevant to her claim. To make Kennedy's immoral behavior matter in this context, the author would have to describe how Kennedy's affairs with women kept him from the business of the presidency.

More relevant to the author's point are Kennedy's hidden health problems and the medications he was forced to take. Painkillers are notorious for clouding a person's ability to think clearly, so they *may* have interfered with Kennedy's performance. But this potential piece of supporting evidence needs to be connected or related to the opening opinion

---

[†]Camelot: according to legend, King Arthur's royal court. Now it's an allusion used to suggest a longed-for time when the world was a better place.

to be convincing. The author needs to cite, for example, some instance in which President Kennedy's presidential decisions were affected by the drugs he took for his health problems. Just telling you Kennedy had health problems isn't enough.

Circular Reasoning

It's easy to determine the opinion expressed in the following paragraph: The U.S. government should regulate night-shift hours. What's not as clear is why the author takes this position. Much of the paragraph simply repeats the opening opinion. That's why it's an example of **circular reasoning**: The opinion and the reason for holding it are one and the same.

Before a disaster occurs, the government of the United States should regulate the number of hours a worker can put in on a night shift. It is a disgrace that this has not been done already. The United States is one of only six industrialized countries that do not regulate night-shift hours. This lack of regulation is a dangerous and costly oversight that will one day prove disastrous.

But imagine now that the author had recognized his failure to provide an argument and revised the above paragraph to make it more persuasive.

In this example, the author follows the opening opinion with evidence— studies showing that loss of sleep is dangerous.

Before a disaster occurs, the government of the United States should regulate the number of hours a worker can put in on a night shift. According to studies completed by the National Commission on Sleep Disorders in 2012, the loss of sleep, whether voluntary or involuntary, is a dangerous and, sometimes, deadly threat. In studies of sleep disorders, the commission has repeatedly concluded that literally millions of accidents are caused every year by people trying to function normally on too little sleep. Earlier studies have come up with similar results. A study by the Congressional Office of Technology, completed in 1991, pointed to the importance that changes in the sleep cycle play in human errors within the workplace. Likewise, a 2007 study by Harvard's Medical School suggested that people are more likely to make errors in judgment if they have not slept seven to eight hours within the last twenty-four hours. They are also more likely to become more emotionally unstable.

The author interprets the studies to make it clear that they are evidence for the opening opinion.

These studies strongly suggest that limits be placed on disturbances of the human sleep cycle. Although the government cannot determine how many hours employees sleep, it can and should place limits on the number of hours they spend on night shifts.

In this paragraph, the author now anticipates and answers the question she rightly assumes readers might pose: "Why should I take this opinion seriously?" To argue that opinion and make it persuasive, the author identifies several studies that describe the possible dangers that can result from lack of sleep. Although thoughtful readers might not immediately embrace the author's opinion as their own, they would certainly seriously consider it, given the support provided.

Offering False Alternatives

Authors who have let bias interfere with logic often insist that there are only two possible alternatives or answers to a problem or question when, in fact, there are several. Here's an example:

Opening claim says product placement is a must.

The other alternative is not good and can't be considered, making product placement a necessity.

Moviemakers intent on creating a realistic atmosphere are forced to engage in *product placement*—the use of brand names in exchange for a fee. Were an actor in a scene to open a can simply labeled tuna, the audience's attention would be distracted by the label, and the effect of the scene would be destroyed. People are used to seeing brand names such as Chicken of the Sea and Bumble Bee. Filmmakers who want realism in their films aren't doing anything wrong when they engage in product placement.

According to this author's reasoning, either moviemakers must accept fees for using brand names or they will be forced to use general name labels that distract the audience. Left out of this reading are two other alternatives: (1) arrange the scene so that audiences don't see labels or (2) invent brand names and labels that resemble the real ones. Faced with the above either-or thinking, critical readers would start looking for other alternatives. As soon as the writer tells you there are only two choices, you can usually count on discovering that others actually do exist.

Making Careless Comparisons

Be wary of authors who use comparisons not to illustrate a point but to prove it. Often the differences between the two things compared are more crucial than the similarities. Here, for example, the author compares producers who get paid for product placement with athletes who get paid to wear their sponsor's clothing:

> Filmmakers who accept fees for using brand names in their films are just like athletes who are paid to wear brand names in public.

Although that reasoning might sound convincing at first, the differences between the two practices may, in fact, be more important than the similarities. Certainly that is what the writer of the following passage believes:

> Product placement and celebrity endorsements are not the same at all. Highly publicized celebrity contracts have made the public fully aware that athletes are paid large sums of money to sport a sponsor's clothing or footwear. In contrast, the average moviegoer is not as knowledgeable about the fees paid to filmmakers using brand names. Thus, the effects of product placement in films work on a far more subconscious level. Audience members have no idea they are seeing paid advertising.

As the author of this passage points out, there are some crucial differences between athletes who wear brand-name clothing and filmmakers who use brand names in their movies. Those differences considerably weaken the first author's argument for product placement.

SUMMING UP THE KEY POINTS

1. To be taken seriously, opinions need to be backed by relevant reasons and evidence. They need to be part of a solid argument that offers readers a basis for sharing the opinion put forth in the reading.

2. Particularly when they are convinced that they are right beyond all doubt, writers can get careless and offer readers shaky evidence that doesn't provide adequate support for their opinion or claim.

3. Hasty generalizations cover large numbers of people, experiences, and ideas, while offering only one or two examples as proof—for instance, "Getting a college degree is worthless. My aunt dropped out of high school, and she owns her own company."

4. Irrelevant evidence is related in some way to the topic at hand but has nothing to do with backing up the opinion being put forth—for instance, "Despite swindling numerous people out of their pensions, the broker should not pay for his crimes with a prison term. After all, he founded several organizations that take care of abandoned animals."

5. Circular arguments restate the opinion being proposed in different language, and the restatement is supposed to function as evidence—for example, "Ten years from now, there will no longer be print books; everything will be digitalized. It's bound to happen because books composed of paper are going to disappear and e-books are going to take their place."

6. Writers using false alternatives insist that a problem with several solutions actually has only two—for example, "The only choice we have where swine flu is concerned is to either slaughter every single pig in countries where the disease emerges or face the death of millions around the world."

7. Careless comparisons use the similarities between two groups, experiences, or ideas to prove a point. Although comparisons are a useful step in an analysis, they are often shaky as evidence because the differences usually outweigh the similarities. For example, "Why is there always so much talk about the corruption of politics through campaign contributions? Campaign donations are just like speech. They are another form of self-expression."

◆ **EXERCISE 7**   **Recognizing Shaky Arguments**

DIRECTIONS   The following passages all present arguments in favor of an opinion. But each one reveals flawed logic. Circle the appropriate letter to identify the error.

EXAMPLE   In far too many American cities, homelessness has become a major problem. In some cities, whole families live on the street. In a country this rich, homelessness is a national disgrace. In response to this social problem, Americans must dig more deeply into their pockets to support the work of local charities, or the number of homeless people will continue to grow.

a. irrelevant evidence

b. false alternatives *(circled)*

c. careless comparison

d. hasty generalization

e. circular reasoning

EXPLANATION   The author insists that we have only two choices about how to treat the homeless: give to local charities or allow the problem of homelessness to increase. It doesn't take a sociologist to realize that there are other alternatives as well.

1. Stephen King is an underrated artist who is every bit as gifted as Shakespeare. Evidence of King's greatness can be found by examining the similarities in the work of both authors. Shakespeare often wrote about love and relationships. An excellent example of this is his play *Romeo and Juliet.* Stephen King also writes about relationships. *The Stand* and *It* both focus on the importance of love and the power of friendship. Both authors examine issues of morality and are interested in the power of evil.

a. irrelevant evidence

b. false alternatives

c. careless comparison

d. hasty generalization

e. circular reasoning

2. The works of Ernest Hemingway should no longer be part of the high school curriculum. His novels and short stories are too dated and of little interest to a modern generation. Although Hemingway is still beloved by high school English teachers, he writes about a world that is obsolete and to which people, particularly young people, can no longer respond. Everyone now knows about the destructive power of war and the impossibility of fulfilling the rigid masculine role. Hemingway doesn't tell young people anything they need to know anymore, although he might have done so when his first novel was published in 1926. But that was a long time ago.

The bullfight played an important role in one of Hemingway's most famous novels, *The Sun Also Rises.*

a. irrelevant evidence

b. false alternatives

c. careless comparison

d. hasty generalization

e. circular reasoning

3. Sociologists have long claimed that a lack of daily or weekly contact with a parent has few negative effects on the children of divorce; however, new research shows that a lack of regular contact with one of the parents is actually destructive. In one study, fifty college freshmen with divorced parents completed a questionnaire about their experiences and feelings. A number of the students who were geographically separated from one of their parents following a divorce admitted to having a more difficult time adjusting. In comparison to those whose parents continued to live near each other after divorcing, this group also claimed to feel more hostility.

a. irrelevant evidence

b. false alternatives

c. hasty generalization

d. careless comparison

e. circular reasoning

4. Elementary school teachers often keep classroom pets such as gerbils, hamsters, guinea pigs, and reptiles. The teachers claim that these animals help young children learn about both responsibility and biology. However, animals in the classroom should be outlawed for ethical and health reasons. According to People for the Ethical Treatment of Animals and the American Society for the Prevention

of Cruelty to Animals, keeping animals in cages for education or enjoyment teaches youngsters that cruelty to animals is acceptable if it serves human interests. Therefore, either we put a stop to keeping animals in the classroom or we destroy young peoples' compassion for the other creatures of our world.

a. irrelevant evidence

b. false alternatives

c. hasty generalization

d. careless comparison

e. circular reasoning

5. The growing movement toward using social media in the classroom is a misguided one at best. Students have enough trouble concentrating while they are in school; they don't need the lure of Facebook or Twitter to further distract them. Teachers enthusiastic about using social media in the classroom should look at studies from the PEW Internet and American Life Project. When people use Facebook, they spend their time looking at friends' photographs, searching for former friends and classmates, and liking or not liking the posts they read. There is no way to connect these frivolous activities to learning in school.

a. irrelevant evidence

b. false alternatives

c. hasty generalization

d. careless comparison

e. circular reasoning

VOCABULARY ROUND UP

Below are ten words introduced in pages 619–43. The words are accompanied by more detailed definitions, the page on which they originally appeared, and additional sample sentences. Spend time reviewing the words and their meanings because you will see them again in review tests at the end of the chapter. Use the online dictionary Wordnik to find additional sentences illustrating the words in context. (*Note*: If you know of another dictionary with as many examples of words in context feel free to use that one instead.)

1. **retention** (p. 619): keeping something in one's memory; holding on to or maintaining. (1) "Long-term *retention* only occurs when the information is thoroughly understood." (2) "The company is known for long-term *retention* of its employees."

2. **reparations** (p. 626): payments for a wrong that's been done, compensation, amends. "After World War II, the Allied Powers demanded heavy *reparations* from the German and Japanese governments."

3. **memoir** (p. 631): life story, written account of a person or an event. "Andre Dubus III's *memoir* of what it was like to turn from an angry brawler into a writer like his famous father is called *Townie*."

4. **vile** (p. 632): disgusting, despicable, morally low. "The television character Dexter is a *vile* serial killer, who, nevertheless, has a certain charm."

5. **ineluctably** (p. 634): inescapably, unavoidably, incapable of being resisted. "Without their knowing it, Marie Antoinette and her husband, Louis XVI, were moving *ineluctably* toward a meeting with death by the guillotine."

6. **euphemistically** (p. 635): expressed positively despite having negative connotations, substituting a mild term for a more direct one. "People tend to speak *euphemistically* when the subject of death comes up, preferring to say that someone passed away or passed on instead of died."

7. **discreet** (p. 635): careful, tactful, selective about what's said, respectful of privacy. "The celebrity lovers were married to other people, but that didn't seem to concern them, and they were not very *discreet* in their expressions of affection."

8. **infirmity** (p. 635): weakness, illness. "*Infirmity* does not necessarily come with age; some people stay remarkably healthy until the day they die."

9. **oratory** (p. 638): speech making; the art of public speaking. (1) "Any chance she got, the candidate would soar into flights of *oratory* that answered no questions but sounded important." (2) "In ancient Rome, *oratory* was part of a standard education for the upper classes."

10. **forensic** (p. 643): related to courts of law and criminal investigations. "The medical examiner was conducting a *forensic* investigation into the murder that had shocked the small, sleepy town."

DIGGING Critical Thinking and Pseudo-Psychologies—
DEEPER Palms, Planets, and Personality

Looking Ahead Psychologist and professor Dennis Coon believes that most people are not skeptical enough about what he calls pseudo-psychologies. To discover what they are and find out why many of us are all too ready to believe in them, read the selection drawn from Professor Coon's textbook *Essentials of Psychology*.

Getting Focused As you read, make sure you understand how the author defines the key terms in the title, *critical thinking and pseudo-psychologies*. Make sure as well that you understand the different ways believers in astrology maintain their belief despite a lack of any scientific evidence.

1 Most of us would be skeptical when buying a used car. But all too often, we may be tempted to "buy" outrageous claims about topics such as "channeling," dowsing,[†] the occult, the Bermuda Triangle, hypnosis, numerology, and so forth. Likewise, most of us easily accept our ignorance of sub-atomic physics. But because we all deal with human behavior every day, we tend to think that we already know what is true and what is false in psychology.

Despite shaky scientific support, people have been using divining rods since the sixteenth century, and they are still using them today.

Peter Essick/Aurora/Getty Images.

2 For these, and many more reasons, learning to think critically is one of the lasting benefits of a college education. **Critical thinking** refers to

[†]dowsing: the use of a divining rod to search for underground water or minerals.

an ability to evaluate, compare, analyze, critique, and synthesize information. Critical thinkers are willing to ask the hard questions, including those that challenge conventional wisdom.

Pseudo-Psychologies

3   A **pseudo-psychology** (SUE-doe-psychology) is any dubious and unfounded system that resembles psychology. Many pseudo-psychologies offer elaborate systems that give the appearance of science but are actually false. (*Pseudo* means "false.") Like most pseudo-sciences, pseudo-psychologies change little over time because their followers do not actively seek new data. In fact, they often go to great lengths to avoid evidence that contradicts their beliefs. Scientists, in contrast, actively look for contradictions as a way to advance knowledge.

4   Unlike the real thing, pseudo-psychologies are not based on empirical[†] observation or scientific testing. **Palmistry**, for instance, claims that lines in the hand reveal personality and predict a person's future. Despite the overwhelming evidence against this, palmists can still be found separating the gullible from their money in many cities. A similar false system is **phrenology**, popularized in the nineteenth century by Franz Gall, a German anatomy teacher. Gall believed that personality is revealed by the shape of the skull. However, modern research has shown that bumps on the head have nothing to do with talents or abilities. In fact, the area of the brain that controls hearing was listed on phrenology charts as the center for "combativeness" and "destructiveness"!

5   At first glance, a pseudo-psychology called **graphology** may seem more reasonable. Graphologists believe that they can identify personality traits and predict job performance from handwriting. Graphology is moderately popular in the United States, where at least three thousand companies use handwriting analysis to evaluate job applicants. This is troubling to psychologists because studies show that graphologists score close to zero in tests of accuracy in rating personality (Ben-Shakhar et al., 1986). In fact, studies have long shown that graphologists do no better than untrained college students in rating personality and job performance (Neter & Ben-Shakhar, 1989; Rafaeli & Klimoski, 1983). (By the way, graphology's failure at revealing personality should be separated from its proven value for detecting forgeries.)

6   If pseudo-psychologies have no scientific basis, how do they survive and why are they popular? There are several reasons, all of which can be demonstrated by looking at astrology.

---

†empirical: based on observation or experiment; verifiable by such means.

7 **Problems in the Stars** Astrology is probably the most popular pseudo-psychology. Astrologers assume that the position of the stars and planets at the time of a person's birth determines personality traits and affects behavior. Like other pseudo-psychologies, astrology has repeatedly been shown to have no scientific validity (Crowe, 1990). The objections to astrology are numerous and devastating, as shown by the following:

8 1. The zodiac has shifted by one full constellation since astrology was first set up. However, most astrologers simply ignore this shift. (In other words, if astrology calls you a Scorpio you are really a Libra, and so forth.)
2. There is no connection between the "compatibility" of the astrological signs of couples and their marriage and divorce rates.
3. Studies have found no connection between astrological signs and leadership, physical characteristics, career choice, or personality traits.
4. The force of gravity exerted by the obstetrician's body at the moment of birth is greater than that exerted by the stars. Also, astrologers have failed to explain why the moment of birth should be more important than the moment of conception.
5. A study of over three thousand predictions by famous astrologers found that only a small percentage were fulfilled. These "successful" predictions tended to be vague ("There will be a tragedy somewhere in the eastern United States in the spring.") or easily guessed from current events ("Astrology and Astronomy," 1983; Culver & Ianna, 1979; Pasachoff, 1981; Randi, 1980).

9 In short, astrology has no scientific basis and cannot tell you anything about your current or future life. But then why do so many people believe in it? The following discussion answers that question.

10 **Uncritical Acceptance** If you have ever had your astrological chart done, you may have been impressed with its seeming accuracy. Careful reading shows many such charts to be made up of mostly flattering traits. Naturally, when your personality is described in *desirable* terms, it is hard to deny that the description has the "ring of truth." How much acceptance would astrology receive if the characteristics of a birth sign read like this?

Virgo: You are the logical type and hate disorder. Your nitpicking is unbearable to your friends. You are cold, unemotional, and usually fall asleep while making love. Virgos make good doorstops.

11   **Positive Instances**   Even when an astrological description of personality contains a mixture of good and bad traits it may seem accurate. Its apparent accuracy is an illusion based on the **fallacy[†] of positive instances**, in which a person remembers or notices things that confirm his or her expectations and forgets the rest. The pseudo-psychologies thrive on this effect. For example, you can always find "Leo characteristics" in a Leo. If you looked, however, you could also find "Gemini characteristics," "Scorpio characteristics," and so forth.

12   **The Barnum Effect**   P. T. Barnum, the famed circus showman, had a formula for success: "Always have a little something for everybody." Like the all-purpose personality description, palm readings, fortunes, horoscopes, and other products of pseudo-psychology are stated in such *general* terms that they can hardly miss. There is always "a little something for everybody." If you doubt this, read *all* twelve of the daily horoscopes found in newspapers for several days. You will find that predictions for other signs fit events as well as those for your own sign do. (Adapted from Coon, *Essentials of Psychology*, 9th ed., pp. 43–44.)

Sharpening Your Skills

> **DIRECTIONS**   Answer the questions by filling in the blanks or circling the letter of the correct response.

1. What's the main idea of the entire reading?

   _____

   _____

2. What word part gives away the meaning of the word *pseudo-psychology*?

   _____

3. What inference does the author expect readers to add to the opening paragraph?

[†]fallacy: error.

a. We think we know a lot about psychology because we deal with human behavior all the time, but we don't know as much as we think we do.

b. We don't mind being ignorant about physics because, for some reason, ignorance of science is accepted in our culture.

c. Our everyday dealings with other human beings do, in fact, teach us everything we need to know about psychology.

d. Being knowledgeable about physics is more important than being knowledgeable about psychology.

4. Paragraph 4 opens with the phrase "unlike the real thing." What is the "thing" referred to?

_____

5. The author opens paragraph 5 with this sentence: "At first glance, a pseudo-psychology called **graphology** may seem more reasonable." What does the phrase "at first glance" suggest about the message that follows?

_____

_____

6. What is the function of paragraph 6?

a. It sums up the main idea of the reading.

b. It acts as a transition.

c. It's a major supporting detail.

7. What other paragraph in the reading fulfills the same function?

_____

8. Paragraphs 10 and 11 rely primarily on which organizational pattern?

a. comparison and contrast

b. classification

c. time order

d. definition

9. In your own words, paraphrase the definition for the fallacy of positive instances.

_____

Why is the fallacy of positive instances mentioned in the reading?

_____

10. What is the purpose of the reading?

   a. to inform
   b. to persuade

Share Your Thoughts Imagine that you have just met someone you like at a party. After you express a strong opinion, he or she says to you, "You must be a Leo. Leos are very strong willed." Having read the previous excerpt, what would you think about that comment?

WEB QUEST
What's the famous quote attributed to P. T. Barnum that he apparently never said?

_____

▶ **TEST 1**   **Reviewing Key Concepts**

DIRECTIONS   Answer the following questions by filling in the blanks.

1. How is determining the author's purpose similar to identifying organizational patterns?

   _____

   _____

2. The key difference between a fact and an opinion is that statements of fact can be _____.

3. While facts rely on _____ language, opinions are likely to employ _____ language.

4. Unlike facts, opinions can't be _____, but they can be _____. They can be labeled _____

   _____.

5. How can a writer blend an opinion into a largely factual statement?

   _____

   _____

6. When an author's purpose is to persuade, you should expect the author to give you an _____.

7. Tone in writing is the _____

   _____.

8. If an author provides facts or reasons unrelated to the point of an argument, then he or she is using _____. But if the author restates the point of an argument as evidence why

readers should share his or her point of view, then the reasoning is

_____.

9. If the author tells you that children in elementary school are not learning to read and offers as evidence the example of his neighbor's child who, at the age of eight, still can't read, then you are

dealing with a _____.

10. If the author insists that there are only two ways to handle the situation described in a persuasive reading, then the chances are good

that you are being presented with _____.
But if the author tells you that the government's handling of finances is no different from how ordinary people have to balance their budgets, then you are being confronted with

a _____, because the government can print its own money. We can't.

▶ **TEST 2** **Identifying Fact, Opinion, or Both**

DIRECTIONS Label each sentence *F* for fact, *O* for opinion, or *M* for a mix of both.

1. Alan Mathison Turing (1912–1954) was an English mathematician whose brilliant career was senselessly destroyed when it was discovered that he was a homosexual.

    _____

2. A carcinogen is any agent that increases the chances of a cell becoming cancerous.

    _____

3. During World War I, Chile remained neutral.

    _____

4. Home shopping networks encourage viewers to engage in mindless consumerism.

    _____

5. Although most people don't realize it, eyewitnesses to crimes are extremely unreliable.

    _____

6. Reality television shows appeal to people who have no lives of their own.

    _____

7. A new species of land mammal has been discovered in the forests of Vietnam.

    _____

8. Son of an African-drummer father and a gourmet-chef mother, the talented rapper Lupe Fiasco was born Wasalu Muhammad Jaco.

   _____

9. Bruce Springsteen's 2012 album *Wrecking Ball* is probably the angriest record Springsteen has ever made, as he condemns with a vengeance those who have made fortunes at the expense of others.

   _____

10. The Japanese mushrooms called *maitake* sometimes grow as big as footballs.

    _____

▶ **TEST 3**   **Identifying Tone**

DIRECTIONS Circle the appropriate letter to identify the tone of each passage.

1. In August 2006, the *New York Times* published an article titled "Tale of the Tapeworm (Squeamish Readers Stop Here)." Readers who didn't take the warning seriously made a huge mistake. What the article reported on was the story of a woman who had, in the course of making gefilte fish, ingested a tapeworm, and here's where the squeamish should have stopped reading. When the tapeworm was removed from the woman's body, it turned out to be three feet long. The source of numerous and vague symptoms like fatigue and indigestion, the worm had been happily living in the woman's stomach for who knows how long. Disgusting as the idea may be, tapeworms can, in fact, do just that: take up residence in your body without your knowing it. Unless the body gets irritated by its guest and produces some symptoms, the tapeworm can make use of it for as long as twenty years. As if that thought weren't gross enough, tapeworms can, if undetected, grow as long as thirty feet. Consider that the next time you think about eating sushi.

   The tone is

   a. humorous.
   b. horrified.
   c. neutral.
   d. lighthearted.

2. Chimpanzees, who share nearly 99 percent of our DNA, are almost human, but you would never know it from the way we treat them. As photographer Michael Nichols has shown in his disturbing book *Brutal Kinship*, we use and abuse them at will for medical research, for entertainment, or simply out of personal greed. Determined to remain blind to their suffering, we refuse to grasp how like us they are. Chimpanzees nurture their young and mourn their dead. They have distinct personalities and can express a variety of emotions, from love to rage. Yet for all their similarities, we appear to think little of their pain and suffering if our interests are served. Leafing through the pages of Nichols's book, which is filled with images of

chimps in cages or lying vacant-eyed with tubes dangling from their arms, it's practically impossible to understand how we can torture and maim creatures who look and behave so much like ourselves.

The tone is

a. disgusted.

b. confident.

c. ironic.

d. neutral.

3. I'm on the couch because the dog on the blanket gets worried at night. During the day she sleeps the catnappy sleep of the elderly, but when it gets dark her eyes open and she is agitated.† I'm next to her. We are in this together, the dying game, and I read for hours in the evening with one foot on her back, getting up only to open a new can of beer or take blankets to the basement. At some point I stretch out on the vinyl couch and close my eyes, one hand hanging down, touching her side. By morning the dog arm has become a nerveless club that doesn't come around until noon. My friends think I am nuts. (Jo Ann Beard, "The Fourth State of Matter," *The Best American Essays 1997*, ed. Ian Frazier and Robert Atwan, p. 12.)

The tone is

a. angry.

b. grieving.

c. irritated.

d. neutral.

4. I'm afraid I have noticed an alarming development at our house. The dog is trying to talk. He is not at all interested in remaining The Creature in the Household Who Barks, which, I have explained to him again and again, is the only role for which he is suited. Oh, I've done all the right things to raise his self-esteem about this: I've assured him that forever and ever he will be the only one in the house who is permitted to bark, and that, in fact, is why we hired him as the family dog in the first place, so he would bark and maybe

---

†agitated: nervous.

protect us. I even told him that we *respect* him for his bark. You know what he says to this? "*Oowwww....*" (Sandi Shelton, *You Might as Well Laugh*, Bankcroft Press, 1997, p. 74.)

The tone is

a. surprised.

b. neutral.

c. comic.

d. angry.

5. For years, critics have argued about the ancient Greek play *Oedipus Rex*. Some have claimed that Oedipus knows nothing of his guilt until the end of the play, when it is revealed that he murdered his own father. Others have insisted that Oedipus is aware all along of his guilt. According to this point of view, Oedipus, the brilliant solver of riddles, could not possibly have ignored the mounting evidence that he was the king's murderer. Just how or why this debate has raged for so many years remains a mystery. The correct interpretation is so obvious. Oedipus knows from the beginning that he is guilty. He just pretends to be ignorant of the truth. For example, when a servant tells the story of the king's murder, he uses the word *bandits*. But when Oedipus repeats this story, he uses the singular form *bandit*. Sophocles provides clues like this throughout the play. Thus, it's hard to understand why anyone would think that Oedipus does not know the truth about his crime.

The tone is

a. lighthearted.

b. confident.

c. neutral.

d. outraged.

▶ **TEST 4** **Getting to the Point of an Argument**

DIRECTIONS Read each selection and identify the point of view the writer wants readers to share. Then circle the appropriate letter to identify the author's tone.

1. Do These Parents Talk to Their Kids?

1 According to a report of the National Campaign to Prevent Teen Pregnancy, 20 percent of adolescents have had sex before their fifteenth birthday. The report also revealed that only a third of these adolescents' parents know their children are sexually active. Such alarming statistics should cause us to wonder why parents aren't communicating more with their children.

2 Communication between parents and children is important, and far too many parents seem to be falling down on the job. How can two-thirds of them not know what their own children are doing? And why aren't they talking to their kids and making them understand the risks of becoming sexually active? Are these parents that oblivious to the temptations bombarding modern young people? Or are the parents simply too lazy or self-absorbed to concern themselves with how their own kids are spending their free time?

3 Whatever the reason for parents' apathy and ignorance, it's the kids who will ultimately pay the price. One in seven sexually active fourteen-year-old girls gets pregnant. And sexually experienced adolescents are far more likely than virgins to smoke, drink alcohol, and use drugs. Thanks to parents who won't get their heads out of the sand and watch their own kids, America's young people are growing up much too fast.

The author would like readers to agree that _____

_____.

The tone of the passage is

a. irate.

b. solemn.

c. ironic.

d. cautious.

2. The Genius of Camille Claudel

1 Camille Claudel (1864–1943) was an extraordinarily talented French sculptor, who initially was remembered largely for being the model, assistant, and mistress of the legendary artist Auguste Rodin, creator of the famous sculpture *The Kiss*. Camille Claudel, however, was a gifted sculptor in her own right. She created gorgeous marble and bronze sculptures such as *The Waltz*, *Wave*, and *The Age of Maturity*, which left even Rodin in awe of her talent.

2 These masterpieces have won Claudel posthumous, critical acclaim from many of today's art critics and historians. Yet, sadly, it took almost three-quarters of a century for her to get the recognition she fully deserved. For many years after her death, the genius she showed as a young artist was largely forgotten by all but a few art historians.

3 Some of those historians have argued that Claudel's talent was unfairly eclipsed by that of her teacher and lover. The respected and popular Rodin occupied a prominent place in French culture, and even though Claudel established her own reputation, she never quite managed to emerge from his shadow, especially during a time when being an artist was still considered a masculine calling.

4 After Claudel, pregnant with Rodin's child, lost their baby, she suffered serious bouts of depression. Her behavior became increasingly unstable and she was plagued by persecution fantasies. In despair because Rodin would not leave his wife, Claudel left Rodin in 1898 to strike out on her own, but her mental condition only worsened.

5 Tragically, Claudel's family, embarrassed by her free-wheeling lifestyle as an artist, used Claudel's depressed state to have her institutionalized in 1913 after her father died. However, her mother and brother refused all medical advice about providing Claudel with effective treatment, preferring to keep her locked away in order to protect the family name. While living on her own, Claudel had become notorious for insisting that she wanted to create her sculptures from nude models. That male artists used nude models was understood. But for a female artist of the time, it was a shocking demand. Her mother and brother seem not to have forgiven Claudel her "wild" behavior, and it was their preference that she be hospitalized for the rest of her life, which she was.

6 Claudel spent thirty years in an institution, forbidden to have any visitors except members of her family. During that time, she destroyed most of what she had accomplished during her years of confinement.

However, close to one hundred pieces of her work have survived. They are the basis of the acclaim she began to receive in the 1980s when feminist art historians began writing about her work and a film was made of her tragic but artistically productive and creative life.

The author would like readers to agree that _____

_____.

The tone of the passage is

a. critical.
b. cool.
c. sarcastic.
d. admiring.

▶ **TEST 5** **Identifying the Author's Point, Purpose, and Tone**

DIRECTIONS Read each selection and answer the questions that follow.

1. The Triumph of Maya Lin

1   When architectural student Maya Lin won the contest to design the Vietnam Veterans Memorial in 1981, many people—especially veterans—were shocked and angry. Her design, a long black wall inscribed with the names of those who died, was described as a "black gash of shame," and the resulting opposition and controversy came close to preventing Lin's design from ever being built.

2   However, when people now visit Lin's completed monument, they see a black granite wall that, while making no political statement about the war, cuts into the earth like the shiny scar of a deep wound. The wall lists the names of all of the men and women who lost their lives in the conflict. It is long and low, and every name is within reach. In its effect, the memorial invites the living to reach out and touch the names of the dead.

3   When visitors look at the wall, its polished mirrored surface reflects the ghosts of their own faces behind the names of fallen friends and loved ones. As a result, many visitors openly grieve, demonstrating the monument's ability to evoke powerful emotional responses that can help assuage grief. Even the memorial's opponents have changed their initial opinion about its design. They now agree that the wall is a moving tribute, which encourages visitors to reflect on the price of war while still honoring those who served. The pity is that it took so long for Lin's critics to recognize her achievement.

What is the author's point? _____

_____

What is the author's purpose? _____

How would you describe the author's tone? _____

_____

2. Columbus Revisited

1 When Columbus set sail in 1492, King Ferdinand and Queen Isabella of Spain wanted him to spread Christianity while fulfilling his promise of finding a route to Asia. Columbus, as it turned out, did neither, and it's a wonder why we have given him a national holiday.

2 When Columbus first sighted land, he thought he was somewhere in the East Indies, but he was actually stepping on shore of what is now Barbados. Claiming everything in sight as the property of Spain, Columbus demanded that the native population pay tribute, preferably in gold. If they refused outright or seemed to be making insufficient efforts to pay, their hands were chopped off per order of Columbus.

3 In 1493, as the governor of Hispaniola, now Haiti and the Dominican Republic, Columbus gifted the New World population with imported European diseases, malnutrition, overwork, and painful punishment for any failure to follow his orders. Eventually, Columbus's rule and its aftermath took a terrible toll, reducing the population to a mere 22,000 people.

4 With time even the Spanish missionaries, sent to help Columbus spread God's word, were alarmed by his behavior. One missionary reported that Columbus was guilty of "robbing and destroying the land." The missionary was appalled because Columbus thought nothing of cutting down a whole forest in order to have enough wood for heat and building construction. By 1500, even his Spanish sponsors knew their man was a failure. Stripped of his authority, Columbus was returned to Spain in chains at the command of the new governor.

5 In the light of his failures, we have to wonder about those people who claim that Columbus's voyage began a new era of exploration and that his great achievement is worthy of a federal holiday.

What is the author's point? _____

_____

What is the author's purpose? _____

How would you describe the author's tone? _____

_____

▶ TEST 6   Locating Errors in Logic

DIRECTIONS   Read each selection and then circle the appropriate letter or letters to identify the error in logic.

1. Fast food restaurants such as McDonald's, Burger King, and Taco Bell should be required to display warning notices about the fat content of the foods they sell. Animal studies have suggested that eating fatty foods seems to provoke addictive behavior. For example, rats fed a diet high in sugar exhibit signs of anxiety when the sugar is removed. Other research suggests that high-fat foods may stimulate the brain's pleasure centers, producing an effect similar to that of drugs such as nicotine and heroin. As a result, consumers have the right to be informed that eating fast food is just like getting hooked on drugs. The government requires cigarette manufacturers to print warning labels on every pack to inform consumers that smoking is an addictive habit that causes cancer and death. It stands to reason, then, that every fast food wrapper and carton should be similarly labeled to make it clear that their addictive contents will lead to obesity and death.

   a. irrelevant evidence

   b. careless comparison

   c. false alternatives

   d. hasty generalization

   e. circular reasoning

2. Kids today are being assigned far too much homework, so schools should require teachers to limit their after-school assignments to a maximum of one hour's worth of work. When children are forced to spend school nights doing hours of homework, they quickly learn to dislike both school and learning. Kids burn out quickly if their free time is filled up with assignments and projects. Children need their evenings free to play and relax. Plus, now more than ever, children should be spending quality time with their families in the evenings. If kids are always doing homework instead of bonding with family members, how can they possibly grow up with any sense of family values? Either we limit homework now, or kids will grow up believing

that academic achievement is more important than cultivating family relationships.

a. irrelevant evidence

b. careless comparison

c. false alternatives

d. hasty generalization

e. circular reasoning

3. George Balanchine, the Russian-born choreographer and dance teacher, founded the School of American Ballet in 1934. Best known as the prime mover at the New York City Ballet from 1948 to 1983, Balanchine has been called one of the finest creators of ballets the world has ever known. But if we examine his career without the blinders of hero worship, it's obvious that Balanchine possessed neither enormous talent nor great artistic vision. Out of the studio, Balanchine ignored dancers he had trained for years, pretending not to recognize members of his troupe when he bumped into them in restaurants or stores. Even Balanchine's fellow choreographers had to endure rude treatment: He was so self-centered he could scarcely remember their names.

a. irrelevant evidence

b. careless comparison

c. false alternatives

d. hasty generalization

e. circular reasoning

4. According to an American Management Association report, 78 percent of U.S. firms monitor their employees' communications in some way, and 47 percent read their workers' e-mail messages. Companies may argue that they monitor their workers only to guard company secrets or to protect themselves from potential lawsuits over harassment and other violations. But the fact remains that employers are spying on Americans whose privacy is protected by the U.S. Constitution. Yet employers record telephone conversations and videotape employees with surveillance cameras. Employees should be outraged by their employers' attempts to monitor their every

move. They should speak out against attempts to infringe upon their privacy. What's more, companies themselves should realize that stooping to snoop on their workers sends a bad message about how little trust or respect they have for their employees.

a. irrelevant evidence

b. careless comparison

c. false alternatives

d. hasty generalization

e. circular reasoning

5. Today's zookeepers claim to have learned the lessons of the past and are creating habitats for animals that take into account the animals' needs. Unfortunately, though, no matter how many plants, trees, rocks, and waterfalls are added to create more naturalistic settings, the creatures confined in zoo exhibits are still suffering from mistreatment. They may not be cruelly locked up in cramped cages as in the past, but they are still neglected and even beaten. When an elephant handler at the Oregon Zoo inflicted 176 gashes and cuts upon one of the beasts in his care, the truth became clear. The pretty, naturalistic settings of modern zoos do nothing more than camouflage the animal abuse occurring in these lovely locations.

a. irrelevant evidence

b. careless comparison

c. false alternatives

d. hasty generalization

e. circular reasoning

▶ **TEST 7**   **Reviewing Chapter 12 Vocabulary**

DIRECTIONS   Fill in the blank at the end of each sentence with a vocabulary word that could replace the underlined word or phrase.

vile	reparation	ineluctably	memoir	infirmity
discreet	euphemistically	oratory	forensics	retention

1. The last ten years seems to be the decade of the <u>personal life story</u>, when countless people, the famous, the infamous, and the generally unknown, have written about their private lives in great detail.

   _____

2. Periodic reviews will improve <u>the ability to remember new information long term.</u> _____

3. After meeting the divorcee Wallis Simpson, the King of England[†] knew he was moving <u>unavoidably</u> toward losing the throne. _____

4. The prisoner was very <u>careful</u> about handing his lawyer the letter he wanted sent without the authorities seeing what was in it.

   _____

5. The administrator expressed his displeasure <u>in a nice way</u> but still made it clear he was not happy with the team's performance.

   _____

6. For several years, the president made every effort to hide his <u>medical problem</u>, but the concealment and the painkillers had taken their toll. _____

_____

[†]In 1936, Edward VIII gave up his throne to marry a divorcee and a commoner, Wallis Simpson. Madonna made a movie about the romance called *W.E.*

7. The author Mark Twain loved making fun of people who were fond of <u>giving speeches</u>. _____

8. The head of the laboratory did not know the first thing about <u>scientific techniques used in the investigation of crimes</u>, so he hired people who did. _____

9. The concentration camp guard was a <u>disgusting</u> example of humanity. _____

10. The young district attorney tried to offer some form of <u>compensation</u> for the harm he had done. _____

Putting It All Together

The extended readings that follow give you a chance to review everything you have learned in Chapters 1–12. There are three sets of questions for each reading. *Getting the Gist* focuses on the kinds of questions that you might take on a standardized test in order to show that you have a general grasp of the material covered. The questions in *Taking a Closer Look* concentrate on both the content of the reading as well as the textual clues to meaning that writers have purposely left to help keep their readers on the right track. *Reading with a Critical Eye* tests your ability to evaluate what you have read and includes questions about word choice, fact and opinion, purpose, argument, and tone.

© Ulrich Flemming from *Found Art Around the World.*

◆ **READING 1** Communication and Identity

Ronald B. Adler and Russell F. Proctor

Looking Ahead This selection comes from a communications textbook titled *Looking Out/Looking In.* Each chapter of the book targets a particular aspect of how we present ourselves to the world in both one-on-one and group situations. Keep that larger context in mind as you read.

Word Watch Some of the more difficult words in the reading are defined below. The number in parentheses indicates the paragraph in which the word appears. An asterisk marks its first appearance in the reading. Preview the definitions before you begin reading and watch for the words while you read.

Topic

1ST Sen - M. I.

2ND Sen - Major Details

> **fundamental (5):** essential, basic
>
> **hypothetical (6):** in theory rather than practice, imagined but not yet real
>
> **genetic (9):** related to the genes that we inherit from our parents
>
> **extroversion (9):** a tendency to turn outward toward others, the inclination to be sociable
>
> **spectrum (10):** range
>
> **appraisals (13):** evaluations
>
> **metaphor (14):** implied comparison of two seemingly different things that actually share a similarity

Getting Focused The title is a strong clue to the content of the reading. By the time you finish it, make sure you can explain how self-concept influences communication.

> **TEXTBOOK TIP** Textbooks that explain how people think and behave—for instance, psychology, sociology, and communications texts—are very likely to introduce key theories by identifying the person or group who first publicly described or named the theory. When a name is introduced outside of parentheses or a footnote, check to see if a theory or term is associated with it. Record the name of the person along with the theory or definition in your notes.

Note how both the title and the questionnaire suggest the authors are writing about a topic like self-concept or personal identity.

Introduction: Defining Who You Are

1   Who are you? Take a moment now to answer this question and let the following list guide your answer. Try to include all the characteristics that describe you:

Your moods or feelings (for example, happy, angry, excited)
Your appearance (for example, attractive, short)
Your social traits (for example, friendly, shy)
Talents you have or do not have (for example, musical, nonathletic)
Your intellectual capacity (for example, school smart, street smart)
Your strong beliefs (for example, religious, environmental)
Your social roles (for example, parent, girlfriend)

2   Now take a look at what you've written. How did you define yourself? As a student? A man or woman? By your age? Your religion? Your occupation? There are many ways of identifying yourself. List as many ways as you can. You'll probably see that the words you've chosen represent a profile of what you view as your most important characteristics. In other words, if you were required to describe the "real you," this list ought to be a good summary.

The heading connects self-concept to communication, so be on the lookout for paragraphs that link the two.

Note the definition of self-concept, which is in boldface. It's a good idea to paraphrase key terms that aren't too technical.

What distinction is the author making in paragraph 6 between what and what?

Communication and the Self-Concept

3   What you've done in developing this list is to give a partial description of your **self-concept**: the relatively stable set of perceptions you hold of yourself. If a special mirror existed that reflected not only your physical features but also other aspects of yourself—emotional states, talents, likes, dislikes, values, roles, and so on—the reflection you'd see would be your self-concept. . . .

4   Of course, not every item on your self-concept list is equally important. For example the most significant part of one person's self-concept might consist of social roles, and for another person it might be physical appearance, health, friendships, accomplishments, or skills.

5   Whatever aspect of your self-concept you consider fundamental,* the concept of self is perhaps our most basic possession. Knowing who we are is essential because without a self-concept, it would be impossible to relate to the world.

6   **Self-esteem** is the part of the self-concept that involves evaluations of self-worth. A hypothetical* communicator's self-concept might include being quiet, argumentative, or serious. His or her self-esteem would be

determined by how he or she felt about these qualities: "I am glad that I am quiet," or "I am embarrassed about being so quiet," for example.

At the beginning of paragraph 7 the authors make a key connection between what two topics?

7   Figure 1 shows the relationship between self-esteem and communication behavior. People who feel good about themselves have positive expectations about how they will communicate. These expectations increase the chance that communication will be successful, and successes contribute to positive self-evaluations that reinforce self-esteem. Of course, the same principle can work in a negative way with communicators who have low self-esteem.

Figure 1   The Relationship Between Self-Esteem and Communication Behavior

Biological and Social Roots of the Self

8   How did you become the kind of communicator you are? Were you born that way? Are you a product of your environment? As you'll now see, the correct answer to the last two of these questions is "yes."

What is the relationship between the content of this heading and the previous chapter section?

9   **Biology and the Self**   Take another look at the "Who Am I?" list you developed at the beginning of the chapter. You will almost certainly find some terms that describe your personality—characteristic ways that you think and behave across a variety of situations. Your personality tends to be stable throughout your life. Often it grows more pronounced over time. Research suggests that personality is, to a large degree, part of our genetic* makeup. For example, people who were judged shy as children will show a distinctive reaction in their brains as adults when they encounter new situations. In fact, biology accounts for as much as half of some communication-related personality traits, including extroversion,* shyness, assertiveness, verbal aggression, and overall willingness to communicate. In other words, to some degree, we come "programmed" to communicate in certain ways. . . .

Note how the authors are using the phrase "genetic makeup" as a synonym for biology.

What in paragraph 9 would cause readers to worry in paragraph 10 that they are "stuck with a personality"?

The transition "second" signals continuation of the thought from the previous paragraph. The author is still saying "don't be distressed."

10   But before you become distressed about being stuck with a personality that makes communication difficult, keep two important points in mind. First realize that these traits are a matter of degree, not an either-or matter. It's an over-simplification to think of yourself as shy *or* sociable, argumentative *or* agreeable, self-controlled *or* spontaneous. It's more accurate to realize that almost everyone's personality fits at some point on a spectrum* for each trait. You may be somewhat shy, a little argumentative, or moderately self-controlled.

11   Second, while you may have a disposition toward traits like shyness or aggressiveness, you can do a great deal to control how you actually communicate. Even shy people can learn to reach out to others. And those with aggressive tendencies can learn to communicate in more sociable ways.

12   Finally, realize that although your personality may shape the way you communicate to a degree, your self-concept determines how you feel about the way you relate to others. Consider how different self-concepts can lead to very different ways of thinking about your method of communication:

Quiet	"I'm a coward for not speaking up."
	"I enjoy listening more than talking."
Argumentative	"I'm pushy, and that's obnoxious."
	"I stand up for my beliefs."
Self-controlled	"I'm too cautious."
	"I think carefully before I say or do things."

As you will soon see, our self-concept and self-esteem are shaped to a great extent by both the messages we receive from others and the way we think about ourselves.

Note how the heading serves to move the reader away from biological/ genetic explanations.

13   **Socialization and the Self-Concept**   How important are others in shaping our self-concept? Imagine growing up on a deserted island, with no one to talk to or share activities. How would you know how smart you are—or aren't? How would you gauge your attractiveness? How would you decide if you're short or tall, kind or mean, skinny or fat? Even if you could view your reflection in a mirror, you still wouldn't know how to evaluate your appearance without appraisals* from others or people with whom to compare yourself. In fact, the messages we receive from the people in our lives play the most important role in shaping how we regard ourselves.

Remember the opening textbook tip. Paragraph 14 gives you a chance to apply it.

C. Cooley-"reflected Appraisal" (1912)

14   As early as 1912, sociologist Charles Cooley used the ~~metaphor*~~ of a mirror to identify the process of **reflected appraisal**: the fact that each of us develops a self-concept that reflects the way we believe others see us. In other words, we are likely to feel less valuable, lovable, and capable to the degree that others have communicated ego-busting signals; and we will probably feel good about ourselves to the degree that others affirm our value. The principle of reflected appraisal will become clear when you realize that the self-concept you described in the list at the beginning of this chapter is a product of the positive and negative messages you have received throughout your life.

Look what you have broken now! How can you be so clumsy!

© Ulrich Flemming.

Notice how paragraph 15 opens with an introduction that identifies the function of the paragraph.

15   To illustrate this point further, let's start at the beginning. Children aren't born with any sense of identity. They learn to judge themselves only through the way others treat them. As children learn to speak and understand language, verbal messages contribute to a developing self-concept. Each day a child is bombarded with scores of messages about him- or herself. Some of these are positive: "You're so cute!" "I love you." "What a big girl." Other messages are negative: "What's the matter with you? Can't you do anything right?" "You're a bad boy." "Leave me alone. You're driving me crazy!" Evaluations like these are the mirror by which we know ourselves; and because children are trusting souls who have no other way of viewing themselves, they accept at face value both the positive and negative evaluations of the apparently all-knowing and all-powerful adults around them.

In paragraph 16, what does the phrase "this same principle" refer to?

16   This same principle in the formation of the self-concept continues in later life, especially when messages come from what sociologists term *significant others*—people whose opinions we especially value. Family

members are the most obvious type of significant others. Friends, teachers, and acquaintances, though, can also be significant others. To see the importance of significant others, ask yourself how you arrived at your opinion of yourself as a student, as a person attractive to others, as a competent worker, and you'll see that these self-evaluations were probably influenced by the way others regarded you. (Adapted from Adler and Proctor, *Looking Out/Looking In*, 12th ed., pp. 41–48. From Adler/Proctor/Towne, Freedom LL Version: *Looking Out/Looking In* (with CD-ROM and InfoTrac), 11th ed., © 2006 Cengage Learning.)

Close Up on Visual Aids

♦

In visual aids, the arrows are always important. The arrows in Figure 1 on page 686, help send a message to readers. Moving in a circle and pointing in the same direction, the arrows suggest which of the following?

a. High self-esteem leads to good behavior while low self-esteem leads to bad behavior.

b. Low self-esteem can produce negative thoughts and behavior that further contribute to low self-esteem.

c. Both positive and negative self-esteem affect how well we communicate and how well we communicate further raises or lowers our self-esteem.

Monitoring Your Comprehension

Review the marginal annotations and answer any questions posed. If you can't answer a question, mark the sentence or passage referred to and reread it before turning to the comprehension and critical reading questions.

GETTING THE GIST These questions are the kind you might encounter on a standardized reading test.

DIRECTIONS Identify the general gist, or point, of the authors' words by circling the appropriate letter.

1. According to the authors, what's the relationship between our self-concept and communication?

a. Until we develop a positive self-concept, it's unlikely that we would be good communicators.

b. How we view ourselves has a strong influence on how well or how effectively we communicate.

c. Communicating with others is a way of figuring out how they see us.

d. The ability to communicate only develops after we have a sense of self.

2. According to the authors, your self-concept is

a. largely a product of genetic inheritance.

b. developed by your interaction with those who are close to you.

c. a product of both genetic inheritance and interaction with others.

d. the result of parental training.

3. What's the difference between *self-concept* and *self-esteem*?

a. Self-concept refers to our conscience whereas self-esteem refers to our personality.

b. Self-concept is the self we see reflected in the eyes of others whereas self-esteem refers to our positive sense of self.

c. Self-concept refers to the internal image we have of who we are; self-esteem refers to the value we place on ourselves.

4. Which statement best paraphrases the term *reflected appraisal* in paragraph 14?

a. How much success we have in life affects how we see ourselves.

b. Our appraisal of ourselves influences the way we see others.

c. We develop our sense of self by seeing ourselves reflected in the eyes of others.

5. The cartoon with the chicken and the chick that broke the egg appears in the section titled "Socialization and the Self-Concept" to illustrate which of these three statements?

a. "Even if you could view your reflection in a mirror, you still wouldn't know how to evaluate your appearance without appraisals from others or people with whom to compare yourself."

b. "Children are trusting souls who have no other way of viewing themselves; they accept at face value both the positive and negative evaluations of the apparently all-knowing and all-powerful adults around them."

c. "As early as 1912, sociologist Charles Cooley used the metaphor of a mirror to identify the process of **reflected appraisal**."

TAKING A CLOSER LOOK This set of questions focuses on your understanding of the text, both its content and the language used to convey that content.

DIRECTIONS Answer the following questions on the blank lines provided or by circling the letter of the best response.

Paraphrasing
1. How would you paraphrase the author's definition of self-concept in paragraph 3?

_____

_____

Repetition and Reference
2. The title of the first chapter section is "Communication and the Self-Concept." In which paragraph do the authors connect communication with self-concept?

_____

Recognizing the Main Idea
3. In your own words, what is the connection between self-concept and communication?

_____

_____

Recognizing Patterns of Organization
4. What pattern of organization does the main idea of the reading suggest?

_____

Repetition and Reference
5. In paragraph 9, the authors use what word as a synonym for the word *self* introduced in the heading "Biology and the Self"?

_____

Understanding Figurative Language
6. Where's the metaphor in this sentence that appears at the end of paragraph 9, and what two things does it compare? "In other words, to some degree, we come 'programmed' to communicate in certain ways."

_____

_____

What is the point of the metaphor? What is it supposed to tell you about the communication?

_____

_____

Identifying and Evaluating Supporting Details

7. What category word in paragraph 10 helped you identify the major supporting details?

_____

8. Is the information in paragraph 11 essential or nonessential? _____ Please explain the basis for your answer.

_____

_____

Recognizing Sentence Functions

9. Which function does the concluding sentence in paragraph 12 fulfill?

a. It provides a major supporting detail that supports the main idea of the paragraph.

b. It explains how some person or event mentioned in the paragraph changed over time.

c. It provides a transition to specific examples illustrating the main idea.

Recognizing Explanatory Patterns

10. At the beginning of paragraph 13, the authors pose this question: "How important are others in shaping our self-concept?" Where in the paragraph does that question get answered?

_____

Paraphrasing

11. In your own words, how do the authors answer the opening question in paragraph 13?

_____

Understanding
Transitions

12. Paragraph 15 opens with a transitional phrase that tells *readers*

    a. the authors are making a new and different point.

    b. the authors are continuing the same thought but adding an example.

    c. the authors are going to slightly revise what's just been said.

Repetition and
Reference

13. In paragraph 15, the following statements—some positive, some negative—all illustrate what previous phrase in the paragraph? "You're so cute!" "I love you." "What a big girl." "What's the matter with you? Can't you do anything right?" "You're a bad boy."

    _____

14. Paragraph 16 opens with the phrase "This same principle." To what principle are the authors referring?

    _____

Recognizing
Patterns of
Organization

15. What would you say is the primary organizational pattern in this reading?

    _____

READING WITH A CRITICAL EYE The goal here is not to be critical in the negative sense, but rather to understand how fact, opinion, argument, and tone reinforce the authors' apparent purpose.

DIRECTIONS Answer the questions on the blank lines provided or by circling the letter of the correct response.

Fact and Opinion

1. How would you label this statement from paragraph 9? "In fact, biology accounts for as much as half of some communication-related personality traits...."

    a. It's a fact.

    b. It's an opinion.

    c. It's a mix of both.

Analyzing
Arguments

2. In paragraph 13, the image of the deserted island is used to make what point?

_____

_____

3. In paragraph 16, the authors say this: "To see the importance of significant others, ask yourself how you arrived at your opinion of yourself as a student, as a person attractive to others, as a competent worker, and you'll see that these self-evaluations were probably influenced by the way others regarded you." What's the point of the argument?

_____

What's the evidence for that point?

_____

_____

4. How would you evaluate the evidence? Do you consider it solid or shaky? _____

Please explain. _____

_____

Identifying Purpose

5. How would you label the authors' purpose?
   a. purely informative
   b. purely persuasive
   c. primarily informative with some persuasion included
   d. primarily persuasive with some informative writing included

Share Your Thoughts When you were growing up, what kinds of messages do you think you received from the world around you? Do you think those messages had a powerful effect as the authors suggest they do? Please explain why or why not.

From Reader to Writer Describe the person who you believe contributed most significantly to your self-concept. Make sure to explain how that person shaped your sense of self and why he or she was so critical to your personal development.

◆ **READING 2**   # Is Neutralization Necessary?

Larry J. Siegel

Looking Ahead This selection comes from a criminology textbook. But it too deals with the issue of how self-concept and self-esteem affect behavior.

Word Watch Some of the more difficult words in the reading are defined below. The number in parentheses indicates the paragraph in which the word appears. An asterisk marks its first appearance in the reading. Preview the definitions before you begin reading and watch for the words while you read.

> **subterranean (2):** underground
>
> **justifications (4):** explanations as to why behavior is appropriate or right
>
> **novice (4):** new, inexperienced
>
> **inconclusive (4):** not leading to a definite conclusion or eliminating doubt
>
> **norms (6):** rules or standards for social behavior
>
> **data (7):** information
>
> **gleaned (7):** gathered, figured out, gradually understood
>
> **provocation (8):** cause or reason for action
>
> **whim (9):** quickly changing mood or desire
>
> **opportunism (9):** readiness to take advantage of others without regard for the consequences
>
> **universally (10):** done or felt by all people in a group, appearing in all cultures

Getting Focused Make sure you determine what the term *neutralization* in the context of criminology means. Also, since the title questions how necessary it is, there must be some opposition, challenge, or contradiction described in the reading. Be on the lookout for some person or group who doesn't think neutralization is important.

TEXTBOOK TIP Criminology, like communications, sociology, and psychology, focuses on theories of behavior. Only within the context of criminology, the focus is on criminal behavior, rather than the everyday behavior of ordinary life.

Look for the names of the people who came up with theories about why people engage in criminal behavior. Make sure you understand the theory or theories they have proposed and be on the lookout as well for criticism or challenges to the explanations offered. Textbooks likely to offer theoretical explanations are just as likely to offer opposition to or criticisms of those explanations.

1   *Neutralization Theory* is identified with the writings of David Matza and his associate Gresham Sykes. They view the process of becoming a criminal as a learning experience in which potential delinquents and criminals master techniques that enable them to counterbalance or *neutralize* conventional, or traditional, values and drift back and forth between illegitimate and conventional behavior.

Typically for academic writing, the pronoun this *is the link to the previous paragraph.*

2   One reason this is possible is the subterranean* value structure of American society. **Subterranean values** are morally tinged influences that have become entrenched in the culture but are publicly condemned. They exist side by side with conventional values and while condemned in public may be admired or practiced in private. Examples include viewing pornographic films, drinking alcohol to excess, and gambling on sporting events.

3   Matza argues that even the most committed criminals and delinquents are not involved in criminality all the time. They also attend schools, family functions, and religious services. Their behavior can be conceived as falling along a continuum between total freedom and total restraint. This process, which he calls **drift**, refers to the movement from one extreme of behavior to another, resulting in behavior that is sometimes unconventional, free, or deviant, and at other times constrained and sober. Learning techniques of neutralization enable a person to temporarily "drift away" from conventional behavior and get involved in more subterranean values and behaviors, including crime and drug abuse.

What does drift *have to do with neutralization?*

4   Sykes and Matza suggest that people develop a distinct set of justifications* for their law-violating behavior. These techniques of neutralization include the following patterns:

Never ignore a list, especially one with an italicized term after each number. This is practically an announcement

1. *Deny responsibility*. Offenders sometimes claim their unlawful acts were simply not their fault. Criminal acts resulted from forces beyond their control or were accidents.

2. *Deny injury*. Criminals neutralize illegal behavior by denying the wrongfulness of the act. For example, stealing is viewed as borrowing. Vandalism is considered mischief that has gotten out of hand.

for an essay question, "Describe the techniques of neutralization."

3. *Deny the victim*. Criminals sometimes neutralize wrongdoing by maintaining that the victim of crime "had it coming." Vandalism may be directed against a disliked teacher or neighbor; or homosexuals may be beaten up by a gang because their behavior is considered offensive.

4. *Condemn condemners*. An offender views the world as a corrupt place with a dog-eat-dog code. Because police and judges are on the take, teachers show favoritism, and parents take out their frustrations on their kids, it is ironic and unfair for these authorities to condemn his or her misconduct.

5. *Appeal to higher loyalties*. Novice* criminals often argue that they are caught in the dilemma of being loyal to their own peer group while at the same time attempting to abide by the rules of the larger society.

In sum, the theory of neutralization suggests that people who engage in deviant behavior neutralize that behavior with slogans like "I didn't mean to do it." "They had it coming to them." "Everyone is picking on me."

Testing Neutralization Theory

The heading says the author's explanation is changing direction.

5 Attempts have been made to verify the assumptions of neutralization theory. But the results have been inconclusive.* So far the evidence is mixed. Some studies show that law violators approve of criminal behavior. Still others find evidence that even though they may be active participants themselves, criminals voice disapproval of illegal behavior.

Sometimes Being Bad Is Good

6 In their neutralization theory, Sykes and Matza claim that neutralizations provide offenders with a means of preserving a noncriminal self-concept even as they engage in crime and deviance. Sykes and Matza's vision assumes that most criminals believe in conventional norms* and values and must use neutralizations in order to shield themselves from the shame attached to criminal activity.

How does Topalli challenge the theory of neutralization?

7 Recent research by criminologist Volkan Topalli finds that Sykes and Matza may have ignored the influential street culture that exists in highly disadvantaged neighborhoods. Using data* gleaned* from 191 in-depth interviews with active criminals in St. Louis, Missouri, Topalli finds that street criminals living in disorganized, gang-ridden neighborhoods "disrespect authority, lionize honor and violence, and place individual needs above those of all others." Rather than having to neutralize conventional values in order to engage in deviant ones, these offenders do not experience guilt that requires neutralization. They are "guilt free." There is no need for them to "drift" into criminality, Topalli finds, because their

allegiance to nonconventional values and lack of guilt perpetually leave them in a state of openness to crime.

8   Rather than being contrite, or ashamed, the offenders Topalli interviewed took great pride in their criminal activities and abilities. Bacca, a street robber who attacked a long-time neighbor without provocation,* exemplified such sentiments:

> Actually I felt proud of myself just for robbing him, just for doing what I did. I felt proud of myself. I didn't feel like I did anything wrong. I didn't feel like I lost a friend cause the friends I do have … are lost. They're dead. I feel like I don't have anything to lose. I wanted to do just what I wanted to do.

9   Topalli refers to streetwise offenders such as Bacca as "hardcores," who experience no guilt for their actions and operate with little or no regard for the law. They have little contact with agents of formal social control or conventional norms because their crimes are not directed toward conventional society—they rob drug dealers. Most hardcores maintain no permanent home, staying in various residences as their whim* dictates. Their lifestyles are almost entirely dominated by the street ethics of violence, self-sufficiency, and opportunism.* Obsessed with a constant need for cash, drugs, and alcohol in order to "keep the party going," on the one hand and limited by self-defeating and reckless spending habits on the other, they often engage in violent crime to bankroll their street life activities. They do not have to neutralize conventional values because they have none.

What change in attitude toward neutralization is the author outlining here?

10   Rather than neutralizing conventional values, hardcore criminals often have to neutralize deviant values. They are expected to be "bad" and have to explain good behavior. Even if they themselves are the victims of crime, they can never help police or even talk to them, a practice defined as snitching and universally* despised and discouraged. Smokedog, a carjacker and drug dealer, described the anticipated guilt of colluding with the police in this way, "You know I ain't never told on nobody and I ain't never gonna tell on nobody 'cause I would feel funny in the world if I told on somebody. You know, I would have regrets about what I did."

11   Street criminals are expected to seek vengeance if they are the target of theft or violence. If they don't, their self-image is damaged and they look weak and ineffective. If they decide against vengeance, they must neutralize their decision by convincing themselves that they are being merciful, respecting direct appeals by their target's family and friends. T-dog, a young drug dealer and car thief, told Topalli how he neutralized the decision not to seek revenge by allowing his uncle to "calm him

down." The older man, a robber and drug dealer himself, intervened before T-dog could leave his house armed with two 9 mm automatics. "That's basically what he told me. 'Calm down.' He took both my guns and gave me a little .22 to carry when I'm out to put me back on my feet. Gave me an ounce of crack and a pound of weed. That's what made me let it go." In other words, offenders claimed the target was just not worth the effort, reserving their vengeance for those who were worthy opponents.

(Excerpted from Larry Siegel, *Criminology*, 10th ed., pp. 222–25. © 2010 Cengage Learning.)

Monitoring Your Comprehension Review the marginal annotations and answer any questions posed. If you can't answer a question, mark the sentence or passage referred to and re-read it before turning to the comprehension and critical reading questions.

GETTING THE GIST These questions are the kind you might encounter on a standardized reading test.

DIRECTIONS Identify the general gist, or point, of the author's words by circling the appropriate letter.

1. Which statement best expresses the overall main idea of this reading?
   a. The neutralization patterns described by Sykes and Matza seem to be backed by solid evidence.
   b. Some recent research challenges the basis of neutralization theory suggesting that criminals are genetically programmed to commit crimes and are, therefore, not subject to the pangs of conscience.
   c. There are many different theories about the origins of criminal behavior.
   d. While Sykes and Matza suggest that criminals have to somehow neutralize, or justify, their illegal behavior, criminologist Volkan Topalli argues that criminals gain status from deviant behavior and don't have to neutralize it.

2. Which statement best paraphrases the views of criminologist Volkan Topalli?
   a. Criminals never quite overcome their fear of being outside of society and cut off from the life led by law-abiding citizens.
   b. Criminals are not born. They are created by lives that offer no hope for a better future and therefore make criminal behavior, with its immediate rewards, seem more appealing.

    c. Criminals aren't ashamed of their behavior because they are following their own subculture's rules and don't need to neutralize society's rules or their behavior in order to commit a crime.

    d. Criminals are genetically programmed to carry out illegal activities and thus remain untouched by the rules of society and have no need to neutralize deviant behavior.

3. Which definition of *hardcores* fits the definition in the text?

    a. *Hardcores* are people who are addicted to pornography.

    b. *Hardcores* are people who have no heart and no sympathy for others.

    c. *Hardcores* are people who commit crimes and feel no guilt about their behavior.

    d. *Hardcores* commit violent crimes without any hesitation.

4. Criminal culture, as defined in this reading, places a high emphasis on

    a. loyalty.

    b. courage.

    c. vengeance.

    d. secrecy.

5. Which statement best sums up Volkan Topalli's response to the theory of Sykes and Matza?

    a. Neutralization theory doesn't take into account the genetic basis for criminal behavior.

    b. Neutralization theory is just that, a theory without a strong basis in research.

    c. Neutralization theory does not recognize the important role street culture plays in a criminal's value system.

    d. Neutralization theory made more sense before the rise of an urban culture that left people feeling more disconnected from one another.

TAKING A CLOSER LOOK   This set of questions focuses on your understanding of the text, both its content and the language used to convey that content.

DIRECTIONS   Answer the following questions on the blank lines provided or by circling the letter of the best response.

Recognizing Patterns of Organization

1. What organizational pattern is central to the first paragraph?

     _____

Paraphrasing

2. According to Sykes and Matza, what do criminals need to do?

     _____

     _____

Repetition and Reference

3. In the second paragraph, what does the opening pronoun *this* refer to?

     _____

     _____

Paraphrasing

4. In your own words, what is *drift*?

     _____

5. What connection do Sykes and Matza make between drift and neutralization techniques?

     _____

     _____

6. According to the authors, what is Topalli's view of drift?

     _____

Repetition and Reference

7. In the following pair of sentences, the phrase "these techniques of neutralization" refers to what phrase in the first sentence? "Sykes and Matza suggest that people develop a distinct set of justifications for their law-violating behavior. These techniques of neutralization include the following patterns."

     _____

Seeing Transitions **8.** In what paragraph do the authors begin to describe a challenge to the neutralization theory developed by Sykes and Matza?

_____

Monitoring Your **9.** Based on your understanding of paragraph 7, how would you fill in
Comprehension the blanks left in this statement?

According to Topalli, _____ don't have to

_____ their traditional _____
because they don't have them in the first place.

10. What evidence has Topalli offered in support of his claim?

_____

11. In paragraph 8, the story about Bacca is used to support what main idea?

_____

Repetition and **12.** Throughout paragraph 9, what do the pronouns _they_ and _their_
Reference refer to?

_____

Understanding **13.** Smokedog is introduced in paragraph 10 in order to illustrate what
Supporting Details main idea?

_____

_____

14. In paragraph 11, why is the story of T-dog introduced? What point does it support?

_____

_____

_____

_____

Recognizing
Patterns of
Organization

15. Overall, what are the primary patterns of organization in this reading?

a. classification, process, and definition

b. definition and simple listing

c. comparison and contrast, simple listing, and classification

d. comparison and contrast, definition, and cause and effect

READING WITH A CRITICAL EYE The goal here is not to be critical in the negative sense, but rather to understand how fact, opinion, argument, and tone reinforce the author's apparent purpose.

DIRECTIONS Answer the questions on the blank lines provided or by circling the letters of the correct response.

Analyzing
Arguments

1. The reading presents two opposing points of view. Briefly describe each one.

Sykes and Matza: _____

_____

Topalli: _____

_____

2. What evidence do the authors offer for each side of the debate?

Sykes and Matza: _____

_____

_____

Topalli: _____

_____

_____

3. Based on the evidence, which argument to do you find more convincing?

_____

_____

_____

Purpose 4. How would you label the author's purpose?

    a. purely informative

    b. purely persuasive

    c. primarily informative with some persuasion included

    d. primarily persuasive with some informative writing included

Bias 5. Which statement best describes the author's attitude toward the issue discussed in the reading?

    a. The author supports the neutralization theory of Sykes and Matza.

    b. The author favors Topalli's explanation.

    c. It's impossible to determine the author's personal bias.

Share Your Thoughts Which theory described in reading 2 better fits what you learned about self-concept in reading 1?

From Reader to Writer Write a brief paper that opens with a summary of the theory put forth by Sykes and Matza. Then use a reversal transition word, phrase, or sentence to point out how Topalli disagrees. In the last paragraph, explain your own position. Tell your readers which theory seems to make more sense and why.

◆ **READING 3**   Memory, Perception, and Eyewitness Testimony

Douglas A. Bernstein, Louis A. Penner, Alison Clarke-Stewart, and
Edward J. Roy

Looking Ahead Reading 2 talked about crime from the criminal's point of view. This one discusses it from the point of view of the eyewitness. In many criminal cases, defendants are convicted based on what eyewitnesses say they saw. However, in this selection from a psychology textbook, the authors point out the dangers of trusting eyewitness testimony.

Word Watch Some of the more difficult words in the reading are defined below. The number in parentheses indicates the paragraph in which the word appears. An asterisk marks its first appearance in the reading. Preview the definitions before you begin reading and watch for the words while you read.

---

constructive memory (1): the theory that memories can be transformed when the mind adds later experiences to the original remembrance

DNA evidence (1): proof based on the body's DNA molecules, which are like a blueprint for everything in an individual's body; this means that, except in the case of identical twins, DNA evidence is unique to the person from whom it was derived

perceive (2): recognize; absorb into consciousness

stimulus (2): something that causes a response

assumption (4): belief that is considered to be true and therefore does not require proof

prosecution (5): related to the lawyers who make a case against a defendant during legal proceedings

inherent (8): inborn; naturally a part of

amplified (8): made more powerful

miscarriages (11): failures

arrays (12): arrangements

Getting Focused In this selection, the authors are inclined to follow general statements with specific examples. Try paraphrasing the general statements in the margins. Then use arrows to point out the examples. To take your understanding a step deeper, write your own examples in the margins across from the authors' examples.

> **TEXTBOOK TIP** Psychology texts usually include broad general statements about human behavior and thinking. But they seldom generalize without offering specific incidents, examples, or studies that support the general point. Each time you see a general statement about how people are likely to behave or think, make sure you can match the general statement with the proof of its accuracy.

As you read, notice the way references to mistakes have become a constant theme.

Here you have a typical textbook template in which the last sentence of the first paragraph tells readers what the chapter section will do.

1   There are few situations in which accurate retrieval of memories is more important—and constructive memory* is more dangerous—than when an eyewitness testifies in court about a crime. Eyewitnesses provide the most compelling evidence in many trials, but they can sometimes be mistaken. In 1984, for example, a North Carolina college student, Jennifer Thompson, confidently identified Ronald Cotton as the man who had raped her at knifepoint. Mainly on the basis of Thompson's testimony, Cotton was convicted of rape and sentenced to life in prison. After eleven years behind bars, DNA evidence* revealed that he was innocent (and it identified another man as the rapist). The eyewitness victim's certainty had convinced a jury, but her memory had been faulty (O'Neill, 2000). Let's consider the accuracy of eyewitness memory and how it can be distorted.

2   Like the rest of us, eyewitnesses can remember only what they perceive,* and they can perceive only what they attend to. Perception is influenced by a combination of the stimulus* features we find "out there" in the world and what we already know, expect, or want.

After you finish paragraphs 3 and 4, see if you can paraphrase two of the "limits" mentioned here.

3   Witnesses are asked to report exactly what they saw or heard; but no matter how hard they try to be accurate, there are limits to how faithful their reports can be. For one thing, during the time that information is encoded and stored in long-term memory, certain details can be lost. Further, the appearance of new information, including information contained in questions posed by police or lawyers, can alter a witness's memory (Belli & Loftus, 1996). In one study, when witnesses were asked, "How fast were the cars going when they *smashed into* each other?" they were likely to recall a higher speed than when they were asked, "How fast were the cars going when they *hit* each other?" (Loftus & Palmer, 1974). See Figure 2.

Note the category word ways. Make sure you can itemize them by the end of the paragraph.

4   There is also evidence that an object mentioned during questioning about an incident is often mistakenly remembered as having been there during the incident. So if a lawyer says that a screwdriver was lying on the ground (when it was not), witnesses often recall with great certainty having seen it. This *misinformation effect* can occur in several ways. In some cases, hearing new information can make it harder to retrieve the original

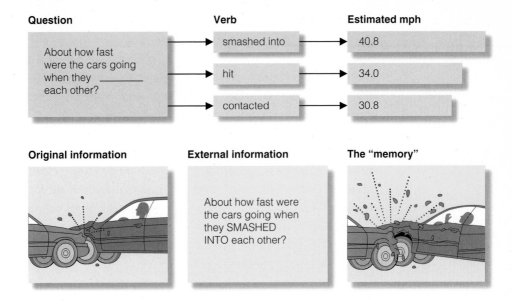

Question	Verb	Estimated mph
About how fast were the cars going when they _____ each other?	smashed into	40.8
	hit	34.0
	contacted	30.8

Original information

External information

About how fast were the cars going when they SMASHED INTO each other?

The "memory"

Figure 2 The Impact of Questioning on Eyewitness Memory

After seeing a filmed traffic accident, people were asked, "About how fast were the cars going when they (smashed into, hit, or contacted) each other?" As shown here, the witnesses' responses were influenced by the verb used in the question; "smashed" was associated with the highest average speed estimates. A week later, people who heard the "smashed" question remembered the accident as being more violent than did people in the other two groups (Loftus & Palmer, 1974).

(From G. R. Loftus and E. F. Loftus, *Human Memory: The Processing of Information*. Copyright 1976. Reprinted with permission of Lawrence Erlbaum Associates, Inc.)

memory. In others, the new information may be integrated into the old memory, making it impossible to distinguish the new information from what was originally seen (Loftus, 1992). In still others, an eyewitness report might be influenced by the person's assumption* that if a lawyer or police officer says an object was there or that something happened, it must be true.

How can the way a witness testifies make a difference?

5   A jury's belief in a witness's testimony often depends as much (or even more) on *how* the witness presents evidence as on the content or relevance of that evidence (Leippe, Manion, & Romanczyk, 1992). Many jurors are impressed, for example, by witnesses who give lots of details about what they saw or heard. Extremely detailed testimony from prosecution* witnesses is especially likely to lead to guilty verdicts, even when the details reported are irrelevant (Bell & Loftus, 1989). When a witness gives highly detailed testimony, such as the exact time of the crime or the color of the criminal's shoes, jurors apparently assume that the witness paid especially close attention or has a particularly accurate memory.

What does "at first glance" suggest about what follows?

6   At first glance, these assumptions seem reasonable. However, the ability to divide attention is limited. As a result, witnesses might be able to focus attention on the crime and the criminal, or on the surrounding details, but probably not on both—particularly if they were emotionally aroused and the crime happened quickly. So witnesses who accurately remember unimportant details of a crime scene may not accurately recall more important ones, such as the criminal's facial features (Backman & Nilsson, 1991).

How can you tell from the first sentence that the authors are continuing the same train of thought?

7   Juries also tend to believe witnesses who are confident. Unfortunately, witnesses' confidence in their testimony often exceeds its accuracy (Shaw, 1996). Repeated exposure to misinformation and the repeated recall of misinformation can increase a witness's confidence in testimony, whether or not it is accurate. In other words, as in the Jennifer Thompson case, even witnesses who are confident about their testimony are not always correct.

What new element has been introduced that adds to the possibility of error?

8   The weaknesses inherent* in eyewitness memory can be amplified* by the use of police lineups and certain other criminal identification procedures (Wells & Olson, 2003). In one study, for example, participants watched a videotaped crime and then tried to identify the criminal from a set of photographs (Wells & Bradfield, 1999). None of the photos showed the person who had committed the crime, but some participants nevertheless identified one of them as the criminal they saw on tape.

9   When these mistaken participants were led to believe that they had correctly identified the criminal, they became even more confident in the accuracy of their false identification. These incorrect, but confident, witnesses became more likely than other participants to claim that it had been easy for them to identify the criminal from the photos because they had had a good view of him and had paid careful attention to him.

Remember Ronald Cotton from the opening of the reading? Why is he referred to now?

10   Since 1973, at least 115 people, including Ronald Cotton, have been released from U.S. prisons in twenty-five states after DNA tests or other evidence revealed that they had been falsely convicted—mostly on the basis of faulty eyewitness testimony (Death Penalty Information Center, 2004; Scheck, Neufeld, & Dwyer, 2000; Wells, Malpass et al., 2000). DNA evidence freed Charles Fain, who had been convicted of murder and spent almost eighteen years on death row in Idaho (Bonner, 2001). Maryland officials approved $900,000 in compensation for Bernard Webster, who served 20 years in prison for rape before DNA revealed that he was innocent (Associated Press, 2003).

11   Frank Lee Smith, too, would have been set free after the sole eyewitness at his murder trial retracted her testimony, but he had already

died of cancer while awaiting execution in a Florida prison. Research on memory and perception helps explain how these miscarriages* of justice can occur, and it is also guiding efforts to prevent such errors in the future.

12   The U.S. Department of Justice has acknowledged the potential for errors in eyewitness evidence, as well as the dangers of asking witnesses to identify suspects from lineups and photo arrays.* The result was *Eyewitness Evidence: A Guide for Law Enforcement* (U.S. Department of Justice, 1999), the first-ever guide for police and prosecutors who work with eyewitnesses. The guide warns these officials that asking leading questions about what witnesses saw can distort their memories. It also suggests that witnesses should examine photos of possible suspects one at a time and points out that false identifications are less likely if witnesses viewing suspects in a lineup are told that the real criminal might not be included. (From Douglas A. Bernstein et al., *Psychology*, 7th ed., © 2006 Cengage Learning.)

Monitoring Your Comprehension Review the marginal annotations and answer any questions posed. If you can't answer the questions, mark the sentence or paragraph referred to and re-read it before turning to the comprehension and critical reading questions.

GETTING THE GIST   These questions are the kind you might encounter on a standardized reading test.

DIRECTIONS   Identify the general gist, or point, of the authors' words by circling the appropriate letter.

1. Which statement best expresses the main idea of the entire reading?
    a. The wording of questions can distort the memories of crime victims and eyewitnesses.
    b. Because eyewitnesses can and do make mistakes, innocent people have been wrongly convicted of crimes.
    c. People's memories are, in general, not very reliable, but eyewitnesses are particularly inclined to distort reality.
    d. Many innocent people have been convicted of crimes they did not commit; fortunately, DNA evidence has been used to exonerate them and set them free.

2. What do the authors say about police procedures used to identify wrongdoers?

   a. Some of the techniques police use are helpful whereas others are not.

   b. Having crime victims look at photographs is an ineffective criminal identification technique.

   c. Procedures that police use to help eyewitnesses identify criminals can encourage distorted memories of events.

   d. Eyewitnesses are intimidated by police authority and tend to say what the police want them to say.

3. Why do the authors mention victim Jennifer Thompson and/or accused rapist Ronald Cotton three times throughout the reading?

   a. They illustrate the authors' point that the wording of questions often distorts eyewitnesses' memories.

   b. Their example supports the idea that, in spite of its flaws, eyewitness testimony is usually accurate.

   c. They illustrate the idea that bystander-eyewitnesses tend to recall details more accurately than victim eyewitnesses do.

   d. Their story supports the idea that an individual can be falsely convicted on the basis of eyewitness testimony.

4. According to the authors, jury members often make the mistake of believing eyewitnesses who

   a. speak clearly and slowly.

   b. are confident and remember lots of details.

   c. correct themselves during their testimony in order to make sure that what they say is accurate.

   d. admit that they were scared during the commission of the crime.

5. According to the authors, the government

   a. shares their point of view about the inaccuracy of eyewitness testimony.

   b. doesn't believe that eyewitness testimony is prone to so much error.

   c. recognizes the potential for error in eyewitness testimony.

   d. has no interest in improving the accuracy of eyewitness testimony.

TAKING A CLOSER LOOK   This set of questions focuses on your understanding of the text, both its content and the language used to convey that content.

DIRECTIONS   Answer the following questions on the blank lines provided or by circling the letter of the best response.

Recognizing Thesis Statements

1. The thesis statement of the reading appears in
   a. paragraph 1.
   b. paragraph 2.
   c. paragraph 3.

   The thesis statement appears
   a. at the beginning of the paragraph.
   b. right after a reversal transition.
   c. at the end.
   d. at the beginning and the end.

Paraphrasing Supporting Details

2. In paragraph 2, the authors say perception is influenced by two factors. In your own words what are those two factors?

   1. _____

   2. _____

Recognizing and Paraphrasing Topic Sentences

3. The topic sentence in paragraph 3 is
   a. the first sentence.
   b. the second sentence.
   c. in the middle of the paragraph.
   d. the last sentence of the paragraph.

4. In your own words, what does that topic sentence of paragraph 3 tell readers?

   _____

   _____

Recognizing
Transitions

5. What two transitions introduce support for the main idea of paragraph 3?

_____

Making Connections

6. Does paragraph 4 continue to develop the main idea from paragraph 3 or does it introduce a new point?

_____

Understanding
Supporting Details

7. Why is a screwdriver mentioned in paragraph 4?

_____

_____

_____

Paraphrasing

8. Which of the following statements accurately paraphrases the *misinformation effect* introduced in paragraph 4?

a. Human memory is limited in the amount of detail it can store and some details of an experience are bound to get forgotten.

b. Information people hear or see after an event has occurred often gets added to the memory of the event.

c. When people are told by an authority figure that something is true, they are inclined to believe it.

Understanding
Supporting Details

9. What category word in paragraph 4 directs readers to the major supporting details? _____

Repetition and
Reference

10. Paragraph 6 opens with the statement, "At first glance, these assumptions seem reasonable." What does the phrase "these assumptions" refer to?

_____

_____

Making Connections

11. What should that opening phrase in paragraph 6 suggest to readers?

_____

Recognizing Topic **12.** In paragraph 8, the topic sentence is
Sentences
a. the first sentence.

b. the second sentence.

c. the concluding sentence.

d. the opening and closing sentences.

Understanding **13.** Why are Ronald Cotton, Charles Fain, Bernard Webster, and Frank
Supporting Details Lee Smith mentioned in paragraphs 10 and 11?

_____

_____

Recognizing **14.** What is the primary organizational pattern in this reading?
Patterns of
Organization _____

Understanding **15.** The reference to *Eyewitness Evidence: A Guide for Law Enforcement*
Supporting Details appears in paragraph 12 to back up what point?

_____

_____

Close Up on Visual Aids

◆

Look closely at Figure 2. Like the figure on page 707, this one makes use of arrows, and the direction of the arrows is important. In your own words what do the arrows indicate about the relationship between *Question*, *Verb*, and *Estimated mph*?

_____

_____

Box by box, explain what the boxes labeled *Original information*, *External information*, and *The "memory"* illustrate for the reader.

1. "Original information" shows _____.

2. "External information" shows _____.

3. "The memory" indicates _____.

_____

READING WITH A CRITICAL EYE The goal here is not to be critical in the negative sense, but rather to understand how fact, opinion, argument, and tone reinforce the authors' apparent purpose.

DIRECTIONS Answer the questions on the blank lines provided or by circling the letter of the correct response.

Fact and Opinion
1. The following statement in paragraph 5 is an opinion: "A jury's belief in a witness's testimony often depends as much (or even more) on *how* the witness presents evidence as on the content or relevance of that evidence." How would you describe this opinion?
   a. informed
   b. uninformed

   Please explain.

   _____

   _____

Recognizing Tone
2. How would you describe the authors' tone?
   a. infuriated
   b. puzzled
   c. argumentative
   d. confident

Identifying Purpose
3. Can you cite passages in the text where the authors suggest an opposing point of view about eyewitness testimony? _____ What does that suggest to you?

   _____

   _____

4. What do you think is the authors' primary purpose?
   a. The authors want to tell readers about the various ways eyewitness testimony can occasionally be inaccurate.
   b. The authors want to convince readers that eyewitness testimony cannot be completely trusted.

Recognizing Bias　5. How would you describe the authors' attitude toward eyewitness testimony?

    a. The authors know that eyewitnesses can make mistakes, but they still have faith in eyewitness testimony as evidence.

    b. The authors think that eyewitness testimony is too flawed to be completely trusted as evidence.

    c. It's impossible to determine what the authors think.

Share Your Thoughts　Did the authors convince you that eyewitness testimony was seriously flawed? Imagine that you are a juror in a murder trial. The prosecutor's case is weak. The only compelling evidence comes from an eyewitness account. When you enter the jury room, you realize that all the jurors are leaning toward conviction. What will you do, agree to convict or discuss the problem of eyewitness testimony with other jury members?

From Reader to Writer　Write two or three paragraphs summarizing the reasons why, according to the authors, eyewitness testimony can't be trusted.

◆ **READING 4**   # Why People Believe Misinformation, Even After It's Corrected

Lee Dye

Looking Ahead   Like the authors of reading 3 on eyewitness testimony, this author also questions the reliability of memory. He describes a study that suggests if we really want to believe something is true, we will. And if confronted with evidence that proves us wrong, we eventually manage to forget it.

Word Watch   Some of the more difficult words in the reading are defined below. The number in parentheses indicates the paragraph in which the word appears. An asterisk marks its first appearance in the reading. Preview the definitions before you begin reading and watch for the words while you read.

> **cognitive (2):** related to the study of thought and memory
>
> **purge (2):** rid, eliminate
>
> **entrenched (5):** established
>
> **regressed (7):** returned, went back to
>
> **cherished (7):** beloved, deeply cared for
>
> **transient (8):** short-lived, not of long duration
>
> **benign (10):** mild, gentle; favorable

Getting Focused   After reading this selection, you should be able to explain why the title claims people believe misinformation even after they know it's wrong. However, you should also be able to say whether or not there is evidence that the determination to hold on to false facts or ideas can ever be altered.

What kind of tone is the author creating by saying the deer and the gerbil stories are a "bunch of bunk"?

1   Have you seen the photo of the dog that's as big as a horse? How about the deer on top of a telephone pole? And do you know about the Hollywood actor who needed emergency medical help because of a gerbil that went where no gerbil had gone before? That's all a bunch of bunk, of course. But we've heard those stories, or seen those photos, so many times that they have become a part of our world, even if they are totally false.

2   These days we are bombarded with information, much of it incorrect, and long after the political campaigns are over a lot of it will still be buried in the part of our brain where we store our memories. And new research shows that the more intensely we believe something to be true, the more likely it will resurface in the future, even if we have learned it was false.

Cognitive* psychologist Andrew Butler of Duke University, a memory and learning specialist, hopes to figure out a way to help us purge* our brains of false data, and he's a little encouraged. But it's probably not going to be easy.

3   Butler's latest research project, conducted with psychologist Lisa Fazio of Carnegie Mellon University and Elizabeth Marsh of Duke [University,] found that it's possible to correct misinformation, but the correction may not last much more than a week. Give it a little time, and that dog will be as big as a horse again.

4   Fifty students participated in the study, in which they were asked 120 basic science questions. (What is stored in a camel's hump? What organ in the human body cleans the bloodstream and produces urine? What class of animals is the closest living relative of the dinosaurs?) The students also ranked their level of confidence in their answers, and they were really sure they had it right, at least some of the time. But in most cases they were dead wrong. And here's the finding that Butler described in a telephone interview as "totally surprising."

5   The more strongly they believed they were right, the more efficient they were at accepting and remembering a correction. "That flies in the face of a lot of memory theory," Butler said. According to memory theory, the brain throws up a wall of interference to protect a "deeply entrenched"* idea or factoid, even if it is wrong. So a person who is highly confident that his understanding is correct should fight any effort to prove it wrong. But that didn't happen here.

6   Half the participants took the same test again immediately after learning the correct answers. And most of those who were so sure they had been right answered the question correctly when asked, for instance, about the closest living relative of dinosaurs. It's birds, not reptiles. And they knew, the second time around, that the kidney cleans the bloodstream and produces urine, not the bladder.

7   In fact, they corrected their mistakes 86 percent of the time on the retest. And they were more likely to get it right the second time if they had really believed their previous answers were correct than if they had less confidence in their facts. The other half of the participants waited one week to take the test a second time. The same pattern persisted, but by then they only corrected their errors 56 percent of the time. In just one week, nearly half the time they regressed* to their cherished,* but untrue, answers.

8   "It seems like a relatively transient* thing," Butler said. "Our results indicate that over time, you are going to shift back to that misconception that

Whenever a researcher talks about results, the passage deserves extra attention.

According to the author, what's the effect of all the connectedness we experience?

you had before." He thinks, however, that it's possible that simply repeating the test, and correcting the answers, over and over will gradually condition the brain to process and retrieve information more efficiently. Maybe, with practice, we can learn how to toss out the bad stuff, and he hopes teachers will take note.

9   But these days the world is a classroom. Through social media, the Internet, email, and all those technologies that link us together tighter than ever before, we are vulnerable to one of the strongest memory enhancers: repetition. "People are exposed (to misinformation) over and over again, so it's no wonder that people come to believe it," Butler said. "When they do, if they believe it very strongly, our study shows it's very easy to correct this in the short term. But as they go on about their lives, over time, they forget it. They remember the misinformation."

10   The Duke study is limited by the fact that the questions were relatively benign.* If the questions were highly emotional, as is so often the case these days on subjects ranging from global climate change to presidential elections, the results might be quite different. "People want to believe or disbelieve certain things," Butler said. "Our research assumes people are open to correction. People who don't want to believe in another candidate, for example, may not be open to even considering that the new information is correct."

11   So let's stick to science, not politics. What is stored in a camel's hump? Water? Wrong. And you probably really believed that. (Lee Dye, "Why People Believe Misinformation, Even After It's Corrected," February 8, 2012, www.abcnews.com. Used by permission of ABCNews Videosource.)

Monitoring Your Comprehension   Review the marginal annotations and answer any questions posed. If you can't answer a question, mark the sentence or paragraph referred to and re-read it before turning to the comprehension and critical reading questions.

GETTING THE GIST   These questions are the kind you might encounter on a standardized reading test.

DIRECTIONS   Identify the general gist, or point, of the author's words by circling the appropriate letter.

1.   Which statement best expresses the main idea of the entire reading?

   a. Because our general understanding of science is so limited, it's easy for misinformation to get anchored in memory.

b. When people really want or need to believe in someone or something, there is nothing anyone can do to convince them otherwise.

c. The more confident people are about what they know, the less likely they are to listen to anyone who shows them they're wrong.

d. A new study suggests that people are initially willing to have misinformation about the world corrected, but as time passes, they return to their former beliefs.

2. In his research, psychologist Andrew Butler asked students questions about

a. their personal lives.

b. history.

c. their religious beliefs.

d. scientific facts.

3. Butler and his colleagues discovered that

a. students highly confident about their beliefs were often correct.

b. students highly confident about their beliefs were often wrong.

c. students had no confidence in their knowledge of science.

d. students had almost no accurate scientific knowledge.

4. As a result of his study, Butler thinks

a. it's hopeless to try to influence what people think about science.

b. repeated testing and correcting of inaccurate information can eventually stop people from clinging to misinformation.

c. that people hold on to misinformation about science because they are too embarrassed to admit they were wrong.

d. that it's possible to correct misinformation about science but all but impossible to correct misinformation about one's favorite (or least favorite) political candidate.

5. One limitation of Butler's study was that

a. the questions were hard to read and based on boring topics.

b. the subjects of the study were not science majors.

c. the questions were too controversial and people got so angry, they couldn't concentrate.

d. the questions didn't evoke emotion or controversy.

TAKING A CLOSER LOOK This set of questions focuses on your understanding of the text, both its content and the language used to convey that content.

DIRECTIONS Answer the following questions on the blank lines provided or by circling the letter of the best response.

Making Connections

1. In the opening paragraph, the references to the dog as big as a horse, the deer on top of the telephone pole, and the gerbil that's gone where no gerbil had gone before are in the reading to help make what point?

_____

_____

Recognizing Patterns of Organization

2. According to paragraph 2, there is a cause and effect relationship between the _____ and

_____ .

Drawing Inferences

3. When the author says in paragraph 3, "Give it a little time, and that dog will be as big as a horse again," he's not really talking about dogs, he's telling readers that _____

_____ .

Recognizing Sentence Functions

4. What is the function of the last sentence in paragraph 4?
a. It introduces the main idea of paragraph 4.
b. It provides a supporting detail for the main idea of paragraph 4.
c. It makes a transition to paragraph 5.

Repetition and Reference

5. What is the "finding" referred to at the end of paragraph 4?

_____

_____

In what paragraph is that finding explained?

_____

Paraphrasing Key Points

6. In paragraph 5, what is the traditional theory of remembering that Butler's research contradicted?

_____

_____

Recognizing Sentence Functions

7. What is the function of the last sentence in paragraph 5?

a. It introduces the main idea of paragraph 5.

b. It provides a supporting detail for the main idea of paragraph 5.

c. It makes a transition to paragraph 6.

Understanding Supporting Details

8. In paragraph 6, the references to birds and the functions of the kidney are evidence for what result of Butler's study?

_____

Recognizing Patterns of Organization

9. What organizational pattern binds paragraphs 6 and 7 together?

a. cause and effect

b. classification

c. simple listing

d. comparison and contrast

Understanding Supporting Details

10. How does the information provided in paragraphs 6 and 7 support the first two sentences of paragraph 8?

_____

_____

_____

_____

READING WITH A CRITICAL EYE   The goal here is not to be critical in the negative sense, but rather to understand how fact, opinion, argument, and tone reinforce the author's apparent purpose.

DIRECTIONS   Answer the questions on the blank lines provided or by circling the letter of the correct response.

Recognizing Tone **1.** In the opening two paragraphs, the author presents himself to the reader as

    a. a distant and serious science writer.

    b. a man who can't resist a joke.

    c. an important person who takes himself very seriously.

    d. a smart guy who doesn't necessarily believe what he's told.

2. Can you explain what in the author's language made you see him in this way?

_____

_____

_____

_____

Recognizing Fact and Opinion **3.** How would you label the following sentences, *F* for fact, *O* for opinion, or *M* for a mixture of both?

    a. These days we are bombarded with information, much of it incorrect, and long after the political campaigns are over a lot of it will still be buried in the part of our brain where we store our memories. _____

    b. Cognitive psychologist Andrew Butler of Duke University, a memory and learning specialist, hopes to figure out a way to help us purge our brains of false data, and he's a little encouraged. _____

    c. Fifty students participated in the study, in which they were asked 120 basic science questions. _____

Recognizing Purpose **4.** How would you describe the author's purpose?

    a. He wants to describe for readers a new study on the subject of memory.

    b. He wants to persuade readers that Andrew Butler has found a way to make people change their minds when they discover they are wrong.

    c. He wants to persuade readers that correcting misinformation is possible, but very tough to do.

Determining Bias 5. How would you describe the author's attitude toward the study outlined in this reading?

    a. The author doesn't think the study proves much of anything significant.

    b. The author thinks the study described makes an important contribution to the study of learning and memory.

    c. It's impossible to determine the author's personal feelings about the study's importance.

Share Your Thoughts What do you think? Do people generally resist changing their mind? How do you react to the discovery that something you thought was true is not?

From Reader to Writer Start your paper by paraphrasing Andrew Butler's explanation of how the brain responds to information that challenges a cherished belief. Then briefly summarize the study he conducted. Include only the essential elements of the study.

After the summary, introduce a transitional sentence like this one: "But one doesn't need a formal study to see this principle in action." Then give an example you have experienced or read about that shows people refusing to remember what they don't want to know. If you need help with the last part, type the phrase "cognitive dissonance" into your search engine, and you will get numerous examples of people forgetting or simply not acknowledging anything that challenges their view of the world.

WEB QUEST

What is inside a camel's hump? _____

◆ READING 5   Forget What You Know About Good Study Habits

Benedict Carey

Looking Ahead Here's a reading that returns to the topic of Chapter 1—the importance of good study skills. Written by *New York Times* journalist Benedict Carey, the article describes the research done by some cognitive scientists—people engaged in studying how humans think and learn—who believe that traditional thinking on study skills needs to be revised.

Word Watch Some of the more difficult words in the reading are defined below. The number in parentheses indicates the paragraph in which the word appears. An asterisk marks its first appearance in the reading. Preview the definitions before you begin reading and watch for the words while you read.

---

cognitive (2): related to thinking

retention (3): remembering, or the act of holding on to something

credible (4): trustworthy, believable

utility (4): usefulness

constructive (5): leading to improvement; helping to build up

hallowed (6): sacred

neural (7): related to the central nervous system, especially the brain

prism (9): a solid object that has two identical ends and all flat sides

assumption (12): belief considered to be true and therefore not in need of proof

immersion (12): absorption, complete involvement

assessment (14): evaluation, testing

fundamentally (14): at the most basic level, in the most primary respect

analogy (14): a comparison of two different things in which one thing is used to explain the other

paradoxically (16): seeming to be a contradiction but actually making sense

---

Getting Focused As you read, make sure you understand *why* the researchers Carey interviewed think some traditional advice about study skills needs to be abandoned. Pay close attention as well to the new advice they offer, and read the quotations from the individual researchers very carefully.

1 Every September, millions of parents try a kind of psychological witchcraft, to transform their summer-glazed campers into fall students, their video-bugs into bookworms. Advice is cheap and all too familiar: Clear a quiet work space. Stick to a homework schedule. Set goals. Set boundaries. Do not bribe (except in emergencies). And check out the classroom. Does Junior's learning style match the new teacher's approach? Or the school's philosophy? Maybe the child isn't "a good fit" for the school.

Make sure you know what those techniques are by the time you finish reading.

2 Such theories have developed in part because of sketchy education research that doesn't offer clear guidance. Student traits and teaching styles surely interact; so do personalities and at-home rules. The trouble is, no one can predict how. Yet there are effective approaches to learning, at least for those who are motivated. In recent years, cognitive* scientists have shown that a few simple techniques can reliably improve what matters most: how much a student learns from studying.

3 These findings can help anyone, from a fourth grader doing long division to a retiree taking on a new language. But they directly contradict much of the common wisdom about good study habits, and they have not caught on. For instance, instead of sticking to one study location, simply alternating the room where a person studies improves retention.* So does studying distinct but related skills or concepts in one sitting, rather than focusing intensely on a single thing.

What are "these principles" that the author refers to?

4 "We have known these principles for some time, and it's intriguing that schools don't pick them up, or that people don't learn them by trial and error," said Robert A. Bjork, a psychologist at the University of California, Los Angeles. "Instead, we walk around with all sorts of unexamined beliefs about what works that are mistaken." Take the notion that children have specific learning styles, that some are "visual learners" and others are auditory; some are "left-brain" students, others "right-brain." In a recent review of the relevant research, published in the journal *Psychological Science in the Public Interest*, a team of psychologists found almost zero support for such ideas. "The contrast between the enormous popularity of the learning-styles approach within education and the lack of credible* evidence for its utility* is, in our opinion, striking and disturbing," the researchers concluded.

What does "ditto for teaching styles" mean?

5 Ditto for teaching styles, researchers say. Some excellent instructors caper in front of the blackboard like summer-theater Falstaffs†; others are reserved to the point of shyness. "We have yet to identify the common threads between teachers who create a constructive* learning atmosphere,"

---

†Falstaff: a character in Shakespeare's plays *Henry IV* and *Henry V*. Falstaff amuses his king by making jokes and just generally being a cutup.

said Daniel T. Willingham, a psychologist at the University of Virginia and author of the book "Why Don't Students Like School?"

When the author says, "But individual learning is another matter," what is he saying about individual learning and learning styles?

6   But individual learning is another matter, and psychologists have discovered that some of the most hallowed* advice on study habits is flat wrong. For instance, many study skills courses insist that students find a specific place, a study room or a quiet corner of the library, to take their work. The research finds just the opposite. In one classic 1978 experiment, psychologists found that college students who studied a list of 40 vocabulary words in two different rooms—one windowless and cluttered, the other modern, with a view on a courtyard—did far better on a test than students who studied the words twice, in the same room. Later studies have confirmed the finding, for a variety of topics.

What's the reason why studying in different places is effective?

7   The brain makes subtle associations between what it is studying and the background sensations it has at the time, the authors say, regardless of whether those perceptions are conscious. It colors the terms of the Versailles Treaty† with the wasted fluorescent glow of the dorm study room, say; or the elements of the Marshall Plan† with the jade-curtain shade of the willow tree in the backyard. Forcing the brain to make multiple associations with the same material may, in effect, give that information more neural* scaffolding. "What we think is happening here is that, when the outside context is varied, the information is enriched, and this slows down forgetting," said Dr. Bjork, the senior author of the two-room experiment.

8   Varying the type of material studied in a single sitting—alternating, for example, among vocabulary, reading and speaking in a new language— seems to leave a deeper impression on the brain than does concentrating on just one skill at a time. Musicians have known this for years, and their practice sessions often include a mix of scales, musical pieces and rhythmic work. Many athletes, too, routinely mix their workouts with strength, speed and skill drills.

"Advantages" is an important category word. Make sure you know what the advantages mentioned here are.

9   The advantages of this approach to studying can be striking in some topic areas. In a study recently posted online by the journal *Applied Cognitive Psychology*, Doug Rohrer and Kelli Taylor of the University of South Florida taught a group of fourth graders four equations, each to calculate a different dimension of a prism.* Half of the children learned by studying repeated examples of one equation, say, calculating the number of prism faces when given the number of sides at the base, then moving on to the next type of calculation, studying repeated examples of that. The other half

---

†Versailles Treaty: The treaty that ended World War I.
†Marshall Plan: This plan for delivering aid was put in place to keep the European economy afloat after World War II.

studied mixed problem sets, which included examples of all four types of calculations grouped together. Both groups solved sample problems along the way, as they studied.

10   A day later, the researchers gave all of the students a test on the material, presenting new problems of the same type. The children who had studied mixed sets did twice as well as the others, outscoring them 77 percent to 38 percent. The researchers have found the same in experiments involving adults and younger children.

Note how the opening phrase helps readers get a sense of order in time.

11   When students see a list of problems, all of the same kind, they know the strategy to use before they even read the problem," said Dr. Rohrer. "That's like riding a bike with training wheels." With mixed practice, he added, "each problem is different from the last one, which means kids must learn how to choose the appropriate procedure—just like they had to do on the test." These findings extend well beyond math, even to aesthetic intuitive learning. In an experiment published last month in the journal *Psychology and Aging*, researchers found that college students and adults of retirement age were better able to distinguish the painting styles of 12 unfamiliar artists after viewing mixed collections (assortments, including works from all 12) than after viewing a dozen works from one artist, all together, then moving on to the next painter.

In the context of studying, what is "mixed practice"?

12   The finding undermines the common assumption* that intensive immersion* is the best way to really master a particular genre, or type of creative work, said Nate Kornell, a psychologist at Williams College and the lead author of the study. "What seems to be happening in this case is that the brain is picking up deeper patterns when seeing assortments of paintings; it's picking up what's similar and what's different about them," often subconsciously. Cognitive scientists do not deny that honest-to-goodness cramming can lead to a better grade on a given exam. But hurriedly jam-packing a brain is akin to speed-packing a cheap suitcase, as most students quickly learn—it holds its new load for a while, then most everything falls out. "With many students, it's not like they can't remember the material" when they move to a more advanced class, said Henry L. Roediger III, a psychologist at Washington University in St. Louis. "It's like they've never seen it before."

What causes the brain to pick up the "deeper patterns" mentioned?

13   When the neural suitcase is packed carefully and gradually, it holds its contents for far, far longer. An hour of study tonight, an hour on the weekend, another session a week from now: such so-called spacing improves later recall, without requiring students to put in more overall study effort or pay more attention, dozens of studies have found. No one knows for sure why. It may be that the brain, when it revisits

Consider how forgetting is a "friend" of learning.

material at a later time, has to relearn some of what it has absorbed before adding new stuff—and that that process is itself self-reinforcing. "The idea is that forgetting is the friend of learning," said Dr. Kornell. "When you forget something, it allows you to relearn, and do so effectively, the next time you see it."

This is probably the most difficult passage. Read it twice. If you need to, read it three times. Read it just to understand the point of the illustration.

14   That's one reason cognitive scientists see testing itself—or practice tests and quizzes—as a powerful tool of learning, rather than merely assessment.* The process of retrieving an idea is not like pulling a book from a shelf; it seems to fundamentally* alter the way the information is subsequently stored, making it far more accessible in the future. Dr. Roediger uses the analogy* of the Heisenberg uncertainty principle in physics, which holds that the act of measuring a property of a particle (position, for example) reduces the accuracy with which you can know another property (momentum, for example): "Testing not only measures knowledge but changes it," he says—and, happily, in the direction of more certainty, not less.

What is Dr. Roediger's study meant to prove?

15   In one of his own experiments, Dr. Roediger and Jeffrey Karpicke, who is now at Purdue University, had college students study science passages from a reading comprehension test in short study periods. When students studied the same material twice, in back-to-back sessions, they did very well on a test given immediately afterward, and then began to forget the material. But if they studied the passage just once and did a practice test in the second session, they did very well on one test two days later, and another given a week later. "Testing has such bad connotations; people think of standardized testing or teaching to the test," Dr. Roediger said. "Maybe we need to call it something else, but this is one of the most powerful learning tools we have."

16   Of course, one reason the thought of testing tightens people's stomachs is that tests are so often hard. Paradoxically,* it is just this difficulty that makes them such effective study tools, research suggests. The harder it is to remember something, the harder it is to later forget. This effect, which researchers call "desirable difficulty," is evident in daily life. The name of the actor who played Linc in *The Mod Squad*? Francie's brother in *A Tree Grows in Brooklyn*? The name of the co-discoverer, with Newton, of calculus? The more mental sweat it takes to dig it out, the more securely it will be subsequently anchored.

17   None of which is to suggest that these techniques—alternating study environments, mixing content, spacing study sessions, self-testing or all the above—will turn a grade-A slacker into a grade-A student. Motivation matters. So do impressing friends, making the hockey team

and finding the nerve to text the cute student in social studies. "In lab experiments, you're able to control for all factors except the one you're studying," said Dr. Willingham. "Not true in the classroom, in real life. All of these things are interacting at the same time." But at the very least, the cognitive techniques give parents and students, young and old, something many did not have before: a study plan based on evidence, not schoolyard folk wisdom, or empty theorizing. (Benedict Carey from *The New York Times*, September 6, 2010. Copyright © 2010 The New York Times Co. All rights reserved. Reprinted by permission.)

Monitoring Your Comprehension   Review the marginal annotations and answer any questions posed. If you can't answer a question, mark the sentence or passage referred to and re-read it before turning to the comprehension and critical reading questions.

GETTING THE GIST   These questions are the kind you might encounter on a standardized reading test.

DIRECTIONS   Identify the general gist, or point, of the author's words by circling the appropriate letter.

1. Which of the following statements best expresses the main idea of the entire reading?

     a. Much traditional advice about how to go about studying does not reflect the results of research on human learning carried out by cognitive scientists.

     b. Despite the reality of test anxiety, being tested on new information is actually the best way to store that information in long-term memory.

     c. Whatever kind of learning you need to do, spacing your review sessions out over an extended period of time will help you store information in long-term memory.

     d. Although research into how people learn has provided some new insight into effective learning techniques, much of the traditional wisdom about studying has proven to be accurate.

2. According to the researchers interviewed, students seem to remember more when they

   a. immerse themselves in the material for an extended period of time.

   b. consistently study at the same time and in the same location.

   c. work on varied but related subjects during the same study session.

   d. work in small groups with very little teacher interference.

3. The researchers interviewed in the article think that

   a. instruction geared to individual learning styles plays a big role in how quickly students master new material.

   b. there is no evidence showing that an individual's learning style plays a key role in how well or how poorly someone learns new material.

   c. newer research on the role of individual learning styles will confirm the widely held belief that knowing a student's learning style is essential to effective instruction.

   d. schools have been slow about implementing new research on the importance of matching instruction to a student's individual learning style.

4. According to the researchers interviewed in the article,

   a. effective teachers use humor to hold students' attention.

   b. good teachers make effective use of questions to get students to contribute to discussions.

   c. effective teachers are in constant motion during a class and move around the room in order to hold students' attention.

   d. good teachers have very different styles of instruction, and it's impossible to generalize about which style is most effective.

5. According to the researchers interviewed, implementing their findings can have a profound educational effect on

   a. elementary students.

   b. high school students.

   c. students with attention deficit disorder.

   d. students of any age.

TAKING A CLOSER LOOK This set of questions focuses on your understanding of the text, both its content and the language used to convey that content.

DIRECTIONS Answer the following questions on the blank lines provided or by circling the letter of the best response.

Determining the
Main Idea

1. How much information about the main idea does the title give readers?
   a. the topic
   b. the topic and part of the main idea
   c. the topic and the main idea

Repetition and
Reference

2. Paragraph 2 starts with the phrase "such theories." To what in the previous paragraph does that phrase refer?

   _____

   _____

3. Paragraph 3 opens with the phrase "these findings." To what in the previous paragraph does that phrase refer?

   _____

Identifying
Explanatory
Patterns

4. In this reading, the author starts off by _____
   _____ as a way of introducing _____.

Recognizing Thesis
Statements

5. Which paragraph introduces the thesis statement?
   a. paragraph 1
   b. paragraph 2
   c. paragraph 3

   Does the thesis statement open or conclude the paragraph?

   _____

Drawing
Inferences to Make
Connections

6. Paragraph 5 opens with the phrase, "Ditto for teaching styles." What inference does the writer expect the reader to draw based on this phrase?

_____

Analyzing
Sentences

7. This sentence appears in paragraph 6: "The research finds just the opposite." This is

a. a topic sentence.

b. a supporting detail.

c. a transitional sentence.

Monitoring Your
Comprehension

8. Based on what you read in paragraphs 5, 6, and 7, fill in the blanks left in this statement.

Traditional wisdom on study skills suggests that students should study _____, but research by cognitive scientists suggests that studying the same material in different places is more effective because the brain _____

_____.

Understanding
Supporting Details

9. The studies cited in paragraphs 8, 9, and 10 all support what main idea?

a. It's easier to learn a foreign language if you read, write, and speak in the same study session.

b. Musicians and mathematicians share similar methods of learning new information.

c. Studying different but related subjects or materials in the same learning session is the most effective method of learning.

Understanding
Figurative Language

10. Paragraph 13 is connected to paragraph 12 by a metaphor that compares _____ to _____.

11. The author uses the metaphor to help make what point?

a. As soon as the brain feels overwhelmed by information, the process of forgetting kicks in and shuts down the brain's ability to remember.

b. If you want to create a store of information in long-term memory, add it bit by bit, reviewing it repeatedly over an extended period of time.

c. Information that makes its way into long-term memory is there forever, but the human mind doesn't always know what recall clue to use to make the information available.

12. Paragraph 13 says that "forgetting is the friend of learning." Explain what that means in your own words.

_____

_____

13. Is the statement "forgetting is the friend of learning" an example of a paradox? _____ Please explain.

_____

_____

_____

Repetition and Reference 14. Paragraph 14 opens by saying, "That's one reason . . . testing itself [is] . . . a powerful tool for learning." What is the "one reason" referred to in paragraph 13?

_____

_____

Inferring Main Idea 15. What's the implied main idea of paragraph 16?

_____

_____

READING WITH A CRITICAL EYE The goal here is not to be critical in the negative sense, but rather to understand how fact, opinion, argument, and tone reinforce the author's apparent purpose.

DIRECTIONS Answer the questions on the blank lines provided or by circling the letter of the correct response.

Analyzing Arguments

1. In paragraph 4, what perspective on learning styles in education does the researcher express?

_____

_____

2. What evidence does he supply for that claim? _____

3. Is this an example of a hasty generalization? _____ Please explain.

_____

_____

Identifying Purpose

4. How would you describe the author's purpose?
   a. purely informative
   b. primarily informative with some persuasion included
   c. primarily persuasive

Detecting Bias

5. Which statement best describes the author's attitude toward the ideas in the reading?
   a. The author favors the position of the cognitive scientists interviewed.
   b. The author believes that traditional study skills advice has merit.
   c. It's impossible to determine the author's attitude.

Share Your Thoughts

Do you think reading this article will affect how you study? Why or why not?

From Reader to Writer

Write a sentence or two to define "desirable difficulty" introduced in paragraph 16. Give an example that illustrates how desirable difficulty aids learning.

◆ READING 6   ## The Rise of the New Groupthink

Susan Cain

Looking Ahead   Reading 5 challenges traditional wisdom about study skills. This reading also mounts a challenge. It suggests that the current emphasis on working in teams to get the best results is misguided. Instead, the author argues that more attention needs to be paid to working in solitude because that's where great things get done.

Word Watch   Some of the more difficult words in the reading are defined below. The number in parentheses indicates the paragraph in which the word appears. An asterisk marks its first appearance in the reading. Preview the definitions before you begin reading and watch for the words while you read.

---

in thrall (1): fascinated by, devoted to

gregarious (1): group-oriented, liking to be among people

introverted (2): shy in groups, focused inward

extroverted (2): comfortable in groups, focused outward

catalyst (3): stimulus, motivator

innovation (3): originality, the creation of something new

transcendence (4): going beyond worldly limitations

charisma (4): the power to attract and influence others, charm, magnetic personality

autonomously (11): independently

nuanced (20): having an understanding of subtle differences

Getting Focused   As you read, look for passages that identify the author's objections. Look as well for parts of the reading that support her point of view.

1   Solitude is out of fashion. Our companies, our schools, and our culture are in thrall* to an idea I call the New Groupthink, which holds that creativity and achievement come from an oddly gregarious* place. Most of us now work in teams, in offices without walls, for managers who prize people skills above all. Lone geniuses are out. Collaboration is in.

Note how the opening transitional sentence brings the previous train of thought to a halt.

2   But there's a problem with this view. Research strongly suggests that people are more creative when they enjoy privacy and freedom from interruption. And the most spectacularly creative people in many fields are

often introverted,* according to studies by the psychologists Mihaly Csikszentmihalyi and Gregory Feist. They're extroverted* enough to exchange and advance ideas, but see themselves as independent and individualistic. They're not joiners by nature.

3   One explanation for those findings is that introverts are comfortable working alone—and solitude is a catalyst* to innovation.* As the influential psychologist Hans Eyseneck observed, introversion fosters creativity by "concentrating the mind on the tasks in hand, and preventing the dissipation of energy on social and sexual matters unrelated to work." In other words, a person sitting quietly under a tree in the backyard, while everyone else is clinking glasses on the patio, is more likely to have an apple land on his head. (Newton[†] was one of the world's great introverts: William Wordsworth described him as "A mind for ever/Voyaging through strange seas of Thought, alone.")

What do Picasso, Moses, Jesus, Buddha, and Steve Wozniak all have in common?

4   Solitude has long been associated with creativity and transcendence."* "Without great solitude, no serious work is possible," Picasso said. A central narrative of many religions is the seeker—Moses, Jesus, Buddha—who goes off by himself and brings profound insights back to the community. Culturally, we're often so dazzled by charisma* that we overlook the quiet part of the creative process. Consider Apple. In the wake of Steve Jobs's death, we've seen a profusion of myths about the company's success. Most focus on Mr. Jobs's supernatural magnetism and tend to ignore the other crucial figure in Apple's creation: a kindly, introverted engineering wizard Steve Wozniak, who toiled alone on a beloved invention, the personal computer.

What's the time frame of this paragraph?

5   Rewind to March 1975: Mr. Wozniak believes the world would be a better place if everyone had a user-friendly computer. This seems a distant dream—most computers are still the size of minivans, and many times as pricey. But Mr. Wozniak meets a simpatico band of engineers that call themselves the Homebrew Computer Club. The Homebrewers are excited about a primitive new machine called the Altair 8800. Mr. Wozniak is inspired, and immediately begins work on his own magical version of a computer. Three months later, he unveils his amazing creation for his friend, Steve Jobs. Mr. Wozniak wants to give his invention away free, but Mr. Jobs persuades him to co-found Apple Computer.

Why did the author change the time frame of her discussion?

[†]Isaac Newton: the man who discovered the laws of gravity. According to legend, he discovered gravity when an apple fell from a tree and whizzed by his head as he was sitting in his backyard. The apple's direction supposedly gave him a clue to the nature of gravity. The story may or may not be true.

Notice how the author reverses direction in the middle of the paragraph.

6   The story of Apple's origin speaks to the power of collaboration. Mr. Wozniak wouldn't have been catalyzed by the Altair but for the kindred spirits of Homebrew. And he'd never have started Apple without Mr. Jobs. But it's also a story of solo spirit. If you look at how Mr. Wozniak got the work done—the sheer hard work of creating something from nothing—he did it alone. Late at night, all by himself.

7   Intentionally so. In his memoir, Mr. Wozniak offers this guidance to aspiring inventors: "Most inventors and engineers I've met are like me . . . they live in their heads. They're almost like artists. In fact, the very best of them are artists. And artists work best alone. . . . I'm going to give you some advice that might be hard to take. That advice is: Work alone. . . . Not on a committee. Not on a team."

Why is the information about office space included in the reading?

8   And yet. The New Groupthink has overtaken our workplaces, our schools and our religious institutions. Anyone who has ever needed noise-canceling headphones in her own office or marked an online calendar with a fake meeting in order to escape yet another real one knows what I'm talking about. Virtually all American workers now spend time on teams and some 70 percent inhabit open-plan offices, in which no one has "a room of one's own." During the last decades, the average amount of space allotted to each employee shrank 300 square feet, from 500 square feet in the 1970s to 200 square feet in 2010.

9   Our schools have also been transformed by the New Groupthink. Today, elementary school classrooms are commonly arranged in pods of desks, the better to foster group learning. Even subjects like math and creative writing are often taught as committee projects. In one fourth-grade classroom I visited in New York City, students engaged in group work were forbidden to ask a question unless every member of the group had the very same question.

10   The New Groupthink also shapes some of our most influential religious institutions. Many mega-churches feature extracurricular groups organized around every conceivable activity, from parenting to skateboarding to real estate, and expect worshipers to join in. They also emphasize a theatrical style of worship—loving Jesus out loud, for all the congregation to see. "Often the role of a pastor seems closer to that of church cruise director than to the traditional roles of spiritual friend and counselor," said Adam McHugh, an evangelical pastor and author of "Introverts in the Church."

Why is the word "some" in all capital letters?

11   SOME teamwork is fine and offers a fun, stimulating, useful way to exchange ideas, manage information and build trust. But it's one thing to associate with a group in which each member works autonomously*

on his piece of the puzzle; it's another to be corralled into endless meetings or conference calls conducted in offices that afford no respite from the noise and gaze of co-workers. Studies show that open-plan offices make workers hostile, insecure and distracted. They're also more likely to suffer from high blood pressure, stress, the flu and exhaustion. And people whose work is interrupted make 50 percent more mistakes and take twice as long to finish it.

What change did Backbone Entertainment make and why?

12   Many introverts seem to know this instinctively, and resist being herded together. Backbone Entertainment, a video game development company in Emeryville, Calif., initially used an open-plan office, but found that its game developers, many of whom were introverts, were unhappy. "It was one big warehouse space, with just tables, no walls, and everyone could see each other," recalled Mike Mika, the former creative director. "We switched over to cubicles and were worried about it—you'd think in a creative environment that people would hate that. But it turns out they prefer having nooks and crannies they can hide away in and just be away from everybody."

Why does the author mention the Coding War Games?

13   Privacy also makes us productive. In a fascinating study known as the Coding War Games, consultants Tom DeMarco and Timothy Lister compared the work of more than 600 computer programmers at 92 companies. They found that people from the same companies performed at roughly the same level—but that there was an enormous performance gap between organizations. What distinguished programmers at the top-performing companies wasn't greater experience or better pay. It was how much privacy, personal workspace and freedom from interruption they enjoyed. Sixty-two percent of the best performers said their workspace was sufficiently private compared with only 19 percent of the worst performers. Seventy-six percent of the worst programmers but only 38 percent of the best said that they were often interrupted needlessly.

When writers use studies to make a point, make sure you can paraphrase the methods and results.

Expert opinion is present in a text for a reason. Always know what the expert adds to the writer's point of view.

14   Solitude can even help us learn. According to research on expert performance by the psychologist Anders Ericsson, the best way to master a field is to work on the task that's most demanding for you personally. And often the best way to do this is alone. Only then, Mr. Ericsson told me, can you "go directly to the part that's challenging to you. If you want to improve, you have to be the one who generates the move. Imagine a group class—you're the one generating the move only a small percentage of the time."

15   Conversely, brainstorming sessions are one of the worst possible ways to stimulate creativity. The brainchild of a charismatic advertising

What did Alex Osborn claim?

executive named Alex Osborn who believed that groups produced better ideas than individuals, workplace brainstorming sessions came into vogue in the 1950s. "The quantitative results of group brainstorming are beyond question," Mr. Osborn wrote. "One group produced 45 suggestions for a home-appliance promotion, 56 ideas for a money-raising campaign, 124 ideas on how to sell more blankets."

What did the research show?

16   But decades of research show that individuals almost always perform better than groups in both quality and quantity, and group performance gets worse as group size increases. The "evidence from science suggests that business people must be insane to use brainstorming groups," wrote the organizational psychologist Adrian Furnham. "If you have talented and motivated people, they should be encouraged to work alone when creativity or efficiency is the highest priority."

17   The reasons brainstorming fails are instructive for other forms of group work, too. People in groups tend to sit back and let others do the work; they instinctively mimic others' opinions and lose sight of their own; and, often succumb to peer pressure. The Emory University neuroscientist Gregory Berns found that when we take a stance different from the group's, we activate the amygdala, a small organ in the brain associated with the fear of rejection. Professor Berns calls this "the pain of independence."

What does the phrase "dismal record" refer to?

18   The one important exception to this dismal record is electronic brainstorming, where large groups outperform individuals; and the larger the group the better. The protection of the screen mitigates many problems of group work. This is why the Internet has yielded such wondrous collective creations. Marcel Proust called reading a "miracle of communication in the midst of solitude," and that's what the Internet is, too. It's a place where we can be alone together—and this is precisely what gives it power.

When an author says "My point is not..." the reader should immediately be looking for what?

19   My point is not that man is an island. Life is meaningless without love, trust and friendship. And I'm not suggesting that we abolish teamwork. Indeed, recent studies suggest that influential academic work is increasingly conducted by teams rather than by individuals. (Although teams whose members collaborate remotely, from separate universities, appear to be the most influential of all.) The problems we face in science, economics and many other fields are more complex than ever before, and we'll need to stand on one another's shoulders if we can possibly hope to solve them.

20   But even if the problems are different, human nature remains the same. And most humans have two contradictory impulses: we love

and need one another, yet we crave privacy and autonomy. To harness the energy that fuels both these drives, we need to move beyond the New Groupthink and embrace a more nuanced* approach to creativity and learning. Our offices should encourage casual, cafe-style interactions, but allow people to disappear into personalized, private spaces when they want to be alone. Our schools should teach children to work with others, but also to work on their own for sustained periods of time. And we must recognize that introverts like Steve Wozniak need extra quiet and privacy to do their best work.

Notice how the author concludes by returning to Steve Wozniak and the lesson to be learned from his accomplishment.

21   Before Mr. Wozniak started Apple, he designed calculators at Hewlett-Packard, a job he loved partly because HP made it easy to chat with his colleagues. Every day at 10 a.m. and 2 p.m., management wheeled in doughnuts and coffee, and people could socialize and swap ideas. What distinguished these interactions was how low-key they were. For Mr. Wozniak, collaboration meant the ability to share a doughnut and a brainwave with his laid-back, poorly dressed colleagues—who minded not a whit when he disappeared into his cubicle to get the real work done.

(Susan Cain, "The Rise of the New Groupthink," from *The New York Times*, January 15, 2012.

GETTING THE GIST   These questions are the kind you might encounter on a standardized reading test.

DIRECTIONS   Identify the general gist, or point, of the author's words by circling the appropriate letter.

1. Which of the following statements best expresses the main idea of the entire reading?

   a. We need to put more emphasis on being alone because there isn't always a team nearby when life deals out a hard blow. There are many times when the only person you can rely on is yourself.

   b. Collaboration has taken over our school system, so much so that children have to agree on the questions they want to raise. If they don't agree, the question doesn't get asked.

   c. Collaboration has its rewards, but more emphasis needs to be placed on working alone because creative work gets done when people work in groups *and* get a chance to think on their own with no one else around.

    d. Solitude is the best training there is for the mind. It's when we are alone that we are fully ourselves because we are not being influenced or intimidated, by the thoughts of others.

2. Steve Jobs and Steve Wozniak appear in the reading to make what point?

    a. A smart businessman can always get the best of a technological genius; the genius lives in his or her head and isn't wise to the ways of the world.

    b. Although Apple is always considered the brain child of Steve Jobs, it was Steve Wozniak who made Apple a household name.

    c. Apple's success is a result of both team effort and one man working in solitude.

    d. Apple's success story has mistakenly encouraged the notion that greatness can only be achieved in a group.

3. The author believes that

    a. teamwork would be more effective if someone were always on hand to moderate discussions among members who disagree.

    b. teamwork completely destroys individual creativity.

    c. teamwork has value, but there should be time made as well for individuals to work on their own.

    d. teamwork lets people avoid responsibility for their mistakes and that is the source of its current popularity in the workplace.

4. According to the author, brainstorming is

    a. one of the best ways to generate creative thinking.

    b. one of the worst ways to stimulate creative thinking.

    c. a waste of time unless the group involved is really large.

    d. unlikely to work outside of a corporate setting.

5. The author argues that human beings

    a. have two contradictory impulses, to be alone and to be together.

    b. want to be alone more than they want to be together with other people.

    c. don't know what they want.

    d. need to be in groups in order to see themselves reflected in the eyes of others.

TAKING A CLOSER LOOK This set of questions focuses on your understanding of the text, both its content and the language used to convey that content.

DIRECTIONS Answer the following questions on the blank lines provided or by circling the letter of the best response.

Recognizing
Explanatory
Patterns

1. Which explanatory pattern does the author use to introduce the thesis statement?

   a. The reading starts off with the thesis statement.

   b. The reading starts with an introductory sentence and the next sentence introduces the thesis statement.

   c. The author opens with an introductory paragraph followed by a reversal transition that gets readers ready for the thesis statement.

   d. The last sentence of the first paragraph introduces the thesis statement.

Repetition and
Reference

2. In paragraph 3, the opening phrase "those findings" refers to what from the previous paragraph?

   _____

   _____

Inferring
Connections
Between Sentences

3. In the middle of paragraph 4, the author says, "Consider Apple." Based on what came before those two words, what should readers expect the author to do?

   _____

   _____

Understanding
Transitions

4. The author opens paragraph 5 by saying "Rewind to March 1975." Given what she has said in paragraph 4, why does the author want to take her readers back in time?

   _____

   _____

5. What category of transition is "Rewind to March 1975"?

   a. reversal

   b. comparative

   c. time order

   d. addition

Inferring Main Ideas 6. What's the implied main idea of paragraph 6?

   a. Apple is the perfect example of what collaboration can accomplish.

   b. Apple is the perfect example of how collaboration has to be balanced by work in solitude.

   c. Apple illustrates how Steve Jobs would have been nothing without Steve Wozniak.

Understanding Supporting Details 7. Why does the author quote Steve Wozniak's memoir in paragraph 7?

   _____

Making Connections Between Paragraphs 8. Does paragraph 9 continue the train of thought begun in 8, or does it introduce a new main idea?

   _____

Understanding Supporting Details 9. In paragraph 9, what main idea does the author's visit to a fourth grade classroom support?

   _____

Inferring Main Ideas 10. Which statement best sums up the implied main idea of paragraph 11?

   a. Teamwork has taken over the world of work, and the end result is that no one takes responsibility for what they do or do not accomplish.

   b. Professional teamwork can be both fun and useful, but if employees never get a chance to work on their own and by themselves, they and their work will suffer.

c. Teamwork is supposed to be an effective way of getting things accomplished, but studies show that this method of working wastes an enormous amount of time.

d. People who are forced to work in teams on a constant basis often have a host of stress-related health problems.

Understanding Comparison and Contrast

11. What do the computer programmers and game developers the author mentions in paragraphs 12 and 13 have in common?

_____

Why does the author compare the two?

_____

_____

Understanding Transitions

12. Paragraph 15 opens with the transition *conversely*, which means "just the opposite" or "on the other hand." That transition tells the reader that paragraph 15 will introduce an idea that is *the opposite* of what point made previously?

_____

Organizational Patterns and Paraphrasing

13. Paraphrase the cause and effect relationship described by Gregory Berns in paragraph 17.

_____

_____

Summarizing

14. Write one sentence that summarizes the point of paragraphs 19 and 20.

_____

_____

Drawing Inferences

15. Why does the author end the reading with a story about Hewlett-Packard's doughnut break?

a. The way work was set up at Hewlett-Packard, with a scheduled time for socializing and the freedom to be alone, is what the author considers the best way to get serious, creative work done.

b. Hewlett-Packard, with its policy of forced socializing, is precisely the kind of work arrangement that the author is arguing against.

c. Steve Wozniak was a lonely computer genius, who tried hard to be a social person, but he just could not stand being around a lot of people.

d. The story suggests that really gifted people get their work done while those with fewer gifts waste time on extended coffee breaks.

READING WITH A CRITICAL EYE   The goal here is not to be critical in the negative sense, but rather to understand how fact, opinion, argument, and tone reinforce the author's apparent purpose.

DIRECTIONS   Answer the questions on the blank lines provided or by circling the letter of the correct response.

Analyzing Arguments

1. The author claims that our society needs to put more emphasis on privacy and solitude in order to encourage creative thinking. Given that opinion, what does the discussion of brainstorming contribute to the author's argument?

_____

_____

2. In paragraph 9, the author tells us that our schools have been dramatically influenced by the rise of Groupthink. What specific piece of evidence does she offer as proof?

_____

_____

Is her evidence solid or shaky? _____ Please explain.

_____ .

3. What role does electronic brainstorming, mentioned in paragraph 18, play in her discussion of Groupthink?

_____

_____

4. Which statement best paraphrases the ideas of Anders Ericsson in paragraph 14?

   a. Working alone improves performance because you can decide what area needs your attention and focus on it; you don't have to wait for members of your group to make a decision about what needs additional study and analysis.

   b. Working alone improves performance because it removes distractions. You can focus on the areas that need extra attention and don't have to worry about your concentration failing when someone starts a conversation.

   c. Experts and geniuses need to work alone so that they can be open to inspiration and not be distracted by the chatter of those less brilliant.

   d. Without solitude, there would be no scientific progress; nor would there be any artistic breakthroughs.

   How is Ericsson's point of view relevant to the author's argument?

   _____

   _____

   _____

Understanding Figurative Language and Tone

5. What simile does Adam McHugh, the pastor quoted in paragraph 10, make use of?

   _____

   What's the point of the simile?

   _____

   _____

   Does the simile seem at odds with the author's tone? _____ Please

   explain. _____

   _____

Share Your Thoughts How do you work best, alone or in a group? Can you explain why you work better alone or in a group? Or are you someone who likes to work both alone and in a group depending on the task at hand?

From Reader to Writer Write a few paragraphs describing the different ways you think people respond to being in a group. This would be the perfect opportunity to show your mastery of the classification pattern if you have in mind three or even four different ways people respond to being in a group.

◆ READING 7   The Altruistic Personality

Sharon S. Brehm, Saul M. Kassin, and Steven Fein

Looking Ahead In this reading from a sociology textbook, the authors try to understand what makes some people willing to put the interests of others before their own.

Word Watch Some of the more difficult words in the reading are defined below. The number in parentheses indicates the paragraph in which the word appears. An asterisk marks its first appearance in the reading. Preview the definitions before you begin reading and watch for the words while you read.

---

altruistic (2): exhibiting unselfish concern for the welfare of others

genetically (2): related to biological inheritance

empathy (5): understanding of another person's situation or feelings

fraternal twins (5): developed from two separate eggs (identical twins develop from one egg)

heritable (5): capable of being passed by birth from one generation to the next

variables (9): characteristics, events, or things that can change with time or context

pro-social (10): caring about the welfare of others

collectivist (11): valuing the group's well-being over all else

individualist (11): valuing the individual person's well-being over all else

extroversion (11): interest in other people, interest in the world outside one's own mind

---

Getting Focused The title, "The Altruistic Personality," tells you the topic. But that's just the subject matter. Read to discover what the authors have to say about the altruistic personality. Does it exist? If so, what character traits does it seem to consist of? And what does the research say about the origins of an altruistic personality? Is it inherited or shaped by environment? These are the kinds of questions you should be able to answer once you finish reading.

TEXTBOOK TIP

As much as or even more than psychology texts, sociology textbooks use research to back up their descriptions of how people function in society. In addition to understanding the details of each study mentioned, e.g., who conducted the study, what they were looking for, and what methods were used, make sure you know *why* the study is present in the text. That means knowing what main idea is explained or supported by the studies. Studies are in a text to prove or illustrate a point. Make sure you know what that point is.

Based on the title, preview, and quotation, what do you think this reading will explore?

"The purpose of human life is to serve and to show compassion and the will to help others."

—Albert Schweitzer[†]

1   When we think about extreme acts of helping, or of failing to help, or when we think about long-term, well-planned acts of helping such as volunteering at a clinic or shelter or serving as a Big Brother or Big Sister, we tend to wonder about the nature of the people involved.

2   Researchers have even tried to identify an *altruistic* personality*, one that distinguishes people who help from those who don't. Some research has focused on whether certain people tend to be more helpful across situations than others. Other research has asked whether and to what extent unselfishness and a willingness to give to others might be genetically* based. Several studies have sought to identify what general personality characteristics and traits comprise the altruistic personality.

Are Some People More Helpful Than Others?

As soon as the heading poses a question, start looking for the answer.

3   When Daniel Santos's friends and co-workers learned of his heroics in jumping 150 feet off the Tappan Zee Bridge to save a stranger, they were not surprised. "That's just how he is," said a fellow volunteer firefighter. "If he sees something, he's going to go and try to help out that person." A receptionist at the company where he worked as a mechanic added, "He will help anyone at any place and any time." His sister noted that he leaped into the water even though he's not a strong swimmer. "He has a good heart," she said (Fitz-Gibbon & Siemaszko, 1996, p. 7).

4   Are there people who are generally helpful across all situations? Are there others who are generally unhelpful? Although the specific situation clearly can overwhelm individual differences in influencing helping

---

[†]Albert Schweitzer (1875–1965) was a doctor and philosopher, who devoted himself to medical missionary work.

behaviors, researchers have provided some evidence for individual differences in helping tendencies. These tendencies seem to endure in a variety of settings. People who are more helpful than others in one situation are likely to be more helpful in other situations as well. In addition, a long-term study by Nancy Eisenberg and others (1999) suggests that this individual difference may be relatively stable over time. Specifically, they found that the degree to which preschool children exhibited spontaneous helping behavior predicted how helpful they would be in later childhood and early adulthood.

Remember, if you see a reference to a study, make sure you know both what it proves and what it contributes to the overall main idea.

5   According to J. Philippe Rushton and his colleagues (1984), this individual difference in helpfulness is, in part, genetically based. Studies of twins offer some support for Rushton's argument. Genetically identical twins are more similar to each other in their helpful behavioral tendencies and their helping-related emotions and reactions, such as empathy,* than are fraternal twins* who share only a portion of their genetic make-up. These findings suggest that there may be a heritable* component to helpfulness.

What Is the Altruistic Personality?

6   Even if we identify some people who help others a lot and other people who don't, we have not addressed the question of what distinguishes people who help from those who don't—other than their helpfulness, of course. What are the various components of the altruistic personality? Can we predict who is likely to be altruistic by looking at people's overall personalities?

7   Consider some examples of people who have acted very altruistically. Do they seem to have very similar personality traits and characteristics? Think, for example, about Oskar Schindler† and how he cheated in business and in his marriage. Could anyone have predicted his altruistic actions from his overall personality? It is doubtful.

What do all the people described in paragraphs 7 and 8 have in common?

8   What about more contemporary models of altruism? In 1997, Ted Turner, founder of numerous cable stations and owner of professional sports teams, pledged a personal donation of one billion dollars to the United Nations. Not to be outdone, by July 2000 Microsoft Chairman Bill Gates had pledged 22 billion dollars to charity. Actor Paul Newman donated all of the millions of dollars in profits that were generated by his brands of salad dressing, spaghetti sauce, popcorn, and the like to charities, such as his camp for children living with a fatal disease. And until her

---

†Oskar Schindler (1908–1974): a German businessman famous for helping Jews to escape from Nazi Germany and the subject of the hit film *Schindler's List*.

death in 1997, Mother Teresa devoted her life to the poor in India. These four well-known figures seem quite different from each other in overall personality—except for their concern with helping others.

9   The quest to discover the altruistic personality has not been an easy one. Much of the research conducted over the years has failed to find consistent, reliable personality characteristics that predict helping behavior across situations. Situational variables* have predicted people's helping behaviors much better than personality variables.

10   Some researchers have changed the nature of the quest, however, focusing on personality variables that predict helping in some specific situations rather than across all situations; and their studies have been more successful in identifying traits that predict such behavior (Carlo et al., 1991; Penner et al., 1995). George Knight and his colleagues (1994) have suggested that an interacting group of personality traits influences pro-social* behavior and responses differ depending on the situation. For example, in dangerous emergencies, people who are high in self-confidence and independence are more likely to help than other people, but they are no more likely to help in response to a request to donate money to a charity.

11   Personality variables, or traits, that have been associated with greater helpfulness in some contexts include the following: empathy toward others; a tendency to attribute the causes of events to individual control rather than external circumstances; a collectivist* rather than an individualist* orientation; and extroversion,* openness to experience, and agreeableness (Bierhof et al., 1991; Kosek, 1995; Moorman & Blakely, 1995). And whether or not people have the traits associated with pro-social behavior, if they can be convinced or motivated to believe that they are altruistic, their behavior may follow. For example, labeling someone as a helpful person seems to increase that individual's helpful behavior.

The transition "in sum" is a sign to slow down, here's where a key point will be explicitly stated.

12   In sum, research provides some insight into the traits and characteristics that may be associated with helpful behavioral tendencies. However, more research is needed before a conclusion can be reached about the make-up of the altruistic personality. The research thus far does point to two qualities that seem essential for such a personality: empathy and advanced moral reasoning. (Adapted from Sharon S. Brehm, Saul Kassin, and Steven Fein, *Social Psychology*, 5th ed., © 2002 Cengage Learning.)

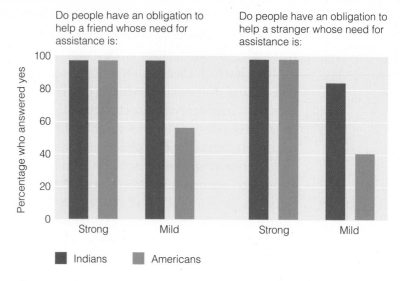

Figure 3 The Sense of Social Responsibility in India Compared to the United States

These results compare the proportion of children and adults in India with the proportion of children and adults in the United States who said that people have an obligation to help others, both friends and strangers. Source of data: J. G. Miller et al., 1990.

Close Up on Visual Aids
◆

Bar graphs like the one shown in this reading help readers make comparisons. They are a visual method of indicating degrees of difference between two groups. Longer bars indicate that one group has more of what's being measured while the group represented by the shorter bar has less. The caption following the figure number will usually tell you what is being measured.

1. In the case of the bar graph accompanying the reading on altruism, what two groups are being compared?

   _____

2. What's being measured?

   _____

3. The first set of bars on the left labeled "Strong" tells readers that

   Indians and Americans _____

   _____.

4. The second set on the left labeled "Mild" indicates that _____

_____

_____ .

5. On the right side of the graph, the bars labeled "Strong" empha-

size _____

_____ The bars labeled "Mild" show that _____

_____

_____ .

Monitoring Your Comprehension Review the marginal annotations and answer any questions posed. If you can't answer a question, mark the sentence or paragraph referred to and re-read it before turning to the comprehension and critical reading questions.

GETTING THE GIST These questions are the kind you might encounter on a standardized reading test.

DIRECTIONS Identify the general gist, or point, of the authors' words by circling the appropriate letter.

1. Which statement best expresses the main idea of the entire reading?
   a. Research has proven that altruistic behavior has no genetic basis.
   b. Research on the altruistic personality suggests that certain personal characteristics and situations do seem to predispose, or encourage, an individual to help others.
   c. So far, researchers have been unable to construct any reliable studies for identifying the characteristics that make up an altruistic personality. However, one characteristic in particular, self-confidence, does seem to be mentioned as significant in several different studies.
   d. People who readily help others all have very similar personalities: They are affectionate by nature and enjoy extending a helping hand even if means discomfort or danger for themselves.

2. According to the reading, researchers have discovered that

   a. we are all equally capable of altruism, but we don't all get the same chance to express it.

   b. we would all grow up to be hopelessly self-centered and self-absorbed if adults didn't model altruistic behavior for us.

   c. people differ in their capacity for altruism.

   d. women are more naturally altruistic than men.

3. Why do the authors mention Oskar Schindler, Ted Turner, Bill Gates, Paul Newman, and Mother Teresa?

   a. They illustrate the idea that donating large sums of money is a common behavior of people with altruistic personalities.

   b. They are all examples of people who were altruistic from childhood on.

   c. They illustrate the idea that people who behave in altruistic ways can have very different personalities.

   d. They support the authors' point that extremely altruistic people always become famous.

4. According to the reading, research on altruism

   a. has given us a clear picture of the altruistic personality.

   b. has indicated that true altruism does not exist.

   c. has been difficult to carry out for an extended period of time.

   d. hasn't come up with any definite conclusions about what makes a person altruistic.

5. According to the reading, which two characteristics seem likely to be essential to altruistic behavior?

   a. an affectionate nature and a high degree of self-confidence

   b. an outgoing personality and an enthusiastic attitude

   c. a capacity for empathy and advanced moral reasoning

   d. rigidity of character and a tendency to be outspoken

TAKING A CLOSER LOOK   This set of questions focuses on your understanding of the text, both its content and the language used to convey that content.

DIRECTIONS   Answer the following questions on the blank lines provided or by circling the letter of the best response.

Identifying Supporting Details

1. In general, the researchers described in this reading haven't come to many clear conclusions about the nature of altruism, but they haven't come up completely empty either. In your own words, name the three things we now know about altruism as a result of the research described.

   1. _____

   2. _____

   3. _____

   _____

Monitoring Your Comprehension

2. Having read this selection, how would you answer if someone asked you, "Are some people more inclined than others to be altruistic?" _____ What paragraph or paragraphs in the reading would support your answer? _____

3. Paragraph 4 opens with two questions. Where do the answers to these questions appear? _____

Recognizing Main Ideas

4. The work of J. Philippe Rushton supports what main idea about altruism?

   _____

Recognizing Patterns of Organization

5. The heading for paragraph 6, "What Is the Altruistic Personality?" suggests which pattern of organization?

   a. definition

   b. simple listing

   c. classification

   d. comparison and contrast

Constructing
the Main Idea
Statement

6. Which sentence in paragraph 8 could play the role of the topic sentence, as long as the reader added the names of the people discussed in the paragraph?

_____

Paraphrasing

7. Which statement is the best paraphrase of this sentence from paragraph 9? "Situational variables have predicted people's helping behaviors much better than personality variables."

a. People are always ready to reach out to others when a situation is life threatening, but they are much less inclined to do so when financial help is needed.

b. Researchers are more comfortable describing some specific situations that encourage altruism than they are defining the personality trains linked to altruistic behavior.

c. Researchers have been able to determine the personality traits related to altruistic behavior, but they don't know what situations call forth expressions of altruism.

Drawing Inferences
to Add Information

8. To see to it that the opening sentence of paragraph 10 makes sense in terms of the rest of the reading, what word or words does the reader need to add after the word *quest*?

_____

Repetition and
Reference

9. In paragraphs 10 and 11, what phrase do the authors start using to refer to altruistic actions?

_____

Recognizing
Transitions and
Paraphrasing

10. By the end of the reading, the authors describe a shift in what researchers on altruism are looking for. What sentence opening announces that shift?

_____

Describe the shift in your own words.

_____

_____

_____

READING WITH A CRITICAL EYE   The goal here is not to be critical in the negative sense, but rather to understand how fact, opinion, argument, and tone reinforce the authors' apparent purpose.

DIRECTIONS   Answer the questions on the blank lines provided or by circling the letter of the best response.

Fact and Opinion 1. Label the following statements from the reading as *F* for fact, *O* for opinion, or *M* for mix of both.

    a. "A number of researchers have tried to characterize, or describe, an altruistic personality." _____

    b. "The quest to discover the altruistic personality has not been an easy one." _____

    c. "George Knight and his colleagues have suggested that an interacting group of personality traits influences pro-social behavior."

    _____

    d. "Research provides some insight into the traits and characteristics that may be associated with helpful behavioral tendencies."

    _____

Recognizing the Authors' Point of View 2. In paragraph 5, how do the authors indicate that they think researcher J. Philippe Rushton may be on the right track concerning the origins of altruism?

_____

_____

3. In paragraph 10, the authors discuss the research of George Knight. Do they also think that he is on the right track with his research? ___ Please explain.

_____

_____

Purpose 4. What is the authors' primary purpose?

    a. The authors want to describe current research suggesting that altruism may be inborn.

b. The authors want to describe researchers' efforts to discover the nature and origin of altruism.

c. The authors want to encourage their readers to be more altruistic.

d. The authors want to convince readers that altruism has a genetic basis.

Tone 5. How would you describe the authors' tone?

a. confident

b. casual

c. skeptical

d. neutral

Share Your Thoughts Based on the information in this reading, what do you think the authors would say about some preschools' attempts to develop altruism in young children? Would they say that these efforts are useful or that they might not be effective? What statements in the reading led you to your conclusion?

From Reader to Writer Martin Luther King Jr. said, "Every man must decide if he will walk in the light of creative altruism or in the darkness of destructive selfishness." Write two or three paragraphs in which you explain why King called altruism "creative" and "selfishness" destructive. In your final paragraph, explain why you think King was right or wrong in labeling altruism creative and selfishness destructive.

WEB QUEST

Who coined the word *altruism*? _____. How was the word initially defined? _____

_____. Around a century after the word *altruism* first came into being, a novelist and would-be philosopher named Ayn Rand took a stand on altruism. What was her position? _____

_____.

Index